Complete and Return this Card
for a *FREE* Computer Book Catalog

Thank you for purchasing this book! You have purchased a superior computer book written expressly for your needs. To continue to provide the kind of up-to-date, pertinent coverage you've come to expect from us, we need to hear from you. Please take a minute to complete and return this self-addressed, postage-paid form. In return, we'll send you a free catalog of all our computer books on topics ranging from word processing to programming and the internet.

Mr. ☐   Mrs. ☐   Ms. ☐   Dr. ☐

Name (first) ☐☐☐☐☐☐☐☐☐☐☐   (M.I.) ☐   (last) ☐☐☐☐☐☐☐☐☐☐☐☐☐☐☐☐

Address ☐☐☐☐☐☐☐☐☐☐☐☐☐☐☐☐☐☐☐☐☐☐☐☐☐☐☐☐☐☐☐☐☐☐☐☐☐☐

City ☐☐☐☐☐☐☐☐☐☐☐☐☐☐☐☐☐☐   State ☐☐   Zip ☐☐☐☐☐☐☐☐☐

Phone ☐☐☐ ☐☐☐ ☐☐☐☐   Fax ☐☐☐ ☐☐☐ ☐☐☐☐

Company Name ☐☐☐☐☐☐☐☐☐☐☐☐☐☐☐☐☐☐☐☐☐☐☐☐☐☐☐☐☐☐☐☐

E-mail address ☐☐☐☐☐☐☐☐☐☐☐☐☐☐☐☐☐☐☐☐☐☐☐☐☐☐☐☐☐☐☐☐

1. Please check at least (3) influencing factors for purchasing this book.

Front or back cover information on book .... ☐
Special approach to the content .... ☐
Completeness of content .... ☐
Author's reputation .... ☐
Publisher's reputation .... ☐
Book cover design or layout .... ☐
Index or table of contents of book .... ☐
Price of book .... ☐
Special effects, graphics, illustrations .... ☐
Other (Please specify): _____ ☐

2. How did you first learn about this book?

Saw in Macmillan Computer Publishing catalog .... ☐
Recommended by store personnel .... ☐
Saw the book on bookshelf at store .... ☐
Recommended by a friend .... ☐
Received advertisement in the mail .... ☐
Saw an advertisement in: _____ ☐
Read book review in: _____ ☐
Other (Please specify): _____ ☐

3. How many computer books have you purchased in the last six months?

This book only .... ☐   3 to 5 books .... ☐
2 books................... ☐   More than 5 .... ☐

4. Where did you purchase this book?

Bookstore .... ☐
Computer Store .... ☐
Consumer Electronics Store .... ☐
Department Store .... ☐
Office Club .... ☐
Warehouse Club .... ☐
Mail Order .... ☐
Direct from Publisher .... ☐
Internet site .... ☐
Other (Please specify): _____ ☐

5. How long have you been using a computer?

☐ Less than 6 months   ☐ 6 months to a year
☐ 1 to 3 years   ☐ More than 3 years

6. What is your level of experience with personal computers and with the subject of this book?

	With PCs	With subject of book
New	☐	☐
Casual	☐	☐
Accomplished	☐	☐
Expert	☐	☐

Source Code ISBN: 0-7897-1295-4

7. Which of the following best describes your job title?

Administrative Assistant ☐
Coordinator ☐
Manager/Supervisor ☐
Director ☐
Vice President ☐
President/CEO/COO ☐
Lawyer/Doctor/Medical Professional ☐
Teacher/Educator/Trainer ☐
Engineer/Technician ☐
Consultant ☐
Not employed/Student/Retired ☐
Other (Please specify): _____ ☐

8. Which of the following best describes the area of the company your job title falls under?

Accounting ☐
Engineering ☐
Manufacturing ☐
Operations ☐
Marketing ☐
Sales ☐
Other (Please specify): _____ ☐

9. What is your age?

Under 20 ☐
21-29 ☐
30-39 ☐
40-49 ☐
50-59 ☐
60-over ☐

10. Are you:

Male ☐
Female ☐

11. Which computer publications do you read regularly? (Please list)

_____
_____
_____
_____
_____
_____
_____
_____
_____

Comments: _____
_____
_____

Fold here and scotch-tape to mail.

Check out Que® Books on the World Wide Web
http://www.quecorp.com

As the biggest software release in computer history, Windows 95 continues to redefine the computer industry. Click here for the latest info on our Windows 95 books

Make computing quick and easy with these products designed exclusively for new and casual users

Examine the latest releases in word processing, spreadsheets, operating systems, and suites

The Internet, The World Wide Web, CompuServe®, America Online®, Prodigy® —it's a world of ever-changing information. Don't get left behind!

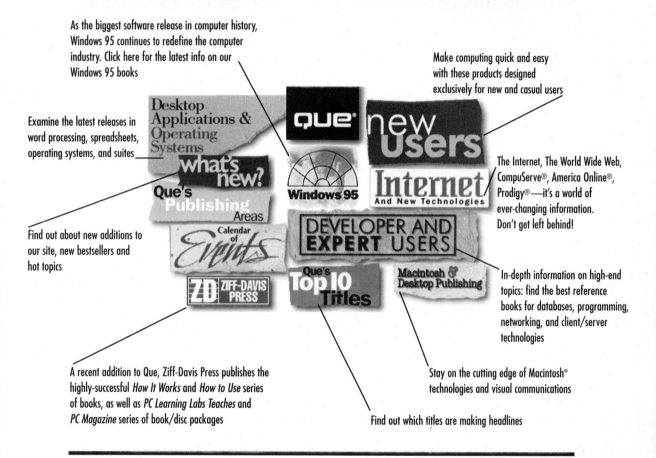

Find out about new additions to our site, new bestsellers and hot topics

In-depth information on high-end topics: find the best reference books for databases, programming, networking, and client/server technologies

A recent addition to Que, Ziff-Davis Press publishes the highly-successful *How It Works* and *How to Use* series of books, as well as *PC Learning Labs Teaches* and *PC Magazine* series of book/disc packages

Stay on the cutting edge of Macintosh® technologies and visual communications

Find out which titles are making headlines

With 6 separate publishing groups, Que develops products for many specific market segments and areas of computer technology. Explore our Web Site and you'll find information on best-selling titles, newly published titles, upcoming products, authors, and much more.

- Stay informed on the latest industry trends and products available
- Visit our online bookstore for the latest information and editions
- Download software from Que's library of the best shareware and freeware

The CD-ROM that accompanies this book will automatically start the install process by using Windows 95's auto-play feature. If you have disabled this feature, or are using Windows 3.x, please see the README files in \ZDBENCH\WB96 (WinBench 96), \ZDBENCH\WS96 (Winstone 96), and ZDBENCH\WS32 (Winstone 32). If you have problems with this disc, please contact Macmillan Technical Support at (317) 581-3833. We can be reached by e-mail at **support@mcp.com**.

License Agreement

This package contains one CD-ROM that includes software described in this book. See applicable chapters for a description of these programs and instructions for their use.

By opening this package you are agreeing to be bound by the following:

Building Internet Firewalls

Building Internet Firewalls

Second Edition

Elizabeth D. Zwicky, Simon Cooper &
D. Brent Chapman

O'REILLY®

Beijing · Cambridge · Farnham · Köln · Paris · Sebastopol · Taipei · Tokyo

Building Internet Firewalls, Second Edition

by Elizabeth D. Zwicky, Simon Cooper, and D. Brent Chapman

Published by O'Reilly & Associates, Inc., 101 Morris Street, Sebastopol, CA 95472.

Editor: Deborah Russell

Production Editor: Nancy Crumpton

Production Coordinator: Madeleine Newell

Cover Designer: Edie Freedman

Printing History:

April 1995:	First Edition.
November 1995:	Minor corrections.
June 2000:	Second Edition.

Library of Congress Cataloging-in-Publication Data

Zwicky, Elizabeth D.
    Building Internet firewalls / Elizabeth D. Zwicky, Simon Cooper & D. Brent Chapman.--
        2nd ed. p. cm.
    ISBN 1-56592-871-7
    1. Computer networks--Security measures. 2. Internet (Computer network)--Security
        measures. I. Cooper, Simon. II. Chapman, D. Brent. III. Title.

TK5105.59.Z85 2000
005.8--dc21   00-039954

ISBN: 1-56592-871-7

[M]

Table of Contents

Preface

This book is a practical guide to building your own firewall. It provides step-by-step explanations of how to design and install a firewall at your site and how to configure Internet services such as electronic mail, FTP, the World Wide Web, and others to work with a firewall. Firewalls are complex, though, and we can't boil everything down to simple rules. Too much depends on exactly what hardware, operating system, and networking you are using at your site, and what you want your users to be able to do and not do. We've tried to give you enough rules, examples, and resources here so you'll be able to do the rest on your own.

What is a firewall, and what does it do for you? A firewall is a way to restrict access between the Internet and your internal network. You typically install a firewall at the point of maximum leverage, the point where your network connects to the Internet. The existence of a firewall at your site can greatly reduce the odds that outside attackers will penetrate your internal systems and networks. The firewall can also keep your own users from compromising your systems by sending dangerous information—unencrypted passwords and sensitive data—to the outside world.

The attacks on Internet-connected systems we are seeing today are more serious and more technically complex than those in the past. To keep these attacks from compromising our systems, we need all the help we can get. Firewalls are a highly effective way of protecting sites from these attacks. For that reason, we strongly recommend you include a firewall in your site's overall Internet security plan. However, a firewall should be only one component in that plan. It's also vital that you establish a security policy, that you implement strong host security, and that you consider the use of authentication and encryption devices that work with the firewalls you install. This book will touch on each of these topics while maintaining its focus on firewalls.

Scope of This Book

This book is divided into five parts.

Part I, *Network Security*, explores the problem of Internet security and focuses on firewalls as part of an effective strategy to address that problem.

- Chapter 1, *Why Internet Firewalls?*, introduces the major risks associated with using the Internet today; discusses what to protect, and what to protect against; discusses various security models; and introduces firewalls in the context of what they can and can't do for your site's security.

- Chapter 2, *Internet Services*, outlines the services users want and need from the Internet, and summarizes the security problems posed by those services.

- Chapter 3, *Security Strategies*, outlines the basic security principles an organization needs to understand before it adopts a security policy and invests in specific security mechanisms.

Part II, *Building Firewalls*, describes how to build firewalls.

- Chapter 4, *Packets and Protocols*, describes the basic network concepts firewalls work with.

- Chapter 5, *Firewall Technologies*, explains the terms and technologies used in building firewalls.

- Chapter 6, *Firewall Architectures*, describes the major architectures used in constructing firewalls, and the situations they are best suited to.

- Chapter 7, *Firewall Design*, presents the process of designing a firewall.

- Chapter 8, *Packet Filtering,* describes how packet filtering systems work, and discusses what you can and can't accomplish with them in building a firewall.

- Chapter 9, *Proxy Systems*, describes how proxy clients and servers work, and how to use these systems in building a firewall.

- Chapter 10, *Bastion Hosts*, presents a general overview of the process of designing and building the bastion hosts used in many firewall configurations.

- Chapter 11, *Unix and Linux Bastion Hosts*, presents the details of designing and building a Unix or Linux bastion host.

- Chapter 12, *Windows NT and Windows 2000 Bastion Hosts*, presents the details of designing and building a Windows NT bastion host.

Part III, *Internet Services*, describes how to configure services in the firewall environment.

- Chapter 13, *Internet Services and Firewalls*, describes the general issues involved in selecting and configuring services in the firewall environment.

- Chapter 14, *Intermediary Protocols*, discusses basic protocols that are used by multiple services.

- Chapter 15, *The World Wide Web*, discusses the Web and related services.

- Chapter 16, *Electronic Mail and News*, discusses services used for transferring electronic mail and Usenet news.

- Chapter 17, *File Transfer, File Sharing, and Printing*, discusses the services used for moving files from one place to another.

- Chapter 18, *Remote Access to Hosts*, discusses services that allow you to use one computer from another computer.

- Chapter 19, *Real-Time Conferencing Services*, discusses services that allow people to interact with each other online.

- Chapter 20, *Naming and Directory Services*, discusses the services used to distribute information about hosts and users.

- Chapter 21, *Authentication and Auditing Services*, discusses services used to identify users before they get access to resources, to keep track of what sort of access they should have, and to keep records of who accessed what and when.

- Chapter 22, *Administrative Services*, discusses other services used to administer machines and networks.

- Chapter 23, *Databases and Games*, discusses the remaining two major classes of popular Internet services, databases and games.

- Chapter 24, *Two Sample Firewalls*, presents two sample configurations for basic firewalls.

Part IV, *Keeping Your Site Secure*, describes how to establish a security policy for your site, maintain your firewall, and handle the security problems that may occur with even the most effective firewalls.

- Chapter 25, *Security Policies*, discusses the importance of having a clear and well-understood security policy for your site, and what that policy should and should not contain. It also discusses ways of getting management and users to accept the policy.

- Chapter 26, *Maintaining Firewalls*, describes how to maintain security at your firewall over time and how to keep yourself aware of new Internet security threats and technologies.

- Chapter 27, *Responding to Security Incidents*, describes what to do when a break-in occurs, or when you suspect that your security is being breached.

Part V, *Appendixes*, consists of the following summary appendixes:

- Appendix A, *Resources*, contains a list of places you can go for further information and help with Internet security: World Wide Web pages, FTP sites, mailing lists, newsgroups, response teams, books, papers, and conferences.

- Appendix B, *Tools*, summarizes the best freely available firewall tools and how to get them.

- Appendix C, *Cryptography*, contains background information on cryptography that is useful to anyone trying to decrypt the marketing materials for security products.

Audience

Who should read this book? Although the book is aimed primarily at those who need to build firewalls, large parts of it are appropriate for everyone who is concerned about Internet security. This list tells you what sections are particularly applicable to you:

System administrators
> You should read the entire book.

Senior managers
> You should read at least Part I of the book. The chapters in Part I will introduce you to the various types of Internet threats, services, and security approaches and strategies. These chapters will also introduce you to firewalls and describe what firewalls can and cannot do to enforce Internet security. You should also read Chapter 5, which provides an overview of firewall technologies. In addition, Appendix A will tell you where to go for more information and resources.

Information technology managers and users
> You should read all of the chapters we've cited for the managers in the previous category. In addition, you should read Part III, which explains the kinds of issues that may arise at your site over time—for example, how to develop a security policy, keep up to date, and react if someone attacks your site.

Although this book provides general concepts of firewalls appropriate to any site, it focuses on "average" sites: small to large commercial or educational sites. If you are setting up a personal firewall, you may wish to read just Part I, Chapter 5, and the service chapters appropriate to the services you wish to run. If you are setting up a firewall for an extremely large site, all of the chapters will be useful to you, but you may find that you need to use additional techniques.

Platforms

To a large extent, this book is platform-independent. Because most of the information provided here consists of general principles, most of it should be applicable to you, regardless of what equipment, software, and networking you are using. The most platform-specific issue is what type of system to use as a bastion host. People have successfully built bastion hosts (which we describe in Chapter 10) using all kinds of computers, including Unix systems, Windows NT machines, Macintoshes, VMS VAXes, and others.

Having said this, we must acknowledge that this book is strongly oriented towards Unix (including Linux), with Windows NT as a major secondary theme. There are several reasons for this orientation. First, these operating systems are the dominant operating systems in the Internet world. Unix is still the predominant operating system for Internet servers, although Windows NT is a strong presence. Another reason is, of course, that our own experience is primarily in the Unix world; we have entered the world of Windows NT only recently, as it started to intersect with the world of the Internet. Although we do speak Windows NT, we do so with a strong Unix accent.

Linux, while it is not strictly speaking Unix, is a close relative of the Unix we have spent our careers working with. In many cases, it is truer to the Unix tradition than commercial operating systems entitled to use the Unix trademark. While we do mention Linux by name in some places, you should bear in mind that all of our statements about Unix are meant to include Linux except when we explicitly state otherwise.

Similarly, when we mention "Windows NT", unless we explicitly mention versions, we mean both Windows NT 4 and Windows 2000. Windows 2000 is a direct descendant of Windows NT 4 and behaves like it in most important respects. We call out differences where appropriate (although you should bear in mind that Windows 2000 was being released as this book went to press; both the operating system and the world's experience with it are bound to have changed by the time you read this).

Products

It's impossible to give a complete list of commercial and publicly available products in this book because new products are constantly being introduced and capabilities are constantly being added to existing products. Instead, we concentrate on discussing generic features and capabilities, and the consequences of having—or not having—particular capabilities, so that you can make your own evaluation of the products currently available to you. We do periodically mention individual products, some commercial and some publicly available, particularly when there are striking features of well-known products. This is not intended to be an endorsement of the products we mention, or a slight to products that we omit.

Examples

Writing a book of this nature requires a large number of examples with host-names and addresses in them. In order to avoid offending or inconveniencing people, we have attempted to use only names and addresses that are not in use. In most cases, we have used names and addresses that are reserved and cannot be publicly registered. In particular, this is why most of the example hosts in this book are in the ".example" domain (reserved for this use in RFC 2606). In a few cases where we needed large numbers of hostnames and felt that using the reserved example namespace would be confusing, we have used names that can be registered; we have attempted to use names that are not currently registered and do not seem likely to be registered. We apologize to anybody who inadvertently uses one of these names and is inconvenienced.

We also apologize to those readers who have memorized the entire reserved IP address space, and find it upsetting that many of our illustrations show reserved IP addresses in use over the Internet. This is, of course, impossible in practice, and we show it only to avoid attracting undesirable attention to addresses that can be accessed over the Internet.

Conventions Used in This Book

The following conventions are used in this book:

Italic
> Used for file and directory names and URLs, and for the first mention of new terms under discussion.

`Constant width`
> Used for code examples.

`Constant width italic`
> In some code examples, indicates an element (e.g., a filename) that you supply.

The following icon is used in this book:

Indicates a tip, suggestion, or general note.

Comments and Questions

We have tested and verified the information in this book to the best of our ability, but you may find that features have changed (or even that we have made mistakes!). Please let us know about any errors you find, as well as your suggestions for future editions, by writing to:

O'Reilly & Associates
101 Morris Street
Sebastopol, CA 95472
800-998-9938 (in the U.S. or Canada)
707-829-0515 (international or local)
707-829-0104 (FAX)

You can also send us messages electronically. To be put on the mailing list or request a catalog, send email to:

info@oreilly.com

To ask technical questions or comment on the book, send email to:

bookquestions@oreilly.com

We have a web site for this book, where we'll list examples, errata, and any plans for future editions. You can access this page at:

http://www.oreilly.com/catalog/fire2

For more information about this book and others, see the O'Reilly web site:

http://www.oreilly.com

Acknowledgments for the Second Edition

As unlikely as it may seem, we still had no idea how much time and effort the second edition would take when we started working on it; what we expected to be a relatively simple effort has turned into a marathon. Even the smallest revision requires many hands, and a fully new edition requires what seems like a cast of thousands.

Thanks to those who reviewed the second edition and made helpful comments: Steve Beaty, David LeBlanc, Phil Cox, Eric Pearce, Chuck Phillips, Greg Rose, and Wietse Venema—and to Bruce Schneier and Diana Smetters who read Appendix C on a four-hour turnaround! Thanks to the entire editorial and production team at O'Reilly, especially project manager Madeleine Newell and production editor Nancy Crumpton.

Elizabeth says: My thanks to my friends, family, and colleagues for their patience and aid; my monomaniacal interest in network protocols coupled with emotional instability and intermittent overwork have required more than a reasonable and customary amount of tolerance. I am particularly indebted to Arnold Zwicky, Diana Smetters, Jeanne Dusseault, and Brent Chapman. Special thanks are due to my second father, Jacques Transue, who required me to take slow and calm breaks from writing. Thanks to Debby Russell and Sue Miller at O'Reilly for their deft, patient, and calm job of editing; and to Simon, who expected a simple writing project, got his life disrupted for more than a year and a half, and kept working anyway, even though we insisted on spelling everything in American instead of proper English. And thanks to the many O'Reilly people who helped to produce this book.

Simon says: I would like to thank my colleagues, my friends, and my family for their understanding and support during this project. Particular thanks go to Beryl Cooper, Mel Pleasant, Landon Curt Noll, Greg Bossert, James R. Martin II, Alesia Bischoff, and Cherry Mill for their encouragement and patience. A special mention goes to my ice hockey teammates—thanks for such an active alternative to writing. Enormous thanks to Elizabeth for asking me to coauthor and for coaching me through the process. Finally, thanks to Debby, Sue, and the staff of O'Reilly for putting this book into the hands of our readers.

Acknowledgments for the First Edition

Note: We've preserved these acknowledgments for the first edition because we continue to be grateful to the people who helped us with that edition. Note, however, that several parts of the first edition (e.g., the foreword and the TCP/IP appendix) are no longer included in the book.

When we set out to write this book, we had no idea that it would consume so much time and energy. We would never have succeeded without the help of many people.

Special thanks to Ed DeHart and Craig Hunt. Ed worked with Brent in the early stages of this book and wrote the foreword to it; we appreciate all that he has done to help. TCP/IP is essential for understanding the basics of firewall construction, and Craig Hunt, author of *TCP/IP Network Administration* (O'Reilly & Associates) has kindly let us excerpt much of that book's Chapters 1 and 2 in this book's Appendix C so readers who do not already have a TCP/IP background can get a jump start.

Thanks to all those who reviewed drafts of the book before publication and made helpful suggestions: Fred Avolio, Steve Bellovin, Niels Bjergstrom, Rik Farrow, Simson Garfinkel, Eliot Lear, Evi Nemeth, Steve Simmons, Steve Romig, Gene Spafford, Phil Trubey, and Mark Verber. Thanks as well to Eric Allman for answering many Sendmail questions and Paul Traina for answering many Cisco questions.

Thanks to all the people at O'Reilly & Associates who turned this manuscript into a finished book: to Mary Anne Weeks Mayo, the wonderful and patient project manager/copyeditor for the book; Len Muellner, Ellen Siever, and Norm Walsh, who converted the book from Word to SGML and contributed their tool-tweaking prowess; Chris Reilley, who created the many excellent diagrams; Edie Freedman, who designed the cover, and Nancy Priest, who designed the interior layout; John Files and Juliette Muellner, who assisted with production; Seth Maislin, who prepared the index; and Sheryl Avruch and Kismet McDonough-Chan, who did the final quality control on the book.

Brent says: I would like to extend personal thanks to my friends and family, for keeping me going for a year and a half while I worked on the book; to my staff at Great Circle Associates, for keeping my business going; to the many hundreds of folks who've attended my Internet Security Firewalls Tutorial, for providing the impetus for this whole endeavor (and for keeping my bills paid!); and to the many thousands of subscribers to the Firewalls mailing list on the Internet, for providing a stimulating environment to develop many of the ideas found in this book. I also owe a lot of thanks to Debby Russell, our editor at O'Reilly & Associates, for all her help and guidance, and to our technical reviewers, for all their wonderful comments and suggestions. Most of all, though, I'd like to thank my very good friend and coauthor, Elizabeth Zwicky, without whose collaboration and encouragement this book probably never would have been finished, and certainly wouldn't have been as good.

Elizabeth says: My thanks go to my friends, my family, and my colleagues at Silicon Graphics, for an almost infinite patience with my tendency to alternate between obsessing about the book and refusing to discuss anything even tangentially related to it. I'd like to particularly thank Arnold Zwicky, Diana Smetters, Greg Rose, Eliot Lear, and Jeanne Dusseault for their expert moral support (often during similar crises of their own). But the most thanks for this effort have to go to Debby and Brent, for giving me a chance to be part of an unexpected but extremely rewarding project.

I

Network Security

This part of the book explores the problem of Internet security and focuses on firewalls as part of an effective strategy to solve that problem. It introduces firewalls, introduces the major services Internet users need, and summarizes the security problems posed by those services. It also outlines the major security principles you need to understand before beginning to build firewalls.

1

Why Internet
Firewalls?

It is scarcely possible to enter a bookstore, read a magazine or a newspaper, or listen to a news broadcast without seeing or hearing something about the Internet in some guise. It's become so popular that no advertisement is complete without a reference to a web page. While nontechnical publications are obsessed with the Internet, the technical publications have moved on and are obsessed with security. It's a logical progression; once the first excitement of having a superhighway in your neighborhood wears off, you're bound to notice that not only does it let you travel, it lets a very large number of strangers show up where you are, and not all of them are people you would have invited.

Both views are true: The Internet is a marvelous technological advance that provides access to information, and the ability to publish information, in revolutionary ways. But it's also a major danger that provides the ability to pollute and destroy information in revolutionary ways. This book is about one way to balance the advantages and the risks—to take part in the Internet while still protecting yourself.

Later in this chapter, we describe different models of security that people have used to protect their data and resources on the Internet. Our emphasis in this book is on the network security model and, in particular, the use of Internet firewalls. A firewall is a form of protection that allows a network to connect to the Internet while maintaining a degree of security. The section later in this chapter called "What is an Internet Firewall?" describes the basics of firewalls and summarizes what they can—and cannot—do to help make your site secure. Before we discuss what you can do with a firewall, though, we want to describe briefly why you need one. What are you protecting on your systems? What types of attacks and attackers are common? What types of security can you use to protect your site?

What Are You Trying to Protect?

A firewall is basically a protective device. If you are building a firewall, the first thing you need to worry about is what you're trying to protect. When you connect to the Internet, you're putting three things at risk:

- Your data: the information you keep on the computers
- Your resources: the computers themselves
- Your reputation

Your Data

Your data has three separate characteristics that need to be protected:

Secrecy
   You might not want other people to know it.

Integrity
   You probably don't want other people to change it.

Availability
   You almost certainly want to be able to use it yourself.

People tend to focus on the risks associated with secrecy, and it's true that those are usually large risks. Many organizations have some of their most important secrets—the designs for their products, financial records, or student records—on their computers. On the other hand, you may find that at your site it is relatively easy to separate the machines containing this kind of highly secret data from the machines that connect to the Internet. (Or you may not; you can't do Internet electronic commerce without having information about orders and money pass through Internet-accessible machines.)

Suppose that you *can* separate your data in this way, and that none of the information that is Internet accessible is secret. In that case, why should you worry about security? Because secrecy isn't the only thing you're trying to protect. You still need to worry about integrity and availability. After all, if your data isn't secret, and if you don't mind its being changed, and if you don't care whether or not anybody can get to it, why are you wasting disk space on it?

Even if your data isn't particularly secret, you'll suffer the consequences if it's destroyed or modified. Some of these consequences have readily calculable costs: if you lose data, you'll have to pay to have it reconstructed; if you were planning to sell that data in some form, you'll have lost sales regardless of whether the data is something you sell directly, the designs from which you build things, or the code for a software product. Intangible costs are also associated with any security incident. The most serious is the loss of confidence (user confidence, customer confidence, investor confidence, staff confidence, student confidence, public confidence) in your systems and data and, consequently, a loss of confidence in your organization.

Has Your Data Been Modified?

Computer security incidents are different from many other types of crimes because detection is unusually difficult. Sometimes, it may take a long time to find out that someone has broken into your site. Sometimes, you'll never know. Even if somebody breaks in but doesn't actually *do* anything to your system or data, you'll probably lose time (hours or days) while you verify that the intruder didn't do anything. In a lot of ways, a brute-force trash-everything attack is a lot easier to deal with than a break-in by somebody who doesn't appear to damage your system. If the intruder trashes everything, you bite the bullet, restore from backups, and get on with your life. But if the intruder doesn't appear to have done anything, you spend a lot of time second-guessing yourself, wondering what he or she might have done to your system or data. The intruder almost certainly has done something—most intruders will start by making sure that they have a way to get back in, before they do anything else.

Although this book is primarily about preventing security incidents, Chapter 27, *Responding to Security Incidents*, supplies some general guidelines for detecting, investigating, and recovering from security incidents.

Your Resources

Even if you have data you don't care about—if you enjoy reinstalling your operating system every week because it exercises the disks, or something like that—if other people are going to use your computers, you probably would like to benefit from this use in some way. Most people want to use their own computers, or they want to charge other people for using them. Even people who give away computer time and disk space usually expect to get good publicity and thanks for it; they aren't going to get it from intruders. You spend good time and money on your computing resources, and it is your right to determine how they are used.

Intruders often argue that they are using only excess resources; as a consequence, their intrusions don't cost their victims anything. There are two problems with this argument.

First, it's impossible for an intruder to determine successfully what resources are excess and use only those. It may look as if your system has oceans of empty disk space and hours of unused computing time; in fact, though, you might be just about to start computing animation sequences that are going to use every bit and every microsecond. An intruder can't give back your resources when you want them. (Along the same lines, I don't ordinarily use my car between midnight and 6 A.M., but that doesn't mean I'm willing to lend it to you without being asked. What if I have an early morning flight the next day, or what if I'm called out to deal with an emergency?)

Second, it's your right to use your resources the way you want to, even if you merely feel some sort of Zen joy at the sight of empty disk space, or if you like the way the blinky lights look when nothing's happening on your computer. Computing resources are not natural resources that belong by right to the world at large, nor are they limited resources that are wasted or destroyed if they're not used.

Your Reputation

An intruder appears on the Internet with your identity. Anything he or she does appears to come from you. What are the consequences?

Most of the time, the consequences are simply that other sites—or law enforcement agencies—start calling you to ask why you're trying to break into their systems. (This isn't as rare an occurrence as it may seem. One site got serious about security when its system administration staff added a line item to their time cards for conversations with the FBI about break-in attempts originating from their site.)

Sometimes, such impostors cost you a lot more than lost time. An intruder who actively dislikes you, or simply takes pleasure in making life difficult for strangers, may change your web site, send electronic mail, or post news messages that purport to come from you. Generally, people who choose to do this aim for maximum hatefulness, rather than believability, but even if only a few people believe these messages, the cleanup can be long and humiliating. Anything even remotely believable can do permanent damage to your reputation.

A few years ago, an impostor posing as a Texas A&M professor sent out hate email containing racist comments to thousands of recipients. The impostor was never found, and the professor is still dealing with the repercussions of the forged messages. In another case, a student at Dartmouth sent out email over the signature of a professor late one night during exam period. Claiming a family emergency, the forged email canceled the next day's exam, and only a few students showed up.

It's possible to forge electronic mail or news without gaining access to a site, but it's much easier to show that a message is a forgery if it's generated from outside the forged site. The messages coming from an intruder who has gained access to your site will look exactly like yours because they *are* yours. An intruder will also have access to all kinds of details that an external forger won't. For example, an intruder has all of your mailing lists available and knows exactly who you send mail to.

Currently, attacks that replace web sites are very popular; one list shows more than 160 successful attacks where sites were replaced, in 18 countries, in a single month. Many of those attacks simply replaced the sites with boasting by the attackers, but a significant portion of them were directed at the content of the sites. A site that should have touted Al Gore's suitability for the U.S. presidency was replaced by a similar anti-Gore site, for instance; political movements in Peru, Mexico, and China put up slogans; and there's no need to feel safe merely because your site concerns frivolity, as pop stars, Pro Wrestling, and the Boston Lyric Opera all suffered as well.

Even if an intruder doesn't use your identity, a break-in at your site isn't good for your reputation. It shakes people's confidence in your organization. In addition, most intruders will attempt to go from your machines to others, which is going to make their next victims think of your site as a platform for computer criminals. Many intruders will also use compromised sites as distribution sites for pirated software, pornography, and/or other stolen information, which is not going to endear you to many folks either. Whether or not it's your fault, having your name linked to other intrusions, software piracy, and pornography is hard to recover from.

What Are You Trying to Protect Against?

What's out there to worry about? What types of attacks are you likely to face on the Internet, and what types of attackers are likely to be carrying them out? And what about simple accidents or stupidity? In the sections that follow, we touch on these topics, but we don't go into any technical detail; later chapters describe different kinds of attacks in some detail and explain how firewalls can help protect against them.

Types of Attacks

There are many types of attacks on systems, and many ways of categorizing these attacks. In this section, we break attacks down into three basic categories: intrusion, denial of service, and information theft.

Intrusion

The most common attacks on your systems are *intrusions*; with intrusions, people are actually able to use your computers. Most attackers want to use your computers as if they were legitimate users.

Attackers have dozens of ways to get access. They range from social engineering attacks (you figure out the name of somebody high up in the company; you call a system administrator, claiming to be that person and claiming to need your password changed right now, so that you can get important work done), to simple guesswork (you try account names and password combinations until one works), to intricate ways to get in without needing to know an account name and a password.

As we describe in this book, firewalls help prevent intrusions in a number of ways. Ideally, they block all ways to get into a system without knowing an account name and password. Properly configured, they reduce the number of accounts accessible from the outside that are therefore vulnerable to guesswork or social engineering. Most people configure their firewalls to use one-time passwords that prevent guessing attacks. Even if you don't use these passwords, which we describe in Chapter 21, *Authentication and Auditing Services*, a firewall will give you a controlled place to log attempts to get into your system, and, in this way, they help you detect guessing attacks.

Denial of service

A *denial of service* attack is one that's aimed entirely at preventing you from using your own computers.

In late 1994, writers Josh Quittner and Michelle Slatalla were the target of an "electronic mail bomb". Apparently in retaliation for an article on the cracker community they'd published in *Wired* magazine, someone broke into IBM, Sprint, and the writers' network provider, and modified programs so their email and telephone service was disrupted. A flood of email messages so overwhelmed their network service that other messages couldn't get through; eventually, their Internet connection was shut down entirely. Their phone service also fell victim to the intruders, who reprogrammed the service so that callers were routed to an out-of-state number where they heard an obscene recording.

Although some cases of electronic sabotage involve the actual destruction or shutting down of equipment or data, more often they follow the pattern of flooding seen in the Quittner-Slatalla case or in the case of the 1988 Morris Internet worm. An intruder so floods a system or network—with messages, processes, or network requests—that no real work can be done. The system or network spends all its time responding to messages and requests, and can't satisfy any of them.

While flooding is the simplest and most common way to carry out a denial of service attack, a cleverer attacker can also disable services, reroute them, or replace them. For example, the phone attack in the Quittner-Slatalla case denied phone service by rerouting their phone calls elsewhere; it's possible to mount the same kind of attack against Internet services.

It's close to impossible to avoid all denial of service attacks. Sometimes it's a "heads, I win; tails, you lose" situation for attackers. For example, many sites set accounts up to become unusable after a certain number of failed login attempts. This prevents attackers from simply trying passwords until they find the right one. On the other hand, it gives the attackers an easy way to mount a denial of service attack: they can lock any user's account simply by trying to log in a few times.

Most often, the risk of denial of service attacks is unavoidable. If you accept things from the external universe—electronic mail, telephone calls, or packages—it's possible to get flooded. The notorious college prank of ordering a pizza or two from every pizzeria in town to be delivered to your least favorite person is a form of denial of service; it's hard to do much else while arguing with 42 pizza deliverers. In the electronic world, denial of service is as likely to happen by accident as on purpose (have you ever had a persistent fax machine try to fax something to your voice line?). The most important thing is to set up services so that if one of them is flooded, the rest of your site keeps functioning while you find and fix the problem.

Flooding attacks are considered unsporting by many attackers, because they aren't very difficult to carry out. For most attackers, they're also pointless, because they don't provide the attacker with the information or the ability to use your computers (the payoff for most other attacks). Intentional flooding attacks are usually the work of people who are angry at your site in particular, and at most sites such people are quite rare.

With the right tools and cooperation, it's fairly easy to trace flood packets back to their source, but that might not help you figure out who is behind the attacks. The attacks almost always come from machines that have themselves been broken into; only a really stupid attacker generates an easily traced flood of packets from their own machine. Sometimes flooding attacks are carried out by remote control. Attackers install remotely controlled flooding software on systems that they break into over the course of many weeks or months. This software lies dormant and undiscovered until some later time, when they trigger many of these remotely controlled installations simultaneously to bombard their victims with massive floods of traffic from many different directions at once. This was the method behind the highly publicized denial of service attacks on Yahoo!, CNN, and other high-profile Internet sites early in the year 2000.

You are far more likely to encounter unintentional flooding problems, as we discuss in the "Stupidity and Accidents" section, later in this chapter.

On the other hand, some denial of service attacks are easier for attackers, and these are relatively popular. Attacks that involve sending small amounts of data that cause machines to reboot or hang are very popular with the same sort of people who like to set off fire alarms in dormitories in the middle of the night, for much the same reason; with a small investment, you can massively annoy a very large number of people who are unlikely to be able to find you afterwards. The good news is that most of these attacks are avoidable; a well-designed firewall will usually not be susceptible to them itself, and will usually prevent them from reaching internal machines that are vulnerable to them.

Information theft

Some types of attacks allow an attacker to get data without ever having to directly use your computers. Usually these attacks exploit Internet services that are intended to give out information, inducing the services to give out more information than was intended, or to give it out to the wrong people. Many Internet services are designed for use on local area networks, and don't have the type or degree of security that would allow them to be used safely across the Internet.

Information theft doesn't need to be active or particularly technical. People who want to find out personal information could simply call you and ask (perhaps pretending to be somebody who had a right to know): this is an *active* information theft. Or they could tap your telephone: this is a *passive* information theft. Similarly, people who want to gather electronic information could actively query for it (perhaps pretending to be a machine or a user with valid access) or could passively tap the network and wait for it to flow by.

Most people who steal information try to get access to your computers; they're looking for usernames and passwords. Fortunately for them, and unfortunately for everybody else, that's the easiest kind of information to get when tapping a network. Username and password information occurs quite predictably at the beginning of many network interactions, and such information can often be reused in the same form.

How would you proceed if you want to find out how somebody answers her telephone? Installing a tap would be an easy and reliable way to get that information, and a tap at a central point in the telephone system would yield the telephone greetings of hundreds or thousands of people in a short period of time.

On the other hand, what if you want to know how somebody spells his or her last name, or what the names and ages of his or her children are? In this case, a telephone tap is a slow and unreliable way to get that information. A telephone tap at a central point in the system will probably yield that information about some people, and it will certainly yield some secret information you could use in interesting ways, but the information is going to be buried among the conversations of hundreds of people setting up lunch dates and chatting about the weather.

Similarly, network taps, which are usually called *sniffers*, are very effective at finding password information but are rarely used by attackers to gather other kinds of information. Getting more specific information about a site requires either extreme dedication and patience, or the knowledge that the information you want will reliably pass through a given place at a given time. For example, if you know that somebody calls the bank to transfer money between his or her checking and savings accounts at 2 P.M. every other Friday, it's worth tapping that phone call to find out the person's access codes and account numbers. However, it's probably not worth tapping somebody else's phone, on the off chance that they too will do such a transfer, because most people don't transfer money over the phone at all.

Network sniffing is much easier than tapping a telephone line. Historically, the connectors used to hook a computer to an Ethernet network were known as *network taps* (that's why the term *tapping* isn't used for spying on a network), and the connectors behave like taps too. In most networks, computers can see traffic that is intended for other hosts. Traffic that crosses the Internet may cross any number of local area networks, any one of which can be a point of compromise. Network service providers and public-access systems are very popular targets for intrusions; sniffers placed there can be extremely successful because so much traffic passes through these networks.

There are several types of protection against information theft. A properly configured firewall will protect you against people who are trying to get more information than you intended to give. Once you've decided to give information out across the Internet, however, it's very difficult to protect against that information's reaching an unintended audience, either through misauthentication (somebody claiming to be authorized, when he or she isn't) or through sniffing (somebody simply reading information as it crosses a correctly authorized channel). For that matter, once you have given the information to somebody, you have no way to prevent that person from distributing it to other people. Although these risks are outside of the protection a firewall can give (because they occur once information has intentionally been allowed to go outside your network), we do discuss them and the methods used to reduce them, as appropriate in this book.

Types of Attackers

This section very briefly describes the types of attackers who are out there on the Internet. There are many ways to categorize these attackers; we can't really do justice to the many variants of attackers we've seen over the years, and any quick summary of this kind necessarily presents a rather stereotyped view. Nevertheless, this summary may be useful in distinguishing the main categories of attackers.

All attackers share certain characteristics. They don't want to be caught, so they try to conceal themselves, their identity and real geographic location. If they gain access to your system, they will certainly attempt to preserve that access, if possible, by building in extra ways to get access (and they hope you won't notice these access routes even if you find the attackers themselves). Most of them have some contact with other people who have the same kinds of interests ("the underground" is not hard to find), and most will share the information they get from attacking your system. A secondary group of attackers may not be as benign.

Joyriders

Joyriders are bored people looking for amusement. They break in because they think you might have interesting data, or because it would be amusing to use your computers, or because they have nothing better to do. They might be out to learn about the kind of computer you have or about the data you have. They're curious but not actively malicious; however, they often damage the system through ignorance or in trying to cover their tracks. Joyriders are particularly attracted to well-known sites and uncommon computers.

Vandals

Vandals are out to do damage, either because they get their kicks from destroying things, or because they don't like you. When one gets to you, you'll know it.

Vandals are a big problem if you're somebody that the Internet underground might think of as The Enemy (for example, the phone company or the government) or if you tend to annoy people who have computers and time (for example, you're a university with failing students, or a computer company with annoyed customers, or you have an aggressively commercial presence on the Internet). You can also become a target simply by being large and visible; if you put a big wall up in certain neighborhoods, people will put graffiti on it no matter how they feel about you.

Fortunately, vandals are fairly rare. People don't like them, even people in the underground who have nothing against breaking into computers in general. Vandals also tend to inspire people to go to great lengths to find them and stop them. Unlike more mundane intruders, vandals have short but splashy careers. Most of them also go for straightforward destruction, which is unpleasant but is relatively easily detected and repaired. In most circumstances, deleting your data, or even ruining your computer equipment, is not the worst thing somebody could do to you, but it is what vandals do. (Actually, introducing subtle but significant changes in programs or financial data would be much harder to detect and fix.)

Unfortunately, it's close to impossible to stop a determined vandal; somebody with a true vendetta against your site is going to get you, sooner or later. Certain attacks are attractive to vandals but not to other types of attackers. For example, denial of service attacks are not attractive to joyriders; while joyriders are around in your system, they are just as interested as you are in having your computers up, running, and available to the Internet.

Scorekeepers

Many intruders are engaging in an updated version of an ancient tradition. They're gaining bragging rights, based on the number and types of systems they've broken into.

Like joyriders and vandals, *scorekeepers* may prefer sites of particular interest. Breaking into something well known, well defended, or otherwise especially cool is usually worth more points to them. However, they'll also attack anything they can get at; they're going for quantity as well as quality. They don't have to want anything you've got or care in the least about the characteristics of your site. They may or may not do damage on the way through. They'll certainly gather information and keep it for later use (perhaps using it to barter with other attackers). They'll probably try to leave themselves ways to get back in later. And, if at all possible, they'll use your machines as a platform to attack others.

These people are the ones you discover long after they've broken in to your system. You may find out slowly, because something's odd about your machine. Or you'll find out when another site or a law enforcement agency calls up because your system is being used to attack other places. Or you'll find out when somebody sends you a copy of your own private data, which they've found on a cracked system on the other side of the world.

Many scorekeepers are what are known as *script kiddies*—attackers who are not themselves technically expert but are using programs or scripts written by other people and following instructions about how to use them. Although they do tend to be young, they're called "kiddies" mostly out of contempt aimed at them by more experienced intruders. Even though these attackers are not innovators, they still pose a real threat to sites that don't keep rigorously up to date. Information spreads very rapidly in the underground, and the script kiddies are extremely numerous. Once a script exists, somebody is almost guaranteed to attack your site with it.

These days, some scorekeepers aren't even counting machines they've broken into but are keeping score on crashed machines. On the one hand, having a machine crash is generally less destructive than having it broken into; on the other hand, if a particular attack gets into the hands of the script kiddies, and thousands of people use it to crash your machine, it's not funny any more.

Spies (industrial and otherwise)

Most people who break into computers do so for the same reason people climb mountains—because they're there. While these people are not above theft, they usually steal things that are directly convertible into money or further access (e.g., credit card, telephone, or network access information). If they find secrets they think they can sell, they may try to do so, but that's not their main business.

As far as anybody knows, serious computer-based espionage is much rarer, outside of traditional espionage circles. (That is, if you're a professional spy, other professional spies are probably watching you and your computers.) Espionage is much more difficult to detect than run-of-the-mill break-ins, however. Information theft need not leave any traces at all, and even intrusions are relatively rarely detected immediately. Somebody who breaks in, copies data, and leaves without disturbing anything is quite likely to get away with it at most sites.

In practical terms, most organizations can't prevent spies from succeeding. The precautions that governments take to protect sensitive information on computers are complex, expensive, and cumbersome; therefore, they are used on only the most critical resources. These precautions include electromagnetic shielding, careful access controls, and absolutely no connections to unsecured networks.

What can you do to protect against attackers of this kind? You can ensure that your Internet connection isn't the easiest way for a spy to gather information. You don't want some kid to break into your computers and find something that immediately appears to be worth trying to sell to spies; you don't want your competitors to be trivially able to get to your data; and you do want to make it expensive and risky to spy on you. Some people say it's unreasonable to protect data from network access when somebody could get it easily by coming to your site physically. We don't agree; physical access is generally more expensive and more risky for an attacker than network access.

Stupidity and Accidents

Most disasters are not caused through ill will; they're accidents or stupid mistakes. One study estimates that 55 percent of all security incidents actually result from naive or untrained users doing things they shouldn't.*

Denial of service incidents, for example, frequently aren't attacks at all. Apple's corporate electronic mail was rendered nonfunctional for several days (and their network provider was severely inconvenienced) by an accident involving a single mail message sent from a buggy mail server to a large mailing list. The mail

---

* Richard Power, *Current and Future Danger: A CSI Primer on Computer Crime and Information Warfare* (San Francisco: Computer Security Institute, 1995).

resulted in a cascade of hundreds of thousands of error messages. The only hostile person involved was the system administrator, who wasn't hostile until he had to clean up the resulting mess.

Similarly, it's not uncommon for companies to destroy their own data or release it to the world by accident. Firewalls aren't designed to deal with this kind of problem. In fact, there is no known way to fully protect yourself from either accidents or stupidity. However, whether people are attacking you on purpose, or are simply making mistakes, the results are quite similar. (Hence the saying, "Never ascribe to malice that which can adequately be explained by stupidity".) When you protect yourself against evildoers, you also help protect yourself against the more common, but equally devastating, unintentional or well-intentioned error.

Theoretical Attacks

It's relatively easy to determine the risk involved in attacks that are currently under way, but what do you do about attacks that are theoretically possible but have not yet been used? It's very tempting to dismiss them altogether—after all, what matters to you is not what might happen to you, but what actually does happen to you. You don't really care if it's possible to do something, as long as nobody ever does it. So why should you worry if somebody produces a proof that an attack is possible, but it's so difficult that nobody is actually doing it?

- Because the limits on what's difficult change rapidly in computing.

- Because problems rarely come in isolation, and one attack that's too difficult may help people find an easier one.

- Because eventually people run out of easier attacks and turn to more difficult ones.

- And most importantly, because attacks move almost instantly from "never attempted" to "widely used".

The moment at which an attack is no longer merely theoretical, but is actually in use against your site, is that time that is technically called "too late". You certainly don't want to wait until then. You'll have a calmer and more peaceful life if you don't wait until the moment when an attack hits the newspaper headlines, either, and that's where a lot of theoretical attacks suddenly end up.

One computer vendor decided that a certain class of attacks, called *stack attacks,* were too difficult to exploit, and it was not worth trying to prevent them. These attacks are technically challenging on any hardware, and more difficult on their machines. It seemed unlikely that attackers would bother to go to the considerable effort necessary, and preventing the attacks required rewriting fundamental parts of the operating system. Thus, the vendor elected to avoid doing tedious and dangerous rewriting work to prevent what was then considered a purely theoretical risk. Six months later, somebody found and exploited one of the vulnerabilities; once the hard work had been done for one, the rest were easy, so that started a landslide of exploits and bad publicity.

Who Do You Trust?

Much of security is about trust; who do you trust to do what? The world doesn't work unless you trust some people to do some things, and security people sometimes seem to take an overly suspicious attitude, trusting nobody. Why shouldn't you trust your users, or rich, famous software vendors?

We all know that in day-to-day life there are various kinds of trust. There are people you would lend a thousand dollars but not tell a secret to; people you would ask to babysit but not lend a book to; people you love dearly but don't let touch the good china because they break things. The same is true in a computer context. Trusting your employees not to steal data and sell it is not the same thing as trusting them not to give it out by accident. Trusting your software vendor not to sell you software designed to destroy your computer is not at all the same thing as trusting the same vendor not to let other people destroy your computer.

You don't need to believe that the world is full of horrible, malicious people who are trying to attack you. You do need to believe that the world has *some* horrible, malicious people who are trying to attack you, and is full of really nice people who don't always pay attention to what they're doing.

When you give somebody private information, you're trusting them two ways. First, you're trusting them not to do anything bad with it; second, you're trusting them not to let anybody else steal it. Most of the time, most people worry about the first problem. In the computer context, you need to explicitly remember to think about the second problem. If you give somebody a credit card number on paper, you have a good idea what procedures are used to protect it, and you can influence them. If carbon sheets are used to make copies, you can destroy them. If you give somebody a credit card electronically, you are trusting not only their honesty but also their skill at computer security. It's perfectly reasonable to worry about the latter even if the former is impeccable.

If the people who use your computers and who write your software are all trustworthy computer security experts, great; but if they're not, decide whether you trust their expertise separately from deciding whether you trust their honesty.

How Can You Protect Your Site?

What approaches can you take to protect against the kinds of attacks we've out-lined in this chapter? People choose a variety of security models, or approaches, ranging from no security at all, through what's called "security through obscurity" and host security, to network security.

No Security

The simplest possible approach is to put no effort at all into security, and run with whatever minimal security your vendor provides you by default. If you're reading this book, you've probably already rejected this model.

Security Through Obscurity

Another possible security model is the one commonly referred to as *security through obscurity*. With this model, a system is presumed to be secure simply because (supposedly) nobody knows about it—its existence, contents, security measures, or anything else. This approach seldom works for long; there are just too many ways to find an attractive target. One of the authors had a system that had been connected to the Internet for only about an hour before someone attempted to break in. Luckily, the operating system that was in the process of being installed detected, denied, and logged the access attempts.

Many people assume that even though attackers can find them, the attackers won't bother to. They figure that a small company or a home machine just isn't going to be of interest to intruders. In fact, many intruders aren't aiming at particular tar-gets; they just want to break into as many machines as possible. To them, small companies and home machines simply look like easy targets. They probably won't stay long, but they will attempt to break in, and they may do considerable dam-age. They may also use compromised machines as platforms to attack other sites.

To function on any network, the Internet included, a site has to do at least a mini-mal amount of registration, and much of this registration information is available to anyone, just for the asking. Every time a site uses services on the network, someone—at the very least, whoever is providing the service—will know they're there. Intruders watch for new connections, in the hope that these sites won't yet have security measures in place. Some sites have reported automated probes apparently based on new site registrations.

You'd probably be amazed at how many different ways someone can determine security-sensitive information about your site. For example, knowing what hard-ware and software you have and what version of the operating system you're run-ning gives intruders important clues about what security holes they might try. They can often get this information from your host registration, or by trying to connect to your computer. Many computers disclose their type of operating system in the greeting you get before you log in, so an intruder doesn't need access to get it.

In addition, you send out all sorts of information when you deal with other sites on the Internet. Whenever you visit a web site, you tell that site what kind of browser you are running, and often what kind of machine you are using. Some email programs include this information in every piece of mail you send out.

Even if you manage to suppress all of these visible sources of information, intruders have scripts and programs that let them use much subtler clues. Although the Internet operates according to standards, there are always loopholes, or questionable situations. Different computers do different things when presented with exceptional situations, and intruders can figure out a lot by creating these situations and seeing what happens. Sometimes it's possible to figure out what kind of machine you're dealing with just by watching the sizes and timings it uses to send out data packets!

If all of that fails, intruders have a lot of time on their hands, and can often avoid having to figure out obscure facts by simply trying all the possibilities. In the long run, relying on obscurity is not a smart security choice.

Host Security

Probably the most common model for computer security is *host security*. With this model, you enforce the security of each host machine separately, and you make every effort to avoid or alleviate all the known security problems that might affect that particular host. What's wrong with host security? It's not that it doesn't work on individual machines; it's that it doesn't scale to large numbers of machines.

The major impediment to effective host security in modern computing environments is the complexity and diversity of those environments. Most modern environments include machines from multiple vendors, each with its own operating system, and each with its own set of security problems. Even if the site has machines from only one vendor, different releases of the same operating system often have significantly different security problems. Even if all these machines are from a single vendor and run a single release of the operating system, different configurations (different services enabled, and so on) can bring different subsystems into play (and into conflict) and lead to different sets of security problems. And, even if the machines are all absolutely identical, the sheer number of them at some sites can make securing them all difficult. It takes a significant amount of up-front and ongoing work to effectively implement and maintain host security. Even with all that work done correctly, host security still often fails due to bugs in vendor software, or due to a lack of suitably secure software for some required functions.

Host security also relies on the good intentions and the skill of everyone who has privileged access to any machine. As the number of machines increases, the number of privileged users generally increases as well. Securing a machine is much more difficult than attaching it to a network, so insecure machines may appear on your network as unexpected surprises. The mere fact that it is not supposed to be possible to buy or connect machines without consulting you is immaterial; people develop truly innovative purchasing and network-connection schemes if they feel the need.

A host security model may be highly appropriate for small sites, or sites with extreme security requirements. Indeed, all sites should include some level of host security in their overall security plans. Even if you adopt a network security model, as we describe in the next section, certain systems in your configuration will benefit from the strongest host security. For example, even if you have built a firewall around your internal network and systems, certain systems exposed to the outside world will need host security. (We discuss this in detail in Chapter 10, *Bastion Hosts*.) The problem is, the host security model alone just isn't cost-effective for any but small or simple sites; making it work requires too many restrictions and too many people.

Network Security

As environments grow larger and more diverse, and as securing them on a host-by-host basis grows more difficult, more sites are turning to a *network security* model. With a network security model, you concentrate on controlling network access to your various hosts and the services they offer, rather than on securing them one by one. Network security approaches include building firewalls to protect your internal systems and networks, using strong authentication approaches (such as one-time passwords), and using encryption to protect particularly sensitive data as it transits the network.

A site can get tremendous leverage from its security efforts by using a network security model. For example, a single network firewall of the type we discuss in this book can protect hundreds, thousands, or even tens of thousands of machines against attack from networks beyond the firewall, regardless of the level of host security of the individual machines.

This kind of leverage depends on the ability to control the access points to the network. At sites that are very large or very distributed, it may be impossible for one group of people to even identify all of those access points, much less control them. At that point, the network security model is no longer sufficient, and it's necessary to use layered security, combining a variety of different security approaches.

Although this book concentrates on network security, please note that we aren't suggesting you ignore host security. As mentioned previously, you should apply the strongest possible host security measures to your most important machines, especially to those machines that are directly connected to the Internet. (This is discussed in more detail in Chapter 10.) You'll also want to consider using host security on your internal machines in general, to address security problems other than attacks from the Internet.

No Security Model Can Do It All

No security model can solve all your problems. No security model—short of "maximum security prison"—can prevent a hostile person with legitimate access from purposefully damaging your site or taking confidential information out of it. To get around powerful host and network security measures, a legitimate user can simply use physical methods. These may range from pouring soda into your computers to carrying sensitive memos home. You can protect yourself from accidents and ignorance internally, and from malicious external acts, but you cannot protect yourself from your legitimate users without severely damaging their ability to use their computers. Spies succeed in breaching government security with depressing regularity despite regulations and precautions well beyond the resources and tolerance of civilians.

No security model can take care of management problems; computer security will not keep your people from wasting time, annoying each other, or embarrassing you. Sites often get sucked into trying to make security protect against these things. When people are wasting time surfing the Web, annoying each other by playing tricks with window systems, and embarrassing the company with horrible email, computer security looks like a promising technological solution that avoids difficult issues. However tempting this may be, a security model won't work here. It is expensive and difficult to even try to solve these problems with computer security, and you are once again in the impossible situation of trying to protect yourself from legitimate users.

No security model provides perfect protection. You can expect to make break-ins rare, brief, and inexpensive, but you can't expect to avoid them altogether. Even the most secure and dedicated sites expect to have a security incident every few years.*

---

* You can impress a security expert by saying you've been broken into only once in the last five years; if you say you've never been broken into, they stop being impressed and decide that either you can't detect break-ins, or you haven't been around long enough for anyone to try seriously!

Why bother, then? Security may not prevent every single incident, but it can keep an incident from seriously damaging or even shutting down your business. At one high-profile company with multiple computer facilities, a manager complained that his computer facility was supposed to be the most secure, but it got broken into along with several others. The difference was that the break-in was the first one that year for his facility; the intruder was present for only eight minutes; and the computer facility was off the Internet for only 12 hours (from 6 P.M. to 6 A.M.), after which it resumed business as usual with no visible interruption in service to the company's customers. For one of the other facilities, it was the fourth time; the intruder was present for months before being detected; recovery required taking the facility down for four days; and they had to inform customers that they had shipped them tapes containing possibly contaminated software. Proper security made the difference between an annoying occurrence and a devastating one.

What Is an Internet Firewall?

As we've mentioned, firewalls are a very effective type of network security. This section briefly describes what Internet firewalls can do for your overall site security. Chapter 5, *Firewall Technologies,* and Chapter 7, *Firewall Design,* define the firewall terms used in this book and describe the various types of firewalls in use today, and the other chapters in Part II and those in Part III describe the details of building those firewalls.

In building construction, a firewall is designed to keep a fire from spreading from one part of the building to another. In theory, an Internet firewall serves a similar purpose: it prevents the dangers of the Internet from spreading to your internal network. In practice, an Internet firewall is more like a moat of a medieval castle than a firewall in a modern building. It serves multiple purposes:

- It restricts people to entering at a carefully controlled point.
- It prevents attackers from getting close to your other defenses.
- It restricts people to leaving at a carefully controlled point.

An Internet firewall is most often installed at the point where your protected internal network connects to the Internet, as shown in Figure 1-1.

All traffic coming from the Internet or going out from your internal network passes through the firewall. Because the traffic passes through it, the firewall has the opportunity to make sure that this traffic is acceptable.

What does "acceptable" mean to the firewall? It means that whatever is being done—email, file transfers, remote logins, or any kinds of specific interactions between specific systems—conforms to the security policy of the site. Security

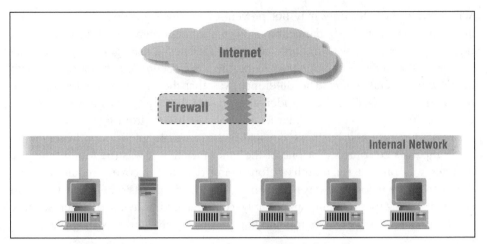

Figure 1-1. A firewall usually separates an internal network from the Internet

policies are different for every site; some are highly restrictive and others fairly open, as we'll discuss in Chapter 25, *Security Policies*.

Logically, a firewall is a separator, a restricter, an analyzer. The physical implementation of the firewall varies from site to site. Most often, a firewall is a set of hardware components—a router, a host computer, or some combination of routers, computers, and networks with appropriate software. There are various ways to configure this equipment; the configuration will depend upon a site's particular security policy, budget, and overall operations.

A firewall is very rarely a single physical object, although some commercial products attempt to put everything into the same box. Usually, a firewall has multiple parts, and some of these parts may do other tasks besides function as part of the firewall. Your Internet connection is almost always part of your firewall. Even if you have a firewall in a box, it isn't going to be neatly separable from the rest of your site; it's not something you can just drop in.

We've compared a firewall to the moat of a medieval castle, and like a moat, a firewall is not invulnerable. It doesn't protect against people who are already inside; it works best if coupled with internal defenses; and, even if you stock it with alligators, people sometimes manage to swim across. A firewall is also not without its drawbacks; building one requires significant expense and effort, and the restrictions it places on insiders can be a major annoyance.

Given the limitations and drawbacks of firewalls, why would anybody bother to install one? Because a firewall is the most effective way to connect a network to the Internet and still protect that network. The Internet presents marvelous opportunities. Millions of people are out there exchanging information. The benefits are obvious: the chances for publicity, customer service, and information gathering. The popularity of the information superhighway is increasing everybody's desire to get out there. The risks should also be obvious: any time you get millions of people together, you get crime; it's true in a city, and it's true on the Internet. Any superhighway is fun only while you're in a car. If you have to live or work by the highway, it's loud, smelly, and dangerous.

How can you benefit from the good parts of the Internet without being overwhelmed by the bad? Just as you'd like to drive on a highway without suffering the nasty effects of putting a freeway off-ramp into your living room, you need to carefully control the contact that your network has to the Internet. A firewall is a tool for doing that, and in most situations, it's the single most effective tool for doing that.

There are other uses of firewalls. For example, they can be used to divide parts of a site from each other when these parts have distinct security needs (and we'll discuss these uses in passing, as appropriate). The focus of this book, however, is on firewalls as they're used between a site and the Internet.

Firewalls offer significant benefits, but they can't solve every security problem. The following sections briefly summarize what firewalls can and cannot do to protect your systems and your data.

What Can a Firewall Do?

Firewalls can do a lot for your site's security. In fact, some advantages of using firewalls extend even beyond security, as described in the sections that follow.

A firewall is a focus for security decisions

Think of a firewall as a choke point. All traffic in and out must pass through this single, narrow choke point. A firewall gives you an enormous amount of leverage for network security because it lets you concentrate your security measures on this choke point: the point where your network connects to the Internet.

Focusing your security in this way is far more efficient than spreading security decisions and technologies around, trying to cover all the bases in a piecemeal fashion. Although firewalls can cost tens of thousands of dollars to implement, most sites find that concentrating the most effective security hardware and software at the firewall is less expensive and more effective than other security measures—and certainly less expensive than having inadequate security.

A firewall can enforce a security policy

Many of the services that people want from the Internet are inherently insecure. The firewall is the traffic cop for these services. It enforces the site's security policy, allowing only "approved" services to pass through and those only within the rules set up for them.

For example, one site's management may decide that certain services are simply too risky to be used across the firewall, no matter what system tries to run them or what user wants them. The firewall will keep potentially dangerous services strictly inside the firewall. (There, they can still be used for insiders to attack each other, but that's outside of the firewall's control.) Another site might decide that only one internal system can communicate with the outside world. Still another site might decide to allow access from all systems of a certain type, or belonging to a certain group. The variations in site security policies are endless.

A firewall may be called upon to help enforce more complicated policies. For example, perhaps only certain systems within the firewall are allowed to transfer files to and from the Internet; by using other mechanisms to control which users have access to those systems, you can control which users have these capabilities. Depending on the technologies you choose to implement your firewall, a firewall may have a greater or lesser ability to enforce such policies.

A firewall can log Internet activity efficiently

Because all traffic passes through the firewall, the firewall provides a good place to collect information about system and network use—and misuse. As a single point of access, the firewall can record what occurs between the protected network and the external network.

A firewall limits your exposure

Although this point is most relevant to the use of internal firewalls, which we describe in Chapter 6, *Firewall Architectures*, it's worth mentioning here. Sometimes, a firewall will be used to keep one section of your site's network separate from another section. By doing this, you keep problems that impact one section from spreading through the entire network. In some cases, you'll do this because one section of your network may be more trusted than another; in other cases, because one section is more sensitive than another. Whatever the reason, the existence of the firewall limits the damage that a network security problem can do to the overall network.

What Can't a Firewall Do?

Firewalls offer excellent protection against network threats, but they aren't a complete security solution. Certain threats are outside the control of the firewall. You need to figure out other ways to protect against these threats by incorporating physical security, host security, and user education into your overall security plan. Some of the weaknesses of firewalls are discussed in the sections that follow.

A firewall can't protect you against malicious insiders

A firewall might keep a system user from being able to send proprietary information out of an organization over a network connection; so would simply not having a network connection. But that same user could copy the data onto disk, tape, or paper and carry it out of the building in his or her briefcase.

If the attacker is already inside the firewall—if the fox is inside the henhouse—a firewall can do virtually nothing for you. Inside users can steal data, damage hardware and software, and subtly modify programs without ever coming near the firewall. Insider threats require internal security measures, such as host security and user education. Such topics are beyond the scope of this book.

A firewall can't protect you against connections that don't go through it

A firewall can effectively control the traffic that passes through it; however, there is nothing a firewall can do about traffic that doesn't pass through it. For example, what if the site allows dial-in access to internal systems behind the firewall? The firewall has absolutely no way of preventing an intruder from getting in through such a modem.

Sometimes, technically expert users or system administrators set up their own "back doors" into the network (such as a dial-up modem connection), either temporarily or permanently, because they chafe at the restrictions that the firewall places upon them and their systems. The firewall can do nothing about this. It's really a people-management problem, not a technical problem.

A firewall can't protect against completely new threats

A firewall is designed to protect against known threats. A well-designed one may also protect against some new threats. (For example, by denying any but a few trusted services, a firewall will prevent people from setting up new and insecure services.) However, no firewall can automatically defend against every new threat that arises. People continuously discover new ways to attack, using previously trustworthy services, or using attacks that simply hadn't occurred to anyone before. You can't set up a firewall once and expect it to protect you forever. (See Chapter 26, *Maintaining Firewalls*, for advice on keeping your firewall up to date.)

A firewall can't fully protect against viruses

Firewalls can't keep computer viruses out of a network. It's true that all firewalls scan incoming traffic to some degree, and some firewalls even offer virus protection. However, firewalls don't offer very good virus protection.

Detecting a virus in a random packet of data passing through a firewall is very difficult; it requires:

- Recognizing that the packet is part of a program
- Determining what the program should look like
- Determining that a change in the program is because of a virus

Even the first of these is a challenge. Most firewalls are protecting machines of multiple types with different executable formats. A program may be a compiled executable or a script (e.g., a Unix shell script or a Microsoft batch file), and many machines support multiple, compiled executable types. Furthermore, most programs are packaged for transport and are often compressed as well. Packages being transferred via email or Usenet news will also have been encoded into ASCII in different ways.

For all of these reasons, users may end up bringing viruses behind the firewall, no matter how secure that firewall is. Even if you could do a perfect job of blocking viruses at the firewall, however, you still haven't addressed the virus problem. You've done nothing about the other sources of viruses: software downloaded from dial-up bulletin-board systems, software brought in on floppies from home or other sites, and even software that comes pre-infected from manufacturers are just as common as virus-infected software on the Internet. Whatever you do to address those threats will also address the problem of software transferred through the firewall.

The most practical way to address the virus problem is through host-based virus protection software, and user education concerning the dangers of viruses and precautions to take against them. Virus filtering on the firewall may be a useful adjunct to this sort of precaution, but it will never completely solve the problem.

A firewall can't set itself up correctly

Every firewall needs some amount of configuration. Every site is slightly different, and it's just not possible for a firewall to magically work correctly when you take it out of the box. Correct configuration is absolutely essential. A misconfigured firewall may be providing only the illusion of security. There's nothing wrong with illusions, as long as they're confusing the other side. A burglar alarm system that consists entirely of some impressive warning stickers and a flashing red light can actually be effective, as long as you don't believe that there's anything else going on. But you know better than to use it on network security, where the warning stickers and the flashing red light are going to be invisible. Unfortunately, many people have firewalls that are in the end no more effective than that, because they've been configured with fundamental problems. A firewall is not a magical protective device that will fix your network security problems no matter what you do with it, and treating it as if it is such a device will merely increase your risk.

What's Wrong with Firewalls?

There are two main arguments against using firewalls:

- Firewalls interfere with the way the Internet is supposed to work, introducing all sorts of problems, annoying users, and slowing down the introduction of new Internet services.

- The problems firewalls don't deal with (internal threats and external connections that don't go through the firewall) are more important than the problems they do deal with.

Firewalls interfere with the Internet

It's true that the Internet is based on a model of end-to-end communication, where individual hosts talk to each other. Firewalls interrupt that end-to-end communication in a variety of ways. Most of the problems that are introduced are the same sorts of problems that are introduced by any security measure. Things are slowed down; things that you want to get through can't; it's hard to introduce changes. Having badge readers on doors introduces the same sorts of problems (you have to swipe the badge and wait for the door to open; when your friends come to meet you they can't get in; new employees have to get badges). The difference is that on the Internet there's a political and emotional attachment to the idea that information is supposed to flow freely and change is supposed to happen rapidly. People are much less willing to accept the sorts of restrictions that they're accustomed to in other environments.

Furthermore, it's truly very annoying to have side effects. There are a number of ways of doing things that provide real advantages and are limited in their spread by firewalls, despite the fact that they aren't security problems. For instance, broadcasting audio and video over the Internet is much easier if you can use multiple simultaneous connections, and if you can get quite precise information about the capabilities of the destination host and the links between you and it. However, firewalls have difficulty managing the connections, they intentionally conceal some information about the destination host, and they unintentionally destroy other information. If you're trying to develop new ways of interacting over the Internet, firewalls are incredibly frustrating; everywhere you turn, there's something cool that TCP/IP is supposed to be able to do that just doesn't work in the real world. It's no wonder that application developers hate firewalls.

Unfortunately, they don't have any better suggestions for how to keep the bad guys out. Think how many marvelous things you could have if you didn't have to

lock your front door to keep strangers out; you wouldn't have to sit at home waiting for the repairman or for a package to be delivered, just as a start. The need for
security is unavoidable in our world, and it limits what we can do, in annoying
ways. The development of the Internet has not changed human nature.

Firewalls don't deal with the real problem

You also hear people say that firewalls are the wave of the past because they
don't deal with the real problems. It's true that firewall or no firewall, intruders get
in, secret data goes out, and bad things happen. At sites with really good firewalls, these things occur by avoiding the firewalls. At sites that don't have really
good firewalls, these things may go on through the firewalls. Either way, you can
argue that this shows that firewalls don't solve the problem.

It's perfectly true, firewalls won't solve your security problem. Once again, the
people who point this out don't really have anything better to offer. Protecting
individual hosts works for some sites and will help the firewall almost anywhere;
detecting and dealing with attacks via network monitoring, once again, will work
for some problems and will help a firewall almost anywhere. That's basically the
entire list of available alternatives. If you look closely at most of the things promoted as being "better than firewalls", you'll discover that they're lightly disguised
firewalls marketed by people with restrictive definitions of what a firewall is.

Religious Arguments

The world is full of "religious arguments", philosophical debates on which people
hold strong and divisive beliefs. Firewalls are no exception to this rule.

Buying Versus Building

Initially, if a site wanted a firewall, they had little choice but to design and build it
themselves (perhaps with their own staff, or perhaps by hiring a consultant or con-
tractor). Over the years, however, more and more commercial firewall offerings
have reached the market. These products continue to grow in number and functionality at an astounding rate, and many sites may find that one of these products
suits their needs. Most sites find that commercial products are at least a valuable
component of their firewall solution.

In deciding whether or not a particular commercial firewall product will meet your
needs, you have to understand what your needs are. Even if you decide to buy a
firewall, you still need to understand a fair bit about how they're built and how
they work in order to make an informed purchasing decision. Many sites spend as
much or more effort evaluating commercial firewall products as they would building their own firewall.

We're not saying that nobody should buy a firewall, or that everybody should build their own. Our point is merely that it's not necessarily any easier to buy than it is to build; it all depends on your particular situation and what resources you have at your disposal. Sites with money to spend but little staff time or expertise available often find buying an attractive solution, while sites with expertise and time but little money often find building more attractive.

Just what expertise do you need to design and build your own firewall? Like everything else, it depends; it depends on what services you want to provide, what platforms you're using, what your security concerns are, and so on. To install most of the tools described in this book, you need basic Internet skills to obtain the tools, and basic system administration skills to configure, compile, and install them. If you don't know what those skills are, you probably don't have them; you can obtain them, but that's beyond the scope of this book.

Some people feel uncomfortable using software that's freely available on the Internet, particularly for security-critical applications. We feel that the advantages outweigh the disadvantages. You may not have the "guarantees" offered by vendors, but you have the ability to inspect the source code and to share information with the large community that helps to maintain the software. In practice, vendors come and go, but the community endures. The packages we discuss in this book are widely used; many of the largest sites on the Internet base their firewalls on them. These packages reflect years of real-life experience with the Internet and its risks.

Other people feel uncomfortable using commercial software for security-critical applications, feeling that you can't trust software unless you can read the code. While there are real advantages to having code available, auditing code is difficult, and few people can do an adequate job on a package of any significant size. Commercial software has its own advantages; when you buy software you have a legal contract with somebody, which may give you some recourse if things go wrong.

Frequently, people argue that open source software is more risky than commercial software because attackers have access to the source code. In practice, the attackers have access to all the source code they need, including commercial source code. If it's not given to them, they steal or reverse-engineer it; they have the motivation and time, and they don't have ethical constraints. There's no distinction between programs on this point.

While it's perfectly possible to build a firewall consisting solely of freely available software or solely of commercial software, there's no reason to feel that it's all or nothing; freely available tools provide a valuable complement to purchased solutions. Buying a firewall shouldn't make you reluctant to supplement with freely

Software, Freedom, and Money

A number of terms are used for various kinds of software that you may (or may not) be able to use without paying money to anybody:

Free software

> This term is unfortunately ambiguous; sometimes it means software that you don't have to pay for ("free software" like "free beer"), and sometimes it refers to software that has been liberated from certain kinds of constraints, by very carefully tying it up with others ("free software" like "free speech"). In practice, you cannot be sure that it means anything at all, although it strongly implies that you will be able to use the software without paying for it (but not necessarily resell it in any form).

Freely available software

> This term clearly means software that you don't have to pay for, although it is sometimes used for software that only some classes of users have to pay for (for instance, software that is free to individuals but costs money for corporations).

Public domain software

> Although this term is often carelessly used, it has a specific legal meaning and refers to software that is free of copyright restrictions and may be used in any way whatsoever without the permission of the author. Software is public domain only if it is clearly marked as such; software that contains a copyright notice or use restrictions is not public domain. You may copy public domain software without paying for it, but because there are no use restrictions, nothing keeps people from charging you money for it anyway.

Open source software

> Open source software is software that you can get the source code for without a fee. In most cases, you may also use it, at least for some purposes, without paying, although licensing restrictions will usually prevent you from selling it to anybody else.

available tools, and building one shouldn't make you reluctant to supplement with purchased tools. Don't rule out a product just because it's commercial, or just because it's freely available. Truly excellent products with great support appear in both categories, as do poorly thought out products with no support.

Unix Versus Windows NT

Building a firewall requires at least one Internet-aware server (and often more than one). Until relatively recently, the only popular platform that provided the necessary services was Unix. These days, Windows NT also has the necessary characteristics; it provides a security-aware and network-aware multi-user operating system and is widely used.

Many people argue violently about which is better, Unix or Windows NT, in every domain. These arguments are particularly vociferous when it comes to firewalls, where Unix people tend to say that Windows NT machines are simply unsuited to building firewalls, and Windows NT people say that this is pure prejudice.

The truth, as always, is somewhere between the two camps. The Unix people who complain about Windows NT are usually working from a basis of both prejudice and ignorance, and have an annoying tendency to misconfigure machines and then complain that they don't work. A properly configured Windows NT machine is a reasonable machine for building a firewall.

On the other hand, Windows NT machines are genuinely more difficult to configure properly for firewalls, for two reasons. The most widely cited Windows NT problem has to do with the way Windows NT implements the TCP/IP networking standards. Unix is one of the earliest systems to do TCP/IP, and many Unix implementations of TCP/IP share a more than 20-year common heritage. In that time, they've seen almost every way you can torture a networking protocol, and they've been made quite reliable. Microsoft reimplemented TCP/IP from scratch for Windows NT, and the resulting code has problems that have faded into distant memories for Unix (or never existed; different programmers make different mistakes). An unstable TCP/IP implementation is a real problem in a firewall, which may be exposed to a lot of hostile or incompetent programs doing eccentric things with TCP/IP.

On the other hand, it's not as big a problem as many people give it credit for. Many ways of designing a firewall put a packet filtering router, built on a specialized, robust, and quickly upgradeable TCP/IP implementation, in front of any general-purpose computer in any case. In these designs, the router can offer some protection to Windows NT machines. Windows NT's TCP/IP implementation is also catching up rapidly, because problems with it tend to be extremely visible (once somebody's crashed a few hundred thousand hosts, people tend to take notice). It is painful to have to upgrade the operating system on your firewall, and the low-level TCP/IP is one of the most risky and painful parts to have to upgrade, so changes that come out after your machines are installed are not very comforting, but it is probable that most of the worst problems have been found already.

The second difficulty in securing Windows NT is more fundamental. Windows NT is designed to be opaque; things are supposed to just work without administrators knowing how they work. This simplifies the process of setting up a machine, as long as you want to set it up to do something expected. It vastly complicates the process of evaluating the machine's security, setting it up to do something unexpected (like run in a highly secure environment), or modifying the way it behaves.

Your average Windows NT machine looks less complex than your average Unix machine but actually supports many more protocols. Unix machines tend to provide a fairly straightforward set of TCP/IP services, while Windows NT machines provide servers and/or clients for most of those, plus support for multiple generations of Microsoft protocols, and optional support for NetWare and AppleTalk. Go to your local bookstore and look at the shelves of books for Windows NT compared to the shelves of books for Unix. Some of the difference is in popularity; some of the difference has to do with the economics of certification; but a lot of the difference is that Windows NT is just more complicated than Unix, and in security, complexity is bad.

Unix administrators who complain about Windows NT's complexities aren't merely ignorant (although the shock of learning a new operating system does have something to do with it), nor are they simply trying the wrong approach. Windows NT really is extremely complicated and difficult to understand, and in a security context, you do need to understand it. Trusting vendors to provide a secure solution is not going to be satisfactory for a site of any significant size.

That doesn't mean Windows NT is entirely unsuited to building firewalls. It may be complicated, but Unix isn't exactly trivial. A firewall is not a good place to learn a new operating system. Even commercial firewalls require some basic competency with the operating system they run on, in order to secure the base operating system and manage the software. If you're already experienced in Windows NT, you're better off using it and learning the previously hidden parts than trying to learn Unix from scratch. If you're experienced in Unix, you are still going to make stupid beginner mistakes trying to run Windows NT, even in a prepackaged commercial firewall.

If you find yourself stuck putting machines of the type you don't understand into your firewall, don't panic. You can survive the experience and come out of it with your security intact, and you might as well do it with as much grace as possible. Expect it to be difficult and confusing, and keep an open mind. You'll need basic training on the operating system as well as this book, which assumes that you are able to do normal administrative tasks already.

That's Not a Firewall!

The world is full of people eager to assure you that something is not a firewall; it's "just a packet filter" or maybe it's "better than a mere firewall". If it's supposed to keep the bad guys out of your network, it's a firewall. If it succeeds in keeping the bad guys out, while still letting you happily use your network, it's a good firewall; if it doesn't, it's a bad firewall. That's all there is to it.

2

Internet Services

In Chapter 1, *Why Internet Firewalls?*, we discussed, in general terms, what you're trying to protect when you connect to the Internet: your data, your resources, and your reputation. In designing an Internet firewall, your concerns are more specific: what you need to protect are those services you're going to use or provide over the Internet.

There are a number of standard Internet services that users want and that most sites try to support. There are important reasons to use these services; indeed, without them, there is little reason to be connected to the Internet at all. But there are also potential security problems with each of them.

What services do you want to support at your site? Which ones can you support securely? Every site is different. Every site has its own security policy and its own working environment. For example, do all your users need electronic mail? Do they all need to transfer files to sites outside your organization? How about downloading files from sites outside the organization's own network? What information do you need to make available to the public on the Web? What sort of control do you want over web browsing from within your site? Who should be able to log in remotely from another location over the Internet?

This chapter briefly summarizes the major Internet services your users may be interested in using. It provides only a high-level summary (details are given in later chapters). None of these services are really secure; each one has its own security weaknesses, and each has been exploited in various ways by attackers. Before you decide to support a service at your site, you will have to assess how important it is to your users and whether you will be able to protect them from its dangers. There are various ways of doing this: running the services only on certain protected machines; using especially secure variants of the standard services; or, in some cases, blocking the services completely to or from some or all outside systems.

This chapter doesn't list every Internet service—it can't. Such a list would be incomplete as soon as it was finished and would include services of interest only to a few sites in the world. Instead, we attempt to list the major services, and we hope this book will give you the background you need to make decisions about new services as you encounter them.

Managers and system administrators together need to decide which services to support at your site and to what extent. This is a continuous process; you will change your decisions as new services become available and as your needs change. These decisions are the single most important factor in determining how secure your site will be, much more important than the precise type of technology you use in implementing them. No firewall can protect you from things you have explicitly chosen to allow through it.

Getting Started with Internet Services

Are you just getting connected? Or, have you been connected for a while but are getting concerned about Internet security? Where should you start? Many system administrators try to be too ambitious. If you attempt to develop and deploy the be-all and end-all of firewall systems right from day one, you probably aren't going to succeed. The field is just too complex, and the technology is changing so fast that it will change out from under you before you get such an endeavor "finished".

Start small. At many sites, it boils down to five basic services. If you can provide these services securely, most of your users will be satisfied, at least for a while.

- World Wide Web access (HTTP).

- Electronic mail (SMTP).

- File transfer (FTP).

- Remote terminal access (Telnet or preferably SSH).

- Hostname/address lookup (DNS): Users generally don't use this service directly, but it underlies the other four services by translating Internet hostnames to IP addresses and vice versa.

All five of these services can be safely provided in a number of different ways, including packet filtering and proxies—firewall approaches discussed in Part II of this book. Providing these services lets your users access most Internet resources, and it buys you time to figure out how to provide the rest of the services they'll be asking for soon.

Secure Services and Safe Services

You will occasionally hear people talk about "secure services". They are referring to services that give two kinds of guarantees:

1. The service cannot be used for anything but its intended purpose, and/or

2. Other people can't read or falsify transactions with the service.

That doesn't actually mean that you can use the service to do anything whatsoever and still be safe. For instance, you can use Secure HTML to download a file, and be sure that you are downloading exactly the file that the site intended you to download, and that nobody else has read it on the way past. But you have no guarantee that the file doesn't contain a virus or an evil program. Maybe the site is run by somebody nasty.

It is also possible to use "insecure" services in secure ways—it just has to be done with more caution. For instance, electronic mail over Simple Mail Transfer Protocol (SMTP) is a classic example of an "insecure" service. However, if you carefully configure your mail servers and encrypt message bodies, you can achieve the goals mentioned previously. (This still won't save you if somebody mails you an evil program and you run it!)

Similarly, chain saws are extremely unsafe objects, but people still use them regularly with appropriate precautions and very little risk. Plastic bags are really quite safe objects, but you can still hurt yourself with one in a variety of ways, ranging from putting it over your head and suffocating, to slipping on one on the stairs and breaking your leg. When you evaluate the security of a service, you should be sure that you're thinking of its security implications to your environment in your intended configurations—whether or not it's "secure" or "safe" in the abstract is not of any great interest. For further information about evaluating services and their security, see Chapter 13, *Internet Services and Firewalls*.

The World Wide Web

These days, the World Wide Web has become so popular that many people think it is the Internet. If you aren't on the Web, you aren't anybody. Unfortunately, although the Web is based primarily on a single protocol (HTTP), web sites often use a wide variety of protocols, downloadable code, and plug-ins, which have a wide variety of security implications. It has become impossible to reliably configure a browser so that you can always read everything on every web site; it has always been insecure to do so.

Many people confuse the functions and origins of the Web, Netscape, Microsoft Internet Explorer, HTTP, and HTML, and the terminology used to refer to these distinct entities has become muddy. Some of the muddiness was introduced intentionally; web browsers attempt to provide a seamless interface to a wide variety of information through a wide variety of mechanisms, and blurring the distinctions makes it easier to use, if more difficult to comprehend. Here is a quick summary of what the individual entities are about:

The Web

The collection of HTTP servers (see the description of HTTP that follows) on the Internet. The Web is responsible, in large part, for the recent explosion in Internet activity. It is based on concepts developed at the European Particle Physics Laboratory (CERN) in Geneva, Switzerland, by Tim Berners-Lee and others. Much of the ground-breaking work on web clients was done at the National Center for Supercomputing Applications (NCSA) at the University of Illinois in Urbana-Champaign. Many organizations and individuals are developing web client and server software these days, and many more are using these technologies for a huge range of purposes. The Internet Engineering Task Force (IETF) is currently responsible for maintaining the HTTP standard, and the World Wide Web Consortium (W3C) is developing successors to HTML (see Appendix A, *Resources*, for more information about these organizations). Nobody "controls" the Web, however, much as nobody "controls" the Internet.

HTTP

The primary application protocol that underlies the Web: it provides users access to the files that make up the Web. These files might be in many different formats (text, graphics, audio, video, etc.), but the format used to provide the links between files on the Web is the HyperText Markup Language (HTML).

HTML

A standardized page description language for creating web pages. It provides basic document-formatting capabilities (including the ability to include graphics) and allows you to specify hypertext links to other servers and files.

Netscape Navigator and Microsoft Internet Explorer

Commonly known as "Netscape" and "Explorer", these commercial products are web browsers (they let you read documents via HTTP and other protocols). There are hundreds of other web browsers, including Lynx, Opera, Slurp, Go!Zilla, and perlWWW, but most estimates show that the vast majority of web users are using Netscape or Explorer. HTTP is only one protocol used by web browsers; web browsers typically also can use at least the FTP, NNTP, SMTP, and POP protocols. Some of them also can use other protocols like WAIS, Gopher, and IMAP. Thus, when users say "we want Explorer" or "we want Netscape", what they really mean, from a protocol level, is that they want access to the HTTP servers that make up the Web, and probably to associated servers running other protocols that the web browsers can use (for instance, FTP, SMTP, and/or NNTP).

Web Client Security Issues

Web browsers are fantastically popular and for good reason. They provide a rich graphical interface to an immense number of Internet resources. Information and services that were unavailable or expert-only before are now easily accessible. In Silicon Valley, you can use the Web to have dinner delivered without leaving your computer except to answer the door. It's hard to get a feel for the Web without experiencing it; it covers the full range of everything you can do with a computer, from the mundane to the sublime with a major side trip into the ridiculous.

Unfortunately, web browsers and servers are hard to secure. The usefulness of the Web is in large part based on its flexibility, but that flexibility makes control difficult. Just as it's easier to transfer and execute the right program from a web browser than from FTP, it's easier to transfer and execute a malicious one. Web browsers depend on external programs, generically called *viewers* (even if they play sounds instead of showing pictures), to deal with data types that the browsers themselves don't understand. (The browsers generally understand basic data types such as HTML, plain text, and JPEG and GIF graphics.) Netscape and Explorer now support a mechanism (designed to replace external viewers) that allows third parties to produce *plug-ins* that can be downloaded to become an integrated and seamless extension to the web browser. You should be very careful about which viewers and plug-ins you configure or download; you don't want something that can do dangerous things because it's going to be running on your computers, as if it were one of your users, taking commands from an external source. You also want to warn users not to download plug-ins, add viewers, or change viewer configurations, based on advice from strangers.

In addition, most browsers also understand one or more extension systems (Java™, JavaScript, or ActiveX, for instance). These systems make the browsers more powerful and more flexible, but they also introduce new problems. Whereas HTML is primarily a text-formatting language, with a few extensions for hypertext linking, the extension systems provide many more capabilities; they can do anything you can do with a traditional programming language. Their designers recognize that this creates security problems. Traditionally, when you get a new program you know that you are receiving a program, and you know where it came from and whether you trust it. If you buy a program at a computer store, you know that the company that produced it had to go to the trouble of printing up the packaging and convincing the computer store to buy it and put it up for sale. This is probably too much trouble for an attacker to go to, and it leaves a trail that's hard to cover up. If you decide to download a program, you don't have as much evidence about it, but you have some. If a program arrives on your machine invisibly when you decide to look at something else, you have almost no information about where it came from and what sort of trust you should give it.

The designers of JavaScript, VBScript, Java, and ActiveX took different approaches to this problem. JavaScript and VBScript are simply supposed to be unable to do anything dangerous; the languages do not have commands for writing files, for instance, or general-purpose extension mechanisms. Java uses what's called a "sandbox" approach. Java does contain commands that could be dangerous, and general-purpose extension mechanisms, but the Java interpreter is supposed to prevent an untrusted program from doing anything unfortunate, or at least ask you before it does anything dangerous. For instance, a Java program running inside the sandbox cannot write or read files without notification. Unfortunately, there have been implementation problems with Java, and various ways have been found to do operations that are supposed to be impossible.

In any case, a program that can't do anything dangerous has difficulty doing anything interesting. Children get tired of playing in a sandbox relatively young, and so do programmers.

ActiveX, instead of trying to limit a program's abilities, tries to make sure that you know where the program comes from and can simply avoid running programs you don't trust. This is done via digital signatures; before an ActiveX program runs, a browser will display signature information that identifies the provider of the program, and you can decide whether or not you trust that provider. Unfortunately, it is difficult to make good decisions about whether or not to trust a program with nothing more than the name of the program's source. Is "Jeff's Software Hut" trustworthy? Can you be sure that the program you got from them doesn't send them all the data on your hard disk?

As time goes by, people are providing newer, more flexible models of security that allow you to indicate different levels of trust for different sources. New versions of Java are introducing digital signatures and allowing you to decide that programs with specific signatures can do specific unsafe operations. Similarly, new versions of ActiveX are allowing you to limit which ActiveX operations are available to programs. There is a long way to go before the two models come together, and there will be real problems even then. Even if you don't have to decide to trust Jeff's Software Hut completely or not at all, you still have to make a decision about what level of trust to give them, and you still won't have much data to make it with. What if Jeff's Software Hut is a vendor you've worked with for years, and suddenly something comes around from Jeff's Software House? Is that the same people, upgrading their image, or is that somebody using their reputation?

Because programs in extension systems are generally embedded inside HTML documents, it is difficult for firewalls to filter them out without introducing other problems. For further discussion of extension systems, see Chapter 15, *The World Wide Web*.

Because an HTML document can easily link to documents on other servers, it's easy for people to become confused about exactly who is responsible for a given document. "Frames" (where the external web page takes up only part of the display) are particularly bad in this respect. New users may not notice when they go from internal documents at your site to external ones. This has two unfortunate consequences. First, they may trust external documents inappropriately (because they think they're internal documents). Second, they may blame the internal web maintainers for the sins of the world. People who understand the Web tend to find this hard to believe, but it's a common misconception: it's the dark side of having a very smooth transition between sites. Take care to educate users, and attempt to make clear what data is internal and what data is external.

Web Server Security Issues

When you run a web server, you are allowing anybody who can reach your machine to send commands to it. If the web server is configured to provide only HTML files, the commands it will obey are quite limited. However, they may still be more than you'd expect; for instance, many people assume that people can't see files unless there are explicit links to them, which is generally false. You should assume that if the web server program is capable of reading a file, it is capable of providing that file to a remote user. Files that should not be public should at least be protected by file permissions, and should, if possible, be placed outside of the web server's accessible area (preferably by moving them off the machine altogether).

Most web servers, however, provide services beyond merely handing out HTML files. For instance, many of them come with administrative servers, allowing you to reconfigure the server itself from a web browser. If you can configure the server from a web browser, so can anybody else who can reach it; be sure to do the initial configuration in a trusted environment. If you are building or installing a web server, be sure to read the installation instructions. It is worthwhile checking the security resources mentioned in Appendix A, *Resources*, for problems.

Web servers can also call external programs in a variety of ways. You can get external programs from vendors, either as programs that will run separately or as plug-ins that will run as part of the web server, and you can write your own programs in a variety of different languages and using a variety of different tools. These programs are relatively easy to write but very difficult to secure, because they can receive arbitrary commands from external people. You should treat all programs run from the web server, no matter who wrote them or what they're called, with the same caution you would treat a new server of any kind. The web server does not provide any significant protection to these programs. A large number of third-party server extensions originally ship with security flaws, generally caused by the assumption that input to them is always going to come from well-behaved forms. This is not a safe assumption; there is no guarantee that people are going to use your forms and your web pages to access your web server. They can send any data they like to it.

A number of software (and hardware) products are now appearing with embedded web servers that provide a convenient graphical configuration interface. These products should be carefully configured if they are running on systems that can be accessed by outsiders. In general, their default configurations are insecure.

Electronic Mail and News

Electronic mail and news provide ways for people to exchange information with each other without requiring an immediate, interactive response.

Electronic Mail

Electronic mail is one of the most popular network services. It's relatively low risk, but that doesn't mean it's risk-free. Forging electronic mail is trivial (just as is forging regular postal mail), and forgeries facilitate two different types of attacks:

- Attacks against your reputation

- Social manipulation attacks (e.g., attacks in which users are sent mail purporting to come from an administrator and advising them to change to a specific password)

Accepting electronic mail ties up computer time and disk space, opening you up to denial of service attacks, although with proper configuration, only the electronic mail service will be denied. Particularly with modern multimedia mail systems, people can send electronic mail containing programs that run with insufficient supervision and may turn out to be Trojan horses (programs that appear to do something interesting or useful but are actually concealing hostile operations).

Although people worry most about deliberate attacks, in practice, the most common problems with electronic mail are inadvertent floods (including chain letters) and people who put entirely inappropriate confidence in the confidentiality of electronic mail and send proprietary data via electronic mail across the Internet. However, as long as users are educated, and the mail service is isolated from other services so that inadvertent or purposeful denial of service attacks shut down as little as possible, electronic mail is reasonably safe.

Simple Mail Transfer Protocol (SMTP) is the Internet standard protocol for sending and receiving electronic mail; mail going between servers on the Internet almost always uses SMTP, and outgoing mail from clients to servers often does. SMTP itself is not usually a security problem, but SMTP servers can be. A program that delivers mail to users often needs to be able to run as any user that might receive mail. This gives it broad power and makes it a tempting target for attackers.

Mail servers, like other programs, have a trade-off between features and security. You probably do not want to use the same server for your internal mail exchange and for exchanging mail with the Internet. Instead, you'll want to use a full-featured server internally and a highly secure server to speak to the Internet. The internal server will run the well-known software you're used to using, while the external server will run specialized software. Because SMTP is designed to pass mail through multiple servers, this is easy to configure.

The most common SMTP server on Unix is Sendmail. Sendmail has been exploited in a number of break-ins, including the Internet worm, which makes people nervous about using it. Many of the available replacements, however, are not clearly preferable to Sendmail; the evidence suggests they are less exploited because they are less popular, not because they are less vulnerable. There are exceptions in programs designed explicitly for security, like Postfix.

The most common SMTP server on Windows NT is Microsoft Exchange, which has also been exploited in a number of ways. Microsoft Exchange has had fewer problems with actual break-ins than Sendmail, but has a troubling reputation for stability problems with SMTP, resulting in denial of service attacks. Like Sendmail, Microsoft Exchange is a useful mail server with some specialized features not available elsewhere, but it is no more suitable than Sendmail as a secure interface to the Internet. For one thing, it supports multiple protocols, making it even larger and more complex; for another, it is a noticeably newer implementation of SMTP.

While SMTP is used to exchange electronic mail between servers, users who are reading electronic mail that has already been delivered to a mail server do not use SMTP. In some cases, they may be reading the electronic mail directly on the server, but these days most users transfer the mail from the server across a network using some protocol. Across the Internet, the most common protocols for this purpose are the Post Office Protocol (POP) and the Internet Message Access Protocol (IMAP). Microsoft Exchange and Lotus Notes have their own proprietary protocols as well, which provide more features.

POP and IMAP have similar security implications; they both normally transfer user authentication data and email without encrypting it, allowing attackers to read the mail and often to get reusable user credentials. It is relatively easy to configure them to conceal the user authentication information, and relatively difficult to protect the email contents. IMAP has more features than POP and correspondingly more security problems. On the other hand, encryption is more widely and interoperably available with IMAP than with POP. The proprietary protocols used by Microsoft Exchange and Lotus Notes have even more functionality and are difficult, if not impossible, to protect adequately across the Internet. (Note that both Microsoft Exchange and Lotus Notes can use nonproprietary protocols as well; see Chapter 16, *Electronic Mail and News*, for more information.)

Usenet News

While electronic mail allows people to communicate, it's most efficient as a way for one person to send a message to another person, or to a small list of people interested in a particular topic. Newsgroups are the Internet counterpart to bulletin boards and are designed for many-to-many communication. Mailing lists also support many-to-many communication but much less openly and efficiently, because there's no easy way to find out about all mailing lists, and every recipient has his own copy of every message. The largest discussion mailing lists (i.e., lists where discussions take place among subscribers, rather than lists used to simply distribute information or announcements to subscribers) have tens of thousands of subscribers; the most popular newsgroups have at least hundreds of thousands. Usenet news is rather like television; there's a lot going on, most of it has little socially redeeming value, and some of it is fantastically amusing or informative.

The risks of news are much like those of electronic mail: your users might foolishly trust information received; they might release confidential information; and you might get flooded. News resembles a flood when it's functioning normally—most sites receive all the news they can stand every day, and the amount is continuously increasing—so you must make absolutely sure to configure news so that floods don't affect other services. Because news is rarely an essential service, denial of service attacks on a single site are usually just ignored. The security risks of news are therefore quite low. You might want to avoid news because you don't have the bandwidth or the disk space to spare, or because you are worried about the content, but it's not a significant security problem.

These days, a number of web sites allow people to access newsgroups from a web browser using HTTP. This is not very efficient if a large number of people are reading news, and it's a poor interface at best for creating news, but if your site has a small number of people who need to read news, the most efficient solution may be to use one of these sites.

Network News Transfer Protocol (NNTP) is used to transfer news across the Internet. In setting up a news server at your site, you'll need to determine the most secure way for news to flow into your internal systems so NNTP can't be used to penetrate your system. Some sites put the news server on the bastion host (described in Chapter 10, *Bastion Hosts*); others on an internal system, as we'll describe in Chapter 16, *Electronic Mail and News*. NNTP doesn't do much, and your external transfers of news will all be with specific other machines (it's not like mail, which you want to receive from everybody), so it's not particularly difficult to secure.

The biggest security issue you'll face with news is what to do with private newsgroups. Many sites create private local newsgroups to facilitate discussions among their users; these private newsgroups often contain sensitive, confidential, or proprietary information. Someone who can access your NNTP server can potentially access these private newsgroups, resulting in disclosure of this information. If you're going to create private newsgroups, be sure to configure NNTP carefully to control access to these groups. (Configuring NNTP to work in a firewall environment is discussed fully in Chapter 16.)

File Transfer, File Sharing, and Printing

Electronic mail transfers data from place to place, but it's designed for small files in human-readable form. Electronic mail transfer protocols are allowed to make changes in a message that are acceptable to humans (for instance, inserting ">" before the word "From" at the beginning of a line, so the mailer doesn't get it confused with a header line) but are unacceptable to programs.[*]

Although electronic mail systems these days include elaborate workarounds for such problems, so that a large binary file may be split into small pieces and encoded on the sending side and decoded and reassembled on the receiving side, the workarounds are cumbersome and error prone. Also, people may want to actively look for files, instead of waiting for someone to send them. Therefore, even when electronic mail is available, it's useful to have a method designed for transferring files on request.

Furthermore, you may not want to transfer files between machines; you may want to have a single copy of a file but use it on multiple machines. This is file sharing. File sharing protocols can be used as file transfer protocols (first you share the file, then you make a local copy of it), but they also allow you to use a file more or less as if it were a local file. File sharing is usually more convenient than file transfer for users, but because it provides more functionality, it is less efficient, less robust, and less secure.

---

[*] Inserting ">" before "From" is so common that some published books still contain the occasional ">From" in the text, where the ">" was inserted as authors exchanged drafts via electronic mail.

Printing is often based on file sharing or file transfer protocols; this makes a certain amount of sense, since you have to transfer the data to the printer somehow.

File Transfer

File Transfer Protocol (FTP) is the Internet standard protocol for file transfers. Most web browsers will support FTP as well as HTTP and will automatically use FTP to access locations with names that begin "ftp:", so many people use FTP without ever being aware of it. In theory, allowing your users to bring in files is not an increase of risk over allowing electronic mail; in fact, some sites offer services allowing you to access FTP via electronic mail. FTP is also nearly interchangeable in risk with HTTP, yet another way of bringing in files. In practice, however, people do use FTP differently from the way they use HTTP and electronic mail, and may bring in more files and/or larger files.

What makes these files undesirable? The primary worry at most sites is that users will bring in Trojan horse software. Although this can happen, actually the larger concern is that users will bring in computer games, pirated software, and pornographic pictures. Although these are not a direct security problem, they present a number of other problems (including wasting time and disk space and introducing legal problems of various sorts), and they are often used as carriers for viruses. If you make sure to do the following, then you can consider inbound FTP to be a reasonably safe service that eases access to important Internet resources:

- Educate your users to appropriately mistrust any software they bring in via FTP.

- Communicate to users your site's guidelines about sexual harassment policies and organizational resource usage.

How about the other side of the coin: allowing other people to use FTP to transfer files from your computers? This is somewhat riskier. Anonymous FTP is an extremely popular mechanism for giving remote users access to files without having to give them full access to your machine. If you run an FTP server, you can let users retrieve files you've placed in a separate, public area of your system without letting them log in and potentially get access to everything on your system. Your site's anonymous FTP area can be your organization's public archive of papers, standards, software, graphics images, and information of other kinds that people need from you or that you want to share with them. FTP makes a nice complement to HTTP, providing easier access to larger files for a wider audience.

To get access to the files you've made available, users log into your system using FTP with a special login name (usually "anonymous" or "ftp"). Most sites request that users enter their own electronic mail address, in response to the password prompt, as a courtesy so that the site can track who is using the anonymous FTP server, but this requirement is rarely enforced (mostly because there is no easy way to verify the validity of an electronic mail address).

In setting up an anonymous FTP server, you'll need to ensure that people who use it can't get access to other areas or files on the system, and that they can't use FTP to get shell-level access to the system itself. Writable directories in the anonymous FTP area are a special concern, as we'll see in Chapter 17, *File Transfer, File Sharing, and Printing*.

You'll also need to ensure that your users don't use the server inappropriately. It can be very tempting for people to put up files that they want specific people to read. Many times people don't realize that anybody on the Internet can read them, or they do realize this but believe in security through obscurity. Unfortunately for these innocents, a number of tools attempt to index anonymous FTP servers, and they succeed in removing most of the obscurity.

You may have heard of other file transfer protocols. Trivial File Transport Protocol (TFTP) is a simplified FTP protocol that diskless machines use to transfer information. It's extremely simple so that it can be built into hardware, and therefore supports no authentication. There's no reason to provide TFTP access outside of your network; ordinary users don't transfer files with TFTP.

Within a Unix site, you may want to use *rcp* to transfer files between systems. *rcp* (described in Chapter 18, *Remote Access to Hosts*, with the rest of the so-called "Berkeley 'r' commands") is a file transfer program that behaves like an extended version of the Unix *cp* command. It is inappropriate for use across the Internet because it uses a trusted host authentication model. Rather than requiring user authentication on the remote machine, it looks at the IP address of the host the request is coming from. Unfortunately, you can't know that packets are really coming from that host. There is an *rcp* replacement called *scp* that provides considerably more security, including user authentication and encryption of the data that passes across the network; it is also discussed in Chapter 18, along with the *ssh* command on which it is based.

File Sharing

Several protocols are available for file sharing, which allow computers to use files that are physically located on disks attached to other computers. This is highly desirable, because it lets people use remote files without the overhead of transferring them back and forth and trying to keep multiple versions synchronized. However, file sharing is much more complicated to implement than file transfer. File sharing protocols need to provide transparency (the file appears to be local, you do not see the file sharing occurring) and rich access (you can do all the things to the remote file that you could do to a local file). These features are what make file sharing desirable for users, but the need to be transparent puts limits on the sort of security that can be implemented, and the need to provide rich access makes the protocols complex to implement. More complexity inevitably leads to more vulnerability.

The most commonly used file sharing protocols are the Network File System (NFS) under Unix, the Common Internet File System (CIFS) under Microsoft Windows, and AppleShare on the Macintosh. CIFS is part of a family of related protocols and has a complex heritage, involving Server Message Block (SMB), NetBIOS/Net-BEUI, and LanManager. You will see all of these names, and some others, used to refer to file sharing protocols on Microsoft operating systems. Although there are differences between these protocols, sometimes with radical security implications, they are interrelated and, for the most part, interoperable, and at the highest level, their security implications are similar. In fact, at the highest level, all of the file sharing protocols have similar implications for firewalls; they are all insecure and difficult to use across the Internet.

NFS was designed for use in local area networks and assumes fast response, high reliability, time synchronization, and a high degree of trust between machines. There are some serious security problems with NFS. If you haven't properly configured NFS (which can be tricky), an attacker may be able to simply NFS-mount your filesystems. The way NFS works, client machines are allowed to read and change files stored on the server without having to log in to the server or enter a password. Because NFS doesn't log transactions, you might not even know that someone else has full access to your files.

NFS does provide a way for you to control which machines can access your files. A file called */etc/exports* lets you specify which filesystems can be mounted and which machines can mount them. If you leave a filesystem out of */etc/exports,* no machine can mount it. If you put it in */etc/exports,* but don't specify what machines can mount it, you're allowing any machine to mount it.

A number of subtler attacks on NFS are also possible. For example, NFS has very weak client authentication, and an attacker may be able to convince the NFS server that a request is coming from a client that's permitted in the *exports* file. There are also situations where an attacker can hijack an existing NFS mount.

These problems are mostly due to the fact that NFS uses host authentication, which is easily spoofed. Because NFS doesn't actually work well across the Internet in any case (it assumes a much faster connection between hosts), there isn't much point in allowing it between your site and the Internet. It creates a security problem without adding functionality.

CIFS and AppleShare both rely on user authentication instead of host authentication, which is a slight improvement in security. However, AppleShare is not capable of supporting flexible methods of user authentication with normal clients. You are limited to using reusable passwords, which means that attackers can simply capture passwords. CIFS can provide good authentication and good protection in recent versions. However, backward compatibility features in CIFS increase its vulnerability, as it attempts to support older clients that have much weaker security. Furthermore, CIFS actually provides an entire family of services, some of them even more vulnerable than file sharing. (For instance, it provides a general-purpose remote procedure call mechanism that can be used to allow arbitrary programs to communicate with each other.) Although it is possible for a firewall to understand CIFS and allow only some operations through (in order to allow CIFS file sharing but not other CIFS-based protocols), this is quite complex, and few firewalls are capable of it. It's also not clear how useful it would be, since file sharing and other services are intertwined; the commands for reading data from files and for reading data from other programs are the same.

There are file sharing protocols designed for use on networks like the Internet; for instance, the Andrew File System (AFS) uses Kerberos for authentication, and optionally encryption, and is designed to work across wide area networks, including the Internet. NFS, CIFS, and AppleShare are all shipped as part of popular operating systems, while AFS is a third-party product. Because of this, and because AFS and Kerberos require significant technical expertise to set up and maintain, AFS is not widely used outside of a small number of large sites. If you have a need to do secure, wide area network filesystems, it may be worth investigating AFS, but it is not covered here.

Printing Systems

Almost every operating system these days provides remote printing—via *lp* or *lpr* on Unix machines, SMB printing on Windows machines, or AppleTalk print services on Macintoshes.* Remote printing allows a computer to print to a printer that is physically connected to a different computer or directly to the network. Obviously, this is highly desirable in a local area network; you shouldn't need as many printers as you have machines. However, all of the remote printing options are insecure and inefficient as ways to transfer data across the Internet. There is no reason to allow them. If you have a need to print at a site across the Internet or to allow another site to use your printers, it's possible to set up special mail aliases that print the mail on receipt. This is the method many companies use even across in-house wide area networks because it's considerably more reliable.

---

* Or recombine the protocols and operating systems in any combination you wish, as all three platforms will support all the protocols if you install enough extra software.

Remote Access

There are many situations in which you would like to run a program on a computer other than the one that you're in front of. For instance, you may be in front of a slow computer because you're travelling with a laptop, or your other computer is a supercomputer, or you're using "thin clients"—purposefully stupid computers—in order to lower maintenance costs and get economies of scale. Originally, remote access meant some form of remote terminal access, which allows you to use character-based applications. These days, character-only access is rarely sufficient. Instead, you may need some form of remote graphics.

The general questions about remote access are the same for all methods:

- Are there appropriate controls on who can access the machine remotely? How are remote users authenticated?

- Can anybody take over a connection that's in progress?

- Can eavesdroppers pick up important information (particularly, authentication information)?

Remote Terminal Access and Command Execution

Originally, programs that provided remote terminal access allowed you to use a remote system as if your computer were a directly attached terminal—an old-fashioned terminal, capable of displaying and generating text. These days, there are computers that support remote terminal access without supporting genuine physical terminals, and there are many computers that can't do much with a text-only interface no matter how it's attached to them.

Telnet is the standard for remote terminal access on the Internet. Telnet allows you to provide remote text access for your users from any Internet-connected site without making special arrangements.

Telnet was once considered a fairly secure service because it requires users to authenticate themselves. Unfortunately, Telnet sends all of its information unencrypted, which makes it extremely vulnerable to sniffing and hijacking attacks. For this reason, Telnet is now considered one of the most dangerous services when used to access your site from remote systems. (Accessing remote systems from your site is *their* security problem, not yours.) Telnet is safe only if the remote machine and all networks between it and the local machine are safe. This means that Telnet is not safe across the Internet, where you can't reliably identify the intervening networks, much less trust them.

There are various kinds of authentication schemes for doing remote logins, which will automatically work with Telnet (in particular, see the discussion of one-time passwords in Chapter 21, *Authentication and Auditing Services*). Unfortunately, even if you protect your password, you may still find that your session can be tapped or hijacked; preventing it requires using an encrypted protocol.

There are two popular ways of doing this. First, you can simply replace Telnet with an encrypted remote terminal access program; the widely accepted Internet standard is the secure shell (SSH), which provides a variety of encrypted remote access services, but a number of other solutions are available. Second, you can create an encrypted network connection (a virtual private network, or VPN) and run normal Telnet across that. See Chapter 5, *Firewall Technologies*, for a discussion of VPN techniques.

Other programs besides Telnet and SSH can be used for remote terminal access and remote execution of programs—most notably *rlogin*, *rsh*, and *on*. These programs are used in a trusted environment to allow users remote access without having to reauthenticate themselves. The host they're connecting to trusts the host they're coming from to have correctly authenticated the user. The trusted host model is simply inappropriate for use across the Internet because you generally cannot trust hosts outside your network. In fact, you can't even be sure the packets are coming from the host they say they are.

rlogin and *rsh* may be appropriate for use within a network protected by a firewall, depending on your internal security policies. *on*, however, places all of its security checks in the client program, and anyone can use a modified client that bypasses these checks, so *on* is completely insecure for use even within a local area network protected by a firewall (it lets any user run any command as any other user). You disable *on* by disabling the *rexd* server, as we'll describe in Chapter 18, *Remote Access to Hosts*. Fortunately, *on* is relatively rare these days; Windows NT, which provides *rlogin* and *rsh* clients, does not provide an *on* client.

Remote Graphic Interfaces for Microsoft Operating Systems

Although Windows NT provides clients for most of the remote execution services described previously, and servers for many of them are available as part of the resource kits or third-party products, remote terminal services in general aren't very interesting on Windows NT. While there are character-oriented programs that will allow you to do many administrative tasks, most of the programs people want to use are graphical.

Microsoft provides remote graphical interfaces as part of Windows 2000 servers, in a package called Terminal Services. This is also available for Windows NT 4 as a special Terminal Server edition of the operating system. Terminal Services and

Terminal Server both use a Microsoft-developed protocol called Remote Desktop Protocol (RDP) to communicate between clients and servers.

A variety of other proprietary protocols are used for remote graphical interfaces to Windows, of which the most capable and widespread is Independent Computing Architecture (ICA) developed by Citrix. ICA has been licensed by a number of vendors, and a wide variety of clients and servers that use it are available, including multi-user Windows NT servers and Java-based clients that can run on any machine with a Java-enabled web browser. ICA plug-ins are available for Terminal Services and Terminal Server.

TCP/IP-based remote access is also available from almost every other remote access program in the Windows market, including LapLink, RemotelyPossible, and PcANYWHERE, to name only a few. There is also the controversial program BO2K, which is a freely available open source program that provides remote access. It is controversial because it is widely distributed as a tool for intruders, designed to provide remote access to outsiders; on the other hand, it is a full-featured and effective tool to provide legitimate remote access as well.

These programs differ widely in their security implications, although most of them are unfortunately insecure. For a full discussion of the issues and approaches, see Chapter 18, *Remote Access to Hosts*.

Network Window Systems

Most Unix machines currently provide window systems based on the X11 window system. X11 servers are also available as third-party applications for almost every other operating system, including all versions of Microsoft Windows and many versions of MacOS. X11 clients are rarer but are available for Windows NT. Network access is an important feature of X11. As more and more programs have graphical user interfaces, remote terminal access becomes less and less useful; you need graphics, not just text. X11 gives you remote graphics.

X11 servers are tempting targets for intruders. An intruder with access to an X11 server may be able to do any of the following types of damage:

Get screen dumps
These are copies of whatever is shown on the users' screens.

Read keystrokes
These may include users' passwords.

Inject keystrokes
They'll look just as if they were typed by the user. Imagine how dangerous this could be in a window in which a user is running a root shell.

Originally, X11 primarily used authentication based on the address that connections came from, which is extremely weak and not suitable for use across the Internet. These days, most X11 servers implement more secure authentication mechanisms. However, just like Telnet, X11 is still vulnerable to hijacking and sniffing, even when the authentication is relatively secure, and solving the overall security problem requires that you encrypt the entire connection via SSH or a VPN solution.

Real-Time Conferencing Services

A number of different real-time conferencing services are available on the Internet, including *talk*, IRC, web chat rooms, and the various services provided over the Multicast Backbone (MBONE). All of these services provide a way for people to interact with other people, as opposed to interacting with databases or information archives. Electronic mail and Usenet news are designed to facilitate asynchronous communications; they work even if the participants aren't currently logged in. The next time they log in, the email messages or news postings will be waiting for them. Real-time conferencing services, on the other hand, are designed for interactive use by online participants.

Internet Relay Chat (IRC) is sort of like Citizens Band (CB) radio on the Internet; it has its own little culture involving lots of people talking at each other. Users access IRC via dedicated IRC clients, or by using Telnet to access a site that provides public IRC client service. IRC servers provide hundreds (sometimes thousands) of named "channels" for users to join. These channels come and go (anyone can create a new channel, and a channel survives as long as there's anyone on it), although some popular channels are more or less permanent. Unlike *talk*, which is limited to a pair of users, any number of people can participate on an IRC channel simultaneously. Some IRC clients allow a user to participate in multiple channels simultaneously (sort of like taking part in two different conversations at once at a party).

There are a number of security problems with IRC; most of the problems aren't with the protocol itself, but with the clients, and with who uses IRC and how. Many of the clients allow servers far more access to local resources (files, processes, programs, etc.) than is wise; a malicious server can wreak havoc with a weak client. Further, many of the most frequent users of IRC are pranksters and crackers who use IRC to pass technical information among themselves and to try to trick other IRC users. Their idea of a fine time is to tell some neophyte IRC user "Hey, give this command to your IRC client so that I can show you this neat new toy I wrote". Then, when the unsuspecting user follows the prankster's directions, the commands trash the system. Anyone using IRC needs a good client program and a healthy dose of wariness and suspicion.

Purely web-based chat rooms have fewer vulnerabilities, but HTTP doesn't lend itself well to chatting, so these tend to be clunky and uncomfortable to use. People therefore have developed a number of hybrid solutions using plug-ins to HTTP clients (for instance, Mirabilis's ICQ and AOL's Messenger). These provide much nicer interfaces but also introduce new vulnerabilities. Like IRC, they have many "bad neighborhoods" where people hang out looking for neophytes they can trick or attack. In addition, the protocols and the plug-ins themselves are often vulnerable.

More complicated systems allow richer conversations. As high-speed network connections become common, full-fledged video conferencing systems have become popular, even across the Internet. The most famous of those systems is Microsoft's NetMeeting. NetMeeting and most other video conferencing systems in wide use are based on a set of International Telecommunications Union standards and protocols for video conferencing. These protocols are extremely difficult to secure. They have almost every feature that makes a protocol difficult to protect, including using multiple data streams, initiating data transfer from both ends of the conversation (instead of having a clearly defined client and server), using connectionless protocols, and dynamically assigning port numbers instead of using well-known port numbers. While they can be very useful, providing them securely requires an extremely specialized firewall. Because video conferencing involves large amounts of data, the firewall also needs good performance.

The MBONE is the source of a new set of services on the Internet, focusing on expanding real-time conference services beyond text-based services like *talk* and IRC to include audio, video, and electronic whiteboard. The MBONE is used to send real-time video of many technical conferences and programs over the Internet (e.g., Internet Engineering Task Force meetings, keynote sessions from USENIX conferences, space shuttle flight operations, and so on). At this point, the commonly used MBONE services appear to be reasonably secure. Although there are theoretical problems, the only reported attacks have been floods, which are easy to deal with. Theoretical problems have a way of eventually becoming actual problems, but these are extremely theoretical (nobody has verified that they are actually exploitable at all) and not very threatening (if they were exploitable, they still wouldn't be catastrophic). Unintentional denial of service can be a real concern with the MBONE, however, because audio and video can use so much bandwidth. The methods used to distribute MBONE across the Internet also present some interesting risks, which are discussed in Chapter 19, *Real-Time Conferencing Services*.

Naming and Directory Services

A naming service translates between the names that people use and the numerical addresses that machines use. Different protocols use different naming services; the primary protocol used on the Internet is the Domain Name System (DNS), which converts between hostnames and IP addresses.

In the early days of the Internet, it was possible for every site to maintain a host table that listed the name and number for every machine on the Internet that it might ever care about. With millions of hosts attached, it isn't practical for any single site to maintain a list of them, much less for every site to do so. Instead, DNS allows each site to maintain information about its own hosts and to find the information for other sites. DNS isn't a user-level service, per se, but it underlies SMTP, FTP, Telnet, and virtually every other service users need, because users want to be able to type "telnet fictional.example" rather than "telnet 10.100.242.32". Furthermore, many anonymous FTP servers will not allow connections from clients unless they can use DNS to look up the client host's name, so that it can be logged.

The net result is that you must both use and provide name service in order to participate in the Internet. The main risk in providing DNS service is that you may give away more information than you intend. For example, DNS lets you include information about what hardware and software you're running, information that you don't want an attacker to have. In fact, you may not even want an attacker to know the names of all your internal machines. Chapter 20, *Naming and Directory Services*, discusses how to configure name service in order to make full information available to your internal hosts, but only partial information to external inquirers.

Using DNS internally and then relying on hostnames for authentication makes you vulnerable to an intruder who can install a deceitful DNS server. This can be handled by a combination of methods, including:

- Using IP addresses (rather than hostnames) for authentication on services that need to be more secure.

- Authenticating users instead of hosts on the most secure services, because IP addresses can also be spoofed.

Windows 2000 networks use DNS in conjunction with the Active Directory service to locate resources. Clients access the Active Directory service via the Lightweight Directory Access Protocol (LDAP), which is a widely used standard for access to directory information.

Older Microsoft Windows networks use Windows Internet Name Service (WINS) to map NetBIOS hostnames to IP addresses. The name is unintentionally misleading; WINS is not an Internet name service (one intended to function on the worldwide Internet) but an internet name service (one intended to function on an internet, a collection of local area networks). The service that WINS extends, NetBIOS name service, functions only on a single local area network. Popular terminology has changed since the service was named, and now it might more appropriately be called Windows Intranet Name Service.

As WINS has evolved, the interrelationship between it and DNS has become ever more complex and confusing. WINS servers can consult DNS servers, and Microsoft DNS servers can consult WINS servers. The important things to remember about WINS are:

- WINS is designed as a purely internal protocol for a single organization.
- There are scaling issues using WINS on large and complex networks, even for a single organization.
- Microsoft is phasing out use of WINS in favor of DNS.
- WINS is less secure than DNS.

WINS has all the security issues that DNS has, and then some. First, WINS contains more information than DNS does. While DNS contains information, like host-names, that you might not want an attacker to have, WINS contains information, like valid usernames and lists of running services, that you definitely don't want an attacker to have. Second, WINS is designed around dynamic registration; not only does it accept queries from hosts, it accepts new data from the network. This makes it much more vulnerable than DNS to hostile clients. Making WINS visible to the Internet is highly dangerous and not at all useful.

Some sites use Sun's Network Information Service (NIS), formerly known as Yellow Pages (YP) to distribute hostname information internally. It is not necessary to do this. You can use DNS clients instead on any platform that supports NIS, but NIS may be more convenient for configuring your internal machines. It is certainly neither necessary nor advisable to provide NIS service to external machines. NIS is designed to administer a single site, not to exchange information between sites, and it is highly insecure. For example, it would not be possible to provide your host information to external sites via NIS without also providing your password file, if both are available internally.

Authentication and Auditing Services

Another important (although often invisible) service is authentication. Authentication services take care of assigning a specific identity to an incoming connection. When you type a username and a password, something is using these to authenticate you—to attempt to determine that you are the user that you say you are. Authentication may occur locally to a machine or may use a service across the network. Network services have the advantage of providing a centralized point of administration for multiple machines, and therefore a consistent level of trustworthiness.

A number of different services provide authentication services, sometimes combined with other functions. Under Unix, the most common authentication services are NIS (which also provides various other administrative databases) and Kerberos (which is specialized for nothing but authentication). Windows NT normally uses NTLM (which is integrated with CIFS logon service), while Windows 2000 uses Kerberos by default, falling back to NTLM only for access to older servers. For various reasons, these protocols can be difficult to use across the Internet or for authenticating people who wish to connect over telephone lines, so two protocols have been developed for just this situation, RADIUS and TACACS. Chapter 21, *Authentication and Auditing Services*, provides additional information.

Administrative Services

A variety of services are used to manage and maintain networks; these are services that most users don't use directly—indeed, that many of them have never even heard of—but they are very important tools for network managers. They are described in detail in Chapter 22, *Administrative Services*.

System Management

Simple Network Management Protocol (SNMP) is a protocol designed to make it easy to centrally manage network devices. Originally, SNMP focused on devices that were purely network-oriented (routers, bridges, concentrators, and hubs, for instance). These days, SNMP agents may be found on almost anything that connects to a network, whether or not it's part of the network infrastructure. Many hosts have SNMP agents; large software packages, like databases, often have specialized SNMP agents; and even telephone switches and power systems have network interfaces with SNMP agents.

SNMP management stations can request information from agents via SNMP. SNMP management stations can also control certain functions of the device. Devices can also report urgent information (for example, that a line has gone down, or that a significant number of errors are occurring on a given line) to management stations via SNMP. Devices vary greatly in the sorts of information they give out via SNMP, and in the parameters that can be changed via SNMP. The network devices that originally spoke SNMP used it for mildly sensitive data, like the number of bytes that had gone through a specific port, or the routing table of a given device. Some of them allowed management stations to do potentially catastrophic things (turning off a network interface, for instance), but most of them didn't (if only because many of them simply failed to implement the "set" command, which is required for a management station to actually change anything).

Modern SNMP agents often contain extremely sensitive data; the default SNMP agent for Windows NT includes the complete list of valid usernames on the machine and a list of currently running services, for instance. Many SNMP agents allow for machine reboots and other critical changes. Unfortunately, they are hardly secured at all. SNMP security currently relies on a cleartext password, known as a *community string*, with a well-known and widely used default. Some SNMP agents implement additional levels of security (for instance, controls over the IP addresses they will accept queries from), but these are still insufficient for extremely sensitive data. Allowing SNMP from the Internet is extremely dangerous.

With the introduction of SNMP v3, which provides better authentication and can encrypt data, it is becoming possible to run SNMP more securely. However, SNMP v3 is not yet widespread.

Routing

Routing protocols like RIP and OSPF are used to distribute information about where packets should be directed. Transactions on the Internet involve hosts distributed across the world, which are added, moved, and deleted, all without a single central authority to control them. The Domain Name System provides part of the information necessary to make this work (the mapping between human-readable names and machine-usable numbers), and another critical part is provided by routing services, which distribute information about which numbers are where and how to get to them.

If you interfere with a host's routing, you interfere with its ability to talk to the rest of the world. You can cut it off altogether or merely steal traffic that was intended to go someplace else. Unfortunately, most routing protocols now in use were designed when the Internet was a less dangerous place, and they don't provide any significant degree of protection.

The good news is that routing information rarely needs to go to any significant number of hosts; in general, you will have at most a few routers that talk to the Internet, and those will be the only hosts that need to talk routing protocols to the Internet. In general, you will not need to pass routing protocols through firewalls, unless you are using internal firewalls inside a site.

Network Diagnostics

The two most common network management tools are *ping* and *traceroute* (also known as *tracert*). Both are named after the Unix programs that were the first implementations, but both are now available in some form on almost all Internet-capable platforms. They do not have their own protocols but make use of the same underlying protocol, the Internet Control Message Protocol (ICMP). Unlike most of the programs we've discussed, they are not clients of distinguishable servers. ICMP is implemented at a low level as a required part of the TCP/IP protocols all Internet hosts use.

ping simply tests reachability; it tells you whether or not you can get a packet to and from a given host, and often additional information like how long it took the packet to make the round trip. *traceroute* tells you not only whether you can reach a given host (and whether it can answer), but also the route your packets take to get to that host; this is very useful in analyzing and debugging network trouble somewhere between you and some destination.

Because there aren't servers for *ping* and *traceroute*, you can't simply decide not to turn the servers on. However, you can use packet filtering to prevent them from reaching your machines. There are few risks for outbound *ping* or *traceroute*, and those risks can be avoided by using them without hostname resolution. Inbound *ping* and *traceroute*, however, pose significant risks. *ping*, in particular, is a frequent basis for denial of service attacks. *ping* and *traceroute* can both be used to determine which hosts at your site exist, as a preliminary step to attacking them. For this reason, many sites either prevent or limit the relevant packets inbound.

Time Service

Network Time Protocol (NTP), an Internet service that sets the clocks on your system with great precision, has clients on most operating systems (including Unix, Windows NT, and MacOS). Synchronizing time among different machines is important in many ways. From a security point of view, examining the precise times noted on the log files of different machines may help in analyzing patterns of break-ins. Having synchronized clocks is also a requirement for preventing attackers from recording an interaction and then repeating it (a playback attack); if timestamps are encoded in the interaction, they will be incorrect the second time the transaction is replayed. Kerberos authentication, for example, which we discuss in Chapter 21, *Authentication and Auditing Services*, depends on time synchronization. From a practical point of view, synchronized clocks are also required to successfully use NFS.

You do not have to use NTP across the Internet; it will synchronize clocks to each other within your site, if that's all you want. The reason that people use NTP from the Internet is that a number of hosts with extremely accurate clocks—radio clocks that receive the time signal from master atomic clocks or from the atomic clocks in the Global Positioning System (GPS) satellites—provide NTP service to make certain that your clocks are not only synchronous with each other but also correct. Without an external time service, you might find that all your computers have exactly the same wrong time. Accepting an external service makes you vulnerable to spoofing, but because NTP won't move the clocks very far very fast, a spoofed external clock is unlikely to make you vulnerable to a playback attack, although it could succeed in annoying you by running all your clocks slow or fast. Radio or GPS clocks suitable for use as NTP time sources are not terribly expensive, however, and if you are using NTP to synchronize clocks for an authentication protocol like Kerberos, you should buy your own and provide all time service internally, instead of using an external reference.

Databases

For a long time, databases were relatively self-contained; most accesses to a database system were from the same machine that was running the software. These days, databases are very rarely self-contained. Instead, they are the data storage for larger, distributed systems; sales information systems, e-commerce systems, even large electronic mail systems all use databases and communicate with them over networks.

This makes secure remote communication with databases more important than ever. Unfortunately, database communication protocols tend to be proprietary and different for each database manufacturer. Furthermore, they've only recently been designed with any concern for security. It is unwise to pass database transactions unprotected across the Internet. Chapter 23, *Databases and Games*, discusses database protocols and ways to configure databases to function with your firewall.

Games

Games produce some special security challenges. Like multimedia protocols, they have characteristics that make them inherently difficult to secure; they're trying to make flexible, high-performance connections. Games also change frequently, are designed by people more interested in attractiveness than security, and are a favorite target of attackers. In general, you should avoid supporting game play through a firewall. There is no network security risk in running multiplayer games internal to a network.

3

Security Strategies

Before we discuss the details of firewalls, it's important to understand some of the basic strategies employed in building firewalls and in enforcing security at your site. These are not staggering revelations; they are straightforward approaches. They're presented here so that you can keep them in mind as you put together a firewall solution for your site.

Least Privilege

Perhaps the most fundamental principle of security (any kind of security, not just computer and network security) is that of *least privilege*. Basically, the principle of least privilege means that any object (user, administrator, program, system, whatever) should have only the privileges the object needs to perform its assigned tasks—and no more. Least privilege is an important principle for limiting your exposure to attacks and for limiting the damage caused by particular attacks.

Some car manufacturers set up their locks so that one key works the doors and the ignition, and a different key works the glove compartment and the trunk; that way, you can enforce least privilege by giving a parking lot attendant the ability to park the car without the ability to get at things stored in the trunk. Many people use splittable key chains, for the same reason. You can enforce least privilege by giving someone the key to your car but not the key to your house as well.

In the Internet context, the examples are endless. Every user probably doesn't need to access every Internet service. Every user probably doesn't need to modify (or even read) every file on your system. Every user probably doesn't need to know the machine's administrative password. Every system administrator probably doesn't need to know the administrative passwords for all systems. Every system probably doesn't need to access every other system's files.

Unlike car manufacturers, most operating system vendors do not configure their operating systems with least privilege by default. It is common for them to be in a "most privileged" mode when connected to a network out of the box or during an operating system installation. Applying the principle of least privilege suggests that you should explore ways to reduce the privileges required for various operations. For example:

- Don't give a user administrative rights for a system if all she needs to do is reset the print system. Instead, provide a way to reset the print system without administrative rights (under Unix, it involves a special program of some sort; under NT, it involves giving that user the privileges required, usually by making the account a member of the Print Operators group).

- Don't make a program run as a user with general privileges if all it needs to do is write to one protected file. Instead, make the file group-writable to some group and make the program run as a member of that group rather than as a highly privileged user.

- Don't have your internal systems trust one of your firewall machines just so it can do backups. Instead, make the firewall machine trust the internal system, or, better yet, put a local tape drive on the firewall machine so that it can do its own backups.

Many of the common security problems on the Internet can be viewed as failures to follow the principle of least privilege. For example, any number of security problems have been and continue to be discovered in Sendmail, which is a big, complex program; any such program is going to have bugs in it. The problem is that Sendmail runs (at least some of the time) *setuid* to root; many of the attacks against Sendmail take advantage of this. Because it runs as root, Sendmail is a high-value target that gets a lot of attention from attackers; the fact that it's a complex program just makes their jobs easier. This implies both that privileged programs should be as simple as possible and that, if a complex program requires privileges, you should look for ways to separate and isolate the pieces that need privileges from the complex parts.[*]

Many of the solutions you'll employ in protecting your site are tactics for enforcing the strategy of least privilege. For example, a packet filtering system is designed to allow in only packets for the services you want. Running insecure programs in an environment where only the privileges the programs absolutely need are available to them (e.g., a machine that's been stripped down in one way or another) is another example; this is the essence of a bastion host.

---

[*] It's important to realize that Sendmail is far from the only example we could cite; you can find similar problems in almost any large, complex, privileged piece of software.

There are two problems with trying to enforce least privilege. First, it can be complex to implement when it isn't already a design feature of the programs and protocols you're using. Trying to add it on may be very difficult to get right. Some of the cars that try to implement least privilege with separate keys for the trunk and the ignition have remote trunk release buttons that are accessible without the keys, or fold-down rear seats that allow you to access the trunk without opening it the traditional way at all. You need to be very careful to be sure that you've actually succeeded in implementing least privilege.

Second, you may end up implementing something less than least privilege. Some cars have the gas cap release in the glove compartment. That's intended to keep parking lot attendants from siphoning off your gas, but if you lend a friend your car, you probably want him or her to be able to fill it up with gas. If you give your friend only the ignition key, you're giving your friend less than the minimum privilege you want him or her to have (because your friend won't be able to fill up the gas tank), but adding the key to the trunk and the glove compartment may give your friend more privilege than you want.

You may find similar effects with computer implementations of least privilege. Trying to enforce least privilege on people, rather than programs, can be particularly dangerous. You can predict fairly well what permissions a mail server is going to need to do its job; human beings are less predictable and more likely to become annoyed and dangerous if they can't do what they want. Be very careful to avoid turning your users into your enemies.

Defense in Depth

Another principle of security (again, any kind of security) is *defense in depth*. Don't depend on just one security mechanism, however strong it may seem to be; instead, install multiple mechanisms that back each other up. You don't want the failure of any single security mechanism to totally compromise your security. You can see applications of this principle in other aspects of your life. For example, your front door probably has both a doorknob lock and a dead bolt; your car probably has both a door lock and an ignition lock; and so on.

Although our focus in this book is on firewalls, we don't pretend that firewalls are a complete solution to the whole range of Internet security problems. Any security—even the most seemingly impenetrable firewall—can be breached by attackers who are willing to take enough risk and bring enough power to bear. The trick is to make the attempt too risky or too expensive for the attackers you expect to face. You can do this by adopting multiple mechanisms that provide backup and redundancy for each other: network security (a firewall), host security (particularly for your bastion host), and human security (user education, careful system administration, etc.). All of these mechanisms are important and can be highly effective, but don't place absolute faith in any one of them.

Your firewall itself will probably have multiple layers. For example, one architecture has multiple packet filters; it's set up that way because the two filters need to do different things, but it's quite common to set up the second one to reject packets that the first one is supposed to have rejected already. If the first filter is working properly, those packets will never reach the second; however, if there's some problem with the first, then with any luck, you'll still be protected by the second. Here's another example: if you don't want people sending mail to a machine, don't just filter out the packets; also remove the mail programs from the machine. In situations in which the cost is low, you should always employ redundant defenses.

These redundant defenses aren't solely, or even primarily, to protect from attackers; they mostly provide protection against failures of one level of defense. In the car example, there's a door lock and an ignition lock, and maybe an alarm system as well, but your average professional car thief can break all of them. The best you can hope for is that the redundancy will slow a thief down some. However, if you're having a bad day and you leave the door unlocked, the ignition lock will still keep casual thieves from driving the car away. Similarly, redundant packet filters probably won't keep a determined attacker out (if you know how to get through the first layer, you'll probably make it through the second). However, when a human or machine error turns off the first layer, you'll still have protection.

Choke Point

A *choke point* forces attackers to use a narrow channel, which you can monitor and control. There are probably many examples of choke points in your life: the toll booth on a bridge, the check-out line at the supermarket, the ticket booth at a movie theatre.

In network security, the firewall between your site and the Internet (assuming that it's the only connection between your site and the Internet) is such a choke point; anyone who's going to attack your site from the Internet is going to have to come through that channel, which should be defended against such attacks. You should be watching carefully for such attacks and be prepared to respond if you see them.

A choke point is useless if there's an effective way for an attacker to go around it. Why bother attacking the fortified front door if the kitchen door around back is wide open? Similarly, from a network security point of view, why bother attacking the firewall if dozens or hundreds of unsecured dial-up lines could be attacked more easily and probably more successfully?

A second Internet connection—even an indirect one, like a connection to another company that has its own Internet connection elsewhere—is an even more threatening breach. Internet-based attackers might not have a modem available, or might not have gotten around to acquiring phone service they don't need to pay for, but they can certainly find even roundabout Internet connections to your site.

A choke point may seem to be putting all your eggs in one basket, and therefore a bad idea, but the key is that it's a basket you can guard carefully. The alternative is to split your attention among many different possible avenues of attack. If you split your attention in this way, chances are that you won't be able to do an adequate job of defending any of the avenues of attack, or that someone will slip through one while you're busy defending another (where the intruder may even have staged a diversion specifically to draw your attention away from the real attack).

Weakest Link

A fundamental tenet of security is that a chain is only as strong as its *weakest link* and a wall is only as strong as its weakest point. Smart attackers are going to seek out that weak point and concentrate their attentions there. You need to be aware of the weak points of your defense so that you can take steps to eliminate them, and so that you can carefully monitor those you can't eliminate. You should try to pay attention equally to all aspects of your security, so that there is no large difference in how insecure one thing is as compared to another.

There is always going to be a weakest link, however; the trick is to make that link strong enough and to keep the strength proportional to the risk. For instance, it's usually reasonable to worry more about people attacking you over the network than about people actually coming to your site to attack you physically; therefore, you can usually allow your physical security to be your weakest link. It's not reasonable to neglect physical security altogether, however, because there's still some threat there. It's also not reasonable, for example, to protect Telnet connections very carefully but not protect FTP connections, because of the similarities of the risks posed by those services.

Host security models suffer from a particularly nasty interaction between choke points and weak links; there's no choke point, which means that there are a very large number of links, and many of them may be very weak indeed.

Fail-Safe Stance

Another fundamental principle of security is that, to the extent possible, systems should *fail safe*; that is, if they're going to fail, they should fail in such a way that they deny access to an attacker, rather than letting the attacker in. The failure may also result in denying access to legitimate users as well, until repairs are made, but this is usually an acceptable trade-off.

Safe failures are another principle with wide application in familiar places. Electrical devices are designed to go off—to stop—when they fail in almost any way. Elevators are designed to grip their cables if they're not being powered. Electric door locks generally unlock when the power fails, to avoid trapping people in buildings.

Most of the applications we discuss automatically fail safely. For example, if a packet filtering router goes down, it doesn't let any packets in. If a proxying program goes down, it provides no service. On the other hand, some host-based packet filtering systems are designed such that packets are allowed to arrive at a machine that runs a packet filtering application and separately runs applications providing services. The way some of these systems work, if the packet filtering application crashes (or is never started at boot time), the packets will be delivered to the applications providing services. This is not a fail-safe design and should be avoided.

The biggest application of this principle in network security is in choosing your site's *stance* with respect to security. Your stance is, essentially, your site's overall attitude towards security. Do you lean towards being restrictive or permissive? Are you more inclined to err in the direction of safety (some might call it paranoia) or freedom?

There are two fundamental stances that you can take with respect to security decisions and policies:

The default deny stance
Specify only what you allow and prohibit everything else.

The default permit stance
Specify only what you prohibit and allow everything else.

It may seem obvious to you which of these is the "right" approach to take; from a security point of view, it's the default deny stance. Probably, it will also seem obvious to your users and management; from their point of view, it's the default permit stance. It's important to make your stance clear to users and management, as well as to explain the reasons behind that stance. Otherwise, you're likely to spend a lot of unproductive time in conflict with them, wondering "How could they be so foolish as to even suggest that?" time and again, simply because they don't understand the security point of view.

Default Deny Stance: That Which Is Not Expressly Permitted Is Prohibited

The *default deny stance* makes sense from a security point of view because it is a fail-safe stance. It recognizes that what you don't know *can* hurt you. It's the obvious choice for most security people, but it's usually not at all obvious to users.

With the default deny stance, you prohibit everything by default; then, to determine what you are going to allow, you:

- Examine the services your users want.

- Consider the security implications of these services and how you can safely provide them.

- Allow only the services that you understand, can provide safely, and see a legitimate need for.

Services are enabled on a case-by-case basis. You start by analyzing the security of a specific service, and balance its security implications against the needs of your users. Based on that analysis and the availability of various remedies to improve the security of the service, you settle on an appropriate compromise.

For one service, you might determine that you should provide the service to all users and can do so safely with commonly available packet filtering or proxy systems. For another service, you might determine that the service cannot be adequately secured by any currently available means, but that only a small number of your users or systems require it. In the latter case, perhaps its use can be restricted to that small set of users (who can be made aware of the risks through special training) or systems (which you may be able to protect in other ways—for example, through host security). The whole key is to find a compromise that is appropriate to your particular situation.

Default Permit Stance: That Which Is Not Expressly Prohibited Is Permitted

Most users and managers prefer the *default permit stance*. They tend to assume that everything will be, by default, permitted, and that certain specific, troublesome actions and services will then be prohibited as necessary. For example:

- NFS is not permitted across the firewall.

- World Wide Web access is restricted to users who have received awareness training about its security problems.

- Users are not allowed to set up unauthorized servers.

They want you to tell them what's dangerous; to itemize those few (they think) things that they can't do; and to let them do everything else. This is definitely not a fail-safe stance.

First, it assumes that you know ahead of time precisely what the specific dangers are, how to explain them so users will understand them, and how to guard against them. Trying to guess what dangers might be in a system or out there on the Internet is essentially an impossible task. There are simply too many possible problems, and too much information (new security holes, new exploitations of old holes, etc.) to be able to keep up to date. If you don't know that something is a problem, it won't be on your "prohibited" list. In that case, it will go right on being a problem until you notice it, and you'll probably notice it because somebody takes advantage of it.

Second, the default permit stance tends to degenerate into an escalating "arms race" between the firewall maintainer and the users. The maintainer prepares defenses against user action or inaction (just keeps saying, "Don't do that!"); the users come up with fascinating new and insecure ways of doing things; and the process repeats, again and again. The maintainer is forever playing catch up. Inevitably, there are going to be periods of vulnerability between the time that a system is set up, the time that a security problem is discovered, and the time that the maintainer is able to respond to the problem. No matter how vigilant and cooperative everyone may be, some things are going to fall through the cracks forever: because the maintainer has never heard about them, never realized the full security consequences, or just plain hasn't had time to work on the problem.

About the only people who benefit from the default permit stance are potential attackers, because the firewall maintainer can't possibly close all the holes, is forever stuck in "fire fighting" mode, and is likely to be far too busy to notice an attacker's activities.

For example, consider the problem of sharing files with collaborators at another site. Your users' first idea will probably be to use the same tool that they use to share files internally—for instance, NFS or Windows file sharing. The problem is, both of these are completely unsafe to allow across a firewall (for reasons discussed in Chapter 2, *Internet Services*, and Chapter 17, *File Transfer, File Sharing, and Printing*). Suppose that your stance is a permissive one, and you haven't specifically told your users that it's not safe to share files across your firewall (or even if you have told them, they don't remember or don't care). In this case, you're probably going to find yourself sharing files across your firewall because it seemed like a good idea to somebody who didn't understand (or care about) the security issues. If your stance is default deny, on the other hand, your users' attempts to set up file sharing will fail. You'll need to explain why to them, suggest alternatives that are more secure (such as FTP), and look for ways to make those more secure alternatives easier to use without sacrificing security.

Universal Participation

In order to be fully effective, most security systems require the *universal participation* (or at least the absence of active opposition) of a site's personnel. If someone can simply opt out of your security mechanisms, then an attacker may be able to attack you by first attacking that exempt person's system and then attacking your site from the inside. For example, the best firewall in the world won't protect you if someone who sees it as an unreasonable burden sets up a back door connection between your site and the Internet in order to circumvent the firewall. This can be as easy as buying a modem, obtaining free PPP or SLIP software off the Internet, and paying a few dollars a month to a local low-end Internet service provider; this is well within the price range and technical abilities of many users and managers.

Much more mundane forms of rebellion will still ruin your security. You need everybody to report strange happenings that might be security-related; you can't see everything. You need people to choose good passwords; to change them regularly; and not to give them out to their friends, relatives, and pets.

How do you get everyone to participate? Participation might be voluntary (you convince everybody that it's a good idea) or involuntary (someone with appropriate authority and power tells them to cooperate or else), or some combination of the two. Obviously, voluntary participation is strongly preferable to involuntary participation; you want folks helping you, not looking for ways to get around you. This means that you may have to work as an evangelist within your organization, selling folks on the benefits of security and convincing them that the benefits outweigh the costs.

People who are not voluntary participants will go to amazing lengths to circumvent security measures. On one voicemail system that required passwords to be changed every month, numerous people discovered that it recorded only six old passwords, and took to changing their passwords seven times in a row (in seven separate phone calls!) in order to be able to use the same password. This sort of behavior leads to an arms race (the programmers limit the number of times you can change your password), and soon numerous people are sucked into a purely internal battle. You have better things to do with your time, as do your users; it's worth spending a lot of energy to convince people to cooperate voluntarily, because you'll often spend just as much to force them, with worse side effects.

Diversity of Defense

Diversity of defense is closely related to depth of defense but takes matters a bit further; it's the idea that you need not only multiple layers of defense, but different kinds of defense. Having a door lock and an ignition lock on a car is depth of defense; adding an alarm system creates not only depth but also diversity, by adding a completely different kind of defense. Now, you are not only trying to keep people from being able to use the vehicle, you're also trying to attract attention to people who're attacking it.

Properly implemented, diversity of defense makes a significant difference to the security of a system. However, many attempts to create diversity of defense are not particularly effective. A popular theory is to use different types of systems—for instance, in an architecture that has two packet filtering systems, you can increase diversity of defense by using systems from different vendors. After all, if all of your systems are the same, somebody who knows how to break into one of them probably knows how to break into all of them.

Using security systems from different vendors may reduce the chances of a common bug or configuration error that compromises them all. There is a trade-off in terms of complexity and cost, however. Procuring and installing multiple different systems is going to be more difficult, take longer, and be more expensive than procuring and installing a single system (or even several identical systems). You're going to have to buy the multiple systems (at reduced discounts from each vendor because you're buying less from them) and multiple support contracts to cover them. It's also going to take additional time and effort for your staff to learn how to deal with these different systems.

If you're not careful, you can create diversity of weakness instead of diversity of defense. If you have two different packet filters, one of them in front of the other, then using different products will help protect you from weaknesses in either one. If you have two different packet filters, each separately allowing traffic to come in, then using different products will merely make you vulnerable to two different sets of problems instead of one.

Worse yet, all these problems caused by differences may not have bought you true diversity. Beware of illusionary diversity. Two systems with different company's names on the front may have more in common than you think:

- Systems of the same type (for instance, packet filters) share the inherent weaknesses of the technology.

- Systems configured by the same people are probably configured with the same weaknesses.

- Many different systems share the same code lineage—code for things like TCP/IP protocol stacks is rarely written from scratch.

- It's not unusual for companies to simply resell other people's technology under their nameplates.

We'll look at each of these issues in the following sections.

Inherent Weaknesses

If an attack gets through your packet filters because it relies on subverting a theoretically safe protocol, it will go through any number of packet filters, regardless of who they're made by. In this case, true diversity of defense is backing up a packet filter with a proxy system, which has some hope of recognizing protocol problems.

Common Configuration

Diverse systems configured by the same person (or group of people) may share common problems if the problems stem from conceptual rather than technological roots. If the problem is a misunderstanding about how a particular protocol works, for example, your diverse systems may all be configured incorrectly in the same way according to that misunderstanding.

Common Heritage

Simply using different vendors' Unix systems probably won't buy you diversity, because most Unix systems are derived from either the BSD or System V source code. Further, most common Unix networking applications (such as Sendmail, *telnet/telnetd*, *ftp/ftpd*, and so on) are derived from the BSD sources, regardless of the platform. Any number of bugs and security problems in the original releases were propagated into most of the various vendor-specific versions of these operating systems; many vendor-specific versions of Unix still have bugs and security problems that were first discovered years ago in other versions from other vendors, and have not yet been fixed. Linux, which has an independently developed kernel, uses many applications derived from the same Unix heritage.

Similarly, Windows NT-based systems inherit any Windows NT weaknesses. Some versions of Windows NT–based firewalls replace Windows NT's IP stack, which removes one major source of common holes but may introduce others.

"Black-box" systems are based on something—usually a version of Unix or a Microsoft operating system—and they inherit weaknesses the same way any other system does.

Skin-Deep Differences

A number of vendors remarket other people's products. This is particularly true in the firewall market, where a number of companies that basically write applications software are trying to provide entire solutions. They do this by buying the underlying computer and operating system from somebody else and doing a more or less subtle job of relabeling it. There usually isn't any desire to mislead people; it's simply a marketing plus to have something that looks unified. In addition, relabeled machines may be acceptable when the originals wouldn't be—a manager who won't have Unix, or a company that won't buy a machine from a direct competitor, may find a "black box" with an innocuous name on the front acceptable. However, this candy-coating may unexpectedly reduce your diversity of defense to diversity of decor if you're not careful.

Conclusion

Although many sites acknowledge that using multiple types of systems could potentially increase their security, they often conclude that diversity of defense is more trouble than it's worth, and that the potential gains and security improvements aren't worth the costs. We don't dispute this; each site needs to make its own evaluation and decision concerning this issue.

Simplicity

Simplicity is a security strategy for two reasons. First, keeping things simple makes them easier to understand; if you don't understand something, you can't really know whether or not it's secure. Second, complexity provides nooks and crannies for all sorts of things to hide in; it's easier to secure a studio apartment than a mansion.

Complex programs have more bugs, any of which may be security problems. Even if bugs aren't in and of themselves security problems, once people start to expect a given system to behave erratically, they'll accept almost anything from it, which kills any hope of their recognizing and reporting security problems when these problems do arise.

You therefore want things as simple and elegant as possible; simple to understand, simple to use, simple to administer. But just as Einstein famously suggested, you don't want it any simpler than possible. Effective security is inherently complex. You want a system you can explain, but you still want it to work. Don't sacrifice security in order to get simplicity.

Security Through Obscurity

Security through obscurity is the principle of protecting things by hiding them. In day-to-day life, people use it all the time. Lock yourself out a lot? Hide a key somewhere. Going to leave a valuable object in your car? Put it out of sight. Want to finish off those cookies yourself? Hide them behind the canned peas. In all of these cases, there's no serious protection; anybody who can find the key, bothers to break your car window, or looks behind the canned peas immediately gets the goodies. But as long as you don't do anything else stupid (hide the key where everyone else does, leave the car unlocked, let somebody see you reaching behind the canned peas), you get a perfectly acceptable level of protection.

In computer terms, all of the following are examples of security through obscurity:

- Putting a machine on the Internet and figuring nobody will try to break into it because you haven't told anybody it's there.

- Developing a new encryption algorithm and not letting anybody look at it.

- Running a server on a different port number from the one it normally uses (providing FTP service, but setting it to port 45 instead of port 20, for instance).

- Setting up your firewall so that outsiders don't see the same information about your hostnames that insiders do.

In general, when people discuss security through obscurity, they do so with contempt. "It's just security through obscurity", they say, or "Why won't you tell me how it works? Everybody knows security through obscurity is bad". In fact, obscurity is a perfectly valid security tactic; it's just not a very strong one. You may notice that in all our noncomputer examples, it was used either in conjunction with much stronger security measures (a locked house, a locked car) or for unimportant risks (it's not really that important if somebody else eats your cookies).

Security through obscurity is bad when:

- It's the only security there is.

- There isn't any real obscurity involved.

- It prevents people from accurately determining what level of security a product provides.

- It gives people irrational confidence.

For instance, making a machine Internet accessible, not securing it, and hoping nobody notices because you aren't advertising it isn't security through obscurity. It's complete insecurity through almost no obscurity. You're protecting something important with absolutely nothing but obscurity, and the obscurity isn't very good.

Not advertising something is not the same as hiding it. This is like protecting your-self from being locked out by locking the front door but leaving the back door open, figuring that nobody will bother to go around and check it.

An encryption algorithm that hasn't been evaluated by experts because it's secret isn't security through obscurity, either; it's arrogance on the part of the algorithm's inventor. Once again, there's not a whole lot of obscurity in most cases. If you get the algorithm as software, it's easy enough to figure out exactly how it works. (Building it into supposedly tamper-proof hardware helps, but it won't keep attackers out forever.) People will attack encryption algorithms; they will figure out how they work; and if the algorithms are insecure, they will break them. It's bet-ter to have experts do it before you actually start using the algorithm.

Running a server on a different port actually does provide some level of obscu-rity, but it's tiny. An attacker has lots of ways of figuring out what port the server is on, including checking all the ports to see what answers, asking somebody at your site how to configure a machine to talk to you, and watching the traffic that's coming to your site. Meanwhile, you pay a high price in other annoyances, as nor-mal clients can't talk to you without reconfiguration and other people's firewall rules won't allow connections to you.

All of these frequent misuses of security through obscurity shouldn't prevent you from making appropriate use of the concept. You don't need to tell people what kind of firewall you're using and exactly how you configure it. The less informa-tion that attackers have, the better. Ignorance won't keep them out, but it may slow them down. The slower they are, the better off you are. Anything that makes it take longer to get into your site increases the chances that the attacker will go away and look for some place easier to break into, that you'll notice the attack and take steps to get rid of them, and that you'll have changed your defenses before the attacker succeeds in compromising them.

You don't want attackers to know:

- Exactly what kind of equipment you're using in your firewall (so that they can target vulnerabilities specific to that equipment).

- What protocols you allow under what conditions (so that they can target those protocols).

- Valid internal hostnames and usernames (so that they can target those hosts or users, or use the information to convince other people to give them access).

- What kind of intrusion detection you're doing (so that they can attack where you're not going to notice).

You can't keep all of this information hidden, but the less of it that gets out, the more work an attacker needs to do. Eventually, an attacker can figure out where your weaknesses are, but there's no need to make it easy.

II

Building Firewalls

This part of the book describes how to build firewalls. It discusses basic network concepts; explains firewall technologies, architectures, and design principles; and describes how packet filtering and proxying systems work. It also presents a general overview of the process of designing and building bastion hosts for firewall configurations, and discusses the specifics of building them in Unix, Linux, Windows NT, and Windows 2000 environments.

4

Packets and Protocols

In order to understand firewall technology, you need to understand something about the underlying objects that firewalls deal with: packets and protocols. We provide a brief introduction to high-level IP* networking concepts (a necessity for understanding firewalls) here, but if you're not already familiar with the topic, you will probably want to consult a more general reference on TCP/IP (for instance, *TCP/IP Network Administration*, by Craig Hunt, published by O'Reilly and Associates).

To transfer information across a network, the information has to be broken up into small pieces, each of which is sent separately. Breaking the information into pieces allows many systems to share the network, each sending pieces in turn. In IP networking, those small pieces of data are called *packets*. All data transfer across IP networks happens in the form of packets.

What Does a Packet Look Like?

To understand packet filtering, you first have to understand packets and how they are layered to build up the TCP/IP protocol stack, which is:

- Application layer (e.g., FTP, Telnet, HTTP)
- Transport layer (TCP or UDP)
- Internet layer (IP)
- Network access layer (e.g., Ethernet, FDDI, ATM)

---

* Unless otherwise noted, we are discussing IP version 4, which is the version currently in common use.

Packets are constructed in such a way that layers for each protocol used for a particular connection are wrapped around the packets, like the layers of skin on an onion.

At each layer (except perhaps at the application layer), a packet has two parts: the header and the body. The header contains protocol information relevant to that layer, while the body contains the data for that layer, which often consists of a whole packet from the next layer in the stack. Each layer treats the information it gets from the layer above it as data, and applies its own header to this data. At each layer, the packet contains all of the information passed from the higher layer; nothing is lost. This process of preserving the data while attaching a new header is known as *encapsulation*.

At the application layer, the packet consists simply of the data to be transferred (for example, part of a file being transferred during an FTP session). As it moves to the transport layer, the Transmission Control Protocol (TCP) or the User Datagram Protocol (UDP) preserves the data from the previous layer and attaches a header to it. At the next layer, the Internet layer, IP considers the entire packet (consisting now of the TCP or UDP header and the data) to be data and now attaches its own IP header. Finally, at the network access layer, Ethernet or another network protocol considers the entire IP packet passed to it to be data and attaches its own header. Figure 4-1 shows how this works.

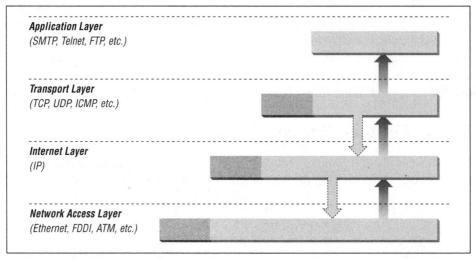

Figure 4-1. Data encapsulation

At the other side of the connection, this process is reversed. As the data is passed up from one layer to the next higher layer, each header (each skin of the onion) is stripped off by its respective layer. For example, the Internet layer removes the IP header before passing the encapsulated data up to the transport layer (TCP or UDP).

In trying to understand packet filtering, the most important information from our point of view is in the headers of the various layers. The following sections look at several examples of different types of packets and show the contents of each of the headers that packet filtering routers will be examining. We assume a certain knowledge of TCP/IP fundamentals and concentrate on discussing the particular issues related to packet filtering.

In the following discussion, we start with a simple example demonstrating TCP/IP over Ethernet. From there, we go on to discuss IP's packet filtering characteristics, then protocols above IP (such as TCP, UDP, and ICMP), protocols below IP (such as Ethernet), and finally non-IP protocols (such as NetBEUI, AppleTalk, and IPX).

TCP/IP/Ethernet Example

Let's consider an example of a TCP/IP packet (for example, one that is part of a Telnet connection) on an Ethernet.* We're interested in four layers here: the Ethernet layer, the IP layer, the TCP layer, and the data layer. In this section, we'll consider them from bottom to top and look at the contents of the headers that the packet filtering routers will be examining.

Ethernet layer

At the Ethernet layer, the packet consists of two parts: the Ethernet header and the Ethernet body. In general, you won't be able to do packet filtering based on information in the Ethernet header. In some situations, you may be interested in Ethernet address information. The Ethernet address is also known as the MAC (Media Access Control) address. Basically, the header tells you:

What kind of packet this is
> We'll assume in this example that it is an IP packet, as opposed to an Apple-Talk packet, a Novell packet, a DECNET packet, or some other kind of packet.

The Ethernet address of the machine that put the packet onto this particular Ethernet network segment
> The original source machine, if it's attached to this segment; otherwise, the last router in the path from the source machine to here.

---

* Ethernet is the most popular networking protocol currently at the link layer; 10-base T and 100-base T networks are almost always Ethernet networks.

The Ethernet address of the packet's destination on this particular Ethernet network segment

> Perhaps the destination machine, if it's attached to this segment; otherwise, the next router in the path from here to the destination machine. Occasionally it's a broadcast address indicating that all machines should read the packet, or a multicast address indicating that a group of subscribing machines should read the packet.

Because we are considering IP packets in this example, we know that the Ethernet body contains an IP packet.

IP layer

At the IP layer, the IP packet is made up of two parts: the IP header and the IP body, as shown in Figure 4-2. From a packet filtering point of view, the IP header contains four interesting pieces of information:

The IP source address

> Four bytes long and typically written as something like 172.16.244.34.

The IP destination address

> Just like the IP source address.

The IP protocol type

> Identifies the IP body as a TCP packet, as opposed to a UDP packet, an ICMP (Internet Control Message Protocol) packet, or some other type of packet.

The IP options field

> Almost always empty; where options like the IP source route and the IP security options would be specified if they were used for a given packet (see the discussion in "IP options", later in this chapter).

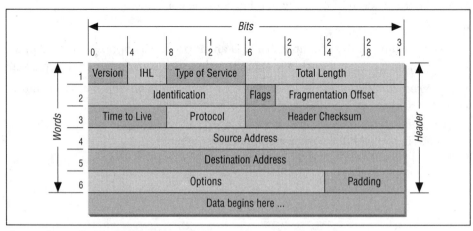

Figure 4-2. IP header and body

Most networks have a limit on the maximum length of a packet, which is much shorter than the limit imposed by IP. In order to deal with this conflict, IP may divide a packet that is too large to cross a given network into a series of smaller packets called *fragments*. Fragmenting a packet doesn't change its structure at the IP layer (the IP headers are duplicated into each fragment), but it may mean that the body contains only a part of a packet at the next layer. (See the discussion in "IP Fragmentation", later in this chapter.)

The IP body in this example contains an unfragmented TCP packet, although it could just as well contain the first fragment of a fragmented TCP packet.

TCP layer

At the TCP layer, the packet again contains two parts: the TCP header and the TCP body. From a packet filtering point of view, the TCP header contains three interesting pieces of information:

The TCP source port
> A two-byte number that specifies what client or server process the packet is coming from on the source machine.

The TCP destination port
> A two-byte number that specifies what client or server process the packet is going to on the destination machine.

The TCP flags field
> This field contains various flags that are used to indicate special kinds of packets, particularly during the process of setting up and tearing down TCP connections. These flags are discussed further in the sections that follow.

The TCP body contains the actual "data" being transmitted—for example, for Telnet the keystrokes or screen displays that are part of a Telnet session, or for FTP the data being transferred or commands being issued as part of an FTP session.

IP

IP serves as a common middle ground for the Internet. It can have many different layers below it, such as Ethernet, token ring, FDDI, PPP, or carrier pigeon.* IP can have many other protocols layered on top of it, with TCP, UDP, and ICMP being by far the most common, at least outside of research environments. In this section, we discuss the special characteristics of IP relevant to packet filtering.

---

* See RFC 1149, dated 1 April 1990, which defines the Avian Transport Protocol; RFCs dated 1 April are usually worth reading.

IP Multicast and Broadcast

Most IP packets are what are called *unicast*; they are sent to an individual destination host. IP packets may also be *multicast* (sent to a group of hosts) or *broadcast* (intended for every host that can receive them). Multicast packets are like memos, which are sent to a group of people ("Employees in the purchasing department" or "People working on the Ishkabibble project" or "Potential softball players"); their destination is a group of hosts that ought to be interested in the information. Broadcast packets are like announcements made on overhead speakers; they are used when everybody needs the information ("The building is on fire, evacuate now") or when the message's sender can't determine which particular destination should get the message, but believes that the destination will be able to figure it out ("The green Honda with license plate 4DZM362 has its lights on").

The purpose of multicasting is to create efficiency. Unlike a memo, a multicast packet is a single object. If 7, or 17, or 70 hosts want the same information, a multicast packet allows you to get it to them by sending just one packet, instead of one packet each. A broadcast packet would give you the same savings in network resources, but it would waste computing time on the uninterested machines that would have to process the packet in order to decide it was irrelevant and reject it.

Note that multicast and broadcast addresses are meant as destination addresses, not as source addresses. A machine may use a broadcast address as a source address only if it does not have a legitimate source address and is trying to get one (see Chapter 22, *Administrative Services*, for more information about DHCP, which may use this mechanism). Otherwise, multicast and broadcast source addresses are generally signs of an attacker who is using a destination machine as an amplifier. If a packet has a broadcast source address and a unicast destination address, any reply to it will have a unicast source address and a broadcast destination; thus, an attacker who uses a broadcast source can cause another machine to do the broadcasting.

This is a good deal for the attacker because it's rare that packets with a broadcast destination are allowed to cross a firewall (or, in fact, any router). The attacker probably wouldn't be able to get at a large number of hosts without using this kind of dirty trick. You don't want broadcast information from other networks; it's not relevant to your life, and it may be dangerous (either because it's incorrect for your network, or because it allows attackers to gather information about your network). Routers are sometimes configured to pass some or all broadcasts between networks that are part of the same organization, because some protocols rely on broadcasts to distribute information. This is tricky to get right and tends to result in overloaded networks and hosts, but it is more acceptable than passing broadcasts to or from the Internet.

Your firewall should therefore refuse to pass packets with broadcast destinations and packets with multicast or broadcast source addresses.

IP Options

As we saw in the previous discussion of the IP layer, IP headers include an options field, which is usually empty. In its design, the IP options field was intended as a place for special information or handling instructions that didn't have a specific field of their own in the header. However, TCP/IP's designers did such a good job of providing fields for everything necessary that the options field is almost always empty. In practice, IP options are very seldom used except for break-in attempts and (very rarely) for network debugging.

The most common IP option a firewall would be confronted with is the IP source route option. Source routing lets the source of a packet specify the route the packet is supposed to take to its destination, rather than letting each router along the way use its routing tables to decide where to send the packet next. Source routing is supposed to override the instructions in the routing tables. In theory, the source routing option is useful for working around routers with broken or incorrect routing tables; if you know the route that the packet should take, but the routing tables are broken, you can override the bad information in the routing tables by specifying appropriate IP source route options on all your packets. In practice though, source routing is commonly used only by attackers who are attempting to circumvent security measures by causing packets to follow unexpected paths.

This is in fact a circular problem; several researchers have proposed interesting uses of source routing, which are impossible to use widely because source routing is commonly disabled—because it's useful for nothing but attacks. This situation interferes considerably with widespread use of most solutions for mobile IP (allowing machines to move from place to place while keeping a fixed IP address).

Some packet filtering systems take the approach of dropping any packet that has any IP option set, without even trying to figure out what the option is or what it means; this doesn't usually cause significant problems.

IP Fragmentation

Another IP-level consideration for packet filtering is fragmentation. One of the features of IP is its ability to divide a large packet that otherwise couldn't traverse some network link (because of limitations on packet size along that link) into smaller packets, called *fragments*, which can traverse that link. The fragments are then reassembled into the full packet by the destination machine (not by the machine at the other end of the limited link; once a packet is fragmented, it normally stays fragmented until it reaches its destination).

Normally, any router can decide to fragment a packet. A flag in the IP header can be used to prevent routers from fragmenting packets. Originally, this wasn't much used, because a router that needs to fragment a packet but is forbidden to do so will have to reject the packet, and communication will fail, which is generally less desirable than having the packet fragmented. However, there is now a system called path maximum transmission unit (MTU) discovery that uses the flag that prevents fragmentation.

Path MTU discovery is a way for systems to determine what is the largest packet that can be sent to another machine without getting fragmented. Large unfragmented packets are more efficient than small packets, but if packets have to be broken up later in the process, this will significantly decrease transfer speed. Therefore, maximum efficiency depends on knowing how big to make the packets, but that depends on all the network links between the machines. Neither machine has any way to know what the answer is (and, in fact, it may vary from moment to moment). In order to discover the limit, systems can send out packets with "don't fragment" set and look for the error response that says that the packet has been dropped because it was too big but could not be fragmented. If there's an error, the machine reduces the packet size; if there's no error, it increases it. This adds some extra expense at the beginning of a connection, but for a connection that transmits a significant amount of data across a network that includes a limited link, the overall transmission time will probably be improved despite the intentionally lost packets. However, path MTU discovery will fail catastrophically if the error messages (which are ICMP messages, discussed later in this chapter) are not correctly returned (for instance, if your firewall drops them).

IP fragmentation is illustrated in Figure 4-3.

From a packet filtering point of view, the problem with fragmentation is that only the first fragment will contain the header information from higher-level protocols, like TCP, that the packet filtering system needs in order to decide whether or not to allow the full packet. Originally, the common packet filtering approach to dealing with fragmentation was to allow any non-first fragments through and to do packet filtering only on the first fragment of a packet. This was considered safe because if the packet filtering decides to drop the first fragment, the destination system will not be able to reassemble the rest of the fragments into the original packet, regardless of how many of the rest of the fragments it receives. If it can't reconstruct the original packet, the partially reassembled packet will not be accepted.

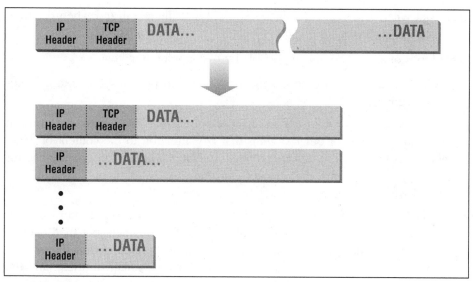

Figure 4-3. Data fragmentation

However, there are still problems with fragmented packets. If you pass all non-first fragments, the destination host will hold the fragments in memory for a while, waiting to see if it gets the missing piece; this makes it possible for attackers to use fragmented packets in a denial of service attack. When the destination host gives up on reassembling the packet, it will send an ICMP "packet reassembly time expired" message back to the source host, which will tell an attacker that the host exists and why the connection didn't succeed.

In addition, attackers can use specially fragmented packets to conceal data. Each fragment contains information about where the data it contains starts and ends. Normally, each one starts after the last one ended. However, an attacker can construct packets where fragments actually overlap, and contain the same data addresses. This does not happen in normal operation; it can happen only when bugs or attackers are involved, and attackers are by far the most likely cause.

Operating systems differ in their response to overlapping fragments. Because overlapping fragments are abnormal, many operating systems respond very badly to them and may reassemble them into invalid packets, with the expected sorts of unfortunate results up to and including operating system crashes. When they are reassembled, there are differences in whether the first or second fragment's data is kept; these differences can be increased by sending the fragments out of order. Some machines prefer the first version received, others the most recent version received, others the numerically first, and still others the numerically last. This makes it nearly impossible for packet filtering or intrusion detection systems to figure out what data the receiving system will actually see if and when the fragments are reassembled.

Three kinds of attacks are made possible by overlapping fragments:

- Simple denial of service attacks against hosts with poor responses to overlapping fragments.

- Information-hiding attacks. If an attacker knows that virus detectors, intrusion detection systems, or other systems that pay attention to the content of packets are in use and can determine what assembly method the systems use for overlapping fragments, the attacker can construct overlapping fragments that will obscure content from the watching systems.

- Attacks that get information to otherwise blocked ports. An attacker can construct a packet with acceptable headers in the first fragment but then overlap the next fragment so that it also has headers in it. Since packet filters don't expect TCP headers in non-first fragments, they won't filter on them, and the headers don't need to be acceptable. Figure 4-4 shows overlapped fragments.

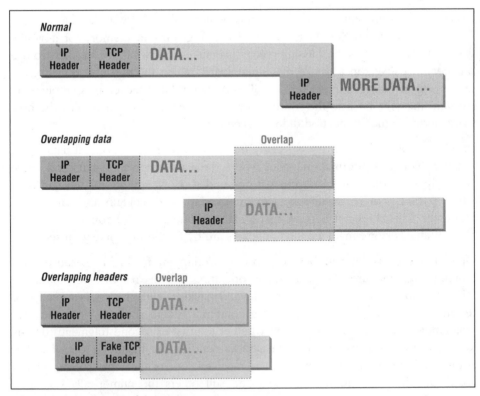

Figure 4-4. Overlapping fragments

There are other, special problems with passing outbound fragments. Outbound fragments could conceivably contain data you don't want to release to the world. For example, an outbound NFS packet would almost certainly be fragmented, and if the file were confidential, that information would be released. If this happens by accident, it's unlikely to be a problem; people do not generally hang around looking at the data in random packets going by just in case there's something interesting in them. You could wait a very long time for somebody to accidentally send a fragment out with interesting data in it.

If somebody inside intentionally uses fragmentation to transmit data, you have hostile users within the firewall, and no firewall can deal successfully with insiders. (They probably aren't very clever hostile users, though, because there are easier ways to get data out.)

However, there is one other situation in which outbound fragments could carry data: if you have decided to deal with some vulnerability by blocking outbound responses to something (instead of attempting to block the original request on the incoming side, which would be a better idea), and the reply is fragmented. In this situation, non-first fragments of the reply will get out, and the attacker has reason to expect them and look for them. You can deal with this by being careful to filter out requests and by not relying on filtering out the replies.

Because of these many and varied problems with fragmentation, you should look for a packet filter that does fragment reassembly; rather than either permitting or denying fragments, the packet filter should reassemble the packet locally (and, if necessary, refragment it before sending it on). This will increase the load on the firewall somewhat, but it protects against all fragmentation-based risks and attacks, except those the firewall itself is vulnerable to (for instance, denial of service attacks based on sending non-first fragments until the firewall runs out of memory).

If you cannot do fragment reassembly, your safest option is to reject all non-first fragments. This may destroy connections that otherwise would have succeeded, but it is the lesser of two evils. Denying fragments will cause some connections to fail mysteriously, which is extremely unpleasant to debug. On the other hand, allowing them will open you to a variety of attacks that are widely exploited on the Internet. Fortunately, fragmented packets are becoming rarer as the use of path MTU discovery increases.

Protocols Above IP

IP serves as the base for a number of different protocols; by far the most common are TCP, UDP, and ICMP. In addition, we briefly discuss IP over IP (i.e., an IP packet encapsulated within another IP packet), which is used primarily for tunneling protocols over ordinary IP networks. This technique has been used in the past to tunnel multicast IP packets over nonmulticast IP networks, and more recently for a variety of virtual private networking systems, IPv6, and some systems for supporting mobile IP. These are the only IP-based protocols that you're likely to see being routed between networks outside a research environment.*

TCP

TCP is the protocol most commonly used for services on the Internet. For example, Telnet, FTP, SMTP, NNTP, and HTTP are all TCP-based services. TCP provides a reliable, bidirectional connection between two endpoints. Opening a TCP connection is like making a phone call: you dial the number, and after a short setup period, a reliable connection is established between you and whomever you're calling.

TCP is *reliable* in that it makes three guarantees to the application layer:

- The destination will receive the application data in the order it was sent.

- The destination will receive all the application data.

- The destination will not receive duplicates of any of the application data.

TCP will kill a connection rather than violate one of these guarantees. For example, if TCP packets from the middle of a session are lost in transit to the destination, the TCP layer will arrange for those packets to be retransmitted before handing the data up to the application layer. It won't hand up the data following the missing data until it has the missing data. If some of the data cannot be recovered, despite repeated attempts, the TCP layer will kill the connection and report this to the application layer, rather than hand up the data to the application layer with a gap in it.

These guarantees incur certain costs in both setup time (the two sides of a connection have to exchange startup information before they can actually begin moving data) and ongoing performance (the two sides of a connection have to keep track of the status of the connection, to determine what data needs to be resent to the other side to fill in gaps in the conversation).

TCP is *bidirectional* in that once a connection is established, a server can reply to a client over the same connection. You don't have to establish one connection from a client to a server for queries or commands and another from the server back to the client for answers.

If you're trying to block a TCP connection, it is sufficient to simply block the first packet of the connection. Without that first packet (and, more importantly, the

---

* You may also see the routing protocols OSPF or IGMP, which are discussed in Chapter 22. However, they are rarely distributed between networks and do not form the basis for other protocols.

connection startup information it contains), any further packets in that connection won't be reassembled into a data stream by the receiver, and the connection will never be made. That first packet is recognizable because the ACK bit in its TCP header is not set; all other packets in the connection, regardless of which direction they're going in, will have the ACK bit set. (As we will discuss later, another bit, called the SYN bit, also plays a part in connection negotiation; it must be on in the first packet, but it can't be used to identify the first packet because it is also on in the second packet.)

Recognizing these "start-of-connection" TCP packets lets you enforce a policy that allows internal clients to connect to external servers but prevents external clients from connecting to internal servers. You do this by allowing start-of-connection TCP packets (those without the ACK bit set) only outbound and not inbound. Start-of-connection packets would be allowed out from internal clients to external servers but would not be allowed in from external clients to internal servers. Attackers cannot subvert this approach simply by turning on the ACK bit in their start-of-connection packets, because the absence of the ACK bit is what identifies these packets as start-of-connection packets.

Packet filtering implementations vary in how they treat and let you handle the ACK bit. Some packet filtering implementations give direct access to the ACK bit— for example, by letting you include "ack" as a keyword in a packet filtering rule. Some other implementations give indirect access to the ACK bit. For example, the Cisco "established" keyword works by examining this bit (established is "true" if the ACK bit is set, and "false" if the ACK bit is not set). Finally, some implementations don't let you examine the ACK bit at all.

TCP options

The ACK bit is only one of the options that can be set; the whole list, in the order they appear in the header, is:

- URG (urgent)
- ACK (acknowledgment)
- PSH (push)
- RST (reset)
- SYN (synchronize)
- FIN (finish)

URG and PSH are supposed to be used to identify particularly critical data; PSH tells the receiver to stop buffering and let some program have the data, while URG more generally marks data that the sender thinks is particularly important (sometimes incorrectly called "out of band" data). In practice, neither of these is reliably implemented, and for most purposes, firewalls do not need to take special action based on them. It can be useful for firewalls to drop packets with URG or PSH set when dealing with protocols that are known not to use these features.

ACK and SYN together make up the famed TCP three-way handshake (so-called because it takes three packets to set up a connection). Figure 4-5 shows what ACK and SYN are set to on packets that are part of a TCP connection.

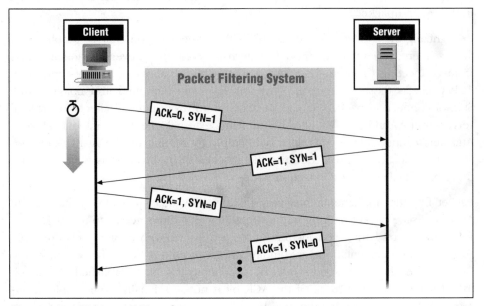

Figure 4-5. ACK bits on TCP packets

SYN is turned on for the first two packets of a connection (one in each direction), in order to set up sequence numbers. The first packet of a connection must have ACK off (since it isn't in response to anything) but SYN on (to give the next packet a number to acknowledge). Sequence numbers are discussed further in the section that follows.

RST and FIN are ways of closing a connection. RST is an ungraceful close, sent to indicate that something has gone wrong (for instance, there's no process listening on the port, or there seems to be something nasty about the packet that came in). FIN is part of a graceful shutdown, where both ends send FIN to each other to say goodbye.

Of this entire laundry list, ACK and RST are the only two of interest to a firewall in normal operation (ACK because it is a reliable way to identify the first packet of connections, and RST because it's a useful way to shut people up without returning a helpful error message). However, there are a number of attacks that involve setting options that don't normally get set. Many TCP/IP implementations respond badly to eccentric combinations of options (for instance, they crash the machine). Others respond but don't log the fact, allowing attackers to scan networks without being noticed. These attacks are discussed further in the section that follows.

TCP sequence numbers

TCP provides a guarantee to applications that they will always receive data in the correct order, but nothing provides a guarantee to TCP that packets will always arrive in the correct order. In order to get the packets back into the correct order, TCP uses a number on each packet, called a *sequence number.* At the beginning of a connection, each end picks a number to start off with, and this number is what's communicated when SYN is set. There are two packets with SYN set (one in each direction), because the two ends maintain separate sequence numbers, chosen independently. After the SYN, for each packet, the number is simply incremented by the number of data bytes in the packet. If the first sequence number is 200, and the first data packet has 80 bytes of data on it, it will have a sequence number of 280.* The ACK is accompanied by the number of the next expected piece of data (the sequence number plus one, or 281 in this case).

In order for an attacker to take over a TCP connection, the attacker needs to get the sequence numbers correct. Since sequence numbers are just incremented during a connection, this is easy for an attacker who can see the traffic. On the other hand, it's much more difficult if you can't see the initial negotiation; the initial sequence number is supposed to be randomly chosen. However, on many operating systems, initial sequence numbers are not actually random. In some TCP/IP implementations, initial sequence numbers are predictable; if you know what initial sequence number one connection uses, you can figure out what initial sequence number the next one will use, because the numbers are simply incremented, either based on number of connections (the number gets bigger by some fixed amount on each connection) or based on time (the number gets bigger by some fixed amount each microsecond).

This may seem like it's not worth worrying about. After all, in order to hijack a connection by predicting sequence numbers, an attacker needs:

1. The ability to forge TCP/IP packets.

2. The initial sequence number for one connection.

3. The knowledge that somebody else has started up a desirable connection (but not the ability to actually see that connection—if the attacker can see the connection, there's no need to predict the sequence number).

---

* The details of how the sequence number is calculated are actually slightly more complex than this, but the end result is as described.

4. Precise information about when the desirable connection started up.

5. Either the ability to redirect traffic so that you receive responses, or the ability to continue the conversation and achieve something without ever getting any of the responses.

In fact, for years this was considered a purely hypothetical attack, something that paranoid minds came up with but that presented no danger in reality. However, it was eventually implemented, and programs are now available that simplify the process. It's still not a technique that's used routinely by casual attackers, but it's available to determined attackers, even if they aren't technically extremely advanced. You should be sure that security-critical hosts have truly random initial sequence numbers by installing an appropriate version of the operating system.

UDP

The body of an IP packet might contain a UDP packet instead of a TCP packet. UDP is a low-overhead alternative to TCP.

UDP is *low overhead* in that it doesn't make any of the reliability guarantees (delivery, ordering, and nonduplication) that TCP does, and, therefore, it doesn't need the mechanism to make those guarantees. Every UDP packet is independent; UDP packets aren't part of a "virtual circuit" as TCP packets are. Sending UDP packets is like dropping postcards in the mail: if you drop 100 postcards in the mail, even if they're all addressed to the same place, you can't be absolutely sure that they're all going to get there, and those that do get there probably won't be in exactly the same order they were in when you sent them. (As it turns out, UDP packets are far less likely to arrive than postcards—but they are far more likely to arrive in the same order.)

Unlike postcards, UDP packets can actually arrive intact more than once. Multiple copies are possible because the packet might be duplicated by the underlying network. For example, on an Ethernet, a packet would be duplicated if a router thought that it might have been the victim of an Ethernet collision. If the router was wrong, and the original packet had not been the victim of a collision, both the original and the duplicate would eventually arrive at the destination. (An application may also decide to send the same data twice, perhaps because it didn't get an expected response to the first one, or maybe just because it's confused.)

All of these things can happen to TCP packets, too, but they will be corrected before the data is passed to the application. With UDP, the application is responsible for dealing with the data exactly as it arrives in packets, not corrected by the underlying protocol.

UDP packets are very similar to TCP packets in structure. A UDP header contains UDP source and destination port numbers, just like the TCP source and destination port numbers. However, a UDP header does not contain any of the flags or sequence numbers that TCP uses. In particular, it doesn't contain anything resembling an ACK bit. The ACK bit is part of TCP's mechanism for guaranteeing reliable delivery of data. Because UDP makes no such guarantees, it has no need for an ACK bit. There is no way for a packet filtering router to determine, simply by examining the header of an incoming UDP packet, whether that packet is a first packet from an external client to an internal server, or a response from an external server back to an internal client.

ICMP

ICMP is used for IP status and control messages. ICMP packets are carried in the body of IP packets, just as TCP and UDP packets are. Examples of ICMP messages include:

Echo request
> What a host sends when you run *ping*.

Echo response
> What a host responds to an "echo request" with.

Time exceeded
> What a router returns when it determines that a packet appears to be looping. A more intuitive name might be *maximum hopcount exceeded* because it's based on the number of routers a packet has passed through, not a period of time.

Destination unreachable
> What a router returns when the destination of a packet can't be reached for some reason (e.g., because a network link is down).

Redirect
> What a router sends a host in response to a packet the host should have sent to a different router. The router handles the original packet anyway (forwarding it to the router it should have gone to in the first place), and the redirect tells the host about the more efficient path for next time.

Unlike TCP or UDP, ICMP has no source or destination ports, and no other protocols layered on top of it. Instead, there is a set of defined ICMP message types; the particular type used dictates the interpretation of the rest of the ICMP packet. Some types also have individual codes that convey extra information (for instance, the "Destination unreachable" type has codes for different conditions that caused the destination to be unreachable, one of which is the "Fragmentation needed and Don't Fragment set" code used for path MTU discovery).

Many packet filtering systems let you filter ICMP packets based on the ICMP message type field, much as they allow you to filter TCP or UDP packets based on the TCP or UDP source and destination port fields. Relatively few of them allow you to filter on codes within a type. This is a problem because you will probably want to allow "Fragmentation needed and Don't Fragment set" (for path MTU discovery) but not any of the other codes under "Destination unreachable", all of which can be used to scan networks to see what hosts are attackable.

Most ICMP packets have little or no meaningful information in the body of the packet, and therefore should be quite small. However, various people have discovered denial of service attacks using oversized ICMP packets (particularly echo packets, otherwise known as "ping" packets after the Unix command normally used to send them). It is a good idea to put a size limit on any ICMP packet types you allow through your filters.

There have also been attacks that use ICMP as a *covert channel,* a way of smuggling information. As we mentioned previously, most ICMP packet bodies contain little or no meaningful information. However, they may contain padding, the content of which is undefined. For instance, if you use ICMP echo for timing or testing reasons, you will want to be able to vary the length of the packets and possibly the patterns of the data in them (some transmission mechanisms are quite sensitive to bit patterns, and speeds may vary depending on how compressible the data is, for instance). You are therefore allowed to put arbitrary data into the body of ICMP echo packets, and that data is normally ignored; it's not filtered, logged, or examined by anybody. For someone who wants to smuggle data through a firewall that allows ICMP echo, these bodies are a very tempting place to put it. They may even be able to smuggle data into a site that allows only outbound echo requests by sending echo responses even when they haven't seen a request. This will be useful only if the machine that the responses are being sent to is configured to receive them; it won't help anyone break into a site, but it's a way for people to maintain connections to compromised sites.

IP over IP and GRE

In some circumstances, IP packets are encapsulated within other IP packets for transmission, yielding so-called *IP over IP*. IP over IP is used for various purposes, including:

- Encapsulating encrypted network traffic; for instance, using the IPsec standard or PPTP, which are described in Chapter 14, *Intermediary Protocols.*

- Carrying multicast IP packets (that is, packets with multicast destination addresses) between networks that do support multicasting over intermediate networks that don't

- Mobile IP (allowing a machine to move between networks while keeping a fixed IP address)
- Carrying IPv6 traffic over IPv4 networks

Multiple different protocols are used for IP over IP, including protocols named Generic Routing Encapsulation (GRE), IP in IP, IP within IP, and swIPe. Currently, GRE appears to be the most popular. The general principle is the same in all cases; a machine somewhere picks up a packet, encapsulates it into a new IP packet, and sends it on to a machine that will unwrap it and process it appropriately.

In some cases (for instance, for multicast and IPv6 traffic), the encapsulation and de-encapsulation is done by special routers. The sending and receiving machines send out their multicast or IPv6 traffic without knowing anything about the network in between, and when they get to a point where the network will not handle the special type, a router does the encapsulation. In this case, the encapsulated packet will be addressed to another router, which will unwrap it. The encapsulation may also be done by the sending machine or the de-encapsulation by the receiving machine.

IP over IP is also a common technique used for creating virtual private networks, which are discussed further in Chapter 5, *Firewall Technologies*. It is the basis for a number of higher-level protocols, including IPsec and PPTP, which are discussed further in Chapter 14, *Intermediary Protocols*.

IP over IP presents a problem for firewalls because the firewall sees the IP header information of the external packet, not the original information. In some cases, it is possible but difficult for the firewall to read the original headers; in other cases, the original packet information is encrypted, preventing it from being read by snoopers, but also by the firewall. This means that the firewall cannot make decisions about the internal packet, and there is a risk that it will pass traffic that should be denied. IP over IP should be permitted only when the destination of the external packet is a trusted host that will drop the de-encapsulated packet if it is not expected and permitted.

Protocols Below IP

It's theoretically possible to filter on information from below the IP level—for example, the Ethernet hardware address. However, doing so is very rarely useful because in most cases, all packets from the outside are coming from the same hardware address (the address of the router that handles your Internet connection). Furthermore, many routers have multiple connections with different lower-level protocols. As a result, doing filtering at lower levels would require configuring different interfaces with different kinds of rules for the different lower-level protocols. You couldn't write one rule to apply to all interfaces on a router that had two Ethernet connections and two FDDI connections because the headers of Ethernet and FDDI packets, while similar, are not identical. In practice, IP is the lowest level protocol at which people choose to do packet filtering.

However, if you are dealing with a network with a small, fixed number of machines on it, filtering based on hardware addresses is a useful technique for detecting and disabling machines that have been added inappropriately. (It is also a useful technique for making yourself look like an idiot when you exchange network boards, and an important machine suddenly and mysteriously stops working—better document it very carefully.) Even on relatively large networks, setting alarms based on hardware addresses will notify you when machines are changed or added. This may not be obvious based on IP address alone, since people who add new machines will often reuse an existing IP address.

Filtering based on hardware addresses is not a reliable security mechanism against hostile insiders. It is trivial to reset the apparent hardware address on most machines, so an attacker can simply choose to use the hardware address of a legitimate machine.

Application Layer Protocols

In most cases, there is a further protocol on top of any or all of the above protocols, specific to the application. These protocols differ widely in their specificity, and there are hundreds, if not thousands, of them (almost as many as there are network-based applications). Much of the rest of this book is about network applications and their protocols.

IP Version 6

The current version of IP (as we write) is officially known as IP Version 4; throughout this book, whenever we talk about IP with no further qualification, that's what we're talking about. There is, however, a new version of IP in the works right now, known as IP Version 6 (IPv6 for short). Why do we need a new version of IP, and how will IPv6 affect you?

The impetus to create IPv6 was one simple problem: the Internet is running out of IP addresses. The Internet has become so popular that there just won't be enough IP network numbers (particularly Class B network numbers, which have proven to be what most sites need) to go around; by some estimates, if nothing had been done, the Internet would have run out of addresses in 1995 or 1996. Fortunately, the problem was recognized, and something was done. Two things, actually—first, the implementation of a set of temporary measures and guidelines to make best possible use of the remaining unassigned addresses, and second, the design and implementation of a new version of IP that would permanently deal with the address exhaustion issue.

If you're going to create a new version of IP in order to deal with address-space exhaustion, you might as well take advantage of the opportunity to deal with a whole raft of other problems or limitations in IP as well, such as encryption, authentication, source routing, and dynamic configuration. (For many people, these limitations are the primary reasons for IPv6, and the addressing problem is merely a handy reason for other people to accept it.) This produces a number of implications for firewalls. According to Steve Bellovin of AT&T Bell Laboratories, a well-known firewalls expert and a participant in the IPv6 design process:[*]

> IPv6 is based on the concept of nested headers. That's how encryption and authentication are done; the "next protocol" field after the IPv6 header specifies an encryption or an authentication header. In turn, their next protocol fields would generally indicate either IPv6 or one of the usual transport protocols, such as TCP or UDP.
>
> Nested IP over IP can be done even without encryption or authentication; that can be used as a form of source routing. A more efficient way is to use the source routing header—which is more useful than the corresponding IPv4 option, and is likely to be used much more, especially for mobile IP.
>
> Some of the implications for firewalls are already apparent. A packet filter must follow down the full chain of headers, understanding and processing each one in turn. (And yes, this can make looking at port numbers more expensive.) A suitably cautious stance dictates that a packet with an unknown header be bounced, whether inbound or outbound. Also, the ease and prevalence of source routing means that cryptographic authentication is absolutely necessary. On the other hand, it is intended that such authentication be a standard, mandatory feature. Encrypted packets are opaque, and hence can't be examined; this is true today, of course, but there aren't very many encryptors in use now. That will change. Also note that encryption can be done host-to-host, host-to-gateway, or gateway-to-gateway, complicating the analysis still more.
>
> Address-based filtering will also be affected, to some extent, by the new autoconfiguration mechanisms. It's vital that any host whose address is mentioned in a filter receive the same address each time. While this is the intent of the standard mechanisms, one needs to be careful about proprietary schemes, dial-up servers, etc. Also, high-order address bits can change, to accommodate the combination of provider-based addressing and easy switching among carriers.
>
> Finally, IPv6 incorporates "flows." Flows are essentially virtual circuits at the IP level; they're intended to be used for things like video, intermediate-hop ATM cir-

---

[*] Steve Bellovin, posting to the Firewalls mailing list, 31 December 1994.

cuit selection, etc. But they can also be used for firewalls, given appropriate authentication: the UDP reply problem might go away if the query had a flow id that was referenced by the response. This, by the way, is a vague idea of mine; there are no standards for how this should be done. The regular flow setup protocol won't work; it's too expensive. But a firewall traversal header might do the job.

As you can see, IPv6 could have a major impact on firewalls, especially with respect to packet filtering. However, IPv6 is not being deployed rapidly. The address exhaustion problem doesn't seem to be as bad as people had feared (under many estimates, the address space ought to have been gone before this edition made it to press). On the other hand, the problem of converting networks from IPv4 to IPv6 has turned out to be worse. The end result is that while IPv6 is still a viable technology that is gaining ground, it's not going to take over from IPv4 in the immediate future; you're going to need an IPv4 firewall for quite some time.

Non-IP Protocols

Other protocols at the same level as IP (e.g., AppleTalk and IPX) provide similar kinds of information as IP, although the headers and operations for these protocols, and therefore their packet filtering characteristics, vary radically. Most packet filtering implementations support IP filtering only and simply drop non-IP packets. Some packages provide limited packet filtering support for non-IP protocols, but this support is usually far less flexible and capable than the router's IP filtering capability.

At this time, packet filtering as a tool isn't as popular and well developed for non-IP protocols, presumably because these protocols are rarely used to communicate outside a single organization over the Internet. (The Internet is, by definition, a network of IP networks.) If you are putting a firewall between parts of your network, you may find that you need to pass non-IP protocols.

In this situation, you should be careful to evaluate what level of security you are actually getting from the filtering. Many packages that claim to support packet filtering on non-IP protocols simply mean that they can recognize non-IP packets as legal packets and allow them through, with minimal logging. For reasonable support of non-IP protocols, you should look for a package developed by people with expertise in the protocol, and you should make sure that it provides features appropriate to the protocol you're trying to filter. Products that were designed as IP routers but claim to support five or six other protocols are probably just trying to meet purchasing requirements, not to actually meet operational requirements well.

Across the Internet, non-IP protocols are handled by encapsulating them within IP protocols. In most cases, you will be limited to permitting or denying encapsulated protocols in their entirety; you can accept all AppleTalk-in-UDP connections, or reject them all. A few packages that support non-IP protocols can recognize these connections when encapsulated and filter on fields in them.

Attacks Based on Low-Level Protocol Details

As we've discussed protocols, we've also mentioned some of the attacks against them. You will often see attacks discussed using the names given to them by the people who wrote the original exploit programs, which are eye-catching but not informative. These names multiply daily, and there's no way for us to document them all here, but we can tell you about a few of the most popular. In fact, although there are dozens and dozens of different attacks, they are pretty much all variations on the same few themes, and knowing the name of the day isn't very important.

Port Scanning

Port scanning is the process of looking for open ports on a machine, in order to figure out what might be attackable. Straightforward port scanning is quite easy to detect, so attackers use a number of methods to disguise port scans. For instance, many machines don't log connections until they're fully made, so an attacker can send an initial packet, with a SYN but no ACK, get back the response (another SYN if the port is open, a RST if it is not), and then stop there. (This is often called a *SYN scan* or a *half open scan*.) Although this won't get logged, it may have other unfortunate effects, particularly if the scanner fails to send a RST when it stops (for instance, it may end up being a denial of service attack against the host or some intermediate device that's trying to keep track of open connections, like a firewall).

Attackers may also send other packets, counting a port as closed if they get a RST and open if they get no response, or any other error. Almost any combination of flags other than SYN by itself can be used for this purpose, although the most common options are FIN by itself, all options on, and all options off. The last two possibilities, sometimes called *Christmas tree* (some network devices show the options with lights, and it makes them all light up like a Christmas tree) and *null*, tend to have unfortunate side effects on weak TCP/IP stacks. Many devices will either crash or disable TCP/IP.

Implementation Weaknesses

Many of the attacks that work at this level are denial of service attacks that exploit weaknesses in TCP/IP implementations to crash machines. For instance, *teardrop* and its relatives send overlapping fragments; there are also attacks that send invalid combinations of options, set invalid length fields, or mark data as urgent when no application would (*winnuke*).

IP Spoofing

In IP spoofing, an attacker sends packets with an incorrect source address. When this happens, replies will be sent to the apparent source address, not to the attacker. This might seem to be a problem, but actually, there are three cases where the attacker doesn't care:

* The attacker can intercept the reply.

* The attacker doesn't need to see the reply.

* The attacker doesn't want the reply; the point of the attack is to make the reply go somewhere else.

The attacker can intercept the reply

If an attacker is somewhere on the network between the destination and the forged source, the attacker may be able to see the reply and carry on a conversation indefinitely. This is the basis of hijacking attacks, which are discussed in more detail later. Figure 4-6 shows an attacker using a forgery this way.

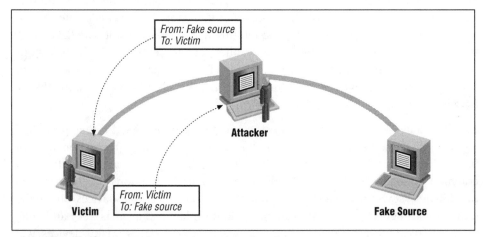

Figure 4-6. Attacker intercepting replies to forged packets

The attacker doesn't need to see the reply

An attacker doesn't always care what the reply is. If the attack is a denial of service, the attacked machine probably isn't going to be able to reply anyway. Even if it isn't, the attacker may be able to make a desired change without needing to see the response. Figure 4-7 shows this kind of attack.

Figure 4-7. Attacker using forged packets for denial of service

The attacker doesn't want the reply

Several attacks rely upon the fact that the reply (or better yet, lots of replies) will go somewhere else. The *smurf* attack uses forged source addresses to attack the host that's the apparent source; an attacker sends a forged packet to some host he or she doesn't like very much (call it "apparentvictim") with a source address of a host that he or she doesn't like at all (call it "realvictim"). "apparentvictim" then replies to "realvictim", tying up network resources at both victim sites but not at the attacker's actual location. The administrators at "apparentvictim" and "realvictim" then start arguing about who is attacking whom and why. This attack has a number of variants using different protocols and methods for multiplying the replies. The most common protocols are ICMP echo and the UDP-based echo service, both of which are discussed in Chapter 22, *Administrative Services*. The most common method of multiplying the replies is to use a broadcast address as the source address. Figure 4-8 shows this kind of attack.

The *land* attack sends a packet with a source identical to the destination, which causes many machines to lock up. Figure 4-9 shows this kind of attack.

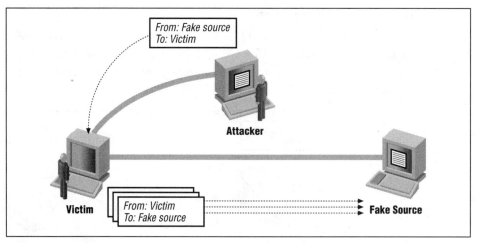

Figure 4-8. Attacker using forged packets to attack a third party

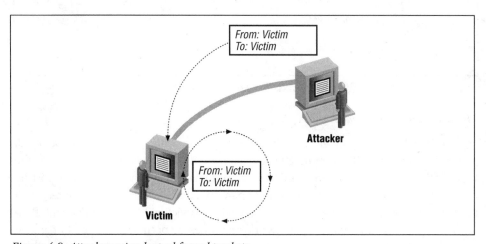

Figure 4-9. Attacker using looped forged packets

Packet Interception

Reading packets as they go by, frequently called *packet sniffing*, is a frequent way of gathering information. If you're passing around important information unencrypted, it may be all that an attacker needs to do.

In order to read a packet, the attacker needs to get the packet somehow. The easiest way to do that is to control some machine that the traffic is supposed to go through anyway (a router or a firewall, for instance). These machines are usually highly protected, however, and don't usually provide tools that an attacker might want to use.

Usually, it's more practical for an attacker to use some less-protected machine, but that means that the attacker needs to be able to read packets that are not addressed to the machine itself. On some networks, that's very easy. An Ethernet network that uses a bus topology, or that uses 10-base T cabling with unintelligent hubs, will send every packet on the network to every machine. Token-ring networks, including FDDI rings, will send most or all packets to all machines. Machines are supposed to ignore the packets that aren't addressed to them, but anybody with full control over a machine can override this and read all the packets, no matter what destination they were sent to.

Using a network switch to connect machines is supposed to avoid this problem. A network switch, by definition, is a network device that has multiple ports and sends traffic only to those ports that are supposed to get it. Unfortunately, switches are not an absolute guarantee. Most switches have an administrative function that will allow a port to receive all traffic. Sometimes there's a single physical port with this property, but sometimes the switch can turn this function on for any port, so that an attacker who can subvert the switch software can get all traffic. Furthermore, switches have to keep track of which addresses belong to which ports, and they only have a finite amount of space to store this information. If that space is exhausted (for instance, because an attacker is sending fake packets from many different addresses), the switch will fail. Some of them will stop sending packets anywhere; others will simply send all packets to all ports; and others provide a configuration parameter to allow you to choose a failure mode.

Some switches offer increased separation of traffic with a facility called a Virtual Local Area Network (VLAN). On a normal switch, all the ports are part of the same network. A switch that supports VLANs will be able to treat different ports as parts of different networks. Traffic is only supposed to go between ports on different VLANs if a router is involved, just as if the ports were on completely separate switches. Normal tricks to confuse switches will compromise only one VLAN. VLANs are a convenient tool in many situations, and they provide a small measure of increased security over a plain switched network. However, you are still running all of the traffic through a single device, which could be compromised. There are known attacks that will move traffic from one VLAN to another in most implementations, and almost any administrative error will compromise the separation. You should not rely on VLANs to provide strong, secure separation between networks.

5

Firewall Technologies

In Part I, we introduced Internet firewalls and summarized what they can and cannot do to improve network security. In this chapter, we present major firewalls concepts. What are the terms you will hear in discussions of Internet firewalls? What are the components that can be put together to build these common firewall architectures? How do you evaluate a firewall design? In the remaining chapters of this book, we'll describe these components and architectures in detail.

Some Firewall Definitions

You may be familiar with some of the following firewall terms, and some may be new to you. Some may seem familiar, but they may be used in a way that is slightly different from what you're accustomed to (though we try to use terms that are as standard as possible). Unfortunately, there is no completely consistent terminology for firewall architectures and components. Different people use terms in different—or, worse still, conflicting—ways. Also, these same terms sometimes have other meanings in other networking fields; the following definitions are for a firewalls context.

Here are some very basic definitions; we describe these terms in greater detail elsewhere:

Firewall
> A component or set of components that restricts access between a protected network and the Internet, or between other sets of networks.

Host
> A computer system attached to a network.

Bastion host

A computer system that must be highly secured because it is vulnerable to attack, usually because it is exposed to the Internet and is a main point of contact for users of internal networks. It gets its name from the highly fortified projections on the outer walls of medieval castles.*

Dual-homed host

A general-purpose computer system that has at least two network interfaces (or homes).

Network address translation (NAT)

A procedure by which a router changes data in packets to modify the network addresses. This allows a router to conceal the addresses of network hosts on one side of it. This technique can enable a large number of hosts to connect to the Internet using a small number of allocated addresses or can allow a network that's configured with illegal or unroutable addresses to connect to the Internet using valid addresses. It is not actually a security technique, although it can provide a small amount of additional security. However, it generally runs on the same routers that make up part of the firewall.

Packet

The fundamental unit of communication on the Internet.

Packet filtering

The action a device takes to selectively control the flow of data to and from a network. Packet filters allow or block packets, usually while routing them from one network to another (most often from the Internet to an internal network, and vice versa). To accomplish packet filtering, you set up a set of rules that specify what types of packets (e.g., those to or from a particular IP address or port) are to be allowed and what types are to be blocked. Packet filtering may occur in a router, in a bridge, or on an individual host. It is sometimes known as *screening.*†

Perimeter network

A network added between a protected network and an external network, in order to provide an additional layer of security. A perimeter network is sometimes called a *DMZ*, which stands for *De-Militarized Zone* (named after the zone separating North and South Korea).

---

* Marcus Ranum, who is generally held responsible for the popularity of this term in the firewalls professional community, says, "Bastions . . . overlook critical areas of defense, usually having stronger walls, room for extra troops, and the occasional useful tub of boiling hot oil for discouraging attackers".

† Some networking literature (in particular, the BSD Unix release from Berkeley) uses the term "packet filtering" to refer to something else entirely (selecting certain packets off a network for analysis, as is done by the *etherfind* or *tcpdump* programs).

Proxy

A program that deals with external servers on behalf of internal clients. Proxy clients talk to proxy servers, which relay approved client requests on to real servers, and relay answers back to clients.

Virtual private network (VPN)

A network where packets that are internal to a private network pass across a public network, without this being obvious to hosts on the private network. In general, VPNs use encryption to protect the packets as they pass across the public network. VPN solutions are popular because it is often cheaper to connect two networks via public networks (for instance, getting them both Internet connections) than via private networks (like traditional leased-line connections between the sites).

The next few sections briefly describe the major technologies associated with firewalls: packet filtering, proxy services, network address translation, and virtual private networks.

There are legitimate questions about how to distinguish between packet filtering and proxying, particularly when dealing with complex packet filtering systems and simple proxies. Many people believe that systems that pay attention to individual protocols and/or modify packets should not be considered packet filters, and may even refer to these systems as *transparent proxies*. In fact, these systems don't behave much like older, simpler packet filtering systems, and it's a good idea not to apply generalizations about packet filtering to them blindly. On the other hand, they don't behave much like proxying systems, either.

Similarly, a number of proxying systems provide *generic proxies,* which essentially function like packet filters, accepting all traffic to a given port without analyzing it. It's advisable to pay close attention to the individual technology a product uses, without making assumptions based on whether it claims to be a packet filter or a proxy. However, many systems still are clearly packet filters or clearly proxies, so it is worth understanding what these technologies are and how they work.

Packet Filtering

Packet filtering systems route packets between internal and external hosts, but they do it selectively. They allow or block certain types of packets in a way that reflects a site's own security policy, as shown in Figure 5-1. The type of router used in a packet filtering firewall is known as a *screening router*.

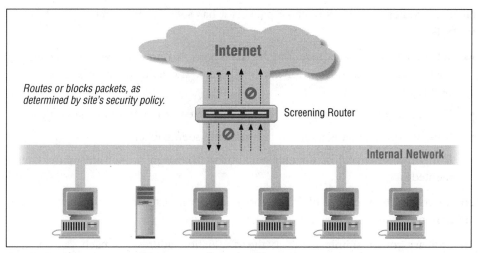

Figure 5-1. Using a screening router to do packet filtering

As we discuss in Chapter 8, *Packet Filtering*, every packet has a set of headers containing certain information. The main information is:

- IP source address

- IP destination address

- Protocol (whether the packet is a TCP, UDP, or ICMP packet)

- TCP or UDP source port

- TCP or UDP destination port

- ICMP message type

- Packet size

The router can also look past the packet headers at data further on in the packet; this allows it, for instance, to filter packets based on more detailed information (like the name of the web page that somebody is requesting) and to verify that packets appear to be formatted as expected for their destination port. The router can also make sure that the packet is valid (it actually is the size that it claims to be and is a legal size, for instance), which helps catch a number of denial of service attacks based on malformed packets.

In addition, the router knows things about the packet that aren't reflected in the packet itself, such as:

- The interface the packet arrives on

- The interface the packet will go out on

Finally, a router that keeps track of packets it has seen knows some useful historical facts, such as:

- Whether this packet appears to be a response to another packet (that is, its source was the destination of a recent packet and its destination is the source of that other packet)

- How many other packets have recently been seen to or from the same host

- Whether this packet is identical to a recently seen packet

- If this packet is part of a larger packet that has been broken into parts (fragmented)

To understand how packet filtering works, let's look at the difference between an ordinary router and a screening router.

An ordinary router simply looks at the destination address of each packet and picks the best way it knows to send that packet towards that destination. The decision about how to handle the packet is based solely on its destination. There are two possibilities: the router knows how to send the packet towards its destination, and it does so; or the router does not know how to send the packet towards its destination, and it forgets about the packet and returns an ICMP "destination unreachable" message, to the packet's source.

A screening router, on the other hand, looks at packets more closely. In addition to determining whether or not it *can* route a packet towards its destination, a screening router also determines whether or not it *should.* "Should" or "should not" are determined by the site's security policy, which the screening router has been configured to enforce.

Packet filtering may also be performed by devices that pay attention only to "should" and "should not" and have no ability to route. Devices that do this are *packet filtering bridges.* They are rarer than packet filtering routers, mostly because they are dedicated security devices that don't provide all the other functions that routers do. Most sites would rather add features to routers that they need anyway, instead of adding a dedicated device. However, being a dedicated device provides advantages for packet filtering bridges; in particular, they are harder to detect and attack than packet filtering routers. They provide the same general features that we discuss for packet filtering routers.

Once it has looked at all the information, a straightforward packet filtering router can do any of the following things:

- Send the packet on to the destination it was bound for.

- Drop the packet—just forget it, without notifying the sender.

- Reject the packet—refuse to forward it, and return an error to the sender.

- Log information about the packet.

- Set off an alarm to notify somebody about the packet immediately.

More sophisticated routers might also be able to do one or more of these things:

- Modify the packet (for instance, to do network address translation).

- Send the packet on to a destination other than the one that it was bound for (for instance, to force transactions through a proxy server or perform load balancing).

- Modify the filtering rules (for instance, to accept replies to a UDP packet or to deny all traffic from a site that has sent hostile packets).

The fact that servers for particular Internet services reside at certain port numbers lets the router block or allow certain types of connections simply by specifying the appropriate port number (e.g., TCP port 23 for Telnet connections) in the set of rules specified for packet filtering. (Chapter 8, *Packet Filtering*, describes in detail how you construct these rules.)

Here are some examples of ways in which you might program a screening router to selectively route packets to or from your site:

- Block all incoming connections from systems outside the internal network, except for incoming SMTP connections (so that you can receive electronic mail).

- Block all connections to or from certain systems you distrust.

- Allow electronic mail and FTP services, but block dangerous services like TFTP, the X Window System, RPC, and the "r" services (*rlogin*, *rsh*, *rcp*, etc.). (See Chapter 13, *Internet Services and Firewalls*, for more information.)

Packet filtering devices that keep track of packets that they see are frequently called *stateful packet filters* (because they keep information about the state of transactions). They may also be called *dynamic packet filters* because they change their handling of packets dynamically depending on the traffic they see. Devices that look at the content of packets, rather than at just their headers, are frequently called *intelligent packet filters*. In practice, almost all stateful packet filters also are capable of looking at the contents of packets, and many are also capable of modifying the contents of packets, so you may see all these capabilities lumped together under the heading "stateful packet filtering". However, something can legitimately be called a "stateful packet filter" without having the ability to do advanced content filtering or modification.

A packet filtering system is also a logical place to provide virtual private network or network address translation services. Since the packet filter is already looking at all of the packets, it can easily identify packets that are intended for a destination that is part of the virtual private network, encrypt those packets, and encapsulate them in another packet bound for the appropriate destination.

Advantages of Packet Filtering

Packet filtering has a number of advantages.

One screening router can help protect an entire network

One of the key advantages of packet filtering is that a single, strategically placed packet filtering router can help protect an entire network. If only one router connects your site to the Internet, you gain tremendous leverage on network security, regardless of the size of your site, by doing packet filtering on that router.

Simple packet filtering is extremely efficient

Because simple packet filtering requires paying attention only to a few packet headers, it can be done with very low overhead. Proxying is a fairly time-consuming operation, and adding proxying means directing connections through another program, usually on a machine that otherwise wouldn't be necessary to the routing process. Packet filtering takes place on a machine that was already in the critical path, and introduces a much smaller delay.

However, there is no free lunch; the more work your packet filters do, the slower they will be. If your packet filters behave like proxies, doing complicated data-driven operations that require keeping track of multiple packets, they will tend to perform like proxies as well.

Packet filtering is widely available

Packet filtering capabilities are available in many hardware and software routing products, both commercial and freely available over the Internet. Most sites already have packet filtering capabilities available in the routers they use.

Most commercial router products include packet filtering capabilities. Packet filtering capabilities are also available for a number of general-purpose computers. These are discussed further in Chapter 8, *Packet Filtering*.

Disadvantages of Packet Filtering

Although packet filtering provides many advantages, there are some disadvantages to using packet filtering as well.

Current filtering tools are not perfect

Despite the widespread availability of packet filtering in various hardware and software packages, packet filtering is still not a perfect tool. The packet filtering capabilities of many of these products share, to a greater or lesser degree, common limitations:

- The packet filtering rules tend to be hard to configure. Although there is a range of difficulty, it mostly runs from slightly mind-twisting to brain-numbingly impossible.

- Once configured, the packet filtering rules tend to be hard to test.

- The packet filtering capabilities of many of the products are incomplete, making implementation of certain types of highly desirable filters difficult or impossible.

- Like anything else, packet filtering packages may have bugs in them; these bugs are more likely than proxying bugs to result in security problems. Usually, a proxy that fails simply stops passing data, while a failed packet filtering implementation may allow packets it should have denied.

Packet filtering reduces router performance

Doing packet filtering places a significant extra load on a router. As we discussed previously, more complex filters place more load on the router, but in some cases, simply turning on packet filtering on a given interface can also cost you a lot of performance on some routers, because the filtering is incompatible with certain caching strategies commonly used for performance enhancement. Cisco's "fastpath" functionality is an example of this; normally, fastpath can perform basic routing functions completely on the interface card, without involving the main CPU, but using some forms of filtering requires involving the main CPU for each packet, which is much slower. What enables/disables fastpath depends on the hardware and software version.

Some policies can't readily be enforced by normal packet filtering routers

The information that a packet filtering router has available to it doesn't allow you to specify some rules you might like to have. For example, packets say what host they come from but generally not what user. Therefore, you can't enforce restrictions on particular users. Similarly, packets say what port they're going to but not what application; when you enforce restrictions on higher-level protocols, you do it by port number, hoping that nothing else is running on the port assigned to that protocol. Malicious insiders can easily subvert this kind of control.

This problem is eased by using more intelligent packet filters; however, in each case, you have to give up some of the advantages of normal packet filtering. For instance, a packet filter can insist that users authenticate themselves before sending packets, and then it can filter packets by username. However, this removes the transparency advantage of normal packet filtering. A packet filter can also do protocol validity checking, but this is less than perfect and also increases filtering overhead.

Proxy Services

In general, a *proxy* is something or someone who does something on somebody else's behalf. For instance, you may give somebody the ability to vote for you by proxy in an election.

Proxy services are specialized application or server programs that take users' requests for Internet services (such as FTP and Telnet) and forward them to the actual services. The proxies provide replacement connections and act as gateways to the services. For this reason, proxies are sometimes known as *application-level gateways.** In this book, when we are talking about proxy services, we are specifically talking about proxies run for security purposes, which are run on a firewall host: either a dual-homed host with an interface on the internal network and one on the external network, or some other bastion host that has access to the Internet and is accessible from the internal machines.

You will also run into proxies that are primarily designed for network efficiency instead of for security; these are *caching proxies,* which keep copies of the information for each request that they proxy. The advantage of a caching proxy is that if multiple internal hosts request the same data, the data can be provided directly by the proxy. Caching proxies can significantly reduce the load on network connections. There are proxy servers that provide both security and caching; in general, they are better at one purpose than the other.

Proxy services sit, more or less transparently, between a user on the inside (on the internal network) and a service on the outside (on the Internet). Instead of talking to each other directly, each talks to a proxy. Proxies handle all the communication between users and Internet services behind the scenes.

Transparency is the major benefit of proxy services. It's essentially smoke and mirrors. To the user, a proxy server presents the illusion that the user is dealing directly with the real server. To the real server, the proxy server presents the illu-

---

* Firewall terminologies differ. Whereas we use the term *proxy service* to encompass the entire proxy approach, other authors refer to *application-level gateways* and *circuit-level gateways.* Although there are small differences between the meanings of these various terms, which we'll explore in Chapter 9, *Proxy Systems,* in general our discussion of proxies refers to the same type of technology other authors mean when they refer to these gateway systems.

sion that the real server is dealing directly with a user on the proxy host (as opposed to the user's real host).

How do proxy services work? Let's look at the simplest case, where we add proxy services to a dual-homed host. (We'll describe these hosts in some detail in the "Dual-Homed Host" section in Chapter 6, *Firewall Architectures.*)

 Proxy services are effective only when they're used in conjunction with a mechanism that restricts direct communications between the internal and external hosts. Dual-homed hosts and packet filtering are two such mechanisms. If internal hosts are able to communicate directly with external hosts, there's no need for users to use proxy services, and so (in general) they won't. Such a bypass probably isn't in accordance with your security policy.

As Figure 5-2 shows, a proxy service requires two components: a proxy server and a proxy client. In this illustration, the *proxy server* runs on the dual-homed host (as we discuss in Chapter 9, *Proxy Systems*, there are other ways to set up a proxy server). A *proxy client* is a special version of a normal client program (e.g., a Telnet or FTP client) that talks to the proxy server rather than to the "real" server out on the Internet; in some configurations, normal client programs can be used as proxy clients. The proxy server evaluates requests from the proxy client and decides which to approve and which to deny. If a request is approved, the proxy server contacts the real server on behalf of the client (thus the term *proxy*) and proceeds to relay requests from the proxy client to the real server, and responses from the real server to the proxy client.

In some proxy systems, instead of installing custom client proxy software, you'll use standard software but set up custom user procedures for using it. (We'll describe how this works in Chapter 9.)

There are also systems that provide a hybrid between packet filtering and proxying where a network device intercepts the connection and acts as a proxy or redirects the connection to a proxy; this allows proxying without making changes to the clients or the user procedures.

The proxy server doesn't always just forward users' requests on to the real Internet services. The proxy server can control what users do because it can make decisions about the requests it processes. Depending on your site's security policy, requests might be allowed or refused. For example, the FTP proxy might refuse to let users export files, or it might allow users to import files only from certain sites. More sophisticated proxy services might allow different capabilities to different hosts, rather than enforcing the same restrictions on all hosts.

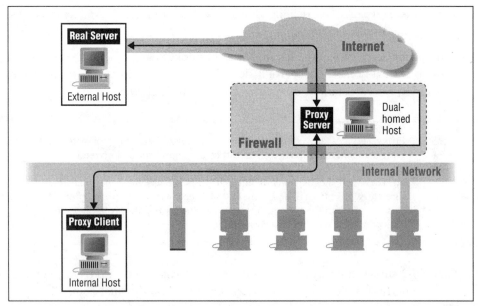

Figure 5-2. Using proxy services with a dual-homed host

Some proxy servers do in fact just forward requests on, no matter what they are. These may be called *generic proxies* or *port forwarders*. Programs that do this are providing basically the same protections that you would get if you had a packet filter in place that was allowing traffic on that port. You do not get any significant increase in security by replacing packet filters with proxies that do exactly the same thing (you gain some protection against malformed packets, but you lose by adding an attackable proxying program).

Some excellent software is available for proxying. SOCKS is a proxy construction toolkit, designed to make it easy to convert existing client/server applications into proxy versions of those same applications. The Trusted Information Systems Internet Firewall Toolkit (TIS FWTK) includes proxy servers for a number of common Internet protocols, including Telnet, FTP, HTTP, *rlogin*, X11, and others; these proxy servers are designed to be used in conjunction with custom user procedures. See the discussion of these packages in Chapter 9, *Proxy Systems*.

Many standard client and server programs, both commercial and freely available, now come equipped with their own proxying capabilities or with support for generic proxy systems like SOCKS. These capabilities can be enabled at runtime or compile time.

Most proxy systems are used to control and optimize outbound connections; they are controlled by the site where the clients are. It is also possible to use proxy systems to control and optimize inbound connections to servers (for instance, to balance connections among multiple servers or to apply extra security). This is sometimes called *reverse proxying.*

Advantages of Proxying

There are a number of advantages to using proxy services.

Proxy services can be good at logging

Because proxy servers can understand the application protocol, they can allow logging to be performed in a particularly effective way. For example, instead of logging all of the data transferred, an FTP proxy server can log only the commands issued and the server responses received; this results in a much smaller and more useful log.

Proxy services can provide caching

Since all requests are passing through the proxy service anyway, the proxy can provide caching, keeping local copies of the requested data. If the number of repeat requests is significant, caching can significantly increase performance and reduce the load on network links.

Proxy services can do intelligent filtering

Since a proxy service is looking at specific connections, it is frequently able to do filtering more intelligently than a packet filter. For instance, proxy services are much more capable of filtering HTTP by content type (for instance, to remove Java or JavaScript) and better at virus detection than packet filtering systems.

Proxy systems can perform user-level authentication

Because a proxy system is actively involved in the connection, it is easy for it to do user authentication and to take actions that depend on the user involved. Although this is possible with packet filtering systems, it is much more difficult.

Proxy systems automatically provide protection for weak or faulty IP implementations

As a proxy system sits between a client and the Internet, it generates completely new IP packets for the client. It can therefore protect clients from deliberately malformed IP packets. (You just need a proxy system that isn't vulnerable to the bad packets!)

Disadvantages of Proxying

There are also some disadvantages to using proxy services.

Proxy services lag behind nonproxied services

Although proxy software is widely available for the older and simpler services like FTP and Telnet, proven software for newer or less widely used services is harder to find. There's usually a distinct lag between the introduction of a service and the availability of proxying servers for it; the length of the lag depends primarily on how well the service is designed for proxying. This makes it difficult for a site to offer new services immediately as they become available. Until suitable proxy software is available, a system that needs new services may have to be placed outside the firewall, opening up potential security holes. (Some services can be run through generic proxies, which will give at least minimal protection.)

Proxy services may require different servers for each service

You may need a different proxy server for each protocol, because the proxy server may need to understand the protocol in order to determine what to allow and disallow, and in order to masquerade as a client to the real server and as the real server to the proxy client. Collecting, installing, and configuring all these various servers can be a lot of work. Again, you may be able to use a generic proxy, but generic proxies provide only the same sorts of protection and functionality that you could get from packet filters.

Products and packages differ greatly in the ease with which they can be configured, but making things easier in one place can make it harder in others. For example, servers that are particularly easy to configure can be limited in flexibility; they're easy to configure because they make certain assumptions about how they're going to be used, which may or may not be correct or appropriate for your site.

Proxy services usually require modifications to clients, applications, or procedures

Except for services designed for proxying, you will need to use modified clients, applications, and/or procedures. These modifications can have drawbacks; people can't always use the readily available tools with their normal instructions.

Because of these modifications, proxied applications don't always work as well as nonproxied applications. They tend to bend protocol specifications, and some clients and servers are less flexible than others.

Network Address Translation

Network address translation (NAT) allows a network to use one set of network addresses internally and a different set when dealing with external networks. Network address translation does not, by itself, provide any security, but it helps to conceal the internal network layout and to force connections to go through a choke point (because connections to untranslated addresses will not work, and the choke point does the translation).

Like packet filtering, network address translation works by having a router do extra work. In this case, not only does the router send packets on, but it also modifies them. When an internal machine sends a packet to the outside, the network address translation system modifies the source address of the packet to make the packet look as if it is coming from a valid address. When an external machine sends a packet to the inside, the network address translation system modifies the destination address to turn the externally visible address into the correct internal address. The network address translation system can also modify the source and destination port numbers (this is sometimes called Port and Address Translation or PAT). Figure 5-3 shows a network address translation system modifying only addresses, while Figure 5-4 shows port and address translation.

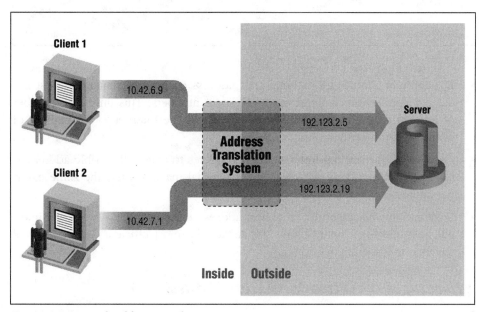

Figure 5-3. Network address translation

Network address translation systems can use different schemes for translating between internal and external addresses:

- Allocate one external host address for each internal address and always apply the same translation. This provides no savings in address space, and it slows down connections; it is normally a temporary measure used by sites that have been using illegal address spaces but are in the process of moving to using valid addresses.

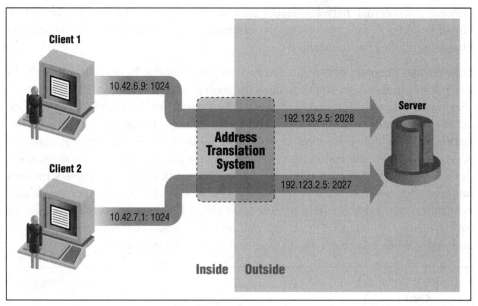

Figure 5-4. Port and address translation

- Dynamically allocate an external host address each time an internal host initiates a connection, without modifying port numbers. This limits the number of internal hosts that can simultaneously access the Internet to the number of available external addresses.

- Create a fixed mapping from internal addresses to externally visible addresses, but use port mapping so that multiple internal machines use the same external addresses.

- Dynamically allocate an external host address and port pair each time an internal host initiates a connection. This makes the most efficient possible use of the external host addresses.

Advantages of Network Address Translation

The main purpose of network address translation is to economize on address space, but it can also have some security advantages.

Network address translation helps to enforce the firewall's control over outbound connections

Since individual hosts have addresses that won't work on the external network, they require the assistance of the network address translation system to connect. If a host finds a way to connect to the Internet without going through the address translation, the connection won't work.

Network address translation can help restrict incoming traffic

Depending on how you configure a network address translation system, it can provide stronger restrictions on incoming traffic than packet filtering. A network address translation system that's doing dynamic translation will allow only packets that are part of a current interaction initiated from the inside. This is similar to the protection that a dynamic packet filter offers, but the changing IP addresses put stronger time constraints on attackers. Not only can they attack only certain ports, but if they wait too long, the address translation will have gone away, and the entire address will have disappeared or been given to another host.

Many people assume that all network address translation systems provide this sort of protection, but this is not true. If you configure a network address translation system to do static translations, it may provide no restrictions at all on incoming traffic. Even doing dynamic translations, the simplest implementations allocate an entire externally visible address to the internal host and translate all traffic sent to that address. This does limit the time that an attacker has, but otherwise provides no protection at all.

*Network address translation helps to conceal the internal
network's configuration*

The less an attacker knows about you, the better off you are. A network address translation system makes it much more difficult for an attacker to determine how many computers you have, what kind of machines they are, and how they're arranged on the network. Note, however, that many protocols leak useful information (for instance, they may include the client's IP address or hostname in places where the network address translation system doesn't need to change it). When we discuss the network address translation properties of protocols, we attempt to mention leaks of this sort.

Disadvantages of Network Address Translation

While network address translation is a very useful way of conserving network address space, it presents some problems.

*Dynamic allocation requires state information
that is not always available*

It is very easy for a network address translation system to tell whether or not a host has stopped using a TCP connection, but there's no way to know at the packet header level whether a UDP packet is part of an ongoing conversation or is an isolated event. This means that a network address translation system has to guess how long it should keep a particular translation. If it guesses incorrectly, responses may be lost or delivered to unexpected hosts.

Embedded IP addresses are a problem for network address translation

Network address translation systems normally translate the addresses in the headers of packets (see Chapter 4, *Packets and Protocols*, for more information about packet layout). Some protocols also hide addresses in other places, and in order to find those addresses, the network address translator has to understand the protocol enough to find and modify the address, while preserving the validity of the packet. Most network address translation systems are capable of doing this for at least some protocols (for instance, FTP) but not for all protocols.

Network address translation interferes with some encryption and authentication systems

Systems for encrypting data often attempt to ensure the integrity of the data, so that the systems that are communicating know that packets have not been tampered with in transit. Network address translation is a form of tampering with the data in transit. If the protocol that's being translated does not protect the data that the network address translation system modifies, it will work. Otherwise, the integrity checking will be violated, and connections will fail. In most cases, protocols that do not have embedded IP addresses are compatible (the packet headers are not part of the protocol's protected data). The major exception to this rule is IPsec, which protects the entire packet, including headers. Network address translation is almost guaranteed to fail for protocols that combine embedded IP addresses with data integrity protection.

Dynamic allocation of addresses interferes with logging

If you are logging information after the network address translation happens, the logs will show the translated addresses, and you will have to correlate the logs with information from the network address translation system to figure out what internal system is actually involved. For instance, if you have a screened subnet architecture (discussed in Chapter 6, *Firewall Architectures*), and you are doing network address translation on the interior router, the translated addresses will be in logs from the exterior router or from a caching web proxy server on the screened subnet. Although log correlation is theoretically possible, it may be difficult, and clock synchronization will be critical.

Dynamic allocation of ports may interfere with packet filtering

Packet filtering systems pay attention to source and destination port numbers in order to try to figure out what protocol a packet should be using. Changing the source port may change the packet's acceptability. In most cases, this is not a problem because address translation systems are translating for clients, which are usually allowed to use any port above 1023. However, if ports above 1023 are translated to ports below 1023, traffic may be dropped.

Virtual Private Networks

A *virtual private network* (VPN) is a way of employing encryption and integrity protection so that you can use a public network (for instance, the Internet) as if it were a private network (a piece of cabling that you control). Making a private, high-speed, long-distance connection between two sites is much more expensive than connecting the same two sites to a public high-speed network, but it's also much more secure. A virtual private network is an attempt to combine the advantages of a public network (it's cheap and widely available) with some of the advantages of a private network (it's secure).

Fundamentally, all virtual private networks that run over the Internet employ the same principle: traffic is encrypted, integrity protected, and encapsulated into new packets, which are sent across the Internet to something that undoes the encapsulation, checks the integrity, and decrypts the traffic.

Virtual private networks are not exactly a firewall technology, but we discuss them here for several reasons:

- If you're using virtual private networking, you need to be careful about how it interacts with the firewall. In many cases, the firewall can't control traffic that comes in over the virtual network, which makes it a way to avoid the firewall controls and open new insecurities.

- A firewall is a convenient place to add virtual private networking features.

- We will frequently mention virtual private networking as a way to provide remote services that cannot be provided securely using other firewall techniques.

Where Do You Encrypt?

Virtual private networks depend on encryption. That encryption can be done as a transport method, where a host decides to encrypt traffic when it is generated, or as a tunnel, where traffic is encrypted and decrypted somewhere in between the source and the destination. The question of where you do the encryption and decryption relative to your packet filtering is an important one. If you do the encryption and decryption inside the packet filtering perimeter (i.e., on your internal net), then the filters just have to allow the encrypted packets in and out. This is especially easy if you're doing tunneling, because all the tunneled packets will be addressed to the same remote address and port number at the other end of the tunnel (the decryption unit). On the other hand, doing the encryption and decryption inside your filtering perimeter means that packets arriving encrypted are not subject to the scrutiny of the packet filters. This leaves you vulnerable to attack from the other site if that site has been compromised.

If you do the encryption and decryption outside the packet filtering perimeter (i.e., on your perimeter net or in your exterior router), then the packets coming in from the other site can be subjected to the full scrutiny of your packet filtering system. On the other hand, they can also be subjected to the full scrutiny of anyone who can read traffic on your perimeter net, including intruders.

Key Distribution and Certificates

As with any encryption and integrity protection system, key distribution can be a very sticky problem. A number of choices are available, including sharing keys or using a public key system; see Appendix C, *Cryptography*, for descriptions of these systems and the advantages and disadvantages of each.

Advantages of Virtual Private Networks

Most of the advantages of virtual private networks are economic; it's cheaper to use shared public networks than it is to set up dedicated connections, whether those are leased lines between sites or modem pools that allow individual machines to connect to a central site. On the other hand, virtual private networks also provide some security advantages.

Virtual private networks provide overall encryption

A virtual private network conceals all the traffic that goes over it. Not only does it guarantee that all the information is encrypted, but it also keeps people from knowing which internal machines are being used and with what protocols. You can protect information from snooping by using individual encrypted protocols, but attackers will still have some idea what machines are talking and what kind of information they're exchanging (for instance, if you use an encrypted mail protocol, they will know that things are being mailed). A virtual private network conceals more information.

Virtual private networks allow you to remotely use protocols that are difficult to secure any other way

Some protocols are extremely difficult to provide securely through a firewall. For instance, a number of protocols used on Microsoft systems are based on SMB, which provides a wide variety of services with different security implications over the same ports and connections. Packet filtering and proxying both have trouble adding security to SMB. Virtual private networking provides a way to give remote access for these protocols without letting people attack them from the Internet at large.

Disadvantages of Virtual Private Networks

Although virtual private networks are an important security tool, they also present problems in a firewall environment.

Virtual private networks involve dangerous network connections

A virtual private network runs over an actual network, which is presumably not a private network. The hosts on the virtual private network must be connected to that actual network, and if you're not careful, they will be vulnerable to attack from that network. For instance, if you use a virtual private network to provide connectivity to your internal network for mobile users who connect to the Internet, their machines may be attacked from the Internet.

Ideally, a virtual private network system will disable all other uses of the network interface. It's important to choose a system that will allow you to force this on the remote system. It's not good enough to have a system where the remote system is able to turn off other uses because the user on the remote system may turn networking back on. It's very tempting as a way to get rapid access to Internet resources.

Virtual private networks extend the network you must protect

When you attach something via a virtual private network, you are making it part of your internal network. If a machine on the virtual private network is broken into, the attacker will then be able to use the virtual private network to attack the rest of your site, from something that's treated as if it were inside of your local network. Virtual private networking is commonly used to give access to machines that are much more vulnerable than those that are physically on the network—for instance, laptops that are carried around in public, home machines that curious children have physical access to, and machines owned by other sites with interests and policies that are not identical to yours.

Even if the virtual private network disables other uses of the network interface it is running over, the machine may have other network interfaces. This can make it into a gateway between your network and others, inside your network's security perimeter.

Because of this, you want to be careful how you attach the virtual private network to your real private network, and how you secure the remote end. It may not be appropriate to make the virtual private network a seamless part of your internal network. Consider putting in a subsidiary firewall or at least special intrusion detection to watch for problems.

6

Firewall Architectures

This chapter describes a variety of ways to put firewall components together, and discusses their advantages and disadvantages. We'll tell you what some appropriate uses are for each architecture.

Single-Box Architectures

The simplest firewall architectures have a single object that acts as the firewall. In general, the security advantage of *single-box architectures* is that they provide a single place that you can concentrate on and be sure that you have correctly configured, while the disadvantage is that your security is entirely dependent on a single place. There is no defense in depth, but on the other hand, you know exactly what your weakest link is and how weak it is, which is much harder with multiple layers.

In practice, the advantages of single-box architectures are not in their security but in other practical concerns. Compared to a multiple-layer system that's integrated with your network, a single-box architecture is cheaper, easier to understand and explain to management, and easier to get from an external vendor. This makes it the solution of choice for small sites. It also makes it a tempting solution for people who are looking for magic security solutions that can be put in once and forgotten about. While there are very good single-box firewalls, there are no magic firewalls, and single-box solutions require the same difficult decisions, careful configuration, and ongoing maintenance that all other firewalls do.

Screening Router

It is possible to use a packet filtering system by itself as a firewall, as shown in Figure 6-1, using just a *screening router* to protect an entire network. This is a low-cost system, since you almost always need a router to connect to the Internet anyway, and you can simply configure packet filtering in that router. On the other hand, it's not very flexible; you can permit or deny protocols by port number, but it's hard to allow some operations while denying others in the same protocol, or to be sure that what's coming in on a given port is actually the protocol you wanted to allow. In addition, it gives you no depth of defense. If the router is compromised, you have no further security.

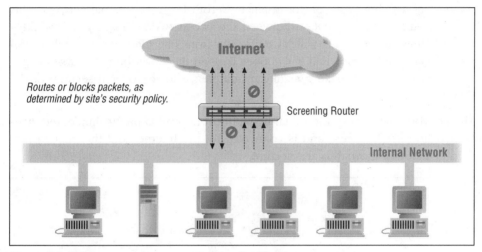

Figure 6-1. Using a screening router to do packet filtering

Appropriate uses

A screening router is an appropriate firewall for a situation where:

- The network being protected already has a high level of host security.

- The number of protocols being used is limited, and the protocols themselves are straightforward.

- You require maximum performance and redundancy.

Screening routers are most useful for internal firewalls and for networks that are dedicated to providing services to the Internet. It's not uncommon for Internet service providers to use nothing but a screening router between their service hosts and the Internet, for instance.

Dual-Homed Host

A *dual-homed host architecture* is built around the dual-homed host computer, a computer that has at least two network interfaces. Such a host could act as a router between the networks these interfaces are attached to; it is capable of routing IP packets from one network to another. However, to use a dual-homed host as a firewall, you disable this routing function. Thus, IP packets from one network (e.g., the Internet) are not directly routed to the other network (e.g., the internal, protected network). Systems inside the firewall can communicate with the dual-homed host, and systems outside the firewall (on the Internet) can communicate with the dual-homed host, but these systems can't communicate directly with each other. IP traffic between them is completely blocked.

Some variations on the dual-homed host architecture use IP to the Internet and some other network protocol (for instance, NetBEUI) on the internal network. This helps to enforce the separation between the two networks, making it less likely that host misconfigurations will let traffic slip from one interface to another, and also reducing the chance that if this does happen there will be vulnerable clients. However, it does not make a significant difference to the overall security of the firewall.

The network architecture for a dual-homed host firewall is pretty simple: the dual-homed host sits between, and is connected to, the Internet and the internal network. Figure 6-2 shows this architecture.

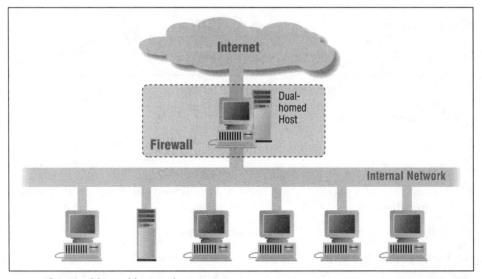

Figure 6-2. Dual-homed host architecture

Dual-homed hosts can provide a very high level of control. If you aren't allowing packets to go between external and internal networks at all, you can be sure that any packet on the internal network that has an external source is evidence of some kind of security problem.

On the other hand, dual-homed hosts aren't high-performance devices. A dual-homed host has more work to do for each connection than a packet filter does, and correspondingly needs more resources. A dual-homed host won't support as much traffic as an equivalent packet filtering system.

Since a dual-homed host is a single point of failure, it's important to make certain that its host security is absolutely impeccable. An attacker who can compromise the dual-homed host has full access to your site (no matter what protocols you are running). An attacker who crashes the dual-homed host has cut you off from the Internet. This makes dual-homed hosts inappropriate if being able to reach the Internet is critical to your business.

You are particularly vulnerable to problems with the host's IP implementation, which can crash the machine or pass traffic through it. These problems exist with packet filtering routers as well, but they are less frequent and usually easier to fix. Architectures that involve multiple devices are usually more resilient because multiple different IP implementations are involved.

A dual-homed host can provide services only by proxying them, or by having users log into the dual-homed host directly. You want to avoid having users log into the dual-homed host directly. As we discuss in Chapter 10, *Bastion Hosts*, user accounts present significant security problems by themselves. They present special problems on dual-homed hosts, where users may unexpectedly enable services you consider insecure. Furthermore, most users find it inconvenient to use a dual-homed host by logging into it.

Proxying is much less problematic but may not be available for all services you're interested in. Chapter 9, *Proxy Systems*, discusses some workarounds for this situation, but they do not apply in every case. Using a dual-homed host as your only network connection actually slightly eases some problems with proxying; if the host pretends to be a router, it can intercept packets bound for the outside world and transparently proxy them without anybody else's cooperation.

Proxying is much better at supporting outbound services (internal users using resources on the Internet) than inbound services (users on the Internet using resources on the internal network). In a dual-homed host configuration, you will normally have to provide services to the Internet by running them on the dual-homed host. This is not usually advisable because providing services to the Internet is risky, and the dual-homed host is a security-critical machine that you don't want to put risky services on. It might be acceptable to put a minimally functional web server on the dual-homed host (for instance, one that was only capable of providing HTML files and had no active content features, additional protocols, or forms processing), but it would clearly be extremely dangerous to provide a normal web server there.

The screened subnet architecture we describe in a later section offers some extra options for providing new, untrusted, or inbound services (e.g., you can add a worthless machine to the screened subnet that provides only an untrusted service).

Appropriate uses

A dual-homed host is an appropriate firewall for a situation where:

* Traffic to the Internet is small.
* Traffic to the Internet is not business-critical.
* No services are being provided to Internet-based users.
* The network being protected does not contain extremely valuable data.

Multiple-Purpose Boxes

Many single-box firewalls actually provide some combination of proxying and packet filtering. This gives you many of the advantages of both; you can allow some protocols at high speed while still having detailed control. It also gives you many of the disadvantages of both; you are vulnerable to problems where protocols that you thought were forced through the proxies are simply passed on by the packet filters. In addition, you have all the normal risks of having only a single entity between you and the great outside world.

Appropriate uses

A single machine that does both proxying and packet filtering is appropriate for a situation where:

* The network to be protected is small.
* No services are being provided to the Internet.

Screened Host Architectures

Whereas a dual-homed host architecture provides services from a host that's attached to multiple networks (but has routing turned off), a *screened host architecture* provides services from a host that's attached to only the internal network, using a separate router. In this architecture, the primary security is provided by packet filtering. (For example, packet filtering is what prevents people from going around proxy servers to make direct connections.)

Figure 6-3 shows a simple version of a screened host architecture. The bastion host sits on the internal network. The packet filtering on the screening router is set up in such a way that the bastion host is the only system on the internal network that hosts on the Internet can open connections to (for example, to deliver incoming email). Even then, only certain types of connections are allowed. Any external system trying to access internal systems or services will have to connect to this host. The bastion host thus needs to maintain a high level of host security.

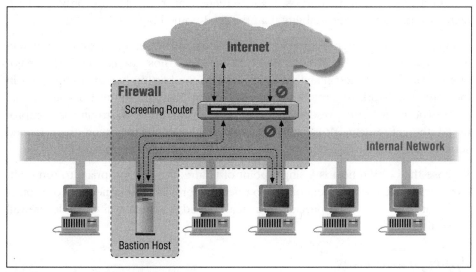

Figure 6-3. Screened host architecture

Packet filtering also permits the bastion host to open allowable connections (what is "allowable" will be determined by your site's particular security policy) to the outside world. The "Bastion Host" section in the "Screened Subnet Architectures" discussion, later in this chapter, contains more information about the functions of bastion hosts, and Chapter 10, *Bastion Hosts*, describes in detail how to build one.

The packet filtering configuration in the screening router may do one of the following:

* Allow other internal hosts to open connections to hosts on the Internet for certain services (allowing those services via packet filtering, as discussed in Chapter 8, *Packet Filtering*)

* Disallow all connections from internal hosts (forcing those hosts to use proxy services via the bastion host, as discussed in Chapter 9, *Proxy Systems*)

You can mix and match these approaches for different services; some may be allowed directly via packet filtering, while others may be allowed only indirectly via proxy. It all depends on the particular policy your site is trying to enforce.

Because this architecture allows packets to move from the Internet to the internal networks, it may seem more risky than a dual-homed host architecture, which is designed so that no external packet can reach the internal network. In practice, however, the dual-homed host architecture is also prone to failures that let packets actually cross from the external network to the internal network. (Because this type of failure is completely unexpected, there are unlikely to be protections against attacks of this kind.) Furthermore, it's easier to defend a router than it is to defend a host. For most purposes, the screened host architecture provides both better security and better usability than the dual-homed host architecture.

Compared to other architectures, however, such as the screened subnet architecture, there are some disadvantages to the screened host architecture. The major one is that if an attacker manages to break in to the bastion host, nothing is left in the way of network security between the bastion host and the rest of the internal hosts. The router also presents a single point of failure; if the router is compromised, the entire network is available to an attacker. For this reason, the screened subnet architecture, discussed next, has become increasingly popular.

Because the bastion host is a single point of failure, it is inappropriate to run high-risk services like web servers on it. You need to provide the same level of protection to it that you would provide to a dual-homed host that was the sole firewall for your site.

Appropriate Uses

A screened host architecture is appropriate when:

- Few connections are coming from the Internet (in particular, it is *not* an appropriate architecture if the screened host is a public web server).

- The network being protected has a relatively high level of host security.

Screened Subnet Architectures

The *screened subnet architecture* adds an extra layer of security to the screened host architecture by adding a perimeter network that further isolates the internal network from the Internet.

Why do this? By their nature, bastion hosts are the most vulnerable machines on your network. Despite your best efforts to protect them, they are the machines most likely to be attacked because they're the machines that *can be* attacked. If, as in a screened host architecture, your internal network is wide open to attack from your bastion host, then your bastion host is a very tempting target. No other defenses are between it and your other internal machines (besides whatever host security they may have, which is usually very little). If someone successfully breaks into the bastion host in a screened host architecture, that intruder has hit the jackpot. By isolating the bastion host on a perimeter network, you can reduce the impact of a break-in on the bastion host. It is no longer an instantaneous jackpot; it gives an intruder some access but not all.

With the simplest type of screened subnet architecture, there are two screening routers, each connected to the perimeter net. One sits between the perimeter net and the internal network, and the other sits between the perimeter net and the external network (usually the Internet). To break into the internal network with this type of architecture, an attacker would have to get past *both* routers. Even if the attacker somehow broke in to the bastion host, he'd still have to get past the interior router. There is no single vulnerable point that will compromise the internal network.

Figure 6-4 shows a possible firewall configuration that uses the screened subnet architecture. The next few sections describe the components in this type of architecture.

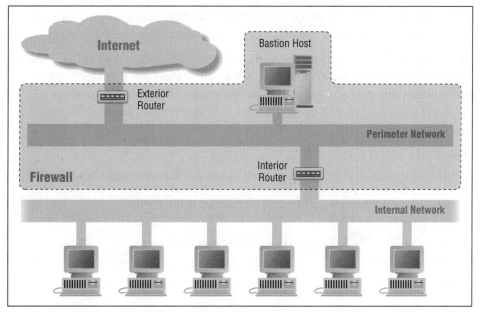

Figure 6-4. Screened subnet architecture (using two routers)

Perimeter Network

The perimeter network is another layer of security, an additional network between the external network and your protected internal network. If an attacker successfully breaks into the outer reaches of your firewall, the perimeter net offers an additional layer of protection between that attacker and your internal systems.

Here's an example of why a perimeter network can be helpful. In many network setups, it's possible for any machine on a given network to see the traffic for every machine on that network. This is true for most Ethernet-based networks (and Ethernet is by far the most common local area networking technology in use today); it is also true for several other popular technologies, such as token ring and FDDI. Snoopers may succeed in picking up passwords by watching for those used during Telnet, FTP, and *rlogin* sessions. Even if passwords aren't compromised, snoopers can still peek at the contents of sensitive files people may be accessing, interesting email they may be reading, and so on; the snooper can essentially "watch over the shoulder" of anyone using the network. A large number of tools are available that attackers use to do this sort of snooping and to conceal that it's being done.

With a perimeter network, if someone breaks into a bastion host on the perimeter net, they'll be able to snoop only on traffic on that net. All the traffic on the perimeter net should be either to or from the bastion host, or to or from the Internet. Because no strictly internal traffic (that is, traffic between two internal hosts, which is presumably sensitive or proprietary) passes over the perimeter net, internal traffic will be safe from prying eyes if the bastion host is compromised.

Obviously, traffic to and from the bastion host, or the external world, will still be visible. Part of the work in designing a firewall is ensuring that this traffic is not itself confidential enough that reading it will compromise your site as a whole.

Bastion Host

With the screened subnet architecture, you attach a bastion host (or hosts) to the perimeter net; this host is the main point of contact for incoming connections from the outside world; for example:

- For incoming email (SMTP) sessions to deliver electronic mail to the site
- For incoming FTP connections to the site's anonymous FTP server
- For incoming Domain Name System (DNS) queries about the site

and so on.

Outbound services (from internal clients to servers on the Internet) are handled in either of these ways:

- Set up packet filtering on both the exterior and interior routers to allow internal clients to access external servers directly.
- Set up proxy servers to run on the bastion host (if your firewall uses proxy software) to allow internal clients to access external servers indirectly. You would also set up packet filtering to allow the internal clients to talk to the proxy servers on the bastion host and vice versa, but to prohibit direct communications between internal clients and the outside world.

In either case, packet filtering allows the bastion host to connect to, and accept connections from, hosts on the Internet; which hosts, and for what services, are dictated by the site's security policy.

Much of what the bastion host does is act as proxy server for various services, either by running specialized proxy server software for particular protocols (such as HTTP or FTP), or by running standard servers for self-proxying protocols (such as SMTP).

Chapter 10, *Bastion Hosts*, describes how to secure a bastion host, and the chapters in Part III, *Internet Services*, describe how to configure individual services to work with the firewall.

Interior Router

The *interior router* (sometimes called the *choke router* in firewalls literature) protects the internal network both from the Internet *and* from the perimeter net.

The interior router does most of the packet filtering for your firewall. It allows selected services outbound from the internal net to the Internet. These services are the services your site can safely support and safely provide using packet filtering rather than proxies. (Your site needs to establish its own definition of what "safe" means. You'll have to consider your own needs, capabilities, and constraints; there is no one answer for all sites.) The services you allow might include outgoing HTTP, Telnet, FTP, and others, as appropriate for your own needs and concerns. (For detailed information on how you can use packet filtering to control these services, see Chapter 8, *Packet Filtering*.)

The services the interior router allows between your bastion host (on the perimeter net itself) and your internal net are not necessarily the same services the interior router allows between the Internet and your internal net. The reason for limiting the services between the bastion host and the internal network is to reduce the number of machines (and the number of services on those machines) that can be attacked from the bastion host, should it be compromised.

You should limit the services allowed between the bastion host and the internal net to just those that are actually needed, such as SMTP (so the bastion host can forward incoming email), DNS (so the bastion host can answer questions from internal machines, or ask them, depending on your configuration), and so on. You should further limit services, to the extent possible, by allowing them only to or from particular internal hosts; for example, SMTP might be limited only to connections between the bastion host and your internal mail server or servers. Pay careful attention to the security of those remaining internal hosts and services that can be contacted by the bastion host, because those hosts and services will be what an attacker goes after—indeed, will be all the attacker *can* go after—if the attacker manages to break in to your bastion host.

Exterior Router

In theory, the *exterior router* (sometimes called the *access router* in firewalls literature) protects both the perimeter net and the internal net from the Internet. In practice, exterior routers tend to allow almost anything outbound from the perimeter net, and they generally do very little packet filtering. The packet filtering rules to protect internal machines would need to be essentially the same on both the interior router and the exterior router; if there's an error in the rules that allows access to an attacker, the error will probably be present on both routers.

Frequently, the exterior router is provided by an external group (for example, your Internet provider), and your access to it may be limited. An external group that's maintaining a router will probably be willing to put in a few general packet filtering rules but won't want to maintain a complicated or frequently changing rule set. You also may not trust them as much as you trust your own routers. If the router breaks and they install a new one, are they going to remember to reinstall the filters? Are they even going to bother to mention that they replaced the router so that you know to check?

The only packet filtering rules that are really special on the exterior router are those that protect the machines on the perimeter net (that is, the bastion hosts and the internal router). Generally, however, not much protection is necessary, because the hosts on the perimeter net are protected primarily through host security (although redundancy never hurts).

The rest of the rules that you could put on the exterior router are duplicates of the rules on the interior router. These are the rules that prevent insecure traffic from going between internal hosts and the Internet. To support proxy services, where the interior router will let the internal hosts send some protocols as long as they are talking *to* the bastion host, the exterior router could let those protocols through as long as they are coming *from* the bastion host. These rules are desirable for an extra level of security, but they're theoretically blocking only packets that can't exist because they've already been blocked by the interior router. If they do exist, either the interior router has failed, or somebody has connected an unexpected host to the perimeter network.

So, what does the exterior router actually need to do? One of the security tasks that the exterior router *can* usefully perform—a task that usually can't easily be done anywhere else—is the blocking of any incoming packets from the Internet that have forged source addresses. Such packets claim to have come from within the internal network but actually are coming in from the Internet.

The interior router could do this, but it can't tell if packets that claim to be from the perimeter net are forged. While the perimeter net shouldn't have anything fully trusted on it, it's still going to be more trusted than the external universe; being able to forge packets from it will give an attacker most of the benefits of compromising the bastion host. The exterior router is at a clearer boundary. The interior router also can't protect the systems on the perimeter net against forged packets. (We discuss forged packets in greater detail in Chapter 4, *Packets and Protocols*.)

Another task that the exterior router can perform is to prevent IP packets containing inappropriate source addresses from leaving your network. All traffic leaving your network should come from one of your source addresses. If not, then either you have a serious configuration problem, or somebody is forging source addresses.

Although filtering inappropriate source addresses outbound doesn't provide any network protection to you, it prevents an intruder from using your systems to launch certain types of attacks on other sites. If the exterior router is configured to alert you when forged source addresses are seen, this may be just the early warning alarm you need in order to detect a serious network problem. The practice of being a good network citizen may also be enough to keep the name of your site out of a possibly embarrassing news headline.

Appropriate Uses

A screened subnet architecture is appropriate for most uses.

Architectures with Multiple Screened Subnets

Some networks will need more than one screened subnet. This happens when there are multiple things that need to happen on a screened subnet that have different security implications.

Split-Screened Subnet

In a *split-screened subnet*, there is still a single interior router and an exterior router, but multiple networks are between the two routers. In general, the screened networks are connected to each other by one or more dual-homed hosts, not by yet another router.

Some sites use this architecture purely to provide defense in depth, protecting a proxy host with the routers. The routers provide protection from forgery, and protection from failures where the dual-homed host starts to route traffic. The dual-homed host provides finer controls on the connections than packet filtering. This is a belt-and-suspenders firewall, providing excellent multilayered protection, although it requires careful configuration on the dual-homed host to be sure you're taking full advantage of the possibilities. (There's no point in running simple, straight-through proxies.) Figure 6-5 shows this configuration.

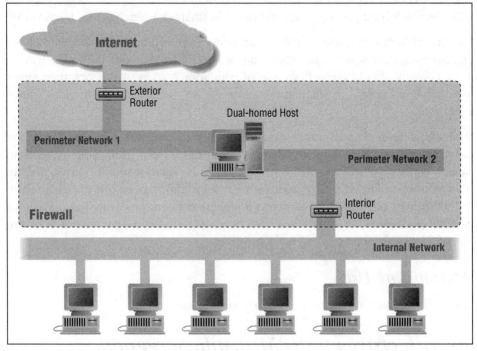

Figure 6-5. Split-screened subnet with dual-homed host

Others use this architecture to provide administrative access to machines that also provide service to the Internet. This allows administrators to use protocols that are too dangerous to allow to the Internet on a sensitive machine (for instance, the NT-native protocols used for remote User Manager and Performance Monitor use) without relying solely on the exterior router as protection. It also may be useful for performance reasons on machines making intense use of the network; it prevents administrative traffic from using bandwidth that could be used to serve user requests. Figure 6-6 shows this sort of architecture.

In fact, machines that can drive multiple high-speed network interfaces at full speed may benefit from having three network interfaces; one to speak to the external users, one to speak to the internal administrators, and one with no connections to other networks that is used for backups and/or communications among bastion hosts. Figure 6-8 shows this sort of architecture.

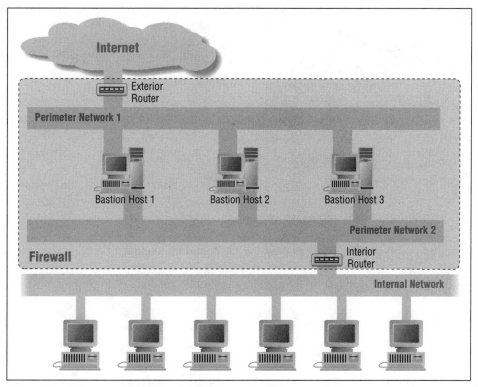

Figure 6-6. Split-screened subnet with no through traffic

Appropriate uses

Split-screened subnets are appropriate for networks that need high security, particularly if they are providing services to the Internet.

Independent Screened Subnets

In some cases you will want to have multiple, *independent screened subnets,* with separate exterior routers. Figure 6-7 shows this configuration.

You might put in multiple perimeter nets to provide redundancy. It doesn't make much sense to pay for two connections to the Internet, and then run them both through the same router or routers. Putting in two exterior routers, two perimeter nets, and two interior routers ensures that no single point of failure is between you and the Internet.[*]

---

[*] Providing, of course, that your two Internet providers are actually running on different pieces of cable, in different conduits. Never underestimate the destructive power of a backhoe or a jackhammer.

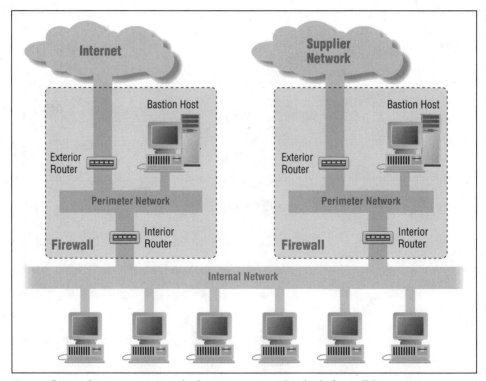

Figure 6-7. Architecture using multiple perimeter nets (multiple firewalls)

You might also put in multiple perimeter nets for privacy, so that you can run moderately confidential data across one, and an Internet connection across the other. In that case, you might even attach both perimeter nets to the same interior router.

You might also want to use multiple perimeter nets to separate inbound services (services that you provide to the Internet, like publicly accessible web servers) from outbound services (services that allow your users to get to the Internet, like a caching web proxy). It is much easier to provide truly strong security to these functions if you separate them, and if you use a split perimeter net for the inbound services.

Having multiple perimeter nets is less risky than having multiple interior routers sharing the same internal net, but it's still a maintenance headache. You will probably have multiple interior routers, presenting multiple possible points of compromise. Those routers must be watched very carefully to keep them enforcing appropriate security policies; if they both connect to the Internet, they need to enforce the same policy. Figure 6-8 shows the sort of firewall an Internet service provider might use, with many perimeter nets and multiple connections to the Internet.

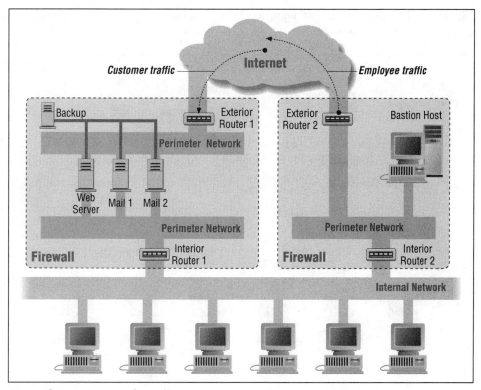

Figure 6-8. An intricate firewall setup

Appropriate uses

Independent screened subnets are appropriate in networks with a particularly strong need for redundancy, or with high security requirements and several independent uses of the Internet.

Variations on Firewall Architectures

We've shown the most common firewall architectures in Figures 6-2 through 6-8. However, there is a lot of variation in architectures. There is a good deal of flexibility in how you can configure and combine firewall components to best suit your hardware, your budget, and your security policy. This section describes some common variations and their benefits and drawbacks.

It's OK to Use Multiple Bastion Hosts

Although we tend to talk about a single bastion host in this book, it may make sense to use multiple bastion hosts in your firewall configuration, as we show in

Figure 6-9. Reasons you might want to do this include performance, redundancy, and the need to separate data or servers.

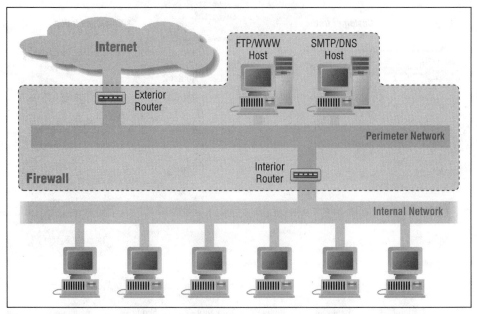

Figure 6-9. Architecture using two bastion hosts

You might decide to have one bastion host handle the services that are important to your own users (such as SMTP servers, proxy servers, and so on), while another host handles the services that you provide to the Internet, but which your users don't care about (for example, your public web server). In this way, performance for your own users won't be dragged down by the activities of outside users.

You may have performance reasons to create multiple bastion hosts even if you don't provide services to the Internet. Some services, like Usenet news, are resource-intensive and easily separated from others. It's also possible to provide multiple bastion hosts with the same services for performance reasons, but it can be difficult to do load balancing. Most services need to be configured for particular servers, so creating multiple hosts for individual services works best if you can predict usage in advance.

How about redundancy? If your firewall configuration includes multiple bastion hosts, you might configure them for redundancy, so that if one fails, the services can be provided by another, but beware that only some services support this approach. For example, you might configure and designate multiple bastion hosts as DNS servers for your domain (via DNS NS [Name Server] records, which specify the name servers for a domain), or as SMTP servers (via DNS MX [Mail Exchange] records, which specify what servers will accept mail for a given host or domain), or both. Then, if one of the bastion hosts is unavailable or overloaded, the DNS and SMTP activity will use the other as a fallback system.

You might also use multiple bastion hosts to keep the data sets of services from interfering with each other. In addition to the performance issues discussed earlier, there may be security reasons for this separation. For example, you might decide to provide one HTTP server for use by your customers over the Internet, and another for use by the general public. By providing two servers, you can offer different data to customers, and possibly better performance, by using a less loaded or more powerful machine.

You could also run your HTTP server and your anonymous FTP server on separate machines, to eliminate the possibility that one server could be used to compromise the other. (For a discussion of how this might be done, see the description of HTTP server vulnerabilities in Chapter 15, *The World Wide Web*.)

It's OK to Merge the Interior Router and the Exterior Router

You can merge the interior and exterior routers into a single router, but only if you have a router sufficiently capable and flexible. In general, you need a router that allows you to specify both inbound and outbound filters on each interface. In Chapter 8, *Packet Filtering*, we discuss what this means, and we describe the packet filtering problems that may arise with routers that have more than two interfaces and don't have this capability.

If you merge the interior and exterior routers, as we show in Figure 6-10, you'll still have a perimeter net (on one interface of the router) and a connection to your internal net (on another interface of the router). Some traffic would flow directly between the internal net and the Internet (the traffic that is permitted by the packet filtering rules set up for the router), and other traffic would flow between the perimeter net and the Internet, or the perimeter net and the internal net (the traffic that is handled by proxies).

This architecture, like the screened host architecture, creates a single point of failure. Since now only one router is between the inside and the outside, if that router is compromised, the entire site is compromised. In general, routers are easier to protect than hosts, but they are not impenetrable.

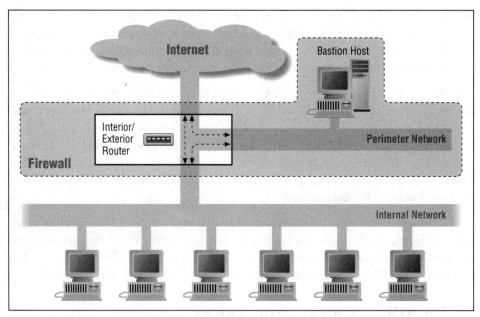

Figure 6-10. Architecture using a merged interior and exterior router

It's OK to Merge the Bastion Host and the Exterior Router

There might be cases in which you use a single dual-homed machine as both your bastion host and your exterior router. Here's an example: suppose you only have a dial-up SLIP or PPP connection to the Internet. In this case, you might run PPP on your bastion host, and let it act as both bastion host and exterior router. This is functionally equivalent to the three-machine configuration (bastion host, interior router, exterior router) described for the screened subnet architecture shown earlier in this chapter.

Using a dual-homed host to route traffic won't give you the performance or the flexibility of a dedicated router, but you don't need much of either for a single low-bandwidth connection. Depending on the operating system and software you're using, you may or may not have the ability to do packet filtering. Several of the available interface software packages have quite good packet filtering capabilities. However, because the exterior router doesn't have to do much packet filtering anyway, using an interface package that doesn't have good packet filtering capabilities is not that big a problem.

Unlike merging the interior and exterior routers, merging the bastion host with the exterior router, as shown in Figure 6-11, does not open significant new vulnerabilities. It does expose the bastion host further. In this architecture, the bastion host is more exposed to the Internet, protected only by whatever filtering (if any) its own interface package does, and you will need to take extra care to protect it.

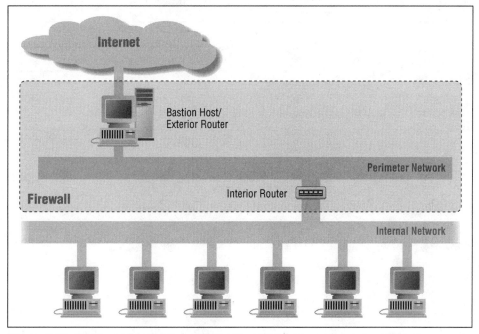

Figure 6-11. Architecture using a merged bastion host and exterior router

It's Dangerous to Merge the Bastion Host and the Interior Router

While it is often acceptable to merge the bastion host and the exterior router, as we discussed in the previous section, it's not a good idea to merge the bastion host and the interior router, as we show in Figure 6-12. Doing so compromises your overall security.

The bastion host and the exterior router each perform distinct protective tasks; they complement each other but don't back each other up. The interior router functions in part as a backup to the two of them.

If you merge the bastion host and the interior router, you've changed the firewall configuration in a fundamental way. In the first case (with a separate bastion host and interior router), you have a screened subnet firewall architecture. With this type of configuration, the perimeter net for the bastion host doesn't carry any strictly internal traffic, so this traffic is protected from snooping even if the bastion host is successfully penetrated; to get at the internal network, the attacker still must get past the interior router. In the second case (with a merged bastion host and interior router), you have a screened host firewall architecture. With this type of configuration, if the bastion host is broken into, there's nothing left in the way of security between the bastion host and the internal network.

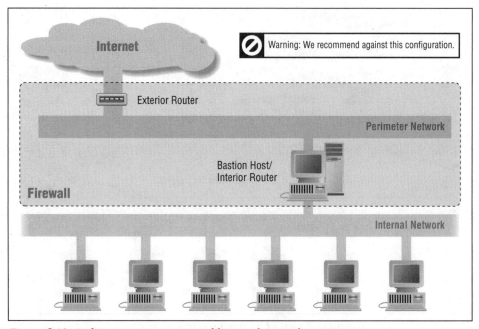

Figure 6-12. Architecture using a merged bastion host and interior router

One of the main purposes of the perimeter network is to prevent the bastion host from being able to snoop on internal traffic. Moving the bastion host to the interior router makes all of your internal traffic visible to it.

It's Dangerous to Use Multiple Interior Routers

Using multiple interior routers to connect your perimeter net to multiple parts of your internal net can cause a lot of problems and is generally a bad idea.

The basic problem is that the routing software on an internal system could decide that the fastest way to another internal system is via the perimeter net. If you're lucky, this approach simply won't work because it will be blocked by the packet filtering on one of the routers. If you're unlucky, it will work, and you'll have sensitive, strictly internal traffic flowing across your perimeter net, where it can be snooped on if somebody has managed to break in to the bastion host.

It's also difficult to keep multiple interior routers correctly configured. The interior router is the one with the most important and the most complex set of packet filters, and having two of them doubles your chances of getting the rule sets wrong.

Nevertheless, you may still end up wanting to do this. Figure 6-13 shows the basic architecture using multiple interior routers. On a large internal network, having a single interior router may be both a performance problem and a reliability problem. If you're trying to provide redundancy, that single point of failure is a major annoyance. In that case, the safest (and most redundant) thing to do is to set up each interior router to a separate perimeter net and exterior router; this configuration is discussed earlier in this chapter. This configuration is more complex and more expensive, but it increases both redundancy and performance, as well as making it highly unlikely that traffic will try to go between the interior routers (if the Internet is the shortest route between two parts of your internal network, you have much worse problems than most sites) and extraordinarily unlikely that it will succeed (four sets of packet filters are trying to keep it out).

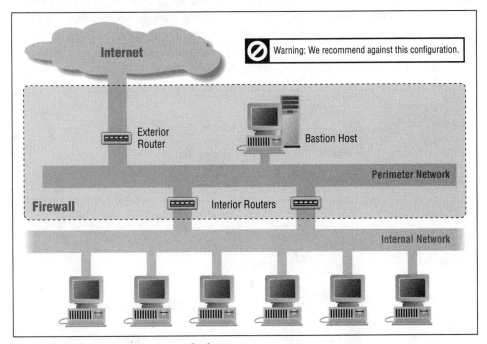

Figure 6-13. Architecture using multiple interior routers

If performance problems alone are motivating you to look at multiple interior routers, it's hard to justify the expense of separate perimeter networks and exterior routers. In most cases, however, the interior router is not the performance bottleneck. If it is, then one of the following cases is occurring:

- A lot of traffic going to the perimeter net is not then going to the external network.

- Your exterior router is much faster than your interior router.

In the first case, you have probably misconfigured something; the perimeter net may take occasional traffic that isn't destined for the external world in some configurations (for example, DNS queries about external hosts when the information is cached), but that traffic should never be significant. In the second case, you should seriously consider upgrading the interior router to match the exterior router, instead of adding a second one.

Another reason for having multiple interior routers is that you have multiple internal networks, which have technical, organizational, or political reasons not to share a single router. The simplest way to accommodate these networks would be to give them separate interfaces on a single router, as shown in Figure 6-14. This complicates the router configuration considerably (how considerably depends a great deal on the router in question, as discussed in Chapter 8, *Packet Filtering*) but doesn't produce the risks of a multiple interior router configuration. If there are too many networks for a single router, or if sharing a router is unpalatable for other reasons, consider making an internal backbone and connecting it to the perimeter network with a single router, as shown in Figure 6-15.

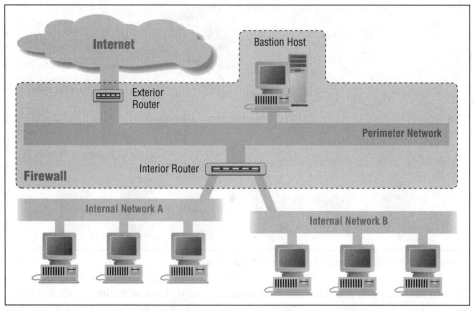

Figure 6-14. Multiple internal networks (separate interfaces in a single router)

You may find that an effective way to accommodate different security policies among different internal networks is to attach them to the perimeter through separate routers (e.g., one network wants to allow connections that others consider insecure). In this case, the perimeter network should be the *only* interconnection between the internal networks; there should be no confidential traffic passing

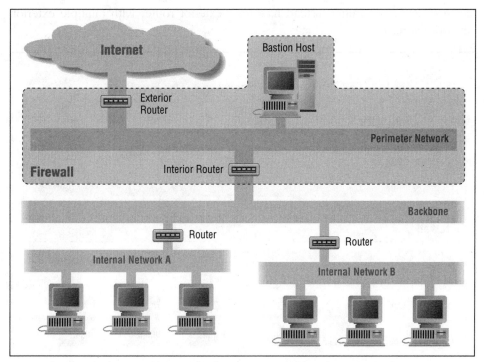

Figure 6-15. Multiple internal networks (backbone architecture)

between them; and each internal network should treat the other as an untrusted, external network. This is likely to be extremely inconvenient for some users on each network, but anything else will either compromise the security of the site as a whole or remove the distinction that caused you to set up the two routers in the first place.

If you decide that you are willing to accept the risks of having multiple interior routers, you can minimize those risks by having all the interior routers managed by the same group (so conflicting security policies aren't being enforced). You should also keep a careful watch for internal traffic crossing the perimeter network and act promptly to cure the sources of it.

It's OK to Use Multiple Exterior Routers

In some cases, it makes sense to connect multiple exterior routers to the same perimeter net, as we show in Figure 6-16. Examples are:

*   You have multiple connections to the Internet (for example, through different service providers, for redundancy).
*   You have a connection to the Internet plus other connections to other sites.

In these cases, you might instead have one exterior router with multiple exterior network interfaces.

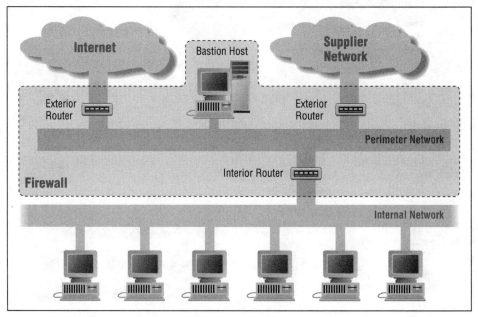

Figure 6-16. Architecture using multiple exterior routers

Attaching multiple exterior routers that go to the same external network (e.g., two different Internet providers) is not a significant security problem. They may have different filter sets, but that's not critical in exterior routers. There is twice the chance that one will be compromisable, but a compromise of an exterior router usually is not particularly threatening.

Things are more complex if the connections are to different places (for example, one is to the Internet and one is to a site you're collaborating with and need more bandwidth to). To figure out whether such an architecture makes sense in these cases, ask yourself this question: what traffic could someone see if they broke into a bastion host on this perimeter net? For example, if an attacker broke in, could he snoop on sensitive traffic between your site and a subsidiary or affiliate? If so, then you may want to think about installing multiple perimeter nets instead of multiple exterior routers on a single perimeter net. (This case is shown in the next section.)

Other significant problems are involved in setting up connections to external networks with which you have special relationships, which are discussed later in this chapter, in the "Internal Firewalls" section.

It's Dangerous to Use Both Screened Subnets and Screened Hosts

If you have a screened subnet, you should not allow connections from the Internet directly onto your internal networks. This may seem intuitively obvious (what's the point in having a screened subnet if you're not going to use it?), but you'd be surprised how many people end up making exceptions. These sorts of exceptions are extremely dangerous. Once you have a screened subnet, you're going to be concentrating your protections there, and it's almost impossible to properly protect both a screened subnet and a screened host on an internal network.

There are two common situations in which people ask for exceptions. First, people providing services to Internet users find that the interior router interferes with either administration of the services or communication between components (for instance, a web server that needs to talk to an internal database server). Second, people with tools for accessing new protocols (proxy servers for the latest multimedia 3D all-singing all-dancing tool, for instance) don't want to go to the trouble of putting them in somebody else's carefully protected space and are completely convinced that they're so safe you can just let traffic through to them.

Chapter 23, *Databases and Games*, discusses the positioning of web servers and their associated components in detail, but the short summary is that putting the web server itself on the internal network is extremely risky, even if you are sure that only web traffic can get to it. If you are having problems allowing administrative protocols through, Chapter 11, *Unix and Linux Bastion Hosts*, and Chapter 12, *Windows NT and Windows 2000 Bastion Hosts*, discuss methods for safely administering bastion hosts.

As for the theoretically safe brand-new protocols, there's a lot to consider before you hand over control of an experimental bastion host. Make sure that:

- No other bastion hosts trust the experimental one.
- The experimental bastion host cannot snoop on important network traffic.
- The machine starts out in a secure configuration.
- You will be able to detect break-ins on the experimental bastion host.

Then hand it over and let people play with it. It's better for them to experiment in a controlled way where you can keep an eye on them than to succeed in working around the firewall altogether. If you have the resources, you may want to put a separate screened subnet in place just for experimentation.

Terminal Servers and Modem Pools

Another issue that is only somewhat related to firewalls (but that the security folks putting up firewalls are often asked to address) is where to locate the terminal servers and modem pools within a site's network. You definitely need to pay as much attention to the security of your dial-up access ports as you do to the security of your Internet connection. However, dial-up security (authentication systems, callback systems, etc.) is a whole topic of its own, separate from firewalls. We'll therefore restrict our comments to those related to firewalls.

The big firewall question concerning terminal servers and modem pools is where to put them: do you put them inside your security perimeter, or outside? (This is similar to the question of where to put encryption endpoints in a virtual private network, discussed earlier.) Our advice is to put them on the inside and to protect them carefully. You'll not only be doing yourself a favor, you'll also be a good neighbor. Putting open terminal servers on the Internet is a risk to other people's sites as well as your own.

If the modem ports are going to be used primarily to access internal systems and data (that is, employees working from home or on the road), then it makes sense to put them on the inside. If you put them on the outside, you'd have to open holes in your perimeter to allow them access to the internal systems and data— holes that an attacker might be able to take advantage of. Also, if you put them on the outside, then an attacker who has compromised your perimeter (broken into your bastion host, for example) could potentially monitor the work your users do, essentially looking over their shoulders as they access private, sensitive data. If you do put the modems on the inside, you'll have to protect them very carefully, so they don't become an easier break-in target than your firewall. It doesn't do any good to build a first-class firewall if someone can bypass it by dialing into an unprotected modem connected to the internal network.

On the other hand, if the modem ports are going to be used primarily to access external systems (that is, by employees or guests who mainly use your site as an access point for the Internet), then it makes more sense to put them on the outside. There's no sense in giving someone access to your internal systems if he or she doesn't need it. This external modem pool should be treated just as suspiciously as the bastion host and the other components of your firewall.

If you find that you need both types of access, then you might want to consider two modem pools: one on the inside, carefully protected, to access internal systems, and another on the outside to access the Internet.

If your terminal servers and modem pools are being used to support dial-up network connections from homes or other sites, you should make sure you enforce any implicit assumptions you have about that usage. For instance, people setting up PPP accounts on terminal servers generally assume that the PPP account is going to be used by a single remote machine running standalone. More and more machines, however, are part of local area networks, even at home (Dad's PC is in the den, Mom's in the living room). That PPP connection could be used not just by the machine you set it up for, but by anything that machine is connected to, and anything those machines are connected to, and so forth. The machine that uses the PPP account might be connected to a local area network, with any number of other machines on it; any of them might be connected (via other PPP connections, for example) to another site or an Internet service provider. If you don't do anything to prevent it, traffic could flow from the Internet, to the second PC, to the "legitimate" PC, and finally into your own net, completely bypassing your firewall.

You can prevent this problem by simply enabling packet filtering on the PPP connection that limits what it *can* do to what you *expect* it to do (i.e., that limits packets on the connection to only packets to or from the machine you expect to be at the other end of the connection).

Some sites with significant dial-up networking activity take the approach of building a separate firewall just for that activity. See the previous discussion of multiple perimeter networks.

We discuss remote access protocols further in Chapter 14, *Intermediary Protocols*, and we discuss the authentication protocols generally used to protect modem pools and terminal servers in Chapter 21, *Authentication and Auditing Services*.

Internal Firewalls

The assumption in most of the discussions in this book is that you are building a firewall to protect your internal network from the Internet. However, in some situations, you may also be protecting parts of your internal network from other parts. There are a number of reasons why you might want to do this:

- You have test or lab networks with strange things going on there.

- You have networks that are less secure than the rest of your site—for example, demonstration or teaching networks where outsiders are commonly present.

- You have networks that are more secure than the rest of your site—for example, secret development projects or networks where financial data or grades are passed around.

This is another situation where firewalls are a useful technology. In some cases, you will want to build *internal firewalls*; that is, firewalls that sit between two parts of the same organization, or between two separate organizations that share a network, rather than between a single organization and the Internet.

It often makes sense to keep one part of your organization separate from another. Not everyone in an organization needs the same services or information, and security is frequently more important in some parts of an organization (the accounting department, for example) than in others.

Many of the same tools and techniques you use to build Internet firewalls are also useful for building these internal firewalls. However, there are some special considerations that you will need to keep in mind if you are building an internal firewall. Figure 6-17 shows this architecture.

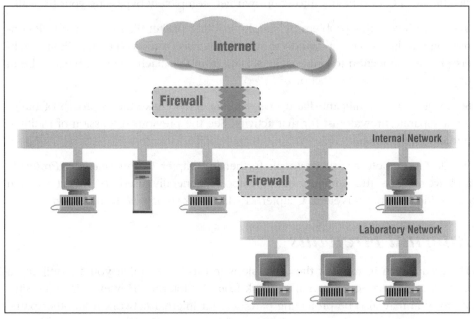

Figure 6-17. Firewall architecture with an internal firewall

Laboratory Networks

Laboratory and test networks are often the first networks that people consider separating from the rest of an organization via a firewall (usually as the result of some horrible experience where something escapes the laboratory and runs amok). Unless people are working on routers, this type of firewall can be quite simple. Neither a perimeter net nor a bastion host is needed, because there is no worry about snooping (all users are internal anyway), and you don't need to provide many services (the machines are not people's home machines). In most cases, you'll want a packet filtering router that allows any connection inbound to the test network but only known safe connections from it. (What's safe will depend on what the test network is playing with, rather than on the normal security considerations.)

In a few cases (for example, if you are testing bandwidth on the network), you may want to protect the test network from outside traffic that would invalidate tests, in which case you'll deny inbound connections and allow outbound connections.

If you are testing routers, it's probably wisest to use an entirely disconnected network; if you don't do this, then at least prevent the firewall router from listening to routing updates from the test network. You can do this in a number of ways, depending on your network setup, what you're testing, and what routers you have available. You might do any of the following:

- Use a different routing protocol from the one under test and entirely disable the protocol under test.

- Tell the router not to accept any routing updates from the interface under test and to filter out packets in the routing protocol.

- Specify which hosts the router will accept updates from.

If you have a number of test networks, you may find it best to set up a perimeter net for them and give each one a separate router onto the perimeter net, putting most of the packet filtering in the router between the perimeter and the main network. That way, if one test network crashes its router, the rest still have their normal connectivity.

If your testing involves external connections, the test network has to be treated as an external network itself; see the "Joint Venture Firewalls" section, later in this chapter.

Insecure Networks

Test networks are dangerous but not necessarily less secure than other networks. Many organizations also have some networks that are intrinsically less secure than most. For example, a university may consider networks that run through student dormitories to be particularly insecure; a company may consider demonstration networks, porting labs, and customer training networks to be particularly insecure. Nevertheless, these insecure networks need more interaction with the rest of the organization than does a purely external network.

Networks like dormitory networks and porting labs, where external people have prolonged access and the ability to bring in their own tools, are really as insecure as completely external networks and should be treated that way. Either position them as a second external connection (a new connection on your exterior router or a new exterior router) or set up a separate perimeter network for them. The only advantage these networks offer over purely external networks is that you can specify particular software to be run on them, which means you can make use of encryption effectively.

External people may also be able to gain access to your internal network if you use wireless networking devices. These network devices provide more accessibility and less security than traditional fixed networking. In particular, they often have a range that extends outside of your physical building, and they provide little or no authentication. This can allow anyone who owns a compatible device to connect to your network by sitting in the parking lot or in an adjacent building. Even if the range of the wireless device does not extend outside of your facilities, they make it much harder to notice a visitor attempting to gain access to your network. Some wireless networking devices provide stronger authentication and encryption facilities that prevent eavesdropping and unauthorized access. In most cases, however, you should treat a wireless network as an untrusted network and place a firewall between it and the rest of your network.

Demonstration and training labs, where external people have relatively brief, supervised access and cannot bring in tools, can be more trusted (as long as you are sure that people really do have relatively brief, supervised access and cannot bring in tools!). You still need to use a packet filtering router or a dual-homed host to prevent confidential traffic from flowing across those networks. You will also want to limit those networks to connections to servers you consider secure. However, you may be willing to provide NFS service from particular servers, for example, which you wouldn't do to a purely untrusted network. One of your main concerns should be preventing your trusted users from doing unsafe things while working on those networks (for example, logging into the machines on their desks and forgetting to log out again, or reading confidential electronic mail). This should be done with a combination of training and force (ensuring that the most insecure uses fail).

This is a place where a dual-homed host can be quite useful, even with no proxies on it; the number of people who need to use the host is probably small, and having to log into it will ensure that they see warning messages. The host will also be unable to provide some tempting but highly insecure services; for example, you won't be able to run NFS except from the dual-homed host, and people won't be able to mount their home machine's filesystems.

Extra-Secure Networks

Just as most organizations have points where they're particularly insecure, most of them have points where they're particularly security-conscious, such as:

- Particularly exciting research projects
- New products under development

- The accounting, personnel, and finance machines
- The registrar's office at a university
- Unclassified but sensitive government work
- Joint work with other organizations

Many countries have legal requirements for the protection of personal data, which are likely to apply to anywhere that employee, student, client, or patient records are kept. Some unclassified government work also requires extra protections.

Networks for doing classified work—at any level of classification—not only need to be more secure, but also need to meet all relevant government regulations. Generally speaking, they will have to be separated from unclassified networks. In any case, they are outside of the scope of this book. If you need to set one up, consult your security officer; traditional firewalls will not meet the requirements.*

You can choose to meet your requirements for extra security either by encrypting traffic that passes over your regular internal networks, or by setting up separate networks for the secure traffic. Separate networks are technically easier as long as separate machines are on them. That is, if you have a secure research project that owns particular computers, and if people log into them to work on that project, it's reasonably simple to set up a straightforward single-machine firewall (a packet filtering router, most likely). That firewall will treat your normal network as the insecure external universe. Because the lab machines probably don't need many services, a bastion host is unnecessary, and a perimeter net is needed only for the most secret ventures.

If you are dealing with people whose day-to-day work is secure, and who don't have separate machines for that work, a separate network becomes harder to implement. If you put their machines onto a more secure network, they can't work easily with everybody else at the site, and they need a number of services. In this case, you'll need a full bastion host and therefore probably a perimeter net to put it on. It's tempting to connect their machines to *two* networks, the secure net and the insecure net, so they can transmit confidential data over one and participate with the rest of the site on the other, but this is a configuration nightmare. If they're attached to both at once, each host is basically a dual-homed host firewall, with all the attendant maintenance problems. If they can be attached to only one at a time, things are more secure. However, configuring the machines is unpleasant for you, and moving back and forth is unpleasant for the user.

---

* If you don't have a security officer, you're not going to have a classified network, either.

At a university, where there are sharp distinctions between different organizations, putting the registrar's office and the financial people on secure networks, firewalled from the rest of the university, will probably work. At a company or government office, where most people work in the same environment, look into using encryption in your applications instead.

Joint Venture Firewalls

Sometimes, organizations come together for certain limited reasons, such as a joint project; they need to be able to share machines, data, and other resources for the duration of the project. For example, look at the decision of IBM and Apple to collaborate on the PowerPC; undertaking one joint project doesn't mean that IBM and Apple have decided to merge their organizations or to open up all their operations to each other.

Although the two parties have decided to trust each other for the purposes of this project, they are still competitors. They want to protect most of their systems and information from each other. It isn't just that they may distrust each other; it's also that they can't be sure how good the other's security is. They don't want to risk that an intruder into their partner's system might, through this joint venture, find a route into their system as well. This security problem occurs even if the collaborators aren't competitors.

You may also want to connect to an external company because it is an outside vendor to you. A number of services depend on information transfer, from shipping (you tell them what you want to ship; they tell you what happened to your shipment), to architecture (you give them specifications; they give you designs), to chip fabrication (you send them the chip design, they give you status on the fabrication process). These outside vendors are not competitors in any sense, but they frequently also work for competitors of yours. They are probably aware of confidentiality issues and try to protect the information they are supposed to have, to the best of their ability. On the other hand, if there are routing slip-ups, and data you're not explicitly sending to them crosses their networks, they are probably going to be completely unconscious of it, and the data will be at risk.

This may seem far-fetched, but it turns out to be a fairly routine occurrence. One company was mystified to discover routes on its network for a competitor's internal network, and still more baffled to discover traffic using these routes. It turned out that the shortest route between them and their competitor was through a common outside vendor. The traffic was not confidential because it was all traffic that would have gone through the Internet. On the other hand, the connection to the outside vendor was not treated as if it were an Internet connection (the outside vendor itself was not Internet-connected, and nobody had considered the possibility of its cross-connecting Internet-connected clients). Both companies had sudden, unexpected, and unprotected vulnerabilities.

An internal firewall limits exposure in such a situation. It provides a mechanism for sharing some resources, while protecting most of them. Before you set out to build an internal firewall, be sure you're clear on what you want to share, protect, and accomplish. Ask these questions:

- What exactly do you want to accomplish by linking your network with some other organization's network? The answer to this question will determine what services you need to provide (and, by implication, what services should be blocked).

- Are you trying to create a full work environment for a joint project in which team members from both organizations can work together and yet still have access to their own "home" systems (which need to be protected from the other organization)? In such a case, you might actually need two firewalls: one between the joint project net and each of the home organizations.

Exactly what you're trying to accomplish, and what your security concerns are, will determine what firewall technologies are going to be useful to you.

A Shared Perimeter Network Allows an "Arms-Length" Relationship

Shared perimeter networks are a good way to approach joint networks. Each party can install its own router under its own control, onto a perimeter net between the two organizations. In some configurations, these two routers might be the only machines on the perimeter net, with no bastion host. If this is the case, then the "net" might simply be a high-speed serial line (e.g., a 56 Kbps or T1/E1 line) between the two routers, rather than an Ethernet or another type of local area network.

This is highly desirable with an outside vendor. Most of them are not networking wizards, and they may attempt to economize by connecting multiple clients to the same perimeter network. If the perimeter net is an Ethernet or something similar, any client that can get to its router on that perimeter network can see the traffic for all the clients on that perimeter network—which, with some providers, is almost guaranteed to be confidential information belonging to a competitor. Using a point-to-point connection as the "perimeter net" between the outside vendor and each client, rather than a shared multiclient perimeter net, will prevent them from doing this, even accidentally.

An Internal Firewall May or May Not Need Bastion Hosts

You might not actually need to place a bastion host on the perimeter network between two organizations. The decision about whether you need a bastion host depends on what services are required for your firewall and how much each organization trusts the other. Bastion hosts on the perimeter net are rarely required for relationships with outside vendors; usually you are sending data over one particular protocol and can adequately protect that as a screened host.

If the organizations have a reasonable amount of trust in each other (and, by extension, in each other's security), it may be reasonable to establish the packet filters so that clients on the other side can connect to internal servers (such as SMTP and DNS servers) directly.

On the other hand, if the organizations distrust each other, they might each want to place their own bastion host, under their own control and management, on the perimeter net. Traffic would flow from one party's internal systems, to their bastion host, to the other party's bastion host, and finally to the other party's internal systems.

7

Firewall Design

In previous chapters, we've discussed the technologies and architectures that are usually used to build firewalls. Now we can discuss how you put them together to get a solution that's right for your site. The "right solution" to building a firewall is seldom a single technology; it's usually a carefully crafted combination of technologies to solve different problems. This chapter starts the discussion of how to come up with the combination that's right for you. Which problems you need to solve depend on what services you want to provide your users and what level of risk you're willing to accept. Which techniques you use to solve those problems depend on how much time, money, and expertise you have available.

When you design a firewall, you go through a process that you will then repeat over time as your needs change. The basic outline is as follows:

1. Define your needs.
2. Evaluate the available products.
3. Figure out how to assemble the products into a working firewall.

Define Your Needs

The first step in putting together a firewall is to figure out exactly what you need. You should do this before you start to look at firewall products, because otherwise you risk being influenced more by advertising than by your own situation. This is inevitable, and it has nothing to do with being gullible. If you don't know clearly what you need, the products that you look at will shape your decisions, no matter how suspicious you are.

You may need to re-evaluate your needs if you find that there are no products on the market that can meet them, of course, but at least you'll have some idea of what you're aiming for.

What Will the Firewall Actually Do?

First, you need to determine what the firewall needs to do, in detail. Yes, you're trying to make your site secure, but how secure does it need to be?

Your first starting point will be your security policy. If you don't have a security policy, see Chapter 25, *Security Policies*, for some suggestions on how to go about setting one up. You can't just do without a policy because a firewall is an enforcement device; if you didn't have a policy before, you do once you have a firewall in place, and it may not be a policy that meets your needs.

What services do you need to offer?

You need to know what services are going to go between your site and the Internet. What will your users do on the Internet? Are you going to offer any services to users on the Internet (for instance, will you have a web site)? Are you going to let your users come into your site from the Internet (if not, how are you providing your users with remote access)? Do you have special relationships with other companies that you're going to need to provide services for?

How secure do you need to be?

Many decisions have to do with relative levels of security. Are you trying to protect the world from destruction by protecting nuclear secrets, or do you want to keep from looking silly? Note that looking silly is not necessarily a trivial problem; if you look silly on the front page of a major newspaper, it can be a real disaster for the organization, at least. Many banks and financial institutions regard being "above the fold" (in the top half of the front page of the newspaper) as a significantly worse problem than losing money. One large organization in a small country found that any time they appeared on the front page of the newspaper looking silly, their nation's currency dropped in value. You need to know what level of security you're aiming for.

How much usage will there be?

What kinds of network lines do you have? How many users will you have, and what will they do?

How much reliability do you need?

If you are cut off from the network, what will happen? Will it be an inconvenience or a disaster?

What Are Your Constraints?

Once you've determined what you need the firewall to do, your next job is to determine what the limits are.

What budget do you have available?

How much money can you spend, and what can you spend it on? Does personnel time count in the budget? How about consulting time? If you use a machine that you already own, what does that do to your budget? (Can you use one somebody else has and make his or her budget pay to replace it?) The budget is often the most visible constraint, but it tends to be the most flexible as well (as long as the organization you are building the firewall for actually has money somewhere).

What personnel do you have available?

How many people do you have and what do they know? Personnel is much harder to change than budget—even if you get agreement to hire people, you have to find them and integrate them. Therefore, your first effort should be to fit the firewall to the available resources. If you have 47 Windows NT administrators and one Unix person, start looking at Windows NT-based firewalls. If you have only one person to run the firewall, and that's in addition to a full-time job he or she is already doing, get a commercial firewall and a consultant to install it.

What is your environment like?

Do you have political constraints? Are there forbidden operating systems or vendors, or preferred ones? It is sometimes possible to work around these, but not always; for instance, if you work for a company that sells firewalls, it is probably never going to be acceptable to run somebody else's firewall anywhere visible.

What country or countries are you going to need to install the firewall in? Firewalls often involve encryption technology, and laws about encryption and its export and import vary from country to country. If you are going to need to install multiple firewalls in different countries, you may need to use the lowest common denominator or develop an exception policy and strategy to deal with the situation.

Evaluate the Available Products

When you know what you need to do, and what constraints you have, you can start looking at the products available to you. At this stage, people often ask "What's the best firewall?", to which the standard answer is "How long is a piece of string?"—a sarcastic way of suggesting that the answer is, as always, "It depends". Here are some things to keep in mind as you go through the process of determining what's best for your situation.

Scalability

As your site gets larger, or your Internet usage gets larger, how are you going to grow the solution? Can you increase the capacity without changing anything fundamental (for instance, by adding more memory, more CPUs, a higher-speed interface, an additional interface)? Can you duplicate pieces of the configuration to get extra capacity, or will that require reconfiguring lots of client machines, or break functionality?

For instance, if you are using proxying, it may be difficult to add a second proxy host because clients will need to be reconfigured. If you are using stateful packet filtering, it may be impossible to add a second packet filter. Stateful packet filtering relies on having the packet filter see all the packets that make up a connection; if some packets go through one filter, but other packets don't, the two filters will have different state and make different decisions. Either the packet filters need to exchange state, or you need to scale up by making a single packet filter larger.

Reliability and Redundancy

In many situations, a firewall is a critical piece of the network; if it stops passing traffic, important parts of your organization may be unable to function. You need to decide how important the firewall you're designing is going to be, and if it requires high availability, you need to evaluate solutions on their ability to provide high reliability and/or redundancy. Can you duplicate parts? Can you use high-availability hardware?

Auditability

How are you going to tell whether the firewall is doing what you want? Is there a way to set up accurate logging? Can you see details of the configuration, or is your only access through a graphical user interface that gives only an overview? If you are putting multiple pieces in multiple places, can you see what's going on from a single centralized place?

Price

The price of specialized components is the most visible part of a firewall's price, and often the most visible criterion in the entire evaluation. However appallingly high it may seem, it's not the entire price. Like any other computer system, a firewall has significant costs besides the initial purchase price:

Hardware price

    If you are buying a software solution, what hardware do you need to run it on? If the initial price includes hardware, will you require any additional hardware? Do you need a UPS system, a backup system, additional power or air-conditioning, new networking hardware?

Software price

    Are you going to need anything besides the firewall software itself? Do you need backup software or an operating system license? What is the licensing scheme on the software? Is it a fixed price, a price per outgoing connection, or a price per machine connected to your networks?

Support and upgrades

    What support contracts do you need and how much do they cost? Will there be a separate fee for upgrades? Remember that you may need separate contracts for software, hardware, and the operating system—on each component.

Administration and installation

    How much time is it going to take to install and run, and whose time is it? Can it be done in-house, or will you have to pay consultants? Is installation time included in the purchase price? Will you need training for the people who are going to administer it, and how much will the training cost?

Management and Configuration

In order for a firewall to be useful, you need to be able to configure it to meet your needs, change that configuration as your needs change, and do day-to-day management of it. Who is going to do the configuration? What sort of management and configuration tools are available? Do they interface well with your existing environment?

Adaptability

Your needs will change over the lifetime of the firewall, and the firewall will need to change to meet them. What will happen when you need to add new protocols? What will happen if new attacks come out based on malformed packets? If the firewall can adapt, do you have the expertise to make the needed changes, or will you need assistance from the vendor or a consultant?

Appropriateness

One size does not fit all; these days, even clothing manufacturers have revised the motto to "One size fits most". It's not clear that even that statement holds true for firewalls. The sort of solution that's appropriate for a small company that does minimal business over the Internet is not appropriate for a small company that does all of its business over the Internet, and neither of those solutions will be appropriate for a medium or large company. A university of any size will probably need a different solution from a company.

You are not looking for the perfect firewall; you are looking for the firewall that best solves your particular problem. (This is good, because there is no perfect firewall, so looking for it is apt to be unrewarding.) You should not pay attention to absolute statements like "Packet filtering doesn't provide enough security" or "Proxying doesn't provide enough performance". On a large network, the best solution will almost always involve a combination of technologies. On a small network, the best solution may well involve something that's said to be "insecure" or "low performance" or "unmaintainable"—maybe you don't need that much security, or performance, or maintainability.

You can think of it two ways. Either there are no bad firewalls, only good firewalls used in silly ways, or there are no good firewalls, only bad firewalls used in places where their weaknesses are acceptable. Either way, the trick is to match the firewall to the need.

Put Everything Together

Once you have determined what the basic components of your firewall are, an unfortunate number of details still have to be determined. You need to figure out how you're actually going to assemble the pieces, and how you're going to provide the support services that will keep them functioning.

Where will logs go, and how?

Logging is extremely important for a firewall. The logs are your best hope of detecting attacks against your site and your best source of information about what happened when an attack succeeds. You will need to keep logs separate from the firewall, where an intruder can't destroy the logs as soon as he or she compromises the firewall. If you have a firewall composed of multiple machines, or you have multiple firewalls, you'll also want to bring all of the logs together to simplify the process of using them. Logging is discussed further in Chapter 10, *Bastion Hosts*, and Chapter 26, *Maintaining Firewalls*.

How will you back up the system?

You will need to keep backups of all the parts of your firewalls. These will let you rebuild systems in an emergency, and they will also give you evidence when you discover an attack, allowing you to compare before and after states.

Unfortunately, when you do backups between two machines, they become vulnerable to each other. The machine that you use for backing up your firewall is part of the firewall and needs to be treated appropriately. You may find it more appropriate to do local backups, with a device that's attached to each computer that makes up part of the firewall (be sure to use removable media and remove it; otherwise, a disaster or compromise will take the backups along with the originals). If you have a large and complex firewall, you may want to add a dedicated backup system to the firewall. This system should be part of the firewall system, treated like any other bastion host. It should not have access to internal networks or data, and it should be secured like other bastion hosts.

What support services does the system require?

You should carefully examine all cases where the firewall is getting information from external machines, get rid of as many dependencies as possible, and move other services into the firewall wherever possible.

For instance, is the firewall dependent on other machines for name service? If so, interfering with the name service may cause problems with the firewall (even if the firewall only uses name service to write hostnames into logs, problems with the name service can make it unusably slow). If you can, configure firewall machines so that they never use name service for any purpose; if you can't, protect your name server as part of your firewall (though you will still be vulnerable to forged name service packets).

Similarly, if you are using a time service to synchronize clocks on firewall machines, it should use authentication and come from a protected source. Firewall machines should not require or accept routing updates unless they can be authenticated and their sources protected.

How will you access the machines?

You will need to do some routine maintenance tasks on the machines (upgrade them, change configurations, add or remove user accounts, reboot them). Are you going to physically go to the machines to do this, or will you use some kind of remote access? If you're going to do it remotely, how are you going to do it securely? Chapter 11, *Unix and Linux Bastion Hosts*, and Chapter 12, *Windows NT and Windows 2000 Bastion Hosts*, discuss remote administration options for Unix and Windows NT.

Where will routine reports go, and how?

You will need some sort of reporting on the machine, so that you know it's still functioning normally. Exactly what you need will depend on the administration infrastructure that you have in place, but you will need some way of getting regular log summaries and reports from security auditing systems. You may also want to use a monitoring system that will show you status on a regular basis.

Where will alarms go, and how?

When things go wrong, the firewall should send emergency notifications. The mechanism that is used should be one that attackers can't easily interfere with. For instance, if the firewall machines need to send network traffic to provide emergency notification, it's easy for an attacker to simply take down the network interface. (In some configurations, this may also remove the attacker's access, but if the attack is a denial of service, that isn't important.) Either machines should have ways of sending alarms that are not dependent on the network (for instance, by using a modem), or alarms should be generated by independent monitoring machines that are not on the same network and will produce alarms if they lose contact.

8

Packet Filtering

Packet filtering is a network security mechanism that works by controlling what data can flow to and from a network. The basic device that interconnects IP networks is called a *router*. A router may be a dedicated piece of hardware that has no other purpose, or it may be a piece of software that runs on a general-purpose computer running Unix, Windows NT, or another operating system (MS-DOS, Windows 95/98, Macintosh, or other). Packets traversing an internetwork (a network of networks) travel from router to router until they reach their destination. The Internet itself is sort of the granddaddy of internetworks—the ultimate "network of networks".

A router has to make a routing decision about each packet it receives; it has to decide how to send that packet on towards its ultimate destination. In general, a packet carries no information to help the router in this decision, other than the IP address of the packet's ultimate destination. The packet tells the router where it wants to go but not how to get there. Routers communicate with each other using *routing protocols* such as the Routing Information Protocol (RIP) and Open Shortest Path First (OSPF) to build *routing tables* in memory to determine how to get the packets to their destinations. When routing a packet, a router compares the packet's destination address to entries in the routing table and sends the packet onward as directed by the routing table. Often, there won't be a specific route for a particular destination, and the router will use a *default route;* generally, such a route directs the packet towards smarter or better-connected routers. (The default routes at most sites point towards the Internet.)

In determining how to forward a packet towards its destination, a normal router looks only at a normal packet's destination address and asks only *"How* can I forward this packet?" A packet filtering router also considers the question *"Should* I forward this packet?" The packet filtering router answers that question according to the security policy programmed into the router via the packet filtering rules.

Some machines do packet filtering without doing routing; that is, they may accept or reject packets destined for them before they do further processing.

 Some unusual packets do contain routing information about how they are to reach their destination, using the "source route" IP option. These packets, called *source-routed packets*, are discussed in the "IP Options" section, in Chapter 4, *Packets and Protocols.*

What Can You Do with Packet Filtering?

If you put enough work into it, you can do anything you want to with packet filtering; all of the information that crosses the Internet has to go into a packet at some point, after all. But some things are very much easier to do than others. For instance, operations that require detailed protocol knowledge or prolonged tracking of past events are easier to do in proxy systems. Operations that are simple but need to be done fast and on individual packets are easier to do in packet filtering systems.

The main advantage of packet filtering is leverage: it allows you to provide, in a single place, particular protections for an entire network. Consider the Telnet service as an example. If you disallow Telnet by turning off the Telnet server on all your hosts, you still have to worry about someone in your organization installing a new machine (or reinstalling an old one) with the Telnet server turned on. On the other hand, if Telnet is not allowed by your filtering router, such a new machine would be protected right from the start, regardless of whether or not its Telnet server was actually running. This is an example of the kind of "fail safe" stance we discussed in Chapter 3, *Security Strategies.*

Routers also present a useful choke point (also discussed in Chapter 3) for all of the traffic entering or leaving a network. Even if you have multiple routers for redundancy, you probably have far fewer routers, under much tighter control, than you have host machines.

Certain protections can be provided *only* by filtering routers, and then only if they are deployed in particular locations in your network. For example, it's a good idea to reject all external packets that have internal source addresses—that is, packets that claim to be coming from internal machines but that are actually coming in from the outside—because such packets are usually part of address-spoofing attacks. In such attacks, an attacker is pretending to be coming from an internal machine. You should also reject all internal packets that have external source addresses; once again, they are usually part of address-spoofing attacks. Decision-making of this kind can be done only in a filtering router at the perimeter of your network. Only a filtering router in that location (which is, by definition, the boundary between "inside" and "outside") is able to recognize such a packet, by looking at the source address and whether the packet came from the inside (the internal network connection) or the outside (the external network connection). Figure 8-1 illustrates this type of source address forgery.

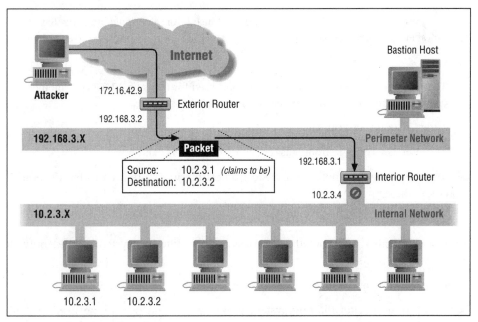

Figure 8-1. Source address forgery

Filtering routers are also good at detecting and filtering out illegal packets. Many denial of service attacks depend on sending misformatted packets of one sort or another. Routers in general have very reliable TCP/IP implementations (so they are not vulnerable to these attacks) and are well placed to prevent these attacks. General-purpose computers being used as packet filters are more likely to be vulnerable to these attacks, but at least it is easier to fix them than it is to fix all your internal machines.

Basic Packet Filtering

The most straightforward kind of packet filtering lets you control (allow or disallow) data transfer based on:

*   The address the data is (supposedly) coming from

- The address the data is going to

- The session and application ports being used to transfer the data

Basic packet filtering systems don't do anything based on the data itself; they don't make content-based decisions. Straightforward packet filtering will let you say:

> Don't let anybody use the port used by Telnet (an application protocol) to log in from the outside.

or:

> Let everybody send us data over the port used for electronic mail by SMTP (another application protocol).

or even:

> That machine can send us data over the port used for news by NNTP (yet another application protocol), but no other machines can do so.

However, it won't let you say:

> This user can Telnet in from outside, but no other users can do so.

because "user" isn't something a basic packet filtering system can identify. And it won't let you say:

> You can transfer these files but not those files.

because "file" also isn't something a basic packet filtering system can identify. It won't even let you say:

> Only allow people to send us electronic mail over the port used by SMTP.

because a basic packet filtering system looks only at the port being used; it can't tell whether the data is good data, conforming to the protocol that's supposed to use that port, or whether somebody is using the port for some other purpose.

More advanced packet filtering systems will let you look further into the data of a packet. Instead of paying attention only to headers for lower-level protocols, they also understand the data structures used by higher-level protocols, so they can make more detailed decisions.

Stateful or Dynamic Packet Filtering

Slightly more advanced packet filtering systems offer state tracking and/or protocol checking (for well-known protocols). State tracking allows you to make rules like the following:

> Let incoming UDP packets through only if they are responses to outgoing UDP packets you have seen.

or:

Accept TCP packets with SYN set only as part of TCP connection initiation.

This is called *stateful packet filtering* because the packet filter has to keep track of the state of transactions. It is also called *dynamic packet filtering* because the behavior of the system changes depending on the traffic it sees. For instance, if it's using the preceding rule, you can't look at an incoming UDP packet and say that it will always be accepted or rejected.

Different systems keep track of different levels of state information. Some people are willing to call something a stateful packet filtering system if it enforces TCP state rules (which control the flags used during startup and teardown of TCP sessions), even if the packet filtering system provides no further stateful features. While TCP state enforcement is nice to have (it helps to prevent some forms of port scanning and denial of service), it does not allow you to support additional protocols, and we do not consider it stateful packet filtering.

Figure 8-2 illustrates dynamic packet filtering at the UDP layer.

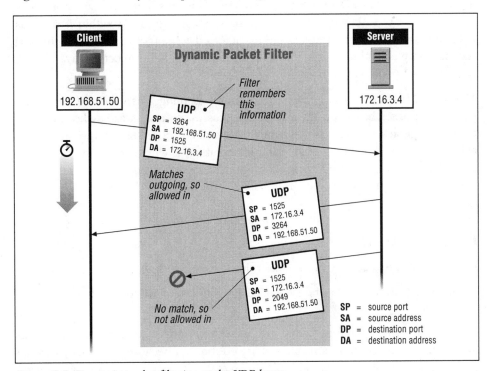

Figure 8-2. Dynamic packet filtering at the UDP layer

State tracking provides the ability to do things that you can't do otherwise, but it also adds complications. First, the router has to keep track of the state; this increases the load on the router, opens it to a number of denial of service attacks, and means that if the router reboots, packets may be denied when they should have been accepted. If a packet may go through redundant routers, they all need to have the same state information. There are protocols for exchanging this information, but it's still a tricky business. If you have redundant routers only for emergency failover, and most traffic consistently uses the same router, it's not a problem. If you are using redundant routers simultaneously, the state information needs to be transferred between them almost continuously, or the response packet may come through before the state is updated.

Second, the router has to keep track of state without any guarantee that there's ever going to be a response packet. Not all UDP packets have responses. At some point, the router's going to have to give up and get rid of the rule that will allow the response. If the router gives up early, it will deny packets that should have been accepted, causing delays and unneeded network traffic. If the router keeps the rule too long, the load on the router will be unneccessarily high, and there's an increased chance that packets will be accepted when they should have been denied. Some protocol specifications provide guidelines, but those are not necessarily useful. For instance, DNS replies are supposed to arrive within 5 seconds, but reply times for name service queries across the Internet can be as high as 15 seconds; implementing to the protocol specification will almost always deny a response that you wanted to accept.

This sort of filtering is also vulnerable to address forging; it is validating that packets are responses based on their source addresses, so an attacker who intercepts an outgoing packet can forge the appropriate source address and return an acceptable "reply" (or, depending on the implementation, a whole bunch of packets all of which will be accepted as replies). Nonetheless, this provides a reasonable degree of security for some UDP-based protocols that would otherwise be extremely difficult to protect.

Protocol Checking

Protocol checking allows you to make rules like:

> Let in packets bound for the DNS port, but only if they are formatted like DNS packets.

Protocol checking therefore helps you avoid situations where somebody has set up an unsafe service on a port that is allowed through because it normally belongs to a safe service. It can also help avoid some attacks that involve sending misformatted packets to perfectly genuine servers. Protocol checking is normally fairly rudimentary and still can be circumvented by a determined insider. It also gives you no guarantee that the data is good, so it will catch only a fairly small number of attacks that involve sending hostile data to genuine servers. However, it still provides a useful degree of sanity checking.

The most advanced packet filtering systems will allow you to specify all sorts of data-specific rules for well-known protocols. For instance, you can say:

Disconnect any FTP connection where the remote username is "anonymous".

or:

Do not allow HTTP transfers to these sites.

In order to do this, these packet filters have to have a deep understanding of the application protocol. In general, they can provide this level of control only for a few popular protocols, and there is a significant cost to provide it, since they have to process larger amounts of data. Furthermore, it is often possible to circumvent this sort of control. For instance, there are numerous ways of getting to a site via HTTP without having the site's name appear in the outgoing HTTP request, including using an IP address instead of a hostname and using an anonymizing site set up to provide this sort of service.

Stateful packet filters may also look at protocol-specific details to make state changes. Some protocols contain information about what ports transactions will use. For instance, the file transfer protocol FTP often uses a connection that is started from the server to the client, and the two ends negotiate the port number that will be used for this connection. A stateful packet filter that understands the FTP protocol can watch this negotiation and allow the new connection to be made, without allowing other connections of the same sort.

Configuring a Packet Filtering Router

To configure a packet filtering router, you first need to decide what services you want to allow or deny, and then you need to translate your decisions into rules about packets. In reality, you probably don't care about the details of packets at all. What you want is to get your work done. For example, you want to receive mail from the Internet, and whether that's managed by packets or by Murphy's ghost is irrelevant to you. The router, on the other hand, cares only about packets, and only about very limited parts of them. In constructing the rules for your routers, you have to translate the general statement "Receive mail from the Internet" into a description of the particular kinds of packets you want the router to allow to pass.

The following sections outline the general concepts you need to keep in mind when translating decisions about services into rules about packets. The specific details for each service are described in Part III of this book.

Protocols Are Usually Bidirectional

Protocols are usually bidirectional; they almost always involve one side's sending an inquiry or a command, and the other side's sending a response of some kind. When you're planning your packet filtering rules, you need to remember that packets go both ways. For example, it doesn't do any good to allow outbound Telnet packets that carry your keystrokes to a remote host, if you don't also allow the incoming packets for that connection that carry the screen display back to you.

Conversely, it also won't do you any good to block only half a connection. Many attacks can be carried out if attackers can get packets into your network, even if the attackers can't get any responses back. This can be possible for several reasons. For instance, attackers may only be interested in issuing a particular command which does not require a response (like "shut down your network interface" for a denial of service attack, using an SNMP set command). Or, the responses may be predictable enough to allow attackers to carry on their side of the conversation without having to actually see the responses at all. If the responses are predictable, an attacker doesn't need to see them. They won't be able to extract any information directly if they don't see the responses, but they may be able to do something that gives them the data indirectly. For example, even if they can't see your */etc/passwd* file directly, they can probably issue a command to mail a copy.

Be Careful of "Inbound" Versus "Outbound" Semantics

When you're planning your packet filtering strategy, you need to be careful in your discussions of "inbound" versus "outbound". You need to carefully distinguish between inbound and outbound *packets,* and inbound and outbound *services.* An outbound service (e.g., the Telnet service mentioned previously) involves both outbound packets (your keystrokes) and inbound packets (the responses to be displayed on your screen). Although most people habitually think in terms of *services*, you need to make sure you think in terms of *packets* when you're dealing with packet filtering. When you talk to others about filtering, be sure to communicate clearly whether you're talking about inbound versus outbound packets, or inbound versus outbound services.

Default Permit Versus Default Deny

In Chapter 3, *Security Strategies*, we distinguished between the two stances you can choose in putting together your security policy: the default deny stance (that which is not expressly permitted is prohibited) and the default permit stance (that which is not explicitly prohibited is permitted). From a security point of view, it is far safer to take the attitude that things should be denied by default. Your packet filtering rules should reflect this stance. As we discussed earlier, start from a position of denying everything and then set rules that allow only protocols that you need, that you understand the security implications of, and that you feel that you can provide safely enough (according to your own particular definition of "safely enough") for your purposes.

The default deny stance is much safer and more effective than the default permit stance, which involves permitting everything by default and trying to block those things that you know are problems. The reality is that with such an approach, you'll never know about all the problems, and thus you'll never be able to do a complete job.

In practical terms, the default deny stance means that your filtering rules should be a small list of specific things that you allow, perhaps with a few very specific things you deny scattered throughout to make the logic come out right, followed by a default deny that covers everything else. We'll explain in detail how these rules work later in this chapter.

What Does the Router Do with Packets?

Once a packet filtering router has finished examining a specific packet, what can it do with that packet? There are two choices:

Pass the packet on
> Normally, if the packet passes the criteria in the packet filtering configuration, the router will forward the packet on towards its destination, just as a normal router (not a packet filtering router) would do.

Drop the packet
> The other obvious action to take is to drop the packet if it fails the criteria in the packet filtering configuration.

Logging Actions

Regardless of whether the packet is forwarded or dropped ("permitted" or "denied" in some packet filtering implementations), you might want the router to log the action that has been taken. This is especially true if you drop the packet because it runs afoul of your packet filtering rules. In this case, you'd like to know what's being tried that isn't allowed.

You probably aren't going to log every packet that is allowed, but you might want to log some of these packets. For example, you might want to log start-of-connection TCP packets, so that you can keep track of incoming and outgoing TCP connections. Not all packet filters will log allowed packets.

Filtering by Interface

One key piece of information is useful when you are making a packet filtering decision, but it can't be found in the headers of the packet; this is the interface on which the packet came into the router or is going out of the router. This is important information because it allows the router to detect forged packets.

If the sole router between your internal net and the external world receives a packet with an internal source address from the internal interface, there is no problem; all packets coming from the inside will have internal source addresses. If, however, the router receives a packet with an internal source address from the external interface, it means either that someone is forging the packet (probably in an attempt to circumvent security), or that something is seriously wrong with your network configuration.

You can get these packets without forgery. For example, someone might have set up a second connection between your net and the outside world, such as a dial-up PPP link from a user's desk, probably with little or no thought to security. As a result, the traffic that should be staying internal to your net is "leaking" out through this second connection, going across the Internet, and trying to come back in through your "front door". There's little you can do to detect such illicit "back door" connections except by detecting internal packets arriving from the outside; about the best you can do is have a strong and well-publicized policy against them, and provide as many as possible of the services your users desire through the front door (the firewall), so that they don't feel a compelling need to create their own back door.

These packets should be logged and treated as urgent issues. If someone is forging them, that person is attacking you with some seriousness. If the packets are leaked from a back door, you have a security problem because of the extra Internet connection. You may also have a routing problem: a host that claims to be internal and advertises routes for itself is in danger of getting all of your internal network's traffic. This is bad if it's a PPP link, which is probably not going to handle the load. It's much worse if it's not connected to your network at all because some or all of your network's traffic is going to disappear.

Different packet filtering implementations support different forms of logging. Some will log only specific information about a packet, and others will forward or log an entire dropped packet. Generally, your packet filter will need to be configured to log to a host somewhere via the *syslog* service. You don't want the only copy of the logs to be on the packet filter if it is compromised. Most packet filtering also occurs on dedicated routers, which rarely have large amounts of disk space to dedicate to logging. See the discussion of setting up logging in Chapter 10, *Bastion Hosts*, and Chapter 26, *Maintaining Firewalls*.

Returning Error Codes

When a packet is dropped, the router can send back an ICMP error code indicating what happened (in this case, many packages will refer to the packet as having been "rejected" instead of merely dropped). Sending back an ICMP error code has the effect of warning the sending machine not to retry sending the packet, thereby saving some network traffic and some time for the user on the remote side. (If you send back an ICMP error code, the user's connection attempt will fail immediately; otherwise, it will time out, which may take several minutes.)

There are two sets of relevant ICMP codes to choose from:

- The generic "destination unreachable" codes—in particular, the "host unreachable" and "network unreachable" codes.

- The "destination administratively unreachable" codes—in particular, the "host administratively unreachable" and "network administratively unreachable" codes.

The first pair of ICMP error codes that the router might return, "host unreachable" and "network unreachable", were designed to indicate serious network problems: the destination host is down or something in the only path to the host is down. These error codes predate firewalls and packet filtering. The problem with returning one of these error codes is that some hosts (particularly if they're running older versions of Unix) take them quite literally. If these machines get back a "host unreachable" for a given host, they will assume that the host is totally unreachable and will close all currently open connections to it, even if the other connections were working perfectly well.

The second set of ICMP error codes the router might return, "host administratively unreachable" and "network administratively unreachable", were added to the official list of ICMP message types later, specifically to give packet filtering systems something to return when they dropped a packet. Even though they're in the standard, they're not implemented everywhere. Theoretically, this is not a problem; the RFCs specify that a host that gets an ICMP code it doesn't understand should simply ignore the packet. In practice, not all systems will handle this gracefully. The best the standard can do for you is ensure that it is officially not your fault if somebody else's system crashes when you send it an ICMP packet it doesn't understand.

There are several issues to consider when you are deciding whether or not your packet filtering system should return ICMP error codes:

- Which message should you send?

- Can you afford the overhead of generating and returning error codes?

- Will returning these codes enable attackers to get too much information about your packet filtering?

Which set of error codes makes sense for your site? Returning the old "host unreachable" and "network unreachable" codes is technically incorrect (remember that the host may or may not be unreachable, according to the packet filtering policy, depending on what host is attempting to access what service). Also, these error codes can cause many systems to react excessively (shutting down all connections to that host or network).

Returning the new "host administratively unreachable" or "network administratively unreachable" codes advertises the fact that there is a packet filtering system at your site, which you may or may not want to do. These codes may also cause excessive reactions in faulty IP implementations.

There is another consideration as well. Generating and returning ICMP error codes takes a certain small amount of effort on the part of the packet filtering router. An attacker could conceivably mount a denial of service attack by flooding the router with packets the router would reject and for which it would try to generate ICMP error packets. The issue isn't network bandwidth; it's CPU load on the router. (While it's busy generating ICMP packets, it's not able to do other things as quickly, like make filtering decisions.) On the other hand, not returning ICMP error codes will cause a small amount of excess network traffic, as the sending system tries and retries to send the packet being dropped. This traffic shouldn't amount to much, because the number of packets blocked by a packet filtering system should be a fraction of the total number of packets processed. (If it's not a small fraction, you've got more serious problems because people are apparently trying lots of things that "aren't allowed".)

If your router returns an ICMP error code for every packet that violates your filtering policy, you're also giving an attacker a way to probe your filtering system. By observing which packets evoke an ICMP error response, attackers can discover what types of packets do and don't violate your policy (and thus what types of packets are and are not allowed into your network). You should not give this information away because it greatly simplifies the attacker's job. The attacker knows that packets that don't get the ICMP error are going somewhere and can concentrate on those protocols where you actually have vulnerabilities. You'd rather that the attacker spent plenty of time sending you packets that you happily throw away. Returning ICMP error codes speeds up attack programs; if they get back an ICMP error for something they try, they don't have to wait for a timeout.

All in all, the safest thing to do seems to be to drop packets without returning any ICMP error codes. If your router offers enough flexibility, it might make sense to configure it to return ICMP error codes to internal systems (which would like to know immediately that something is going to fail, rather than wait for a timeout) but not to external systems (where the information would give an attacker a means to probe the filtering configuration of the firewall). Even if your router doesn't seem to offer such flexibility, you may be able to accomplish the same result by specifying packet filtering rules to allow the relevant inbound ICMP packets and disallow the relevant outbound ICMP packets.

Some packet filtering systems also allow you to shut off TCP connections without using ICMP, by responding with a TCP reset, which aborts the connection. This is the response that a machine would normally give if it received a TCP packet bound for a port where nothing was listening. Although TCP resets give away less information than ICMP error codes, they still speed up attack programs.

There is one case where you do not usually want to drop packets without an error. A number of systems use the authorization service implemented by *identd* to attempt to do user authentication on incoming connections (usually on mail and IRC connections). If you are not running *identd* or another server that provides information via the Auth protocol, it is advisable to return errors on these attempts, in order to speed up mail delivery to systems using this kind of authorization. If you drop packets without errors, the other system will have to wait for its request to time out before continuing the process of accepting the mail. This can significantly increase the load on your mail system if you need to deliver large amounts of mail. Auth and *identd* are discussed further in Chapter 21, *Authentication and Auditing Services.*

Making Changes

More complicated packet filtering systems may take more complicated actions. In addition to deciding whether or not to forward the packet, they can decide to forward the packet to something other than its original destination, to change states, or to change the contents of the packet itself.

A packet filter can change the destination of the packet either by changing the destination information in the packet (for instance, as part of network address translation or load balancing between servers), or by encapsulating the packet inside another one (this allows a packet filtering router to cooperate with another machine to provide transparent proxying).

When a stateful packet filter gets a packet, it decides not only whether to forward or drop the packet, but also whether to modify its state based on the packet. For instance, if the packet is an outbound UDP packet, the packet filter may change state to allow inbound packets that appear to be replies. If the packet is the first packet in a TCP connection (it has the SYN bit set but no ACK, see Chapter 4, *Packets and Protocols*, for more details), the packet filter may change state to expect a packet with both the SYN bit and the ACK bit set. When it gets that second packet, it will then change state to expect packets with the ACK bit but not the SYN bit set. This enforces a correct TCP handshake, getting rid of some attacks involving interesting settings of header bits.

Some packet filtering systems will also modify parts of packets besides the destination. This is the basis of packet filtering systems that provide network address translation; they need to modify not only destination information, but also source information and sometimes embedded IP addresses further into the packet.

Packet Filtering Tips and Tricks

Packet filtering systems are complicated, and administering them has some subtlety. Here are some ways to deal with them more effectively and make them more secure.

Edit Your Filtering Rules Offline

The filter-editing tools on most systems are usually pretty minimal. Also, it's not always clear how new rules will interact with existing rule sets. In particular, it's often difficult to delete rules, or to add new rules in the middle of an existing rule set.

You might find it more convenient to keep your filters in a text file on one of your Unix or PC systems, so that you can edit them there with the tools you're familiar with, and then load the file on the filtering system as if it contained commands you were typing at the console. Different systems support various ways of doing this. For example, on Cisco products, you can use TFTP to obtain command files from a server. (Be careful of where you enable a TFTP server, though. See the discussion of TFTP in Chapter 17, *File Transfer, File Sharing, and Printing*, and think about using something like TCP Wrapper to control what hosts can activate that TFTP server.)

An added advantage of keeping the filters elsewhere as a file is that you can keep comments in the file (stripping them out of the copy sent to the router, if necessary). Most filtering systems discard any comments in the commands they're given; if you later go look at the active filters on the system, you'll find that the comments aren't retained.

Reload Rule Sets from Scratch Each Time

The first thing the file should do is clear all the old rules, so that each time you load the file you're rebuilding the rule set from scratch; that way, you don't have to worry about how the new rules will interact with the old. Next, specify the rules you want to establish, followed by whatever commands are necessary to apply those rules to the appropriate interfaces.

When you clear the old filtering rules, many filtering systems will default to allowing all packets through. If you have any problems loading the new filtering rules, your filtering system could be allowing everything through while you sort out the problems with the new rules. Therefore, it's a good idea to temporarily disable or shut down the external interface while you update filtering rules, then re-enable it when you're done updating the rules. Make sure that you aren't connecting to the filtering system and doing the update through the external interface, or you'll cut yourself off in mid-session when you shut down the external interface.

Replace Packet Filters Atomically

Sometimes you want to update filtering rules without temporarily shutting off all access (as was discussed previously). This is possible, as long as:

- Your packet filtering system allows you to identify a rule set and then assign the rule set to an interface, replacing the rule set previously assigned to the interface. (Some systems do not allow you to identify rule sets; others do not allow you to assign a rule set to an interface that already has one assigned.)

- When a rule set assignment fails, the packet filtering system reverts to the rule set previously in use. (Some systems will remove all rules in this case, which is unsafe.)

If your system meets both of these conditions, you can update rules with the following system:

1. Load the new rules with an unused identifier.

2. Assign the new rules to the interface.

3. Verify that the new rules are in place and working correctly.

4. Delete the old rules.

5. In order to keep your configuration consistent, load the new rules again with the original identifier and assign them to the interface again. (This doesn't change the rule set, but it returns you to your normal identifier.)

6. Update any offline copies of the configuration with the new rules.

It is possible to automate and script this process if copious and very pessimistic error checking is performed.

Always Use IP Addresses, Never Hostnames

Always specify hosts and networks in filtering rules by IP address, never by hostname or by network name (if your filtering product even supports that). If you specify filtering rules by hostname, your filtering could be subverted if someone accidentally or intentionally corrupts the name-to-address translation (e.g., by feeding false data to your DNS server).

Password Protect Your Packet Filters

Packet filtering systems have to be configured, and many provide ways to do this interactively over the network, perhaps using Telnet or SNMP. If the packet filtering system is based upon a general-purpose computer, then you should take the same remote access precautions as you would when configuring a bastion host. For specialized packet filtering systems, you should take very similar precautions. In particular, if the system stores a master password, even if it is hashed, in a configuration file and attackers can obtain that information, they can use password-cracking tools to guess or break the password. Some packet filtering systems have different password modes; be sure to consult vendor documentation and use a mode that cannot be trivially broken.

If Possible, Use Named Access Lists

Some packet filtering systems allow names to be assigned to sets of rules. In addition, these names may get included in log messages. Using meaningful names can be very useful for both debugging and parsing error log files.

Conventions for Packet Filtering Rules

The rest of this chapter and the chapters in Part III show the kinds of rules you can specify for your packet filtering router in order to control what packets can and cannot flow to and from your network. There are a few things you need to know about these rules.

To avoid confusion, the example rules are specified with abstract descriptions, rather than with real addresses, as much as possible. Instead of using real source and destination addresses (e.g., 172.16.51.50), we use "internal" or "external" to identify which networks we're talking about. Actual packet filtering systems usually require you to specify address ranges explicitly; the syntax varies from router to router.

In all of our packet filtering examples, the assumption is that, for each packet, the router goes through the rules in order until it finds one that matches, and then it takes the action specified by that rule. We assume an implicit default "deny" if no rules apply, although it's a good idea to specify an explicit default (and we generally do).

The syntax used in our filtering examples specifies the number of bits significant for comparison to other addresses after a slash character (/). Thus, 10.0.0.0/8 matches any address that starts with 10; it's equivalent to 10.0.0.0 with a Unix netmask of 255.0.0.0, or 10.0.0.0 with a Cisco wildcard mask of 0.255.255.255, or (if it is a filename) 10.*.*.*. Please note that it is also equivalent to 10.255.255.255/8 or 10.1.27.32/8. The last three octets are simply ignored. Although the examples in this book systematically use "0" for ignored numbers or omit them entirely, that will not be true of all configurations you see in real life, and this is a common source of errors.

Although we try to be as specific as possible in these examples, it's impossible to tell you precisely what you have to specify for your particular packet filtering product. The exact mechanism for specifying packet filtering rules varies widely from product to product. Some products allow you to specify a single set of rules that are applied to all packets routed by the system. Others allow you to specify rules for particular interfaces. Still others allow you to specify sets of rules and then apply sets by name to particular interfaces (so that you might define one set of rules that is shared by a number of different interfaces, for example, and put the rules that are unique to a given interface into a different set).

Here's a simple example to illustrate the differences. We chose these systems because they represent somewhat different ways of specifying filters, not because of any particular preference for them; in general, other systems are similar to these.

Let's say that you want to allow all IP traffic between a trusted external host (host 172.16.51.50) and hosts on your internal network (Class C net 192.168.10.0). In our examples, we would show this case as follows.

Rule	Direction	Source Address	Dest. Address	ACK Set	Action
A	Inbound	Trusted external host	Internal	Any	Permit
B	Outbound	Internal	Trusted external host	Any	Permit
C	Either	Any	Any	Any	Deny

On a Cisco router, you specify rules as sets, and apply the relevant sets to the right direction on the right interface. If your external interface is named "serial1", your rules would look like this:

```
access-list 101 permit ip 172.16.51.50 0.0.0.0 192.168.10.0 0.0.0.255
access-list 101 deny ip 0.0.0.0 255.255.255.255 0.0.0.0 255.255.255.255
interface serial 1
access-group 101 in

access-list 102 permit ip 192.168.10.0 0.0.0.255 172.16.51.50 0.0.0.0
access-list 102 deny ip 0.0.0.0 255.255.255.255 0.0.0.0 255.255.255.255
interface serial 1
access-group 102 out
```

The Linux *ipchains* rules (assuming that eth0 is the internal interface and eth1 is the external interface) would look like this:

```
ipchains -P input DENY
ipchains -P output DENY
ipchains -P forward DENY
ipchains -A input -i eth0 -s 192.168.10.0/24 -d 172.16.51.50 -j ACCEPT
ipchains -A input -i eth1 -s 172.16.51.50 -d 192.168.10.0/24 -j ACCEPT
ipchains -A input -l -j DENY
ipchains -A output -i eth1 -s 192.168.10.0/24 -d 172.16.51.50 -j ACCEPT
ipchains -A output -i eth0 -s 172.16.51.50 -d 192.168.10.0/24 -j ACCEPT
ipchains -A output -l -j DENY
ipchains -A forward -b -s 172.16.51.50 -d 192.168.10.0/24 -j ACCEPT
ipchains -A forward -l -j DENY
```

The rules for *ipfilter*, which would be placed in *ipf*'s configuration file (assuming that le0 is the internal interface and le1 is the external interface) look like this:

```
pass in quick on le0 from 192.168.10.0/24 to 172.16.51.50
pass in quick on le1 from 172.16.51.50 to 192.168.10.0/24
pass out quick on le1 from 192.168.10.0/24 to 172.16.51.50
pass out quick on le0 from 172.16.51.50 to 192.168.10.0/24
block in all
block out all
```

Using Windows NT's Routing and Remote Access Service filtering, you would add two rules:

- Source address 192.168.10.0 and mask 255.255.255.0, destination address 172.16.51.50 and mask 255.255.255.255, protocol any

- Source address 172.16.51.50 and mask 255.255.255.255, destination address 192.168.10.0 and mask 255.255.255.0, protocol any

and then select "Drop all except listed below".

For detailed information on the syntax of a particular package or product, consult the documentation for that package or product. Once you understand the syntax for the particular system you are using, you shouldn't have too much difficulty translating from our tables to that system's syntax.

Watch out for implicit defaults. Different filtering systems have different default actions they take if a packet doesn't match any of the filtering rules specified. Some systems deny all such packets. Other systems make the default the opposite of the last rule; that is, if the last rule was a "permit", the system default is to "deny", and if the last rule was a "deny", the default is to "permit". In any case, it's a good idea to put an explicit default rule at the end of your list of packet filtering rules, so you don't have to worry about (or even remember) which implicit default your system is going to use.

Filtering by Address

The simplest, although not the most common, form of packet filtering is filtering by address. Filtering in this way lets you restrict the flow of packets based on the source and/or destination addresses of the packets without having to consider what protocols are involved. Such filtering can be used to allow certain external hosts to talk to certain internal hosts, for example, or to prevent an attacker from injecting forged packets (packets handcrafted so they appear to come from somewhere other than their true source) into your network.

For example, let's say that you want to block incoming packets with forged source addresses; you would specify the following rule.

Rule	Direction	Source Address	Dest. Address	Action
A	Inbound	Internal	Any	Deny

Note that Direction is relative to your internal network. In the router between your internal network and the Internet, you could apply an inbound rule either to incoming packets on the Internet interface or to outgoing packets on the internal interface; either way, you will achieve the same results for the protected hosts. The difference is in what the router itself sees. If you filter outgoing packets, the router is not protecting itself.

Risks of Filtering by Source Address

It's not necessarily safe to trust source addresses because source addresses can be forged. Unless you use some kind of cryptographic authentication between you and the host you want to talk to, you won't know if you're really talking to that host, or to some other machine that is pretending to be that host. The filters we've discussed previously will help you if an external host is claiming to be an internal host, but they won't do anything about an external host claiming to be a different external host.

There are two kinds of attacks that rely on forgery: source address and man in the middle.

In a basic *source address* forgery attack (shown earlier in Figure 8-1), an attacker sends you packets that claim to be from someone you trust in some way, hoping to get you to take some action based on that trust, without expecting to get any packets back from you. If the attacker doesn't care about getting packets back from you, it doesn't matter where the attacker is. In fact, your responses will go to whomever the attacker is pretending to be, not to the attacker. However, if the attacker can predict your responses, it doesn't matter that they're going some-where else. Many (if not most) protocols are predictable enough for a skilled attacker to be successful at this. Plenty of attacks can be carried out without the attacker's needing to see the results directly. For example, suppose an attacker issues a command to your system that causes it to mail back your password file; if your system is going to send the attacker the password file in the mail, there is no need to see it during the attack itself.

In many circumstances—particularly those involving TCP connections—the real machine (that the attacker is pretending to be) will react to your packets (packets that are attempting to carry on a conversation it knows nothing about) by trying to reset the bogus connection. Obviously, the attacker doesn't want this to happen. Therefore, the attack must complete before the real machine gets the packets you're sending, or before you get the reset packets from the real machine. There are a number of ways to ensure this—for example:

- Carrying out the attack while the real machine is down
- Crashing the real machine so the attack can be carried out
- Flooding the real machine while the attack is carried out
- Confusing the routing between the real machine and the target
- Using an attack where only the first response packet is required, so that the reset doesn't matter

Attacks of this kind used to be considered a theoretical problem with little real-world effect, but they are now common enough to be considered a serious threat.*

The *man in the middle* forgery attack depends on being able to carry out a com-plete conversation while claiming to be the trusted host. In order to do this, the

---

* In general, it's not a good idea to dismiss theoretical attacks completely because they eventually become actual attacks. This kind of attack was known as a theoretical possibility for many years before it actually occurred, yet many people didn't bother to protect against it.

attacking machine needs to be able to not only send you packets, but also intercept the packets you reply with. To do this, the attacker needs to do one of the following:

- Insinuate the attacking machine into the path between you and the real machine. This is easiest to do near the ends of the path, and most difficult to do somewhere in the middle, because given the nature of modern IP networks, the path through "the middle" can change at any second.

- Alter the path between the machines so it leads through the attacking machine. This may be very easy or very difficult, depending on the network topology and routing system used by your network, the remote network, and the Internet service providers between those networks.

Although this kind of attack is called "man in the middle", it's relatively rare for it to actually be carried out in the middle (external to the sites at each end) because nobody but a network provider is in a position to carry it out in that way, and network providers are rarely compromised to that extent. (People who compromise network providers tend to be working on quantity. Packet sniffing will give them many hosts rapidly, but man in the middle attacks give them only one site at a time.) These attacks tend to be problems only if one of the involved sites has hostile users who have physical access to the network (for example, this might be the case if one site is a university).

So, who *can* you trust? At the extreme, nobody, unless you trust the machines involved at both ends and the path between them. If you trust the machines but not the path, you can use encryption and integrity protection to give you a secure connection over an insecure path.

Filtering by Service

Blocking incoming forged packets, as discussed previously, is just about the only common use of filtering solely by address. Most other uses of packet filtering involve filtering by service, which is somewhat more complicated.

From a packet filtering point of view, what do the packets associated with particular services look like? As an example, we're going to take a detailed look at Telnet. Telnet allows a user to log in to another system, as if the user had a terminal directly connected to that system. We use Telnet as an example because it is fairly common, fairly simple, and from a packet filtering point of view, representative of several other protocols such as SMTP and NNTP. We show both outbound and inbound Telnet service.

For detailed discussions of the packet filtering characteristics of other protocols, see the chapters in Part III, *Internet Services*.

Outbound Telnet Service

Let's look first at outbound Telnet service, in which a local client (a user) is talking to a remote server. We need to handle both outgoing and incoming packets. (Figure 8-3 shows a simplified view of outbound Telnet.)

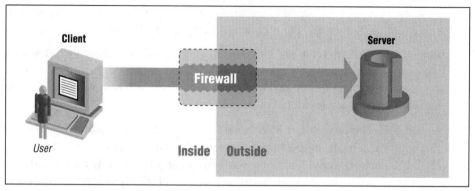

Figure 8-3. Outbound Telnet

The outgoing packets for this outbound service contain the user's keystrokes and have the following characteristics:

- The IP source address of the outgoing packets is the local host's IP address.

- The IP destination address is the remote host's IP address.

- Telnet is a TCP-based service, so the IP packet type is TCP.

- The TCP destination port is 23; that's the well-known port number Telnet servers use.

- The TCP source port number (which we'll call "Y" in this example) is some seemingly random number greater than 1023.

- The first outgoing packet, establishing the connection, will not have the ACK bit set; the rest of the outgoing packets will.

The incoming packets for this outbound service contain the data to be displayed on the user's screen (for example, the "login:" prompt) and have the following characteristics:

- The IP source address of the incoming packets is the remote host's IP address.

- The IP destination address is the local host's IP address.

- The IP packet type is TCP.

- The TCP source port is 23; that's the port the server uses.

- The TCP destination port is the same "Y" we used as the source port for the outgoing packets.

- All incoming packets will have the ACK bit set (again, only the first packet, establishing a connection, has the ACK bit off; in this example, that first packet was an outgoing packet, not an incoming packet).

Note the similarities between the header fields of the outgoing and incoming packets for Telnet. The same addresses and port numbers are used; they're just exchanged between source and destination. If you compare an outgoing packet to an incoming packet, the source and destination addresses are exchanged, and the source and destination port numbers are exchanged.

Why is the client port—the source port for the outgoing packets, and the destination port for the incoming packets—restricted to being greater than 1023? This is a legacy of the BSD versions of Unix, the basis for almost all Unix networking code. BSD Unix reserved ports from 0 to 1023 for local use only by root. These ports are normally used only by servers, not clients, because servers are run by the operating system as privileged users, while clients are run by users. (The major exceptions are the BSD "r" commands like *rcp* and *rlogin*, as we'll discuss in Chapter 18, *Remote Access to Hosts*.) Because TCP/IP first became popular on Unix, this convention spread to other operating systems, even those that don't have a privileged root user (for instance, Macintosh and MS-DOS systems). No actual standard requires this behavior, but it is still consistent on almost every TCP/IP implementation. When client programs need a port number for their own use, and any old port number will do, the programs are assigned a port above 1023. Different systems use different methods to allocate the numbers, but most of them are either pseudo-random or sequential.

Inbound Telnet Service

Next, let's look at inbound Telnet service, in which a remote client (a remote user) communicates with a local Telnet server. Again, we need to handle both incoming and outgoing packets.

The incoming packets for the inbound Telnet service contain the user's keystrokes and have the following characteristics:

- The IP source address of these packets is the remote host's address.

- The IP destination address is the local host's address.

- The IP packet type is TCP.

- The TCP source port is some random port number greater than 1023 (which we'll call "Z" in this example).

- The TCP destination port is 23.

- The TCP ACK bit will not be set on the very first inbound packet, establishing the connection, but it will be set on all other inbound packets.

The outgoing packets for this inbound Telnet service contain the server responses (the data to be displayed for the user) and have the following characteristics:

- The IP source address is the local host's address.

- The IP destination address is the remote host's address.

- The IP packet type is TCP.

- The TCP source port is 23 (these packets are from the Telnet server).

- The TCP destination port is the same random port "Z" that was used as the source port for the inbound packets.

- The TCP ACK bit will be set on all outgoing packets.

Again, note the similarities between the relevant headers of the incoming and the outgoing packets: the source and destination addresses are exchanged, and the source and destination ports are exchanged.

Telnet Summary

The following table illustrates the various types of packets involved in inbound and outbound Telnet services.

Service Direction	Packet Direction	Source Address	Dest. Address	Packet Type	Source Port	Dest. Port	ACK Set
Outbound	Outgoing	Internal	External	TCP	Y	23	a
Outbound	Incoming	External	Internal	TCP	23	Y	Yes
Inbound	Incoming	External	Internal	TCP	Z	23	a
Inbound	Outgoing	Internal	External	TCP	23	Z	Yes

a The TCP ACK bit will be set on all but the first of these packets, which establishes the connection.

Note that Y and Z are both random (from the packet filtering system's point of view) port numbers above 1023.

If you want to allow outgoing Telnet, but nothing else, you would set up your packet filtering as follows.

Rule	Direction	Source Address	Dest. Address	Protocol	Source Port	Dest. Port	ACK Set	Action
A	Out	Internal	Any	TCP	>1023	23	Either	Permit
B	In	Any	Internal	TCP	23	>1023	Yes	Permit
C	Either	Any	Any	Any	Any	Any	Either	Deny

- Rule A allows packets out to remote Telnet servers.

- Rule B allows the returning packets to come back in. Because it verifies that the ACK bit is set, rule B can't be abused by an attacker to allow incoming TCP connections from port 23 on the attacker's end to ports above 1023 on your end (e.g., an X11 server on port 6000).

- Rule C is the default rule. If none of the preceding rules apply, the packet is blocked. Remember from our previous discussion that any blocked packet should be logged, and that it may or may not cause an ICMP message to be returned to the originator.

Risks of Filtering by Source Port

Making filtering decisions based on source port is not without its risks. There is one fundamental problem with this type of filtering: you can trust the source port only as much as you trust the source machine.

Suppose you mistakenly assume that the source port is associated with a particular service. Someone who is in control of the source machine (e.g., someone with root access on a Unix system, or anyone at all with a networked PC) could run whatever client or server he or she wanted on a "source port" that you're allowing through your carefully configured packet filtering system. Furthermore, as we've discussed previously, you can't necessarily trust the source address to tell you for certain what the source machine is; you can't tell for sure if you're talking to the real machine with that address, or to an attacker who is pretending to be that machine.

What can you do about this situation? You want to restrict the local port numbers as much as possible, regardless of how few remote ports you allow to access them. If you only allow inbound connections to port 23, and if port 23 has a Telnet server on it that is trustworthy (a server that will only do things that a Telnet client should be able to tell it to do), it doesn't actually matter whether or not the program that is talking to it is a genuine Telnet client. Your concern is to limit inbound connections to only ports where you are running trustworthy servers, and to be sure that your servers are genuinely trustworthy. Part III discusses how you can achieve these goals for various services.

This problem is particularly bad for servers that use ports above 1023 because you need to allow packets in to those ports in order to let in traffic bound for clients. For instance, in the preceding example, we allow inbound packets for any port over 1023 from source port 23. This would allow an attacker to run anything at all on port 23 (for instance, an X Window System client) and send packets to any server above port 1023 (for instance, an X Window System server). We avoided this problem in our example by using the ACK bit to accept inbound packets but not inbound connections. With UDP, you have no such option, because there is no equivalent to the ACK bit. Fortunately, relatively few important UDP-based protocols are used across the Internet. (The notable exception is DNS, which is discussed further in Chapter 20, *Naming and Directory Services.*)

Choosing a Packet Filtering Router

A number of packet filtering routers are available, some good and some not so good. Almost every dedicated router supports packet filtering in some form. In addition, packet filtering packages are available for many general-purpose Unix and PC platforms you might want to use as routers.

How do you choose the best packet filtering router for your site? This section outlines the most important capabilities a filtering router should have. You should determine which of these capabilities are important to you and select a filtering system that offers at least those capabilities.

It Should Have Good Enough Packet Filtering Performance for Your Needs

Many people worry unnecessarily about packet filtering performance. In most Internet firewalls, in fact, the limiting factor on performance is the speed of your connection to the Internet, not the speed of the packet filtering system. The right question to ask about a packet filtering system is not "How fast is it?" The right question is "Is it fast enough for my needs?"

Internet connections are commonly either 56-Kbps or 1.544-Mbps (T-1) lines. Packet filtering is a per-packet operation. Therefore, the smaller the packets, the more packets will be handled every second and the more filtering decisions a packet filtering system will have to make every second. The smallest possible IP packet—a bare packet containing only an IP header and no data whatsoever—is 20 bytes (160 bits) long. Thus, a line capable of 56 Kbps can carry at most 350 packets per second, and a line capable of 1.544 Mbps (a T-1 line, for example) can carry at most 9,650 packets per second, as shown in the following table. (Cable modems and DSL are variable-rate technologies; depending on the provider, the price you're willing to pay, your location, and the number of other users, speeds may vary from a few hundred kilobits a second to tens of megabits. It's generally safe to assume that theoretical 10-base T speeds are an effective maximum for both.)

Connection Type	Bits/Second (Approximate)	Packets/Second (20-byte Packets)	Packets/Second (40-byte Packets)
V.32bis modem	14,400	90	45
V.90 modem or 56-Kbps leased line	56,000	350	175

Connection Type	Bits/Second (Approximate)	Packets/Second (20-byte Packets)	Packets/Second (40-byte Packets)
ISDN	128,000	800	400
T-1 leased line	1,544,000	9,650	4,825
10-base T or Ethernet (practical)	3,000,000	18,750	9,375
10-base T or Ethernet (theoretical)	10,000,000	62,500	31,250
T-3 leased line	45,000,000	281,250	140,625
FDDI or 100-base T	100,000,000	625,000	312,500

In fact, though, you will rarely see bare IP packets; there is always something in the data segment (e.g., a TCP, UDP, or ICMP packet). A typical packet crossing a firewall would be a TCP/IP packet because most Internet services are TCP-based. The minimum possible TCP/IP packet size, for a packet containing only the IP header and TCP header and no actual data, is 40 bytes, which cuts the maximum packet rates in half, to 175 packets per second for a 56-Kbps line and 4,825 packets per second for a 1.544-Mbps line. Real packets containing real data are going to be larger still, reducing the packet-per-second rates still further.

These per-second packet rates are well within the capabilities of many of the packet filtering systems, both commercial and freely available off the Internet, that are available today. Some can go much faster.

Many manufacturers of firewalls cite speeds in Mbps in order to provide numbers that are comparable to network speeds. These numbers can be highly misleading because firewall performance is dependent on packets per second, not bits per second. Two firewalls that claim to process packets at exactly the same speed may show dramatically different bits per second rates, depending on the assumptions their manufacturers have made about average packet sizes. Ask for rates in packets per second, and compare that to data about your incoming packet rates. If this information is not directly available, insist on knowing what assumptions were made about packet sizes, so that you can make reasonable comparisons.

In addition, firewall performance depends on the complexity of packet filters. You should be sure that the speeds you are quoted are speeds with a reasonable filter set (some manufacturers quote the speed achieved with packet filtering enabled but no filters set, for instance). Stateful packet filtering, intelligent packet filtering, and reassembly of fragmented packets will all slow down performance.

Do not assume that firewall performance will depend on processor speed. The speed of a router (and a packet filter is just a special kind of router) tends to be much more dependent on other factors, including the amount of available memory, the performance of the network interfaces themselves, and the speed and bandwidth of internal connections. Upgrading a machine's processor often has little or no effect on its speed at processing network traffic.

Speed is likely to be more of an issue in a firewall that is internal to an organization's network. Such a firewall will need to run at local area network speeds, which are usually theoretically at least 10 Mbps, and may be much higher. (Firewalls are not practical within a gigabit-per-second network at this point. Fortunately, from a firewalls perspective, such networks are fairly rare at present.) In addition, internal firewalls often require more complex filter sets and support for a larger number of protocols, which will further reduce their performance.

A firewall with more than two connections may also have higher speed requirements. With two connections, the maximum required speed is that of the slowest connection. With three connections, the required speed can rise. For example, if you put a second Internet connection onto an external router, it now needs to drive both at full speed if it's not going to be a limiting factor. If you put two internal networks onto it, it's going to need to achieve the higher speed of those networks to route between them.

If you have a truly high-speed connection to the Internet (because you have a lot of internal Internet users, a lot of services that you're offering to the Internet, or both), router performance may be a real issue. In fact, many really large sites require more performance and more reliability than any single router can provide. In this situation, it's appropriate to worry a great deal about performance. The fewer routers you use to connect to the Internet, the better. Each independent Internet connection is another possible hole in your security. If you must use multiple routers, get the best performance you can, so as to use as few routers as possible. In some cases, this may require carefully designing your network so that you simplify the filtering rules on routers that have to support large amounts of traffic.

It Can Be a Single-Purpose Router or a General-Purpose Computer

Don't expect a single device to serve as your packet filtering router and also to do something that's not part of your firewall. (You may have a device that's doing packet filtering and proxying, or packet filtering and selected bastion host services, or even all three.) In a practical sense, you should expect to be using a dedicated packet filtering router. This doesn't mean you have to buy a single-purpose router, however. You might choose to use either a traditional, single-purpose router, or a general-purpose computer dedicated to routing. What are the pros and cons of each choice?

If you have a large number of networks or multiple protocols, you will probably need a single-purpose router. Routing packages for general-purpose computers usually do not have the speed or flexibility of single-purpose routers, and you may find that you will need an inconveniently large machine to accommodate the necessary interface boards.

On the other hand, if you are filtering a single Internet link, you may not need to do any more than route IP packets between two Ethernets. This is well within the capabilities of a reasonable 486-based (or comparable) computer, and such a machine will certainly be cheaper than a single-purpose router. (It may even be free, if you already have one available within your organization.) Routing and filtering packages are available for Windows NT and many other Microsoft operating systems, as well as most variants of Unix. (See Appendix B for information about available packages.)

Whatever device you use for your filtering router, firewalling should be all the router does. For example, if possible, don't use one device as both your filtering router and the backbone router that ties together multiple separate internal networks. Instead, use one device to tie together your internal networks and a separate (much smaller) device as your filtering router. The more complex the filtering router and its configuration, the more likely it is that you'll make a mistake in its configuration, which could have serious security implications. Filtering also has a significant speed impact on a router and may slow the router down to the point where it has difficulty achieving acceptable performance for the internal networks.

Some commercial firewall packages combine packet filtering with proxying on a machine that behaves like a single-purpose router. Others combine packet filtering with proxying or bastion host services on a high-powered general-purpose computer. This is fine, although it will increase your speed requirements. Don't expect to use a small machine to do this. Depending on what machines you have available, this may either be a good bargain (you buy a single large machine instead of multiple medium-sized ones) or a bad one (you buy a single large machine instead of adding a small machine to an existing configuration). As we've said in Chapter 6, *Firewall Architectures*, combining the bastion host with the external packet filter is a reasonable thing to do from a security perspective.

It Should Allow Simple Specification of Rules

You want to be able to specify the rules for your packet filtering as simply as possible. Look for this feature in any device you select. From a conceptual point of view, packet filtering is complicated to begin with, and it's further complicated by the details and quirks of the various protocols. You don't want your packet filtering system to add any more complexity to the complications you already have to deal with.

In particular, you want to be able to specify rules at a fairly high level of abstraction. Avoid any packet filtering implementations that treat packets as simply unstructured arrays of bits and require you to state rules in terms of the offset and state of particular bits in the packet headers.

On the other hand, you do not want the packet filter to entirely hide the details. You should also avoid packet filtering implementations that require you turn on protocols by name, without specifying exactly what ports this will allow in what directions.

As we discussed before, you'll also probably want to be able to download the rules from another machine if you're using a single-purpose router. Nevertheless, you need a user interface that allows you to create and edit the rules without extreme pain, because you may periodically have to do so.

It Should Allow Rules Based on Any Header or Meta-Packet Criteria

You want to be able to specify rules based on any of the header information or meta-packet information available for your packets. Header information includes the following:

- IP source and destination address

- IP options

- Protocol, such as TCP, UDP, or ICMP

- TCP or UDP source and destination port

- ICMP message type

- Start-of-connection (ACK bit) information for TCP packets

and similar information for any other protocols you're filtering on. Meta-packet information includes any information about the packet that the router knows but that isn't in the headers themselves (e.g., which router interface the packet came in on or is going out on). You want to be able to specify rules based on combinations of these header and meta-packet criteria.

For various reasons, many filtering products don't let you look at the TCP or UDP source port in making packet filtering decisions; they let you look only at the TCP or UDP destination port. This makes it impossible to specify certain kinds of filters. Some manufacturers who omit TCP/UDP source ports from packet filtering criteria maintain that such filtering isn't useful anyway, or that its proper use is "too dangerous" for customers to understand (because, as we've pointed out previously, source port information is not reliable). We believe that this is a fallacy and that such decisions are better left to well-informed customers.

It Should Apply Rules in the Order Specified

You want your packet filter to apply, in a predictable order, the rules you specify for it. By far the simplest order is the order in which you, the person configuring the router, specify the rules. Unfortunately, some products, instead of applying rules in the order you specify, try to reorder and merge rules to achieve greater efficiency in applying the rules. (One innovative vendor even touts this as a user interface benefit, because you no longer have to worry about what order to specify the rules in!) This causes several problems:

- Reordering rules makes it difficult for you to figure out what's going on, and what the router is going to do with a particular set of filtering instructions. Configuring a packet filtering system is already complicated enough, without having a vendor add additional complications by merging and reordering rule sets.

- If any quirks or bugs are in the merging or reordering of rule sets (and there often are because it's something that's very difficult for the vendors to test), it becomes impossible to figure out what the system is going to do with a given set of filters.

- Most importantly, reordering rules can break a rule set that would work just fine if it had not been reordered.

Let's consider an example. Imagine that you're in a corporation, working on a special project with a local university. Your corporate Class B network is 172.16 (i.e., your IP addresses are 172.16.0.0 through 172.16.255.255). The university owns Class A net 10 (i.e., their IP addresses are 10.0.0.0 through 10.255.255.255).*

For the purposes of this project, you're linking your network directly to the university's, using a packet filtering router. You want to disallow all Internet access over this link (Internet access should go through your Internet firewall). Your special project with the university uses the 172.16.6 subnet of your Class B network (i.e., IP addresses 172.16.6.0 through 172.16.6.255). You want all subnets at the university to be able to access this project subnet. The university's eight-bit 10.1.99 subnet has a lot of hostile activity on it; you want to ensure that this subnet can only reach your project subnet.

How can you meet all these requirements? You could try the following three packet filtering rules. (In this example, we are considering only the rules for traffic incoming to your site; you'd need to set up corresponding rules for outgoing traffic.)

Rule	Source Address	Dest. Address	Action
A	10.0.0.0/8	172.16.6.0/24	Permit
B	10.1.99.0/24	172.16.0.0/16	Deny
C	Any	Any	Deny

---

* 172.16 and 10 are both reserved network numbers, which no company or university could have. They're used for example purposes only. Not all the IP addresses in a network's range are valid host addresses; addresses where the host portion is all ones or all zeros are reserved and cannot be allocated to hosts, making the range of host addresses on 172.16 actually 172.16.0.1 through 172.16.255.254.

- Rule A permits the university to reach your project subnet.

- Rule B locks the hostile subnet at the university out of everything else on your network.

- Rule C disallows Internet access to your network.

Now let's look at what happens in several different cases, depending on exactly how these rules are applied.

If the rules are applied in the order ABC

If the rules are applied in the order ABC—the same order specified by the user—the following table shows what happens with a variety of sample packets.

Packet	Source Address	Dest. Address	Desired Action	Actual Action (by Rule)
1	10.1.99.1	172.16.1.1	Deny	Deny (B)
2	10.1.99.1	172.16.6.1	Permit	Permit (A)
3	10.1.1.1	172.16.6.1	Permit	Permit (A)
4	10.1.1.1	172.16.1.1	Deny	Deny (C)
5	192.168.3.4	172.16.1.1	Deny	Deny (C)
6	192.168.3.4	172.16.6.1	Deny	Deny (C)

- Packet 1 is from a machine at the university on the hostile subnet to a random machine on your network (not on the project subnet); you want it to be denied; it is, by rule B.

- Packet 2 is from a machine at the university on the hostile subnet to a machine on your project subnet; you want it to be permitted; it is, by rule A.

- Packet 3 is from a random machine at the university to a machine on your project subnet; you want it to be permitted; it is, by rule A.

- Packet 4 is from a random machine at the university to one of your non-project machines; you want it to be denied; it is, by rule C.

- Packet 5 is from a random machine on the Internet to one of your nonproject machines; you want it to be denied; it is, by rule C.

- Packet 6 is from a random machine on the Internet to one of your project machines; you want it to be denied; it is, by rule C.

Thus, if the rules are applied in the order ABC, they accomplish what you want.

If the rules are applied in the order BAC

What would happen if the router reordered the rules by the number of significant bits in the source address, so that more specific rules are applied first? In other words, rules applying to more specific IP source addresses (i.e., rules that apply to a smaller range of source addresses) would be applied before rules applying to less specific IP source addresses. In this case, the rules would be applied in the order BAC.

Rule	Source Address	Dest. Address	Action
B	10.1.99.0/24	172.16.0.0/16	Deny
A	10.0.0.0/8	172.16.6.0/24	Permit
C	Any	Any	Deny

Here are the same six sample packets, with the new outcomes if the rules are applied in the order BAC; in bold face, we show how the actions differ from the previous case (in which rules are applied in the order specified by the user).

Packet	Source Address	Dest. Address	Desired Action	Actual Action (by Rule)
1	10.1.99.1	172.16.1.1	Deny	Deny (B)
2	**10.1.99.1**	**172.16.6.1**	**Permit**	**Deny (B)**
3	10.1.1.1	172.16.6.1	Permit	Permit (A)
4	10.1.1.1	172.16.1.1	Deny	Deny (C)
5	192.168.3.4	172.16.1.1	Deny	Deny (C)
6	192.168.3.4	172.16.6.1	Deny	Deny (C)

If the rules are applied in the order BAC, then packet 2, which should be permitted, is improperly denied by rule B. Now, denying something that should be permitted is safer than permitting something that should be denied, but it would be better if the filtering system simply did what you wanted it to do.

You can construct a similar example for systems that reorder rules based on the number of significant bits in the destination address, which is the most popular other reordering criteria.

Rule B is actually not necessary

If you consider this example carefully, you can see that the discussion about the hostile subnet, which is the reason for rule B, is redundant and isn't necessary to achieve the desired results. Rule B is intended to limit the hostile subnet to accessing only your project subnet. Rule A, however, already restricts the entire university—including the hostile subnet—to accessing only your project subnet. If you omit rule B, then the rules will be applied in order AC regardless of whether or not the system reorders based on the number of significant bits in the IP source address. The following tables show what happens in either case.

Rule	Source Address	Dest. Address	Action
A	10.0.0.0/8	172.16.6.0/24	Permit
C	Any	Any	Deny

Packet	Source Address	Dest. Address	Desired Action	Actual Action (by Rule)
1	10.1.99.1	172.16.1.1	Deny	Deny (C)
2	10.1.99.1	172.16.6.1	Permit	Permit (A)
3	10.1.1.1	172.16.6.1	Permit	Permit (A)
4	10.1.1.1	172.16.1.1	Deny	Deny (C)
5	192.168.3.4	172.16.1.1	Deny	Deny (C)
6	192.168.3.4	172.16.6.1	Deny	Deny (C)

Packet filtering rules are tricky

The point here is that getting filtering rules right is tricky. In this example, we are considering a relatively simple situation, and we've still managed to come up with a rule set that had a subtle error in it. Real-life rule sets are significantly more complex than these, and often include tens or hundreds of rules. Considering the implications and interactions of all those rules is nearly impossible, unless they are simply applied in the order specified. So-called "help" from a router, in the form of reordering rule sets, can easily turn an over-specified but working rule set into a nonworking rule set. You should make sure that the packet filtering router you select doesn't reorder rule sets.

It's OK if the router does optimization, as long as the optimization doesn't change the effect of the rules. Pay close attention to what kind of optimizations your packet filtering implementation tries to do. If a vendor will not or cannot tell you what order rules are applied in, do not buy that vendor's product.

It Should Apply Rules Separately to Incoming and Outgoing Packets, on a Per-Interface Basis

For maximum flexibility, capability, and performance, you want to be able to specify a separate rule set for incoming and outgoing packets on each interface. In this section, we'll show an example that demonstrates the problems you can run into with routers that aren't that flexible.

A limitation unfortunately shared by many packet filtering systems is that they let you examine packets only as they are leaving the system. This limitation leads to three problems:

- The system is always "outside" its own filters.

- Detecting forged packets is difficult or impossible.

- Configuring such systems is extremely difficult if they have more than two interfaces.

Let's look at the first problem. If a router lets you look only at outgoing packets, then packets directed to the router itself are never subjected to packet filtering. The result is that the filtering doesn't protect the router itself. This is usually not too serious a problem because there are typically few services on the router that could be attacked, and there are other ways to protect those services. Telnet is an example of a service that can be attacked in this way, but you can usually get around the routing problem by disabling the Telnet server, or by controlling from where it will accept incoming connections. SNMP is another commonly available and vulnerable service.

Now consider the second problem. If a router can filter only outgoing packets, it's difficult or impossible to detect forged packets being injected from the outside (that is, packets coming in from the outside but that claim to have internal source addresses), as is illustrated in Figure 8-1. Forgery detection is most easily done when the packet enters the router, on the inbound interface. Detecting forgeries on the outbound interface is complicated by packets generated by the router itself (which will have internal source addresses if the router itself has an internal address) and by legitimate internal packets mistakenly directed to the router (packets that should have been sent directly from their internal source to their internal destinations but were instead sent to the filtering router, for instance, by systems following a default route that leads to the filtering router).

The third problem with outbound-only filtering is that it can be difficult to configure packet filtering on such a router when it has more than two interfaces. If it has only two interfaces, then being able to do only outbound filtering on each interface is no big deal. There are only two paths through the router (from the first interface to the second, and vice versa). Packets going one way can be filtered as outgoing packets on one interface, while packets going the other way can be filtered as outgoing packets on the other interface. Consider, on the other hand, a router with four interfaces: one for the site's Internet connection, one for a finance network, and two for engineering networks. In such an environment, it wouldn't be unreasonable to impose the following policy:

- The two engineering networks can communicate with each other without restrictions.

- The two engineering networks and the Internet can communicate with each other with certain restrictions.

- The two engineering networks and the finance network can communicate with each other with certain restrictions—restrictions that are different from those between the engineering nets and the Internet.

- The finance network cannot communicate with the Internet under any circumstances.

Figure 8-4 illustrates this environment.

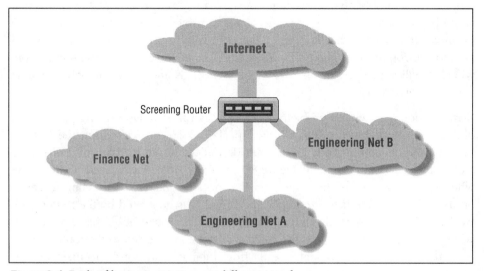

Figure 8-4. Packet filtering restrictions on different interfaces

There are 12 paths through this router, from each of four interfaces to each of three other interfaces (in general, there are N * (N–1) paths through an N-interface router). With an outbound-only filtering system, you would have to establish the following filtering on each interface:

Engineering Net A
    Internet filters, finance net filters, engineering net B filters

Engineering Net B
    Internet filters, finance net filters, engineering net A filters

Finance Net
    Internet filters, engineering net A filters, engineering net B filters

Internet
    Engineering net A filters, engineering net B filters, finance net filters

Merging multiple filtering requirements in a single interface like this can be very tricky. Depending on the complexity of the filters and the flexibility of the filtering system, it may actually be impossible in some situations.

A more subtle problem with such a setup is that it imposes packet filtering overhead between the two engineering networks (which may result in a significant performance problem). With this setup, the router has to examine all the packets flowing between the two engineering nets, even though it will never decide to drop any of those packets.

Now look at the same scenario, assuming that the packet filtering system has both inbound and outbound filters. In this case, you could put:

- All the filters related to the Internet (regardless of whether they apply to the engineering nets or the finance net) on the Internet interface

- All the filters related to the finance net (regardless of whether they apply to the engineering nets or the Internet) on the finance interface

- No filters at all on the engineering interfaces (thus allowing maximum performance for traffic between the engineering nets because it wouldn't pass through any filters)

What if a packet filtering system had inbound-only filters, rather than outbound-only filters? A system of this kind would address the first and second problems we described in this section: a router with inbound-only filters *can* be protected by its own filters and can detect forged packets. However, such a system would not address the third and most serious problem; you still have problems merging filtering rules on routers with more than two interfaces.

What if the packet filtering system had both kinds of filters but didn't allow you to specify individual interfaces? This kind of system has all the problems of an outbound-only system (you have to merge all of the rules into a single set and incur packet filtering overhead even on unfiltered connections). In addition, it becomes very difficult to detect forged source addresses. Most such systems have special configurations to deal with forged source addresses, but these are less flexible than the controls you can get by directly specifying rules. In particular, they may protect you from external forgeries without detecting internal forgeries.

It Should Be Able to Log Accepted and Dropped Packets

Make sure the packet filtering router gives you the option of logging all of the packets it drops. You want to know about any packets that are blocked by your packet filtering rules. These rules reflect your security policy, and you want to know when somebody attempts to violate that policy. The simplest way to learn about these attempted violations is through such a log.

You'd also like to be able to log selected packets that were accepted. For example, you might want to log the start of each TCP connection. Logging all accepted packets is going to be too much data in normal operation but may be worth it occasionally for debugging and for dealing with attacks in progress. Although you will probably be doing some logging at the packet destination, that logging won't work if the destination host has been compromised, and won't show packets that make it through the packet filter but don't have a valid destination. Those packets are interesting because they may be probes from an attacker. Without information from the router, you won't have the complete picture of what the attacker is doing.

The specific information that is logged is also important and packet filtering routers have widely varying capabilities. You will want information about which rule and packet caused the log entry to be made. Ideally, you would like to know the definition of the rule, but a name or other constant identifier would be sufficient. A rule number which changes every time you edit the rule set is the least useful rule identifier, although it's better than no information at all.

You will also want information about the packet itself. At a minimum you will want to see source and destination IP addresses and protocol. For TCP and UDP packets you will want to see source and destination port numbers (and the flags for TCP packets). For ICMP you will want to see the type and code. Without this information it can be very difficult to debug rulesets or, when you are being attacked, trace or block packets from an unwanted source. In some situations, it is preferable to log the entire packet, instead of a summary.

The logging should be flexible; the packet filter should give you the ability to log via *syslog* and to a console or a local file. It would also be helpful if the logging included the ability to generate SNMP traps on certain events. Some packet filters also have various alerting capabilities (they can page an administrator or send email). These capabilities are useful but are less flexible than a generalized alerting system based on SNMP. If the packet filtering machine has a modem directly attached, and is capable of completing a page independently, paging capabilities provide a useful alerting mechanism of last resort, where the machine can call for help if it is unable to send any network traffic at all. Otherwise, paging on the packet filter is not of much interest; you would be better served by an alert sent to a general-purpose system.

It Should Have Good Testing and Validation Capabilities

An important part of establishing a firewall is convincing yourself (and others within your organization) that you've done the job right and haven't overlooked anything. To do that, you need to be able to test and validate your configuration.

Most of the packet filtering packages currently available have little or nothing in the way of testing and validation capabilities.

Testing and validation come down to two related questions:

- Have you properly told the router to do what you want?

- Is the router doing what you've told it to?

Unfortunately, with many products available today, both of these questions tend to be difficult to answer. In the few products that provide any kinds of testing capabilities, what the test says it will do with a given packet and what it actually does with such a packet are sometimes different, often because of subtle caching and optimization bugs. Some sites (and, we hope, some vendors!) have constructed filtering test beds, where they can generate test packets on one side of a filtering router and watch to see what comes through to the other side, but that's beyond the capabilities and resources of most sites. About the best you can do is pick something with a good reputation for not having many problems and good support for when it inevitably does have problems.

Packet Filtering Implementations for General-Purpose Computers

These days, a number of operating systems provide packet filtering features, independent of firewall products. Many Unix variants come with packet filtering, as does Windows NT.

There are two major reasons why you might want to use packet filtering implementations on general-purpose computers. First, you may want to use a general-purpose computer as a router (either providing only packet filtering, or as a single-box firewall that provides both packet filtering and proxying). In this case, you are using the general-purpose computer to provide the same sort of packet filtering services that a router would provide. Second, you may be using the general-purpose computer as a bastion host, and you may want to use packet filtering on the computer as a security measure to protect the computer itself.

Linux ipchains and Masquerading

The Linux kernel includes a packet filtering system called *ipchains*, which provides powerful packet filtering capabilities. This system provides the same sorts of capabilities that you would get from a modern packet filtering router and is suitable for using where you'd use a router. Because it's part of the standard Linux kernel source, it should be present in all up-to-date Linux distributions, although it may not be enabled by default.

Earlier Linux kernels used a filtering system called *ipfw* (which was a port of a BSD filtering system) and a configuration utility called *ipfwadm*. *ipchains* is a new filtering system, which provides more functionality than *ipfw*. *ipchains* allows you to convert configuration files from *ipfwadm* to *ipchains*.

The filtering performed by *ipchains* is done entirely in the kernel, and it requires only a single external utility to initialize the filtering rules. This means that it is possible to build a complete Linux filtering system that will fit on a single 1.44 MB floppy disk. The Linux Router Project is doing exactly this (see Appendix A, *Resources*, for more information about the Linux Router Project).

Linux also has a facility called *masquerading*, which is used with *ipchains* to provide network address translation for both TCP and UDP. Masquerading keeps track of TCP connection state and supports timeout-based UDP requests and responses. Because it must be used with packet filtering, it can be considered a dynamic packet filtering system. In addition to providing straightforward network address translation for simple TCP and UDP protocols, Linux masquerading allows additional kernel modules to be loaded for more complicated protocols (for instance, FTP and RealAudio, which require reverse TCP connections or additional UDP ports).

ipchains

ipchains is designed around the concept of a chain of rules. Each rule specifies a condition and an action to take if the condition is met, called a *target*. The rules in a chain are used in order; a packet is checked against each rule in turn, and if the packet matches the condition, the specified action is taken.

There are three standard chains, called the input, output, and forward chains. All packets coming in to the machine are passed through the *input chain*, and all packets going out of the machine are passed though the *output chain*. The *forward chain* is used for packets that need to be sent to a different network interface from the one they were received on. Thus, if a packet is received for the machine, it's matched against the input chain; if the machine generates a packet, it's matched against the output chain. If the machine is acting as a router and gets a packet addressed to some other machine, the packet will be matched against all three chains.

The standard chains each have a default policy, which is applied when no rules match. It is also possible to create additional, user-defined, chains. If no rules match when checking a user-defined chain, processing will continue at the point where the chain was called.

The conditions in a rule can be based on any of the following:

- The IP protocol number (e.g., TCP, UDP, ICMP, or IGMP).

- The source and destination IP addresses. Addresses can be specified as a variable-length subnet (e.g., 192.168.8.0/22) or a network address with a mask, and negation is allowed (you can specify "all addresses except those that match this address and mask").

- The source and destination TCP and UDP port numbers. Port numbers can be specified with ranges or masks, and negation is allowed.

- The ICMP type and code.

- Whether the packet is an IP fragment.

- Whether the packet is a TCP start-of-connection packet.

- The network interface. This is the interface the packet came in on for the input chain and the destination interface for the output and forward chains.

Each rule in a chain has a target action that is applied when the rule matches. The target of a rule decides what next happens to a packet. The allowed targets are:

- Deny: Drop the packet without generating a response.

- Reject: Don't process the packet, but generate an ICMP response (which will be passed though the output chain).

- Accept: Process the packet.

- Masq: Perform masquerading. This target is only valid in the forward chain.

- Redirect: Forward the packet to a different port on the local machine.

- Return: Apply the default policy for a built-in chain or continue processing at the point where a user-defined chain was called.

- A user-defined chain.

Because a user-defined chain can be the target of a rule, it is possible to build complex filters or make *ipchains* behave like other packet filtering systems.

A rule can also make a log entry, which contains information about the action that was taken, the time, and a summary of the packet headers. Logging is performed by *syslog*.

Testing ipchains rules

ipchains has a very useful feature that allows the kernel-filtering rules to be tested. The *ipchains* command allows you to specify IP header values to be tested against the currently loaded kernel filtering rules. Using the standard target names, the command prints how the kernel would react if the packet had really been sent to the firewall. At the time of writing, it is not possible to generate and test arbitrary packets.

Masquerading

Linux masquerading is a network address translation system. Because it is capable of working at higher protocol levels, and doing more intricate modifications than simple address changes, it's also called a *transparent proxying system*. What it does could be considered either proxying or packet filtering; it's somewhere in between the two.

The IP address of the firewall is used in communicating with remote services. For simple protocols, masquerading alters only IP header information, including IP addresses, port numbers, and TCP sequence and acknowledgment numbers. Masquerading uses the IP address of the host doing the masquerading as the externally visible address, and maps the port number into one from a pool of 4096 ports starting at 61000. This fixed allocation of ports does limit Linux masquerading to 4096 simultaneous TCP connections and 4096 UDP ports. At the time of writing, Linux kernels allocate only ports less than 32768, so the ports used for masquerading will never conflict with ports used for other purposes.

Linux masquerading is also capable of dealing with more complicated protocols, such as FTP or RealAudio, which might require reverse TCP connections or additional UDP ports. Support for new protocols can be added by dynamically loading new kernel modules.

How masquerading works

Masquerading works by intercepting packets that are being forwarded by the Linux kernel. Masquerading for simple protocols works much like simple network address translation, as described in Chapter 5, *Firewall Technologies*. IP addresses and port numbers are modified on outgoing packets. For TCP connections, a new sequence number is generated. The process is reversed for incoming packets. Figure 8-5 is an example of this working for a client connecting to a remote HTTP server, and shows the IP address and ports for each half of the connection. The masquerading firewall will continue to pass packets back to the client as long as the client maintains the outgoing half of the TCP connection. In the case of UDP, the firewall will pass packets back to the client only for a configurable time period, which is typically set to 15–30 seconds.

In addition to handling outgoing traffic, masquerading can be used to forward incoming ports to internal services. The ability to masquerade incoming ports is configured statically for each port that is to be forwarded. Once a port is forwarded, it can no longer be used to connect to a service on the firewall. Figure 8-6 shows a masquerading firewall configured to forward SSH to an internal destina-

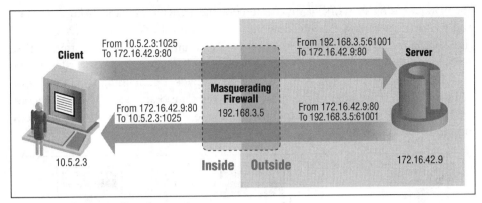

Figure 8-5. Masquerading for simple outgoing protocols

tion and includes the IP addresses and port numbers for each half of the connection. It's possible to forward the same port to multiple destinations if the masquerading firewall is configured to listen to multiple IP addresses.

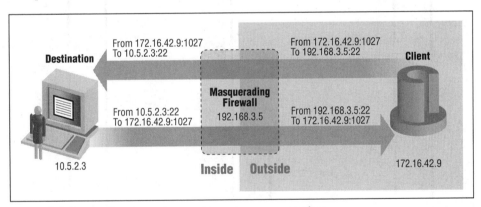

Figure 8-6. Forwarding incoming services using masquerading

For more complicated protocols, masquerading can set up additional listening TCP and UDP ports based upon the contents of packets that have been seen. Masquerading can even rewrite the contents of data packets in order to replace IP addresses and port numbers.

This is best explained by describing how the masquerading module for FTP works. As we discuss in Chapter 17, *File Transfer, File Sharing, and Printing*, FTP is a tricky protocol to support through a firewall because it normally involves a connection from the server to the client. An FTP client opens a control channel to a desired FTP server. At the point where data is to be transferred, the client issues a PORT command that contains the client IP address and a port number the client expects to receive the data on. The FTP server uses this information to open a new TCP connection to the client in order to transfer the data.

For masquerading to work, it must intercept the PORT command from the client. The FTP masquerading module does this by listening to the commands sent over all FTP control channels. When it sees a PORT command, it does two things; first, it sets up a temporary port on the masquerading host, which is forwarded to the port the client specified. Next, it rewrites the IP packet containing the PORT command with the IP address of the firewall and the temporary port. When an incoming connection to the temporary port is made, it is forwarded to the client. Figure 8-7 describes this process.

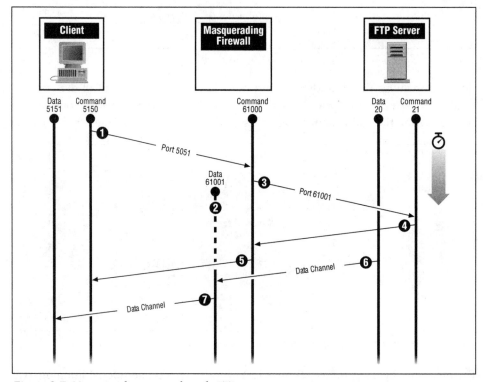

Figure 8-7. Masquerading normal-mode FTP

Available specialized masquerading modules

A number of specialized masquerading modules are available. At the time of writing, they can be split into three categories: multimedia, games, and access to internal services. An up-to-date list of modules and their availability can be found in the Linux MASQUERADING-HOWTO. See Appendix A, *Resources*, for information on how to obtain Linux HOWTO documents.

Using ipchains (including masquerading)

To use *ipchains*, you must compile it into the kernel you are using. The actual kernel compilation flags for turning it on are different in different Linux releases; you should either consult help for your Linux kernel configuration utility or use the Linux IPCHAINS-HOWTO. See Appendix A for information on obtaining Linux HOWTO documents.

We also recommend that you turn on fragment reassembly. See Chapter 4, *Packets and Protocols*, for information on IP fragmentation and why this is important.

Masquerading is included as a standard part of Linux 2.1 and 2.2 kernel source code. It does need to be enabled when the kernel is compiled, and it also depends on the Linux firewalling code. The kernel compile-time option for enabling Linux masquerading is CONFIG_IP_MASQUERADE=Y.

In order to use all of the facilities of *ipchains* and masquerading, you will also need the *ipchains* and *ipmasqadm* commands used to define the filtering and masquerading rules.

ipchains rules are built incrementally; when the machine boots, it installs the rules in order, so there will be a brief period while it is initializing when the chain is not fully built, and the default policy will be used before the end of the chain has been configured. If the default policy is to accept packets, you may accept packets that you would otherwise have denied. You should therefore put in an initial explicit default policy that denies packets.

One tempting way to avoid this problem is to build the chains before you actually configure the network interfaces (if you can't receive the packets, there's no need to worry about what you do with them). In most situations, this won't work because rules will be rejected if they refer to network interfaces that haven't been configured. If you have a configuration of the kind we recommend, you will have to configure the network interface before you can build the chains you are actually going to use. Thus, you will end up using two bootup scripts for the *ipchains* configuration. The first script will initialize default deny policies for each chain; the second will load the rules you wish to use. When combined with the network interface configuration scripts, this will result in the following three-stage process:

1. Load default deny polices that do not specify an interface.

2. Configure the network interfaces.

3. Load the real *ipchains* rules you're going to use.

Since the default policy does not do any logging, it is often useful to duplicate it with a final rule that will also log denied traffic. In other packet filtering situations, we recommend doing this for documentation purposes; in this case, you have already documented the default with the initial default policy, but you need both in order to combine security and logging.

When masquerading is operating, the standard Unix *netstat* program does not list masqueraded ports. This means that the machine will be accepting packets for ports that don't show up when you run *netstat,* which may be disconcerting to experienced network administrators.

ipfilter

ipfilter is another packet filtering system for Unix. It works on the free BSD implementations (FreeBSD, OpenBSD, and NetBSD) and has also been ported to and tested on other Unix operating systems including Solaris and previous versions of SunOS, IRIX, and Linux.

ipfilter uses a list of rules contained in a single configuration file. Unlike *ipchains,* *ipfilter* checks all rules in sequence, and the last rule that successfully matches determines the fate of a packet. This can be a great source of confusion. Imagine a filtering configuration file containing only the following rules:

```
block in all
pass in all
```

This will pass all packets because the second rule is the last rule that matches. Fortunately an *ipfilter* rule can specify the "quick" keyword, which if the rule matches, will terminate the rule checking at that point. The following rules would block all traffic:

```
block in quick all
pass in all
```

Rules may be arranged into groups, which allows you to make more complicated configurations quite easily. A group has a head rule, which is checked to determine whether the rest of the rules in the group are executed. If the group is executed, the rules in it are handled in the normal way. At the end of the group, processing continues at the next line.

The conditions in a rule can be based on any of the following:

- The IP protocol number (for example TCP, UDP, ICMP, or IGMP).

- The IP options that are set.

- The source and destination IP addresses. Addresses can be specified as a variable-length subnet (for example 192.168.8.0/22) or a network address with a mask, and negation is allowed (you can specify "all addresses except those that match this address and mask").

- The source and destination TCP and UDP port numbers. Port numbers can be specified with ranges or masks, and negation is allowed.

- The ICMP type and code.

- Whether the packet is an IP fragment. Fragments that are too short to contain port numbers, and thus could prevent port rules from being applied, can be explicitly handled.

- The TCP flags that are set (for instance, the ACK and SYN bits that let you identify a start of connection packet).

- The network interface the packet came in on.

The actions *ipfilter* can take are:

- Drop the packet without generating a response.

- Don't process the packet, but return an ICMP response (you can specify what ICMP response to return).

- Don't process the packet, but return a TCP reset.

- Process the packet.

- Process the packet, keeping state information to make sure that all TCP packets are part of a valid TCP conversation, with appropriate settings of SYN and ACK and appropriate sequence numbers.

- Change IP address and/or port number information in the packet using a static mapping (this is a simple form of network address translation).

- Send the packet or a copy of it to a specified network interface or address for logging purposes.

- Log information about the packet via *syslog*.

ipfilter also has the ability to do some more complicated packet rewriting to support protocols that cannot be handled by straightforward network address translation. However, there are relatively few supported protocols. The rewriting system in *ipfilter* is not dynamically extensible; rewriting capabilities are set at compile time and cannot be added on the fly.

Comparing ipfilter and ipchains

ipfilter and *ipchains* provide roughly the same functionality; in many cases, people choose between them based on the operating system they're using, using *ipchains* on Linux and *ipfilter* on other operating systems. On the other hand, they do have distinct strengths and weaknesses.

ipchains is much stronger as a network address translation system. The network address translation functionality provided by *ipfilter* is minimal and is not dynamically updatable. *ipchains* is also provided as part of Linux, so that it doesn't require separate integration.

ipfilter provides filtering capabilities that *ipchains* does not (allowing you to filter on IP options and providing more flexible handling of TCP options, for instance), and it is more flexible about the responses it gives to blocked packets. Its packet duplication features are useful for feeding packets to intrusion detection systems.

The architecture of *ipchains* makes it much easier to extend than *ipfilter*, so it's likely that the extra *ipfilter* features will eventually show up in *ipchains*. However, *ipchains* is relatively tightly integrated with the Linux kernel, which will slow down its spread to other operating systems.

Linux netfilter

At this writing, the Linux packet filtering and network address translation systems are being rewritten. The new filtering system is called *netfilter*, and it has several goals. One is to reduce the number of points in the Linux kernel where filtering occurs. Another is to have a clean separation of filtering from network address translation. As a result of this separation, *netfilter* is no longer capable of modifying packets. Some of the concepts from *ipchains* still exist in *netfilter*, in particular, lists of filtering rules are built into named chains. The significant features that have been added to *netfilter* are:

- The ability to filter on both the input and output interface in the forward chain
- The ability to pass packets to user-level processes for handling

If you are using *ipchains* only for packet filtering, you can use *netfilter* with the same filtering rules. However, if you use the masquerading chain, you will need to convert to using the new network address translation tools in order to use *netfilter*.

Windows NT Packet Filtering

Windows NT 4 comes with a very limited ability to do packet filtering, suitable only for protecting the machine itself, and that only in some circumstances. From the Network control panel, when you are configuring TCP/IP properties, you can go to the IP address tab and select Advanced. You have two different ways of doing filtering:

- The Enable PPTP Filtering button will restrict the interface to only using PPTP.*
- The Configure button under Enable Security will let you configure filtering by TCP port, UDP port, or IP protocol.

---

* See Chapter 14, *Intermediary Protocols*, for more information about PPTP.

Windows 2000 provides the latter filtering also, as part of the Advanced TCP/IP Settings; it is under the Options tab and is called TCP/IP filtering. You may specify that you wish to allow everything, or you may provide a list of what you will allow, by individual port number (that is, if you wish to allow ports above 1023, you will have to enter each number from 1024 to 65536 separately).

This packet filtering is extremely minimal, and there are very few situations where it's possible to use it. It is useful for machines that are using PPTP, or that are bastion hosts providing single services like HTTP. Some of the problems with it are not immediately obvious and are frequently unpleasant surprises to people trying to use this packet filtering:

- It controls only incoming packets without ACK set; it will not limit outbound connections.

- The "IP protocol" entries do not control UDP and TCP; if you wish to deny UDP and TCP, you must set the TCP and UDP entries to allow only specified ports and then avoid specifying any ports.

- It will not deny ICMP, even if you set the IP protocol to allow only specified ports and avoid including ICMP.

If you install the Routing and Remote Access Service for Windows NT 4 or Windows 2000, which is a no-cost option, you get much more flexible packet filtering, allowing both inbound and outbound filters by protocol, source and destination address, and source and destination port. This filtering still doesn't compete with full-fledged packet filtering implementations; it doesn't allow specifications of port ranges, it doesn't give you any control over what's done with denied packets, and it doesn't allow you to combine allow and deny rules.

Windows 2000 provides packet filtering in a third place as part of its implementation of IPsec (IPsec is discussed further in Chapter 14, *Intermediary Protocols*). This packet filtering is comparable to the Routing and Remote Access Service filtering for Windows NT 4, except that it is possible to combine filters into sets (allowing you to mix allow and deny rules), and a rule can apply four possible actions:

- Permit all packets that match, regardless of their IPsec status.

- Block all packets that match, regardless of their IPsec status.

- Request IPsec protections on all packets that match, but accept them if IPsec is not available.

- Require IPsec protections on all packets that match, and reject them if IPsec is not available.

If you are using packet filtering as part of IPsec, we strongly recommend that you avoid configuring any of the other possible sorts of packet filtering. Use only one packet filtering package at a time; otherwise, you risk configuring conflicting filtering rules. Whether or not the computer gets confused, its maintainers certainly will.

Ironically, the most powerful packet filtering package that Microsoft makes available for Windows NT is actually part of Microsoft's Proxy Server. While it still does not provide all of the features that a packet filtering router would provide, it does include alerting and logging options, specification of port ranges, and filtering of fragments. As of this writing, a new version of Proxy Server is due out shortly, and it is expected to have still more packet filtering features.

Where to Do Packet Filtering

If you look at the various firewall architectures outlined in Chapter 6, *Firewall Architectures*, you see that you might perform packet filtering in a variety of places. Where should you do it? The answer is simple: anywhere you can.

Many of the architectures (e.g., the screened host architecture or the single-router screened subnet architecture) involve only one router. In those cases, that one router is the only place where you could do packet filtering, so there's not much of a decision to be made.

However, other architectures, such as the two-router screened subnet architecture, and some of the architectural variations, involve multiple routers. You might do packet filtering on any or all of these routers.

Our recommendation is to do whatever packet filtering you can wherever you can. This is an application of the principle of least privilege (described in Chapter 3, *Security Strategies*). For each router that is part of your firewall, figure out what types of packets should legitimately be flowing through it, and set up filters to allow only those packets and no more. You may also want to put packet filters on destination hosts, using a host-based packet filtering system like the ones discussed previously, or using special-purpose software designed for filtering on destination hosts.This is highly advisable for bastion hosts, and destination host filtering packages are discussed further in the chapters about bastion hosts (Chapters 10, 11, and 12).

This may lead to duplication of some filters on multiple routers; in other words, you may filter out the same thing in more than one place. That's good; it's redundancy, and it may save you some day if you ever have a problem with one of your routers—for example, if something was supposed to be done but wasn't (because of improper configuration, bugs, enemy action, or whatever). It provides defense in depth and gives you the opportunity to fail safely—other strategies we outlined in Chapter 3, *Security Strategies.*

If filtering is such a good idea, why not filter on all routers, not just those that are part of the firewall? Basically, because of performance and maintenance issues. Earlier in this chapter, we discussed what "fast enough" means for a packet filtering system on the perimeter of your network. However, what's fast enough at the edge of your network (where the real bottleneck is probably the speed of the line connecting you to the Internet) is probably not fast enough within your network (where you've probably got many busy local area networks of Ethernet, FDDI, or perhaps something even faster). Further, if you put filters on all your routers, you're going to have to maintain all those filter lists. Maintaining filter lists is a manageable problem if you're talking about one or a handful of routers that are part of a firewall, but it gets out of hand in a hurry as the number of routers increases. This problem is worsened if some of the routers are purely internal. Why? Because you probably want to allow more services within your network than you allow between your network and the Internet. This is going to either make your filter sets longer (and thus harder to maintain), or make you switch from a "default deny" stance to a "default permit" stance on those internal filters (which is going to seriously undermine the security they provide anyway). You reach a point of diminishing returns fairly quickly when you try to apply filtering widely within a local area network, rather than just at its perimeter.

You may still have internal packet filtering routers at boundaries within the local area network (between networks with different security policies, or networks that belong to different organizations). As long as they're at clearly defined boundaries, and they're up to the performance requirements, that's not a problem. Whether or not you duplicate the external rules on these internal packet filters is going to depend on how much you trust the external packet filters, and how much complexity and overhead the external rules are going to add.

In some cases, you may also be able to run packet filtering packages on bastion hosts. If this is not a performance problem, it can provide additional security in the event that a packet filtering router is compromised or misconfigured.

Some people argue against putting packet filters on routers when you also have a firewall inside the router, on the grounds that allowing packets to reach the firewall system gives you a single logging point, making it easier to detect attacks. If an attack involves some packets that are filtered out at the router, and others that are rejected at an internal firewall, the internal firewall may not be successful at detecting the attack. This is not a convincing argument; the internal firewall will still be successful at detecting any attack that has any chance of succeeding against it, and any reasonable logging configuration will let you correlate the logs from the packet filters with the logs from the internal firewall and do intrusion detection on the union of them in any case. The increased detection benefit from allowing the packets is more than outweighed by the decrease in security.*

What Rules Should You Use?

Clearly, most of the rules that you will put into your packet filtering system will be determined by the kinds of traffic you want to accept. There are certain rules you will almost always want to use, however.

We've already discussed these rules in various places, but here's a summary list of some standard protections that you should automatically apply unless you have a strong reason to do otherwise:

- Set up an explicit default deny (with logging) so that you are sure that the default behavior is to reject packets.

- Deny inbound traffic that appears to come from internal addresses (this is an indication of forged traffic or bad network configurations).

- Deny outbound traffic that does not appear to come from internal addresses (again, such traffic is either forged or symptomatic of network misconfigurations).

- Deny all traffic with invalid source addresses (including broadcast and multicast source addresses; see Chapter 4, *Packets and Protocols*, for more information about broadcast, multicast, and source addresses).

- Deny all traffic with source routes or IP options set.

- Deny ICMP traffic over a reasonable size (a few kilobytes). ICMP filtering rules are discussed further in Chapter 22, *Administrative Services*.

- Reassemble fragments into entire packets.

Putting It All Together

This section works through a few more examples to show how many of the concepts we've talked about in this chapter come together in the real world. For detailed discussions of the packet filtering characteristics of particular protocols, see the chapters in Part III.

This section is designed to demonstrate the process of developing a filter set; filters are elaborated as we go on, rather than being produced in final form. We aren't attempting to show a complete filter set for any site. Every site is different, and you can get burned by packet filtering if you don't understand all the details

---

* We have also heard the argument that "the firewall is more secure than the packet filter, so you should use it instead." This is relevant only if you can't use both at the same time. Clearly, the firewall is not more secure than the combination of the firewall and the packet filter!

and implications of its use in your particular environment. We want people to carefully consider and understand what they're doing—not blindly copy something out of a book (even ours!) without a careful consideration of how relevant and appropriate it is for their own situation. In any case, a full solution for a site requires considering packet filtering, proxying, and configuration issues. That process is illustrated in Chapter 24, *Two Sample Firewalls*.

Let's start with a simple example: allowing inbound and outbound SMTP (so that you can send and receive electronic mail) and nothing else. You might start with the following rule set.

Rule	Direction	Source Address	Dest. Address	Protocol	Dest. Port	Action
A	In	External	Internal	TCP	25	Permit
B	Out	Internal	External	TCP	>1023	Permit
C	Out	Internal	External	TCP	25	Permit
D	In	External	Internal	TCP	>1023	Permit
E	Either	Any	Any	Any	Any	Deny

- Rules A and B allow inbound SMTP connections (incoming email).

- Rules C and D allow outbound SMTP connections (outgoing email).

- Rule E is the default rule that applies if all else fails.

 We assume in this example that, for each packet, your filtering system looks at the rules in order. It starts at the top until it finds a rule that matches the packet, and then it takes the action specified.

Now, let's consider some sample packets to see what happens. Let's say that your host has IP address 172.16.1.1, and that someone is trying to send you mail from the remote host with IP address 192.168.3.4. Further, let's say the sender's SMTP client uses port 1234 to talk to your SMTP server, which is on port 25. (SMTP servers are always assumed to be on port 25; see the discussion of SMTP in Chapter 16, *Electronic Mail and News*).

Packet	Direction	Source Address	Dest. Address	Protocol	Dest Port	Action (Rule)
1	In	192.168.3.4	172.16.1.1	TCP	25	Permit (A)
2	Out	172.16.1.1	192.168.3.4	TCP	1234	Permit (B)

Figure 8-8 shows this case.

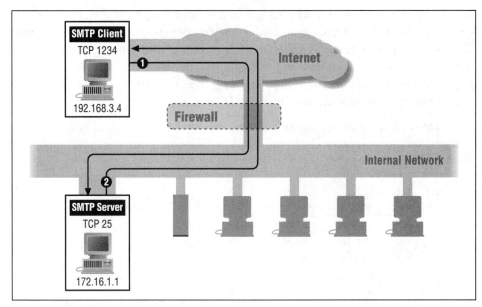

Figure 8-8. Packet filtering: inbound SMTP (sample packets 1 and 2)

In this case, the packet filtering rules permit your incoming email:

- Rule A permits incoming packets from the sender's SMTP client to your SMTP server (represented by packet number 1 in the preceding table).

- Rule B permits the responses from your server back to the sender's client (represented by packet number 2 in the preceding table).

What about outgoing email from you to them? Let's say that your SMTP client uses port 1357 to talk to their SMTP server, as follows.

Packet	Direction	Source Address	Dest. Address	Protocol	Dest. Port	Action (Rule)
3	Out	172.16.1.1	192.168.3.4	TCP	25	Permit (C)
4	In	192.168.3.4	172.16.1.1	TCP	1357	Permit (D)

Figure 8-9 shows this case.

Again, in this case, the packet filtering rules permit your outgoing email:

- Rule C permits outgoing packets from your SMTP client to their SMTP server (represented by packet number 3 above).

- Rule D permits the responses from their server back to your client (represented by packet number 4 above).

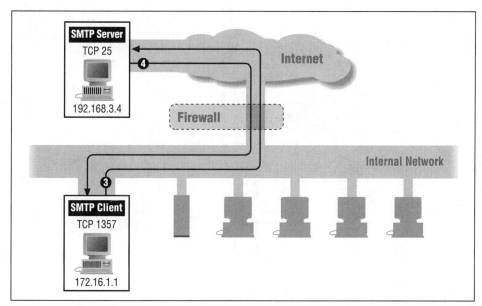

Figure 8-9. Packet filtering: outbound SMTP (sample packets 3 and 4)

Now, let's stir things up. What happens if someone in the outside world (for example, someone on host 10.1.2.3) attempts to open a connection from port 5150 on his end to the web proxy server on port 8080 on one of your internal systems (for example, 172.16.3.4) in order to carry out an attack? (See Chapter 15, *The World Wide Web*, for a discussion of web proxy servers and their vulnerabilities.)

Packet	Direction	Source Address	Dest. Address	Protocol	Dest. Port	Action (Rule)
5	In	10.1.2.3	172.16.3.4	TCP	8080	**Permit (D)**
6	Out	172.16.3.4	10.1.2.3	TCP	5150	**Permit (B)**

Figure 8-10 shows this case.

The preceding rule set allows this connection to take place! In fact, this rule set allows any connection to take place as long as both ends of the connection are using ports above 1023. Why?

- Rules A and B together do what you want to allow inbound SMTP connections.

- Rules C and D together do what you want to allow outbound SMTP connections.

- But Rules B and D together end up allowing *all* connections where both ends are using ports above 1023, and this is certainly not what you intended.

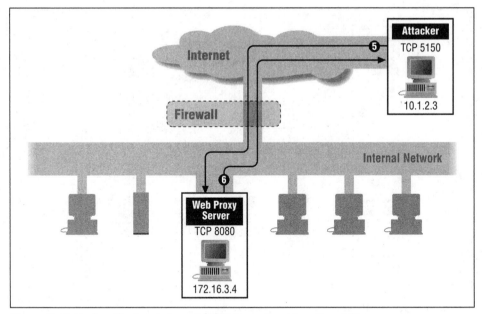

Figure 8-10. Packet filtering: inbound SMTP (sample packets 5 and 6)

Lots of vulnerable servers are probably listening on ports above 1023 at your site. Examples are web proxy servers (port 8080), X11 (port 6000), databases (Sybase, Oracle, Informix, and other databases commonly use site-chosen ports above 1023), and so on. This is why you need to consider a rule set as a whole, instead of assuming that if each rule or group of rules is OK, the whole set is also OK.

What can you do about this? Well, what if you also looked at the source port in making your filtering decisions? Here are those same five basic rules with the source port added as a criterion.

Rule	Direction	Source Address	Dest. Address	Protocol	Source Port	Dest. Port	Action
A	In	External	Internal	TCP	>1023	25	Permit
B	Out	Internal	External	TCP	25	>1023	Permit
C	Out	Internal	External	TCP	>1023	25	Permit
D	In	External	Internal	TCP	25	>1023	Permit
E	Either	Any	Any	Any	Any	Any	Deny

And here are those same six sample packets, filtered by the new rules.

Packet	Direction	Source Address	Dest. Address	Protocol	Source Port	Dest. Port	Action (Rule)
1	In	192.168.3.4	172.16.1.1	TCP	1234	25	Permit (A)
2	Out	172.16.1.1	192.168.3.4	TCP	25	1234	Permit (B)

Packet	Direction	Source Address	Dest. Address	Protocol	Source Port	Dest. Port	Action (Rule)
3	Out	172.16.1.1	192.168.3.4	TCP	1357	25	Permit (C)
4	In	192.168.3.4	172.16.1.1	TCP	25	1357	Permit (D)
5	In	10.1.2.3	172.16.3.4	TCP	5150	8080	Deny (E)
6	Out	172.16.3.4	10.1.2.3	TCP	8080	5150	Deny (E)

As you can see, when the source port is also considered as a criterion, the problem packets (numbers 5 and 6, representing an attack on your web proxy server) no longer meet any of the rules for packets to be permitted (rules A through D). The problem packets end up being denied by the default rule.

OK, now what if you're dealing with a slightly smarter attacker? What if the attacker uses port 25 as the client port on his end (he might do this by killing off the SMTP server on a machine he controls and using its port, or by carrying out the attack from a machine that never had an SMTP server in the first place, like a PC) and then attempts to open a connection to your web proxy server? Here are the packets you'd see.

Packet	Direction	Source Address	Dest. Address	Protocol	Source Port	Dest. Port	Action (Rule)
7	In	10.1.2.3	172.16.3.4	TCP	25	8080	**Permit (D)**
8	Out	172.16.3.4	10.1.2.3	TCP	8080	25	**Permit (C)**

Figure 8-11 shows this case.

As you can see, the packets would be permitted, and the attacker would be able to make connections through your proxy server (as we discuss in Chapter 15, *The World Wide Web*, this would certainly be annoying and could be disastrous).

So what can you do? The solution is to also consider the ACK bit as a filtering criterion. Again, here are those same five rules with the ACK bit also added as a criterion.

Rule	Direction	Source Address	Dest. Address	Protocol	Source Port	Dest. Port	ACK Set	Action
A	In	External	Internal	TCP	>1023	25	Any	Permit
B	Out	Internal	External	TCP	25	>1023	Yes	Permit
C	Out	Internal	External	TCP	>1023	25	Any	Permit
D	In	External	Internal	TCP	25	>1023	Yes	Permit
E	Either	Any	Any	Any	Any	Any	Any	Deny

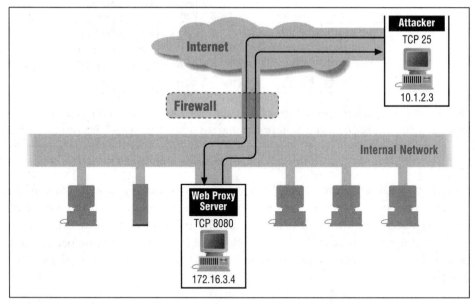

Figure 8-11. Packet filtering: inbound SMTP (sample packets 7 and 8)

Now, packet 7 (the attacker attempting to open a connection to your web proxy server) will fail, as follows.

Packet	Direction	Source Address	Dest. Address	Protocol	Source Port	Dest. Port	ACK Set	Action (Rule)
7	In	10.1.2.3	172.16.3.4	TCP	25	8080	No	Deny (E)

The only differences in this rule set are in rules B and D. Of these, rule D is the most important because it controls incoming connections to your site. Rule B applies to connections outgoing from your site, and sites are generally more interested in controlling incoming connections than outgoing connections.

Rule D now says to accept incoming packets from things that are supposedly SMTP servers (because the packets are coming from port 25) only if the packets have the ACK bit set; that is, only if the packets are part of a connection started from the inside (from your client to his server).

If someone attempts to open a TCP connection from the outside, the very first packet that he or she sends will not have the ACK bit set; that's what's involved in "opening a TCP connection". (See the discussion of the ACK bit in the "TCP" section of the "Protocols Above IP" discussion in Chapter 4, *Packets and Protocols.*) If you block that very first packet (packet 7 in the preceding example), you block the whole TCP connection. Without certain information in the headers of the first packet—in particular, the TCP sequence numbers—the connection can't be established.

Why can't an attacker get around this by simply setting the ACK bit on the first packet? Because the packet will get past the filters, but the destination will believe the packet belongs to an existing connection (instead of the one with which the packet is trying to establish a new connection). When the destination tries to match the packet with the supposed existing connection, it will fail because there isn't one, and the packet will be rejected.

 As a basic rule of thumb, any filtering rule that permits incoming TCP packets for outgoing connections (that is, connections initiated by internal clients) should require that the ACK bit be set.

At this point, you now have a simple rule set that allows the traffic you set out to allow, and only that traffic. It's not a full rule set (it doesn't include the default rules we discussed earlier), and it's not a very interesting rule set (you almost certainly want to allow more protocols than just SMTP). But it's a functioning rule set that you understand precisely, and from here you can build a configuration that actually meets your needs, using the information in the rest of this book.

9

Proxy Systems

Proxying provides Internet access to a single host, or a very small number of hosts, while appearing to provide access to all of your hosts. The hosts that have access act as proxies for the machines that don't, doing what these machines want done.

A proxy server for a particular protocol or set of protocols runs on a dual-homed host or a bastion host: some host that the user can talk to, which can, in turn, talk to the outside world. The user's client program talks to this proxy server instead of directly to the "real" server out on the Internet. The proxy server evaluates requests from the client and decides which to pass on and which to disregard. If a request is approved, the proxy server talks to the real server on behalf of the client and proceeds to relay requests from the client to the real server, and to relay the real server's answers back to the client.

As far as the user is concerned, talking to the proxy server is just like talking directly to the real server. As far as the real server is concerned, it's talking to a user on the host that is running the proxy server; it doesn't know that the user is really somewhere else.

Since the proxy server is the only machine that speaks to the outside world, it's the only machine that needs a valid IP address. This makes proxying an easy way for sites to economize on address space. Network address translation can also be used (by itself or in conjunction with proxying) to achieve this end.

Proxying doesn't require any special hardware, but something somewhere has to make certain that the proxy server gets the connection. This might be done on the client end by telling it to connect to the proxy server, or it might be done by intercepting the connection without the client's knowledge and redirecting it to the proxy server.

Proxy systems are effective only when they are used in conjunction with some method of restricting IP-level traffic between the clients and the real servers, such as a screening router or a dual-homed host that doesn't route packets. If there is IP-level connectivity between the clients and the real servers, the clients can bypass the proxy system (and presumably so can someone from the outside).

Why Proxying?

There's no point in connecting to the Internet if your users can't access it. On the other hand, there's no safety in connecting to the Internet if there's free access between it and every host at your site. Some compromise has to be applied.

The most obvious compromise is to provide a single host with Internet access for all your users. However, this isn't a satisfactory solution because these hosts aren't transparent to users. Users who want to access network services can't do so directly. They have to log in to the dual-homed host, do all their work from there, and then somehow transfer the results of their work back to their own workstations. At best, this multiple-step process annoys users by forcing them to do multiple transfers and work without the customizations they're accustomed to.

The problem is worse at sites with multiple operating systems; if your native system is a Macintosh, and the dual-homed host is a Unix system, the Unix system will probably be completely foreign to you. You'll be limited to using whatever tools are available on the dual-homed host, and these tools may be completely unlike (and may seem inferior to) the tools you use on your own system.

Dual-homed hosts configured without proxies therefore tend to annoy their users and significantly reduce the benefit people get from the Internet connection. Worse, they usually don't provide adequate security; it's almost impossible to adequately secure a machine with many users, particularly when those users are explicitly trying to get to the external universe. You can't effectively limit the available tools because your users can always transfer tools from internal machines that are the same type. For example, on a dual-homed host, you can't guarantee that all file transfers will be logged because people can use their own file transfer agents that don't do logging.

Proxy systems avoid user frustration and the insecurities of a dual-homed host. They deal with user frustration by automating the interaction with the dual-homed host. Instead of requiring users to deal directly with the dual-homed host, proxy systems allow all interaction to take place behind the scenes. The user has the illusion of dealing directly (or almost directly) with the server on the Internet, with a minimum of direct interaction with the dual-homed host. Figure 9-1 illustrates the difference between reality and illusion with proxy systems.

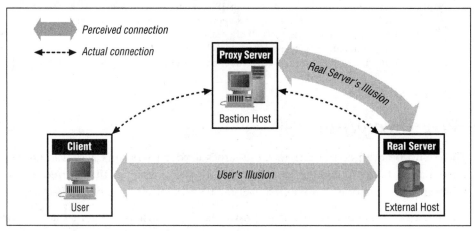

Figure 9-1. Proxies—reality and illusion

Proxy systems deal with the insecurity problems by avoiding user logins on the dual-homed host and by forcing connections through controlled software. Because the proxy software works without requiring user logins, the host it runs on is safe from the randomness of having multiple logins. It's also impossible for anybody to install uncontrolled software to reach the Internet; the proxy acts as a control point.

How Proxying Works

The details of how proxying works differ from service to service. Some services provide proxying easily or automatically; for those services, you set up proxying by making configuration changes to normal servers. For most services, however, proxying requires appropriate proxy server software on the server side. On the client side, it needs one of the following:

Proxy-aware application software
> With this approach, the software must know how to contact the proxy server instead of the real server when a user makes a request (for example, for FTP or Telnet), and how to tell the proxy server what real server to connect to.

Proxy-aware operating system software
> With this approach, the operating system that the client is running on is modified so that IP connections are checked to see if they should be sent to the proxy server. This mechanism usually depends on dynamic runtime linking

(the ability to supply libraries when a program is run). This mechanism does not always work and can fail in ways that are not obvious to users.

Proxy-aware user procedures

With this approach, the user uses client software that doesn't understand proxying to talk to the proxy server and tells the proxy server to connect to the real server, instead of telling the client software to talk to the real server directly.

Proxy-aware router

With this approach, nothing on the client's end is modified, but a router intercepts the connection and redirects it to the proxy server or proxies the request. This requires an intelligent router in addition to the proxy software (although the routing and the proxying can co-exist on the same machine).

Using Proxy-Aware Application Software for Proxying

The first approach is to use proxy-aware application software for proxying. There are a few problems associated with this approach, but it is becoming easier as time goes on.

Appropriate proxy-aware application software is often available only for certain platforms. If it's not available for one of your platforms, your users are pretty much out of luck. For example, the *Igateway* package from Sun (written by Jim Thompson) is a proxy package for FTP and Telnet, but you can use it only on Sun machines because it provides only precompiled Sun binaries. If you're going to use proxy software, you obviously need to choose software that's available for the needed platforms.

Even if software is available for your platforms, it may not be software your users want. For example, dozens of FTP client programs are on the Macintosh. Some of them have really impressive graphical user interfaces. Others have other useful features; for example, they allow you to automate transfers. You're out of luck if the particular client you want to use, for whatever reason, doesn't support your particular proxy server mechanism. In some cases, you may be able to modify clients to support your proxy server, but doing so requires that you have the source code for the client, as well as the tools and the ability to recompile it. Few client programs come with support for any form of proxying.

The happy exception to this rule is web browsers like Netscape, Internet Explorer, and Lynx. Many of these programs support proxies of various sorts (typically SOCKS and HTTP proxying). Most of these programs were written after firewalls and proxy systems had become common on the Internet; recognizing the environment they would be working in, their authors chose to support proxying by design, right from the start.

Using application changes for proxying does not make proxying completely transparent to users. The application software still needs to be configured to use the appropriate proxy server, and to use it only for connections that actually need to be proxied. Most applications provide some way of assisting the user with this problem and partially automating the process, but misconfiguration of proxy software is still one of the most common user problems at sites that use proxies.

In some cases, sites will use the unchanged applications for internal connections and the proxy-aware ones only to make external connections; users need to remember to use the proxy-aware program in order to make external connections. Following procedures they've become accustomed to using elsewhere, or procedures that are written in books, may leave them mystified at apparently intermittent results as internal connections succeed and external ones fail. (Using the proxy-aware applications internally will work, but it can introduce unnecessary dependencies on the proxy server, which is why most sites avoid it.)

Using Proxy-Aware Operating System Software

Instead of changing the application, you can change the environment around it, so that when the application tries to make a connection, the function call is changed to automatically involve the proxy server if appropriate. This allows unmodified applications to be used in a proxied environment.

Exactly how this is implemented varies from operating system to operating system. Where dynamically linked libraries are available, you add a library; where they are not, you have to replace the network drivers, which are a more fundamental part of the operating system.

In either case, there may be problems. If applications do unexpected things, they may go around the proxying or be disrupted by it. All of the following will cause problems:

- Statically linked software
- Software that provides its own dynamically linked libraries for network functions
- Protocols that use embedded port numbers or IP addresses
- Software that attempts to do low-level manipulation of connections

Because the proxying is relatively transparent to the user, problems with it are usually going to be mysteries to the user. The user interface for configuring this sort of proxying is also usually designed for the experienced administrator, not the naive user, further confusing the situation.

Using Proxy-Aware User Procedures for Proxying

With the proxy-aware procedure approach, the proxy servers are designed to work with standard client software; however, they require the users of the software to follow custom procedures. The user tells the client to connect to the proxy server and then tells the proxy server which host to connect to. Because few protocols are designed to pass this kind of information, the user needs to remember not only what the name of the proxy server is, but also what special means are used to pass the name of the other host.

How does this work? You need to teach your users specific procedures to follow for each protocol. Let's look at FTP. Imagine that Amalie Jones wants to retrieve a file from an anonymous FTP server (e.g., *ftp.greatcircle.com*). Here's what she does:

1. Using any FTP client, she connects to your proxy server (which is probably running on the bastion host—the gateway to the Internet) instead of directly to the anonymous FTP server.

2. At the username prompt, in addition to specifying the name she wants to use, Amalie also specifies the name of the real server she wants to connect to. If she wants to access the anonymous FTP server on *ftp.greatcircle.com*, for example, then instead of simply typing "anonymous" at the prompt generated by the proxy server, she'll type "anonymous@ftp.greatcircle.com".

Just as using proxy-aware software requires some modification of user procedures, using proxy-aware procedures places limitations on which clients you can use. Some clients automatically try to do anonymous FTP; they won't know how to go through the proxy server. Some clients may interfere in simpler ways, for example, by providing a graphical user interface that doesn't allow you to type a username long enough to hold the username and the hostname.

The main problem with using custom procedures, however, is that you have to teach them to your users. If you have a small user base and one that is technically adept, it may not be a problem. However, if you have 10,000 users spread across four continents, it's going to be a problem. On the one side, you have hundreds of books, thousands of magazine articles, and tens of thousands of Usenet news postings, not to mention whatever previous training or experience the users might have had, all of which attempt to teach users the standard way to use basic Internet services like FTP. On the other side is your tiny voice, telling them how to use a procedure that is at odds with all the other information they're getting. On top of that, your users will have to remember the name of your gateway and the details of how to use it. In any organization of a reasonable size, this approach can't be relied upon.

Using a Proxy-Aware Router

With a proxy-aware router, clients attempt to make connections the same way they normally would, but the packets are intercepted and directed to a proxy server instead. In some cases, this is handled by having the proxy server claim to be a router. In others, a separate router looks at packets and decides whether to send them to their destination, drop them, or send them to the proxy server. This is often called *hybrid proxying* (because it involves working with packets like packet filtering) or *transparent proxying* (because it's not visible to clients).

A proxy-aware router of some sort (like the one shown in Figure 9-2) is the solution that's easiest for the users; they don't have to configure anything or learn anything. All of the work is done by whatever device is intercepting the packets, and by the administrator who configures it.

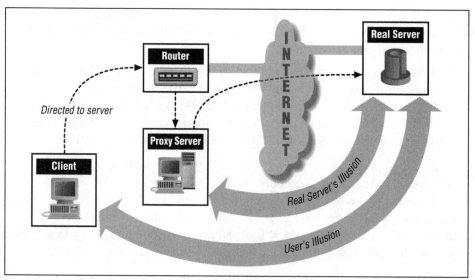

Figure 9-2. A proxy-aware router redirecting connections

On the good side, this is the most transparent of the options. In general, it's only noticeable to the user when it doesn't work (or when it does work, but the user is trying to do something that the proxy system does not allow). From the user's point of view, it combines the advantages of packet filtering (you don't have to worry about it, it's automatic) and proxying (the proxy can do caching, for instance).

From the administrator's point of view, it combines the disadvantages of packet filtering with those of proxying:

- It's easy for accidents or hostile actions to make connections that don't go through the system.

- You need to be able to identify the protocol based on the packets in order to do the redirection, so you can't support protocols that don't work with packet filtering. But you also need to be able to make the actual connection from the proxy server, so you can't support protocols that don't work with proxying.

- All internal hosts need to be able to translate all external hostnames into addresses in order to try to connect to them.

Proxy Server Terminology

This section describes a number of specific types of proxy servers.

Application-Level Versus Circuit-Level Proxies

An *application-level proxy* is one that knows about the particular application it is providing proxy services for; it understands and interprets the commands in the application protocol. A *circuit-level proxy* is one that creates a circuit between the client and the server without interpreting the application protocol. The most extreme version of an application-level proxy is an application like Sendmail, which implements a store-and-forward protocol. The most extreme version of a circuit-level proxy is an application like *plug-gw*, which accepts all data that it receives and forwards it to another destination.

The advantage of a circuit-level proxy is that it provides service for a wide variety of different protocols. Most circuit-level proxy servers are also generic proxy servers; they can be adapted to serve almost any protocol. Not every protocol can easily be handled by a circuit-level proxy, however. Protocols like FTP, which communicate port data from the client to the server, require some protocol-level intervention, and thus some application-level knowledge. The disadvantage of a circuit-level proxy server is that it provides very little control over what happens through the proxy. Like a packet filter, it controls connections on the basis of their source and destination and can't easily determine whether the commands going through it are safe or even in the expected protocol. Circuit-level proxies are easily fooled by servers set up at the port numbers assigned to other services.

In general, circuit-level proxies are functionally equivalent to packet filters. They do provide extra protection against problems with packet headers (as opposed to the data within the packets). In addition, some kinds of protections (protection against packet fragmentation problems, for instance) are automatically provided by even the most trivial circuit-level proxies but are available only from high-end packet filters.

Generic Versus Dedicated Proxies

Although "application-level" and "circuit-level" are frequently used terms in other documents, we more often distinguish between "dedicated" and "generic" proxy servers. A *dedicated proxy server* is one that serves a single protocol; a *generic proxy server* is one that serves multiple protocols. In practice, dedicated proxy servers are application-level, and generic proxy servers are circuit-level. Depending on how you argue about shades of meaning, it might be possible to produce a generic application-level proxy server (one that understands a wide range of protocols) or a dedicated circuit-level proxy server (one that provides only one service but doesn't understand the protocol for it). Neither of these ever occur, however, so we use "dedicated" and "generic" merely because we find them somewhat more intuitive terms than "application-level" and "circuit-level".

Intelligent Proxy Servers

A proxy server can do a great deal more than simply relay requests; one that does is an *intelligent proxy server*. For example, almost all HTTP proxy servers cache data, so that multiple requests for the same data don't go out across the Internet. Proxy servers (particularly application-level servers) can provide better logging and access controls than those achieved through other methods, although few existing proxy servers take full advantage of the opportunities. As proxy servers mature, their abilities are increasing rapidly. Now that there are multiple proxy suites that provide basic functionality, they're beginning to compete by adding features. It's easier for a dedicated, application-level proxy server to be intelligent; a circuit-level proxy has limited abilities.

Proxying Without a Proxy Server

Some services, such as SMTP, NNTP, and NTP, naturally support proxying. These services are all designed so that transactions (email messages for SMTP, Usenet news postings for NNTP, and clock settings for NTP) move between servers, instead of going directly from a client to a final destination server. For SMTP, the messages are forwarded towards an email message's destination. NNTP forwards messages to all neighbor servers. NTP provides time updates when they're requested but supports a hierarchy of servers. With these schemes, each intermediate server is effectively acting as a proxy for the original sender or server.

If you examine the "Received:" headers of incoming Internet email (these headers trace a message's path through the network from sender to recipient), you quickly discover that very few messages travel directly from the sender's machine to the recipient's machine. It's far more common these days for the message to pass through at least four machines:

- The sender's machine

- The outgoing mail gateway at the sender's site (or the sender's Internet service provider)

- The incoming mail gateway at the recipient's site

- Finally, the recipient's machine

Each of the intermediate servers (the mail gateways) is acting as a proxy server for the sender, even though the sender may not be dealing with them directly. Figure 9-3 illustrates this situation.

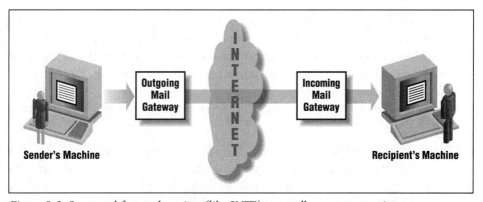

Figure 9-3. Store-and-forward services (like SMTP) naturally support proxying

Using SOCKS for Proxying

The SOCKS package, originally written by David Koblas and Michelle Koblas, and subsequently maintained by Ying-Da Lee, is an example of the type of proxy system that can support both proxy-aware applications and proxy-aware clients. A reference implementation of SOCKS is freely available, and it has become the de facto standard proxying package on the Internet. It is also a proposed official Internet standard, documented in RFC 1928. Appendix B, *Tools*, tells you how to get the freely available version of SOCKS; multiple commercial versions are also available.

Versions of SOCKS

Two versions of the SOCKS protocol are currently in use, SOCKS4 and SOCKS5. The two protocols are not compatible, but most SOCKS5 servers will detect attempts to use SOCKS4 and handle them appropriately. The main additions in SOCKS5 are:

- User authentication

- UDP and ICMP

- Hostname resolution at the SOCKS server

SOCKS4 does no real user authentication. It bases its decisions on whether to allow or deny connections on the same sort of information that packet filters use (source and destination ports and IP addresses). SOCKS5 provides support for several different ways of authenticating users, which gives you more precise control and logging.

SOCKS4 works only for TCP-based clients; it doesn't work for UDP-based clients or ICMP functions like *ping* and *traceroute*. If you are using a UDP-based client, you will need to get another package. You can either use SOCKS5 or the UDP Packet Relayer. This program serves much the same function for UDP-based clients as SOCKS serves for TCP-based clients. Like SOCKS, the UDP Packet Relayer is freely available on the Internet. SOCKS5 is the only widely used freely available proxy for ICMP.

SOCKS4 requires the client to be able to map hostnames to IP addresses. With SOCKS5, the client can provide the hostname instead of the IP address, and the socks server will do the hostname resolution. This is convenient for sites that do what is called "fake root" DNS, where internal hosts use a purely internal name server that does not communicate with the Internet. (This configuration is discussed further in Chapter 20, *Naming and Directory Services.*)

SOCKS Features

In order to make it easy to support new clients, SOCKS is extremely generic. This limits the features that it can provide. SOCKS doesn't do any protocol-specific control or logging.

SOCKS does log connection requests on the server; provide access control by user, by source host and port number, or by destination host and port number; and allow configurable responses to access denials. For example, it can be configured to notify an administrator of incoming access attempts and to let users know why their outgoing access attempts were denied.

The prime advantage of SOCKS is its popularity. Because SOCKS is widely used, server implementations and SOCKS-ified clients (i.e., versions of programs like FTP and Telnet that have already been converted to use SOCKS) are commonly available, and help is easy to find. This can be a double-edged sword; cases have been reported where intruders to firewalled sites have installed their own SOCKS-knowledgeable clients.

SOCKS Components

The SOCKS package includes the following components:

- The SOCKS server. This server must run on a Unix system, although it has been ported to many different variants of Unix.
- The SOCKS client library for Unix machines.
- SOCKS-ified versions of several standard Unix client programs such as FTP and Telnet.
- SOCKS wrappers for *ping* and *traceroute.*
- The *runsocks* program to SOCKS-ify dynamically linked programs at runtime without recompiling.

In addition, client libraries for Macintosh and Windows systems are available as separate packages.

Figure 9-4 shows the use of SOCKS for proxying.

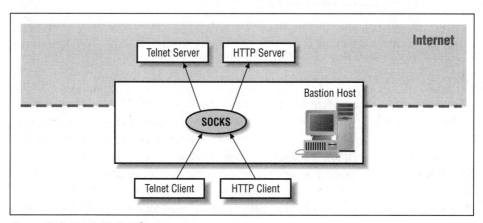

Figure 9-4. Using SOCKS for proxying

Converting Clients to Use SOCKS

Many Internet client programs (both commercial and freely available) already have SOCKS support built in to them as a compile-time or a runtime option.

How do you convert a client program to use SOCKS? You need to modify the program so it talks to the SOCKS server, rather than trying to talk to the real world directly. You do this by recompiling the program with the SOCKS library.

Converting a client program to use SOCKS is usually pretty easy. The SOCKS package makes certain assumptions about how client programs work, and most client programs already follow these assumptions. For a complete summary of these assumptions, see the file in the SOCKS release called *What_SOCKS_expects*.

To convert a client program, you must replace all calls to standard network functions with calls to the SOCKS versions of those functions. Here are the calls.

Standard Network Function	SOCKS Version
connect()	Rconnect()
getsockname()	Rgetsockname()
bind()	Rbind()
accept()	Raccept()
listen()	Rlisten()
select()	Rselect()

You can usually do this simply by including the file *socks.h*, included in the SOCKS distribution. If not, you can use the older method of adding the following to the `CFLAGS=` line of the program's Makefile:

```
-Dconnect=Rconnect
    -Dgetsockname=Rgetsockname
    -Dbind=Rbind
    -Daccept=Raccept
    -Dlisten=Rlisten
    -Dselect=Rselect
```

Then, recompile and link the program with the SOCKS client library.

The client machine needs to have not only the SOCKS-modified clients, but also something to tell it what SOCKS server to contact for what services (on Unix machines, the */etc/socks.conf* file). In addition, if you want to control access with Auth, the client machines must be running an Auth server (for instance, *identd*, which will allow the SOCKS server to identify what user is controlling the port that the connection comes from. Because there's no way for the SOCKS server to verify that the Auth server is reliable, Auth can't be trusted if anybody might intentionally be circumventing it; we recommend using SOCKS5 with user authentication instead. See Chapter 21, *Authentication and Auditing Services*, for more information about Auth.

Using the TIS Internet Firewall Toolkit for Proxying

The free firewalls toolkit (TIS FWTK), from Trusted Information Systems, includes a number of proxy servers of various types. TIS FWTK also provides a number of other tools for authentication and other purposes, which are discussed where appropriate in other chapters of this book. Appendix B, *Tools*, provides information on how to get TIS FWTK.

Whereas SOCKS attempts to provide a single, general proxy, TIS FWTK provides individual proxies for the most common Internet services (as shown in Figure 9-5). The idea is that by using small separate programs with a common configuration file, it can provide intelligent proxies that are provably safe, while still allowing central control. The result is an extremely flexible toolkit and a rather large configuration file.

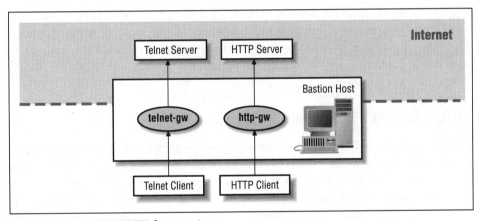

Figure 9-5. Using TIS FWTK for proxying

FTP Proxying with TIS FWTK

TIS FWTK provides FTP proxying either with proxy-aware client programs or proxy-aware user procedures (*ftp-gw*). If you wish to use the same machine to support proxied FTP and straight FTP (for example, allowing people on the Internet to pick up files from the same machine that does outbound proxying for your users), the toolkit will support it, but you will have to use proxy-aware user procedures.

Using proxy-aware user procedures is the most common configuration for TIS FWTK. The support for proxy-aware client programs is somewhat half-hearted (for example, no proxy-aware clients or libraries are provided). Because it's a dedicated FTP proxy, it provides logging, denial, and extra user authentication of particular FTP commands.

Telnet and rlogin Proxying with TIS FWTK

TIS FWTK Telnet (*telnet-gw*) and *rlogin* (*rlogin-gw*) proxies support proxy-aware user procedures only. Users connect via Telnet or *rlogin* to the proxy host, and instead of getting a "login" prompt for the proxy host, they are presented with a prompt from the proxy program, allowing them to specify what host to connect to (and whether to make an X connection if the *x-gw* software is installed, as we describe in the "Other TIS FWTK Proxies" section that follows).

Generic Proxying with TIS FWTK

TIS FWTK provides a purely generic proxy, *plug-gw*, which requires no modifications to clients, but supports a limited range of protocols and uses. It examines the address it received a connection from and the port the connection came in on, and it creates a connection to another host on an appropriate port. You can't specify which host it should connect to while making that connection; it's determined by the incoming host. This makes *plug-gw* inappropriate for services that are employed by users, who rarely want to connect to the same host every time. It provides logging but no other security enhancements, and therefore needs to be used with caution even in situations where it's appropriate (e.g., for NNTP connections).

Other TIS FWTK Proxies

TIS FWTK proxies HTTP and Gopher via the *http-gw* program. This program supports either proxy-aware clients or proxy-aware procedures. Most HTTP clients support proxying; you just need to tell them where the proxy server is. To use *http-gw* with an HTTP client that's not proxy-aware, you add *http://firewall/* in front of the URL. Using it with a Gopher client that is not proxy-aware is slightly more complex, since all the host and port information has to be moved into the path specification.

x-gw is an X gateway. It provides some minimal security by requiring confirmation from the user before allowing a remote X client to connect. The X gateway is started up by connecting to the Telnet or *rlogin* proxy and typing "x", which displays a control window.

Using Microsoft Proxy Server

Logically enough, Microsoft Proxy Server is Microsoft's proxying package. It is part of Microsoft's Back Office suite of products and is Microsoft's recommended solution for building small firewalls on Windows NT. The Proxy Server package includes both proxying and packet filtering, in order to support a maximum number of protocols.

Proxy Server provides three types of proxying; an HTTP proxy, a SOCKS proxy, and a WinSock proxy. HTTP proxying, which will also support several other common protocols used by web browsers, including HTTPS, Gopher, and FTP, is discussed further in Chapter 15, *The World Wide Web*.

Proxy Server and SOCKS

Proxy Server includes a SOCKS server, which implements SOCKS Version 4.3a. Because it is a SOCKS4 server, it supports only TCP connections and only Auth authentication. On the other hand, it does provide name resolution service (which most SOCKS4 servers do not). You can use Proxy Server's SOCKS server with any SOCKS4 client (not just Microsoft applications).

Proxy Server and WinSock

The WinSock proxy is specialized for the Microsoft environment. It uses a modified operating environment on the client to intercept Windows operating system calls that open TCP/IP sockets. It supports both TCP and UDP. Because of the architecture of the networking code, WinSock will proxy only native TCP/IP applications like Telnet and FTP; it won't work with Microsoft native applications like file and printer sharing, which work over TCP/IP by using an intermediate protocol (NetBT, which is discussed further in Chapter 14, *Intermediary Protocols*). On the other hand, WinSock proxying will provide native TCP/IP applications with Internet access even when the machines reach the proxy by protocols other than TCP/IP. For instance, a machine that uses NetBEUI or IPX can use a WinSock proxy to FTP to TCP/IP hosts on the Internet.

Using a WinSock proxy requires installing modified WinSock libraries on all the clients that are going to use it. For this reason, it will work only with Microsoft operating systems, and it creates some administrative difficulties on them (the modified libraries must be reinstalled any time the operating system is installed, upgraded, or patched). In addition, trying to use WinSock and SOCKS at the same time on the same client machine will create confusion, as both of them attempt to proxy the same connection.

What If You Can't Proxy?

You might find yourself unable to proxy a service for one of three reasons:

- No proxy server is available.

- Proxying doesn't secure the service sufficiently.

- You can't modify the client, and the protocol doesn't allow you to use proxy-aware procedures.

We describe each of these situations in the following sections.

No Proxy Server Is Available

If the service is proxyable, but you can't find a proxy-aware-procedure server or proxy-aware clients for your platform, you can always do the work yourself. In many cases, you can simply use the dynamic libraries to wrap existing binaries.

If you can't use dynamic libraries, modifying a normal TCP client program to use SOCKS is relatively trivial. As long as the SOCKS libraries are available for the platform you're interested in, it's usually a matter of changing a few library calls and recompiling. You do have to have the source for the client.

Writing your own proxy-aware-procedure server is considerably more difficult because it means writing the server from scratch.

Proxying Won't Secure the Service

If you need to use a service that's inherently insecure, proxying can't do much for you. You're going to need to set up a victim machine, as described in Chapter 10, *Bastion Hosts*, and let people run the service there. This may be difficult if you're using a dual-homed nonrouting host to make a firewall where all connections must be proxied; the victim machine is going to need to be on the Internet side of the dual-homed host.

Using an intelligent application-level server that filters out insecure commands may help but requires extreme caution in implementing the server and may make important parts of the service nonfunctional.

Can't Modify Client or Procedures

There are some services that just don't have room for modifying user procedures (for example *ping* and *traceroute*). Fortunately, services that don't allow the user to pass any data to the server tend to be small, stupid, and safe. You may be able to safely provide them on a bastion host, letting users log in to a bastion host but giving them a shell that allows them to run only the unproxyable services you want to support. If you have a web server on a bastion host, a web frontend for these services may be easier and more controllable than allowing users to log in.

10

Bastion Hosts

A *bastion host* is your public presence on the Internet. Think of it as the lobby of a building. Outsiders may not be able to go up the stairs and may not be able to get into the elevators, but they can walk freely into the lobby and ask for what they want. (Whether or not they will get what they ask for depends upon the building's security policy.) Like the lobby in your building, a bastion host is exposed to potentially hostile elements. The bastion host is the system that any outsiders—friends or possible foes—must ordinarily connect with to access your systems or services.

By design, a bastion host is highly exposed because its existence is known to the Internet. For this reason, firewall builders and managers need to concentrate security efforts on the bastion host. You should pay special attention to the host's security during initial construction and ongoing operation. Because the bastion host is the most exposed host, it also needs to be the most fortified host.

Although we sometimes talk about a single bastion host in this chapter and elsewhere in this book, remember that there may be multiple bastion hosts in a firewall configuration. The number depends on a site's particular requirements and resources, as discussed in Chapter 7, *Firewall Design*. Each is set up according to the same general principles, using the same general techniques.

Bastion hosts are used with many different firewall approaches and architectures; most of the information in this chapter should be relevant regardless of whether you're building a bastion host to use with a firewall based on packet filtering, proxying, or a hybrid approach. The principles and procedures for building a bastion host are extensions of those for securing any host. You want to use them, or variations of them, for any other host that's security critical, and possibly for hosts that are critical in other ways (e.g., major servers on your internal network).

This chapter discusses bastion hosts in general; the two following chapters give more specific advice for Unix and Windows NT bastion hosts. When you are building a bastion host, you should be sure to read both this chapter and the specific chapter for the operating system you are using.

General Principles

There are two basic principles for designing and building a bastion host:

Keep it simple

The simpler a bastion host is, the easier it is to secure.

Any service a bastion host offers could have software bugs or configuration errors in it, and any bugs or errors may lead to security problems. Therefore, you want a bastion host to do as little as possible. It should provide the smallest set of services with the least privileges it possibly can, while still fulfilling its role.

Be prepared for bastion hosts to be compromised

Despite your best efforts to ensure the security of a bastion host, break-ins can occur. Don't be naive about it. Only by anticipating the worst, and planning for it, will you be most likely to avert it. Always keep the question, "What if this bastion host is compromised?" in the back of your mind as you go through the steps of securing the machine and the rest of the network.

Why do we emphasize this point? The reason is simple: bastion hosts are the machines most likely to be attacked because they're the machines most accessible to the outside world. They're also the machines from which attacks against your internal systems are most likely to come because the outside world probably can't talk to your internal systems directly. Do your best to ensure that each bastion host *won't* get broken into, but keep in mind the question, "What if it does?"

In case a bastion host is broken into, you don't want that break-in to lead to a compromise of the entire firewall. You can prevent it by not letting internal machines trust bastion hosts any more than is absolutely necessary for the bastion hosts to function. You will need to look carefully at each service a bastion host provides to internal machines and determine, on a service-by-service basis, how much trust and privilege each service really needs to have.

Once you've made these decisions, you can use a number of mechanisms to enforce them. For example, you might install standard access control mechanisms (passwords, authentication devices, etc.) on the internal hosts, or you might set up packet filtering between bastion hosts and internal hosts.

Special Kinds of Bastion Hosts

Most of this chapter discusses bastion hosts that are screened hosts or service-providing hosts on a screened network. There are several kinds of bastion hosts, however, that are configured similarly but have special requirements.

Nonrouting Dual-Homed Hosts

A *nonrouting dual-homed host* has multiple network connections but doesn't pass traffic between them. Such a host might be a firewall all by itself, or might be part of a more complex firewall. For the most part, nonrouting dual-homed hosts are configured like other bastion hosts but need extra precautions, discussed in the sections that follow, to make certain they truly are nonrouting. If a nonrouting dual-homed host is your entire firewall, you need to be particularly paranoid in its configuration and follow the normal bastion host instructions with extreme care.

Victim Machines

You may want to run services that are difficult to provide safely with either proxying or packet filtering, or services that are so new that you don't know what their security implications are. For that purpose, a *victim machine* (or *sacrificial goat*) may be useful. This is a machine that has nothing on it you care about, and that has no access to machines that an intruder could make use of. It provides only the absolute minimum necessary to use it for the services you need it for. If possible, it provides only one unsafe or untested service, to avoid unexpected interactions.

Victim machines are configured much as normal bastion hosts are, except that they almost always have to allow users to log in. The users will almost always want you to have more services and programs than you would configure on a normal bastion host; resist the pressure as much as possible. You do not want users to be comfortable on a victim host: they will come to rely on it, and it will no longer work as designed. The key factor for a victim machine is that it is disposable, and if it is compromised, nobody cares. Fight tooth and nail to preserve this.

Internal Bastion Hosts

In most configurations, the main bastion host has special interactions with certain internal hosts. For example, it may be passing electronic mail to an internal mail server, coordinating with an internal name server, or passing Usenet news to an internal news server. These machines are effectively secondary bastion hosts, and they should be configured and protected more like the bastion host than like normal internal hosts. You may need to leave more services enabled on them, but you should go through the same configuration process.

External Service Hosts

Bastion hosts that exist solely to provide services to the Internet (for instance, web servers used to provide service to customers) have special concerns. They are extremely visible, which makes them popular targets for attack, and increases the visibility of successful attacks. If a machine that provides mail service for internal users is compromised, it's not going to be immediately obvious to outsiders, and it's unlikely to make it into the newspaper. If your web site is replaced by somebody else's page, or a clever satire of your web site, that's something people outside your site will notice and care about.

Although these machines have increased needs for security, they have some features that make them easier to secure. They need only limited access to the internal network; they usually provide only a few services, with well-defined security characteristics; and they don't need to support internal users (often, they don't need to support any users at all).

One-Box Firewalls

If the machine you're building is an entire firewall, instead of a part of a firewall, it is even more vulnerable. You are betting your entire site's security on this one machine. It is worth almost any amount of inconvenience and trouble to be absolutely certain that it's a secure machine. You may want to consider having a duplicate machine that you use for testing, so that you can check out new configurations without risking your Internet connection.

Choosing a Machine

The first step in building a bastion host is to decide what kind of machine to use. You want reliability (if a bastion host goes down, you lose most of the benefit of your Internet connection), supportability, and configurability. This section looks at which operating system you should run, how fast a bastion host needs to be, and what hardware configuration should be supported.

What Operating System?

A bastion host should be something you're familiar with. You're going to end up customizing the machine and the operating system extensively; this is not the time to learn your way around a completely new system. Because a fully configured bastion host is a very restricted environment, you'll want to be able to do development for it on another machine, and it helps a great deal to be able to exchange its peripherals with other machines you own. (This is partly a hardware issue, but it doesn't do you any good to be able to plug your Unix-formatted SCSI disk into a Macintosh SCSI chain: the hardware interoperates, but the data isn't readable.)

You need a machine that reliably offers the range of Internet services you wish to provide your users, with multiple connections simultaneously active. If your site is completely made up of MS-DOS, Windows, or Macintosh systems, you may find yourself needing some other platform (perhaps Unix, perhaps Windows NT, perhaps something else) to use as your bastion host. You may not be able to provide or access all the services you desire through your native platform because the relevant tools (proxy servers, packet filtering systems, or even regular servers for basic services such as SMTP and DNS) may not be available for that platform.

Unix is the operating system that has been most popular in offering Internet services, and tools are widely available to make bastion hosts on Unix systems. If you already have Unix machines, you should seriously consider Unix for your bastion host. If you have no suitable platforms for a bastion host and need to learn a new operating system anyway, we recommend you try Unix, because that's where you'll find the largest and most extensive set of tools for building bastion hosts.

The other popular operating system for this purpose is Windows NT. If you are already running Windows NT machines as servers, it makes sense to use Windows NT machines as bastion hosts as well. However, you should bear in mind that Windows NT machines are more complex than Unix machines. If you are familiar with both, we recommend using Unix rather than Windows NT for bastion hosts wherever practical. If you are familiar only with Windows NT, use it for bastion hosts; you are more likely to make mistakes securing a new operating system.

If all of your existing multiuser, IP-capable machines are something other than Unix or Windows NT machines (such as VMS systems, for example), you have a hard decision to make. You can probably use a machine you are familiar with as a bastion host and get the advantages of familiarity and interchangeability. On the other hand, solid and extensive tools for building bastion hosts are not likely to be available, and you're going to have to improvise. You might gain some security through obscurity (don't count on it; your operating system probably isn't as obscure as you think), but you may lose as much or more if you don't have the history that Unix-based bastion hosts offer. With Unix or Windows NT, you have the advantage of learning through other people's mistakes as well as your own.

Most of this book assumes that you will be using some kind of Unix or Windows NT machine as your bastion host. This is because most bastion hosts *are* Unix or Windows NT machines, and some of the details are extremely operating system dependent. See Chapter 11, *Unix and Linux Bastion Hosts*, and Chapter 12, *Windows NT and Windows 2000 Bastion Hosts*, for these details. The principles will be the same if you choose to use another operating system, but the details will vary considerably.

How Fast a Machine?

Most bastion hosts don't have to be fast machines; in fact, it's better for them not to be especially powerful. There are several good reasons, besides cost, to make your bastion host as powerful as it needs to be to do its job, but no more so. It doesn't take much horsepower to provide the services required of most bastion hosts.

Many people use machines in the medium desktop range as their bastion hosts, which is plenty of power for most purposes. The bastion host really doesn't have much work to do. What it needs to do is mostly limited by the speed of your connection to the outside world, not by the CPU speed of the bastion host itself. It just doesn't take that much of a processor to handle mail, DNS, FTP, and proxy services for a 56 Kbps or even a T-1 (1.544 Mbps) line. You may need more power if you are running programs that do compression/decompression (e.g., NNTP servers) or searches (e.g., full-featured web servers), or if you're providing proxy services for dozens of users simultaneously.

You may also need more power to support requests from the Internet if your site becomes wildly popular (e.g., if you create something that everybody and their mothers want to access, like the Great American Web Page or a popular and well-stocked anonymous FTP site). At that point, you might also want to start using multiple bastion hosts, as we describe in Chapter 6, *Firewall Architectures.* A large company with multiple Internet connections and popular services may need to use multiple bastion hosts *and* large, powerful machines.

There are several reasons not to oversize a bastion host:

- A slower machine is a less inviting target. There's no prestige for somebody who brags, "Hey, I broke into a Sun 3/60!" or some other slow (to an attacker, at least) machine. Far more prestige is involved in breaking into the latest, greatest hardware. Don't make your bastion host something with high prestige value (a supercomputer, for example, would be a poor choice of a bastion host).

- If compromised, a slower machine is less useful for attacking internal systems or other sites. It takes longer to compile code; it's not very helpful for running dictionary or brute-force password attacks against other machines; and so on. All of these factors make the machine less appealing to potential attackers, and that's your goal.

- A slower machine is less attractive for insiders to compromise. A fast machine that's spending most of its time waiting for a slow network connection is effectively wasted, and the pressure from your own users to use the extra power for other things (for example, as a compilation server, rendering server, or database server) can be considerable. You can't maintain the security of a bastion host while using it for other purposes. Extra capacity on the bastion host is an accident waiting to happen.

Web servers are an exception to this rule. You might as well size your web server optimistically, because as web sites evolve they tend to increase drastically and rapidly in both size and CPU usage. Changes in client technology also tend to increase the load on web servers (for instance, many clients open multiple connections in order to download several images at the same time, thereby increasing the performance the user sees at the cost of increasing the load on the server).

What Hardware Configuration?

You want a reliable hardware configuration, so you should select a base machine and peripherals that aren't the newest thing on the market. (There's a reason people call it "bleeding edge" as well as "leading edge" technology.) You also want the configuration to be supportable, so don't choose something so old you can't find replacement parts for it. The middle range from your favorite manufacturer is probably about right.

While a desktop-class machine probably has the horsepower you need, you may be better off with something in server packaging; machines packaged as servers are generally easier to exchange disks in, as well as being more possible to mount in racks when you have lots of them. They're also harder to steal, and less likely to get turned off by people who need another outlet to plug the vacuum cleaner into.

While you don't need sheer CPU power, you do need a machine that keeps track of a number of connections simultaneously. This is memory intensive, so you'll want a large amount of memory and probably a large amount of swap space as well. Caching proxies also need a large amount of free disk space to use for the caches.

Here are some suggestions about tape and disk needs:

- The bastion host can't reasonably use another host's tape drive for backups, as we'll discuss later in this chapter, so it needs its own tape drive of a size suitable to back itself up.

- A CD-ROM drive also comes in handy for operating system installation and possibly for keeping checksums on (or for comparing your current files to the original files on the CD-ROM). You may only need the CD-ROM drive initially when you first install and configure the machine, so an external drive that you "borrow" from another machine temporarily may be sufficient. In any case, it should be a CD-ROM or single-session CDW (write) drive, not a drive that will write rewritable or multisession CDs; one of the purposes of this drive is to hold data that you know the bastion host cannot modify, even by adding data!

- You should be able to easily add another disk temporarily to the configuration for maintenance work.

- The boot disk should remove easily and attach to another machine—again, for maintenance work.

Both of the disk considerations mentioned suggest that the bastion host should use the same type of disks as your other machines. For example, it should not be the only machine at your site running IDE disks.

The bastion host doesn't need interesting graphics and shouldn't have them. This is a network services host; nobody needs to see it. Attach a dumb terminal (the dumber the better) as the console. Having graphics will only encourage people to use the machine for other purposes and might encourage you to install support programs (like the X Window System and its derivatives) that are insecure. If you are using a Windows NT machine, which requires a graphics console, use a cheap and ugly VGA display or a console switch.

Most bastion hosts are critical machines and should have appropriate high-availability hardware, including redundant disks and uninterruptible power.

Choosing a Physical Location

The bastion host needs to be in a location that is physically secure.* There are two reasons for this:

- It is impossible to adequately secure a machine against an attacker who has physical access to it; there are too many ways the attacker can compromise it.

- The bastion host provides much of the actual functionality of your Internet connection, and if it is lost, damaged, or stolen, your site may effectively be disconnected. You will certainly lose access to at least some services.

Never underestimate the power of human stupidity. Even if you don't believe that it's worth anyone's time and trouble to get physical access to the machine in order

---

* *Practical UNIX & Internet Security* by Simson Garfinkel and Gene Spafford (second edition, O'Reilly & Associates, 1996) contains an excellent and extensive discussion of physical security.

to break into it, secure it to prevent well-meaning people within your organization from inadvertently making it insecure or nonfunctional.

Your bastion hosts should be in a locked room, with adequate air conditioning and ventilation. If you provide uninterruptible power for your Internet connection, be sure to provide it for all critical bastion hosts as well.

Locating Bastion Hosts on the Network

Bastion hosts should be located on a network that does not carry confidential traffic, preferably a special network of their own.

Most Ethernet and token ring interfaces can operate in "promiscuous mode". In this mode, they are able to capture *all* packets on the network the interfaces are connected to, rather than just those packets addressed to the particular machine the interface is a part of. Other types of network interfaces, such as FDDI, may not be able to capture all packets, but depending on the network architecture, they can usually capture at least some packets not specifically addressed to them.

This capability has a useful purpose: for network analysis, testing, and debugging, for example, by programs like Network Manager, *etherfind,* and *tcpdump.* Unfortunately, it can also be used by an intruder to snoop on all traffic on a network segment. This traffic might include Telnet, FTP, or *rlogin* sessions (from which logins and passwords can be captured), confidential email, NFS accesses of sensitive files, and so on. You need to assume the worst: bastion hosts can be compromised. If a bastion host is compromised, you don't want it to snoop on this traffic.

One way to approach the problem is to not put bastion hosts on internal networks; instead, put them on a perimeter network. As we've discussed in earlier chapters, a perimeter network is an additional layer of security between your internal network and the Internet. The perimeter network is separated from the internal network by a router or bridge. Internal traffic stays on the internal net and is not visible on the perimeter net. All a bastion host on a perimeter network can see are packets that are either to or from itself, or to or from the Internet. Although this traffic might still be somewhat sensitive, it's likely to be a lot less sensitive than your typical internal network traffic, and there are other places (for instance, your Internet service provider) that can already see much of it.

Using a perimeter net with a packet filtering router between it and the internal network gives you some additional advantages. It further limits your exposure, if a bastion host is compromised, by reducing the number of hosts and services the compromised bastion host can access.

If you can't put bastion hosts on a perimeter network, you might consider putting them on a network that's not susceptible to snooping. For example, you might put them on an intelligent 10-base T hub, an Ethernet switch, or an ATM network. If this is all you do, then you need to take additional care to make sure that nothing trusts those bastion hosts, because no further layer of protection is between it and the internal network. Using such a network technology for your perimeter network is the best of both worlds: bastion hosts are isolated from internal systems (as with a traditional perimeter network) but can't snoop on traffic on the perimeter network.

Be careful about how much trust you place in the ability to prevent hosts from snooping the network. Even with an intelligent or switched hub, broadcast traffic will be visible to all nodes, and this traffic may include data that is useful to an attacker. For instance, networks that use Microsoft directory services will include a lot of useful information about machine and filesystem names and types in broadcast traffic. There may also be information that is sensitive in multicast traffic, which any node can ask to receive. Finally, hubs of this type frequently offer an administrative capability that can control the reception of all traffic. That may be limited to a specific port or available to all ports. You should be sure that this is appropriately secured on any hub that bastion hosts are attached to; otherwise, an attacker may be able to simply ask for all traffic and get it, removing the theoretical advantages of using a hub.

Whatever networking devices you use, you should be careful to protect the networking devices to the same degree that you protect the computers. Many network devices support remote administration, often with a wide variety of interfaces (for instance, a switch may provide a Telnet server, SNMP management, and a web management interface). An intruder who can reconfigure networking devices can certainly keep your network from working and may also be able to compromise other machines. Consider disabling all remote management features (with the possible exception of remote logging of errors) and configuring network devices the old-fashioned way, with a terminal and a serial cable.

Selecting Services Provided by a Bastion Host

A bastion host provides any services your site needs to access the Internet, or wants to offer to the Internet—services you don't feel secure providing directly via packet filtering. (Figure 10-1 shows a typical set.) You should not put any services on a bastion host that are not intended to be used to or from the Internet. For example, it shouldn't provide booting services for internal hosts (unless, for some reason, you intend to provide booting services for hosts on the Internet). You have to assume that a bastion host will be compromised, and that all services on it will be available to the Internet.

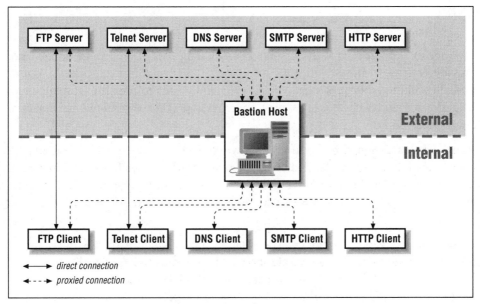

Figure 10-1. The bastion host may run a variety of Internet services

You can divide services into four classes:

Services that are secure
Services in this category can be provided via packet filtering, if you're using this approach. (In a pure-proxy firewall, *everything* must be provided on a bastion host or not provided at all.)

Services that are insecure as normally provided but can be secured
Services in this category can be provided on a bastion host.

Services that are insecure as normally provided and can't be secured
These services will have to be disabled and provided on a victim host (discussed earlier) if you absolutely need them.

Services that you don't use or that you don't use in conjunction with the Internet
You must disable services in this category.

We'll discuss individual services in detail in later chapters, but here we cover the most commonly provided and denied services for bastion hosts.

Electronic mail (SMTP) is the most basic of the services bastion hosts normally provide. You may also want to access or provide information services such as:

FTP
File transfer

HTTP
Hypertext-driven information retrieval (the Web)

NNTP

   Usenet news

In order to support any of these services (including SMTP), you must access and provide Domain Name System (DNS) service. DNS is seldom used directly, but it underlies all the other protocols by providing the means to translate hostnames to IP addresses and vice versa, as well as providing other distributed information about sites and hosts.

Many services designed for local area networks include vulnerabilities that attackers can exploit from outside, and all of them are opportunities for an attacker who has succeeded in compromising a bastion host. Basically, you should disable anything that you aren't going to use, and you should choose what to use very carefully.

Bastion hosts are odd machines. The relationship between a bastion host and a normal computer on somebody's desktop is the same as the relationship between a tractor and a car. A tractor and a car are both vehicles, and to a limited extent they can fulfill the same functions, but they don't provide the same features. A bastion host, like a tractor, is built for work, not for comfort. The result is functional, but mostly not all that much fun.

For the most part, we discuss the procedures to build a bastion host with the maximum possible security that allows it to provide services to the Internet. Building this kind of bastion host out of a general-purpose computer means stripping out parts that you're used to. It means hearing people say "I didn't think you could turn that off!" and "What do you mean it doesn't run any of the normal tools I'm used to?", not to mention "Why can't I just log into it?" and "Can't you turn on the software I like just for a little while?" It means learning entirely new techniques for administering the machine, many of which involve more trouble than your normal procedures.

Multiple Services or Multiple Hosts?

In an ideal world, you would run one service per bastion host. You want a web server? Put it on a bastion host. You want a DNS server? Put it on a different bastion host. You want outgoing web access via a caching proxy? Put it on a third bastion host. In this situation, each host has one clear purpose, it's difficult for problems to propagate from one service to another, and each service can be managed independently.

In the real world, things are rarely this neat. First, there are obvious financial difficulties with the one service, one host model—it gets expensive fast, and most services don't really need an entire computer. Second, you rapidly start to have administrative difficulties. What's the good in having one firewall if it's made up of 400 separate machines?

You are therefore going to end up making trade-offs between centralized and distributed services. Here are some general principles for grouping services together into sensible units:

Group services by importance

> If you have services that your company depends on (like a customer-visible web site) and services you could live without for a while (like an IRC server), don't put them on the same machine.

Group services by audience

> Put services for internal users (employees, for instance) on one machine, services for external users (customers, for instance) on another, and housekeeping services that are only used by other computers (like DNS) on a third. Or put services for faculty on one machine and services for students on a different one.

Group services by security

> Put trusted services on one machine, and untrusted services on another. Better yet, put the trusted services together and put each untrusted service on a separate machine, since they're the ones most likely to interfere with other things.

Group services by access level

> Put services that deal with only publicly readable data on one machine, and services that need to use confidential data on another.

Sometimes these principles will be redundant (the unimportant services are used by a specific user group, are untrustworthy, and use only public data). Sometimes, unfortunately, they will be conflicting. There is no guarantee that there is a single correct answer.

Disabling User Accounts on Bastion Hosts

If at all possible, don't allow any user accounts access to bastion hosts. For various reasons, bastion hosts may know about users, but users should not have accounts that actually allow them to use the host. Keeping such accounts off bastion hosts will give you the best security. There are several reasons why, including:

- Vulnerabilities of the accounts themselves
- Vulnerabilities of the services required to support the accounts
- Reduced stability and reliability of the machine

- Inadvertent subversion of the bastion host's security by users

- Increased difficulty in detecting attacks

User accounts provide relatively easy avenues of attack for someone who is intent on breaking into a bastion host. Each account usually has a reusable password* that can be attacked through a variety of means, including dictionary searches, brute force searches, or capture by network eavesdropping. Multiply this by many users, and you have a disaster in the making.

Supporting user accounts in any useful fashion requires a bastion host to enable services (for example, printing and local mail delivery services) that could otherwise be disabled on the bastion host. Every service that is available on a bastion host provides another avenue of attack, through software bugs or configuration errors.

Having to support user accounts also can reduce the stability and reliability of the machine itself. Machines that do not support user accounts tend to run predictably and are stable. Many sites have found that machines without users tend to run pretty much indefinitely (or at least until the power fails) without crashing.

Users themselves can contribute to security problems on bastion hosts. They don't (usually) do it deliberately, but they can subvert the system in a variety of ways. These range from trivial (e.g., choosing a poor password) to complex (e.g., setting up an unauthorized information server that has unknown security implications). Users are seldom trying to be malicious; they're normally just trying to get their own jobs done more efficiently and effectively.

It's usually easier to tell if everything is "running normally" on a machine that doesn't have user accounts muddying the waters. Users behave in unpredictable ways, but you want a bastion host to have a predictable usage pattern, in order to detect intrusions by watching for interruptions in the pattern.

If you need to allow user accounts on a bastion host, keep them to a minimum. Add accounts individually, monitor them carefully, and regularly verify that they're still needed.

There is one circumstance where you should have user accounts. Every person who needs to log into a bastion host for administrative purposes should have an individual account and should log in with that account. Nobody should log into the machine directly as "administrator" or "root" if there is any other way for them to get work done. These accounts should be kept to a minimum and closely controlled. It should be made impossible to reach these accounts from the Internet

---

* We discuss ways to support nonreusable passwords in Chapter 21, *Authentication and Auditing Services.*

with a reusable password (if the capability is there, some administrator will use it). In fact, it's better not to allow access to the accounts from the Internet at all, and you might want to consider disallowing network logins altogether. (Note that *whitehouse.gov* was broken into because its administrators, who knew better, succumbed to temptation and logged into it across the Internet to do administration.) We will discuss appropriate mechanisms for remote administration in the following chapters about specific operating systems.

Building a Bastion Host

Now that you've figured out what you want your bastion host to do, you need to actually build the bastion host. This process of configuring a machine to be especially secure and resistant to attack is generally known as *hardening*. The basic hardening process is as follows:

1. Secure the machine.
2. Disable all nonrequired services.
3. Install or modify the services you want to provide.
4. Reconfigure the machine from a configuration suitable for development into its final running state.
5. Run a security audit to establish a baseline.
6. Connect the machine to the network it will be used on.

You should be very careful to make sure the machine is not accessible from the Internet until the last step. If your site isn't yet connected to the Internet, you can simply avoid turning on the Internet connection until the bastion host is fully configured. If you are adding a firewall to a site that's already connected to the Internet, you need to configure the bastion host as a standalone machine, unconnected to your network.

If the bastion host is vulnerable to the Internet while it is being built, it may become an attack mechanism instead of a defense mechanism. An intruder who gets in before you've run the baseline audit will be difficult to detect and will be well positioned to read all of your traffic to and from the Internet. Cases have been reported where machines have been broken into within minutes of first being connected to the Internet; while rare, it can happen.

Take copious notes on every stage of building the system. Assume that sometime in the future, a compromise will occur that causes the machine to burst into flames and be destroyed. In order to rebuild your system, you will need to be able to follow all of the steps you took previously.

You will also need all of the software that you used, so you should be sure to securely store all of the things you need to do the installation, including:

- The disks, CDs, or tapes you install software from

- The source code for any software you build from source

- The environment you used to build software from source, if it's different from the one you're installing; this includes the operating system, compiler, and header files (and a machine they run on)

- The manuals and documents you were working from

The following sections briefly describe each of the main steps involved in building a bastion host; these steps will be covered in more detail in the following separate chapters for Unix and Windows NT. They also touch briefly on ongoing maintenance and protection of the bastion host; note, though, that maintenance issues are discussed primarily in Chapter 26, *Maintaining Firewalls.*

Securing the Machine

To start with, build a machine with a standard operating system, secured as much as possible. Start with a clean operating system and follow the procedures we describe in this section:

1. Start with a minimal clean operating system installation.

2. Fix all known system bugs.

3. Use a checklist.

4. Safeguard the system logs.

Start with a Minimal Clean Operating System Installation

Start with a clean operating system installation, straight from vendor distribution media. If you do this, you will know exactly what you're working with. You won't need to retrofit something that may already have problems. Using such a system will also make later work easier. Most vendor security patches you later obtain, as well as the vendor configuration instructions and other documentation, assume that you're starting from an unmodified installation.

While you're installing the operating system, install as little as you can get away with. It's much easier to avoid installing items than it is to delete them completely later on. For that matter, once your operating system is minimally functional, it's not hard to add components if you discover you need them. Don't install any optional subsystems unless you know you will need them.

If you are reusing a machine that has already had an operating system installed on it, be sure to erase all data from the disks before doing the reinstall. Otherwise, you cannot guarantee that all traces of the old system are gone.

Fix All Known System Bugs

Get a list of known security patches and advisories for your operating system; work through them to determine which are relevant for your own particular system, and correct all of the problems described in the patches and advisories. You can get this information from your vendor sales or technical support contacts, or from the user groups, newsgroups, or electronic mailing lists devoted to your particular platform.

In addition, be sure to get from the Computer Emergency Response Team Coordination Center (CERT-CC) any advisories relevant to your platform, and work through them. (For information on how to contact CERT-CC and retrieve its information, see the list of resources in Appendix A, *Resources.*)

Many operating systems have both recommended and optional patches or have periodic patch sets (called *service packs* for Windows NT) with individual patches issued in between (Microsoft calls these *hot fixes*). You should install the current recommended patch set, plus all other security-related patches that are relevant to your installation.

Use a Checklist

To be sure you don't overlook anything in securing your bastion host, use a security checklist. Several excellent checklists are around. Be sure to use one that corresponds to your own platform and operating system version.

Safeguard the System Logs

As a security-critical host, the bastion host requires considerable logging. The next step in building the bastion host is to make sure that you have a way of safeguarding the system logs for the bastion host. The system logs on the bastion host are important for two reasons:

- They're one of the best methods of determining if your bastion host is performing as it should be. If everything the bastion host does is logged (and it should be), you should be able to examine the logs to determine exactly what it's doing and decide if that's what it's supposed to be doing. Chapter 26, *Maintaining Firewalls*, describes the use of system logs in maintaining your firewall.

- When (not if!) someday someone does successfully break in to the bastion host, the system logs are one of the primary mechanisms that determine exactly what happened. By examining the logs and figuring out what went wrong, you should be able to keep such a break-in from happening again.

Where should you put the system logs? On the one hand, you want the system logs to be somewhere convenient; you want them to be where they can be easily examined to determine what the bastion host is doing. On the other hand, you want the system logs to be somewhere safe; this will keep them from any possible tampering in case you need to use them to reconstruct an incident.

The solution to these seemingly contradictory requirements is to keep two copies of the system logs—one for convenience, the other for catastrophes. The details of the logging services are operating-system dependent and are discussed in the chapters on individual operating systems.

System logs for convenience

The first copy of the system logs is the one you'll use on a regular basis to monitor the ongoing activity of the machine. These are the logs against which you run your daily and weekly automated analysis reports. You can keep these logs either on the bastion host itself or on some internal host.

The advantage of keeping them on the bastion host is simplicity: you don't have to set up logging to go to some other system, nor do you have to configure the packet filters to allow this. The advantage to keeping them on an internal host is ease of access: you don't have to go to the bastion host, which doesn't have any tools anyway, to examine the logs. Avoid logging in to the bastion host, in any case.

System logs for catastrophes

The second copy of the system logs is the one you'll use after a catastrophe. You can't use your convenience logs at a time like this. Either the convenience logs won't be available, or you won't be sure of their integrity any longer.

These logs need to be kept separate from the bastion host and kept for a long time. Sometimes you will discover an intruder a long time after the original compromise (among other things, it's not unusual for an intruder to break into a bunch of machines and install back doors for later use; a compromised machine may be left alone for months).

If you have a write-once device available to you, use that device; doing so is probably the technically easiest way to keep the logs, especially if your write-once device can emulate a filesystem. Be sure you can trust the write-once feature. Some magneto-optical drives are capable of both multiple-write and write-once operations and keep track of the mode they're in via software. If the system is compromised, it may be possible to overwrite or damage previously written parts of the supposedly write-once media.

The other methods available to you will differ depending on the operating system you are using and are discussed in Chapter 11, *Unix and Linux Bastion Hosts*, and Chapter 12, *Windows NT and Windows 2000 Bastion Hosts*.

Logging and time

Knowing the time (within minutes and sometimes seconds) when something occurred can be very useful when dealing with break-ins. You will need date and time information if you (or law enforcement agencies) need to request information from other sites. You should make sure that your bastion hosts have accurate and synchronized times in their logs. See Chapter 22, *Administrative Services*, for more information about time synchronization protocols.

Choosing what to log

Choosing the information you want to log is a delicate business. You don't want gigantic logs full of routine events; that just wastes space and time and makes it harder to find important information. On the other hand, you do want logs that are general enough that you can debug problems and figure out what intruders did.

What you would like to do is to log everything except events that are frequent and nonthreatening. Don't try to limit your logging to dangerous or interesting events because it's hard to successfully predict which those are going to be. Instead, log everything you can stand, eliminating only the known clutter.

For instance, Windows NT provides the ability to log all accesses to files. You don't want to turn this on for all files on a bastion host; you'll drown in routine accesses to files that are accessed as it provides services. On the other hand, you probably do want to log all accesses to system files that aren't accessed by the services. These files shouldn't be touched often, and the nuisance caused by the log entries when you do maintenance work will be compensated for by the number of attacks you can detect.

Disabling Nonrequired Services

Once you've completed the basic process of securing your bastion host, go on to the next step: disabling any services that aren't absolutely necessary for the bastion host to provide. You will want to disable all services except the ones you have decided to provide, and the supporting services necessary for those to run, as described earlier. You may not always know which services are the required support services, particularly because service names tend to be cryptic and uninformative.

How do you know which services to disable? There are three simple rules to apply:

- If you don't need it, turn it off.

- If you don't know what it does, turn it off (you probably didn't need it anyway).

- If turning it off causes problems, you now know what it does, and you can either turn it back on again (if it's really necessary) or figure out how to do without it.

Any service provided by the bastion host might have bugs or configuration problems that could lead to security problems. Obviously, you'll have to provide some services that users need, as long as your site's security policy allows them. But if the service isn't absolutely necessary, don't borrow trouble by providing it. If a service isn't provided by the bastion host, you won't have to worry about possible bugs or configuration problems.

If you can live without a service, it should be turned off. It's worth suffering some inconvenience. This means that you're going to need to think very carefully about services. You'll be disabling not just services you never heard of and never used, but also services you've purposefully enabled on other machines (and, unfortunately, services you've never heard of because they're considered too basic ever to do anything to). Look at every service and ask yourself "How could I avoid enabling this? What do I lose if I turn it off?"

How to Disable Services

The first step in disabling services is ensuring that you have a way to boot the machine if you accidentally disable a critical service. This could be a second hard disk with a full boot partition on it or a CD-ROM drive with the operating system install disk. It could even be a second installation of the operating system on the same hard disk. You need to be ruthless; if you can't reboot when you delete the wrong thing, at best you're going to be over-cautious about deleting things, and at worst you're going to end up with an unusable computer. (These fallback operating systems are also useful places to copy files from or compare files to if things go wrong.)

Second, you must save a clean copy of every file before you modify it. Even when you're just commenting things out, every so often your fingers slip, and you delete something you didn't mean to, or you change a critical character. If you are using a user interface to change things instead of directly modifying files, you may not know what files are actually being changed, so you may need to simply back up the entire system. If possible, do this with another disk, rather than with a standard program and a tape; if you have to back out a change, you will want to be able to replace just the files that are actually involved, and that's easiest to determine by comparing things on disk. On Windows NT, you should note that the registry is not backed up or copied by normal procedures; be sure that you include it. You will also want to build a new Emergency Repair Disk (which includes the most important parts of the registry) immediately before you begin the reconfiguration.

When you disable a service, you should also disable all services that depend on it. This will prevent nasty warning messages and will also mean that reenabling a service will not result in a cascade of unfortunate surprises as other services are also turned on.

Finally, we've said it before and we'll say it again: you should not connect a machine to a hostile network until it has been fully configured. That means that all of your work on disabling services should be done with the machine either entirely disconnected from the network, or on a safe test network. The reason that you are disabling services is that they are unsafe, and if you are connected to a hostile network, they may be exploited before you finish disabling them.

Next steps after disabling services

In general, you'll need to reboot your machine after you have changed the configuration files. The changes won't take effect until you do so.

After you have rebooted and tested the machine, and you are comfortable that the machine works without the disabled services, you may want to remove the executables for those services (as long as they are not used by other services). If the executables are lying around, they may be started by somebody—if not you, some other system administrator, or an intruder. A few services may even be executable by nonroot users if they use nonstandard ports.

If you feel uncertain about removing executables, consider encrypting them instead. You should use a program that provides genuinely strong encryption. The Unix *crypt* program is not appropriate; neither are many of the available packages for Microsoft systems. Instead, use a more secure encryption program like *snuffle* or something that uses the DES or IDEA algorithm. Choose a secure key; if you forget the key, you're no worse off than if you'd deleted the files, but if an intruder gets the key, you're considerably worse off.

Running Services on Specific Networks

In some cases, you want to run services that need to respond to only one network on a machine with multiple network interfaces. You may be able to limit those services to just the networks you wish to use them on. Under Unix, this usually means specifying which IP addresses and/or network interfaces you want the service to respond to as part of the service's startup options; this will be slightly different for every service, and not all services provide this facility. Under Windows NT, only a few basic services can be controlled this way. In the Networking control panel, go to the Bindings tab and set it to show bindings for all adapters. Select the services that you wish to turn off and press the Disable button.

Turning Off Routing

If you have a dual-homed host that is not supposed to be a router, you will need to specifically disable routing. In order to act as an IP router, a dual-homed host needs to accept packets that are addressed to other machines' IP addresses, and send them on appropriately. This is known as *IP forwarding*, and it's usually implemented at a low level in the operating system kernel. An IP-capable host with multiple interfaces normally does this automatically, without any special configuration.

Other machines have to know that the dual-homed host is a router in order to use it as such. Sometimes this is done simply by configuring those machines to always route packets for certain networks to the dual-homed host (this is called *static routing*). More often, however, the dual-homed host is configured to broadcast its routing capabilities via a routing protocol such as Routing Information Protocol (RIP). Other machines hear these routing broadcasts and adjust their own routing tables accordingly (this is called *dynamic routing*). This broadcast of routing information by the dual-homed host is usually done by an additional program (for example, *routed* or *gated* on a Unix system), which often has to be turned on explicitly.

To use a dual-homed host as a firewall, you need to convert it to a nonrouting dual-homed host; you take a machine that has two network interfaces, and you configure it so it *can't* act as a router between those two interfaces. This is a two-step process:

1. Turn off any program that might be advertising it as a router; this is usually relatively straightforward.

2. Disable IP forwarding; this can be equally easy or considerably more difficult, and may require modifying the operating system kernel.

Unfortunately, turning off IP forwarding does not always turn off all routing. On some systems, you can turn off IP forwarding, but the IP source-routing option usually remains a security hole.

What is *source routing?* Normal IP packets have only source and destination addresses in their headers, with no information about the route the packet should take from the source to the destination. It's the job of the routers in between the source and the destination to determine the most efficient route. However, source-routed IP packets contain additional information in the IP header that specifies the route the packet should take. This additional routing information is specified by the source host—thus the term "source-routed".

When a router receives a source-routed packet, it follows the route specified in the packet, instead of determining the most efficient route from source to destination. The source-routing specification overrides the ordinary routing. Because of the way the routing code is implemented in many operating systems, turning off IP forwarding does *not* disable forwarding of source-routed packets. It's implemented completely separately and must be turned off separately, often by completely different (and more difficult) mechanisms.

Source-routed packets can easily be generated by modern applications like the Telnet client that's freely available on the Internet as part of the BSD 4.4 release. Unless you block source-routed packets somewhere else, such as in a router between the dual-homed host and the Internet, source-routed packets can blow right past your dual-homed host and into your internal network.

Worse still, source routing goes both ways. Once source-routed packets make their way to an internal system, the system is supposed to reply with source-routed packets that use the inverse of the original route. The reply from your internal system back to the attacker will also blow right through your dual-homed host, allowing two-way connection through a firewall that was supposed to block all communications across it.

Fortunately, it is now common practice for firewalls to ignore all source routing, either by dropping packets with source routing or by stripping the source routing itself. In addition, systems that will accept source routes will rarely include them on the return packet.

If you are not going to screen your dual-homed host, you will need to patch your operating system so that it rejects source-routed packets. Consult your vendor, and/or appropriate security mailing lists (discussed in Appendix A, *Resources*) for information on how to do this on your platform.

Controlling Inbound Traffic

As we discussed in Chapter 8, *Packet Filtering*, many general-purpose computers are provided with packet filtering packages. Even when these packages are not adequate for building packet filtering routers, they can provide an extra level of protection for bastion hosts. If packet filtering is available to you, you should set it up so that it allows only the traffic that you intend to support. In most configurations, this will be multiply redundant; it will duplicate protections provided on routers, and most of the rules will prevent connections to services that don't exist anyway. This is a useful kind of redundancy, which will help to protect you from configuration errors.

Packet filters will also keep you from successfully adding new services to the machine. You should document the filters carefully to avoid puzzling failures later.

Installing and Modifying Services

Some of the services you want to provide may not be provided with your operating system. Others may be provided with servers that are inappropriate for use in a secure environment or are missing features you probably want (for example, stock *fingerd* and *ftpd*). Even those few remaining services that are provided, secure, and up to date in your vendor's operating system release usually need to be specially configured for security.

For information on general schemes for protecting services in the operating system you are using, see Chapter 11, *Unix and Linux Bastion Hosts*, and Chapter 12, *Windows NT and Windows 2000 Bastion Hosts*, as appropriate. For detailed information about individual services, including advice on selecting HTTP, NNTP, and FTP servers, see the chapters relevant to the services you want to provide (for instance, Chapter 15, *The World Wide Web*, for HTTP; Chapter 16, *Electronic Mail and News*, for NNTP; and Chapter 17, *File Transfer, File Sharing, and Printing*, for FTP).

Reconfiguring for Production

Now it's time to move the machine from the configuration that was useful to you when you were building it to the best configuration for running it. You'll need to do several things:

1. Finalize the operating system configuration.

2. Remove all unnecessary programs.

3. Mount as many filesystems as possible as read-only.

Finalize the operating system configuration

Once you've deleted all the services that aren't used on a day-to-day basis, you'll find that it is very difficult to work on the bastion host—for example, when you need to install new software packages or upgrade existing ones. Here are some suggestions for what to do when you find it necessary to do extensive work on the bastion host:

- Write all the tools to tape before deleting them, and then restore them from tape when needed. Don't forget to delete them each time after you're done.

- Set up a small, external, alternate boot disk with all the tools on it. Then, plug the disk in and boot from it when you need the tools. Don't leave the disk connected during routine operations, however; you don't want an attacker to be able to mount the disk and use the tools against you.

You don't want an intruder to attack the machine while you're working on it. To keep that from happening, follow these steps:

1. Either disconnect the bastion host from the network or disconnect your network from the Internet before you begin.

2. Give the bastion host back the tools you'll need to use (as we've described earlier).

3. After you've finished your work on the machine, return it to its normal (stripped down) operating condition.

4. Reconnect the bastion host to the network or your network to the Internet.

You may find it easier to simply remove the bastion host's disk and attach it to an internal host as a nonsystem disk; you can then use the internal host's tools without fear of having them remain available when the bastion host is returned to service. This procedure also guarantees that the bastion host is not vulnerable to compromise from the outside while you are doing the work, since it is entirely nonfunctional while its disk is removed and not susceptible to accidental reconnection.

Mount filesystems as read-only

Once you've got the bastion host configured, you don't want anybody (particularly an attacker) to be able to change the configuration. To guard against this happening, mount the filesystems on the bastion host as read-only if possible (particularly the filesystems that contain program binaries) to protect against tampering.

It's much better if you can use hardware write-protect; an attacker may be able to remount disks with write permission without getting physical access to the machine, but it's not going to do any good if the hardware write-protect on the disk is on. Many SCSI disks have a "write-disable" jumper or switch you can set. If you find powering the disk down and removing it from the case unacceptable as a way to get write access, you could wire this jumper to an external switch on the drive enclosure.

Running a Security Audit

Once you've got the bastion host reconfigured, the next step is to run a security audit. There are two reasons for doing this. First, it gives you a way to ensure you haven't overlooked anything during system setup. Second, it establishes a "baseline", or a basis for comparison, against which you can compare future audits. In this way, you'll be able to detect any tampering with the machine.

Auditing packages

Most auditing packages have two basic purposes:

Checking for well-known security holes
> These are holes that have been uncovered by system administrators, exploited by attackers in system break-ins, or documented in computer security books and papers.

Establishing a database of checksums of all files on a system
> Doing this allows a system administrator to recognize future changes to files— particularly unauthorized changes.

Several very good automated auditing packages are freely available on the Internet.

How do you use the various auditing packages to audit your system? The details of what you do depend upon which package you're using. (See the documentation provided with the packages for detailed instructions.) This section provides some general tips.

You will need to do some configuration. Don't just install the program, run it, and expect you'll get reasonable results. Expect to go through several iterations of running the auditing package, getting warnings, and reconfiguring your machine or the auditing package to get rid of warnings. When you get warnings, you have to decide whether the auditing package is wrong, or you are. There will be some cases where the right thing to do is to turn off checks, but it shouldn't be your automatic response.

Once you've used the tools described in the previous section to create your initial baseline, store a copy of the tools and these initial audit results somewhere safe. Under no circumstances should you store the only copy of the baseline or the tools on the bastion host. Prepare for the worst: if someone were to break into the bastion host and tamper with the only copy of the baseline audit, this would compromise your ability to use the audit later on to detect illicit changes on the system. If intruders can change the auditing software, it doesn't matter whether they can change the baseline; they could simply set up the auditing software to reproduce the baseline. Keeping a copy of the baseline audit on a floppy disk or magnetic tape that's locked up some place safe is a good way to protect against such a compromise. Preferably, you don't want an intruder to even read the audit results; why tell them what you expect the system to look like and what files you aren't watching?

Periodically, (e.g., daily or weekly, depending on your own site's needs and capabilities), audit the machine once again and compare the new audit to the baseline. Make sure you can account for any differences you find. Ideally, you should automate this periodic reaudit so it happens regularly and reliably. Unfortunately, this is easier said than done. It can be difficult to arrange automatic audits that can't be defeated by "replay" attacks. In a replay attack, an attacker who has compromised your auditing system simply sends you a recording of a prior good audit whenever your system invokes the automatic auditing capability. The most practical defense against this is to run your automated auditing system often enough that it's unlikely an attacker could break in, discover the auditing system, and subvert it (covering his tracks) before the next audit runs. This suggests that you should run an audit at least daily. It may help to run the audit at random intervals, although it can be difficult to automate this well. It is better to run the audit at frequent but predictable intervals than to rely on human beings remembering to run it by hand.

If you start receiving warnings from the auditing system and you decide that they are incorrect, you should immediately reconfigure the auditing system or the operating system so that the warnings go away. If you get used to getting warnings, you will end up ignoring important new messages. Also, if you go on vacation, your replacement may not realize that the messages are benign and may take drastic action to remedy nonproblems.

Use cryptographic checksums for auditing

Checksums are very helpful in auditing. An intruder who changes a program or configuration file will almost certainly correct the modification dates afterwards, so you can't use these dates as a reliable index. Comparing every file to a baseline copy avoids that problem but takes a lot of time and requires that you store a copy of every single file, effectively doubling your storage requirements. Storing checksums is probably your best bet.

A checksum is a number calculated on data that is designed to detect changes to the data. This is useful for a communications channel; if a sender calculates a checksum as data is being sent and a receiver does the same, then the two can simply compare checksums to see if the data was changed during transmission. You can also do exactly the same checksum calculation for files, but instead of sending the file elsewhere, you recalculate and compare the checksum at a later time. Calculating checksums can be time consuming because you have to read the contents of every file, but it is not as time consuming as reading everything twice and doing a bit-by-bit compare. In addition, storing a checksum takes up much less space than storing an entire file. However, checksums are not full representations of the file, and every checksum algorithm has cases where it will give the same checksum for two different files. This is called a *collision*, and checksum algorithms are designed to make this unlikely to occur for the differences they are designed to detect.

In order for a checksum to be useful in detecting unauthorized changes to files, it must have several characteristics:

- It must be practically impossible to deliberately create a file that has a checksum that matches another. This can be achieved by designing the algorithm so that it cannot be reversed and run backwards (you can't start with a checksum and use a known method to create a file that produces that checksum).

- The checksum must be of a large enough size so that you cannot create a list of files, one for each value the checksum can have, and match a given checksum that way. In practical terms, this means that a useful checksum should be larger than 128 bits in size.

- If you change something only very slightly in the file, the checksum must change by a large amount.

A checksum algorithm that has these characteristics is sometimes called a *cryptographic checksum*. Cryptographic checksums are discussed further in Appendix C, *Cryptography*.

You will sometimes hear rumors that these algorithms are vulnerable to the same sort of trickery that can be used with standard checksums. This is not true; there are no known incidents where anybody has managed to subvert a cryptographic checksum. These rumors are based on three grounds:

1. They're due to confusions with CRC-style checksums, which are in fact often subverted.

2. They're due to incidents in which people have missed changes when using cryptographic checksums because intruders have been able to rewrite the checksum database or replace the checksumming program.

3. They're due to misunderstanding of some technical arguments about the security of early cryptographic checksums. Such algorithms are no longer used

because of theoretical weaknesses, but those weaknesses were never exploited and are not present in current cryptographic checksums.

It is important not to run checksums on files that are supposed to change and to update checksum data promptly when you make intentional changes. If there are frequent false warnings from the checksum system, you will miss genuine problems.

Connecting the Machine

Now that you have the machine fully secured, you can finally connect it to its destination network and run it. You want to do this when you're going to be around to see what happens; don't make it the last thing you do before that long overdue vacation.

Operating the Bastion Host

Once you put the bastion host into production, your job has only just begun. You'll need to keep a close watch on the operations of the bastion host. Chapter 26, *Maintaining Firewalls*, provides more information on how to do this; this section discusses specific concerns for bastion hosts.

Learn What the Normal Usage Profile Is

If you're going to monitor the bastion host, looking for abnormalities that might indicate break-ins or other types of system compromise, you will need to first develop an understanding of what the "normal" usage profile of the bastion host is. Ask these questions and others like them:

- How many jobs tend to be running at any one time?
- How much CPU time do these jobs consume relative to each other?
- What is the typical load at different times throughout the day?

Your goal is to develop an almost intuitive grasp of what your system normally runs like, so you'll be able to recognize—and investigate—anomalous activity very quickly.

Consider Using Software to Automate Monitoring

Doing a thorough job of system monitoring is tough. Although the logs produced by your system provide lots of useful information, it's easy to get overwhelmed by the sheer volume of logging data. The important information may often be buried.

Too often, the logs end up being used only *after* a break-in, when, in fact, they could be used to detect—and thus perhaps stop—a break-in while it is occurring.

Because each operating system and site is different, each bastion host is configured differently, and each site has different ideas about what the response of a monitoring system should be. For example, some want electronic mail; some want the output fed to an existing SNMP-based management system, some want the systems to trip the pagers of the system administrators, and so on. Monitoring tends to be very site- and host-specific in the details.

A large and growing number of monitoring packages is available for Unix, including both freely available and commercial options. Among the freely available options, NOCOL and NetSaint are both popular, extensible systems that provide the ability to watch logs, to test to make certain machines are still running and providing services, and to alert people when things go wrong (see Appendix B, *Tools*, for information about how to get them).

MRTG is a special sort of monitoring package, which provides graphing services but not alerting services. It is extremely useful for watching trends. Furthermore, MRTG makes very impressive web pages with very little effort, so you not only find out what's going on, you also get an important public relations tool for convincing people that you know what's going on. Information about MRTG is also available in Appendix B, *Tools*.

Normally, monitoring of Windows NT systems is done with the Performance Monitor. Unfortunately, Performance Monitor is yet another tool based on SMB transactions, which cannot be used without enabling all of SMB. Furthermore, Performance Monitor is fairly limited as a monitoring solution for critical systems; it doesn't provide all of the alarm and process-monitoring features you may want.

You will probably want to use an SNMP-based monitoring tool. Windows NT provides an SNMP server, so all you will need to add is the monitoring tool. Some public domain monitoring tools are now available for Windows NT, although fewer than there are for Unix. Some tools that were originally available only under Unix have now been ported to Windows NT (for instance, MRTG). Unix-based monitoring tools will monitor Windows NT systems without problems. In addition, there are a large number of commercial SNMP-based tools you can use.

Protecting the Machine and Backups

Once the bastion host has been fully configured and is in operation, protect the physical machine and make sure that its backups are protected from theft or other compromise.

Watch Reboots Carefully

How will you know if someone has breached security? Sometimes, it's painfully obvious. But sometimes, you'll have to draw conclusions from the behavior of the system. Unexplained reboots or downtime on the system may be a clue. Many attacks (e.g., modifying a kernel) can't succeed unless the system is rebooted.

On the bastion host, crashes and reboots should be rare occurrences. Once the bastion host has been fully configured and is in production, it should be a very stable system, often running for weeks or months at a stretch without a crash or a reboot. If a crash or a reboot does occur, investigate it immediately to determine whether it was caused by some legitimate problem or might have been the result of some kind of attack.

You might want to consider configuring the bastion host so that it doesn't bring itself up automatically after an attempted reboot. That way, if someone does manage to crash or force a reboot of the machine, you'll know about it: the machine will sit there waiting for you to reboot it. The machine won't be able to come back up until you decide it should do so. Many machines treat crashes and explicit reboots differently, and while most of them will let you disable an automatic reboot on a crash, it may be harder to disable an automatic reboot after a clean shutdown that requests a reboot. Even if your machine does not appear to allow you to disable autobooting, you can usually cause autoboots to fail under Unix by configuring the machine to autoboot from a nonexistent disk. (Be sure to leave instructions on how to boot the machine by hand with the machine.) Under Windows NT, you can simply edit *boot.ini* to set the timeout to -1, and it will wait forever for a human being to specify what operating system to boot. This has the advantage of being self-explanatory to an operator sitting in front of the console.

Do Secure Backups

Backups on a bastion host are tricky because of trust issues. Who can you trust?

You definitely don't want internal machines to trust the bastion host enough for it to dump to their tape drives. If the bastion host has somehow been compromised, this could be disastrous. You also don't want the bastion host to trust the internal machines; this could lead to subversion of the bastion host by (well-intentioned) internal users, or to attack from some host pretending to be an internal system.

Common remote backup mechanisms (for example, those used by the BSD *dump* and *rdump* programs) will probably be blocked by packet filtering between the bastion host and the internal systems anyway. Therefore, you will normally want to do backups to a tape device attached directly to the bastion host. Under no circumstances should you rely on backing up the bastion host to disks that remain attached to the bastion host. You must do backups that are removed from the bastion host so they cannot be accessed by an attacker who compromises it.

Fortunately, because the bastion host is an infrequently changing machine, you won't have to do frequent backups. Once the bastion host is fully configured and in production, it should be very stable. A weekly or even monthly manual backup will probably be sufficient.

Backups of the bastion host aren't done just to guard against normal system catastrophes like disk crashes. They're also a tool that you can use later to investigate a break-in or some other security incident. They give you a way to compare what's currently on the bastion host's disk with what was there before the incident.

If you're only doing weekly or monthly backups, how you handle logging becomes an issue. If the bastion host is not being backed up daily, you *must* do your logging to some system other than the bastion host itself. If an incident does occur, the logs are going to be critical in reconstructing what happened. If it turns out that your only copy of the logs was on the (compromised) bastion host, and backups of the logs haven't been done for three weeks, you're going to be severely hampered in your investigative efforts.

As with all backups on all systems, you need to guard your bastion host backups as carefully as you guard the machine itself. The bastion host backups contain all the configuration information for the bastion host. An attacker who gets access to these backups would be able to analyze the security of your bastion host without ever touching it. The information these backups provide might possibly include a way to break in without setting off any of the alarms on the bastion host.

Other Objects to Secure

In addition to securing the backups, you will need to physically secure anything else that contains important data about the machine. This includes:

- The log files
- Any alternate boot disks you use to do maintenance
- The Emergency Repair Disks for Windows NT bastion hosts (including account data!)
- The documentation for the details of the bastion host configuration

Although secrecy is not sufficient to give you security, it's an important part of maintaining security. You should treat the configuration details of your bastion hosts as proprietary information, available only to people you trust. Anybody who has this information can compromise your firewall.

11

Unix and Linux Bastion Hosts

This chapter discusses the details of configuring Unix for use in a firewall environment, building on the principles discussed in Chapter 10, *Bastion Hosts*. You should be sure to read both chapters before attempting to build a bastion host. As usual, we use the word "Unix" for both Unix and Linux, except when we explicitly say otherwise.

It's impossible to give complete instructions on how to configure any given machine; the details vary greatly depending on what version of Unix you're running and exactly what you intend to do with the machine. This chapter is intended to give you an outline of what needs to be done, and how to figure out how to do it. For more complete configuration details, you will need to look at resources that are specific to your platform.

Which Version of Unix?

Which version of Unix should you choose? You want to balance what you're familiar with against which tools are available for which versions. If your site already uses one version of Unix, you will most likely want to use that version. If your site has some familiarity with several versions of Unix, and the relevant tools (discussed throughout this chapter) and support are available for all of them, use the *least* popular one that you still like. Doing so maximizes your happiness and minimizes the likelihood that attackers have precompiled ways of attacking your bastion host. If you have no Unix familiarity, choose any version you like, provided that it is in reasonably widespread use (you don't want "Joe's Unix, special today $9.95"). As a rule of thumb, if your chosen version of Unix has a user's group associated with it, it's probably well-known enough to rely on.

Useful Unix Capabilities

Every operating system has certain special capabilities or features that can be useful in building a bastion host. We can't describe all these capabilities for all systems, but we'll tell you about a few special features of Unix because it's a common bastion host platform:

setuid/setgid

Every Unix user has a numeric user identification (*uid*) in addition to his or her login name and belongs to one or more groups of users, also identified by numbers (*gids*). The Unix kernel uses the *uid* and the various *gids* of a particular user to determine what files that user has access to. Normally, Unix programs run with the file access permissions of the user who executes the program. The *setuid* capability allows a program to be installed so that it always runs with the permissions of the owner of the program, regardless of which user is running the program. The *setgid* capability is similar; it allows the program temporarily (while running the program) to grant membership in a group to users who are not normally members of that group.

chroot

The *chroot* mechanism allows a program to irreversibly change its view of the filesystem by changing the program's idea of where the root of the filesystem is. Once a program *chroots* to a particular piece of the filesystem, that piece becomes the whole filesystem as far as the program is concerned; the rest of the filesystem ceases to exist from the program's point of view. This can provide a very high level of protection, but it is by no means perfect. Programs may not need access to the filesystem to achieve nefarious ends, particularly if they have large numbers of other permissions.

Environmental modifications, such as those made by *setuid/setgid* and *chroot,* are inherited by any subsidiary processes a program starts. A common way of restricting what the programs on a bastion host can do is to run the programs under "wrapper" programs; the wrapper programs do whatever *setuid/setgid, chroot,* or other environmental change work is necessary, and then start the real program. *chrootuid* is a wrapper program for this purpose; Appendix B, *Tools,* gives information on how to get it.

Although Unix suppliers differ vastly in their openness about security issues, the difference in the actual security between different general-purpose versions of Unix is much smaller. Don't assume that the publicity given to security holes reflects the number of security holes; it's a more accurate reflection of the popularity of the operating system and the willingness of a vendor to admit and fix security problems. Don't assume that proprietary versions of Unix are more secure than open source versions, either; paying money to a vendor doesn't guarantee that they care about security, only that they care about money. Ironically, the operating systems with the most worrisome tales may be the most secure ones, because they're the ones getting fixed.

Some versions of Unix are particularly designed for security and are therefore particularly suited for use in bastion hosts. "Designed for security" means different things to different vendors. It ranges from relatively minor changes to the packages that are installed (for instance, the Debian Linux distribution tries to install securely, and the SuSE Linux distribution provides a post installation security script) to major changes to the internals (for instance, OpenBSD has made significant changes to all parts of the operating system).

Several commercial vendors offer secure versions of their operating systems that are designed to meet government security needs. These versions usually lag behind the main releases (the government approval process is slow) and may not support all the add-on products that the main releases do. On the other hand, the auditing capabilities they offer are useful for bastion hosts. If you can afford the extra cost and the delayed release schedule, these operating systems are a good choice for bastion hosts.

Securing Unix

Once you have chosen a machine, you need to make sure that it has a reasonably secure operating system installation. The first steps in this process are the same as for any other operating system and were discussed in Chapter 10, *Bastion Hosts*. They are:

1. Start with a minimal clean operating system installation. Install the operating system from scratch onto empty disks, selecting only the subsystems you need.

2. Fix known bugs. Consult CERT-CC, your vendor, and any other sources of security information you may have to make certain that you have all appropriate patches, and only the appropriate patches, installed.

3. Use a checklist to configure the system. *Practical UNIX & Internet Security*, by Simson Garfinkel and Gene Spafford (O'Reilly & Associates, 1996), contains an extensive checklist that covers most Unix platforms. More specific checklists for particular operating system releases are often available through the formal or informal support channels for those platforms; check with your vendor support contacts, or the user groups, newsgroups, or mailing lists that are devoted to the platform.

Setting Up System Logs on Unix

On a Unix system, logging is handled through *syslog*. The *syslog* daemon records log messages from various local and remote clients (programs with messages they want logged). Each message is tagged with facility and priority codes: the facility code tells *syslog* what general subsystem this message is from (for example, the mail system, the kernel, the printing system, the Usenet news system, etc.), and the priority code tells *syslog* how important the message is (ranging from debugging information and routine informational messages through several levels up to emergency information). The */etc/syslog.conf* file controls what *syslog* does with messages, based on their facility and priority. A given message might be ignored, logged to one or more files, forwarded to the *syslog* daemon on another system, flashed onto the screens of certain or all users who are currently logged in, or any combination.

When you configure *syslog* to record messages to files, you could configure it to send all messages to a single file, or to split messages up to multiple files by facility and priority codes. If you split messages by facility and priority codes, each log file will be more coherent, but you'll have to monitor multiple files. If you direct everything to a single file, on the other hand, you'll have only a single file to check for all messages, but that file will be much larger.

Many non-Unix systems, particularly network devices such as routers, can be configured to log messages via *syslog*. If your systems have that capability, configuring them so they all log to your bastion host provides a convenient way to collect all their messages in a single place.

Be aware that remote logging via *syslog* (e.g., from a router to your bastion host, or from your bastion host to some internal host) is not 100 percent reliable. For one thing, *syslog* is a UDP-based service, and the sender of a UDP packet has no way of knowing whether or not the receiver got the packet unless the receiver tells the sender (*syslog* daemons don't confirm receipt to their senders). Some *syslog* variants can be made to remotely log using TCP. Unfortunately, you still cannot absolutely depend on them not to lose messages; what if the receiving system was down or otherwise unavailable? One solution is to have a local method to reliably capture all *syslog* messages. (See the "System logs for catastrophe" section, later in this chapter.)

syslog will accept messages from anywhere and does no checking on the data that it receives. This means that attackers can use *syslog* for denial of service attacks or can hide important *syslog* messages in a blizzard of fake ones. Some *syslog* daemons can be configured not to accept messages over the network. If this option is available to you, you should use it on all systems except those that you intend to use as log servers.

Despite its weaknesses, though, *syslog* is a useful service; you should make extensive use of it.

syslog Linux example

Most versions of *syslog* are derived from the original BSD version. Example 11-1 is taken from Linux, which includes some enhancements. It allows wildcards for either the facility or the priority and also allows a facility to be ignored by using the syntax *facility.none*. One peculiar feature of almost all *syslog* daemons is that they require the use of the Tab character to delimit fields. The use of spaces can cause a *syslog* line to be silently ignored.

Example 11-1. Linux syslog.conf Example

```
# Log anything (except mail) of level info or higher.
# Don't log private authentication messages!
*.info;mail.none;authpriv.none /var/log/messages

# The authpriv file has restricted access.
authpriv.* /var/log/secure

# Log all the mail messages in one place.
mail.debug  /var/log/maillog

# Everybody gets emergency messages, plus log them on another
# machine.
*.emerg *
*.emerg  @logger.greatcircle.com
```

System logs for catastrophe

One of the simplest ways to create catastrophe logs is to attach a line printer to one of the bastion host's serial ports, and simply log a copy of everything to that port. There are some problems with this approach, though. First, you have to keep the printer full of paper, unjammed, and with a fresh ribbon. Second, once the logs are printed, you can't do much with them except look at them. Because they aren't in electronic form, you have no way to search or analyze them in an automated fashion.

If you have a write-once device available to you, direct logs to that device; that will give you reasonably trustworthy logs in an electronic form. Be sure you can trust the write-once feature. Some magneto-optical drives are capable of both multiple-write and write-once operations, and keep track of the mode they're in via software. If the system is compromised, it may be possible to overwrite or damage previously written parts of the supposedly write-once media.

Some operating systems (notably BSD 4.4-Lite and systems derived from it, such as current releases of BSDI, FreeBSD, and NetBSD) support append-only files. These are not an advisable alternative to write-once media. Even if you can trust the implementation of append-only files, the disk that they're on is itself writable, and there may be ways to access it outside of the filesystem, particularly for an intruder who wants to destroy the logs.

Disabling Nonrequired Services

When you have a secure machine, you can start to set up the services on it. The first step is to remove the services that you don't want to run. Consult Chapter 10, *Bastion Hosts*, for more information about deciding which services you don't want to run. The main idea is to remove all services that you don't actually need for the machine to do the work it's designed to do, even if they seem convenient or harmless.

How Are Services Managed Under Unix?

On Unix machines, most services are managed in one of two ways:

*   By controlling when they start and who can use them
*   By service-specific configuration files

There are two ways services get started on Unix systems:

*   At boot time from a machine's configuration files (for example in */etc/inittab* and */etc/rc* files or directories)
*   On demand by the *inetd* daemon (which is itself started at boot time)

A few services—for example, Sendmail—can be configured to run under either or both mechanisms, but most of them strongly prefer one of the two options.

Services started by /etc/rc files or directories

Services in the first category are designed to run indefinitely. They are started once (when the machine boots), and they are never supposed to exit. (Of course, sometimes they do exit, either because they're killed by a system administrator, or because they trip over a bug or some other error.) Servers are written in this way if they need to handle small transactions quickly, or if they need to "remember" information. Writing them in this way avoids the delays associated with starting a new copy of the server to handle each request made to it.

Servers of this kind are started from a Unix system's */etc/rc* files, which are shell scripts executed when the machine boots. Examples of servers typically started from */etc/rc* files are those that handle NFS, SMTP, and DNS. In BSD-based versions of Unix, there are customarily a few files in */etc* with names that start with "rc". (for example */etc/rc.boot*). In other versions of Unix, there are customarily directories in */etc* instead of files (for instance, */etc/rc0.d*); the directories contain the various startup commands, each in its own little file.

In either case, you need to be careful to look at all of the startup scripts and all of the scripts they call, recursively. Usually, more than one script is run in the process of bringing a system all the way up. On modern Unix systems, those scripts often call others, sometimes through multiple levels of indirection. For example, you may find that a startup script calls another script to start up networking, and that one calls yet another script to start up file service. You may also find that startup scripts use mystical options to familiar commands (e.g., they often run *ifconfig* with little-used options that cause *ifconfig* to pick up configuration information from obscure places). Be sure that you understand these options and that you replace any that tell the machine to pick up information about itself from the network (or from services it normally provides but that you are going to turn off).

Linux and some versions of Unix have a utility called *chkconfig* that is used to determine whether or not services are started up. When a service is installed on a system that's using *chkconfig*, a startup script is also installed and always runs, but the startup script uses the *chkconfig* command to determine whether or not it should actually start the service. Administrators also use the *chkconfig* command to change or check the status of services. Different versions of the *chkconfig* system use different methods of storing the configuration status; some of them create files, while others store the status in the startup scripts themselves.

Some versions of Unix and Linux have a file called */etc/inittab*. On these systems, the *init* process uses information in this file to control how the boot process is performed and to keep a number of system processes running. Normally the processes configured to be run from */etc/inittab* allow interactive logins from terminal and workstation console devices. The *init* process will start and monitor these processes and, if configured to do so, will restart them when they terminate or die. Disabling these processes can usually be performed by commenting out the configuration line or by instructing *init* not to start them at all. If you change the contents of */etc/inittab*, there is usually a special and operating system–dependent way to signal the *init* process to re-read the file.

In some versions of Unix, one of the servers that is run from the startup files is designed to restart other servers if they fail. If such a program exists on a system, it will try to start the other servers if they are removed from the startup files but not from its configuration file. Either turn off this program or be sure to remove from the program's configuration file any servers removed from the startup files. You'll notice the program when you work through the startup files.

Services started by inetd

Some servers are designed to be started "on demand" and to exit after they provide the requested service. Such servers are typically used for services that are requested infrequently, for services that aren't sensitive to delays in starting a new server from scratch, and for services that require a new server process to deal with each request (for example, Telnet or FTP sessions, where a separate server is used for each active session).

Servers of this kind are usually run from the *inetd* server. (The *inetd* server itself, because it runs indefinitely, is started from the */etc/rc* files, as described in the previous section.) The *inetd* server listens for requests for services specified in the */etc/inetd.conf* configuration file. When it hears such a request, it starts the right server to process the request.

Disabling Services Under Unix

As we discussed in Chapter 10, *Bastion Hosts*, there are four general precautions to take when disabling services:

* Make sure that you have a way to boot the machine if you disable a critical service (for instance, a secondary hard disk with a full operating system image or a bootable CD-ROM).

* Save a clean copy of everything you modify so that you know how to put it back the way it was if you do something wrong.

* When you disable a service, disable everything that depends on it.

* Don't connect the machine you are trying to protect to a hostile network before you have completed the process of disabling services. It is possible for the machine to be compromised while you are preparing it.

Once you've set up your alternate boot process, check the startup files and directories for your system. This should be done line by line, making sure you know exactly what each line does—including any command-line options.

In a perfect world, you would like to disable everything, and then enable only the services you need. Unfortunately, if you do this, you may find that the machine is no longer able to boot. It is slightly easier to work from the other direction by disabling services you definitely don't need, and then examining the rest of the boot process and adjusting it slowly so that the machine will always boot.

One way to start this process is to take a snapshot of all the services that are running on your machine by using the *netstat* utility. This utility allows you to list all of the open network connections and, with additional options, the TCP and UDP network ports that have a service configured to listen or accept datagrams. The

Linux *netstat* utility has a very useful feature that allows you to directly list the numeric process identifier and name associated with each network port. Other versions of Unix are supplied with tools, such as *fuser,* which will map the network ports to the numeric process identifier. You can also use the *lsof* utility (see Appendix B for information on where to get *lsof*). Once the process name is known, it can be used to search through the configuration files to find where it is started.

As mentioned before, some versions of Unix and Linux include the *chkconfig* program that can administratively enable and disable services. The command can be used to test whether a service is turned on, to list the services that can be controlled, and to enable or disable services. These systems work because the startup file checks to see if the service should be run. Disabling a service can be as simple as using *chkconfig* to turn the service off. This is a convenient and standard way to disable a service, but it doesn't leave any documentation of why the service is off, and it's very easy to re-enable a service that's been disabled this way.

Although it's more work, it's a good idea to comment out the code that starts the service or to remove the startup file altogether. This will prevent people from simply turning it back on with *chkconfig*, and will give you a good place to put comments about why you've disabled the service. If you do disable services with *chkconfig*, you should be sure to keep a list in a standard place that says what services are supposed to be disabled and why. This will help keep people from re-enabling them by mistake, and it will also allow you to easily reconfirm the list if you upgrade, patch, or reinstall software, which may change the *chkconfig* status of services.

On other versions of Unix, you will have no choice; you will have to comment out or delete the lines that start services you don't need. You will frequently see services that are started after a check for some configuration file. If you don't want the service to run, comment out the entire code block. Don't leave the code active simply because the configuration file doesn't currently exist and the service won't currently be started. Someone or something might create the configuration file some time in the future. Commenting out the entire thing is more secure and less risky.

Commenting out lines is preferable to removing them because it leaves evidence of your intent. When you comment something out, add a comment about why you have commented it out. If you delete something, replace it with a comment about why you have deleted it. Make sure that the next person to look at the files knows that you got rid of things on purpose and doesn't helpfully "fix" it for you. If you comment out a call to another script, add a comment in that script indicating that it's not supposed to be started and why. Renaming it or commenting out its contents are also good ways to help ensure that it won't accidentally reappear.

For every service that you leave enabled, apply the same line-by-line procedure to the service's configuration files. Obviously, you want to pay particular attention to *inetd*'s configuration file. On most systems, this file is called */etc/inetd.conf.* (On other systems, this file might be called */etc/servers* or something else; check your manual pages for *inetd*). If you have a daemon-watcher and have decided to leave it on, its configuration files are also particularly important.

This process will need to be repeated if you install new software or a patch, because sometimes the startup scripts are modified or replaced. Installation scripts often assume that you will want to run all the software you are installing, and will helpfully turn it on for you, in its default, insecure configuration, even when you are upgrading an old installation on which it was turned off. You will want to have good documentation about your desired configuration to refer to when you install upgrades, patches, or new software. In any case, you should certainly disconnect the system from any hostile networks before performing any software installation or patching.

Which Services Should You Leave Enabled?

Certain services are essential to the operation of the machine, and you'll probably need to leave these enabled, no matter what else the machine is configured to do. On a Unix system, these processes include:

init, swap, and page
> The three kernel pseudo-processes used to manage all other processes.

cron
> Runs other jobs at fixed times, for housekeeping and so on.

syslogd
> Collects and records log messages from the kernel and other daemons. If the *syslog* daemon is only going to send messages, check to see if it is possible to disable the ability to log remote *syslog* events.

inetd
> Starts network servers (such as *telnetd* and *ftpd*) when such services are requested by other machines.

In addition, you'll obviously need server processes for the services that you've decided to provide on your bastion host (e.g., real or proxy Telnet, FTP, SMTP, and DNS servers). You will also need servers for any protocols you intend to use for remote administration of the machine (usually, *sshd*).

You should audit the configuration files for the services you leave enabled, to be sure that they are configured appropriately. The manual page for a service is a good place to find out which configuration files are used. In the preceding list, we have already discussed the configuration files for *syslogd* and *inetd*. Checking the configuration files for the *cron* service is frequently overlooked. Vendors typically provide a number of housekeeping functions that are not suitable for a bastion host. In particular, you should check for places where the system log files are rotated. You will typically find that *cron* will attempt to rotate log files on a weekly basis and may discard information older than two weeks. We suggest that you check these housekeeping rules and bring them into alignment with your policy on how long to keep log files.

Specific Unix Services to Disable

You will want to disable all unneccessary services, but some are particularly dangerous and particularly unlikely to be needed on a firewall.

NFS and related services

Start with NFS and related network services. You aren't going to need them. No internal machine should trust your bastion host enough to let the bastion host mount the internal machine's disks via NFS. Besides that, there probably won't be anything on the bastion host that you'll want to export via NFS. NFS is very convenient, but it's incredibly insecure.

NFS services are provided by a whole set of servers; the specific set of servers, and the names of the individual servers, varies slightly from one version of Unix to the next. Look for these names or names like them:

- *nfsd*
- *biod*
- *mountd*
- *statd*
- *lockd*
- *automount*
- *keyserv*
- *rquotad*
- *amd*

Most of these services are started at boot time from the */etc/rc* files, although some are started on demand by *inetd*. *mountd* is somewhat peculiar in that it is often started at boot time *and* is listed in the *inetd* configuration file, apparently so that it will be restarted if the copy that was started at boot time crashes for some reason.

Other RPC services

You should also disable other services based on the Remote Procedure Call (RPC) system. The most critical of these is NIS, a service that is provided by the following servers:

- *ypserv*
- *ypbind*
- *ypupdated*

These servers are generally started at boot time from the */etc/rc* files.

Also disable these RPC-based services:

- *rexd* (the remote execution service, started by *inetd*)
- *walld* (the "write all", or *wall* daemon, started by *inetd*)

All RPC-based services depend on a single service usually called *portmap* (on some machines it is known as *rpcbind*). If you've disabled all of the RPC-based services, you can (and should) also disable the *portmap* service. How can you tell if you've disabled all the RPC-based services? Before disabling *portmap*, but after disabling what you think are the rest of the RPC-based services, reboot the machine and then issue a *rpcinfo -p* command. If the output of that command shows only entries for *portmap* itself, this means that no other RPC services are running. On the other hand, if the output shows that other RPC services are still running, you will need to investigate further to determine what and why. If you decide to provide any RPC-based services, you must also provide the *portmap* service. In that case, consider using Wietse Venema's replacement *portmap*, which is more secure than the versions shipped with most Unix systems (see Appendix B for information on where to find it).

Booting services

Your bastion host should probably not provide booting services; nothing should trust the host enough to be willing to boot from it. This means that, in most cases, you should disable these services:

- *tftpd*
- *bootd*
- *bootpd*
- *dhcpd*

BSD "r" command services

These should all be disabled. The servers for these services are typically named *rshd, rlogind,* and *rexecd* and are typically started by *inetd.* The remaining "r" services are based on them and will not run without them.

routed

Another server that your bastion host probably doesn't need is *routed.* This server is started at boot time from the */etc/rc* files, listens to routing information broadcasts, and updates the kernel routing table based on what it hears.

You probably don't need *routed* on your bastion host because your bastion host is probably located on the perimeter of your network, where routing should be fairly simple. A more secure approach is to create static routes pointing to your internal networks and a default route pointing to your Internet gateway router. You do this at boot time by adding appropriate "route add" commands to the */etc/rc* files.

If you must do dynamic routing on your bastion host, obtain and use a routing daemon that will provide some sort of authentication on the source of routing information. Either it should filter routes based on their source address, or it should support an authenticated routing protocol like RIP v2. If you want to use an authenticated routing protocol, be sure that your routers also support it; if you want to filter on source address, be sure to actually configure the daemon to do so. Traditionally, the most popular routing daemon of this type has been GateD, but others are now available, including Zebra. Appendix B, *Tools,* has information on how to get these daemons.

fingerd

The *finger* server supplies information about existing accounts and accounts on Unix systems. This server is started on demand by *inetd.* The information provided by *fingerd* can be valuable to attackers; it tells them information about potential targets, such as:

Which accounts exist
  This tells them which accounts they should try to guess passwords for.

Personal information about the people with accounts
  This tells them what passwords to start guessing with.

Which accounts are in use
  This tells them which accounts should be avoided, at least until they're not in use.

Which accounts haven't been used lately
   This tells them which accounts are good targets for attack because the owners probably won't notice that the accounts are being used.

On the other hand, Internet users often use *finger* (the program that talks to your *fingerd* daemon) quite legitimately. *finger* is helpful in locating email addresses and telephone numbers. Instead of simply disabling *fingerd*, you might want to replace it with a program that obtains information from a more basic source of contact information for your site; the information might include:

- Your main phone number

- Who to contact if they have questions about your site's products or services

- Sample email addresses if standardized aliases such as *Firstname_Lastname* are maintained for users at your site

- Who to contact in case of network or security problems involving your site

You can provide this kind of generic information to anybody who uses *finger* to check on your site, regardless of what specific information they've requested. The easiest way to accomplish this is to put the information in a file (for example, */etc/finger_info*) and then replace the part of the */etc/inetd.conf* entry for *fingerd* that specifies the program to run with something like */bin/cat /etc/finger_info*. Doing this causes the contents of the */etc/finger_info* file to be returned to anyone contacting your *fingerd* server.

For example, here is the old */etc/inetd.conf* line from Great Circle Associate's system:

```
finger stream tcp nowait nobody /usr/libexec/fingerd fingerd
```

and here is the new */etc/inetd.conf* line:

```
finger stream tcp nowait nobody /bin/cat cat /etc/finger_info
```

and here are the contents of the */etc/finger_info* file:

```
Great Circle Associates
Phone: +1 415 555 0841
Email: Info@GreatCircle.COM

For more information, or to report system problems, please
send email or call.
```

ftpd

If you're going to provide anonymous FTP service on your bastion host, you need to reconfigure the FTP server appropriately. You should replace the *ftpd* program with one more suited to providing anonymous FTP service than the standard *ftpd* programs shipped by most Unix vendors. (See Chapter 17, *File Transfer, File Sharing, and Printing,* for information about providing anonymous FTP service.)

If you're *not* going to provide anonymous FTP, you can probably disable your FTP server entirely; it's started on demand by *inetd.*

Even if you've disabled the FTP server on your bastion host, you can still use the FTP client program (typically called simply *ftp*) on the bastion host to transfer files to and from other systems. You'll just have to do the work from the bastion host, instead of from the other systems.

Other services

There are lots of other services you probably don't need and should disable. Although the specific list depends on your own site's security policy and needs, and on the platform you're using, it should probably include the following:

uucpd
> UUCP over TCP/IP

rwhod
> Sort of like *fingerd,* in that it tells you who's currently logged in on the system

lpd
> The BSD printer daemon or other printing services

Running Services on Specific Networks

In some cases, you want to run some services that need to respond to only one network on a machine with multiple network interfaces. You may be able to limit those services to just the networks you wish to use them on. Under Unix, this usually means specifying which IP addresses and/or network interfaces you want the service to respond to as part of the service's startup options; this will be slightly different for every service, and not all services provide this facility.

Turning Off Routing

As we discussed in Chapter 10, *Bastion Hosts,* most machines with more than one network interface will automatically attempt to route traffic between interfaces. You do not normally want a bastion host to do this. If you are not trying to configure a bastion host that is also a router, you should turn off routing, which is a three-part process:

1. Turn off services that advertise the system as a router.

2. Turn off IP forwarding, which actually does the routing.

3. If necessary, turn off source routing separately.

We discussed turning off routing services in Chapter 10. If you have decided to leave these services running (perhaps you are running *routed* or GateD because the bastion host is in a complex and changeable routing environment), you will need to explicitly configure these services not to advertise the machine as a router.

You will also need to turn off IP forwarding. Turning off routing services merely keeps the machine from advertising itself as a router; it doesn't keep the machine from routing packets. Preventing the machine from routing packets requires modifications to the kernel. Fortunately, these days most Unix vendors provide supported parameters for turning off IP forwarding. Even for vendors that don't, it's about as easy as kernel patches get on most machines: turning off IP forwarding requires a change in the value of only a single kernel variable. You need to consult your vendor to find out how to turn off IP forwarding on your machines.

On some machines, turning off normal IP forwarding will not also turn off source routing; it will still be possible for an attacker to get packets through the machine. (Source routing is discussed further in Chapter 10, *Bastion Hosts*.) If you are not screening out all source routed packets before they reach the bastion host, you should consult your vendor to find out how to disable source routing in addition to normal IP forwarding.

Installing and Modifying Services

Some of the services you want to provide may not be provided with your operating system (for example, web servers generally are not). Others may be provided in versions that are inappropriate for use in a secure environment or that are missing features you probably want (for example, stock *fingerd* and *ftpd*). Even those few remaining services that are provided, secure, and up to date in your vendor's operating system release should be protected with the TCP Wrapper package or the *netacl* program from TIS FWTK to improve security and provide logging. (Although TCP Wrapper and *netacl* will increase security, they're not perfect; they rely on the source IP address to identify hosts, and IP addresses can be forged.)

For detailed information about individual services, including advice on selecting HTTP, NNTP, and FTP servers, see the chapters in Part III, *Internet Services*.

Whatever services you do leave enabled should also be protected to the extent possible by the TCP Wrapper package or the *netacl* program, as we describe in the following sections. For example, you might want to set up your bastion host so that it accepts Telnet connections from only one specific machine, such as the workstation you normally use.

Using the TCP Wrapper Package to Protect Services

The TCP Wrapper package, written by Wietse Venema, monitors incoming network traffic and controls network activity. It is a simple but very effective piece of publicly available software set up to run whenever certain ports (corresponding to certain services) are connected. TCP Wrapper provides simple access control list protection, as well as improved logging, for services that are started by *inetd*.

Using the TCP Wrapper package is easy. Here's what you do:

1. Install the package and set up a pair of simple access control files that define which hosts and networks are allowed to access which services.

2. Reconfigure your *inetd* to run the main TCP Wrapper program (called *tcpd*) instead of the "real" server.

3. When a request for a service comes in, *inetd* starts *tcpd*, which evaluates the request against the TCP Wrapper configuration files. This program decides whether or not to log the request, and whether or not to carry out the request.

4. If *tcpd* decides that the request is acceptable, it starts the "real" server to process the request.

TCP Wrapper example

For example, if you want to allow Telnet connections from a specific host (e.g., 172.16.1.2) to your machine, but deny Telnet connections from all other hosts, you would change the line for *telnetd* in your */etc/inetd.conf* file to say something like:

```
telnet stream tcp nowait root /usr/local/libexec/tcpd telnetd
```

You would also need to create an */etc/hosts.allow* file that tells the TCP Wrapper package (the *tcpd* program) which host to allow connections from:

```
telnetd : 172.16.1.2
```

And finally, you'd need to create an */etc/hosts.deny* file to tell the TCP Wrapper package to deny all connections from all hosts by default, and to send email to root about each probe:

```
ALL : ALL : (/usr/local/etc/safe_finger -l @%h | \
    /usr/ucb/Mail -s "PROBE %d from %c" root)&
```

Note that the */etc/hosts.deny* file only applies to services protected by the TCP Wrapper package (that is, services for which you've configured *inetd* to run *tcpd* instead of the real server). If you don't tell *inetd* to run the TCP Wrapper package (the *tcpd* program) for a given service, then the TCP Wrapper package won't do anything regarding that service.

Despite its name, the TCP Wrapper package supports UDP-based services in addition to TCP-based services. Be aware, however, that the TCP Wrapper package can only control when to *start* UDP-based servers; it cannot control access to those servers once they're started, and many UDP-based servers are designed to process requests for some period of time beyond the initial startup request. Many eventually time out and exit, but once they've been started through a legitimate request, they're vulnerable to illegitimate requests.

In addition, TCP Wrapper relies on the source IP address for authentication. It is relatively difficult to spoof source IP addresses when TCP is used, because the connection setup process requires a dialog between the source and the destination. It is much easier to spoof source IP addresses when using UDP, so TCP Wrapper provides less protection.

Using netacl to protect services

The *netacl* component of TIS FWTK (described in some detail in Chapter 9, *Proxy Systems*) provides much the same capability as the TCP Wrapper package. To implement the same example as the one shown in the previous section (except for the ability to trace probes from unauthorized systems) using *netacl*, you would change the line for *telnetd* in your */etc/inetd.conf* file to:

```
telnet stream tcp nowait root /usr/local/lib/netacl telnetd
```

Then, you would add the following lines to your FWTK *netperm* configuration file (wherever that is on your system):

```
netacl-telnetd: permit-hosts 172.16.1.2 -exec /usr/libexec/telnetd
```

Evaluating and Configuring Unix Services

If you need to install a new service on a bastion host, you will want to secure it as much as possible. You should not assume that services are safe; reputable software companies often ship unsafe packages, and in many cases, their worst problems are easy to find and repair.

Install a test copy of the service on a machine that is otherwise stable and will not change while you are doing the installation. Use *find* to identify all the files that were changed during the installation, and check to make sure that those files are acceptable. In particular:

- Make sure that file permissions are as restrictive as possible; arbitrary users shouldn't be able to write to any executables, configuration files, or temporary directories. If possible, limit read and execute permissions as well.

- Closely check all programs that have the *setuid* bit set, particularly if they are *setuid* to root. If they can run without *setuid*, or if it is at all possible to avoid running them, remove *setuid* permissions.

- If the program installs a user account, make sure that the password is set to something other than the program's default. If possible, change the account name to something other than the program's default; attackers will often focus on well-known account names.

- Make sure that all programs are run by users with appropriate permissions. Do not run services as root unless they need to be run as root (for instance, to use ports below 1024). If you must run services as root, try to run them under *chroot* to control what they can access.

- If you add special user accounts for services, make sure that they cannot be used as normal login accounts; both the password and shell entries should be invalid, so that attackers cannot use the accounts as entry points.

- Check any additions the program has made to startup files or *crontab* files.

Reconfiguring for Production

Now it's time to move the machine from the configuration that was useful to you when you were building it to the best configuration for running it. You'll need to do several things:

1. Reconfigure and rebuild the kernel.

2. Remove all nonessential programs.

3. Mount as many filesystems as possible as read-only.

Reconfigure and Rebuild the Kernel

The first step in this phase of building your bastion host is to rebuild the operating system kernel to remove kernel capabilities you don't need. This may sound intimidating, but it's generally a relatively straightforward operation; it needs to be, because you'll be using the same capabilities you'd use to install a new type of device on your system. Every Unix system, as shipped, contains some form of configuration support (they range considerably in how kernel reconfiguration is supported and in what you can do). Besides reducing the size of your kernel (and thereby making more memory available for other purposes), rebuilding the kernel denies to attackers the chance to exploit these capabilities.

Some capabilities are particularly dangerous. In particular, you should probably remove the following capabilities or device drivers:

- NFS and related capabilities

- Anything that enables network sniffing—for example, Network Interface Tap (NIT) or Berkeley Packet Filter (BPF)

Although NIT and BPF are provided for testing and debugging purposes, they are frequently used by attackers. NIT and BPF are dangerous because they let the machine grab all packets off the Ethernet it's attached to, instead of only the packets addressed to it. Disabling these capabilities may prevent you from using the machine as a packet filtering system, so you may not be able to delete them in all architectures.

If your bastion host is a dual-homed host, this is the time to disable IP forwarding.

You have to be more careful when you disable kernel capabilities than when you disable services started by *inetd* or at boot time from the */etc/rc* files (as described earlier). There are a lot of interdependencies between kernel capabilities. For this reason, it's sometimes hard to determine exactly what a given capability is used for. The consequences of disabling a capability that is actually needed can be severe—for example, the new kernel might not boot.

Make sure you follow your vendor's instructions for building and installing new kernels. Always keep a backup copy of your old kernel. If you have a backup, you can boot from it if you find out that something is wrong with the new kernel. Some boot systems need all the kernels to reside in the same partition, or they may need to be configured with the names of all the kernels you wish to boot. Either way, be sure that you have a backup kernel, that it's possible to boot that kernel, and that you know how to do so, all before you change the working kernel.

When you know you can safely reboot the machine, go through the kernel configuration files the same way you went through the startup files, checking every single line to make certain that it's something you want. Again, watch for places where one configuration file contains another, and check your documentation to be sure that you've looked at all the configuration files that are consulted. Often there is one file for including device drivers and one or more for parameters; IP forwarding will be in the latter.

Once you've got a working kernel, you'll probably want to delete or encrypt your old "full function" kernel. Replace it with a backup copy of the working minimal kernel. Doing so will keep an attacker who somehow manages to break into your machine from simply using that old kernel to reboot, and thereby restore all of the services you so carefully disabled. For similar reasons, you'll probably also want to delete the files and programs needed to build a new kernel.

If your kernel uses loadable modules, it may be difficult to determine when they're used. You will want to delete or encrypt all the ones that you don't want used, but because they're not always explicitly loaded, you may not know which those are. Keeping an alternate boot medium handy, try moving them out of the directory for loadable modules. Run the machine through its paces before you finally remove or encrypt them.

Beware! Your vendor may have provided copies of "generic" kernels (which typically have every possible capability enabled) in unexpected locations for use during the installation of the machine and its (nonexistent) client machines. Poke around in all the directories where installation files are kept and all the directories for clients. The documentation generally tells you where client kernels are but rarely tells you about the internals of the install process. Check the documentation for disaster recovery advice, which may helpfully tell you where to locate spare kernel images.

Remove Nonessential Programs

The next step is to remove all of the programs that aren't essential for day-to-day operation. If a program isn't there, an attacker can't exploit any bugs that it might contain. This is especially true for *setuid/setgid* programs, which are a very tempting target for an attacker. You should remove programs you normally think of as being essential. Remember that the bastion host is purely providing Internet services; it does not need to be a comfortable environment in which to work.

Window systems and compilers are examples of major programs you can get rid of. Attackers find these programs very useful: window systems are fertile ground for security problems, and compilers can be used to build the attacker's own tools. Graphical system administration programs are also usually powerful, vulnerable, and frequently unnecessary; however, on some platforms, they may be impossible to remove. Documentation and help systems (including manual pages) are at best an education for attackers, and at worst another source of vulnerabilities. Attackers have been known to hide programs and files among manual pages. Make sure that you have the information internally, but remove it from all bastion hosts.

Before deleting programs like compilers, make sure you've finished using them yourself; make sure you've built, installed, and tested everything you're going to need on this machine, such as the tools for auditing the system (discussed in the section "Running a Security Audit," later in this chapter).

Instead of simply deleting key tools you'd expect an attacker to use, such as the compiler, you might want to replace them with programs that raise an alarm (for example, sending electronic mail or tripping your pager) when someone tries to run them. You might even want to have the programs halt the system after raising the alarm, if you believe it's better for the machine to be down than under attack. This is a prime way to humiliate yourself, however; you yourself are probably the one person most likely to forget where you are when you try to run a forbidden command. It's also a good way to set yourself up for denial of service attacks.

You'll want to do two scans looking for things to delete:

1. Walk through all the standard directories for binaries on your system (everything that's in root's path or in the default user path). If you're unsure whether a program is needed, turn off execute permission on it for a while (a few days) before you remove or encrypt it and see what happens. You may also want to run the machine for a while before you do the scan and check the access times on files to see if they've been used.

2. Use *find* to look for every file on the system that has the *setuid* or *setgid* bit turned on. The arguments to *find* differ radically from system to system, but you will probably want something like this:

   ```
   find / -type f \( -perm -04000 -o -perm -02000 \) -ls
   ```

   Some versions of *find* provide special primitives for identifying *setuid* and *setgid* files.

If your operating system provides a list of installed packages, you'll also want to look at that list, which may include things that have been stashed in interesting places.

Mount Filesystems as Read-Only

Once you've configured a bastion host, you don't want it to change, so you should mount as many filesystems as possible as read-only. How much of the machine you can protect this way will depend on the version of Unix that you're running and the services that you're providing. A machine that you're using as a packet filtering router may be able to run with all of its disk space protected; a machine that's providing mail service will need space to keep temporary files in, if nothing else.

On a service host, you have to provide a certain amount of writable filesystem space for things like scratch space, system logs, and the mail spool. You might be able to use a RAM disk for this; however, you'll have to be sure that your operating system supports it, that you have enough RAM, and that you think you can afford to lose the contents of the RAM disk (for example, email in transit between internal hosts and the Internet) whenever your machine reboots.

With most versions of Unix, you'll also have to either provide writable disk space for memory swapping or turn off swapping. Many versions of Unix do not allow you to turn off swapping; however, they will usually allow you to use a separate disk for swap space, and that disk can safely be left writable. Using a RAM disk will increase your memory usage to the point where you will probably need swap space.

Systems based on BSD 4.4-Lite (for instance, current releases of NetBSD, FreeBSD, and the BSDI product) have a new immutable attribute that can be set on a per-file basis. If a file is marked "immutable", the file cannot be changed, not even by root, unless the system is running in single-user mode. If your operating system provides this capability, use it to protect your programs and configuration files from tampering by an attacker. (We recommend this approach only if you cannot use hardware write protection, or as an additional layer of security to use with hardware write protection. Because it's implemented in software, it is more likely to be compromisable.)

Running a Security Audit

Several very good automated auditing packages are freely available on the Internet. The four most commonly used are these:

COPS
> The Computer Oracle and Password System, developed by Dan Farmer and Gene Spafford

SATAN
> Security Administrator's Tool for Analyzing Networks (also known as SANTA), developed by Dan Farmer and Wietse Venema

Tiger
> Developed as part of the TAMU package by Texas A&M University

Tripwire
> Developed by Gene H. Kim and Gene Spafford

COPS and Tiger both check for well-known security holes on the host they are run on. There is significant overlap in what COPS and Tiger check; however, they're both free, so it's a good idea to obtain and run both of them to get the best possible coverage. Tripwire is a filesystem integrity checker. It is strictly a tool for dealing with checksum databases; it is much better at this than either COPS or Tiger (which both have basic checksum database capabilities) but has no ability to check for well-known security holes. SATAN is a network-based application which tests hosts other than the one it is running on. These packages are independent of each other; there's nothing to prevent you from using all of them in combination on your bastion host, and that would probably be a good idea. Appendix B, *Tools*, gives you information on how to get all four packages.

Because the well-known security holes tend to be somewhat operating system-specific, the effectiveness of the packages that check for these security holes is very dependent on which operating system you have, and which version of the operating system it is. If it's an operating system and version the package knows about, that's great. If it isn't, then the package has to grope around blindly, trying to guess what holes might exist. (Fortunately, attackers will usually have the same problem, if not to the same extent.) In some cases, packages will report holes that don't exist when they're run on unfamiliar systems.

Commercial packages that perform similar functions are now available. In general, the security scanning products are similar to PC virus software in that they require periodic updates in order to keep up with the latest vulnerabilities.

When you are doing security audits, you should be sure to use an appropriate checksum program. The standard Unix checksum programs (*/bin/sum*, for example) use a 16-bit cyclic redundancy check (CRC) algorithm that is designed to catch a sequence of random bit errors during data transfers. This does not work for detecting unauthorized changes to files because it is possible to reverse the CRC algorithm. This is known to attackers, and they have programs that manipulate the unused bytes in a file (particularly an executable binary file) to make the checksum for that file come out to whatever they want it to be. They can make a modified copy of */bin/login* that produces the same checksum, and *sum* will not be able to detect any difference.

For real security, you need to use a "cryptographic" checksum algorithm like MD5 or Snefru; these algorithms produce larger and less predictable checksums that are much more difficult to spoof. The COPS, Tiger, and Tripwire auditing packages mentioned earlier all include and use such algorithms in place of the normal Unix checksum programs.

The IRIX operating system from Silicon Graphics uses a process called *re-quick-starting* (RQS) to precalculate data needed for loading binaries and to speed up start time. RQS is run automatically as a part of most installations and can update every system binary. This should not be a problem on a bastion host, where software should not be installed regularly in any case. However, you should be aware that small installations may have wide-ranging effects and will require the recalculation of all checksums.

12

Windows NT and Windows 2000 Bastion Hosts

This chapter discusses the details of configuring Windows NT for use in a firewall environment, building on the principles discussed in Chapter 10, *Bastion Hosts*. You should be sure to read both chapters before attempting to build a bastion host. This chapter is not a complete introduction to Windows NT security, which is a complex subject. Instead, it attempts to cover those issues that are specific to bastion hosts, and that are not covered in most Windows NT security texts. As usual, we use the term "Windows NT" for both Windows NT and Windows 2000, except where we explicitly say otherwise.

Just as with Unix, it's impossible to give complete instructions on how to configure any given machine; the details vary greatly depending on what version of Windows NT you're running and exactly what you intend to do with the machine. This chapter is intended to give you an outline of what needs to be done, and how to figure out how to do it.

Approaches to Building Windows NT Bastion Hosts

There are two major approaches to building bastion hosts under Windows NT. As usual, people hold very strong opinions about which one is correct.

One method of building Windows NT bastion hosts is to take the same approach that we recommend for Unix machines: you disable all normal administration tools, remove the machine from all forms of resource and information sharing, and run it as an island unto itself, where nothing is quite the same as it is on the mainland. This is a very secure approach, but it makes the machines quite difficult to administer.

The other method of building Windows NT bastion hosts is to use a split administrative network, as described in Chapter 6, *Firewall Architectures*, and build the machines as relatively normal Windows machines that can participate in domains, use standard administrative tools, and otherwise behave pretty much the way everybody expects. In this configuration, the machine has two network interfaces, and services are disabled only for the externally visible interface. The machine is configured with higher security than normal but not with the extreme measures that make it impossible to administer normally.

Partisans describe the first configuration as "impossible to use" and the second as "impossible to secure". The truth is, of course, somewhere between the two. The first configuration can be used and administered, but it's difficult and peculiar. It's not appropriate for machines that need to change often and provide large numbers of services. The second configuration can be secured, but it's relatively fragile; small accidents can make services available on the external interface. It's not appropriate for the highest security environments, or environments where there are no other protections for the machines.

This chapter is primarily aimed at the first kind of configuration. This is the more extreme configuration, and the one which is not adequately covered by other sources of information. If you want to build the second kind of configuration, you will follow the same basic procedures we describe, but you will leave many more services enabled.

Which Version of Windows NT?

Once you have decided to use Windows NT, you have to decide which version to run. In most cases, you will want to use a version designed to be a server: Windows NT 4 Server rather than Windows NT 4 Workstation, Windows 2000 Server rather than Windows 2000 Professional. Although the differences are not always gigantic, versions intended to be servers support more network connections and more powerful hardware, and often come with more software. In addition, machines that are part of a firewall are, in fact, servers, and Microsoft will attempt to discourage you from running Workstation on them by means that vary from release to release. Don't assume that software intended for workstations is a long-term solution just because it will meet your needs today; if you need to install new software, upgrade your hardware, or upgrade your operating system, you may well find yourself forced to move to versions intended for servers.

You will want the most recent, stable, fully released version of Windows NT. Because Microsoft tends to have very long prerelease periods (beta versions of the operating system now called Windows 2000 were in circulation for at least two years before the final release), it becomes tempting to avoid future upgrades by using prerelease operating systems. Don't do it. It isn't going to significantly improve the upgrade situation, and it will mean that you're running critical systems on unsupported software.

In addition to the Windows NT software itself, you will want to get the most recent version of the relevant Resource Kit, which contains useful documentation and tools. These resources are essential for all Windows NT administrators but will be even more reassuring if you come from a Unix background, since they include many command-line oriented tools that will be familiar to Unix people.

Securing Windows NT

Once you have chosen a machine, you need to make sure that it has a reasonably secure operating system installation. The first steps in this process are the same as for any other operating system and were discussed in Chapter 10, *Bastion Hosts*. They are:

1. Start with a minimal clean operating system installation. Install the operating system from scratch onto empty disks, selecting only the subsystems you need.

2. Fix known bugs. Consult CERT-CC, Microsoft, your hardware vendor, and any other sources of security information you may have to make certain that you have all appropriate hot fixes and service packs installed. (Note that you may need to reapply hot fixes and service packs after you install software.)

3. Use a checklist to configure the system. Microsoft's security web site, located at *http://www.microsoft.com/security,* provides links for checklists.

Setting Up System Logs Under Windows NT

Under Windows NT, logging is done by the Event Logger, and logs are read with the Event Viewer. This poses a number of problems:

- The Event Logger keeps information only locally and doesn't support remote logging.

- No way is provided to reduce the amount of information in the active log automatically without destroying information.

- The Event Viewer doesn't provide a very flexible or powerful way of looking at events.

By default, Windows NT keeps a log of a fixed size, and when the log is full, old events are deleted to make room for new ones. This is not a secure configuration; an attacker can create a lot of unimportant events to force crucial ones to be removed from the log. You'll notice that something's wrong, but you won't know what.

You can set up Windows NT so that it does not delete old items when the log fills. However, if you do so, it will simply stop logging items when the log fills, which is even worse for security. If you're really confident about your ability to keep the log small by hand, you can set the machine up so that if the log fills up, it will not only stop logging, it will also shut the machine down. This approach is very radical; it does not do a graceful shutdown but simply crashes, probably losing information in open files. On the other hand, as long as the machine isn't set to autoboot, it will make sure that you don't lose logging information.

If you are very careful, you can get an Event Logger set up that is relatively secure but that requires considerable maintenance. To do so, you'll need to configure the Event Logger for a large log that does not overwrite old events, have it shut down the machine if the log fills, turn off autobooting, and then regularly save the log to removable media and clear the logs. This still leaves you vulnerable to denial of service attacks and to attackers who modify the logs before you copy them. You can add some security by changing the location to which Event Logger writes and putting the log on write-once media.

To keep events from being overwritten, use the Event Viewer, go to the Log menu, select Log Settings, and select Do Not Overwrite Events (Clear Log Manually). To shut down the machine when the log fills up, set the registry key

```
\HKEY_LOCAL_MACHINE\System\CurrentControlSet\Control\Lsa\CrashOnAuditFail
```

to 1. To change the location where files are stored, look in:

```
\HKEY_LOCAL_MACHINE\System\CurrentControlSet\Services\EventLog
```

You will find an entry for each of the three Windows NT logs (application, system, and security), each of which has a key named "File". Change the value of this key to change the files used to store event logs.

You are better advised to use an add-on product to copy events out of the Event Logger as they are logged. You can then let old events be deleted, since you'll be working from the other copies. Microsoft sells a program that turns events into SNMP traps as they are logged as part of the System Management Service; you can also get programs that will make *syslog* entries for events (see Chapter 11, *Unix and Linux Bastion Hosts*, for more information about *syslog*). The Windows NT Resource Kit provides a utility called *dumpel* that will dump the event log to a text file, which can also be handy for saving event log information. None of these systems are perfect; they have a significant risk of losing or duplicating events. You will therefore want to protect the original event logs as well.

Although Microsoft does not provide tools for rotating event logs, there is a programming interface to the event logger that would allow you to write your own. If you do this, you should still leave the machine set to crash when the log fills, so that you are protected in case of rotation problems.

You will also want to be careful about the amount of logging you do. Logging takes a significant amount of effort under Windows NT, and logging large numbers of events can noticeably slow down a server, particular if you are running add-on software that requires every event to be logged twice. The auditing system can log immense amounts of data if you are incautious about what you turn on.

Disabling Nonrequired Services

When you have a secure machine, you can start to set up the services on it. The first step is to remove the services that you don't want to run. Consult Chapter 10, *Bastion Hosts*, for more information about deciding which services you don't want to run. The main idea is to remove all services that you don't actually need for the machine to do the work it's designed to do, even if they seem convenient or harmless.

How Are Services Managed Under Windows NT?

There are two parts to service management. First, the administrative interfaces, which you use to install, remove, and configure services, and to manually start and stop them. Second, the underlying mechanisms, which automatically handle services and make them continuously available. You do not normally need to know about these mechanisms in order to administer a machine. We discuss them here for two reasons:

- If you end up building a particularly specialized bastion host, you may need a very fine degree of comprehension and control over the services, in which case you will need this information.

- People who are accustomed to administering Unix hosts expect to have this level of information, and will attempt to control services at this level, only to become confused and hostile when they run into some of the more obscure side effects of the differences between the two operating systems.

Under Windows NT, the tool that is normally used to install services that are provided by Microsoft is the Networking control panel. Services that are provided by other vendors will come with their own installation programs. Some services are configured from the Networking control panel, while others have their own configuration and management programs.

The tool that is used to manually start and stop services is the Services control panel. The Services control panel can also set up some generic configuration information for services, but any service-specific parameters have to be managed separately. Windows 2000 gives more information and control from the Services control panel than Windows NT 4; a number of things are accessible only from the registry in Windows NT 4 but are nicely presented in the user interface in Windows 2000 (for instance, information about which services depend on each other).

The rest of this section discusses the underlying mechanisms; you may feel free to ignore it if you do not need control of services beyond that presented by the user interface.

Services under Windows NT are always started by the Service Control Manager (SCM). (The SCM is unfortunately completely different from the user-visible Services control panel.) Services can be started as part of the boot process or on demand. Services started during boot can start at any time from the very beginning (for services with a "boot" startup type) to after users are already able to log in (for services with an "autostart" type). While Unix boot mechanisms specify an explicit order for services to start up in, Windows NT services specify their dependencies and type, and the operating system figures out what order to start them in. This is in general more effective at letting you add new services and get them started correctly but makes it harder to calculate the order that services actually start in.

"On demand" can also cover a range of situations. Most commonly, it means that the service starts when a user starts an application that needs the service.* "On demand" services can also be started explicitly from the Services control panel, or any other application that talks to the Service Control Manager (for instance, the SQL Service Manager). Services that are RPC providers (directly or through DCOM) will be started if there is a request for them. Finally, services can have dependency information, and a demand service can be started because a service that depends on it attempts to start. This can create a situation where a service is marked as demand but actually starts at boot time, because a service that depends on it is marked as autostart.

Not everything that you think of as a service will appear in the Services control panel. Some things that behave like services are implemented entirely or in part as drivers that are loaded into the operating system and do not run as separate processes at all. These are not actually services from the operating system's point of view, and they are listed in the Devices control panel instead of the Services con-

---

* Note that this depends on the application explicitly attempting to start the service; "on demand services" will not be started simply because an application demands them, despite the name.

trol panel. They are, however, listed as services in the registry, with registry entries in the following:

```
HKEY_LOCAL_MACHINE\System\CurrentControlSet\Services
```

This lists all services in alphabetical order, and you will have to look at the value for "Start" to see if they are turned on and when they start up.

Not everything in the Services section of the registry is a network server; the registry also includes normal device drivers and filesystem drivers in this section, and some things that function as servers in the context of the local machine function as clients in the Internet context. That is, they provide a centralized service for programs running on the local machine, but they do not accept requests from other hosts. For instance, a DHCP service is installed by default; it acts as a client, requesting information from a DHCP server. However, it then distributes this information to other processes on the machine, which makes it a service from the operating system's point of view. There is no straightforward way to tell whether something is a purely local service or a network service, or whether something marked as a filesystem driver is a genuine filesystem driver or part of a network service.

Just to add a final note of confusion, there is no need for one Windows NT service to be implemented as one executable. For performance reasons, multiple Windows NT services may be implemented in the same executable (for instance, the simple TCP/IP services, DHCP, and Berkeley LPD print service are all in the same executable). What the executable does will be controlled by the registry entries for the relevant services. It's also possible for one service to be made up of more than one file, with one running as a kernel driver for maximum speed and the other running as a normal service to avoid burdening the kernel too far. And, in fact, it's not at all uncommon for both these things to happen at once, so that a service is split into a kernel driver and a standard service, and the standard service shares an executable with several others.

Note that the kernel drivers by themselves do not provide services. They are simply an efficient way of providing data to the actual servers. Unix people who are attempting to disable services on Windows NT often disable the actual service, note that the port is not listed as open in *netstat*, and then become severely distressed when port scans show that something is listening to the port. This is a symptom of split service that's using a kernel driver, not of some horrible secret way that the operating system is preventing you from turning off the server and then lying about it. The server is off; the port is not bound; but the kernel driver is picking up the data and throwing it away. No significant security problem is involved, and if you wish to get rid of the apparent problem, you can use the Devices control panel to disable the relevant device.

The Resource Kit provides a command named *sc* that presents information about the running services and drivers; this gives you a much more usable interface than the registry and removes the large amounts of information about services and drivers that aren't in use.

There is no standard way of giving options to individual services under Windows NT, aside from a few parameters dealing with startup order and dependencies, which are in well-defined places in the registry. You will have to research each server separately. In general, service parameters are stored somewhere in the registry—the Microsoft-approved locations are in:

```
HKEY_LOCAL_MACHINE\System\CurrentControlSet\Services\ServiceName\Parameters
```

or

```
HKEY_LOCAL_MACHINE\Software\CompanyName\ServiceName
```

but servers are free to put them anywhere they can write to, in or out of the registry. Normally, service authors should provide a management interface in the form of a control panel or a plug-in for the Microsoft Management Console, which will modify some or all of the parameters.

Registry keys

Here is an overview of the registry keys for services and their use in determining what services do in order to secure a bastion host:

DependOnGroup

A list of service groups that this service depends on. This is relatively rarely set. The main group of interest for networking purposes is "TDI", which is the group that contains base network interface drivers.

DependOnService

A list of services that this service depends on. A service that depends on LanmanServer is almost certainly a network server. Services that depend on LanmanWorkstation are probably not network servers but are clients. Services that depend on one of the other networking groups (NetDDE, TCPIP, NetBT, or AppleTalk, for instance) may be either servers or clients, but your suspicions should be aroused.

DisplayName

This is the name shown in the Services or Devices control panel.

ErrorControl

This shows what to do if this service won't run. Check here before you disable the service! If this is set to 0x02 or 0x03, and you disable the service, the machine will reenable it by restoring the previous configuration. If that doesn't work, at 0x03, it will refuse to boot. Possible values are shown here.

Value	Meaning
0x00	Ignore failure; continue without doing anything.
0x01	Produce a warning dialog box.
0x02	Switch to the last known good configuration if one is available; otherwise, boot anyway.
0x03	Count this boot as a failure, switch to the last known good configuration if one is available, and fail to boot if not.

Group

This is the group name that is used in DependOnGroup. Anything in TDI or Network is networking related.

ImagePath

This is the location of the executable, which tells you what to remove or rename if you want to be sure that the service cannot be easily reenabled.

ObjectName

This is actually the name of the account that the service runs under, if it runs as an independent process. Almost all services run as LocalSystem (which is the most privileged account on the system). In order to run as any other user, the service needs to provide a password for the user, which is stored separately, in the Secrets section of the registry. If the service is a kernel driver, this specifies which kernel object will load it.

PlugPlayServiceType

This indicates whether or not it is a Plug and Play service, and if so, what kind. Normally, network services are not Plug and Play.

Start

This key indicates when the service should be started. Possible variables are as follows.

Value	Meaning
0x00	Boot
0x01	System
0x02	Autoload
0x03	On demand
0x04	Disabled (filesystem drivers will load anyway)

Tag

This specifies what order services in the same group start in; lowest value goes first.

Type

The type of service. 0x100 will be added if the service is capable of interacting directly with the user. Possible values are as follows.

Value	Meaning
0x01	Kernel-mode device driver
0x02	Filesystem driver
0x04	Arguments to network adapter
0x10	Server, standalone process
0x20	Server, can share address space

Subkeys

The only useful subkey is the Parameters subkey, which may contain parameters to the service. Many services have parameters controllable here that are not documented elsewhere.

Other ways to start programs under Windows NT

All the descriptions in the previous section are about official Windows NT services. There are several other ways to automatically start programs under Windows NT, and you may run into "services" that use one of these other methods. In general, this is an extremely bad sign. These are not genuine Windows NT services; they are almost certainly originally written to run under other operating systems, and there is very little chance that they will be either secure or reliable. If at all possible, you should avoid running such programs on bastion hosts, or for that matter, other security-critical hosts.

The following registry key:

```
HKEY_LOCAL_MACHINE\System\CurrentControlSet\Control\SessionManager\BootExecute
```

contains a command line that is executed at boot time. This is normally used to run autocheck to do filesystem checking and, as far as we know, is never used by legitimate services. Because it runs early in the boot process, it would be a tempting place to hide a virus.

The following registry key:

```
HKEY_LOCAL_MACHINE\Software\Microsoft\Windows\CurrentVersion
```

contains three keys that are used to start programs at user login: Run, RunOnce, and RunServices. These are normal ways to start persistent programs under Windows 95/98 and may be used by legitimate programs that are designed for that environment. Some programs may also still use a model where they configure a persistent program to autostart when a particular user logs in, under the expectation that the machine will be set up to log that user in automatically at bootup.

Programs started in these ways may behave like services from the user's point of view, but they are not services from the operating system's point of view and are not managed by the Service Control Manager. This gives them very different security models. In particular, unless otherwise configured, the SCM runs services using the System account, which has the odd property that it is all-powerful on the local machine but is incapable of using the network. Programs started at user login will run as the user who just logged in, which will make significant changes to the permissions they have. A regular user will have more access to the network and to user files than the System account, but less access to operating system files and capabilities (meaning that a program that is auto-started at login instead of being a service will have more opportunities to be hostile and fewer to be useful).

Run models that require a user to be logged in are a significant security problem under Windows NT, because having a user logged in adds vulnerabilities. If you can't avoid servers like these, try to convert them to services using the Resource Kit's *srvany.exe.*

How to Disable Services Under Windows NT

As we discussed in Chapter 10, *Bastion Hosts*, there are four general precautions to take when disabling services:

- Make sure that you have a way to boot the machine if you disable a critical service (for instance, a secondary hard disk with a full operating system image or a bootable CD-ROM).

- Save a clean copy of everything you modify so that you know how to put it back the way it was if you do something wrong. Since it's hard to identify modified files precisely on Windows NT, you should have a full backup of the system, including a dump of the registry.

- When you disable a service, disable everything that depends on it.

- Don't connect the machine you are trying to protect to a hostile network before you have completed the process of disabling services. It is possible for the machine to be compromised while you are preparing it.

Once you've set up your alternate boot process, start by going into the Networking control panel's Services tab and removing the things you don't need, which will probably be most, if not all, of them. The "Specific Windows NT Services to Disable" section, later in this chapter, provides more information about which services you should remove. The advantage of disabling services by removing them from the Services tab is that if possible, it removes the services altogether, and the only way to turn them on will be to reinstall them.

You can also disable services by setting them to the startup status "Disabled" from the Services control panel. This is very easy to undo later, which may not be desirable. On the other hand, doing anything more permanent involves untraditional and relatively risky moves. For instance, you can remove the registry keys for services you have disabled. Without the registry keys, the Service Control Manager can't start them, and you have to know what the keys should be in order to put them back. Removing the relevant executables is another solution, but as noted earlier, it's common for multiple Windows NT services to run as part of the same executable. If you want any of the services provided by a given executable, you will have to leave it.

Some Microsoft documentation claims that some services can be disabled by stopping them (from the Services control panel or the "net stop" command). This is not true; a stopped service will be restarted at boot time unless it is also disabled.

Next Steps After Disabling Services

You will need to reboot the machine after you change the service configuration. When it has been rebooted, you should check to make certain that the services are actually off and that the machine is still functional. One way to check that a service is turned off is to use the *netstat* utility to list the network ports the machine is listening on.

After you have rebooted and tested the machine, and you are comfortable that the machine works without the disabled services, you may want to remove the executables for those services (as long as they are not used by other services). If the executables are lying around, they may be started by somebody—if not you, some other system administrator or an intruder.

If you feel uncertain about removing executables, consider encrypting them instead. Use an encryption program that has a stable implementation of a standard algorithm, like Network Associates' version of PGP (see Appendix B, *Tools*, for information about how to get this package).

Which Services Should You Leave Enabled?

Certain services are essential to the operation of the machine, and you'll probably need to leave these enabled, no matter what else the machine is configured to do. On a Windows NT system, nothing in the Services tab of the Networking control panel is actually required for basic functionality. In the Services control panel, the critical services include:

EventLog
   This is what puts things in the event log, even for local programs.

NT LM Security Support Provider
   This is required if the machine will be running services that need to authenticate users (for instance, FTP or HTTP servers).

Protected Storage
> This is part of the encrypted filesystem support and should be left enabled.

Remote Procedure Call (RPC)
> Many servers use loopback RPC calls and will not work if RPC is not available.

In some circumstances you will also need these services:

IPSEC Policy Agent (Windows 2000)
> This is required if you're using IPsec to secure network connections.

Net Logon
> This is required if the machine will be authenticating accounts for other machines or from other machines (for instance, if it's a member server in a domain or a primary domain server for a domain that contains other servers). A bastion host should use only local accounts, in which case this service is not required.

Plug and Play
> This is either pointless or critical, depending on your hardware configuration. It is not network-accessible in either case. Note that it is even required for correct functioning of peripherals on some server configurations that have no hot-swappable components.

Smart Card (Windows 2000)
> This is required if you have a smart card reader and want to use it for authentication; it depends on Plug and Play.

Spooler
> This is needed for printing (even local printing) to work. You can remove it if you are not going to print.

In addition, you'll obviously need server processes for the services that you've decided to provide on your bastion host (e.g., real or proxy Telnet, FTP, SMTP, and DNS servers).

Specific Windows NT Services to Disable

As discussed earlier, there are three separate places where you can disable services for Windows NT:

- The Services tab of the Networking control panel
- The Services control panel
- The registry

You need to disable services from the registry only in very exceptional cases; you should be able to do everything you need from the Networking and Services control panels.

The Networking control panel

In general, nothing in the Services tab of the Networking control panel is actually required, and you should disable all of the services if possible. Here we list services with special considerations:

Microsoft DNS server (Server)

You do not normally want to run a DNS server on a bastion host unless that bastion host is dedicated to name service. You will therefore turn this off on most bastion hosts.

If you are building a bastion host to be a name server, the Microsoft DNS server is a reasonable choice for a DNS server to run, but in a bastion host configuration, you will need to keep two things in mind. First, you do not want a bastion host to rely on data from a WINS server on another machine, so the DNS server should not be configured to fall back to WINS unless the WINS server is on the same bastion host. Second, the DNS Manager (which is often used to configure the DNS server) relies on NetBT, which may not be available on a bastion host, so you may not be able to use it except at the console.

Microsoft TCP/IP printing (Server and Workstation)

Microsoft's implementation of *lpr*. Although *lpr* is not a secure protocol, it is often safer than using SMB printing, which cannot be enabled without enabling more dangerous services at the same time. Therefore, if you want to be able to print from a Windows NT bastion host, but do not have the resources to dedicate a printer, your best choice may be to install the Microsoft TCP/IP Printing subsystem on the bastion host and the print server and then disable the *lpd* server on the bastion host. (Do not use a bastion host as a print server, via any protocol; if you directly attach a printer to the bastion host, resign yourself to having it be a dedicated printer for that single host.)

NetBIOS interface (Default Server and Workstation)

The base for many of the Microsoft-native services. You will need it if you intend to use normal Microsoft networking. Ideally, you should avoid this service on bastion hosts.

Remote Access Service (Server and Workstation)

This provides networking either over phone lines or via PPTP (which is discussed further in Chapter 14, *Intermediary Protocols*). It should not be installed unless the machine will provide or use dial-up networking or virtual private networking services.

Server (Default Server and Workstation)

This is the server for inbound NetBIOS connections, including SMB connections. This includes file sharing, printer sharing, and remote execution of the Registry Editor, Event Viewer, and User Manager. You should probably remove it, although the machine will then be inaccessible via all normal Windows NT networking. If you need to use normal Windows NT networking (this is practically everything but FTP, HTTP, and SMTP), you should be sure that NetBT access is blocked at some other point and/or that the Server is unbound from high-risk network interfaces (see the discussion of configuring services to run on specific network interfaces).

Because of the way that NetBT name service works, a machine that has no Server service running will register its name correctly at boot time but won't be able to defend itself if another machine tries to claim the name. This may seem unimportant (who cares what happens to the NetBT name if the machine doesn't speak NetBT anyway?), but in fact, most Microsoft machines will look for a NetBT name before a DNS name, and attempts to reach the machine via HTTP or FTP from local clients will use NetBT resolution. If it's important to reach the machine from internal Microsoft machines, you need to protect it from masquerades. There are two ways to do this. If you have a reliable WINS configuration with a limited number of WINS servers, you can configure a static mapping for the name in each WINS server. If that is impractical, give the machine a name at least 16 characters long, and NetBT name resolution will be impossible, forcing clients to fall back to DNS, which is not vulnerable to the same sorts of trivial and/or accidental masquerading.

Simple TCP/IP services (Server and Workstation)

This package consists of *echo, chargen, discard, daytime,* and *quotd,* which are discussed further in Chapter 22, *Administrative Services.* The standard advice is to avoid it unless you need one of the services; it is hard to imagine how you could possibly need any of them. Do not install it.

SNMP service (Server and Workstation)

SNMP is a dangerous service that provides a great deal of information and control with very little security, and you should normally avoid it. Many references will advise you to install SNMP in order to get TCP/IP performance statistics in the Performance Monitor. If you install SNMP for this reason, you will also have installed the SNMP agent service, which you do not need to run and which should be disabled from the Services control panel.

If you do wish to run the SNMP agent, you must run a version of Windows NT later than 4.0 Service Pack 4; versions before that do not correctly handle settings and will provide read and write access to the "public" community.

You should also be sure to configure the SNMP Security Properties (available from the Network control panel in Services → SNMP Service → Security):

1. If you have an SNMP monitoring station, leave Send Authentication Trap on, and configure the correct address for the station into the Traps panel. This will cause the machine to send a warning message if it receives a request with an invalid community name in it. (This is all this option does; it does not actually enable any authentication beyond SNMP's default method, which uses the community name as a form of cleartext password.)

2. Edit the Accepted Community Names so that "public" is no longer accepted, and the only accepted value is an unguessable name unique to your site. *Do not leave this field blank!* If this field is blank, any community name will be accepted, and all SNMP requests will be valid.

3. Set Only Accept SNMP Packets from These Hosts. You must include a host here; put in your SNMP monitoring station's address if you intend to use one, or use 127.0.0.1 (the loopback address). Note that this relies on authenticating by source address. If attackers can forge an accepted address on an incoming packet, they can reset important networking parameters. This is especially dangerous because it is an attack that does not require reply packets to be useful. Do not use an SNMP monitoring station unless you can prevent forged packets with its address from reaching the machine.

The Services control panel

Once you have removed the services you don't want, there should be relatively little left in the Services control panel. You will probably want to disable all but the necessary services previously discussed and the services you intend to provide. You should be particularly careful to disable the UPS service and the Schedule service unless you are absolutely certain that they are required and you have taken steps to protect them from misuse. Both of these services have known vulnerabilities.

Turning Off Routing

As we discussed in Chapter 10, *Bastion Hosts*, most machines with more than one network interface will automatically attempt to route traffic between interfaces. You do not normally want a bastion host to do this. If you are not trying to configure a bastion host that is also a router, you should turn off routing, which is a three-part process:

1. Turn off services that advertise the system as a router.

2. Turn off IP forwarding, which actually does the routing.

3. If necessary, turn off source routing separately.

Under Windows NT, turning off IP forwarding can be done either from the Networking control panel (under Protocols → TCP/IP → Routing), by unchecking Enable IP Forwarding or from the registry by setting the following key to 0:

```
HKEY_LOCAL_MACHINE\SYSTEM\CurrentControlSet\Services\Tcpip\Parameters\IPEnableRouter
```

It will automatically be off if there is only one network interface. If you later add a second network interface, Windows NT may helpfully turn it on for you. Be sure to turn it off after you install all the interfaces you intend to have on the machine. In addition, the TCP/IP Properties dialog will not inform you if the registry change it is trying to make fails; you should verify by exiting and returning to the dialog to make certain that your change is still shown, or better yet by simply checking the value in the registry.

As Microsoft points out, the ease with which this can be changed is not particularly comforting from a security point of view:

> A major concern with [using a dual-interface Windows NT machine with routing turned off as a firewall] is that the separation between the Internet and your intranet depends on a single option in the TCP/IP configuration (or in the associated Registry entry)... An individual familiar with Windows NT configuration tools and administrative permissions can find and change the Router check box in a matter of minutes.
>
> —*Microsoft Windows NT Resource Kit Internet Guide*, Chapter 3

This is a major understatement on their part; an individual who actually remembers where to find it ought to be able to change it in well under a minute. In order to slow down an attacker, and also decrease your chances of accidentally reenabling IP forwarding yourself, set the permissions on the Parameters key so that Administrator has the same Special Access rights that Everyone has (Query Value, Create Subkey, Enumerate Subkeys, Notify, and Read Control) and additionally has Write DAC (so that if you want to change things later you can).* Note that this will create one situation in which TCP/IP Properties appears to work, but your changes silently disappear; in this situation, this is not necessarily a bad thing.

Installing and Modifying Services

Some of the services you want to provide may not be provided with your operating system. Others may be provided in versions that are inappropriate for use in a secure environment or are missing features you probably want. You will have to choose servers to provide these services and install them.

---

* If Everyone has Full Access permissions, you have failed to install current service packs on the machine. You are likely to have severe security problems.

Windows NT does not have an equivalent to the Unix TCP wrappers (which provide global controls that can be enforced on most services). Instead, you will need to secure every service separately. You should not assume that services are safe; reputable software companies often ship unsafe packages, and in many cases, their worst problems are easy to find and repair.

Install a test copy of the service on a machine that is otherwise stable and will not change while you are doing the installation. Use Find to identify all the files that were changed during the installation, and check to make sure that those files are acceptable. In particular:

- Make sure that file permissions are as restrictive as possible; arbitrary users shouldn't be able to write to any executables, configuration files, or temporary directories. If possible, limit read and execute permissions as well.

- Verify the permissions on all registry entries to make sure that arbitrary users can't change them. Again, you will probably want to limit read permissions as well. In particular, many services store passwords in registry keys, sometimes with extremely weak protection. You do not want these keys to be readable!

- If the program installs a user account, make sure that the password is set to something other than the program's default. If possible, change the account name to something other than the program's default.

- Make sure that all programs are run by users with appropriate permissions. Do not run services as Administrator unless they need to be run as Administrator. If you add special user accounts for services, make sure that they cannot be used as normal login accounts.

Note that many services have interesting interactions with hot fixes and service packs. Services, hot fixes, and service packs all have a tendency to change system files. You will need to install them in the correct order to make sure that you have the most desirable version of the system files. In general, this means installing the services first and then the hot fixes or service packs that you need. In a few cases, you may need to install hot fixes or service packs both before and after you install a service (for instance, if the service requires a particular service pack, you will have to install that service pack, install the service, and then install the service pack you want to run). Extremely rarely, you need to install the service after the hot fix or service pack (which means that you will need to reinstall the service if you install a new hot fix or service pack).

III

Internet Services

This part of the book describes the details of how to configure Internet services in a firewall environment. It presents general principles and then describes the details for nearly a hundred specific services. It concludes with two extended examples of configurations for sample firewalls.

13

Internet Services and Firewalls

This chapter gives an overview of the issues involved in using Internet services through a firewall, including the risks involved in providing services and the attacks against them, ways of evaluating implementations, and ways of analyzing services that are not detailed in this book.

The remaining chapters in Part III describe the major Internet services: how they work, what their packet filtering and proxying characteristics are, what their security implications are with respect to firewalls, and how to make them work with a firewall. The purpose of these chapters is to give you the information that will help you decide which services to offer at your site and to help you configure these services so they are as safe and as functional as possible in your firewall environment. We occasionally mention things that are not, in fact, Internet services but are related protocols, languages, or APIs that are often used in the Internet context or confused with genuine Internet services.

These chapters are intended primarily as a reference; they're not necessarily intended to be read in depth from start to finish, though you might learn a lot of interesting stuff by skimming this whole part of the book.

At this point, we assume that you are familiar with what the various Internet services are used for, and we concentrate on explaining how to provide those services through a firewall. For introductory information about what particular services are used for, see Chapter 2, *Internet Services*.

Where we discuss the packet filtering characteristics of particular services, we use the same abstract tabular form we used to show filtering rules in Chapter 8, *Packet Filtering*. You'll need to translate various abstractions like "internal", "external", and so on to appropriate values for your own configuration. See Chapter 8 for an explanation of how you can translate abstract rules to rules for particular products and packages, as well as more information on packet filtering in general.

Where we discuss the proxy characteristics of particular services, we rely on concepts and terminology discussed in Chapter 9, *Proxy Systems.*

Throughout the chapters in Part III, we'll show how each service's packets flow through a firewall. The following figures show the basic packet flow: when a service runs directly (Figure 13-1) and when a proxy service is used (Figure 13-2). The other figures in these chapters show variations of these figures for individual services. If there are no specific figures for a particular service, you can assume that these generic figures are appropriate for that service.

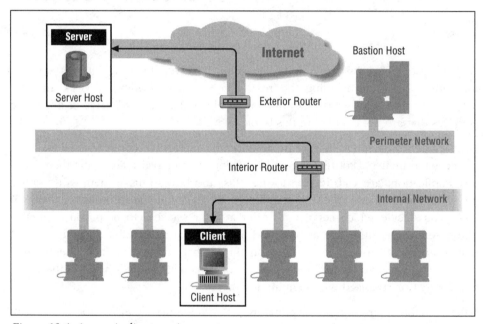

Figure 13-1. A generic direct service

 We frequently characterize client port numbers as "a random port number above 1023". Some protocols specify this as a requirement, and on others, it is merely a convention (spread to other platforms from Unix, where ports below 1024 cannot be opened by regular users). Although it is theoretically allowable for clients to use ports below 1024 on non-Unix platforms, it is extraordinarily rare: rare enough that many firewalls, including ones on major public sites that handle clients of all types, rely on this distinction and report never having rejected a connection because of it.

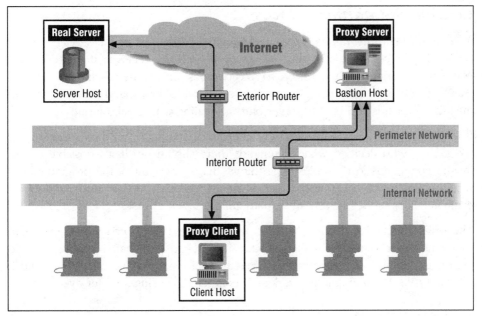

Figure 13-2. A generic proxy service

Attacks Against Internet Services

As we discuss Internet services and their configuration, certain concepts are going to come up repeatedly. These reflect the process of evaluating exactly what risks a given service poses. These risks can be roughly divided into two categories—first, attacks that involve making allowed connections between a client and a server, including:

- Command-channel attacks
- Data-driven attacks
- Third-party attacks
- False authentication of clients

and second, those attacks that get around the need to make connections, including:

- Hijacking
- Packet sniffing
- Data injection and modification
- Replay
- Denial of service

Command-Channel Attacks

A *command-channel attack* is one that directly attacks a particular service's server by sending it commands in the same way it regularly receives them (down its command channel). There are two basic types of command-channel attacks; attacks that exploit valid commands to do undesirable things, and attacks that send invalid commands and exploit server bugs in dealing with invalid input.

If it's possible to use valid commands to do undesirable things, that is the fault of the person who decided what commands there should be. If it's possible to use invalid commands to do undesirable things, that is the fault of the programmer(s) who implemented the protocol. These are two separate issues and need to be evaluated separately, but you are equally unsafe in either case.

The original headline-making Internet problem, the 1988 Morris worm, exploited two kinds of command-channel attacks. It attacked Sendmail by using a valid debugging command that many machines had left enabled and unsecured, and it attacked *finger* by giving it an overlength command, causing a buffer overflow.

Data-Driven Attacks

A data-driven attack is one that involves the data transferred by a protocol, instead of the server that implements it. Once again, there are two types of data-driven attacks; attacks that involve evil data, and attacks that compromise good data. Viruses transmitted in electronic mail messages are data-driven attacks that involve evil data. Attacks that steal credit card numbers in transit are data-driven attacks that compromise good data.

Third-Party Attacks

A third-party attack is one that doesn't involve the service you're intending to support at all but that uses the provisions you've made to support one service in order to attack a completely different one. For instance, if you allow inbound TCP connections to any port above 1024 in order to support some protocol, you are opening up a large number of opportunities for third-party attacks as people make inbound connections to completely different servers.

False Authentication of Clients

A major risk for inbound connections is *false authentication*: the subversion of the authentication that you require of your users, so that an attacker can successfully masquerade as one of your users. This risk is increased by some special properties of passwords.

In most cases, if you have a secret you want to pass across the network, you can encrypt the secret and pass it that way. That doesn't help if the information doesn't have to be understood to be used. For instance, encrypting passwords will not work because an attacker who is using packet sniffing can simply intercept and resend the encrypted password without having to decrypt it. (This is called a *playback attack* because the attacker records an interaction and plays it back later.) Therefore, dealing with authentication across the Internet requires something more complex than encrypting passwords. You need an authentication method where the data that passes across the network is nonreusable, so an attacker can't capture it and play it back.

Simply protecting you against playback attacks is not sufficient, either. An attacker who can find out or guess what the password is doesn't need to use a playback attack, and systems that prevent playbacks don't necessarily prevent password guessing. For instance, Windows NT's challenge/response system is reasonably secure against playback attacks, but the password actually entered by the user is the same every time, so if a user chooses to use "password", an attacker can easily guess what the password is.

Furthermore, if an attacker can convince the user that the attacker is your server, the user will happily hand over his username and password data, which the attacker can then use immediately or at leisure. To prevent this, either the client needs to authenticate itself to the server using some piece of information that's not passed across the connection (for instance, by encrypting the connection) or the server needs to authenticate itself to the client.

Hijacking

Hijacking attacks allow an attacker to take over an open terminal or login session from a user who has been authenticated and authorized by the system. Hijacking attacks generally take place on a remote computer, although it is sometimes possible to hijack a connection from a computer on the route between the remote computer and your local computer.

How can you protect yourself from hijacking attacks on the remote computer? The only way is to allow connections only from remote computers whose security you trust; ideally, these computers should be at least as secure as your own. You can apply this kind of restriction by using either packet filters or modified servers. Packet filters are easier to apply to a collection of systems, but modified servers on individual systems allow you more flexibility. For example, a modified FTP server might allow anonymous FTP from any host, but authenticated FTP only from specified hosts. You can't get this kind of control from packet filtering. Under Unix, connection control at the host level is available from Wietse Venema's TCP Wrapper or from wrappers in TIS FWTK (the *netacl* program); these may be easier to configure than packet filters but provide the same level of discrimination—by host only.

Hijacking by intermediate sites can be avoided using end-to-end integrity protection. If you use end-to-end integrity protection, intermediate sites will not be able to insert authentic packets into the data stream (because they don't know the appropriate key and the packets will be rejected) and therefore won't be able to hijack sessions traversing them. The IETF IPsec standard provides this type of protection at the IP layer under the name of "Authentication Headers", or AH protocol (RFC 2402). Application layer hijacking protection, along with privacy protection, can be obtained by adding a security protocol to the application; the most common choices for this are Transport Layer Security (TLS) or the Secure Socket Layer (SSL), but there are also applications that use the Generic Security Services Application Programming Interface (GSSAPI). For remote access to Unix systems the use of SSH can eliminate the risk of network-based session hijacking. IPsec, TLS, SSL, and GSSAPI are discussed further in Chapter 14, *Intermediary Protocols*. *ssh* is discussed in Chapter 18, *Remote Access to Hosts*.

Hijacking at the remote computer is quite straightforward, and the risk is great if people leave connections unattended. Hijacking from intermediate sites is a fairly technical attack and is only likely if there is some reason for people to target your site in particular. You may decide that hijacking is an acceptable risk for your own organization, particularly if you are able to minimize the number of accounts that have full access and the time they spend logged in remotely. However, you probably do not want to allow hundreds of people to log in from anywhere on the Internet. Similarly, you do not want to allow users to log in consistently from particular remote sites without taking special precautions, nor do you want users to log in to particularly secure accounts or machines from the Internet.

The risk of hijacking can be reduced by having an idle session policy with strict enforcement of timeouts. In addition, it's useful to have auditing controls on remote access so that you have some hope of noticing if a connection is hijacked.

Packet Sniffing

Attackers may not need to hijack a connection in order to get the information you want to keep secret. By simply watching packets pass—anywhere between the remote site and your site—they can see any unencrypted information that is being transferred. *Packet sniffing* programs automate this watching of packets.

Sniffers may go after passwords or data. Different risks are associated with each type of attack. Protecting your passwords against sniffing is usually easy: use one of the several mechanisms described in Chapter 21, *Authentication and Auditing Services*, to use nonreusable passwords. With nonreusable passwords, it doesn't matter if the password is captured by a sniffer; it's of no use to them because it cannot be reused.

Protecting your data against sniffers is more difficult. The data needs to be encrypted before it passes across the network. There are two means you might use for this kind of encryption; encrypting files that are going to be transferred, and encrypting communications links.

Encrypting files is appropriate when you are using protocols that transfer entire files (you're sending mail, using the Web, or explicitly transferring files), when you have a safe way to enter the information that will be used to encrypt them, and when you have a safe way to get the recipient the information needed to decrypt them. It's particularly useful if the file is going to cross multiple communications links, and you can't be sure that all of them will be secured, or if the file will spend time on hosts that you don't trust. For instance, if you're writing confidential mail on a laptop and using a public key encryption system, you can do the entire encryption on the machine you control and send on the entire encrypted file in safety, even if it will pass through multiple mail servers and unknown communications links.

Encrypting files won't help much if you're logging into a machine remotely. If you type in your mail on a laptop and encrypt it there, you're relatively safe. If you remotely log into a server from your laptop and then type in the mail and encrypt it, an attacker can simply watch you type it and may well be able to pick up any secret information that's involved in the encryption process.

In many situations, instead of encrypting the data in advance, it's more practical to encrypt the entire conversation. Either you can encrypt at the IP level via a virtual private network solution, or you can choose an encrypted protocol (for instance, SSH for remote shell access). We discuss virtual private networks in Chapter 5, *Firewall Technologies*, and we discuss the availability of encrypted protocols as we describe each protocol in the following chapters.

These days, eavesdropping and encryption are both widespread. You should require encryption on inbound services unless you have some way to be sure that no confidential data passes across them. You may also want to encrypt outbound connections, particularly if you have any reason to believe that the information in them is sensitive.

Data Injection and Modification

An attacker who can't successfully take over a connection may be able to change the data inside the connection. An attacker that controls a router between a client and a server can intercept a packet and modify it, instead of just reading it. In rare cases, even an attacker that doesn't control a router can achieve this (by sending the modified packet in such a way that it will arrive before the original packet).

Encrypting data won't protect you from this sort of attack. An attacker will still be able to modify the encrypted data. The attacker won't be able to predict what you'll get when you decrypt the data, but it certainly won't be what you expected. Encryption will keep an attacker from intentionally turning an order for 200 rubber chickens into an order for 2,000 rubber chickens, but it won't keep the attacker from turning the order into garbage that crashes your order input system. And you can't even be sure that the attacker won't turn the order into something else meaningful by accident.

Fully protecting services from modification requires some form of message integrity protection, where the packet includes a checksum value that is computed from the data and can't be recomputed by an attacker. Message integrity protection is discussed further in Appendix C, *Cryptography*.

Replay

An attacker who can't take over a connection or change a connection may still be able to do damage simply by saving up information that has gone past and sending it again. We've already discussed one variation of this attack, involving passwords.

There are two kinds of *replays*, ones in which you have to be able to identify certain pieces of information (for instance, the password attacks), and ones where you simply resend the entire packet. Many forms of encryption will protect you from attacks where the attacker is gathering information to replay, but they won't help you if it's possible to just reuse a packet without knowing what's in it.

Replaying packets doesn't work with TCP because of the sequence numbers, but there's no reason for it to fail with UDP-based protocols. The only protection against it is to have a protocol that will reject the replayed packet (for instance, by using timestamps or embedded sequence numbers of some sort). The protocol must also do some sort of message integrity checking to prevent an attacker from updating the intercepted packet.

Denial of Service

As we discussed in Chapter 1, *Why Internet Firewalls?*, a *denial of service* attack is one where the attacker isn't trying to get access to information but is just trying to keep anybody else from having access. Denial of service attacks can take a variety of forms, and it is impossible to prevent all of them.

Somebody undertaking a denial of service attack is like somebody who's determined to keep other people from accessing a particular library book. From the attackers' point of view, it's very desirable to have an attack that can't be traced back and that requires a minimum of effort (in a library, they implement this sort of effect by stealing all the copies of the book; on a network, they use source address forgery to exploit bugs). These attacks, however, tend to be preventable (in a library, you put in alarm systems; in a network, you filter out forged addresses). Other attacks require more effort and caution but are almost impossible to prevent. If a group of people bent on censorship coordinate their efforts, they can simply keep all the copies of a book legitimately checked out of the library. Similarly, a distributed attack can prevent other people from getting access to a service while using only legitimate means to reach the service.

Even though denial of service attacks cannot be entirely prevented, they can be made much more difficult to implement. First, servers should not become unavailable when invalid commands are issued. Poorly implemented servers may crash or loop in response to hostile input, which greatly simplifies the attacker's task. Second, servers should limit the resources allocated to any single entity. This includes:

- The number of open connections or outstanding requests
- The elapsed time a connection exists or a request is being processed
- The amount of processor time spent on a connection or request
- The amount of memory allocated to a connection or request
- The amount of disk space allocated to a connection or request

Protecting Services

How well does a firewall protect against these different types of attacks?

Command-channel attacks

A firewall can protect against command-channel attacks by restricting the number of machines to which attackers can open command channels and by providing a secured server on those machines. In some cases, it can also filter out clearly dangerous commands (for instance, invalid commands or commands you have decided not to allow).

Data-driven attacks

A firewall can't do much about data-driven attacks; the data has to be allowed through, or you won't actually be able to do anything. In some cases, it's possible to filter out bad data. For instance, you can run virus scanners over email and other file transfer protocols. Your best bet, however, is to educate users to the risks they run when they bring files to their machine and when they send data out, and to provide appropriate tools allowing them to protect their computers and data. These include virus checkers and encryption software.

Third-party attacks

Third-party attacks can sometimes be prevented by the same sort of tactics used against command-channel attacks: limit the hosts that are accessible to ones where you know only the desired services are available, and/or do protocol checking to make certain that the commands you're getting are for the service you're trying to allow.

False authentication of clients

A firewall cannot prevent false authentication of clients. It can, however, limit incoming connections to ones on which you enforce the use of nonreusable passwords.

Hijacking

A firewall can rarely do anything about hijacking. Using a virtual private network with encryption will prevent it; so will protocols that use encryption with a shared secret between the client and the server, which will keep the hijacker from being able to send valid packets. Using TCP implementations that have highly unpredictable sequence numbers will decrease the possibility of hijacking TCP connections. It will not protect you from a hijacker that can see the legitimate traffic. Even somewhat unpredictable sequence numbers will help; hijacking attempts will create a burst of invalid packets that may be detectable by a firewall or an intrusion detection system. (Sequence numbers and hijacking are discussed in more detail in Chapter 4, *Packets and Protocols*.)

Packet sniffing

A firewall cannot do anything to prevent packet sniffing. Virtual private networks and encrypted protocols will not prevent packet sniffing, but they will make it less damaging.

Data injection and modification

There's very little a firewall can do about data injection or modification. A virtual private network will protect against it, as will a protocol that has message integrity checking.

Replay

Once again, a firewall can do very little about replay attacks. In a few cases, where there is literally a replay of exactly the same packet, a stateful packet filter may be able to detect the duplication; however, in many cases, it's perfectly reasonable for that to happen. The primary protection against replay attacks is using a protocol that's not vulnerable to them (one that involves message integrity and includes a timestamp, for instance).

Denial of service

Firewalls can help prevent denial of service attacks by filtering out forged or malformed requests before they reach servers. In addition, they can sometimes provide assistance by limiting the resources available to an attacker. For instance, a firewall can limit the rate with which it sends traffic to a server, or control the balance of allowed traffic so that a single source cannot monopolize services.

Evaluating the Risks of a Service

When somebody requests that you allow a service through your firewall, you will go through a process of evaluation to decide exactly what to do with the service. In the following chapters, we give you a combination of information and analysis, based on our evaluations. This section attempts to lay out the evaluation process for you, so that you can better understand the basis for our statements, and so that you can make your own evaluations of services and servers we don't discuss.

When you evaluate services, it's important not to make assumptions about things beyond your control. For instance, if you're planning to run a server, you shouldn't assume that the clients that connect to it are going to be the clients it's designed to work with; an attacker can perfectly well write a new client that does things differently. Similarly, if you're running a client, you shouldn't assume that all the servers you connect to are well behaved unless you have some means of controlling them.

What Operations Does the Protocol Allow?

Different protocols are designed with different levels of security. Some of them are quite safe by design (which doesn't mean that they're safe once they've been implemented!), and some of them are unsafe as designed. While a bad implementation can make a good protocol unsafe, there's very little that a good implementation can do for a bad protocol, so the first step in evaluating a service is evaluating the underlying protocol.

This may sound dauntingly technical, and indeed it can be. However, a perfectly useful first cut can often be done without any actual knowledge of the details of how the protocol works, just by thinking about what it's supposed to be doing.

What is it designed to do?

No matter how little else you know about a protocol, you know what it's supposed to be able to do, and that gives you a powerful first estimate of how risky it must be. In general, the less a protocol does, the safer it is.

For instance, suppose you are going to invent a protocol that will be used to talk to a coffee maker, so that you can put your coffee maker on the Web. You could, of course, build a web server into the coffee maker (or wait for coffee makers to come with web servers, which undoubtedly will happen soon) or use an existing protocol,* but as a rugged individualist you have decided to make up a completely new protocol. Should you allow this protocol through your firewall?

Well, if the protocol just allows people to ask the coffee maker how much coffee is available and how hot it is, that sounds OK. You probably don't care who has that information. If you're doing something very secret, maybe it's not OK. What if the competition finds out you're suddenly making coffee in the middle of the night? (The U.S. government discovered at one point that journalists were tracking important news stories by watching the rates at which government agencies ordered pizza deliveries late at night.)

What if the protocol lets people make coffee? Well, that depends. If there's a single "make coffee" command, and the coffee maker will execute it only if everything's set up to make coffee, that's still probably OK. But what if there's a command for boiling the water and one for letting it run through the coffee? Now your competitors can reduce your efficiency rate by ensuring your coffee is weak and undrinkable.

What if you decided that you wanted real flexibility, so you designed a protocol that gave access to each switch, sensor, and light in the machine, allowing them to be checked and set, and then you provided a program with settings for making weak coffee, normal coffee, and strong coffee? That would be a very useful protocol, providing all sorts of interesting control options, and a malicious person using it could definitely explode the coffee machine.

Suppose you're not interested in running the coffee machine server; you just want to let people control the coffee machine from your site with the coffee machine controller. So far, there doesn't seem to be much reason for concern (particularly if you're far enough away to avoid injury when the coffee machine explodes). The server doesn't send much to the client, just information about the state of the coffee machine. The client doesn't send the server any information about itself, just instructions about the coffee machine.

You could still easily design a coffee machine client that would be risky. For instance, you could add a feature to shut down the client machine if the coffee machine was about to explode. It would make the client a dangerous thing to run without changing the protocol at all.

---

* An appropriate choice would be the Hyper Text Coffee Pot Control Protocol (HTCPCP), defined in RFC 2324, April 1, 1998, but like most RFCs issued on April 1st, it is rarely implemented.

While you will probably never find yourself debating coffee-making protocols, this discussion covers the questions you'll want to ask about real-life protocols; what sort of information do they give out and what can they change? The following table provides a very rough outline of things that make a protocol more or less safe.

Safer	Less Safe
Receives data that will be displayed only to the user	Changes the state of the machine
Exchanges predefined data in a known format	Exchanges data flexibly, with multiple types and the ability to add new types
Gives out no information	Gives out sensitive information
Allows the other end to execute very specific commands	Allows the other end to execute flexible commands

Is the level of authentication and authorization it uses appropriate for doing that?

The more risky an operation is, the more control you want to have over who does it. This is actually a question of authorization (who is allowed to do something), but in order to be able to determine authorization information, you must first have good authentication. It's no point being able to say "Cadmus may do this, but Dorian may not", if you can't be sure which one of them is trying to do what.

A protocol for exchanging audio files may not need any authentication (after all, we've already decided it's not very dangerous), but a protocol for remotely controlling a computer definitely needs authentication. You want to know exactly who you are talking to before you decide that it's okay for them to issue the "delete all files" command.

Authentication can be based on the host or on the user and can range considerably in strength. A protocol could give you any of the following kinds of information about clients:

- No information about where a connection comes from
- Unverifiable information (for instance, the client may send a username or hostname to the server expecting the server to just trust this information, as in SMTP)
- A password or other authenticator that an attacker can easily get hold of (for instance, the community string in SNMP or the cleartext password used by standard Telnet)
- A nonforgeable way to authenticate (for instance, an SSH negotiation)

Once the protocol provides an appropriate level of authentication, it also needs to provide appropriate controls over authorization. For instance, a protocol that allows both harmless and dangerous commands should allow you to give some users permission to do everything, and others permission to do only harmless things. A protocol that provides good authentication but no authorization control is a protocol that permits revenge but not protection (you can't keep people from doing the wrong thing; you can only track them down once they've done it).

Does it have any other commands in it?

If you have a chance to actually analyze a protocol in depth, you will want to make sure that there aren't any hidden surprises. Some protocols include little-used commands that may be more risky than the commands that are the main purpose of the protocol. One example that occurred in an early protocol document for SMTP was the TURN command. It caused the SMTP protocol to reverse the direction of flow of electronic mail; a host that had originally been sending mail could start to receive it instead. The intention was to support polling and systems that were not always connected to the network. The protocol designers didn't take authentication into account, however; since SMTP has no authentication, SMTP senders rely on their ability to control where a connection goes to as a way to identify the recipient. With TURN, a random host could contact a server, claim to be any other machine, and then issue a TURN to receive the other machine's mail. Thus, the relatively obscure TURN command made a major and surprising change in the security of the protocol. The TURN command is no longer specified in the SMTP protocol.

What Data Does the Protocol Transfer?

Even if the protocol is reasonably secure itself, you may be worried about the information that's transferred. For instance, you can imagine a credit card authorization service where there was no way that a hostile client could damage or trick the server and no way that a hostile server could damage or trick the client, but where the credit card numbers were sent unencrypted. In this case, there's nothing inherently dangerous about running the programs, but there is a significant danger to the information, and you would not want to allow people at your site to use the service.

When you evaluate a service, you want to consider what information you may be sharing with it, and whether that information will be appropriately protected. In the preceding TURN command example, you would certainly have been alert to the problem. However, there are many instances that are more subtle. For instance, suppose people want to play an online game through your firewall—no important private information could be involved there, right? Wrong. They might need to give usernames and passwords, and that information provides important clues for attackers. Most people use the same usernames and passwords over and over again.

In addition to the obvious things (data that you know are important secrets, like your credit card number, the location the plutonium is hidden in, and the secret formula for your product), you will want to be careful to watch out for protocols that transfer any of the following:

- Information that identifies individual people (Social Security numbers or tax identifiers, bank account numbers, private telephone numbers, and other information that might be useful to an impersonator or hostile person)

- Information about your internal network or host configuration, including software or hardware serial numbers, machine names that are not otherwise made public, and information about the particular software running on machines

- Information that can be used to access systems (passwords and usernames, for instance)

How Well Is the Protocol Implemented?

Even the best protocol can be unsafe if it's badly implemented. You may be running a protocol that doesn't contain a "shutdown system" command but have a server that shuts down the system anyway whenever it gets an illegal command.

This is bad programming, which is appallingly common. While some subtle and hard-to-avoid attacks involve manipulating servers to do things that are not part of the protocol the servers are implementing, almost all of the attacks of this kind involve the most obvious and easy ways to avoid errors. The number of commercial programs that would receive failing grades in an introductory programming class is beyond belief.

In order to be secure, a program needs to be very careful with the data that it uses. In particular, it's important that the program verify assumptions about data that comes from possibly hostile sources. What sources are possibly hostile depends on the environment that the program is running in. If the program is running on a secured bastion host with no hostile users, and you are willing to accept the risk that any attacker who gets access to the machine has complete control over the program, the only hostile data source you need to worry about is the network.

On the other hand, if there are possibly hostile users on the machine, or you want to maintain some degree of security if an attacker gets limited access to the machine, then all incoming data must be untrusted. This includes command-line arguments, configuration data (from configuration files or a resource manager), data that is part of the execution environment, and all data read from the network. Command-line arguments should be checked to make sure they contain only valid characters; some languages interpret special characters in filenames to mean "run the following program and give me the output instead of reading from the file". If an option exists to use an alternate configuration file, an attacker might be able to construct an alternative that would allow him or her greater access. The execution environment might allow override variables, perhaps to control where temporary files are created; such values need to be carefully validated before using them. All of these flaws have been discovered repeatedly in real programs on all kinds of operating systems.

An example of poor argument checking, which attackers still scan for, occurred in one of the sample CGI programs that were originally distributed with the NCSA HTTP server. The program was installed by default when the software was built and was intended to be an example of CGI programming. The program used an external utility to perform some functions, and it gave the utility information that was specified by the remote user. The author of the program was even aware of problems that can occur when running external utilities using data you have received. Code had been included to check for a list of bad values. Unfortunately, the list of bad values was incomplete, and that allowed arbitrary commands to be run by the HTTP server. A better approach, based upon "That Which Is Not Expressly Permitted Is Prohibited", would have been to check the argument for allowable characters.

The worst result of failure to check arguments is a "buffer overflow", which is the basis for a startlingly large number of attacks. In these attacks, a program is handed more input data than its programmer expected; for instance, a program that's expecting a four-character command is handed more than 1024 characters. This sort of attack can be used against any program that accepts user-defined input data and is easy to use against almost all network services. For instance, you can give a very long username or password to any server that authenticates users (FTP, POP, IMAP, etc.), use a very long URL to an HTTP server, or give an extremely long recipient name to an SMTP server. A well-written program will read in only as much data as it was expecting. However, a sloppily written program may be written to read in all the available input data, even though it has space for only some of it.

When this happens, the extra data will overwrite parts of memory that were supposed to contain something else. At this point, there are three possibilities. First, the memory that the extra data lands on could be memory that the program isn't allowed to write on, in which case the program will promptly be killed off by the operating system. This is the most frequent result of this sort of error.

Second, the memory could contain data that's going to be used somewhere else in the program. This can have all sorts of nasty effects; again, most of them result in the program's crashing as it looks up something and gets a completely wrong answer. However, careful manipulation may get results that are useful to an attacker. For instance, suppose you have a server that lets users specify what name they'd like to use, so it can say "Hi, Fred!" It asks the user for a nickname and then writes that to a file. The user doesn't get to specify what the name of the file is; that's specified by a configuration file read when the server starts up. The name of the nickname file will be in a variable somewhere. If that variable is overwritten, the program will write its nicknames to the file with the new value as its name. If the program runs as a privileged user, that file could be an important part of the operating system. Very few operating systems work well if you replace critical system files with text files.

Finally, the memory that gets overwritten could be memory that's not supposed to contain data at all, but instead contains instructions that are going to be executed. Once again, this will usually cause a crash because the result will not be a valid sequence of instructions. However, if the input data is specifically tailored for the computer architecture the program is running on, it can put in valid instructions. This attack is technically difficult, and it is usually specific to a given machine and operating system type; an attack that works on a Sun running Solaris will not work on an Intel machine running Solaris, nor will an attack that works on the same Intel machine running Windows 95. If you can't move a binary program between two machines, they won't both be vulnerable to exactly the same form of this attack.

Preventing a "buffer overflow" kind of attack is a matter of sensible programming, checking that input falls within expected limits. Some programming languages automatically include the basic size checks that prevent buffer overflows. Notably, C does not do this, but Java does.

Does it have any other commands in it?

Some protocol implementations include extra debugging or administrative features that are not specified in the protocol. These may be poorly implemented or less well thought out and can be more risky than those specified in the protocol. The most famous example of this was exploited by the 1988 Morris worm, which issued a special SMTP debugging command that allowed it to tell Sendmail to execute anything the intruder liked. The debugging command is not specified in the SMTP protocol.

What Else Can Come in If I Allow This Service?

Suppose somebody comes up with a perfect protocol—it protects the server from the client and vice versa, it securely encrypts data, and all the known implementations of it are bullet proof. Should you just open a hole for that protocol to any machine on your network? No, because you can't guarantee that every internal and external host is running that protocol at that port number.

There's no guarantee that traffic on a port is using the protocol that you're interested in. This is particularly true for protocols that use large numbers of ports or ports above 1024 (where port numbers are not assigned to individual protocols), but it can be true for any protocol and any port number. For instance, a number of programs send protocols other than HTTP to port 80 because firewalls frequently allow all traffic to port 80.

In general, there are two ways to ensure that the packets you're letting in belong to the protocol that you want. One is to run them through a proxy system or an intelligent packet filter that can check them; the other is to control the destination hosts they're going to. Protocol design can have a significant effect on your ability to implement either of these solutions.

If you're using a proxy system or an intelligent packet filter to make sure that you're allowing in only the protocol that you want, it needs to be able to tell valid packets for that protocol from invalid ones. This won't work if the protocol is encrypted, if it's extremely complex, or if it's extremely generic. If the protocol involves compression or otherwise changes the position of important data, validating it may be too slow to be practical. In these situations, you will either have to control the hosts that use the ports, or accept the risk that people will use other protocols.

Analyzing Other Protocols

In this book, we discuss a large number of protocols, but inevitably there are some that we've left out. We've left out protocols that we felt were no longer popular (like FSP, which appeared in the first edition), protocols that change often (including protocols for specific games), protocols that are rarely run through firewalls (including most routing protocols), and protocols where there are large numbers of competitors with no single clear leader (including remote access protocols for Windows machines). And those are just the protocols that we intentionally decided to leave out; there are also all the protocols that we haven't heard about, that we forgot about, or that hadn't been invented yet when we wrote this edition.

How do you go about analyzing protocols that we don't discuss in this book? The first question to ask is: Do you really need to run the protocol across your firewall? Perhaps there is some other satisfactory way to provide or access the service desired using a protocol already supported by your firewall. Maybe there is some way to solve the underlying problem without providing the service across the firewall at all. It's even possible that the protocol is so risky that there is no satisfactory justification for running it. Before you worry about how to provide a protocol, analyze the problem you're trying to solve.

If you really need to provide a protocol across your firewall, and it's not discussed in later chapters, how do you determine what ports it uses and so on? While it's sometimes possible to determine this information from program, protocol, or standards documentation, the easiest way to figure it out is usually to ask somebody else, such as the members of the Firewalls mailing list* (see Appendix A, *Resources*).

If you have to determine the answer yourself, the easiest way to do it is usually empirically. Here's what you should do:

1. Set up a test system that's running as little as possible other than the application you want to test.

2. Next, set up another system to monitor the packets to and from the test system (using *etherfind*, Network Monitor, *netsnoop, tcpdump,* or some other package that lets you watch traffic on the local network). Note that this system must be able to see the traffic; if you are attaching systems to a switch, you will need to put the monitoring system on an administrative port, or otherwise rearrange your networking so that the traffic can be monitored.

3. Run the application on the test system and see what the monitoring system records.

You may need to repeat this procedure for every client implementation and every server implementation you intend to use. There are occasionally unpredictable differences between implementations (e.g., some DNS clients always use TCP, even though most DNS clients use UDP by default).

You may also find it useful to use a general-purpose client to connect to the server to see what it's doing. Some text-based services will work perfectly well if you simply connect with a Telnet client (see Chapter 18, *Remote Access to Hosts*, for more information about Telnet). Others are UDP-based or otherwise more particular, but you can usually use *netcat* to connect to them (see Appendix B, *Tools*, for information on where to find *netcat)*. You should avoid doing this kind of testing on production machines; it's not unusual to discover that simple typing mistakes are sufficient to cause servers to go haywire. This is something useful to know before you allow anybody to access the server from the Internet, but it's upsetting to discover it by crashing a production system.

This sort of detective work will be simplified if you have a tool that allows you to match a port number to a process (without looking at every running process). Although *netstat* will tell you which ports are in use, it doesn't always tell you the processes that are using them. A popular tool for this purpose on Windows NT is

---

* But make sure you check the archives first, to see if the question has already been asked and answered.

Finding Assigned Port Numbers

Port numbers are officially assigned by the Internet Assigned Number Authority (IANA). They used to be documented in an IETF RFC; a new assigned numbers RFC was issued every few years (generally carefully timed to be a round number). These days, this would be an extremely large document, so instead, all numbers assigned by IANA are documented by files at an FTP site:

> *ftp://ftp.isi.edu/in-notes/iana/assignments*

Port numbers are found in the file named *port-numbers*. Not all protocols use well-defined and legally assigned port numbers, and the names that protocols are given in the assignments list are sometimes misleading (for instance, there are numerous listed protocols with names like "sqlnet" and "sql-net", none of which is Oracle's SQL*Net). Nonetheless, this is a useful starting place for clues about the relationship between protocols and port numbers.

---

inzider. Under Unix, this is usually done with *fuser*, which is provided with the operating system on most systems; versions of Unix that do not have *fuser* will probably have an equivalent with some other name. Another useful Unix tool for examining ports and the programs that are using them is *lsof*. Information on finding *inzider* and *lsof* is in Appendix B.

What Makes a Good Firewalled Service?

The ideal service to run through a firewall is one that makes a single TCP connection in one direction for each session. It should make that connection from a randomly allocated port on the client to an assigned port on the server, the server port should be used only by this particular service, and the commands it sends over that connection should all be secure. The following sections look at these ideal situations and some that aren't so ideal.

TCP Versus Other Protocols

Because TCP is a connection-oriented protocol, it's easy to proxy; you go through the overhead of setting up the proxy only once, and then you continue to use that connection. UDP has no concept of connections; every packet is a separate transaction requiring a separate decision from the proxy server. TCP is therefore easier to proxy (although there are UDP proxies). Similarly, ICMP is difficult to proxy because each packet is a separate transaction. Once again, ICMP is harder to proxy than TCP but not impossible; some ICMP proxies do exist.

The situation is much the same for packet filters. It's relatively easy to allow TCP through a firewall and control what direction connections are made in; you can use filtering on the ACK bit to ensure that you allow internal clients only to initiate connections, while still letting in responses. With UDP or ICMP, there's no way to easily set things up this way. Using stateful packet filters, you can watch for packets that appear to be responses, but you can never be sure that a packet is genuinely a response to an earlier one, and you may be waiting for responses to packets that don't require one.

One Connection per Session

It's easy for a firewall to intercept the initial connection from a client to a server. It's harder for it to intercept a return connection. With a proxy, either both ends of the conversation have to be aware of the existence of the proxy server, or the server needs to be able to interpret and modify the protocol to make certain the return connection is made correctly and uniquely. With plain packet filtering, the inbound connection has to be permitted all the time, which often will allow attackers access to ports used by other protocols. Stateful packet filtering, like proxying, has to be able to interpret the protocol to figure out where the return connection is going to be and open a hole for it.

For example, in normal-mode FTP the client opens a control connection to the server. When data needs to be transferred:

1. The client chooses a random port above 1023 and prepares it to accept a connection.
2. The client sends a PORT command to the server containing the IP address of the machine and the port the client is listening on.
3. The server then opens a new connection to that port.

In order for a proxy server to work, the proxy server must:

1. Intercept the PORT command the client sends to the server.
2. Set up a new port to listen on.
3. Connect back to the client on the port the client specified.
4. Send a replacement PORT command (using the port number on the proxy) to the FTP server.
5. Accept the connection from the FTP server, and transfer data back and forth between it and the client.

It's not enough for the proxy server to simply read the PORT command on the way past because that port may already be in use. A packet filter must either allow all inbound connections to ports above 1023, or intercept the PORT command and create a temporary rule for that port. Similar problems are going to arise in any protocol requiring a return connection.

Anything more complex than an outbound connection and a return is even worse. The *talk* service is an example; see the discussion in Chapter 19, *Real-Time Conferencing Services*, for an example of a service with a tangled web of connections that's almost impossible to pass through a firewall. (It doesn't help any that *talk* is partly UDP-based, but even if it were all TCP, it would still be a firewall designer's nightmare.)

One Session per Connection

It's almost as bad to have multiple sessions on the same connection as it is to have multiple connections for the same session. If a connection is used for only one purpose, the firewall can usually make security checks and logs at the beginning of the connection and then pay very little attention to the rest of the transaction. If a connection is used for multiple purposes, the firewall will need to continue to examine it to see if it's still being used for something that's acceptable.

Assigned Ports

For a firewall, the ideal thing is for each protocol to have its own port number. Obviously, this makes things easier for packet filters, which can then reliably identify the protocol by the port it's using, but it also simplifies life for proxies. The proxy has to get the connection somehow, and that's easier to manage if the protocol uses a fixed port number that can easily be redirected to the proxy. If the protocol uses a port number selected at configuration time, that port number will have to be configured into the proxy or packet filter as well. If the protocol uses a negotiated or dynamically assigned port, as RPC-based protocols do, the firewall has to be able to intercept and interpret the port negotiation or lookup. (See Chapter 14, *Intermediary Protocols*, for more information about RPC.)

Furthermore, for security it's desirable for the protocol to have its very own assigned port. It's always tempting to layer things onto an existing protocol that the firewall already permits; that way, you don't have to worry about changing the configuration of the firewall. However, when you layer protocols that way, you change the security of the firewall, whether or not you change its configuration. There is no way to let a new protocol through without having the risks of that new protocol; hiding it in another protocol will not make it safer, just harder to inspect.

Protocol Security

Some services are technically easy to allow through a firewall but difficult to secure with a firewall. If a protocol is inherently unsafe, passing it through a firewall, even with a proxy, will not make it any safer, unless you also modify it. For example, X11 is mildly tricky to proxy, for reasons discussed at length in Chapter 18, *Remote Access to Hosts*, but the real reason it's difficult to secure through firewalls has nothing to do with technical issues (proxy X servers are not uncommon as ways to extend X capabilities). The real reason is that X provides a number of highly insecure abilities to a client, and an X proxy system for a firewall needs to provide extra security.

The two primary ways to secure inherently unsafe protocols are authentication and protocol modification. *Authentication* allows you to be certain that you trust the source of the communication, even if you don't trust the protocol; this is part of the approach to X proxying taken by SSH. *Protocol modification* requires you to catch unsafe operations and at least offer the user the ability to prevent them. This is reasonably possible with X (and TIS FWTK provides a proxy called *x-gw* that does this), but it requires more application knowledge than would be necessary for a safer protocol.

If it's difficult to distinguish between safe and unsafe operations in a protocol, or impossible to use the service at all if unsafe operations are prevented, and you cannot restrict connections to trusted sources, a firewall may not be a viable solution. In that case, there may be no good solution, and you may be reduced to using a victim host, as discussed in Chapter 10, *Bastion Hosts*. Some people consider HTTP to be such a protocol (because it may end up transferring programs that are executed transparently by the client).

Choosing Security-Critical Programs

The world of Internet servers is evolving rapidly, and you may find that you want to use a server that has not been mentioned here in a security-critical position. How do you figure out whether or not it is secure?

My Product Is Secure Because...

The first step is to discount any advertising statements you may have heard about it. You may hear people claim that their server is secure because:

* It contains no publicly available code, so it's secret.
* It contains publicly available code, so it's been well reviewed.

- It is built entirely from scratch, so it didn't inherit any bugs from any other products.

- It is built on an old, well-tested code base.

- It doesn't run as root (under Unix) or as Administrator or LocalSystem (under Windows NT).

- It doesn't run under Unix.

- It doesn't run on a Microsoft operating system.

- There are no known attacks against it.

- It uses public key cryptography (or some other secure-sounding technology).

None of these things guarantees security or reliability. Horrible security bugs have been found in programs with all these characteristics.

It contains no publicly available code, so it's secret

People don't need to be able to see the code to a program in order to find problems with it. In fact, most attacks are found by trying attack methods that worked on similar programs, watching what the program does, or looking for vulnerabilities in the protocol, none of which require access to the source code. It is also possible to reverse-engineer an application to find out exactly how it was written. This can take a considerable amount of time, but even if you are not willing to spend the time, it doesn't mean that attackers feel the same way. Attackers are also unlikely to obey any software license agreements that prohibit reverse engineering.

In addition, some vendors who make this claim apply extremely narrow definitions of "publicly available code". For instance, they may in fact use licensed code that is distributed in source format and is free for noncommercial use. Check copyright acknowledgments—a program that includes copyright acknowledgments for the University of California Board of Regents, for instance, almost certainly includes code from some version of the Berkeley Unix operating system, which is widely available. There's nothing wrong with that, but if you want to use something based on secret source code, you deserve to get what you're paying for.

It contains publicly available code, so it's been well reviewed

Publicly available code could be well reviewed, but there's no guarantee. Thousands of people can read publicly available code, but most of them don't. In any case, reviewing code after it's written isn't a terribly effective way of ensuring its security; good design and testing are far more efficient.

People also point out that publicly available code gets more bug fixes and more rapid bug fixes than most privately held code; this is true, but this increased rate of change also adds new bugs.

It is built entirely from scratch, so it didn't inherit any bugs from any other products

No code is bug free. Starting from scratch replaces the old bugs with new bugs. They might be less harmful or more harmful. They might also be identical; people tend to think along the same lines, so it's not uncommon for different programmers to produce the same bug. (See Knight, Leveson, and St. Jean, "A Large-Scale Experiment in N-Version Programming," Fault-Tolerant Computing Systems Conference 15, for an actual experience with common bugs.)

It is built on an old, well-tested code base

New problems show up in old code all the time. Worse yet, old problems that hadn't been exploited yet suddenly become exploitable. Something that's been around for a long time probably isn't vulnerable to attacks that used to be popular, but that doesn't predict much about its resistance to future attacks.

It doesn't run as root/Administrator/LocalSystem

A program that doesn't run as one of the well-known privileged accounts may be safer than one that does. At the very least, if it runs amok, it won't have complete control of your entire computer. However, that's a very long distance from actually being safe. For instance, no matter what user is involved, a mail delivery system has to be able to write mail into users' mailboxes. If the mail delivery system can be subverted, it can be used to fill up disks or forge email, no matter what account it runs as. Many mail systems have more power than that.

There are two separate problems with services that are run as "unprivileged" users. The first is that the privileges needed for the service to function carry risks with them. A mail system must be able to deliver mail, and that's inherently risky. The second is that few operating systems let you control privileges so precisely that you can give a service exactly the privileges that it needs. The ability to deliver mail often comes with the ability to write files to all sorts of other places, for instance. Many programs introduce a third problem by creating accounts to run the service and failing to turn off default privileges that are unneeded. For instance, most programs that create special accounts to run the service fail to turn off the ability for their special accounts to log in. Programs rarely need to log in, but attackers often do.

It doesn't run under Unix, or it doesn't run on a Microsoft operating system

People produce dozens of reasons why other operating systems are less secure than their favorite one. (Unix source code is widely available to attackers! Microsoft source code is too big! The Unix root concept is inherently insecure! Windows NT's layered model isn't any better!) The fact is, almost all of these arguments have a grain of truth. Both Unix and Windows NT have serious design flaws as secure operating systems; so does every other popular operating system.

Nonetheless, it's possible to write secure software on almost any operating system, with enough effort, and it's easy to write insecure software on any operating system. In some circumstances, one operating system may be better matched to the service you want to provide than another, but most of the time, the security of a service depends on the effort that goes into securing it, both at design and at deployment.

There are no known attacks against it

Something can have no known attacks without being at all safe. It might not have an installed base large enough to attract attackers; it might be vulnerable but usually installed in conjunction with something easier to attack; it might just not have been around long enough for anybody to get around to it; it might have known flaws that are difficult enough to exploit that nobody has yet implemented attacks for them. All of these conditions are temporary.

It uses public key cryptography (or some other secure-sounding technology)

As of this writing, public key cryptography is a popular victim for this kind of argument because most people don't understand much about how it works, but they know it's supposed to be exciting and secure. You therefore see firewall products that say they're secure because they use public key cryptography, but that don't say what specific form of public key cryptography and what they use it for. This is like toasters that claim that they make perfect toast every time because of "digital processing technology". They can be digitally processing anything from the time delay to the temperature to the degree of color-change in the bread, and a digital timer will burn your toast just as often as an analog one.

Similarly, there's good public key cryptography, bad public key cryptography, and irrelevant public key cryptography. Merely adding public key cryptography to some random part of a product won't make it secure. The same is true of any other technology, no matter how exciting it is. A supplier who makes this sort of claim should be prepared to back it up by providing details of what the technology does, where it's used, and how it matters.

Their Product Is Insecure Because...

You'll also get people who claim that other people's software is insecure (and therefore unusable or worse than their competing product) because:

- It's been mentioned in a CERT-CC advisory or on a web site listing vulnerabilities.
- It's publicly available.
- It's been successfully attacked.

It's been mentioned in a CERT-CC advisory or on a web site listing vulnerabilities

CERT-CC issues advisories for programs that are supposed to be secure, but that have known problems for which fixes are available from the supplier. While it's always unfortunate to have a problem show up, if there's a CERT-CC advisory for it, at least you know that the problem was unintentional and the vendor has taken steps to fix it. A program with no CERT-CC advisories might have no problems; but it might also be completely insecure by design, be distributed by a vendor who never fixes security problems, or have problems that were never reported to CERT-CC. Since CERT-CC is relatively inactive outside of the Unix world, problems on non-Unix platforms are less likely to show up there, but they still exist.

Other lists of vulnerabilities are often a better reflection of actual risks, since they will list problems that the vendor has chosen to ignore and problems that are there by design. On the other hand, they're still very much a popularity contest. The "exploit lists" kept by attackers, and people trying to keep up with them, focus heavily on attacks that provide the most compromises for the least effort. That means that popular programs are mentioned often, and unpopular programs don't get much publicity, even if the popular programs are much more secure than the unpopular ones.

In addition, people who use this argument often provide big scary numbers without putting them in context; what does it mean if you say that a given web site lists 27 vulnerabilities in a program? If the web site is carefully run by a single administrator, that might be 27 separate vulnerabilities; if it's not, it may be the same 9 vulnerabilities reported three times each. In either case, it's not very interesting if competing programs have 270!

It's publicly available

We've already argued that code doesn't magically become secure by being made available for inspection. The other side of that argument is that it doesn't magically become insecure, either. A well-written program doesn't have the kind of bugs that make it vulnerable to attack just because people have read the code.

(And most attackers don't actually read code any more frequently than defenders do—in both cases, the conscientious and careful read the code, and the vast majority of people just compile it and hope.)

In general, publicly available code is modified faster than private code, which means that security problems are fixed more rapidly when they are found. This higher rate of change has downsides, which we discussed earlier, but it also means that you are less likely to be vulnerable to old bugs.

It's been successfully attacked

Obviously, you don't want to install software that people already know how to attack. However, what you should pay the most attention to is not attacks but the response to them. A successful attack (even a very high-profile and public successful attack) may not be important if the problem was novel and rapidly fixed. A pattern where variations on the same problem show up repeatedly or where the supplier is slow to fix problems is genuinely worrisome, but a single successful attack usually isn't, even if it makes a national newspaper.

Real Indicators of Security

Any of the following things should increase your comfort:

- Security was one of the design criteria.
- The supplier appears to be aware of major types of security problems and can speak to how they have been avoided.
- It is possible for you to review the code.
- Somebody you know and trust actually has reviewed the code.
- A process is in place to distribute notifications of security problems and updates to the server.
- The server fully implements a recent (but accepted) version of the protocol.
- The program uses standard error-logging mechanisms (*syslog* under Unix, the Event Viewer under Windows NT).
- There is a secure software distribution mechanism.

Security was one of the design criteria

The first step towards making a secure program is trying to make one. It's not something you can achieve by accident. The supplier should have convincing evidence that security was kept in mind at the design stage, and that the kind of security they had in mind is the same kind that you have in mind. It's not enough for "security" to be a checkbox item on a list somewhere. Ask what they were try-ing to secure, and how this affected the final product.

For instance, a mail system may list "security" as a goal because it incorporates anti-spamming features or facilitates encryption of mail messages as they pass across the Internet. Those are both nice security goals, but they don't address the security of the server itself if an attacker starts sending it evil commands.

The supplier can discuss how major security problems were avoided

Even if you're trying to be secure, you can't get there if you don't know how. Somebody associated with your supplier and responsible for the program should be able to intelligently discuss the risks involved, and what was done about them. For instance, if the program takes user-supplied input, somebody should be able to explain to you what's been done to avoid buffer overflow problems.

It is possible for you to review the code

Security through obscurity is often better than no security at all, but it's not a via-ble long-term strategy. If there is no way for anybody to see the code, ever, even a bona-fide expert who has signed a nondisclosure agreement and is acting on behalf of a customer, you should be suspicious. It's perfectly reasonable for peo-ple to protect their trade secrets, and it's also reasonable for people to object to having sensitive code examined by people who aren't able to evaluate it anyway (for instance, it's unlikely that most people can do an adequate job of evaluating the strength of encryption algorithms). However, if you're willing to provide some-body who's competent to do the evaluation, and to provide strong protection for trade secrets, you should be allowed to review the code. Code that can't stand up to this sort of evaluation will not stand the test of time, either.

You may not be able and willing to review the code under appropriate condi-tions. That's usually OK, but you should at least verify that there is some proce-dure for code review.

Somebody you know and trust actually has reviewed the code

It doesn't matter how many people could look at a piece of software if nobody ever does. If it's practical to do so, it's wise to make the investment to have some-body reasonably knowledgeable and trustworthy actually look at the code. While anybody could review open source, very few people do. It's relatively cheap and easy, and any competent programmer can at least tell you whether it's well-writ-ten code. Don't assume that somebody else has done this.

There is a security notification and update procedure

All programs eventually have security problems. A well-defined process should be in place for notifying the supplier of security problems and for getting notifications and updates from them. If the supplier has been around for any significant amount of time, there should be a positive track record, showing that they react to reported problems promptly and reasonably.

The server implements a recent (but accepted) version of the protocol

You can have problems with protocols, not just with the programs that implement them. In order to have some confidence in the security of the protocol, it's helpful to have an implementation of an accepted, standard protocol in a relatively recent version. You want an accepted and/or standard protocol so that you know that the protocol design has been reviewed; you want a relatively recent version so that you know that old problems have been fixed. You don't want custom protocols, or experimental or novel versions of standard protocols, if you can avoid them. Protocol design is tricky, few suppliers do a competent job in-house, and almost nobody gets a protocol right on the first try.

The program uses standard error-logging mechanisms

In order to secure something, you need to manage it. Using standard logging mechanisms makes programs much easier to manage; you can simply integrate them into your existing log management and alerting tools. Nonstandard logging not only interferes with your ability to find messages, it also runs the risk of introducing new security holes (what if an attacker uses the logging to fill your disk?).

There is a secure software distribution mechanism

You should have some confidence that the version of the software you have is the correct version. In the case of software that you download across the Internet, this means that it should have a verifiable digital signature (even if it is commercial software!).

More subtly, if you're getting a complex commercial package, you should be able to trust the distribution and release mechanism, and know that you have a complete and correct version with a retrievable version number. If your commercial vendor ships you a writable CD burned just for you and then advises you to FTP some patches, you need to know that some testing, integration, and versioning is going on. If they don't digitally sign everything and provide signatures to compare to, they should at least be able to provide an inventory list showing all the files in the distribution with sizes, dates, and version numbers.

Controlling Unsafe Configurations

As we've discussed in earlier sections, your ability to trust a protocol often depends on your ability to control what it's talking to. It's not unusual to have a protocol that can be perfectly safe, as long as you know that it's going to specific clients with specific configurations, or otherwise horribly unsafe. For instance, the Simple Mail Transport Protocol (SMTP) is considered acceptable at most sites, as long as it's going to a machine with a reliable and well-configured server on it. On the other hand, it's extremely dangerous when talking to a badly configured server.

Normally, if you want to use a protocol like this, you will use bastion hosts, and you will allow the protocol to come into your site only when it is destined for a carefully controlled and configured machine that is administered by your trusted security staff. Sometimes you may not be able to do this, however; you may find that you need to allow a large number of machines, or machines that are not directly controlled by the staff responsible for the firewall. What do you do then?

The first thing to be aware of is that you cannot protect yourself from hostile insiders in this situation. If you allow a protocol to come to machines, and the people who control those machines are actively trying to subvert your security, they will succeed in doing so. Your ability to control hostile insiders is fairly minimal in the first place, but the more protocols you allow, the more vulnerable you are.

Supposing that the people controlling the machines are not hostile but aren't security experts either, there are measures you can take to help the situation. One option is to attempt to increase your control over the machines to the point where they can't get things wrong; this means forcing them to run an operating system like Windows NT or Unix where you can centralize account administration and remove access to globally powerful accounts (root or Administrator). This is rarely possible, and when it is possible, it sometimes doesn't help much. This approach will generally allow you to forcibly configure web browsers into safe configurations, for instance, but it won't do much for web servers. Enough access to administer a web server in any useful way is enough access to make it insecure.

Another option is to attempt to increase your control over the protocol until you're certain that it can't be used to attack a machine even it's misconfigured. For instance, if you can't turn off support for scripting languages in web browsers, you can filter scripting languages out of incoming HTTP. This is at best an ongoing war—it's usually impossible to find a safe but useful subset of the protocol, so you end up removing unsafe things as they become known. At worst, it may be impossible to do this sort of control.

If you can't actually control either the clients or the protocol, you can at least provide peer pressure and social support to get programs safely configured. You can use local installations under Unix or profiles under Windows NT to supply defaults that you find acceptable (this will work best if you also provide localizations that are useful to the user). For instance, you can supply configuration information for web browsers that turns off scripting languages and that also correctly sets proxying information and provides bookmarks of local interest. You want to make it easier and more pleasant to do things securely than insecurely.

You can also provide a security policy that makes clear what you want people to do and why. In particular, it should explain to people why it matters to them, since few people are motivated to go to any trouble at all to achieve some abstract notion of security. (See Chapter 25, *Security Policies*, for more information on security policies.)

No matter how you end up trying to manage these configuration issues, you will want to be sure that you are monitoring for vulnerabilities. Don't fool yourself; you will never get perfect compliance using policies and defaults. (You'll be very lucky to get perfect compliance even when you're using force, since it requires perfect enforcement!)

14

Intermediary Protocols

Earlier we discussed TCP, UDP, and other protocols directly based on IP. Many application protocols are based directly on those protocols, but others use intermediary protocols. Understanding these intermediary protocols is important to understanding the applications that are built on them. This chapter discusses various general-purpose protocols that are used to build numerous applications or higher-level protocols.

We discuss intermediary protocols here because they form the basis for many of the protocols we discuss later. However, intermediary protocols are usually invisible, and they are often complex. If you are not already familiar with network protocols, you may want to skip this chapter initially, and come back to it as needed.

Remote Procedure Call (RPC)

The term "RPC", or remote procedure call, can be used for almost any mechanism that lets a program do something that looks to the programmer like making a simple procedure call but that actually contacts another program. However, it's also the name of some particular protocols for this purpose, which are extremely widespread.

Multiple remote procedure call protocols are known as RPCs. In particular, on Unix systems, the protocol normally known as "RPC" is one developed by Sun and later standardized as Open Network Computing RPC. On Microsoft systems, the protocol normally known as "RPC" is compatible with a descendent of Sun's RPC standardized by the Open Systems Foundation (OSF) as part of its Distributed Computing Environment (DCE). For clarity, we will call these "Sun RPC" and "Microsoft RPC". It is arguably more correct to call them "ONC RPC" and "DCE

RPC"; however, we find that in this case, correctness and clarity are at odds with each other.

Other remote procedure call mechanisms are used on particular implementations, but these two account for most of the market, and the other RPC mechanisms are similar in concept and difficulties. For simplicity, when we are making statements that refer to all protocols we know of that anybody calls "RPC", we'll say just "RPC".

Sun RPC and Microsoft RPC are quite similar and are related, but they do not interoperate. Microsoft RPC is an implementation of DCE RPC and can interoperate with other DCE RPC implementations. Some Unix machines support both Sun RPC and DCE RPC (usually Sun RPC is a default, and DCE RPC is an option or an add-on product). In practice, even if you run DCE RPC on a Unix machine, you will very rarely notice any interoperability with Microsoft RPC. The DCE RPC standard covers only a small amount of functionality, and most applications use features that are not in the base set. These features are not guaranteed to be interoperable between implementations. Since DCE RPC is relatively little used on Unix, Unix applications often stick to base features. Microsoft, however, makes extensive use of RPC and needs more functionality. They therefore almost always use incompatible features (mostly by using DCOM, which is discussed later). This is the main reason for our stubborn insistence on referring to "Microsoft RPC"; we are attempting to avoid the suggestion that Microsoft applications that use RPC can be expected to work with other DCE RPC servers or clients.

Like TCP and UDP, the RPCs are used as general-purpose transport protocols by a variety of application protocols; on Unix machines, this includes NFS and NIS, and on Windows NT machines, it includes Microsoft Exchange and the administrator applications for a number of services, including DHCP and Exchange. NFS and NIS are vulnerable services from a network security point of view. An attacker with access to your NFS server can probably read any file on your system. An attacker with access to your NIS server can probably obtain your password file and then run a password-cracking attack against your system. The Windows NT applications that use RPC are less security-critical but by no means safe. While it's not immediately fatal to have an attacker controlling your mail server, it's not pleasant either.

In the TCP and UDP protocols, port numbers are two-byte fields. This means that there are only 65,536 possible port numbers for TCP and UDP services. There aren't enough ports to be able to assign a unique well-known port number to every possible service and application that might want one. Among other things, RPC addresses this limitation. Each RPC-based service is assigned a unique four-byte *RPC service number*. This allows for 4,294,967,296 different services, each with a unique number. That's more than enough to assign a unique number to every possible service and application you'd need.

RPC is built on top of TCP and UDP, so there needs to be some way of mapping the RPC service numbers of the RPC-based servers in use on a machine to the particular TCP or UDP ports those servers are using. This is where the location server comes in. On Unix machines, the location server is a program called *portmapper*; under Windows NT, it's the RPC Locator service. The functions and characteristics of the two are the same.

The location server is the only RPC-related server that is guaranteed to run on a particular TCP or UDP port number (for Sun RPC, it is at port number 111 on both; for Microsoft RPC, it is at port number 135 on both). When an RPC-based server such as an NFS or NIS server starts, it allocates a TCP and/or UDP (some use one, some the other, some both) port for itself. Then, it contacts the location server on the same machine to "register" its unique RPC service number and the particular port(s) it is using at the moment.

Servers usually choose arbitrary port numbers, but they can consistently choose the same port number every time if they wish. There is no guarantee that a server that does this will be able to register itself; some other server may have gotten there first, in which case the registration will fail. Obviously, if every server requests a fixed port number, there's not much point in using RPC at all. One of the major features of RPC is that it provides access that is not based on fixed port numbers.

An RPC-based client program that wishes to contact a particular RPC-based server on a machine first contacts the location server on that machine (which, remember, always runs on both TCP and UDP port 111 or 135). The client tells the location server the unique RPC service number for the server it wishes to access, and the location server responds with a message saying, in effect, either "I'm sorry, but that service isn't available on this machine at the moment", or "That service is currently running on TCP (or UDP) port *n* on this machine at the moment". At that point, the client contacts the server on the port number it got from the location server and continues its conversation directly with the server, without further involvement from the location server. (Figure 14-1 shows this process.)

The Sun RPC location service also implements an optimization of this process that allows an RPC client to send a service lookup request and an RPC call in a single request. The location service not only returns the information, but also forwards the RPC call to the appropriate service. The service that receives the request will see the IP address of the local machine instead of the IP address of the machine that sent the query. This has caused a number of security problems for RPC

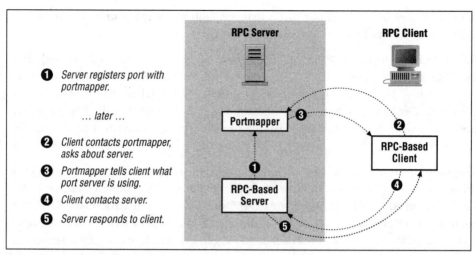

Figure 14-1. RPC and the portmapper

services, since many of them perform authentication based upon the source IP addresses of the request. This feature should normally be disabled.

Sun RPC Authentication

In Sun RPC, each server application chooses what kind of authentication it wants. Two authentication schemes are available in normal Sun RPC, known as "AUTH_NONE" and "AUTH_UNIX". If you have a Kerberos installation and a recent implementation of Sun RPC, applications can use "AUTH_KERB" to do Kerberos authentication.

Logically enough, "AUTH_NONE" means that there is no authentication at all. Applications that use AUTH_NONE are available to all users and ask for no authentication data. "AUTH_UNIX" could more appropriately be called "AUTH_ALMOST_NONE". Applications that use "AUTH_UNIX" ask the client to provide the numeric Unix user and group IDs for the user and enforce the permissions appropriate to those user and group IDs on the server machine. This information is completely forgeable; a hostile client can provide any user or group ID that seems desirable.

RPC servers are free to implement their own authentication schemes, but Sun RPC does not normally provide any reliable authentication for them except through Secure RPC. You do not want to allow access to RPC services unless you are sure that they do have their own, reliable authentication. (In general, this means simply disabling remote access to RPC altogether.)

Secure RPC provides another authentication scheme, known as "AUTH_DES". Secure RPC is an extension to Sun RPC that improves user authentication. Secure RPC has become available much more slowly than normal Sun RPC; for many years, Sun was effectively the only vendor that supported it, and it is still relatively rare and difficult to use in large heterogeneous networks.

This is partly because Secure RPC requires more infrastructure than regular RPC, and this infrastructure is often annoyingly visible to the user. Logically, Secure RPC is a classic combination of public key cryptography and secret key cryptography; Diffie-Hellman public key cryptography is used to securely determine a shared secret used for encryption with the DES algorithm. Cryptography, Diffie-Hellman, and the DES algorithm are discussed further in Appendix C, *Cryptography*.

Secure RPC is based upon using a public key algorithm that has a maximum key size of only 192 bits in length. This size of key is too small and is considered to make Secure RPC vulnerable to factoring attacks, where an attacker can discover the private key from computations based upon captured key exchange data. An attacker would have to use considerable computing resources to break a key, but once a key was broken, it could be used to impersonate the user at any place those credentials were used.

There are two major difficulties: distributing information about public keys, and getting private keys for human beings. Public and private keys are both big numbers, and they're security critical. If somebody can change the database of public keys, that person can put his or her public key in place of some other public key, and authenticate as any entity he or she would like to be. If somebody can read a private key, he or she can then authenticate as the entity that owns that private key. Normally, you might deal with this by not storing the private key on the computer, but human beings are very bad at providing large numbers on demand.

The Secure RPC infrastructure can deal with the public key information in a number of ways. On Suns, the normal method is to use NIS+, which has a credentials database. You can also distribute the same information as a regular NIS map or as a file. If you put the information in a file, you then have to distribute the file, which is normally done with NFS. As we discuss in Chapter 20, *Naming and Directory Services*, normal NIS is not secure; therefore, if you distribute the public key information this way, it will be vulnerable to replacement by attackers. As we discuss in Chapter 17, *File Transfer, File Sharing, and Printing*, normal NFS isn't secure, either. To secure it, you run NFS over Secure RPC, which isn't going to work if you need to have access to NFS before you can get Secure RPC running. If you're going to rely on Secure RPC, you must ensure that the public keys are distributed via a secure method (which will generally be NIS+). NIS+ itself uses Secure RPC, but because it is authenticating as the machine (instead of as a particular user, which is necessary for NFS), and is communicating with a known server, it can locally store the information necessary to start up a connection to the NIS+ service, avoiding the bootstrapping problem.

The private key information is also handled by NIS or NIS+. It is distributed in an encrypted form and decrypted using a user-supplied password.

Microsoft RPC Authentication

Microsoft RPC does provide an authentication system, but not all operating systems support it (in particular, it is supported on Windows NT, but not on Windows 95 or Windows 98). As a result, very few applications actually use RPC authentication, since it limits the platforms the application can run on and requires extra programming effort. Instead, applications that need security with Microsoft RPC usually use RPC over SMB instead of using RPC directly over TCP/IP, and use SMB authentication. (SMB is described later in this chapter.)

Packet Filtering Characteristics of RPC

It's very difficult to use packet filtering to control RPC-based services because you don't usually know what port the service will be using on a particular machine— and chances are that the port used will change every time the machine is rebooted. Blocking access to the location server isn't sufficient. An attacker can bypass the step of talking to the location server and simply try all TCP and/or UDP ports (the 65,536 possible ports can all be checked on a particular machine in a matter of minutes), looking for the response expected from a particular RPC-based server like NFS or NIS.

Direction	Source Addr.	Dest. Addr.	Protocol	Source Port	Dest. Port	ACK Set	Notes
In	Ext	Int	UDP	>1023	111	a	Request, external client to internal Sun RPC location server
Out	Int	Ext	UDP	111	>1023	a	Response, internal Sun RPC location server to external client
Out	Int	Ext	UDP	>1023	111	a	Request, internal client to external Sun RPC location server
In	Ext	Int	UDP	111	>1023	a	Response, external Sun RPC location server to internal client
In	Ext	Int	TCP	>1023	111	b	Request, external client to internal Sun RPC location server
Out	Int	Ext	TCP	111	>1023	Yes	Response, internal Sun RPC location server to external client
Out	Int	Ext	TCP	>1023	111	b	Request, internal client to external Sun RPC location server
In	Ext	Int	TCP	111	>1023	Yes	Response, external Sun RPC location server to internal client
In	Ext	Int	UDP	>1023	135	a	Request, external client to internal Microsoft/DCE RPC location server

Direction	Source Addr.	Dest. Addr.	Protocol	Source Port	Dest. Port	ACK Set	Notes
Out	Int	Ext	UDP	135	>1023	a	Response, internal Microsoft/DCE RPC location server to external client
Out	Int	Ext	UDP	>1023	135	a	Request, internal client to external Microsoft/DCE RPC location server
In	Ext	Int	UDP	135	>1023	a	Response, external Microsoft/DCE RPC location server to internal client
In	Ext	Int	TCP	>1023	135	b	Request, external client to internal Microsoft/DCE RPC location server
Out	Int	Ext	TCP	135	>1023	Yes	Response, internal Microsoft/DCE RPC location server to external client
Out	Int	Ext	TCP	>1023	135	b	Request, internal client to external Microsoft/DCE RPC location server
In	Ext	Int	TCP	135	>1023	Yes	Response, external Microsoft/DCE RPC location server to internal client
In	Ext	Int	UDP	>1023	Any	a	Request, external client to internal RPC server
Out	Int	Ext	UDP	Any	>1023	a	Response, internal RPC server to external client
Out	Int	Ext	UDP	>1023	Any	a	Request, internal client to external RPC server
In	Ext	Int	UDP	Any	>1023	a	Response, external RPC server to internal client
In	Ext	Int	TCP	>1023	Any	b	Request, external client to internal RPC server
Out	Int	Ext	TCP	Any	>1023	Yes	Response, internal RPC server to external client
Out	Int	Ext	TCP	>1023	Any	b	Request, internal client to external RPC server
In	Ext	Int	TCP	Any	>1023	Yes	Response, external RPC server to internal client

a UDP has no ACK equivalent.
b ACK will not be set on the first packet (establishing connection) but will be set on the rest.

Some newer packet filtering products can talk to the location server to determine what services are where and filter on that basis. Note that this has to be verified on a per-packet basis for UDP-based services. The packet filter will have to contact the location server every time it receives a packet, because if the machine has rebooted, the service may have moved. Because TCP is connection-oriented, the port number has to be verified only on a per-connection basis. Using this mechanism to allow UDP-based services is going to result in high overhead and is probably not wise for applications that perform a lot of RPC.

Even though it is not sufficient, you should still block access to the location server because some versions of the location server are capable of being used as proxies for an attacker's clients.

So, what do you do to guard RPC-based services? A couple of observations: First, it turns out that most of the "dangerous" RPC-based services (particularly NIS and NFS) are offered by default over UDP. Second, most services you'd want to access through a packet filter are TCP-based, *not* UDP-based; the notable exceptions are DNS, NTP, and *syslog*. These twin observations lead to the common approach many sites take in dealing with RPC using packet filtering: block UDP altogether, except for specific and tightly controlled "peepholes" for DNS, NTP, and *syslog*. With this approach, if you wish to allow any TCP-based RPC service in a given direction, you'll need to allow them all, or use a packet filter that can contact the location service.

Windows NT provides more control over the ports used by RPC. This will help if you want to allow remote clients to access your servers, but it will not help you allow internal clients to access external servers (unless you can talk the owners of the servers into modifying their machines). Most uses of RPC are actually uses of DCOM, which provides a user interface to configuring ports that is discussed later in this chapter. You can also control the size of the port range used by RPC directly. To limit the size of the port range, modify the following registry key:

    HKEY_LOCAL_MACHINE\Software\Microsoft\RPC

so that the "Ports" key is set to the port range you wish to use, the "PortsInternet-Available" key is set to "Y", and "UseInternetPorts" is also set to "Y".

The procedure for setting the port for a given service varies from service to service. It is sometimes documented in the manuals, and the Microsoft web site gives instructions on setting RPC ports for services that are particularly frequently used through firewalls. Again, most RPC services are DCOM services, and there is a user interface for changing DCOM parameters. It is worth checking the DCOM interface even if you see documentation that advises you to edit the registry directly.

If you set the port that a service uses, be sure to pick a port that is not in use by another server, and a port that is not at the beginning of the RPC port range. Since most servers choose the first free number in the RPC port range, a server that asks for a number very close to the beginning of the port range is quite likely to find it already in use. At this point, either the server will fail to start at all, because the RPC registration fails, or the server will select a random port and start on it. In either case, remote clients who are relying on the server being at a fixed port number will be unable to access it.

Proxying Characteristics of RPC

RPC is difficult to proxy for many of the same reasons that make it difficult to protect with packet filtering. Using RPC requires using the location service, and the proxy server needs to proxy both the location service and the specific service that is being provided. Figure 14-2 shows the process that an RPC proxy needs to go through.

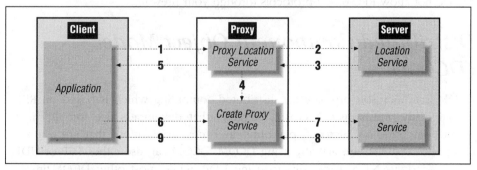

Figure 14-2. Proxying RPC

Normal modified-client proxy systems, like SOCKS, do not support RPC, and no modified-procedure proxies are available for it. This means that there's no external way for the proxy to determine what server the client is trying to contact. Either the client has to be configured to speak RPC to the proxy server, which then always connects to the same actual server, or the proxy server must run as a transparent proxy service, where a router intercepts traffic, complete with server addresses, and hands them to the proxy.

A number of transparent proxy servers do support Sun RPC; a smaller number are now adding support for DCE/Microsoft RPC. Products vary in the amount of support they provide, with some providing all-or-none support, and others allowing you to specify which RPC services you wish to allow.

Network Address Translation Characteristics of RPC

None of the RPC versions uses embedded IP addresses; there is no inherent problem using them with network address translation systems that modify only host addresses. On the other hand, the information returned by the location service does include port numbers. Using RPC with a network address translation system that modifies port numbers will require a system that's able to interpret and modify the responses from the location server so that they show the translated port numbers. In addition, protocols built on top of RPC are free to exchange IP addresses or pay attention to source IP addresses as well as RPC information, so there is no guarantee that all RPC applications will work. In particular, both NIS and NFS use IP source addresses as authenticators and will have to be carefully configured to work with the translated addresses. As discussed in the next section, DCOM, which is the primary user of Microsoft RPC, uses embedded source addresses and will not work with network address translation.

Summary of Recommendations for RPC

* Do not allow RPC-based protocols through your firewall.

Distributed Component Object Model (DCOM)

DCOM is a Microsoft protocol for distributed computing which is based on RPC. DCOM is the mechanism Microsoft suggests that developers use for all client-server computing on Microsoft platforms, and most applications that are listed as using Microsoft RPC are actually using DCOM. DCOM can use either TCP or UDP; under Windows NT 4, it defaults to using UDP, while most other DCOM implementations default to using TCP. If the default version of RPC does not work, servers will use the other.

Although DCOM is based on RPC, it adds a number of features with important implications for firewalls. On the positive side, DCOM adds a security layer to RPC; applications can choose to have integrity protection, confidentiality protection, or both.

On the negative side, DCOM transactions are more complicated to support through firewalls than straightforward RPC transactions. DCOM transactions include IP addresses, so DCOM cannot be straightforwardly used with firewall mechanisms that obscure the IP address of the protected machines (for instance, proxying or network address translation). DCOM servers also may use callbacks, where the server initiates connections to clients, so for some services, it may be insufficient to allow only client-to-server connections.

Microsoft has produced various ways to run DCOM over HTTP. These methods allow you to pass DCOM through a firewall without the problems associated with opening all the ports used by Microsoft RPC. On the other hand, if you use these methods to provide for incoming DCOM access, you are making all your DCOM servers available to the Internet. DCOM services are not written to be Internet accessible and should not be opened this way.

You can control DCOM security configuration and the ports used by DCOM with the *dcomcnfg* application. The Endpoints tab in *dcomcnfg* will let you set the port range used for dynamically assigned ports, and if you edit the configuration for a particular DCOM service, the Endpoints tab will allow you to choose a static port for it. This is safer than editing the registry directly, but you should still be careful about the port number you choose; if port numbers conflict, services will not work correctly. Do not statically assign services to port numbers that are low in the port range (these will frequently be dynamically assigned) or to port numbers that are statically assigned to other services.

NetBIOS over TCP/IP (NetBT)

Although Microsoft supports a number of services that are directly based on TCP/IP, many older services are based on NetBIOS and use NetBT on TCP/IP networks. This provides an additional layer of portability for the services, which can run on TCP/IP networks or NetBEUI networks without the difference being visible to the application.

NetBT provides three services:

- NetBIOS name service
- Datagram service
- Session service

Name service is at UDP port 137 and is used to do name resolution; see Chapter 20, *Naming and Directory Services*, for more information. NetBT datagram service is at UDP port 138 and is the NetBT equivalent of UDP, used for connectionless transactions. NetBT session service is at TCP port 139. NetBT datagram and session service are both used primarily for protocols based on Server Message Block (SMB), which is discussed later in this chapter.

NetBT doesn't actually provide much by itself. NetBT is simply a way of running NetBIOS over TCP/IP, and almost all interesting work is done by higher-level protocols (nearly always SMB). NetBT session connections do provide an extremely minimal level of security. A requester must specify the NetBIOS name and the TCP/IP address that it wants to connect to, as well as the requester's NetBIOS name and TCP/IP address. The connection can't be made unless some program has registered to respond to the specified NetBIOS name. NetBT applications could perform authorization based on the requester's NetBIOS name and/or TCP/IP address, but in practice, this is rare. (Since both of these are trivially forgeable in any case, it's just as well.)

NetBT session service can also act as a sort of locator service. An application that's registering to respond to a name can specify another IP address and port number. When a client attempts to connect, it will initially talk to a NetBT session at port 139, but the NetBT session server will provide another IP address and port number. The client will then close the initial connection and open a new connection (still using the NetBT session protocol) to the new IP address and port number. This is intended to support operating systems where open TCP/IP connections can't be transferred between applications, so that the NetBT session server can't simply transfer the connection to a listener. It is not a feature in widespread use.

NetBT datagram service also includes a source and destination NetBIOS name (although not TCP/IP address information). NetBT datagrams may be broadcast, multicast, or sent to a specific destination. The receiving host looks at the destination NetBIOS name to decide whether or not to process the datagram. This feature is sometimes used instead of name resolution. Rather than trying to find an address for a particular name, clients of some protocols send a broadcast packet and assume that the relevant host will answer. This will work only if broadcast traffic from the client can reach the server. We point out protocols where this feature is commonly used.

Packet Filtering Characteristics of NetBT

NetBT name service is covered in Chapter 20, *Naming and Directory Services.* NetBT datagram service uses UDP port 138; session service uses TCP port 139.* NetBT session service is always directed to a specific host, but NetBT datagram service may be broadcast. If redirection is in use, NetBT session connections may legitimately be made with any destination port. Fortunately, this is rare and will not happen on Windows NT or Unix NetBT servers.

Direction	Source Addr.	Dest. Addr.	Protocol	Source Port	Dest. Port	ACK Set	Notes
In	Ext	Int	UDP	>1023	138	a	Request, external client to internal NetBT datagram server
Out	Int	Ext	UDP	138	>1023	a	Response, internal NetBT datagram server to external client
Out	Int	Ext	UDP	>1023	138	a	Request, internal client to external NetBT datagram server
In	Ext	Int	UDP	138	>1023	a	Response, external NetBT datagram server to internal client
In	Ext	Int	TCP	>1023	139	b	Request, external client to internal NetBT session server
Out	Int	Ext	TCP	139	>1023	Yes	Response, internal NetBT session server to external client
Out	Int	Ext	TCP	>1023	139	b	Request, internal client to external NetBT session server
In	Ext	Int	TCP	139	>1023	Yes	Response, external NetBT session server to internal client

a UDP has no ACK equivalent.
b ACK will not be set on the first packet (establishing connection) but will be set on the rest.

---

* TCP port 138 and UDP port 139 are also registered for use by NetBT but are not actually used.

Proxying Characteristics of NetBT

NetBT session service would be quite easy to proxy, and NetBT datagram service is designed to be proxied. Proxying NetBT will not increase security much, although it will allow you to avoid some sorts of forgery and probably some denial of service attacks based on invalid NetBT datagrams.

Network Address Translation Characteristics of NetBT

Although NetBT does have embedded IP addresses, they do not usually pose a problem for network address translation systems. There are two places where IP addresses are embedded: session service redirections and datagrams. Session service redirection is almost never used, and the embedded IP addresses in datagrams are supposed to be used only for client identification, and not for communication. Replies are sent to the IP source address, not the embedded source.

In some situations, changes in port numbers can be a problem because some implementations respond to port 138 for datagram service, ignoring both the IP source port and the embedded NetBT source port. Fortunately, these older implementations are becoming rare.

Summary of Recommendations for NetBT

- Do not allow NetBT across your firewall.

Common Internet File System (CIFS) and Server Message Block (SMB)

The Common Internet File System (CIFS) is a general-purpose information-sharing protocol formerly known as Server Message Block (SMB). SMB is a message-based protocol developed by Microsoft, Intel, and IBM. SMB is best known as the basis for Microsoft's file and printer sharing, which is discussed further in Chapter 17, *File Transfer, File Sharing, and Printing*. However, SMB is also used by many other applications. The CIFS standard extends Microsoft's usage of SMB.

SMB is normally run on top of NetBT. Newer implementations also support SMB over TCP/IP directly; in this configuration, it is almost always called CIFS. Note that whatever this protocol is called, it is the exact same protocol whether it is run over NetBT or over TCP/IP directly, and that it was called CIFS even when it did not run over TCP/IP directly. We refer to it as "SMB" here mostly because it is used for a variety of things in addition to file sharing, and we find it misleading to refer to it as a filesystem in this context.

The SMB protocol provides a variety of different operations. Many of these are standard operations for manipulating files (open, read, write, delete, and set attributes, for instance), but there are also specific operations for other purposes (messaging and printing, for instance) and several general-purpose mechanisms for doing interprocess communication using SMB. SMB allows sharing not only of standard files, but also of other things, including devices, named pipes, and mailslots. (Named pipes and mailslots are mechanisms for interprocess communication; named pipes provide a data stream, while mailslots are message-oriented.) It therefore provides suitable calls for manipulating these other objects, including support for device controls (I/O controls, or *ioctls*) and several general-purpose transaction calls for communication between processes. It is also sometimes possible to use the same file manipulation calls that are used on normal files to manipulate special files.

In practice, there are two major uses for SMB; file sharing and general-purpose remote transactions. General-purpose remote transactions are implemented by running DCE RPC over SMB, through the sharing of named pipes. In general, any application is using DCE RPC over SMB if it says it uses named pipes; if it relies on *PIPE**something_or_other*, *Named Pipe**something_or_other*, or IPC$; if it requires port 138, 139, or 445; or if it mentions SMB or CIFS transactions. Applications that normally use this include NTLM authentication, the Server Manager, the Registry Editor, the Event Viewer, and print spooling.

Any time that you provide SMB access to a machine, you are providing access to all of the applications that use SMB for transactions. Most of these applications have their own security mechanisms, but you need to be sure to apply those. If you can't be sure that host security is excellent, you should not allow SMB access.

SMB introduces an additional complication for firewalls. Not only do multiple different protocols with very different security implications use SMB (thereby ending up on the same port numbers), but they can all use the very same SMB connection. If two machines connect to each other via SMB for one purpose, that connection will be reused for all other SMB protocols. Therefore, connection-oriented SMB must be treated like a connectionless protocol, with every packet a separate transaction that must be evaluated for security.

For instance, if a client connects to a server in order to access a filesystem, it will start an SMB session. If the client then wants to print to a printer on that server, or run an SMB-based program (like the User Manager or the Event Viewer) on that server, the existing connection will be reused.

In the most common uses of SMB, a client makes a NetBT session connection to a host and then starts an SMB session. At the beginning of the SMB session, the server and the client negotiate a dialect of SMB. Different dialects support different SMB features. Once the dialect has been negotiated, the client authenticates if the dialect supports authentication at this point, and then requests a resource from the server with what is called a *tree connect*. When the client creates the initial SMB connection and authenticates, it gets an identifier called a *user ID* or *UID*. If the client wants another resource, the client will reuse the existing connection and merely do an additional tree connect request. The server will determine whether the client is authorized to do the tree request by looking at the permissions granted to the UID. Multiple resource connections may be used at the same time; they are distinguished by an identifier called a *tree ID* or *TID*.

Not all SMB commands require a valid UID and TID. Obviously, the commands to set up connections don't require them, but others can be used without them, including the messaging commands, the echo command, and some commands that give server information. These commands can be used by anybody, without authentication.

Authentication and SMB

Because SMB runs on a number of machines with different authentication models, it supports several different levels of security. Two different types of authentication are possible, commonly called *share level* and *user level*. Samba, which is a popular SMB implementation for Unix, also refers to "server-level" authentication; this is a Samba-specific term used when user-level authentication is in effect but the Samba server is not authenticating users locally. This is not visible to the client. Samba is discussed further in Chapter 17, *File Transfer, File Sharing, and Printing*.

Share-level authentication

In share-level authentication, the initial SMB connection does not require authentication. Instead, each time you attach to a resource, you provide a password for that particular resource. This authentication is meant for servers running under operating systems that don't actually have a concept of users. Since it requires all users who wish to use a resource to have the same password, it's inherently insecure, and you should avoid it. It uses the same mechanisms to exchange passwords that are used for user-level authentication (which are described in detail in Chapter 21, *Authentication and Auditing Services*), but it does the password exchange during the tree connect instead of during session setup.

User-level authentication

User-level authentication occurs at the beginning of the SMB session, after dialect negotiation. If the negotiated dialect supports user-level authentication, the client provides authentication information to the server. The authentication information that's provided is a username and password; the method that's used to send it depends on the dialect. The password may be sent in cleartext or established via challenge-response. User-level authentication is discussed in detail in Chapter 21, *Authentication and Auditing Services*, because it is used for logon authentication as well as for authenticating users who are connecting to file servers.

Many SMB servers that do user-level authentication provide guest access and will give guest access to clients that fail to authenticate for any reason. This is meant to provide backward compatibility for clients that cannot do user-level authentication. In most configurations, it will also provide access to a number of files to anybody that is able to ask. You should either disable guest access or carefully control file permissions.

Packet Filtering Characteristics of SMB

SMB is generally done over NetBT session service at TCP port 139. It is theoretically possible to run it over NetBT datagram service at UDP port 138, but this is extremely rare. As of Windows 2000, SMB can also be run directly over TCP/IP without involving NetBT, in which case it uses TCP or UDP port 445 (again, although UDP is a theoretical possibility, it does not appear to occur in practice).

Direction	Source Addr.	Dest. Addr.	Protocol	Source Port	Dest. Port	ACK Set	Notes
In	Ext	Int	TCP	>1023	139, 445	a	Incoming SMB/TCP connection, client to server
Out	Int	Ext	TCP	139, 445	>1023	Yes	Incoming SMB/TCP connection, server to client
In	Ext	Int	UDP	>1023	138, 445	b	Incoming SMB/UDP connection, client to server
Out	Int	Ext	UDP	138, 445	>1023	b	Incoming SMB/UDP connection, server to client
Out	Int	Ext	TCP	>1023	139, 445	a	Outgoing SMB/TCP connection, client to server
In	Ext	Int	TCP	139, 445	>1023	Yes	Outgoing SMB/TCP connection, server to client
Out	Int	Ext	UDP	>1023	138, 445	b	Outgoing SMB/UDP connection, client to server
In	Ext	Int	UDP	138, 445	>1023	b	Outgoing SMB/UDP connection, server to client

a ACK is not set on the first packet of this type (establishing connection) but will be set on the rest.
b UDP has no ACK equivalent.

Clients of any SMB protocol will often attempt to reach the destination host via NetBIOS name service as well. SMB will work even if these packets are denied, but you may log large numbers of denied packets. You should be aware of this and should not interpret name service requests from SMB clients as attacks. See Chapter 20, *Naming and Directory Services*, for more information about NetBIOS name service.

Proxying Characteristics of SMB

SMB is not particularly difficult to proxy, but it is difficult to improve its security with a proxy. Because many things are implemented as general-purpose transactions, it's hard for a proxy to know exactly what effect an operation will have on the end machine. The proxy can't just track requests but also needs to track the filenames those requests refer to. In addition, the protocol allows for some operations to be chained together, so that a single transaction may include a tree connect, an open, and a read (for instance). This means that a proxy that is trying to control what files are opened has to do extensive parsing on transactions to make certain that no inappropriate opens are late in the chain. It is not sufficient to simply check the transaction type.

Network Address Translation Characteristics of SMB

SMB is normally run over NetBT, which includes embedded IP addresses but does not generally use them, as discussed earlier. In Windows 2000, it is also possible to run SMB directly over IP. In this mode, it does not have embedded IP addresses and should function with straightforward network address translation.

Summary of Recommendations for SMB

*   Don't allow SMB across your firewall.

Common Object Request Broker Architecture (CORBA) and Internet Inter-Orb Protocol (IIOP)

CORBA is a non-Microsoft-developed object-oriented distributed computing framework. In general, CORBA objects communicate with each other through a program called an Object Request Broker, or *orb*.* CORBA objects communicate with

---

* In a rearguard action against the proliferation of acronyms, CORBA users almost always treat this as a word ("orb") instead of an acronym ("ORB").

each other over the Internet via the Internet Inter-Orb Protocol (IIOP), which is TCP-based but uses no fixed port number.

IIOP provides a great deal of flexibility. It permits callbacks, where a client makes a connection to the server with a request and the server makes a separate connection to the client with the response. It also permits bidirectional use of a connection; if a client makes a connection to the server, the server is not limited to responding to requests from the client but can make requests of its own over the existing connection. IIOP does not provide authentication or encryption services, leaving them up to the application.

All of this flexibility makes it basically impossible to make blanket statements about CORBA's security. Some applications of CORBA are quite secure; others are not. You will have to analyze each CORBA application separately.

In order to help with security, some vendors support IIOPS, which is IIOP over SSL. This protocol provides the basic protections SSL provides, which are discussed later, and therefore will help protect applications that use it from packet-sniffing attacks.

Packet Filtering Characteristics of CORBA and IIOP

Because there is no fixed port number for IIOP or IIOPS, the packet filtering characteristics of CORBA will depend entirely on your implementation. Some orbs come with predefined port numbers for IIOP and IIOPS, and others allow you to allocate your own or allocate ports dynamically. (Some orbs don't support IIOPS at all.) In addition, a number of orbs will allow you to run IIOP over HTTP.

IIOP is extremely difficult to control with packet filtering. A packet filter cannot tell whether an IIOP connection is unidirectional or bidirectional, so it's impossible to keep the server from executing commands on the client using packet filtering. In addition, if your application uses callbacks, you may need to allow connections in both directions anyway, further reducing your control over the situation.

Proxying Characteristics of CORBA and IIOP

There are two different ways of using proxying with IIOP. One of them is to use a proxy-aware orb, which knows how to use a generic proxy like SOCKS or an HTTP proxy server. Another is to use an IIOP-aware proxy server, which can interpret IIOP port and address information. There are multiple implementations of each of these solutions.

Either kind of proxying provides better security than can be managed with packet filtering. Using a generic proxy requires less configuration on the firewall, but it makes your security entirely dependent on the orb and the applications developer. An IIOP-aware proxy server will allow you to add additional protections by using the firewall to control what operation requests can be passed to the orb.

Network Address Translation Characteristics of CORBA and IIOP

IIOP includes embedded IP address and port information and will require a network address translation system that's aware of IIOP and can modify the embedded information.

Summary of Recommendations for CORBA and IIOP

- Do not try to allow all CORBA through your firewall; make specific arrangements for individual CORBA applications.

- For maximum security, develop single-purpose CORBA-aware proxies along with the CORBA application.

ToolTalk

ToolTalk is yet another distributed object system. It is part of the Common Desktop Environment (CDE), a standard produced by a consortium of Unix vendors, which allows desktop tools to communicate with each other. For instance, ToolTalk enables you to drag objects from one application to another with the expected results, and allows multiple applications to keep track of changes to the same file.

Applications using ToolTalk do not communicate with each other directly. Instead, communications are handled by two kinds of ToolTalk servers. A session server, called *ttsession*, handles messages that concern processes, while an object server, called *rpc.ttdbserverd*, handles messages that concern objects. Applications register with the appropriate ToolTalk servers to tell them what kinds of messages they are interested in. When an application has a message to send, it sends the message to the appropriate ToolTalk server, which redistributes it to any interested applications and returns any replies to the sending application. Session servers group together related processes (for instance, all the programs started by a given user will normally be part of one session), and multiple session servers may run on the same machine.

rpc.ttdbserverd is started from *inetd* and runs as root, while *ttsession* is started up as needed and runs as the user that started it. Often, *ttsession* will be started when a user logs in, but that's not required; if an application wants to use ToolTalk but no *ttsession* is available, one will be started up.

ToolTalk is based on Sun RPC. Although ToolTalk provides a range of authentication mechanisms, most ToolTalk implementations use the simplest one, which authorizes requests based on the unauthenticated Unix user information embedded in the request. This is completely forgeable. In addition, there have been a variety of security problems with the ToolTalk implementation, including buffer overflow problems in *rpc.ttdbserverd* and in the ToolTalk client libraries. Several of these problems have allowed remote attackers to run arbitrary programs as root.

Summary of Recommendations for ToolTalk

*   Do not allow RPC through your firewall; since ToolTalk is built on Sun RPC, this will prevent it from crossing the firewall.

*   Remove ToolTalk from bastion host machines (this will remove some desktop functionality, but ideally you should remove all of the graphical user interface and desktop tools anyway).

Transport Layer Security (TLS) and Secure Socket Layer (SSL)

The Secure Socket Layer (SSL) was designed in 1993 by Netscape to provide end-to-end encryption, integrity protection, and server authentication for the Web. The security services libraries that were available at the time didn't provide certain features that were needed for the Web:

*   Strong public key authentication without the need for a globally deployed public key infrastructure.

*   Reasonable performance with the large number of short connections made necessary by the stateless nature of HTTP. State associated with SSL can be maintained, at the server's discretion, across a sequence of HTTP connections.

*   The ability for clients to remain anonymous while requiring server authentication.

Like most network protocols, SSL has undergone a number of revisions. The commonly found versions of SSL are version 2 and version 3. There are known problems with the cryptography in version 2. The cryptography used in SSL version 3 contains some significant differences from its predecessor and is considered to be free of the previous version's cryptographic weaknesses. SSL version 3 also provides a clean way to use new versions of the protocol for forward compatibility.

Unless otherwise noted, this discussion refers to SSL version 3; we suggest that you avoid using SSL version 2.

The SSL protocol is owned by Netscape (and they own a U.S. patent relating to SSL), but they approached the IETF to create an Internet standard. An IETF protocol definition, RFC 2246, is in the process of becoming an Internet standard. The protocol is based very heavily on SSL version 3 and is called Transport Layer Security (TLS). Both TLS and SSL use exactly the same protocol greeting and version extensibility mechanism. This allows servers to be migrated from supporting SSL to TLS, and provisions have been made so that services can be created that support both SSL version 3 and TLS. Netscape has granted a royalty-free license for the SSL patent for any applications that use TLS as part of an IETF standard protocol.

The TLS and SSL Protocols

The TLS and SSL protocols provide server and client authentication, end–to–end encryption, and integrity protection. They also allow a client to reconnect to a server it has already used without having to reauthenticate or negotiate new session keys, as long as the new connection is made shortly after the old one is closed down.

The security of TLS and SSL does not come purely from the fact that they use a specific encryption algorithm, cryptographic hash, or public key cryptography, but from the way the algorithms are used. The important characteristics of a secure private communication session are discussed in Appendix C, *Cryptography*.

Both TLS and SSL meet the characteristics for providing a secure private communication session because:

- The client and server negotiate encryption and integrity protection algorithms.
- The identity of the server a client is connecting to is always verified, and this identity check is performed before the optional client user authentication information is sent.
- The key exchange algorithms that are used prevent man-in-the-middle attacks.
- At the end of the key exchange is a checksum exchange that will detect any tampering with algorithm negotiation.
- The server can check the identity of a client in a number of ways (these mechanisms are discussed in the next section). It is also possible to have anonymous clients.
- All data packets exchanged include message integrity checks. An integrity check failure causes a connection to be closed.

- It is possible, using certain sets of negotiated algorithms, to use temporary authentication parameters that will be discarded after a configurable time period to prevent recorded sessions from being decrypted at a later time.

Cryptography in TLS and SSL

TLS and SSL do not depend on a single algorithm for each of the following: generating keys, encrypting data, or performing authentication. Instead, they can use a range of different algorithms. Not all combinations of algorithms are valid, and both TLS and SSL define suites of algorithms that should be used together. This flexibility provides a number of advantages:

- Different algorithms have different capabilities; supporting multiple ones allows an application to choose one particularly suited to the kind of data and transaction patterns that it uses.

- There is frequently a trade-off between strength and speed; supporting multiple different algorithms allows applications to use faster but weaker methods when security is less important.

- As time goes by, people find ways to break algorithms that were previously considered secure; supporting a range allows applications to stop using algorithms that are no longer considered secure.

The TLS protocol defines sets of algorithms that can be used together. There is only one algorithm suite that an application must implement in order to be called a TLS compliant application. Even then, if a standard for the application prevents it from using this base algorithm suite, it may implement a different one and still be called TLS compliant. The required algorithm suite is a Diffie-Hellman key exchange authenticated with the Digital Signature Standard (DSS) with triple DES used in cipher block-chaining mode with SHA cryptographic hashes. The most important thing to know about this string of cryptographic terms is that at this time, this algorithm suite provides strong encryption and authentication suitable for protecting sensitive information. For more information about specific cryptographic algorithms and key lengths, see Appendix C, *Cryptography*.

Some algorithm suites use public key cryptography which, depending on the application, may require the use of additional network services (such as LDAP for verifying digital certificates) in order to perform server or client authentication.

TLS allows clients to be authenticated using either DSS or RSA public key cryptography. If clients wish to use other forms of authentication, such as a token card or a password, they must authenticate with the server anonymously, and then the application must negotiate to perform the additional authentication. This is the method which a web browser using TLS or SSL uses to perform HTTP basic authentication.

Use of TLS and SSL by Other Protocols

In order for TLS and SSL to be useful, they have to be used in conjunction with some higher-level protocol that actually exchanges data between applications. In some cases, this is done by integrating them into new protocols; for instance, version 2 of the Secure Shell (SSH) protocol uses TLS. However, in other situations it's useful to add TLS or SSL to an existing protocol. There are two basic mechanisms for doing this. One way is to use a new port number for the combination of the old protocol and the encrypting protocol; this is the way SSL and HTTP were originally integrated to create HTTPS. The other common way of integrating TLS or SSL into an existing protocol is to add a command to the protocol that starts up an encrypted session over the existing port; this is the approach taken by ESMTP when using the STARTTLS extension.

Neither of these approaches is perfect. Using a new port number is relatively easy to implement (you don't have to change command parsers) and allows a firewall to easily distinguish between protected and unprotected versions of the protocol (so that you can require the use of TLS, for instance). However, it uses up port numbers (and there are only 1024 in the reserved range to be allocated), and it requires changing firewall configurations to permit TLS-protected connections.

Adding a new command to start up a TLS connection makes more efficient use of port numbers and increases the chances that the upgraded protocol will work through firewalls (it may still be denied by an intelligent proxy that's watching the commands that are used). However, it's harder to implement. In particular, it's hard to make sure that no important data is exchanged before TLS is started up. Furthermore, it's critical for programmers to be cautious about failure conditions. A server or client that supports TLS needs to fail gracefully when talking to one that doesn't. However, if both the server and the client support TLS, it should not be possible for an attacker to force them to converse unprotected by interfering with the negotiation to use TLS.

In addition, once a protocol has upgraded to using TLS, it should restart all protocol negotiation from the beginning. Any information from the unprotected protocol could have been modified by an attacker and cannot be trusted.

Packet Filtering Characteristics of TLS and SSL

Neither TLS nor SSL is associated with an assigned port, although there are a number of ports assigned to specific higher-level protocols running over one or the other. We list these ports along with any other ports assigned to the higher-level protocols (for instance, we list the port assigned to IMAP over SSL in the section on packet filtering characteristics of IMAP in Chapter 16, *Electronic Mail and News*). You will sometimes see port 443 shown as assigned to SSL, but in fact, it is assigned to HTTP over SSL.

TLS and SSL connections will always be straightforward TCP connections, but that does not prevent higher-level protocols that use them from also using other connections or protocols. Because of the end-to-end encryption, it is impossible to do intelligent packet filtering on TLS and SSL connections; there is no way for a packet filter to enforce restrictions on what higher-level protocols are being run, for instance.

Proxying Characteristics of TLS and SSL

Because TLS and SSL use straightforward TCP connections, they work well with generic proxies. Proxying provides very little additional protection with TLS and SSL, because there is no way for a proxy to see the content of packets to do intelligent logging, control, or content filtering; a proxy can only control where connections are made.

Network Address Translation Characteristics of TLS and SSL

TLS and SSL will work well with network address translation. However, the end-to-end encryption will prevent the network address translation system from intercepting embedded addresses. Higher-level protocols that depend on having correct address or hostname information in their data will not work, and it will not be possible for the network address translation system to protect you from inadvertently releasing information about your internal network configuration.

Summary of Recommendations for TLS and SSL

- TLS and SSL version 3 are good choices for adding end-to-end protection to applications.

- Use TLS and SSL version 3 to protect against eavesdropping, session hijacking, and Trojan servers.

- Use TLS or SSL version 3 rather than SSL version 2. TLS should be preferred over SSL version 3.

- When evaluating programs that use TLS or SSL to add protection to existing protocols, verify that the transition to a protected connection occurs before confidential data is exchanged. Ideally any higher-level protocol negotiation should be completely restarted once protection has been established.

The Generic Security Services API (GSSAPI)

The GSSAPI is an IETF standard that provides a set of cryptographic services to an application. The services are provided via a well-defined application programming interface. The cryptographic services are:

- Context/session setup and shutdown

- Encrypting and decrypting messages

- Message signing and verification

The API is designed to work with a number of cryptographic technologies, but each technology separately defines the content of packets. Two independently written applications that use the GSSAPI may not be able to interoperate if they are not using the same underlying cryptographic technology.

There are at least two standard protocol-level implementations of the GSSAPI, one using Kerberos and the other using RSA public keys. In order to understand what is needed to support a particular implementation of the GSSAPI, you also need to know which underlying cryptographic technology has been used. In the case of a Kerberos GSSAPI, you will need a Kerberos Key Distribution Center (see Chapter 21, *Authentication and Auditing Services*, for more information on Kerberos).

The GSSAPI works best in applications where the connections between computers match the transactions being performed. If multiple connections are needed to finish a transaction, each one will require a new GSSAPI session, because the GSSAPI does not include any support for identifying the cryptographic context of a message. Applications that need this functionality should probably be using TLS or SSL.

Because of the lack of context, the GSSAPI does not work well with connectionless protocols like UDP; it is really suited only for use with connection-oriented protocols like TCP.

IPsec

The IETF has been developing an IP security protocol (IPsec) that is built directly on top of IP and provides end-to-end cryptographically based security for both IPv4 and IPv6. IPsec is a requirement for every IPv6 implementation and is an option for IPv4. Since IPv6 provides features that are not available in IPv4, the IPv6 and IPv4 versions of IPsec are implemented slightly differently. Although IPsec is still being standardized, it is sufficiently stable and standard that multiple interoperable implementations are now available and in use on IPv4. Possibly the best known of these is the IPsec implementation for Linux called FreeS/WAN.

Because IPsec is implemented at the IP layer, it can provide protection to any IP protocol including TCP and UDP. The security services that IPsec provides are:

Access control
> The ability to establish an IPsec communication is controlled by a policy—refusal to negotiate security parameters will prevent communication.

Data origin authentication
> The recipient of a packet can be sure that it comes from the sender it appears to come from.

Message integrity
> An attacker cannot modify a packet and have it accepted.

Replay protection
> An attacker cannot resend a previously sent packet and have it accepted.

Confidentiality
> An attacker cannot read intercepted data.

In addition, it provides limited protections against traffic flow analysis. In some cases, it will keep an attacker from figuring out which hosts are exchanging data and what protocols they are using.

IPsec is made up of three protocols, each of which is defined as a framework that defines packet layouts and field sizes and is suitable for use by multiple cryptographic algorithms. The protocols themselves do not define specific cryptographic algorithms to use, although every implementation is required to support a specified set of algorithms. The protocols that make up IPsec are:

- The Authentication Header (AH)
- The Encapsulating Security Payload (ESP)
- The Internet Security Association Key Management Protocol (ISAKMP)

The Authentication Header (AH) protocol provides message integrity and data origin authentication; it can optionally provide anti-replay services as well. The integrity protection that AH provides covers packet header information including source and destination addresses, but there are exceptions for header parameters that are frequently changed by routers, such as the IPv4 TTL or IPv6 hop-count.

The Encapsulating Security Payload (ESP) protocol provides confidentiality (encryption) and limited protection against traffic flow analysis. ESP also includes some of the services normally provided by AH. Both AH and ESP rely on the availability of shared keys, and neither one has a way to move them from one machine to another. Generating these keys is handled by the third IPsec protocol, the ISAKMP.

ISAKMP is also a framework protocol; it doesn't by itself define the algorithms that are used to generate the keys for AH and ESP. The Internet Key Exchange (IKE) protocol uses the ISAKMP framework with specific key exchange algorithms to set up cryptographic keys for AH and ESP. This layering may seem confusing and overly complicated, but the separation of ISAKMP from IKE means that the same basic IPsec framework can be used with multiple different key exchange algorithms (including plain old manual key exchange). The standardization of IKE allows different people to implement the same key exchange algorithms and be guaranteed interoperability. The Linux FreeS/WAN project has an implementation of IKE called Pluto.

In IPv6 the AH and ESP protocols can be used simultaneously, with an IPv6 feature called *header chaining*, to provide authentication modes that ESP alone cannot provide. When they are used in this way it is recommended that ESP be wrapped by the additional AH header. In IPv4, it's not possible to use them both at once (you can have only one header at a time).

IPsec provides two operating modes for AH and ESP, transport and tunnel. In transport mode, AH or ESP occur immediately after the IP header and encapsulate the remainder of the original IP packet. *Transport mode* works only between individual hosts; the packet must be interpreted by the host that receives it. Transport is used to protect host-to-host communications. Hosts can use it to protect all of their traffic to other cooperating hosts, or they can use it much the way TLS is used, as a protection layer around specific protocols.

In *tunnel mode*, the entire original packet is encapsulated in a new packet, and a new IP header is generated. IPsec uses the term *security gateway* for any device that can operate in tunnel mode. This term applies to all devices that can take IP packets and convert them to and from the IPsec protocols, whether they are hosts or dedicated routers. Because the whole IP packet is included, the recipient can forward packets to a final destination after processing. Tunnel mode is used when two security gateways or a gateway and a host communicate, and it is what allows you to build a virtual private network using IPsec.

The AH and ESP protocols each contain a 32-bit value that is called the Security Parameter Index (SPI). This is an identifier that is used to distinguish between different conversations going to the same destination. Every IPsec implementation is required to be able to independently track security parameters for the combination of SPI, destination IP address, and the security protocol that is being used (either AH or ESP). This combination of parameters is called a Security Association (SA). It is the responsibility of the specific ISAKMP key management protocol to negotiate and set the cryptographic parameters, including the SPI, for each Security Association.

An SA is effectively the collection of the cryptographic keys and parameters for use by either AH or ESP:

AH

   The cryptographic keys and algorithm identifiers used for integrity protection and anti-replay parameters

ESP

   The cryptographic keys and algorithm identifiers used for encryption, integrity protection, and anti-replay parameters

Packet Filtering Characteristics of IPsec

The AH and ESP protocols are implemented directly on top of the IP layer. AH is IP protocol 51, and ESP is IP protocol 50. The ISAKMP protocol uses UDP port 500 for both sending and receiving. In order to allow IPsec, you will need a packet filtering system that can filter on IP protocol type. Because IPsec provides end–to–end protections, a firewall will not be able to modify or even be able to inspect the contents of IPsec packets.

Direction	Source Addr.	Dest. Addr.	Protocol	Source Port	Dest. Port	Notes
In	Ext	Int	AH	a	a	Incoming AH, client to server
Out	Int	Ext	AH	a	a	Incoming AH, server to client
In	Ext	Int	ESP	a	a	Incoming ESP, client to server
Out	Int	Ext	ESP	a	a	Incoming ESP, server to client
In	Ext	Int	UDP	500	500	Incoming ISAKMP request
Out	Int	Ext	UDP	500	500	ISAKMP response
Out	Int	Ext	AH	a	a	Outgoing AH, client to server
In	Ext	Int	AH	a	a	Outgoing AH, server to client
Out	Int	Ext	ESP	a	a	Outgoing ESP, client to server
In	Ext	Int	ESP	a	a	Outgoing ESP, server to client
Out	Int	Ext	UDP	500	500	Outgoing ISAKMP request
In	Ext	Int	UDP	500	500	ISAKMP response

a AH and ESP do not have source or destination ports.

You may note that the table does not include information about the setting for the ACK bit. UDP has no equivalent of the TCP ACK bit. When TCP packets are incorporated into AH packets, their flags will still be present; it would be theoretically possible for a firewall that understood AH to use those ACK bits to determine the direction of the TCP connections and to filter using this information. Similarly, TCP and UDP packets in AH will have their original source and destination ports available for filtering.

Proxying Characteristics of IPsec

AH and ESP provide end-to-end message integrity protection that is calculated using data from the IP packet header. Using a proxy will change the header data, thereby causing a message integrity failure. In theory, it is possible for the IPsec architecture to allow the use of intermediary proxies in end-to-end communications if they can participate in the negotiation of integrity protection Security Association parameters. Unfortunately, the details for how this might work have not been defined so it is not currently possible to use IPsec through proxies.

It is, however, possible to use regular IP to the proxy system and have it speak IPsec to the destination. In addition, IPsec could be used with SOCKS. In this configuration, the client would set up communications with the SOCKS server via IPsec, and the SOCKS server would set up a separate IPsec communications channel to the final destination. However, this double use of IPsec may require significant CPU resources to implement.

Network Address Translation Characteristics of IPsec

Both AH and ESP include message integrity protections for the entire packet, including the headers. If you modify the packet at all, even to change the source or destination address, you will make the packet invalid. It is therefore impossible to do network address translation with AH or ESP. On the other hand, it's perfectly possible to do network address translation on packets that are then tunneled in AH or ESP; they don't care what happened to the packet while it was still a standard IP packet.

Therefore, you can combine network address translation and IPsec tunneling, as long as you do the network address translation first and then set up the IPsec tunnel. (Using IPsec parlance, it would be possible to implement network address translation behind or on a security gateway.)

Summary of Recommendations for IPsec

- IPsec is a good choice for building virtual private networks.

Remote Access Service (RAS)

Microsoft's Remote Access Service (RAS) provides a consistent user interface to a wide variety of protocols used to connect a machine in one place to a network in a different place. It is not a single service from a firewall point of view; instead, it uses multiple different services. In Windows NT 4, RAS is available either as an installable package provided with the standard Server operating system or in an enhanced version that is part of the no-cost Routing and Remote Access Service (RRAS) package. In Windows 2000, RAS is always part of RRAS, and it is an indivisible part of the operating system. You may enable it or disable it, but you cannot install or remove it.

RAS can be used in two different modes. In one mode, the RAS client has access only to the RAS server; in the other mode, the RAS server acts as a router, and the RAS client has access to the full network. Allowing access only to the RAS server gives you more control over the client, but it doesn't provide much functionality.

As we mentioned before, RAS clients can use multiple different protocols to connect to RAS servers. Originally, RAS was primarily used to support modems and similar low-level connections, and RAS still supports the use of PPP over a variety of different transports, including most popular modems, ISDN, and X.25. However, RAS is now also frequently used to build virtual private networks over IP connections, using Point-to-Point Tunneling Protocol (PPTP), or in Windows 2000, Layer 2 Transport Protocol (L2TP).

Point-to-Point Tunneling Protocol (PPTP)

PPTP is an encapsulation protocol based on the Point-to-Point Protocol (PPP) and the Generic Routing Encapsulation (GRE) protocol. PPP was originally designed to facilitate using IP and similar protocols over dialup connections and provides a general way to encapsulate protocols at the level of IP. PPTP is an extension of PPP, which takes PPP packets, encrypts them, and encapsulates them in GRE packets. Figure 14-3 shows the layers of encapsulation involved in sending a TCP packet via PPTP. Since PPP supports encapsulating multiple protocols, so does PPTP. It is most often used to provide virtual private networking, tunneling IP over IP, but it can also be used to tunnel non-IP protocols like IPX.

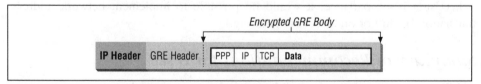

Figure 14-3. PPTP encapsulation of a TCP packet

Since PPTP tunnels packets over IP, there must be an IP-level connection between the hosts. In many situations, that connection allows the hosts to be attacked using other protocols. For instance, if you are using PPTP as a virtual private network across the Internet, the hosts have some sort of Internet connection and will have all the normal vulnerabilities of Internet-connected hosts. You will need to disable all non-PPTP connections or otherwise protect the machines. In particular, we recommend avoiding PPTP products that allow traffic to or from the host to use the underlying network directly.

There's been a great deal of controversy over the security of PPTP. Some of this has been due to weaknesses in Microsoft implementations of PPTP, many of which have been fixed. However, there are some design weaknesses in PPTP as well.

Design Weaknesses in PPTP

Although PPTP is an encrypted protocol, not all the parts of the conversation are encrypted. Before the PPTP server starts accepting the GRE packets, a negotiation takes place over TCP. PPTP encryption protects the information being tunneled but not the negotiation involved in setting up the tunnel. The negotiation is done in cleartext and includes client and server IP addresses, the name and software version information about the client, the username, and sometimes the hashed password used for authentication. All of this information is exposed to eavesdropping.

This negotiation is also done before the client has to authenticate, which makes the server particularly vulnerable to hostile clients. An attacker doesn't have to be able to authenticate in order to engage the server in negotiation, tying up resources and potentially confusing the server.

Implementation Weaknesses in PPTP

As we discussed earlier, PPTP sends authentication information in cleartext. In many versions of Microsoft PPTP, this information can include a LanMan hash of the user's password. As described in Chapter 21, *Authentication and Auditing Services*, it is relatively easy to use a LanMan hash to discover a password. You can disable Lan Manager authentication and should do so on all clients and servers you control. This will force the authentication to use more secure Windows NT password hashes.

Microsoft's implementation also has problems with the encryption. Microsoft offers two levels of encryption, both using the symmetric key encryption algorithm called RC4; one uses a 40-bit key, and the other uses a 128-bit key. (See Appendix C, *Cryptography*, for more information on RC4 and the importance of key length.) The 40-bit RC4 algorithm is not particularly strong to begin with, and Microsoft weakens it further by basing the key on the user's password, so that a user will have multiple sessions with the same key. The longer a key is used, the stronger it needs to be, and the time between password changes may be a very long time indeed.

When 128-bit keys are in use, Microsoft bases the key on the user's password and on a pseudo-random number so that it's different for each connection. This is a major improvement, although using the user's password does reduce the number of probable keys and makes it important for PPTP users to have good passwords.

Most PPTP implementations, including Microsoft's, are susceptible to problems with control negotiations. As we pointed out earlier, these negotiations take place before the client authentication, which means that any attacker can send them. It's therefore extremely important for servers to be able to deal with bad negotiations, but in fact, many servers will crash if they receive garbled negotiations, and some will crash even when sent random garbage that bears no resemblance to a valid negotiation. Although Microsoft offers an option to control PPTP access by source IP address, it's enforced on the GRE tunnel, not on the TCP-based negotiation. If you are doing PPTP from known source addresses, you can protect the PPTP server with a packet filter in front of it; if you are not, you have no choice but to live with these denial of service attacks.

Packet Filtering Characteristics of PPTP

PPTP negotiation takes place on TCP port 1723. The actual tunnel is based on GRE, which is IP protocol 47, and uses GRE protocol hexadecimal 880B (indicating that the tunneled packets are PPP). GRE is discussed further in Chapter 4, *Packets and Protocols.*

Direction	Source Addr.	Dest. Addr.	Protocol	Source Port	Dest. Port	ACK Set	Notes
In	Ext	Int	GRE	a	a	b	Tunnel data, external client to internal server
Out	Int	Ext	GRE	a	a	b	Tunnel reply, internal server to external client
In	Ext	Int	TCP	>1023	1723	c	Setup request, external client to internal server
Out	Int	Ext	TCP	1723	>1023	Yes	Setup response, internal server to external client
Out	Int	Ext	GRE	a	a	b	Tunnel data, internal client to external server
In	Ext	Int	GRE	a	a	b	Tunnel reply, external server to internal client
Out	Int	Ext	TCP	>1023	1723	c	Setup request, internal client to external server
In	Ext	Int	TCP	1723	>1023	Yes	Setup response, external server to internal client

a GRE does not have ports. GRE does have protocol types, and PPTP is protocol type hexadecimal 880B.
b GRE has no ACK equivalent.
c ACK will not be set on the first packet (establishing connection) but will be set on the rest.

Proxying Characteristics of PPTP

It would theoretically be possible to proxy PPTP, as long as you could find a proxy system that supported GRE. It's not clear that there's any point in proxying a tunneling protocol, however. A proxy system can't apply much security, since all of the traffic is encrypted. The only thing a proxy system could protect you from is attacks on the PPTP server over the negotiation protocol.

Network Address Translation Characteristics of PPTP

In general, network address translation won't interfere with PPTP; although there are embedded addresses, they're intended to pass through a tunnel in any case. You will require a network address translation system that supports GRE, as well as TCP and UDP. Network address translation will not conceal any information when used with PPTP, and will not allow you to use PPTP between two networks that are using the same address space, because the original address information will be visible once the PPTP encapsulation is removed.

Summary of Recommendations for PPTP

- Use PPTP with caution; it does not provide as much security as other options for doing virtual private networking but may be an acceptable option if you need to tunnel protocols for reasons other than securing the information they're carrying.

- If you are going to use PPTP, proxying does not give you any significant protection, and you might as well simply pass it through packet filters.

- Configure PPTP clients and servers to use the highest available level of encryption.

Layer 2 Transport Protocol (L2TP)

The Layer 2 Transport Protocol (L2TP) is another generic encapsulation protocol designed to allow you to tunnel IP networking. Like PPTP, it is an extension of PPP. There are two main differences between PPTP and L2TP. First, PPTP always runs on top of IP; it requires that you have an IP connection of some sort. L2TP can run over a number of different protocols, including directly over a phone line (like PPP). Second, PPTP is an encrypted protocol; it encrypts everything except for the initial negotiations. L2TP is not an encrypted protocol; it does not encrypt message bodies. On the other hand, L2TP does do mutual authentication for the initial negotiations and is capable of concealing the information in the initial negotiations.

L2TP is normally used in conjunction with IPsec, so that IPsec can provide the encryption. This results in a heavily layered protocol stack. Figure 14-4 shows the layers of encapsulation involved in sending a TCP packet via LT2P securely over an IP network.

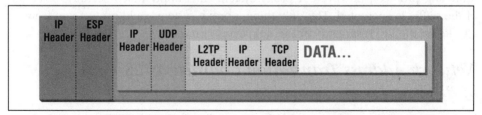

Figure 14-4. L2TP encapsulation of a TCP packet, as normally seen crossing an IP network

Packet Filtering Characteristics of L2TP

When L2TP is layered on top of IP, it uses UDP port 1701. However, in most implementations, L2TP is actually transmitted over IP via IPsec, using ESP encapsulation of UDP; this will have the packet filtering characteristics shown earlier for ESP.

Direction	Source Addr.	Dest. Addr.	Protocol	Source Port	Dest. Port	Notes
In	Ext	Int	UDP	>1023	1701	External client to internal server
Out	Int	Ext	UDP	1701[a]	>1023	Response, internal server to external client
Out	Int	Ext	UDP	>1023	1701	Internal client to external server
In	Ext	Int	UDP	1701[a]	>1023	Response, external server to internal client

[a] The standard does not require L2TP servers to return packets from port 1701; they must receive packets at 1701 but may send them from any port. Many servers will send packets from 1701 to simplify interactions with network address translation and dynamic packet filtering.

Proxying Characteristics of L2TP

It is possible to proxy L2TP, as long as you have a proxy system that supports UDP. It's not clear that there's any point in proxying a tunneling protocol, however. If L2TP is unencrypted, it's insecure regardless of what the proxy does; if it's encrypted, the proxy can't tell what it's doing to apply extra security.

Network Address Translation Characteristics of L2TP

In general, network address translation won't interfere with L2TP; although there are embedded addresses, they're intended to pass through a tunnel in any case. Network address translation will not conceal any information when used with L2TP and will not allow you to use L2TP between two networks that are using the same address space, because the original address information will be visible once the L2TP encapsulation is removed.

If you use an L2TP implementation where the endpoint sends replies from a randomly chosen port, rather than from port 1701, you may have difficulty getting the replies through an address translation system. The translation system will not recognize the packets as replies because the new source port is not the same as the previous destination port.

Summary of Recommendations for L2TP

- Do not use unencrypted L2TP through a firewall; if you need to cross an unsecured network, be sure that L2TP is combined with an encryption transport protocol. Most implementations will use IPsec for this purpose.

- Proxying does not give you any more functionality than packet filtering when used with L2TP.

15

The World Wide Web

The existence of the World Wide Web is a major factor behind the explosive growth of the Internet. (In fact, many of the newcomers to the Internet believe that the Internet and the World Wide Web are the same thing.) Since the first graphical user interface to the Web to gain widespread acceptance, NCSA Mosaic, was introduced in 1993, web traffic on the Internet has been growing at an explosive rate, far faster than any other kind of traffic (SMTP email, FTP file transfers, Telnet remote terminal sessions, etc.). You will certainly want to let your users use a browser to access web sites, and you are very likely to want to run a site yourself, if you do anything that might benefit from publicity. This chapter discusses the underlying mechanisms involved, their security implications, and the measures you can take to deal with them.

The very things that make the Web so popular also make it very difficult to secure. The basic protocols are very flexible, and the programs used for web servers and clients are easy to extend. Each extension has its own security implications, but they are difficult to separate and control.

Most web browsers are capable of using protocols other than HTTP, which is the basic protocol of the Web. For example, these browsers are usually also Gopher and FTP clients or are capable of using your existing Telnet and FTP clients transparently (without it being obvious to the user that an external program is starting). Many of them are also NNTP and SMTP clients. They use a single, consistent notation called a Uniform Resource Locator (URL) to specify connections of various types.

In addition, a number of other protocols are used in conjunction with web browsers. Some of these have other client programs, but most of them are used primarily if not exclusively as a seamless part of web sites.

There are three basic sets of security concerns regarding HTTP:

- What can a malicious client do to your HTTP server?
- What can a malicious HTTP server do to your clients?
- What else can come in, tunneled over HTTP?

The following sections describe these concerns.

HTTP Server Security

A server that supports nothing but the bare HTTP protocol poses relatively few security concerns. An HTTP server with no extensions takes requests and returns files; the only thing it writes to the disk are log files. Therefore, no matter how malicious the user and how badly written the server, the vulnerabilities of an HTTP server by itself are pretty much limited to various sorts of denial of service (the HTTP server crashes, crashes the machine, makes the rest of the machine unusable, fills up the disk...) and inadvertent release of data (a client requests a file you wanted to keep private, but the server gives it out). If the server is sufficiently badly written, an attacker may be able to execute arbitrary commands with the permissions of the HTTP server via a buffer overflow attack. This is unlikely in a simple server and relatively easy to protect against (run the server as an account with no special privileges, and even if an attacker can execute commands he or she won't get any interesting results).

Denial of service is always impossible to protect against completely, but a well-written HTTP server will be relatively immune to it. Normal practices for dealing with bastion hosts (see Chapter 10, *Bastion Hosts*) will also help you avoid and recover from denial of service attacks. Publicly accessible web sites are high-visibility targets and tend to be resource-intensive even when they are not under attack, so it is probably unwise to combine them on the same bastion host with other services.

Inadvertent release of data is a problem that requires more special effort to avoid. You should assume that any file that an HTTP server can read is a file that it will give out. Don't assume that a file is safe because it's not in the document tree, because it's not in HTML, or because you haven't published a link to it. It's easy to get caught out; one of the authors sent out email to a bunch of friends about a web page, only to get an answer back 20 minutes later that said "Interesting, but I don't like the picture of me." "What picture of you? You're not on that web page!" "No, but I always look at the whole directory, and when I saw there was a *.gif* file named after me I had to look at it." That was a combination of a mistake on the author's part (transferring an entire working directory into production instead of just the parts intended to be published) and on the site maintainer's part (it shouldn't have been giving out directory information anyway).

In this case, the effect was benign, but the same sort of mistake can have much more serious consequences. Public web servers frequently make headlines by containing draft or prerelease information erroneously left with information intended to be published; information intended for a small audience but left unprotected in the hope that nobody will notice it; and information used internally by the web server or other processes on the machine but left where the web server can read it and outsiders can request it. That latter category can include everything from Unix password files to customer data (including credit card numbers!).

In order to minimize these exposures:

- Carefully configure the security and access control features of your server to restrict its capabilities and what users can access with it.

- Run the server as an unprivileged user.

- Use filesystem permissions to be sure that the server cannot read files it is not supposed to provide access to.

- Under Unix, use the *chroot* mechanism to restrict the server's operation to a particular section of your filesystem hierarchy. You can use *chroot* either within the server or through an external wrapper program.

- Minimize the amount of sensitive information on the machine.

- Limit the number of people who can put data on the externally visible web sites; educate those people carefully about the implications of publishing data.

- Maintain a clear distinction between production and development servers and specify a cleanup stage before data is moved to the production servers.

HTTP Extensions

In the previous section, we discussed the risks of an HTTP server that processes nothing but the base HTTP protocol and pointed out that they're fairly small. This seems to conflict with the easily observable fact that there are frequent and high-profile break-ins to web sites. The problem is that almost nobody runs an HTTP server without extensions. Almost all HTTP servers make extensive use of external programs or additional protocols. (It used to be that additional protocols were always implemented outside the web server, but for efficiency reasons, it's become common to build extension languages into the web server itself.)

These extensions provide all sorts of capabilities; authoring extensions allow people to add and change web pages using a browser, form-processing extensions allow people to place orders for products, database extensions check the current status of things, active page extensions change the look of a page depending on who's asked for it. Anything that a web server does besides returning an unchanging data file requires some addition to the basic capabilities of the server.

These additions radically change the security picture. Instead of providing an extremely limited interaction, they provide the ability to do all sorts of dangerous things (like write data to the server). Furthermore, many extensions are not simple, limited-function modules; they're general-purpose languages, allowing you to easily add your own insecurity at home. That means that the security of your web server is no longer dependent only on the security of the web server, which you can be relatively confident has been developed by people who know something about security and have a development and debugging process in place, but also on all the add-in programs, which may well have been written in a few minutes by novice programmers with no thoughts about security.

Even if you don't install locally written programs, commercial web server extensions have a long and dark history of security problems. It's pretty easy to write a secure program if it never has to write data. It's hard to write a secure program that actually lets the user change things; it gets harder if the user has to juggle high-value information (for instance, if you're writing a electronic commerce application that is dealing with data that has real-world effects on goods and money). It can become very difficult to evaluate security if you're trying to provide complete flexibility.

The list of companies with serious security problems in their web server extensions doesn't just read like a who's who of the software industry; it's effectively the complete list of companies that provide web servers or extensions! For instance, Microsoft, Sun, Netscape, and Oracle have all had problems, often repeatedly. Lest you think this a commercial problem, we should point out that both the Apache server and the Squid cache server have had their problems as well.

You will often see external programs used with web servers called *CGI scripts*, after the Common Gateway Interface (CGI), which specifies how browsers can pass information to servers. You will also often see *Active Server Pages* (ASP), which is a Microsoft technology for making dynamic pages. New technologies for extensions appear at a rapid rate, but they all have the same sorts of security implications.

There are two things you need to worry about with these extensions:

- Can an attacker trick extensions into doing something they shouldn't?
- Can an attacker run unexpected external programs?

Tricking extensions

Your average HTTP server runs dozens of external programs; they often come from multiple sources and are written in multiple languages. It's not unusual for a single page to involve three or four layers of programs. For instance, the web server calls an external program written in Visual Basic, which uses Jet to access a database server. In many cases, the people writing web pages are using libraries and may not even be aware what other programs are getting run. Figure 15-1 shows one configuration where a simple query to a web server involves multiple programs.

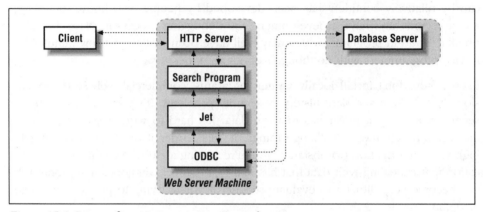

Figure 15-1. Layers of programs running on a web server

This situation is a security nightmare. Effectively, each of these external programs is an Internet-attached server, with all the security implications any other server has. If any one of them has security problems, the entire system may be vulnerable; in the previous example, you are vulnerable to problems in the web server, the external program, the Visual Basic interpreter, Jet, and the database server. Both the Visual Basic interpreter and Jet are invisible in normal circumstances, but there have been security problems with Jet.

In the case of a program that accesses a database server, you may not know exactly how it works, but at least you're probably aware that the program is important to you. But security problems may exist and be important even in programs that you think are too trivial to worry about; for instance, there have been security problems with counter programs (which are used to put up the little signs that say "You are visitor number 437"). These programs appear to be pretty harmless; after all, even if people can manipulate the answer they return, who really cares? The difficulty is that they keep the information in a file somewhere, which means that they are capable of both reading and writing files on the machine. Some counter programs can be manipulated into reading or writing any file they have appropriate permissions for, and overwriting arbitrary files with counter information can do a lot of damage.

In order to minimize the risks created by external programs, treat them as you would any other servers. In particular:

- Install external programs only after you have considered their security implications and tested them on a protected machine.

- Run as few external programs as possible.

- Run external programs with minimal permissions.

- Don't assume that programs will be accessed from pages or CGI forms you provide.

- Develop special bastion host configurations for external programs, going through and removing all unneeded files and double-checking all permissions and placements of files that are read and written.

The most common errors people make are:

- Taking a development tool or web server package and installing it on a production machine without removing sample programs or other development features. These are often proof-of-concept or debugging tools that provide very broad access.

- Running external programs with too many permissions, either by using an overly powerful account (root, under Unix, for instance), or the same account for a number of different external programs, or a default account provided by a software vendor with normal user access to the entire system (such accounts also often have a known name and password).

More conceptually, people are too trusting; they install combinations of commercial, externally and internally produced programs or scripts without considering their implications. Without suitable training, very few programmers are capable of writing secure programs, and all programs run by a web server need to be secure. No external vendor is so large and clever that you can install their software directly onto your production web server and feel sure that you are secure. No web server add-on is so trivial that you can let a novice programmer write it and not worry about its security.

You must treat every single addition to your web server as a new Internet-available server and evaluate its security appropriately. You must also maintain them all, keeping track of any newly discovered vulnerabilities and making appropriate modifications. Allowing people who are not security-aware to put executable programs on your web server is a recipe for disaster.

Running unexpected external programs

The second concern is that attackers might be able to run external programs that you didn't intend to make available. In the worst case, they upload their own external programs and cause your server to run them. How could attackers do this? Suppose the following:

- Your HTTP server and your anonymous FTP server both run on the same machine.

- They can both access the same areas of the filesystem.

- A writable directory is located somewhere in those areas, so that customers can upload crash dumps from your product via FTP for analysis by your programmers, for example.

In this case, the attacker might be able to upload a script or binary to that writable directory using anonymous FTP and then cause the HTTP server to run it.

What is your defense against things like this? Once again, your best bet is to restrict what filesystem areas each server can access (for instance, using *chroot* under Unix) and to provide a restricted environment in which each server can run. Note that this sort of vulnerability is by no means limited to FTP but is present any time that files can be uploaded.

HTTP Client Security

The security problems of HTTP clients are just as complex as those of HTTP servers. There are several problems:

- Inadvertent release of information

- Vulnerabilities in external viewers

- Vulnerabilities in extension systems

Inadvertent Release of Information

There are a number of ways in which web browsers may give away information that you didn't intend to make public. The most common is that they fail to protect passwords and usernames in ways that you might expect. Many web pages pass usernames and passwords around completely unprotected; some of them even embed them into URLs, making it easy to accidentally store them in your bookmarks file or mail them to a friend along with the location of an interesting web page.

The default authentication for web pages is something called *basic authentication*. This is what's happening when you ask for a page, and instead of bringing up the page, your web browser brings up a standard dialog box that asks you for your username and password. There's no encryption protecting that username and password; it's just sent to the server in cleartext. Furthermore, if you ask for another page from the same server, the username and password will be sent again, without any warning, still unencrypted.

A web site can protect the username and password data by telling the browser to use HTTPS, instead of HTTP, to make the connection. (HTTPS is discussed further later in this chapter.) This will encrypt the entire communication, including the authentication information. Unfortunately, you can't usually tell whether or not a web site has done this; although there's a little lock icon to tell you when the page you're looking at is encrypted, most clients don't display it, or any other indication that things have been secured, until the page actually loads, which is after you've already given out the username and password.

That's not the only way in which it's difficult to tell what a web server is going to do with your password. You may be able to tell if the web server is doing something extremely insecure, like embedding the password in cleartext in a URL, but you can't tell if it's storing it properly on the other end. Therefore, while you can sometimes be sure that your password isn't protected, you can never be sure that it is, and you should assume that it isn't. Don't use passwords you've sent over the Web to protect anything you care about deeply. You should use different passwords on different web sites, and they should not be the same passwords that you use anywhere else.

If you're going to send a web site important data, you should be sure that the site has made a legally binding commitment to protect that data appropriately. You should also be sure that you have an encrypted connection to the site.

Cookies

Cookies are a way for a site to track information about you. It can be information that lasts a long time (for instance, information about what you want to see when you come to the site) or information about what you've just done (for instance, information about what items you want to buy in the current transaction). Cookies are important for web sites because it's otherwise extremely difficult to keep track of anything about a web browser. Each time a browser requests a page, it's a new transaction, with no way for the server to know what previous transaction it might be related to. Cookies provide a way for a server to ask a web browser to keep track of and possibly store some data.

A cookie is a fairly simple object; it's a small amount of information to be stored that is associated with an identifying string, an expiration date, and a URL pattern that indicates when the cookie should be sent with HTTP requests. Whenever you visit a web site, the browser checks to see if any unexpired cookies match the URL pattern, and if so, the browser sends them along with your request.

The information that's in a cookie isn't usually of any great interest by itself. Cookies tend to contain customer identifiers or coded lists of preferences—things that make sense only to the site that set the cookie. This is important because cookies are passed across the network unencrypted, and you wouldn't want them to have anything dangerous in them.

On the other hand, once a web site gets a cookie, it may give back information that you do care about. For instance, it might use the cookie to look up the credit card information you used on your last order (in which case somebody with that cookie could order things on your credit card). For that matter, it might just look up your last order and display it along with your name. Since cookies are passed unencrypted, and can be intercepted at any point, it's not good practice to use them for anything critical, but some web sites do.

In addition, many people are worried about situations in which cookies can be used to track patterns of usage. When you use a link on a web page, the site you go to gets information about the page the link was on (this is called the *referrer*). If the site you go to also has a cookie that will identify you, it can build up a history of the places you have come from. This wouldn't be very interesting for most sites, but sites that put up banner advertisements have links on thousands of web pages and can build up a fairly accurate picture of where you come from. Since referrer information includes the entire URL, this will include information about specific search requests and, in the worst cases, may contain password and username information.

There are some controls on the use of cookies. Some browsers don't support cookies at all; others will allow you to control the situations where you give out a cookie, by choosing to reject all cookies, asking you before accepting cookies, or accepting only certain cookies. For instance, cookies are intended to be returned only to the site that set them, but the definition of "site" is unclear. The cookie specifies what hostnames it should be returned to and may give a specific hostname or a broad range of hostnames. Some browsers can be configured so that they will accept only cookies that will be returned to the host that originally set the cookie.

External Viewers

HTTP servers can provide data in any number of formats: plain text files, HTML files, PostScript documents, image files (PNG, JPEG, and GIF), movie files (MPEG), audio files, and so on. The servers use MIME, discussed briefly in Chapter 16, *Electronic Mail and News*, to format the data and specify its type. HTTP clients generally don't attempt to understand and process all of these different data formats. They understand some types (such as HTML, plain text, JPEG, and GIF), and they rely on external programs to deal with the rest. These external programs will display, play, preview, print, or do whatever is appropriate for the format.

For example, web browsers confronted with a PDF file will ordinarily invoke Adobe Acrobat Exchange or Acrobat Reader, and web browsers confronted with a compressed file will ordinarily invoke a decompression program. The user controls (generally via a configuration file) what data types the HTTP client knows about, which programs to invoke for which data types, and what arguments to pass to those programs. If the user hasn't provided a configuration file, the HTTP client generally uses a built-in default or a systemwide default.

These external programs may be obviously separate from the web browser, or they may be *plug-ins*, programs that are not part of the web browser but that integrate with it seamlessly. Plug-ins are simply external programs that can be run by the browser and will display information in windows that the browser controls. There is more than one type of plug-in technology; Microsoft's ActiveX and Netscape's Plug-Ins can both be used to provide seamless integration with a browser. Despite the fact that they look like parts of the browser, they have the same security implications as other external programs.

All of these external programs present two security concerns:

- What are the inherent capabilities of the external programs an attacker might take advantage of?

- What new programs (or new arguments for existing programs) might an attacker be able to convince the user to add to the local configuration?

Let's consider, for example, what an HTTP client is going to do with a PostScript file. PostScript is a language for controlling printers. While primarily intended for that purpose, it is a full programming language, complete with data structures, flow of control operators, and file input/output operators. These operators ("read file", "write file", "create file", "delete file", etc.) are seldom used, except on printers with local disks for font storage, but they're there as part of the language. PostScript previewers (such as GhostScript) generally implement these operators for completeness.

Suppose that a user uses Internet Explorer to pull down a PostScript document. Internet Explorer invokes GhostScript, and it turns out that the document has PostScript commands in it that say "delete all files in the current directory". If GhostScript executes the commands, who's to blame? You can't really expect Internet Explorer to scan the PostScript on the way through to see if it's dangerous; that's an impossible task. You can't really expect GhostScript not to do what it's told in valid PostScript code. You can't really expect your users not to download Post-Script code or to scan it themselves.

Current versions of GhostScript have a safer mode they run in by default. This mode disables "dangerous" operators such as those for file input/output. But what about all the other PostScript interpreters or previewers? And what about the applications to handle all the other data types? How safe are they? Who knows?

Even if you have safe versions of these auxiliary applications, how do you keep your users from changing their configuration files to add new applications, run different applications, or pass different arguments (for example, to disable the safer mode of GhostScript) to the existing applications?

Why would a user do this? Suppose that the user found something on the web that claimed to be something really neat—a game demo, a graphics file, a copy of the hottest new song, whatever. And suppose that this desirable something came with a note that said "Hey, before you can access this Really Cool Thing, you need to modify your browser configuration, because the standard configuration doesn't know how to deal with this thing; here's what you do...." And suppose that the instructions were something like "remove the '-dSAFER' flag from the configuration for files of type PostScript"?

Would your users recognize that they were being instructed to do something dangerous? Even if they recognized it, would they do it anyway (nice, trusting people that they are)?

Extension Systems

Using external viewers is not the only way to extend the capabilities of a web browser. Most browsers also support at least one system that allows web pages to download programs that will be executed by the browser. A variety of different extension systems are supported by different browsers, and they have very different security models and implications. The details of the different systems are discussed in the "Mobile Code and Web-Related Languages" section, later in this chapter. Even though the systems differ, they have a certain number of goals and security implications in common.

These extension systems are very convenient; it is often much more efficient to have the browser do some calculations itself than to have to send data to an HTTP server, have it do some calculations, and get the answer back. In addition, extension languages allow for a much more powerful and flexible interface between the browser and the full capabilities of the computer than you can get by using external viewers.

For instance, if you are filling out a form, it's annoying to have to submit the form to the server and wait for it to come back and tell you that you've omitted a required piece of information. It's preferable for your browser to be able to tell you that immediately. Similarly, if your happiness depends on having penguins dance across the screen, the most efficient way to get that effect is going to be to tell your browser how to draw a dancing penguin and where to move it.

On the other hand, filling out forms and drawing dancing penguins are not all that interesting. In order for extension languages to actually do interesting and useful tasks, they have to have more capabilities, but the more capabilities that are available, the more dangerous a language is.

Of course, normal programming languages have lots of capabilities and therefore lots of dangers, but people don't usually find this worrisome. This is because when you get a program written in a normal programming language, you generally decide that you want the program, you go out looking for it, you have some information about where it comes from, and you explicitly choose to run it. When you get a program as part of a web page, it just shows up and runs; you may be happily watching the dancing penguins and not knowing that anything else is happening.

We discuss the different approaches taken by extension languages in the following sections, as we discuss the specific languages. All of them do attempt to provide security, but none of them is problem free.

What Can You Do?

There is no simple, foolproof defense against the types of problems we've described. At this point in time, you have to rely on a combination of carefully installed and configured client and auxiliary programs, and a healthy dose of user education and awareness training. This is an area of active research and development, and both the safeguards and the attacks will probably develop significantly over the next couple of years.

Content-aware firewalls, whether they are packet filters or proxies, can be of considerable help in reducing client vulnerability. A firewall that pays attention to content can control which extension languages and which types of files are passed through; it is even possible for it to do virus scanning on executables. Unfortunately, it's not possible to do a truly satisfactory job of protection even with a content-aware firewall.

Using *content-based filtering,* you have two options; you can filter out everything that might be dangerous, or you can filter out only those things you know for certain are dangerous. In the first case, you simply filter out all scripting languages; in the second case, you filter out known attacks. Be cautious of products that claim to filter out all hostile code and only hostile code. Accurately determining what code is hostile by simply looking at the code is impossible in the most specific, logical, and mathematical sense of the term. For useful scripting languages, it is equivalent to solving the Turing halting problem (determining whether an arbitrary piece of code ever stops executing), and the proof that it is impossible is one of the most famous and fundamental results in theoretical computer science.

It is possible to recognize particular pieces of hostile code, and sometimes even to recognize patterns that are common to many pieces of hostile code. Most content-based filtering systems rely on recognizing known attacks. Any time somebody comes up with a new attack, you will be vulnerable to it until the filter is updated, which may of course be after you have been attacked. Many content-based filters are easily fooled by trivial changes to the attack. Content filters that try to remove only hostile code fundamentally use the same technology as virus detectors. This has the advantage that it's a well-understood problem for vendors, who know about creating and distributing signatures. It has the disadvantage that it's a well-understood problem for attackers, as well, who have a variety of programs at their disposal for permuting programs to change their signatures.

Using content filtering to remove all scripting languages is safer. Unfortunately, you really do need to remove all scripting languages, since otherwise, it is possible to pass through JavaScript or VBScript programs that create Java code or ActiveX controls. Many web pages are difficult or impossible to use if you filter out all scripting languages (and a significant percentage of them don't detect the problem and are just mysteriously blank or nonfunctional). In addition, using content filtering to remove scripting can interfere with some of the methods that servers use to try to deal with clients that don't support scripting languages. For instance, some servers attempt to determine capabilities of the client by the information the client provides about the browser version, which doesn't provide any information about the filter in the middle. Some pages may also try to use JavaScript to determine if Java is available. This means that pages that work fine if scripting languages are turned off at the browser may still fail miserably when a filter removes the scripts.

As we mention later, content filtering is impossible on some web pages; connections made with HTTPS instead of with HTTP are encrypted, and the firewall cannot tell what is in them to do content filtering.

Internet Explorer and Security Zones

One way for a browser to improve its security is to treat different sites differently. It's reasonable to allow an internal web site to do more risky things than an external one, for instance.

Starting with Internet Explorer 4.0, Microsoft introduced the concept of *security zones* to allow you to configure your browser to do this. Explorer defines multiple security zones and sets different default security policies for them. For instance, there is a security zone for the intranet, which by default accepts all signed ActiveX controls and asks you if you want to allow each unsigned control, and one for the Internet, which by default asks you if you want to accept each signed control and rejects all unsigned controls. (ActiveX controls and signatures are discussed later in this chapter.) There is also a security zone that applies only to data originating on the local machine (this is not supposed to include cached data that was originally loaded from the Internet). The local machine zone is the most trusted zone.

In most cases, Internet Explorer uses the host portion of the URL to determine what zone a page is in. Because the different zones have different security policies, it's important that Internet Explorer get this right. However, there have been several problems with the way that Internet Explorer does this, some of which Microsoft has fixed and some of which are not fixable. In particular, any hostname that does not contain a period is assumed to be in the intranet zone. Originally, there were various ways of referring to Internet hosts by IP address that could force any Internet host to be treated as an intranet host. These problems have been removed, and there is now no known way to write a link that will force Internet Explorer to consider it part of the intranet zone.

However, there are numerous ways for people to set themselves up so that external hosts are considered intranet hosts, and the security implications are unlikely to be clear to them. For instance, adding a domain name to the Domain Suffix Search Order in DNS properties will make all hosts in that domain parts of the intranet zone; for a less sweeping effect, any host that's present in LMHOSTS or HOSTS with a short name is also part of the intranet zone. An internal web server that will act as an intermediary and retrieve external pages will make all those pages parts of the intranet zone. The most notable class of programs that do this sort of thing are translators, like AltaVista's Babelfish (*http://babelfish.altavista.com*), which will translate English to French, among other options, or RinkWorks' Dialectizer (*http://www.rinkworks.com/dialect*), which will show you the page as if it were spoken by the cartoon character Elmer Fudd, among other options.

HTTP

HyperText Transfer Protocol (HTTP) is the protocol that the web is based on. The HTTP protocol itself is a relatively secure protocol and a straightforward one to allow through firewalls.

HTTP Tunneling

HTTP itself is a simple protocol, but it can carry quite complex data. Because HTTP is simple and popular, most people let it through their firewalls. Because it can carry complex data, it's easy to use it to carry other protocols, which can be useful. For instance, as a firewall maintainer, you may prefer having audio data come in over HTTP to having to configure more open ports for audio data (your users may not, since the quality may not be very good).

On the other hand, *tunneling* can also allow inherently insecure protocols to cross your firewall. For this reason, it may be advantageous to use a firewall solution that does content-based checking of HTTP connections, so that you can disallow connections that are actually tunneling other protocols. This can be quite difficult to do.

Different programs use different methods of "tunneling". These range from simply running their normal protocol on port 80, to including support for HTTP proxying using the "CONNECT" method (discussed later in the section about HTTP proxying), to actually using HTTP with a data type that the client handles specially.

Some of these are much easier to filter out than others. For instance, almost any content checking, whether it's an intelligent packet filter or an HTTP-aware proxy, will get rid of people running protocols other than HTTP on port 80. Similarly, most HTTP proxies will let you control what destinations can be used with CONNECT, and you should restrict them carefully to just the destinations that you need.

Tunneling that actually uses HTTP, on the other hand, is very difficult to filter out successfully. In order to get rid of it, you need to do content filtering on the HTTP stream and remove the relevant data types. Relatively few firewalls support this functionality, and it's very difficult to do successfully in any case. The problem is that if you remove only the data types that you know are being used for tunneling, you are setting up a policy that allows connections by default, which is guaranteed to leave you with a continuous stream of new problems. On the other hand, if you accept only data types that you believe to be safe, you are going to have a continuous stream of new complaints from users, because many data types are in use on the web, and they change rapidly.

Fortunately, the uses for tunneling that actually uses HTTP are fairly limited. The HTTP protocol is set up to support interactions that look like normal web browsing; the client sends a query, and the server sends an answer. The client can't send any information except the initial query, which is of limited size. This model works well for tunneling some other protocols (for instance, it's fine for tunneling

RealAudio) but poorly for tunneling protocols that need prolonged interaction between the client and the server. This doesn't prevent people from tunneling any protocol they like over HTTP, but it does at least make it more difficult and less efficient.

There is unfortunately no good solution to the general problem of tunneled protocols. Using proxying to make sure that connections are using HTTP, and controlling the use of CONNECT, will at least limit your exposure.

Special HTTP Servers

We have been discussing web servers, programs that exist purely to provide content via HTTP and related protocols. But HTTP is a straightforward and widely implemented protocol, so a number of things speak HTTP not to provide random content, but for some specialized purpose. The classic example is the administrative interface to normal HTTP servers. If you're administering a web server, you probably have a browser handy, so what's more natural than using the browser to do the administration? For a number of reasons, you don't want the administrative interface built in to the standard server (among other things, common administrative tasks involve stopping and starting the server—stopping it while you're talking to it is one thing, but starting it again is a neat trick if it's not there to talk to). Therefore, there is often a second server that speaks the HTTP protocol but doesn't behave exactly like a normal web server reading information out of files.

These days, other programs and even hardware devices may provide HTTP interfaces. For instance, you can buy a power strip with a built-in web server, allowing you to turn its outlets on and off from a web browser. These servers do not behave like the servers we have been discussing, and the fact that they speak the HTTP protocol doesn't give you any particularly good idea of what their security vulnerabilities may be.

You will have to assess the security of each of these servers separately. Some of the questions you should ask are:

- What information can the web server read? Are there any files that it might unexpectedly reveal?

- How are users authenticated?

- What can be done to the device via the server?

In general, you do not want to allow connections to these servers to cross a firewall.

Packet Filtering Characteristics of HTTP

HTTP is a TCP-based service. Clients use random ports above 1023. Most servers use port 80, but some don't. To understand why, you need some history.

Many information access services (notably HTTP, WAIS, and Gopher) were designed so that the servers don't *have* to run on a fixed well-known port on all machines. A standard well-known port was established for each of these services, but the clients and servers are all capable of using alternate ports as well. When you reference one of these servers, you can include the port number it's running on (assuming that it's not the standard port for that service) in addition to the name of the machine it's running on. For example, an HTTP URL of the form *http:/ /host.domain.example/file.html* is assumed to refer to a server on the standard HTTP port (port 80); if the server were on an alternate port (port 8000, for example), the URL would be written *http://host.domain.example:8000/file.html.*

The protocol designers had two valid reasons for designing these services this way:

- Doing so allows a single machine to run multiple servers for multiple data sets. You could, for example, run one HTTP server that's accessible to the world with data that you wish to make available to the public, and another that has other, nonpublic data on a different port that's restricted (via packet filtering or the authentication available in the HTTP server, for example).

- Doing so allows users to run their own servers (which may be a blessing or a curse, depending on your particular security policy). Because the standard well-known ports are all in the range below 1024 that's reserved for use only by root on Unix machines, unprivileged users can't run their servers on the standard port numbers.

The ability to provide these services on nonstandard ports has its uses, but it complicates things considerably from a packet filtering point of view. If your users wish to access a server running on a nonstandard port, you have several choices:

- You can tell the users they can't do it; this may or may not be acceptable, depending on your environment.

- You can add a special exception for that service to your packet filtering setup. This is bad for your users because it means that they first have to recognize the problem and then wait until you've fixed it, and it's bad for you because you'll constantly have to be adding exceptions to the filter list.

- You can try to convince the server's owner to move the server to the standard port. While encouraging folks to use the standard ports as much as possible is a good long-term solution, it's not likely to yield immediate results.

- You can use some kind of proxied version of the client. This requires setup on your end and may restrict your choice of clients. On the other hand, both Internet Explorer and Netscape Navigator support proxying, and they are by far the most popular clients.

- If you can filter on the ACK bit, you can allow all outbound connections, regardless of destination port. This opens up a wide variety of services, including passive-mode FTP. It also is a noticeable increase in your vulnerability.

The good news is that the vast majority of these servers (probably more than 90 percent of them) use the standard port, and the more widely used and important the server is, the more likely it is to use the standard port. Many servers that use nonstandard ports use one of a few easily recognizable substitutes (800 or 8000, for instance).

Some servers also use nonstandard ports to run secondary servers. Traditionally, HTTP proxies use port 8080, and administrative servers use a port number one higher than the server they're controlling (81 for administering a standard web server and 8081 for administering a proxy server).

Your firewall will probably prevent people on your internal network from setting up their own servers at nonstandard ports (you're not going to want to allow inbound connections to arbitrary ports above 1023). You could set up such servers on a bastion host, but wherever possible, it's kinder to other sites to leave your servers on the standard port.

Direction	Source Addr.	Dest. Addr.	Protocol	Source Port	Dest. Port	ACK Set	Notes
In	Ext	Int	TCP	>1023	80[a]	[b]	Request, external client to internal server
Out	Int	Ext	TCP	80[a]	>1023	Yes	Response, internal server to external client
Out	Int	Ext	TCP	>1023	80[a]	[b]	Request, internal client to external server
In	Ext	Int	TCP	80[a]	>1023	Yes	Response, external server to internal client

[a] 80 is the standard port number for HTTP servers, but some servers run on different port numbers.
[b] ACK is not set on the first packet of this type (establishing connection) but will be set on the rest.

Proxying Characteristics of HTTP

Various HTTP clients (such as Internet Explorer and Netscape Navigator) transparently support various proxying schemes. Some clients support SOCKS; others support user-transparent proxying via special HTTP servers, and some support both. (See the discussion of SOCKS and proxying in general in Chapter 9, *Proxy Systems.*)

HTTP proxies of various kinds are extremely common, and many incorporate caching, which can provide significant performance advantages for most sites. (A caching proxy is one that makes a copy of the requested data, so that if somebody else requests the same data, the proxy can fulfill the request with the copy instead of going back to the original server to request the data again.) In addition, many sites are worried about the content that people access via HTTP and use proxies to control accessibility (for instance, to prevent access to sites containing pornography, stock prices, or sports scores, all of which are common nonbusiness uses of the web by employees).

Clients that are speaking to HTTP proxy servers use HTTP, but they use slightly different commands from the ones they'd normally use. A client that wants to get the document known as "http://amusinginformation.example/foodle" without using a proxy will connect to the host *amusinginformation.example* and send a command much like "GET /foodle HTTP/1.1". In order to use an HTTP proxy, the client will connect to the proxy instead and issue the command as "GET http://amusinginformation.example/foodle HTTP/1.1". The proxy will then connect to *amusinginformation.example* and send "GET /foodle HTTP/1.1" and return the resulting page to the client.

Some HTTP proxy servers support commands that normal HTTP servers don't support. For instance, they may allow a client to issue commands like "FTP ftp://amusinginformation.example/foodle" (to have the proxy server transfer the named file via FTP and return it to the client) or "CONNECT amusinginformation.example: 873" (to have the proxy server make a TCP connection to the named port and relay information between it and the client). There is no standard for these additional commands, although FTP and CONNECT are two of the most common. Most web browsers will support using an HTTP proxy server for FTP and Gopher connections, and common web proxies (for instance, Microsoft Proxy Server) will support FTP and Gopher.

Some clients that are not web browsers will allow you to use an HTTP proxy server for protocols other than HTTP, and most of them depend on using CONNECT, which makes the HTTP proxy server into a generic proxy. For instance, Lotus Notes and *rsync* clients both are able to use HTTP proxies to get to their servers via CONNECT.

Using an HTTP proxy server as a generic proxy in this way is convenient but not particularly secure. Few HTTP proxy servers provide any interesting control or logging on the protocols used with CONNECT. You will want to be very restrictive about what protocols you allow this way.

It's extremely important to prevent external users from connecting to your HTTP proxy servers. If your HTTP proxy server can make inbound connections, external users can use it as a platform to attack internal servers they would not otherwise be able to get to (this is particularly dangerous if they can use CONNECT to get to arbitrary services). Even if the proxy server can't be used this way, it can be used to attack third parties.

People often search actively for open HTTP proxy servers. Some of these people are hostile and want to use the proxy servers as attack platforms, but some of them just want to use the proxy servers to access web sites that would otherwise be unavailable to them because of filtering rules at their site (or in a few cases, filtering imposed by national governments). Either way, it's probably not to your advantage to let them use your site. Being nice to people behind restrictive filters is tempting, but in the long run, it will merely use up your bandwidth and get you added to the list of filtered sites.

Network Address Translation Characteristics of HTTP

HTTP does not use embedded IP addresses as a functional part of the protocol, so network address translation will not interfere with HTTP. Web pages may contain URLs written with IP addresses instead of hostnames, and those embedded IP addresses will not be translated. You should therefore be careful about the content of web pages on servers behind network address translators.

In addition, HTTP clients may provide name and/or IP address information to servers, leaking information about your internal numbering and naming schemes. HTTP clients may provide "From:" headers, telling the server the user's email address (as the user told it to the browser), and proxies may add "Via:" headers indicating the IP addresses of proxies that a request (or response) has passed through.

Securing HTTP

You may hear discussions about secure versions of HTTP and wonder how they relate to firewalls and the configuring of services. Such discussions are mainly focused on the privacy issues of passing information around via HTTP. They don't really help solve the kinds of problems we've been discussing in previous sections.

Two defined protocols actually provide privacy using encryption and strong authentication for HTTP. The one that everyone knows is usually called HTTPS and is denoted by using *https* in the URL. The other, almost unknown protocol, is called Secure HTTP and is denoted by using *shttp* in the URL.

The goal of HTTPS is to protect your communication channel when retrieving or sending data. HTTPS currently uses TLS and SSL to achieve this. Chapter 14, *Intermediary Protocols*, contains more technical information on TLS and SSL.

The goal of Secure HTTP is to protect individual objects rather than the communications channel. This allows, for example, individual pages on a web server to be digitally signed—a web client can check the signature when the page is downloaded. If someone replaces the page without re-signing, then the signature check will fail, causing an alert to be displayed. Similarly, a secure form that is submitted to a web server can be a self-contained digitally signed object. This means that the object can be stored and used later to prove or dispute the transaction.

The use of Secure HTTP could have significant advantages for the consumer in the world of electronic commerce. If a company claims that it has a digitally signed object indicating your desire to purchase 2,000 rubber chickens but the digital signature doesn't match, then you can argue that you did not make the request. If the signature does match, then it can only mean one of two things; either you requested the chickens, or your private key has been stolen. In contrast, when you use HTTPS, your identity is not bound to the transaction but to the communication channel. This means that HTTPS cannot protect you from someone switching your order for rubber chickens to live ones, once it has been made, or just ordering chickens on your behalf.

Packet filtering characteristics of HTTPS and Secure HTTP

HTTPS uses a single TCP connection at port 443. Secure HTTP is designed to operate over port 80 (see the section on HTTP).

Direction	Source Addr.	Dest. Addr.	Protocol	Source Port	Dest. Port	ACK Set	Notes
In	Ext	Int	TCP	>1023	443	a	Request, external client to internal server
Out	Int	Ext	TCP	443	>1023	Yes	Response, internal server to external client
Out	Int	Ext	TCP	>1023	443	a	Request, internal client to external server
In	Ext	Int	TCP	443	>1023	Yes	Response, external server to internal client

a ACK is not set on the first packet of this type (establishing connection) but will be set on the rest.

Proxying characteristics of HTTPS and Secure HTTP

Because HTTPS and Secure HTTP use straightforward TCP connections, they are quite easy to proxy. Most programs that provide HTTP proxying also provide HTTPS and Secure HTTP proxying. However, both HTTPS and Secure HTTP use end-to-end encryption between the client and the server. This means that the data stream is entirely opaque to the proxy system, which cannot do any of the filtering or caching functions it does on normal HTTP connections.

Proxying for HTTPS is normally done using the CONNECT primitive (discussed earlier in the section on proxying HTTP). This allows the real client to exchange certificate information with the server, but it also serves as a generic proxy for any protocol running on the ports that the proxy allows for HTTPS. Since HTTPS is encrypted, the proxy can't do any verification on the contents of the connection. You should be cautious about the ports that you allow for HTTPS.

Network address translation characteristics of HTTPS and Secure HTTP

Like HTTP, HTTPS and Secure HTTP have no embedded IP addresses and will work without problems through a network address translation system. Because of the end-to-end encryption, it will not be possible to correct any IP addresses that occur in the body of secured pages, so you should make sure that such pages use hostnames and not IP addresses.

Summary of Recommendations for HTTP

- If you're going to run an HTTP server, use a dedicated bastion host if possible.

- If you're going to run an HTTP server, carefully configure the HTTP server to control what it has access to; in particular, watch out for ways that someone could upload a program to the system somehow (via mail or FTP, for example) and then trick the HTTP server into executing it.

- Carefully control the external programs your HTTP server can access.

- You can't allow internal hosts to access all HTTP servers without allowing them to access all TCP ports because some HTTP servers use nonstandard port numbers. If you don't mind allowing your users access to all TCP ports, you can use packet filtering to examine the ACK bit to allow outgoing connections to those ports (but not incoming connections from those ports). If you do mind, then either restrict your users to servers on the standard port (80), or use some form of proxying.

- Proxying HTTP is easy, and a caching proxy server offers network bandwidth benefits as well as security benefits.

- Do not allow external connections to HTTP proxy servers.

- Configure your HTTP clients carefully and warn your users not to reconfigure them based on external advice.

Mobile Code and Web-Related Languages

As we mentioned earlier, most web browsers support one or more ways of accepting arbitrary programs from servers. In general, systems that move programs from one machine to another are called *mobile code* systems. Although these systems are commonly implemented in web browsers, they may also be used other places. For instance, some web servers also support running them on the server itself; Java and ActiveX are used entirely independently of the Web for application development; and many web browsers that support using JavaScript and VBScript in web pages also interpret them when included in email or news messages.

Mobile code systems take two fundamental approaches to the security problem. Most of them attempt to keep programs from doing anything dangerous, or at least from doing anything dangerous without asking you about it first. For instance, JavaScript isn't allowed to write files to your disk without your consent; Java isn't allowed to open network connections to any server other than the one that your original connection was to. This approach results in web pages that can't quite do what you want but can still do some things that you don't want.

To avoid this problem, ActiveX takes the second approach and uses digital signatures to attempt to give you some idea where a program comes from, in the hope that this will tell you whether or not to trust it. There are no restrictions on what an ActiveX control can do. This approach results in web pages that you're not certain whether or not to trust. Who is the person who signed it? Do you trust that person to be both well intentioned and competent to write security-critical programs? If a program is not signed, is it because the author is evil, or because the author is lazy, uneducated about digital signatures, or arguing with the signature authority?

These two approaches are being combined, allowing you to decide exactly what a program can do based on what you know about who wrote it. This is still imperfect, but it's the most promising approach, and both Java and ActiveX are moving in this direction.

JavaScript

JavaScript is a scripting language that is completely unrelated to Java and is used as an extension language for web browsers. Microsoft's implementation of JavaScript is called JScript; you may also see Microsoft refer to the language as ECMAScript because it has been standardized by the European Community Manufacturer's Association (ECMA).

JavaScript attempts to provide security by limiting what it's possible to do. For instance, JavaScript does not have commands for reading and writing files. Furthermore, programs written in JavaScript are supposed to be able to access only limited amounts of data: information about user preferences, available plug-ins and capabilities of the browser, and links and forms in the document that contains the script and in windows created by that web page. JavaScript programs can communicate to the outside world only by submitting forms.

A web page with a JavaScript program can contain something that is technically a form without being visible, and JavaScript can fill in that form with any information it can get to and submit it automatically. If your web browser is configured to ask for confirmation before submitting forms, you will see a warning; if not, the entire transaction will be silent. Furthermore, submitting a form simply consists of sending information in a predefined format to a URL, which can specify any IP address and port number. This means that submitting forms effectively lets JavaScript send any information it has to anybody it thinks should have it, possibly without notifying you. This is one of the reasons that web browsers warn you about form submissions, and it is a good reason for leaving these warnings in place.

Most JavaScript security problems fall into one of two categories: denial of service attacks that hang or crash the browser (or, if you're really unlucky, the entire computer), and bugs in the data access limitations that allow JavaScript programs to read arbitrary files and return the data to the site that the page came from. In addition, there have been occasional buffer overflow problems with JavaScript implementations.

The denial of service attacks are, as usual, unavoidable, but they're no worse than annoying. Ones that actually crash the browser or manage to affect the machine are straightforward implementation bugs, and fixes are usually rapidly available. The standard way to hang the browser is to code an infinite loop.

While JavaScript programs cannot directly open files, these programs can cause the web browser to open them by giving the browser local URLs to open (for instance, *file:/etc/passwd*). When the JavaScript security is correctly implemented, this is not a problem, since JavaScript still can't get the data out of the newly opened URLs. However, there have been a series of bugs with the handling of this particular limitation, where the browser becomes confused about the correct context for scripts or data embedded in odd places. For instance, scripts in the titles of pages may be executed in the process of reading bookmarks, and scripts can manage to execute in windows that are supposed to be displaying source code. There have been dozens of bugs in context handling, all of which have roughly similar effects; the script returns data it shouldn't have to the server it was on. That data ranges from information about sites that have been visited recently to the contents of arbitrary files on the disk.

The buffer overflow problems are, strictly speaking, not JavaScript vulnerabilities at all. They occur when the interpreter gets invalid JavaScript and the interpreter itself fails to enforce buffer limitations. There is a known problem with buffer overflows on some JavaScript calls in some versions of Internet Explorer 4.0.

JavaScript can use ActiveX or Java, if they are enabled, to get access to capabilities that JavaScript alone would not have. If ActiveX or Java is enabled in the browser, JavaScript can use them without containing any visible ActiveX or Java objects. This means that filtering out ActiveX and Java is not sufficient to protect a site. You must also filter out scripting languages or disable ActiveX and Java in all browsers.

VBScript

VBScript is a subset of Visual Basic provided by Microsoft as an extension language for web browsers and servers. VBScript provides much the same functionality that JavaScript does—in fact, Microsoft tries to maintain it at the same level. Like JavaScript, VBScript is designed to provide security by avoiding unsafe operations. VBScript is often used in conjunction with ActiveX, and VBScript security is often confused with ActiveX security, but there's no need to enable ActiveX in order to use VBScript (nor do you need VBScript in order to use ActiveX; you can use ActiveX controls from JavaScript just as well).

There don't appear to be any reported VBScript security problems; this does not indicate that VBScript is secure. What it does indicate is that JavaScript is implemented by more browsers than VBScript, while ActiveX is more powerful than VBScript. Therefore, attackers are going to concentrate on JavaScript and ActiveX until they've exhausted their obvious possibilities. Because VBScript provides the same capabilities that JavaScript does, VBScript vulnerabilities are likely to fall into the same sort of categories as JavaScript vulnerabilities, involving mostly denial of service attacks and ways to read data.

Java

Java is a full-fledged programming language that is commonly used as an extension language for web browsers. Java uses what is called a *sandbox* security model, which tries to provide security by limiting the functionality available to a program.

In general, programming languages are divided into interpreted languages and compiled languages. An interpreted language, like Perl or Visual Basic, is one where you write a program, and when you want to run it, you give it to an interpreter in the same form that you wrote it. The interpreter, which is run every time you run a program in the language, is responsible for turning human-readable commands into instructions the computer can execute. A compiled language, like C, is one where you write a program and run it through a compiler once to get an executable. You can then run the executable all by itself; you don't need another program to make it run.

Interpreted languages are machine independent. You have a different interpreter for each kind of machine but run the same programs. Compiled languages, on the other hand, are machine dependent; once you compile a program, the result will run on only one kind of machine. On the other hand, a program that is running through an interpreter is slower than one that has been compiled. In addition, when you give somebody a program in an interpreted language, it's easy for them to modify it and reuse it, while a compiled program is much more difficult to alter.

Java uses an intermediate option, sometimes called *byte compiling.* A program written in Java is compiled into machine-independent Java byte code, which is then turned into computer instructions by an interpreter usually called the Java Virtual Machine. This gives some of the advantages of compiled code (it's faster to run than an interpreted language, and the code is not in an easily modifiable form) and some of the advantages of interpreted code (it's machine independent). It also gives it many of the disadvantages of both; it's slower than compiled code, you have to have an interpreter to do anything with it, and you can have problems with bugs in either the compiler or the interpreter. Just as it is possible for a determined person to write a program directly in machine language, without using a traditional compiler, it's possible for a determined person to write a program directly in Java byte code, without using a Java compiler, and the result may be acceptable to the interpreter even if it couldn't be generated from any program the compiler would accept.

There are security features in both the Java byte-code compiler and the Java runtime interpreter. In general, you should think of the Java compiler as providing security to Java programmers; it helps people write Java programs that cannot be attacked by hostile users. (For instance, Java programs are not susceptible to buffer overflow problems.) The Java interpreter provides security to Java users; it is supposed to keep hostile Java programs from damaging machines. Because people can write Java byte code directly, you can't rely on the compiler to protect you from malicious programs.

Instead, what you're relying on is something called the *security manager,* which is part of the runtime interpreter. The security manager is responsible for determining what a program is allowed to do. It does this by looking at each separate action the program attempts to take and comparing that to the security policy that's in force. Normally, there are two possible security policies: one that covers normal programs, which doesn't put any limitations in place, and one that covers programs that have been downloaded from the network, which restricts what files can be read and written, how much memory and disk space a program can use, and what network connections it can make.

The security manager doesn't directly control the operations that the program performs. Instead, it controls what functions the program can call. For instance, insecure programs are not normally allowed to write to disk, but if there is a library that is supposed to be safe for use by insecure programs, an insecure program can call that library and have the library write to disk. Effectively, this is the same sort of restriction as allowing a child to eat cookies, but only if an adult gets the cookies; you are requiring transactions to go through a theoretically trustworthy intermediary that will impose limits on them.

There are two main risks to this model. First, there is the risk that the security manager will permit something that it should have denied. Second, there is the risk that a theoretically secure library will contain insecure operations. Java has had problems with both of these, but mostly with the security manager. The security manager has a very complex task, and it is extremely difficult to implement correctly. Since the original release of Java, people have found both implementation and design flaws with some regularity. Although these have been rapidly fixed for the most part, and the rate has considerably slowed down, it is reasonable to expect that there will be continuing problems.

ActiveX

ActiveX is not actually a programming language but a way of distributing objects that can then be used by multiple other languages. Unlike the other systems we have discussed, it distributes machine-specific code. A Java, JavaScript, or VBScript program will run on any machine that supports the language; an ActiveX control is an executable program targeted to a specific kind of processor, and you will not be able to run an ActiveX control built for an Intel processor on an Alpha processor, for instance.

ActiveX is an extension and update of Microsoft's Object Linking and Embedding system (OLE). ActiveX controls can be written in any of a number of languages, including C and Visual Basic, and can be accessed from an even wider variety of languages. In the context of the Web, they are usually used from HTML, JavaScript, or VBScript, but they can be used from Java as well. No matter what language is used to access an ActiveX control, it is the ActiveX security model that applies to the control, not the calling language's; this is important because it means that an ActiveX control used in a Java program will not be constrained by the Java sandbox.

ActiveX security is provided in two ways. First, there are limitations on when an ActiveX control can be read in; second, there are limitations on when an existing

ActiveX control can be executed. These limitations are part of the implementation of the current ActiveX interpreters, not part of the language design, so there is no guarantee that future ActiveX implementations will have the same characteristics.

The most famous aspect of ActiveX security is its use of digital signatures, which is part of the security system for reading in ActiveX controls. An ActiveX control may be signed with a digital signature, which theoretically allows you to identify the author of the control and make a decision as to whether or not to allow the control to be loaded. ActiveX controls do not have to be signed, but unsigned controls are normally treated differently from signed controls. (See Appendix C, *Cryptography*, for further discussion of digital signatures and what they mean to you.) By default, unsigned controls from external web pages are rejected, and signed controls request confirmation.

Digital signatures are checked when a control is loaded, but once the control has been loaded, it has to be used in order for anything to happen. The ActiveX model also provides controls over when a control can be run. You can choose to allow controls to run, forbid them from running, or be asked every time something attempts to run a control. By default, controls are allowed to run without confirmation.

In addition, a control can claim to be safe for use with untrusted data and/or safe for use from scripts. By default, a control cannot be run by an external web page unless it claims both these properties. A control that claims both these properties is supposed to be one that will never do anything bad, even if used hostilely. Programs like Internet Explorer that use ActiveX objects look at these properties to decide whether or not to allow a control to be run. Aside from these restrictions, once a control has been loaded for any purpose, it is available from any program.

Note that this means that if a control is present on your local disk, and it claims to be safe for use with untrusted data and safe for use from scripts, any web page can run it, and no request for confirmation will be made before it is run. This can lead to unpleasant surprises. Many vendors have preinstalled ActiveX controls that will allow arbitrary commands to be run and have incorrectly marked them as safe for scripting. Not only have third-party vendors like Compaq shipped machines with dangerous ActiveX controls, but even Microsoft, in Windows 98, provided a control marked as safe for scripting that could be used to run arbitrary programs.

Obviously, the same sort of thing can be done with controls downloaded from web pages. You may download a control from one web site, which is then activated by another. Less obviously, if you go to a page and download a control once, when you revisit the page, it will attempt to download the control again. If you do not let it download the control, you will still have the original copy of the control installed, and the page will happily continue to run that copy, which is presumably not what you had in mind (if you wanted it to run the control, you would have let it download the control). People who have just clicked No on a download dialog box are usually surprised and outraged when the control runs, since the distinction between downloading and running is not normally user-visible.

Cache Communication Protocols

When we discussed proxying and HTTP, we also discussed *caching*, which is one of the primary uses of web proxies. Caching is very important as a way of speeding up transfers and reducing the amount of data transferred across crowded links. Once cache servers are set up, the next logical step is to use multiple cache servers and have them coordinate operations. A lot of active development is going on, and it's not at all clear what protocol is going to win out in the long run.

Internet Cache Protocol (ICP)

ICP is the oldest of the cache management protocols in current use and is supported by the largest number of caches, including Netscape Proxy, Harvest, and Squid. The principle behind ICP is that cache servers operate independently, but when a cache server gets a request for a document that it does not have cached, it asks other cache servers for the document, and retrieves the document from its source only if no other cache server has the document. ICP has a number of drawbacks; it requires a considerable amount of communication between caches, it slows down document retrieval, it provides no security or authentication, and it searches the cache based only on URL, not on document header information, which may cause it to return incorrect document versions. On the other hand, it has the noticeable advantage of being both standardized (it is documented in IETF RFCs 2186 and 2187) and in widespread use.

Packet filtering characteristics of ICP

ICP normally uses UDP; the port number is configurable but defaults to 3130. ICP can also be run over TCP, once again at any port. Caches exchange documents via HTTP. Once again, the port used for HTTP is configurable, but it defaults to 3128.

Direction	Source Addr.	Dest. Addr.	Protocol	Source Port	Dest. Port	ACK Set	Notes
In	Ext	Int	UDP	>1023	3130[a]	b	ICP request or response, external cache to internal cache
Out	Int	Ext	UDP	3130[a]	>1023	b	ICP request or response, internal cache to external cache
In	Ext	Int	TCP	>1023	3128[c]	d	HTTP request, external cache to internal cache

Direction	Source Addr.	Dest. Addr.	Protocol	Source Port	Dest. Port	ACK Set	Notes
Out	Int	Ext	TCP	3128c	>1023	Yes	HTTP response, internal cache to external cache
Out	Int	Ext	TCP	>1023	3128c	d	HTTP request, internal cache to external cache
In	Ext	Int	TCP	3128c	>1023	Yes	HTTP response, external cache to internal cache

a 3130 is the standard port number for ICP, but some servers run on different port numbers.

b UDP has no ACK equivalent.

c 3128 is the standard port number for intercache HTTP servers, but some servers run on different port numbers.

d ACK is not set on the first packet of this type (establishing connection) but will be set on the rest.

Proxying characteristics of ICP

ICP, like SMTP and NNTP, is a self-proxying protocol, one that allows for queries to be passed from server to server. In general, if you are configuring ICP in a firewall environment, you will use this facility and set all internal cache servers to peer with a cache server that's part of the firewall and serves as a proxy.

Since ICP is a straightforward TCP-based protocol, it would also be possible to proxy it through a proxy system like SOCKS; the only difficulty is that you would end up with a one-way relationship, since the external cache would not be able to send queries to the internal cache. This would slow down performance without providing any more security than doing self-proxying, and no current implementations support it.

Network address translation characteristics of ICP

ICP does contain embedded IP addresses, but they aren't actually used for anything. It will work without problems through network address translation systems, as long as you configure a static translation (to allow for requests from other peers) and don't mind the fact that the internal address will be visible to anybody watching traffic.

Cache Array Routing Protocol (CARP)

CARP uses a completely different approach. Rather than having caches communicate with each other, CARP does load balancing between multiple cache servers by having a client or a proxy server use different caches for different requests, depending on the URL being requested and published information about the cache server. The information about available cache servers is distributed through HTTP, so CARP adds no extra protocol complexity. For both packet filtering and proxying, CARP is identical to other uses of HTTP. However, CARP does have difficulties with network address translation, since the documents it uses are guaranteed to have IP addresses in them (the addresses of the cache servers). Netscape and Microsoft both support CARP as well as ICP.

Web Cache Coordination Protocol (WCCP)

WCCP is a protocol developed by Cisco, which takes a third completely different approach. In order to use WCCP, you need a router that is placed so that it can intercept all HTTP traffic that should be handled by your cache servers. The router will detect any packet addressed to TCP port 80 at any destination and redirect the packet to a cache server. The cache server then replies directly to the requestor as if the request had been received normally. WCCP is used for communication between the router and the cache servers, so that the router knows what cache servers are currently running, what load each one is running under, and which URLs should be directed to which servers, and can appropriately balance traffic.

Packet filtering characteristics of WCCP

WCCP uses UDP at port 2048. In addition, routers that use WCCP redirect HTTP traffic to cache servers by encapsulating it in GRE packets (GRE is a form of IP over IP, discussed in Chapter 4, *Packets and Protocols*). WCCP uses GRE protocol type hexadecimal 883E. Note that neither UDP nor GRE uses ACK bits.

Direction	Source Addr.	Dest. Addr.	Protocol	Source Port	Dest. Port	Notes
In	Ext	Int	UDP	a	2048	WCCP update, external participant to internal participant
Out	Int	Ext	UDP	a	2048	WCCP update, internal participant to external participant
In	Ext	Int	GRE	b	b	HTTP query redirected by external router to internal cache server
Out	Int	Ext	GRE	b	b	HTTP query redirected by internal router to external cache server

a The WCCP protocol does not define a source port; it is likely to be 2048.
b GRE does not have source or destination ports, only protocol types. WCCP uses protocol type hexadecimal 883E.

Proxying characteristics of WCCP

Because WCCP uses both UDP and GRE, it is going to be difficult to proxy. Although UDP proxies have become relatively common, GRE is still unknown territory for proxy servers.

Network address translation characteristics of WCCP

WCCP communications include embedded IP addresses and will not work through network address translation. The architecture of WCCP assumes that your router and your cache servers are near each other (in network terms) in any case.

Summary of Recommendations for Cache Communication Protocols

- Cache management should either be private (between internal cache servers) or public (between a bastion host used to access the external world and external caches). Cache management protocols may cross parts of a firewall to reach a bastion host but should not go completely across the firewall between external and internal networks.

Push Technologies

HTTP is a system in which clients ask for the information that they want (this is referred to as a *pull technology*, where the client pulls the information). In some situations, it is desirable for the server to send the information without being asked (this is a *push technology*, where the server pushes the information). For instance, if you want to be informed of some event (a change in a stock price, the outcome of a baseball game, a news item about an area of interest), it's most effective for you to inform the server about your interests once, and then have it send you the information when it becomes available. With standard HTTP, you would have to ask for the information repeatedly to see if it had arrived.

Around 1997, push technologies were predicted as the next big thing on the Web, the most exciting thing to happen since the introduction of TV. They have yet to get much acceptance, for a combination of reasons. First, users have a strong and well-founded suspicion that the main reason that vendors want push technologies is so that they can push advertisements and other information that the user wouldn't have requested. Second, security and network bandwidth considerations cause site administrators to dislike the idea of having incoming unrequested information streams. At this moment, the magic application that would drive people to accept push technologies has not shown up, although there is a significant population that think the existing programs are really cool.

A number of competing programs still claim to be push technologies, although the number has been reduced in recent years. Currently, the popular programs (notably Pointcast and BackWeb) don't actually have to be push-based. Instead, they give an illusion of being push-based by using special HTTP clients that make regular requests for updates to specialized HTTP servers that inform them of changes in the information the user is watching. This polling process is transparent to the user, who sees something that looks like it's push-based.

This approach removes many of the difficulties with true push-based technologies. It doesn't require a new protocol or inbound connections, for instance. On the other hand, it does use bandwidth as the clients check for updates. The specialized clients are generally aware of proxies but may not support all the same features that normal web browsers support (for instance, they don't generally have support for auto-configuration of proxies or for proxy authentication schemes).

The specialized clients don't tend to have the same security implications that traditional web browsers do (they don't support extension languages or external viewers, for instance; they call normal web browsers to deal with complex pages). They do have their own security implications (for instance, the clients are providing information to the server as part of the queries they make and are accepting data from the server).

Some of the traditional web browsers also support things that look like push technology (for instance, Explorer has Active Channels and Netscape has Netcaster). These are in fact based on polling over normal HTTP, sometimes with additional information to optimize the polling. In general, their security implications are identical to those of normal web browsing. Note that if you are pulling web pages that require authentication information, either you will have to provide that information at the start of the download (so much for having it automatically updated while you sleep), or you will have to trust the program to safely store the authentication information. In addition, these services make local copies of the web pages, and you should be sure that those are appropriately protected.

There are also genuine push technologies in use, and both BackWeb and Point-Cast will run as genuine push technologies when they can, using their own protocols. It's not clear what security implications these protocols have, since they're proprietary. However, they accept inbound connections, often return data, and usually have little or no authentication. While there have not been many security problems with them so far, that may simply be because they are not popular enough to attract many attackers. Certainly there seems to be good reason to worry about their security. It is also possible to combine a traditional web browser with a specialized push client using plug-ins, and PointCast provides such a plug-in. The plug-in has the same security implications as the normal PointCast service.

Summary of Recommendations for Push Technologies

- Do not pass push technologies through your firewall.
- Discourage users from using the specialized clients that imitate push technologies using HTTP.

RealAudio and RealVideo

RealAudio and RealVideo are proprietary protocols developed by RealNetworks to provide real-time streaming of audio and video data across the Internet. Although the players for these protocols can run as independent applications, they are most frequently used as plug-ins to web browsers. At this writing, these are the most popular protocols for distributing relatively large amounts of audio or video.

The advantage of using them instead of simply distributing audio or video files is twofold. First, if a web browser encounters an audio or video file, it needs to download the entire file before playing it. This can mean a long and extremely boring wait if the file is eventually going to play for more than a few seconds. Few people are willing to hang around watching a transfer progress meter move for 20 minutes in order to watch a 10-second movie. Second, because the files are downloaded, users are not only able to make their own copies, they're encouraged to do so; once they've waited the 20 minutes, they're certainly not going to delete the local copy of the file! If you want to keep track of who's watching the file when, and you don't want copies of it floating around, this is extremely undesirable.

Protocols for distributing audio and video tend to based on UDP because people are more tolerant of having small amounts of data lost than of having pauses. With TCP, if a packet is lost, there will be a wait for retransmission, which is much more annoying than just going on to the next packet. Audio and video protocols also tend to use multiple ports in order to maximize efficiency. Because of these characteristics, these protocols tend to be difficult to support through firewalls.

Risks of RealServer

Running a server for RealAudio or RealVideo is not inherently dangerous; the protocol is a relatively safe one for the server. On the other hand, RealNetworks has had some problems with security, and both the Windows NT and the Unix server have been distributed with extremely risky installations. Be sure that configuration files are not world-writable, that created accounts have appropriate privileges and passwords, and that programs are not running with more privileges than they need. Since the servers represent a considerable load in any case, you may want to dedicate a bastion host to them; that will also help to contain any security problems.

Risks of RealAudio and RealVideo Clients

The RealAudio and RealVideo clients have relatively limited capabilities and have not had any known security problems. Because of the way the protocols work, it can be difficult to allow the clients to run effectively without opening large holes in your firewall, which is of course risky. However, the clients themselves are relatively low risk if you are able to safely get the data to them.

Packet Filtering Characteristics of RealAudio and RealVideo

RealAudio and RealVideo by default use a system where a TCP connection, initiated by the client, is used for session control, while the actual data is transferred using UDP. Multiple UDP ports may be used for the same session. Because this system is extremely difficult to permit through packet filters without creating significant extra vulnerabilities, it is possible to configure RealVideo and RealAudio clients to use TCP only (on port 7070) or to use TCP accompanied by UDP packets from a single port in the range 6970–7170, specified by the client.

Direction	Source Addr.	Dest. Addr.	Protocol	Source Port	Dest. Port	ACK Set	Notes
In	Ext	Int	TCP	>1023	7070	a	Request, external client to internal server
Out	Int	Ext	TCP	7070	>1023	Yes	Response session control, internal server to external client
Out	Int	Ext	UDP	6970–7170[b]	>1023	c	Response data, internal server to external client
Out	Int	Ext	TCP	>1023	7070	a	Request, internal client to external server
In	Ext	Int	TCP	7070	>1023	Yes	Response session control, external server to internal client
In	Ext	Int	UDP	6970–7170[b]	>1023	c	Response data, external server to internal client

[a] ACK is not set on the first packet of this type (establishing connection) but will be set on the rest.
[b] The client may select a specific port number in this range or may allow the server to choose any port in the range; if the latter, multiple ports may be used for the same session.
[c] UDP has no ACK equivalent.

Proxying Characteristics of RealAudio and RealVideo

RealNetworks provides sample code for RealAudio and RealVideo proxies for use if you would like to have your own. They also have worked with a number of firewall vendors to incorporate the proxy code into products. Using a proxy is the best solution to get reasonable performance of RealAudio and RealVideo through a firewall, since the tricks used to make it allowable through packet filters significantly decrease performance. However, the RealAudio and RealVideo proxies can put a fairly considerable load on a machine.

Network Address Translation Characteristics of RealAudio and RealVideo

RealAudio and RealVideo will work with network translation if they are configured to use TCP only; the UDP-based modes use embedded IP addresses. You will need a network address translation system that understands RealAudio and RealVideo to use UDP, but an appropriate module is available for Linux IP masquerading.

Summary Recommendations for RealAudio and RealVideo

* Unless you need high performance, run RealAudio and RealVideo clients configured to use TCP only, and permit outbound TCP connections on port 7070.

* If you need high performance on RealAudio and RealVideo clients, use Real-Networks' proxies.

* Run RealServer on a dedicated bastion host and configure it carefully.

Gopher and WAIS

Gopher is a menu-driven text-based tool for browsing through files and directories across the Internet. When a user selects a Gopher menu item, Gopher retrieves the specified file and displays it appropriately. This means that if a file is compressed, Gopher automatically uncompresses it; if it's a GIF image, Gopher automatically runs a GIF viewer. Standalone Gopher clients are now rare, but many web browsers support the Gopher protocol, and Gopher servers can be an efficient way of providing access to non-HTML documents for users of web browsers. A Gopher server is provided as part of Microsoft's Internet Information Server (IIS).

WAIS indexes large text databases so that they can be searched efficiently by simple keywords or more complicated Boolean expressions. For example, you can ask for all the documents that mention "firewalls" or all the documents that mention "firewalls" but don't mention "fire marshals". (You might do this to make sure you don't get documents about literal firewalls.) WAIS was originally developed at Thinking Machines as a prototype information service and, for a while, was widely used on the Internet for things like mailing list archives and catalogs of various text-based information (library card catalogs, for example). It is now much more common for people to provide search engines on web pages using CGI, instead of using WAIS directly as an access protocol. Some web browsers will speak the WAIS protocol, but WAIS servers are quite rare these days.

It is unlikely that you will ever want to run a standalone Gopher or WAIS client. Using the support for these protocols that is built in to a web browser adds no additional risk to the risks already posed by HTTP.

You are also unlikely to run a WAIS server, but you might run a Gopher server. Gopher servers present the same basic security concerns as the servers for all of the other common Internet services, such as FTP and HTTP: Can attackers use this server to access something they shouldn't? This is a particularly pressing problem on the Gopher server included as part of IIS, since many sites do not pay much attention to it, and may accidentally leave data where the Gopher server can read it. If you do not intend to run Gopher, turn it off; if you do intend to run it, be sure that it can read only information that you intend to make public.

For servers, you have to worry about what a malicious client can trick you into running. Like HTTP servers, some Gopher servers use auxiliary programs to generate Gopher pages on the fly. Gopher servers are therefore susceptible to the same kinds of problems as HTTP servers:

- Can an attacker trick the auxiliary program?
- Can the attacker upload a new auxiliary program and cause it to be run?

Like HTTP servers, Gopher servers also sometimes live on nonstandard ports, so those concerns are similar to HTTP as well. Some Gopher clients support transparent proxying (via SOCKS or other mechanisms), but many don't.

Packet Filtering Characteristics of Gopher and WAIS

Gopher is a TCP-based service. Gopher clients use ports above 1023. Most Gopher servers use port 70, but some don't; see the discussion of nonstandard server ports in the "Packet Filtering Characteristics of HTTP" section, earlier in this chapter.

Direction	Source Addr.	Dest. Addr.	Protocol	Source Port	Dest. Port	ACK Set	Notes
In	Ext	Int	TCP	>1023	70[a]	[b]	Request, external client to internal server
Out	Int	Ext	TCP	70[a]	>1023	Yes	Response, internal server to external client
Out	Int	Ext	TCP	>1023	70[a]	[b]	Request, internal client to external server
In	Ext	Int	TCP	70[a]	>1023	Yes	Response, external server to internal client

[a] 70 is the standard port number for Gopher servers, but some servers run on different port numbers.
[b] ACK is not set on the first packet of this type (establishing connection) but will be set on the rest.

WAIS is a TCP-based service. WAIS clients use random ports above 1023. WAIS servers usually use port 210, but sometimes don't; see the discussion of nonstandard server ports earlier, in the section on HTTP.

Direction	Source Addr.	Dest. Addr.	Protocol	Source Port	Dest. Port	ACK Set	Notes
In	Ext	Int	TCP	>1023	210[a]	[b]	Request, external client to internal server
Out	Int	Ext	TCP	210[a]	>1023	Yes	Response, internal server to external client
Out	Int	Ext	TCP	>1023	210[a]	[b]	Request, internal client to external server
In	Ext	Int	TCP	210[a]	>1023	Yes	Response, external server to internal client

[a] 210 is the standard port number for WAIS servers, but some servers run on different port numbers.
[b] ACK is not set on the first packet of this type (establishing connection) but will be set on the rest.

Proxying Characteristics of Gopher and WAIS

If you use a proxying Web browser like Netscape Navigator or Internet Explorer to access WAIS or Gopher, you automatically get proxy support using SOCKS and/or HTTP proxying.

In the unlikely event that you wish to use some other Gopher client, the TIS FWTK *http-gw* proxy server can serve Gopher as well as HTTP. SOCKS does not include a modified Gopher client, but Gopher clients are, in general, not difficult to modify to use SOCKS; many of the Gopher clients freely available on the Internet support SOCKS as either a compile-time or runtime option.

As a straightforward single-connection protocol with plenty of user-specified information, WAIS lends itself to both modified-client and modified-procedure proxying. SOCKS support is commonly available in standalone WAIS clients.

Network Address Translation Characteristics of Gopher and WAIS

Gopher and WAIS do not use embedded IP addresses and will work with network address translation without problems.

Summary of Recommendations for Gopher and WAIS

- If you're going to run a Gopher server, carefully configure the Gopher server to control what it has access to; in particular, watch out for ways that someone could upload a program to a Gopher system somehow (via mail or FTP, for example) and then execute it via the Gopher server.

- Carefully control the external programs your Gopher server can access.

- Don't run a WAIS server.

- Use a web browser such as Internet Explorer or Netscape Navigator for your Gopher and WAIS clients, rather than using dedicated clients.

16

Electronic Mail and News

From a user's point of view, electronic mail is one of the most crucial Internet services. Mail, along with news, provides a way for people to hold discussions with other people, singly or in groups. This chapter discusses the security issues related to electronic mail and news protocols, including SMTP, POP, IMAP, MIME, and NNTP.

Electronic Mail

Traditionally, a mail system has three parts, which may be implemented by different programs or by the same program, in any combination:

Mail transfer agent (MTA)
> Accepts mail from external hosts or sends it to external hosts

Mail delivery agent (MDA)
> Puts the mail in the correct mailbox on the local host

Mail user agent (MUA)
> Lets the recipient read the mail and compose outgoing mail

Figure 16-1 shows a large mail system and its parts.

Each of these parts is vulnerable for a different reason:

- The transfer agent directly accepts commands (related to transporting mail) from external hosts; for this reason, if the transfer agent isn't secure, it may end up immediately giving an attacker all the access it has itself.

- The delivery agent needs special permissions because it needs to be able to write into every user's mailbox. Although the delivery agent doesn't need to

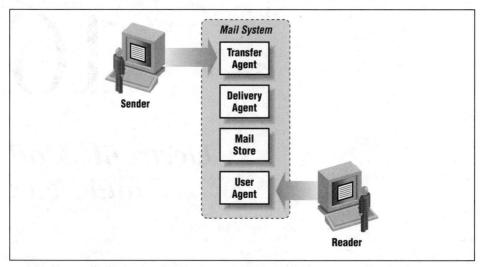

Figure 16-1. The parts of a mail system

talk to the external world, if it can be subverted somehow, the intruder obtains very broad access.

- The user agent runs as one user, and it doesn't talk to the external world, which limits its power and accessibility; however, it can often run arbitrary other programs in response to the data received.

A large modern mail system may involve more than three parts. For instance, it is common for the user agent to be a client speaking POP or IMAP, in which case a POP or IMAP server sits between the delivery agent and the user agent. The delivery agent itself may involve database transactions (and therefore a database server). The basic vulnerabilities remain the same.

With any service that transfers data around, there are three main risks:

- Giving away data that you wanted to keep secret
- Getting information that you didn't want (whether it's illegal, virus-infected, or merely obnoxious)
- Having people directly attack the parts of the server

The last risk is specific to the individual servers and protocols that you use, and we will address it as we talk about particular protocols. The first two, however, have issues that are different for electronic mail than for other kinds of information transfer, but are the same for all mail servers, and we will discuss them here.

Keeping Mail Secret

Most protocols that transfer information use relatively direct connections; the server and the client that talk to each other are usually the original source and final destination of the transfer. That's not true for mail, where messages usually pass through multiple servers between the source and the destination. Figure 16-2 shows a typical mail path.

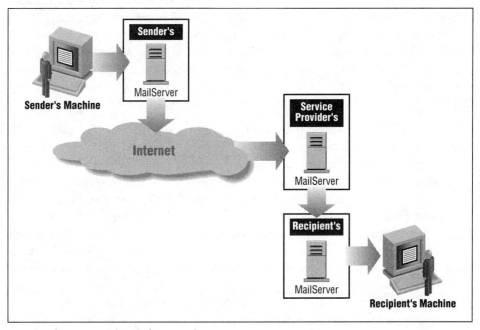

Figure 16-2. A typical path for a mail message

In this situation, protocols that make encrypted connections between a client and a server don't do much good. There are some cases where encryption helps; if you know what route mail follows, and only one part of it is unprotected, and you control the clients and servers on both ends of that link, you can encrypt just that link. For instance, if you are trying to protect internal mail that's being read by a user on the Internet, it's just the last link between the user and your mail server that you're worried about, and you can protect it. If you're trying to securely transfer mail between your company and a subsidiary, you can set up the mail systems so that you know mail goes directly between their server and yours and encrypt that connection. As usual, you can use either an encrypted protocol (ESMTP with STARTTLS or Secure POP, for instance; both of them are discussed later in this chapter) or a virtual private network to protect the connection.

If you're trying to protect mail in a situation where you don't control the servers, the clients, and the mail routing between them, this sort of encryption isn't going to do you any good. You can't guarantee that all the servers involved will use it. You can't even guarantee that you'll be able to authenticate the servers that you need to exchange mail with (you might want to exchange mail with any server on the Internet, and there is currently no infrastructure that allows you to authenticate arbitrary servers).

When you're trying to pass information along a path you don't control, you have to encrypt the message data, instead of using encrypted links. There are a number of systems for doing this; many mail user agents offer encryption features. Most systems require that the sender and the receiver have compatible software, and that they have some way to exchange keys outside of electronic mail. The systems that best address these problems are S/MIME and OpenPGP, discussed later, which are implemented by a number of different user agents and use public key cryptography.

People occasionally advocate the use of self-decrypting archives. To make a self-decrypting archive, you take the file you want to encrypt and use a program that embeds your file into another program. You mail this new program to your correspondent; when it is run, it asks for a password, and if the password is correct, it produces the original file. This removes the need for the recipient to have the decryption program (although not the need for a way to safely communicate the key). Unfortunately, it requires the recipient to have a computer that can run the executable and to be willing to run an unknown executable received in unauthenticated electronic mail. As we discuss later, people should not run executables they get in electronic mail. In addition, it is quite difficult to produce a secure program that will make self-decrypting archives of a reasonable size. Since most security experts are unwilling to have anything to do with self-decrypting archives, finding it unethical to encourage people to associate security with running random unauthenticated executables, it's reasonable to assume that self-decrypting archives are not just a bad idea; they're also insecure.

Undesirable Mail

There are two main kinds of undesirable mail: mail that's merely annoying and mail that's actively hostile.

Junk mail

These days, the most frequent problems with mail servers has to do with something called by a number of names, including the serious "Unsolicited Commercial Email" (UCE) and the frivolous "spam" (which is not a computer-originated acronym, but a reference to a Monty Python skit in which the Hormel meat-product SPAM is undesirable but unavoidable). By any name, this is junk email—advertisements flooding in electronically. This phenomenon arouses great hostility, as well as putting substantial load on the network, so people who create it tend to spread out both the load and the repercussions by routing it through third parties.

Thus, if you run an Internet-attached mail server, you have three concerns about this kind of mail:

- Preventing outsiders from using your mail server to annoy third parties
- Preventing people from annoying your users
- Preventing your users from annoying other people

A variety of techniques are used to achieve these goals. We can't discuss all of them here, as it's a complex and implementation-dependent topic, which fills entire books (for instance, *Stopping Spam* by Alan Schwartz and Simson Garfinkel, O'Reilly & Associates, 1998, which you might want to consult).

Note that these three goals, while they're related, require quite different approaches. When you're evaluating mail servers, you need to pay attention to exactly what sort of protections they offer you; many "anti-spam" features are actually anti-relaying features, designed to prevent outsiders from using your mail server to relay mail to other people. These are useful and important features to have, but they won't be of any immediate use in emptying your mailbox of advertisements for golf balls, pictures of naked people, and completely legal ways to make a million dollars without doing any work.

Viruses and other hostilities

While junk mail is annoying, some mail goes further and actually contains attacks on your machines. This may be because the person the mail seems to come from is trying to attack you, but more likely, it's the fault of some third party who has either forged the mail or tricked the mail's sender. The most important way to control these things is to avoid any situation where you execute code from an electronic mail message without having good authentication (don't accept programs from strangers). This is much more difficult than it sounds.

It's relatively obvious if you receive an attachment that's a normal program executable. It may not be at all obvious to you that HTML files may contain code (in the form of Java, JavaScript, VBScript, or ActiveX controls) or that Microsoft Word documents can also be programs (they can contain Visual Basic macros, which are capable of doing anything other programs can do). In general, don't open any file unless you know exactly where it came from, or you know exactly what the program that opens it can do (and it can't do much). For instance, you certainly don't want to open Microsoft Word documents with Microsoft Word, but you might be willing to open them with the specialized Word Viewer, which can't execute macros.

Furthermore, you don't want to open something just because you know who it comes from, even if you can authenticate the mail. Some programs replicate by reading an infected user's address book and mailing themselves to the addresses in it. They'll appear as perfectly valid mail sent by somebody you know.

Worse yet, you may have to specially configure your mail reader to keep it from executing code automatically. As we discussed in Chapter 15, *The World Wide Web*, some mail readers that are integrated with web browsers will run code in web extension languages even when it is embedded in mail messages. You will want to disable this functionality.

All of this makes it extremely difficult to control hostile mail at the client end. Years of education have not succeeded in getting people to think twice before forwarding chain letters, and they're not going to succeed in the much more difficult task of training people not to even open files to read them. It's therefore a very good idea to do some content filtering of incoming electronic mail to remove known hostile code. You will also need to do the training and filtering on the client end; content filtering on the mail server will not protect you from the many other sources of hostile code; the server is easily deceived by encrypting or otherwise changing the code, and it can detect only known attacks. However, it provides you a single point of control where you can get rid of current problems with one intervention, which can make all the difference in dealing with crises.

If you filter incoming mail, it is both wise and polite to filter your outgoing mail as well. Obviously, it's polite to avoid infecting other people, but it's also a useful way to diagnose and get rid of internal problems; if you're sending out hostile code, you have either infected machines or hostile users, and you want to get rid of them before they do damage to you.

Setting up filtering will depend on the details of your mail server configuration. Virus filters are available for almost all mail servers, as commercial or freely available products. In general, virus filters are most effective when they are running on the same platform they are trying to protect (that is, the Windows NT-based filters are better than the Unix-based filters at protecting Microsoft machines), but it is possible to provide basic protections for any machine from any mail server.

Multimedia Internet Mail Extensions (MIME)

MIME is a set of extensions to the basic Internet electronic mail message format supporting things like:

- Non-ASCII character sets
- Nontext data such as pictures and audio segments

- So-called "rich text" messages (messages containing formatted text, with different fonts and so on, rather than simple single-font unformatted text)

- Multipart messages (messages containing multiple pieces, each piece in its own format)

MIME support is mostly a client issue; to mail servers and transport systems, a MIME message is generally just another message. The question is whether or not a given client can generate outgoing MIME messages, and whether or not it can recognize and cope with incoming MIME messages.

The MIME standards define certain basic data types, such as plain text, formatted text, standard audio, and so on. MIME is designed to be extensible, so that new data types can be added as necessary. MIME-capable mail clients generally understand certain data types (often only multipart messages and plain text) and rely on other programs to handle other data types (for example, graphics programs to display images, and sound programs to play audio clips). The clients generally have a list of external programs to run for particular types of data; this list can be extended or modified by the user.

The issues for email clients are much the same as the issues for web browsers, which are discussed in Chapter 15, *The World Wide Web*. Since you are running additional programs, you are vulnerable to security problems in those programs as well as any security problems that may be present in your mail client.

One difference between MIME support in email clients and web browsers is how data is obtained. With a web browser, the user chooses what data to access; with email, the user accesses whatever anybody sends. In theory, email clients are more vulnerable because you can't control what other people send you by email. In practice, however, the difference isn't that important because it's fairly easy to lure web users into accessing whatever you want them to access. Either way, you need to carefully control what data types your clients understand and how they process that data.

S/MIME and OpenPGP

S/MIME and OpenPGP are extensions to MIME that support encryption and digital signatures (for indentifying the sender of a message or for protecting it from unauthorized modifications). Both S/MIME and OpenPGP are implemented as special MIME data types that use public key encryption to digitally sign and encrypt messages. S/MIME can include certificate information to help senders and receivers establish trust relationships. OpenPGP uses a "web of trust" model, which requires that you have independent access to certificate information. This significantly reduces the overhead added to messages. See Appendix C, *Cryptography*, for more information about public key encryption and certificates. There are several versions of S/MIME; those prior to version 3 do not necessarily provide very strong encryption.

S/MIME version 3 and OpenPGP are being developed as Internet standards, and both require the implementation of strong encryption. Neither requires a license for using patented encryption technology in a commercial environment. There are multiple implementations of both S/MIME and OpenPGP; commercial products typically implement S/MIME, and freely available software tends to implement OpenPGP.

Simple Mail Transfer Protocol (SMTP)

On the Internet, electronic mail exchange between mail servers is handled with SMTP. A host's SMTP server accepts mail and examines the destination address to decide whether to deliver the mail locally or to forward it on to some other machine. If it decides to deliver the mail locally, it recodes the mail headers and delivery address into the proper form for the local delivery program, and it then hands the mail to that program. If it decides to forward the mail to another machine, it modifies the headers and contacts that machine (usually via SMTP, but sometimes via UUCP or another protocol) and forwards the mail.

SMTP is a store-and-forward system, and such systems are well suited to firewall applications, particularly those using proxy services. In Chapter 9, *Proxy Systems*, Figure 9-2 shows how mail sent from an individual user's workstation is directed initially to a gateway system before leaving the user's own network. Mail entering a network goes to a gateway system on that network before being distributed to individual users on other hosts.

Extended SMTP (ESMTP)

Extended SMTP (ESMTP) is an update to SMTP. It runs on the same port as regular SMTP, and ESMTP clients and servers are compatible with SMTP clients and servers. ESMTP is not actually a new protocol but a mechanism for supporting extensions to SMTP. Different mail servers implement different extensions; you can't tell what features a mailer has just by knowing that it supports ESMTP. In fact, since all the ESMTP extensions are optional, there are mail servers that speak ESMTP without implementing any new functions that affect mail handling.

The ESMTP mechanism presents no security advantages or problems different from the ones found with SMTP; it is the individual extensions that are important. From a security perspective, STARTTLS is the most interesting extension, and it is discussed in the next section.

You may want to have an ESMTP-capable server that supports performance and administrative extensions. In that case, you should make certain to pick a mail server for your bastion host that supports the particular extensions that you are interested in.

TLS/SSL, SSMTP, and STARTTLS

SMTP passes all traffic over the network unencrypted. As we discussed earlier, various systems for encrypting and digitally signing message bodies work without changing the SMTP protocol itself. These techniques do not protect message headers, which include the email addresses of the sender and recipients, the time, and frequently the message subject. People have therefore suggested running SMTP over SSL or TLS (TLS and SSL are discussed further in Chapter 14, *Intermediary Protocols*), which would encrypt the entire connection, including all mail headers, and would also authenticate the mail relay machines.

Several methods have been proposed, including using a separate TCP port for a new SSMTP protocol. Although a port has been reserved for use by SSMTP, very few mail servers support it, and it is not a standard. An alternative that is being proposed as a standard is based upon an ESMTP extension called STARTTLS. When a client discovers that an ESMTP server supports the extension, it issues the STARTTLS command and negotiates a TLS session. The client and server then begin a completely new authenticated and encrypted dialog. STARTTLS is supported by some current mail servers, but not many.

As we have already discussed, single-hop encryption and authentication are not very useful for electronic mail. SMTP is no exception, and STARTTLS or SSMTP will be useful to you only in situations where you are directly accepting mail from known, trusted hosts (business partners or your own users, for instance).

Packet Filtering Characteristics of SMTP

SMTP is a TCP-based service. SMTP receivers use port 25. SMTP senders use a randomly selected port above 1023.

Direction	Source Addr.	Dest. Addr.	Protocol	Source Port	Dest. Port	ACK Set	Notes
In	Ext	Int	TCP	>1023	25	[a]	Incoming mail, sender to recipient
Out	Int	Ext	TCP	25	>1023	Yes	Incoming mail, recipient to sender
Out	Int	Ext	TCP	>1023	25	[a]	Outgoing mail, sender to recipient
In	Ext	Int	TCP	25	>1023	Yes	Outgoing mail, recipient to sender

[a] ACK is not set on the first packet of this type (establishing connection) but will be set on the rest.

Normally, you want to configure your packet filters to allow incoming and outgoing SMTP only between external hosts and the bastion host, and between the bastion host and your internal mail servers.

Do not allow external hosts to contact random internal hosts via SMTP. As we've discussed, only specially configured hosts can safely accept SMTP connections.

If you cannot filter on the ACK bit, you cannot safely allow outgoing SMTP connections directly from random internal hosts, as we demonstrate in the final example in Chapter 8, *Packet Filtering*. If you can filter on the ACK bit, you can allow internal hosts to send mail to external hosts, but it isn't advisable to do so. Although it shouldn't increase your vulnerability to direct attacks from the outside, it dramatically increases your vulnerability to internal problems, including Trojan horse programs that users may be running unintentionally. Because port 25 is frequently allowed through packet filtering systems, it is one of the most popular ports to use for Trojan horses and other attempts to subvert firewalls.

Allowing outgoing SMTP from all internal hosts also increases the likelihood that you're going to send misformatted mail, because the mail (mis)configurations of all your machines will be visible to the external world, and the chances that all your internal machines do all the right things with mail headers (particularly in adding fully qualified domain names to addresses and "Message-ID:" lines) are low. Sending outgoing mail via the bastion host allows the bastion host the opportunity to clean up the headers before the mail is loosed upon the world.

Finally, if you allow all internal hosts to send mail to the outside, you are creating a configuration where the same machines handle internal and external mail delivery. The dangers of this sort of configuration are discussed later in the "Configuring SMTP to Work with a Firewall" section.

Proxying Characteristics of SMTP

Because SMTP is a store-and-forward protocol, it's inherently suited to proxying. Since any SMTP server can be a proxy, it's rare to set up separate proxying for it. Instead, most sites direct SMTP connections to a bastion host running a secure SMTP server that is the proxy.

Dedicated firewall products that provide proxying may proxy SMTP (they can't reasonably be expected to run a full SMTP server). This is straightforward to configure because SMTP uses a single connection. In this configuration, it's not unreasonable to continue to direct the proxied SMTP connections to a single secured SMTP server on a bastion host that acts as a second proxy. Proxying protects you from unwanted connections, but not from misuses of connections; you don't want to let external hosts talk to a standard unsecured SMTP server, even through a proxy.

Network Address Translation Characteristics of SMTP

SMTP does not use embedded IP addresses, but outgoing SMTP connections will include the internal hostname as a greeting to the destination server. In addition, some naive mechanisms used to prevent mail relaying will refuse mail unless the IP address matches the host greeting and passes a double-reverse DNS lookup. (Double-reverse DNS lookups are discussed in Chapter 20, *Naming and Directory Services*.) These problems can be avoided by using a small number of servers to relay all mail to the outside, setting up static translations for them, and advertising those names externally with the translated addresses.

Configuring SMTP to Work with a Firewall

Because you want to send all your incoming mail through your bastion host, you need to configure your mail system in a special way. Here are the important steps to follow:

1. Use DNS Mail Exchange (MX) records to specify that all your incoming mail should be directed to your bastion host(s).*

2. Configure the mailer on the bastion host to check the destination address on mail it receives. If the mail is being sent from an internal host to an external host, the bastion host should process the mail as usual; if the mail is to an internal host, the bastion host should simply pass the mail to an internal mail server for processing, rather than attempt to deliver the mail itself. (If the mail is from an external host to an external host, the mailer should reject it altogether; see the section on preventing mail relaying, earlier in this chapter.)

3. Configure your internal systems to send all outgoing mail to the bastion host.

You may also want to configure your mail system so that mail is sent out with a central address, instead of with the name of an individual host, as its return address. For example, you might want mail from your users to appear as *person@bigcompany.example* and not as *person@littlemachine.bigcompany.example*. Because all of the incoming mail (replies to the above addresses in outgoing mail) will be going to the bastion host in any case, this doesn't remove any necessary information. It helps to guarantee that mail will go to the bastion host correctly, even if there are problems with the MX records for individual machines, and it gives more consistent information to the recipients of the mail.

---

* For a detailed discussion of MX records, how they work, and how to use them, see the books *TCP/IP Network Administration*, by Craig Hunt (O'Reilly & Associates, 1998) and *DNS and BIND*, by Paul Albitz and Cricket Liu (O'Reilly & Associates, 1998). Both of these books are also available in specialized versions for Windows NT; further details are in Appendix A, *Resources*.

If you configure your mail servers with an internal server and a bastion host, it is important to keep internal mail from going to the bastion host. The best way of doing this is to use a split DNS system (described in Chapter 20, *Naming and Directory Services*). If the MX record that directs Internet hosts to the bastion host is also visible to internal hosts, they may attempt to deliver mail there. If this is possible, it's a security problem (it passes potentially confidential data through the bastion host unintentionally). If this is not possible, it's a usability problem (mail that should be valid bounces unexpectedly).

Why should you separate internal and external mail servers? By passing the incoming mail to a single internal server for processing, the bastion host is relieved of having to keep track of internal aliases and internal mail configuration, and you don't have to update the mailer configuration on the bastion host nearly as often. If the bastion host passes the incoming mail to a single internal server or small list of internal servers, the filtering system can restrict SMTP connections from the bastion host to just that host or hosts, reducing the number of internal systems that can be attacked via SMTP from the bastion host if the bastion host itself is compromised.

Furthermore, if the same machines handle internal and external mail delivery, an attacker that can spoof DNS information may be able to cause mail that was intended for internal destinations to be delivered to an external host. Most email messages are addressed with hostnames instead of IP addresses, and the SMTP server uses DNS to determine the matching IP address. An attacker who can manipulate DNS responses can redirect mail to a server under the control of the attacker; that server can then copy the mail and return it. This will introduce delays and will usually leave a trail in the logs or message headers, but neither of these events will usually be obtrusive, and you are unlikely to notice them promptly. Therefore, you want to avoid situations where internal and external mail delivery are handled on the machine and internal names are resolved through DNS. The most common bad configuration is one where all machines send mail directly; the easiest good configuration is one in which there is an external mail server and an internal mail server, and the external mail server has the IP address of the internal mail server configured locally (for instance, via a hosts file).

Sendmail

The mailer most commonly used on Unix systems is Sendmail. Sendmail is very powerful, but it also has a long and troubling history of major and minor security problems.

Sendmail's security problems have been widely discussed, while the problems of other mailers have received much less attention. However, the lack of public discussion about other mailers should not lead you to assume these mailers are any more secure than Sendmail. These mailers are simply not as widely used as Sendmail, and therefore, they have fewer people—with both good intentions and bad—who are examining them for security problems.

Sendmail is the devil that everybody knows, which is both an advantage and a disadvantage. On the one hand, problems are going to be found in Sendmail because that's where lots of people are looking for them (because lots of people use Sendmail). On the other hand, what problems are found are likely to be fixed very quickly (again, because lots of people use Sendmail). Sendmail is very actively supported on security issues.

One of the reasons Sendmail has security problems is that it's a very complex and monolithic program. It performs several different functions, and it requires the necessary permissions to perform *all* of those functions. Sendmail needs root privileges for a number of reasons; for example, these privileges allow Sendmail to:

- Listen on port 25 (a privileged port) for incoming SMTP connections
- Operate as a particular user to read *.forward* files and *:include:* alias files owned by that user, and to run programs specified by those files
- Execute certain kernel system calls that (in some versions of Unix) are restricted to programs running as root (for example, to determine the system load in order to decide whether enough capacity is left to process mail)
- Protect files in the mail queue (i.e., messages in transit) from snooping by unprivileged users

These root permissions can be a liability, though, when Sendmail acts as an SMTP server; an attacker who manages to exploit a bug over an SMTP connection is now talking to a process that is running as root. The process can do essentially anything on the target machine at the attacker's bidding. Sendmail tries to be careful to give up its privileges whenever it doesn't really need them, but there have still been quite a number of privilege-related bugs over the years.

On a bastion host, it should be possible to make Sendmail run *setuid* to something other than root. You can use an alternative SMTP server (the *smap* package, discussed later) for incoming SMTP connections, so that Sendmail doesn't need to listen on port 25. You shouldn't have any users receiving mail on the bastion host, so you shouldn't need the ability to operate as particular users to read protected *.forward* and *:include:* files. There probably aren't any privileged system calls on your system that are critical to Sendmail's operation (though you may lose some functionality and/or need to recompile Sendmail from source to prevent it from attempting to use those calls). All you're left with is the need to keep ownership of files in the mail queue consistent and to keep nonprivileged users (which the bastion host shouldn't have anyway) from snooping on messages in transit. Creating a user just for Sendmail and making that user the owner of the queue directory should solve that problem.

Each of these tasks could probably be done in more secure ways, but this would require a major redesign and reimplementation of Sendmail, and nobody has yet stepped up to accept this challenge: among other reasons, out of fear that doing so would probably introduce new problems. Instead, we keep getting patch after patch for problem after problem, so that "the current Sendmail patch" has become something of a running joke in the network security community.

Sendmail has exhibited all of the types of general mailer vulnerabilities we discussed earlier. Patching has eliminated or reduced most of them; for example, it used to be easy to exploit command-line bugs in Sendmail as an unprivileged user, but modern versions strictly limit the options available to unprivileged users. However, as with all programs of any complexity, more problems are sure to be discovered. Also, patches for old problems have sometimes introduced new problems.

Other Freely Available SMTP Servers for Unix

A number of other freely available SMTP servers are available for Unix. The best-known alternative SMTP servers for Unix are all designed to provide security, ease of configuration, and good performance. These include *smail*, Wietse Venema's Postfix, and Dan Bernstein's *qmail*. All of them provide a reasonable level of compatibility with Sendmail and offer similar (but not identical) features in the area of forwarding, aliasing, and mailbox delivery. All of the SMTP alternatives are arguably easier to customize than Sendmail and also support virtual domains, anti-relaying, and unsolicited bulk email protections. If you wish to replace Sendmail with one of these SMTP alternatives, we strongly recommend that you set up a trial for at least a month in order to gain operational experience, unless you are already familiar with the replacement. Users are fanatically unforgiving when it comes to bounced email.

Yet more freely available servers, designed for various purposes, are, of course, available for Unix. Few of them are designed specifically to provide security. You may have reasons to use servers not mentioned here, but you should be careful to evaluate the security that they provide.

smail

*smail** was designed to be a secure replacement for Sendmail. It was originally designed and implemented by Ronald S. Karr and Landon Curt Noll, although it

---

* We are discussing *smail* version 3; there is an earlier mailer also called *smail* with a different lineage.

has now been passed on to other maintainers. *smail* is one of the earliest of the Sendmail replacements; it was released in 1987.

smail can be used as a plug-in replacement for Sendmail as it uses many of the same command-line switches. In fact, it has been used as the SMTP mailer for several Linux distributions.

Many of the security problems with Sendmail stem from its complexity, and *smail* was designed to incorporate only the most commonly used features of Sendmail. However, *smail* is still a monolithic program and requires the same security privileges as Sendmail. Furthermore, the addition of new features and different maintainers has resulted in a small number of security problems. Given the monolithic nature of *smail*, we cannot recommend using this package in a bastion host environment.

Postfix

Postfix was designed and implemented by Wietse Venema as a highly secure and compartmentalized mailer. Rather than being a single program like Sendmail, Postfix is broken up into separate components, each with a specific task. The Postfix design also eliminates problems that can arise from Unix process inheritance; once a message is accepted by Postfix, it is processed by components that are not related to the Unix process ancestry of the submitter. Each component performs defensive data checking and is suspicious of all input data even if it has been read from another component of Postfix. All programs ought to be written in this way, but it is rarely done with enough care. Defensive data checking significantly reduces the chances of buffer overflow problems.

Postfix can be installed to just send mail, to send and receive mail alongside Sendmail, or to completely replace Sendmail. The configuration of Postfix is quite easy. Compatibility with Sendmail is good; it supports the use of user *.forward* files and can also be configured to use a system-wide custom local delivery agent (such as *procmail*). Postfix is supplied with simple, straightforward, and clearly written instructions for compiling and installing Postfix and replacing Sendmail.

Postfix avoids most of the inherent difficulties with the design of Sendmail. It is the exact opposite of a monolithic problem, and does not use any *setuid* program. However, it does require a world-writable directory. This could cause problems on a multiuser system, but it can be eliminated by using a single program that uses the group equivalent of *setuid*, called *setgid*. If you don't want to run Sendmail on your bastion host mail server, then we recommend using either Postfix or *smap/ smapd*, mentioned later in the "Improving SMTP Security with smap and smapd" section.

Qmail

Dan Bernstein wrote Qmail as a secure, reliable, and efficient replacement for Sendmail on typical Internet-connected Unix hosts. Qmail, like Postfix, is a compartmentalized mailer with separate programs for separate tasks. Unlike Postfix, it passes some information through process inheritance (one program starts another, which inherits information from the first). This reduces the separation between the programs.

Qmail is the least Sendmail-compatible SMTP replacement, although over time, it is becoming more compatible. As it is currently distributed, it handles forwarding and aliasing rather differently. In order to completely replace Sendmail and use the recommended mailbox format, you may also need to also replace the local delivery agent and possibly your mail user agents.

The different parts of Qmail run as different users, in order to make sure that each one has only the permissions it needs. Only one of them is *setuid*, and it is *setuid* to one of the special Qmail users, not to root. As long as the permissions and passwords for all of the Qmail users are correct, this is more secure than the widespread use of root made by Sendmail and *smail*.

Commercial SMTP Servers for Unix

In addition to the freely available SMTP servers mentioned previously, there are also a number of commercial SMTP servers for Unix, including the commercial version of Sendmail, Intermail, and Netscape's mail server. These products are mostly designed for volume, rather than for security and, with the exception of Sendmail, should be treated with the same skepticism you would apply to any other commercial network server. You should assume that they are vulnerable until proven otherwise. For more information on evaluating servers, see the comments on choosing security-critical programs in Chapter 13, *Internet Services and Firewalls*. Ironically, because of the high-profile problems with Sendmail, the developers of the commercial Sendmail version are more security-conscious than any of the other developers of commercial mailers.

Improving SMTP Security with smap and smapd

An important step a firewall can take to improve security is to prevent attackers from speaking SMTP directly to a full-featured server and, instead, to use a substitute server. Fortunately, this is feasible. SMTP stands for "Simple Mail Transport Protocol", and it really is simple. An SMTP server needs to implement only about a half-dozen or so commands in the protocol in order to accept incoming mail.

If you are using Unix for handling electronic mail, you may want to consider using the *smap* package that is part of TIS FWTK as a "wrapper" for your SMTP server (particularly if you are using Sendmail). The package includes a pair of programs called *smap* and *smapd*.

smap is a very short, simple program intended solely to handle incoming SMTP connections; unlike Sendmail, which contains about 30,000 lines of code, *smap* contains only about 700 lines. The relative simplicity of *smap* means that, unlike Sendmail, it can be easily be examined and considered in its entirety for security problems. Furthermore, it's designed with least privilege and compartmentaliza-tion in mind. The *smap* program runs without root privileges. It is started by *inetd*, which takes care of binding it to port 25 before starting it, so that *smap* doesn't need to run as root to do that. It runs *chroot*ed to a particular queue directory, and thus can't access anything outside that directory. All it does is accept incoming messages from the Internet via SMTP. It speaks the very minimum necessary set of SMTP commands, and it stores each message it receives in a separate file in the queue directory.

The second program, *smapd*, comes along regularly (typically once a minute) to process the files queued in this directory, normally by handing them to Sendmail for delivery.

The result of using this substitute SMTP server is that an attacker never has a direct SMTP connection to Sendmail or any other complex SMTP server. Such a system does not protect against data-driven security holes, but such holes would be extremely hard for any firewall system to guard against. Fortunately, data-driven holes in Sendmail seem to be very rare anyway; there has only been one instance to date.*

You do give up certain capabilities by using the *smap* package because *smap* quite intentionally handles only the minimum possible set of SMTP commands. In particular, *smap* does not support any ESMTP features.

A potential drawback of *smap,* which has been incorporated into several commer-cial firewalls, is that the original version allowed mail relaying. Although mail relaying is not specifically a security problem, it can easily result in your firewall's running out of resources. If you are using *smap*, make sure that you have a ver-sion that prevents mail relaying.

---

* This is covered in CERT Advisory 93:16. For information on obtaining CERT Advisories, see Appendix A.

biff

Many SMTP mail servers for Unix implement a mail notification service called *biff*.* If a user has *biff* turned on, then every time a message comes in, the user gets a notification that includes a message header summary and the first few lines of the message. The notification service uses UDP port 512 and is associated with the network daemon called *comsat*. Even though it uses a UDP port, it is not intended to be a network-available service; it normally gets packets only from processes running on the same host. This service should be disabled on all bastion hosts because they do not need to provide mail notification to their users (neither the mail nor the users should be local!). Similarly, bastion SMTP mail servers for Unix should be configured not to send the UDP packets. Since *biff* is not actually a network service, there's no reason to try to provide it through a firewall.

SMTP Support in Non-SMTP Mail Systems

Several popular mail systems are not based on SMTP. Lotus Notes and Microsoft Exchange, for instance, provide mail service, among other things, and use proprietary protocols to talk to their native clients. (They are discussed later in this chapter.) They also provide SMTP handling for Internet compatibility.

In general, non-SMTP mail systems are not particularly secure as SMTP servers. They are large systems to start with, designed for relatively secure environments and then improved for use on the Internet, which makes them vulnerable. Adding SMTP support to them merely increases the problem. In addition, their SMTP implementations tend to be at best eccentric and more often simply incorrect in their handling of obscure conditions, leading to various interoperability problems. If at all possible, use a dedicated SMTP mailer to speak and listen to the Internet (preferably Postfix, *smap*, or another security-oriented server).

SMTP Servers for Windows NT

The most widely used SMTP servers for Windows NT are Lotus Notes and Microsoft Exchange, which provide SMTP servers in addition to their other features. However, a number of SMTP servers are available for Windows NT that are designed primarily as SMTP servers. In general, dedicated SMTP servers are both more reliable and more secure than SMTP services added onto other mail systems. In the case of Windows NT SMTP servers, few are actually designed for security, and fewer still with the extensive history that Unix SMTP servers have. In

---

* "Biff" is not an acronym; it is the name of the original programmer's dog, which used to bark at the mailman.

general, they are full-fledged mail server systems including POP and/or IMAP servers, designed for maximum service rather than maximum security.

If you have a mixed environment, you will probably want to run your front-line SMTP server on Unix. If your environment is mostly or entirely Windows NT-based, there can be significant advantages to using a Windows NT-based SMTP server (aside from the normal administrative issues). Using a Windows NT-based server allows you to do virus checking on the SMTP server, for instance (this is possible with Unix servers, but the virus checkers tend to lag behind the versions that are available under Windows NT).

Windows NT systems, like Unix systems, should be set up with a security-conscious server as the Internet-visible server, which then passes the mail to a full-featured server on the inside.

Summary of Recommendations for SMTP

- Use the normal store-and-forward features of SMTP to send all incoming and outgoing mail through a bastion host.

- Use packet filtering to restrict SMTP connections from external hosts to just the bastion host you use as a mail server.

- Use packet filtering to restrict SMTP connections from the bastion host you use as a mail server to a specific internal server or set of servers.

- Use Postfix or *smap* instead of Sendmail as the SMTP server on the bastion host you use as a mail server and probably on your internal mail server as well.

- Keep up to date with patches on delivery agents and user agents.

- Educate your users concerning mail-based scams, such as instructions to run particular programs or to change their passwords to some specified string.

Other Mail Transfer Protocols

SMTP is the standard protocol for mail transfer between servers on the Internet. However, a few other protocols are used for server-server transfer within other mail systems. For instance, both Lotus Notes and Microsoft Exchange, discussed in the following sections, provide email service, among other services. Each of these systems has one proprietary protocol that is used for server-server and server-client mail transfer, as well as other functions. As discussed earlier, both of them are also capable of using SMTP to speak to the Internet.

In addition, the X.400 mail protocol is part of the Open Systems Interconnect (OSI) protocol set. Some mail systems are still running it, and both Lotus Notes and

Microsoft Exchange are also capable of using X.400 to speak to other mail systems. On TCP/IP networks, X.400 is run over TCP port 102. This is actually a general-purpose port that is used to provide OSI's Transport Service Access Protocol (TSAP) and that can carry any higher-level OSI protocol. X.400 and X.500 (directory services) happen to be the only higher-level OSI protocols that are still used to any noticeable extent, but opening up port 102 exposes you to all OSI protocols, not just to these.

Microsoft Exchange

Microsoft Exchange is perhaps best known as a mail server, but it also provides a number of other services, including news, calendar maintenance, contact management, and document exchange.

Both Exchange client-server conversations and the Exchange Administrator use Microsoft RPC, which is discussed in Chapter 14, *Intermediary Protocols*. In addition, depending on how it is configured, Exchange may use SMTP, POP, IMAP, NNTP, LDAP, X.400, and/or LDAP over SSL. SMTP, POP, IMAP, X.400 over TCP/IP and NNTP are discussed in this chapter; LDAP and LDAP over SSL are discussed in Chapter 19, *Real-Time Conferencing Services*.

Microsoft RPC is difficult to safely allow through a firewall using any technology because it involves connections at arbitrary ports and embedded IP addresses. It is difficult to secure with packet filtering and requires protocol-aware proxies or network address translation systems, which are not widely available. Therefore, you should avoid trying to support Exchange through a firewall using Microsoft RPC.

Almost all of the other protocols that Exchange supports are quite easy to allow through a firewall. Using them instead will impose three kinds of restrictions:

• You will not be able to use the Exchange Administrator.

• Server-to-server transactions (other than straightforward mail transfer) will have reduced performance.

• Clients will have mail service but will not have access to all Exchange features.

You can also configure Exchange to provide an HTTP interface to the calendar management features so that clients can use a web browser for scheduling. This is slower than using Exchange's native protocols.

Exchange servers that are speaking to other servers can do all Exchange operations without using Microsoft RPC, using what are called *Connectors* that embed operations in other protocols. You can therefore make server-to-server connections over SMTP without losing functionality, although there will be some performance penalty.

Because Exchange is a large and complicated system, it's relatively risky to allow access from the Internet to an Exchange server, even if you use the more controllable options. If you need to support remote users from anywhere on the Internet, attempt to limit them to mail reading, preferably using IMAP over SSL. If you provide HTTP access, restrict it to a limited range of source addresses.

Administering Exchange is an extremely complex topic, and we cannot do it justice here. You may want to consult a book on Exchange administration (for instance, *Managing Microsoft Exchange Server*, by Paul Robichaux, O'Reilly & Associates, 1999).

Summary of Recommendations for Microsoft Exchange

- Do not run Exchange on a bastion host. Instead use a dedicated SMTP server and forward the mail to your internal Exchange server.

- Do not use Microsoft RPC through a firewall. If a local Exchange server needs to communicate to a remote server via the Internet, use SMTP and forward the mail through your bastion host.

- If clients need to use full Exchange functionality, consider setting up an Exchange server where they can reach it without crossing a firewall and using server-to-server connectors over SMTP to cross the firewall.

Lotus Notes and Domino

Like Exchange, Lotus Notes is not just an electronic mail system; it provides a large number of services, including calendar management and document sharing. In addition, it is integrated with a web server, allowing it to provide forms and documents to web browsers. Although Notes was originally designed to be a groupware product, enabling groups to work together better, current versions also use the web server to provide services to Internet users. The name "Domino" was introduced as part of this change and refers to the new versions of the server (the client software is still known as Lotus Notes). When Domino is used as an Internet web server, it should be treated like any other web server; see Chapter 15, *The World Wide Web*.

Notes clients can use Notes RPC to speak to servers, but in recent versions, they can also use HTTP, SMTP, and/or POP3, to speak to Notes/Domino servers or to other servers. This provides extra options for supporting Notes clients over the Internet.

Notes uses public key encryption for authentication and does not send passwords across the network. By default, Notes does not encrypt other information, but it can be set to use encryption for all network traffic on a given port. This can be forced by the server; if the server is configured to use encryption, the clients will encrypt, regardless of the client setting. In addition, users and application designers can decide to encrypt individual documents, whether or not all network traffic is being encrypted. Notes can use a number of different encryption algorithms (RSA for public key encryption, DES, triple DES, RC2, and RC4 for secret key encryption) and a number of different key lengths depending on the type of encryption in use and the location of servers and clients. Encryption algorithms are discussed further in Appendix C, *Cryptography*.

Notes documents may contain embedded code in a language called "LotusScript". LotusScript does not provide any security controls by itself (it can call external programs and do anything that the user running Notes can do). Originally, Notes clients would execute LotusScript programs received in mail without notification or security controls. Starting in release 4.5, Notes provides controls on what programs can do, based on the digital signature of the document containing the program. Configurations can be set up for specific signatures, for a default that applies to signed documents with unknown signatures, and for unsigned documents. All Notes clients should be configured with maximum restrictions for the default and for unsigned documents.

Packet Filtering Characteristics of Lotus Notes

Native Notes transactions are done over a protocol called Notes RPC using TCP at port 1352. Connections between servers follow the same pattern as client/server connections.

Direction	Source Addr.	Dest. Addr.	Protocol	Source Port	Dest. Port	ACK Set	Notes
In	Ext	Int	TCP	>1023	1352	a	Incoming Notes connection, client to server
Out	Int	Ext	TCP	1352	>1023	Yes	Incoming Notes connection, server to client
Out	Int	Ext	TCP	>1023	1352	a	Outgoing Notes connection, client to server
In	Ext	Int	TCP	1352	>1023	Yes	Outgoing Notes connection, server to client

a ACK is not set on the first packet of this type (establishing connection) but will be set on the rest.

Proxying Characteristics of Lotus Notes

As of release 4.5, Lotus Notes clients are shipped with support for SOCKS v4. Lotus also has what they call a *Passthru server*, which is an application-aware proxy server; you can use this as a modified-procedure proxy by having the client connect to the Passthru server by name. You can also configure a Notes client to tunnel Notes RPC using an HTTP proxy, either using CONNECT or using a special Notes server that does HTTP. Some commercial firewalls also include Notes proxies.

You can also use a generic proxy, but this requires modifying the client configuration. Notes clients expect that the greeting from the server will match the name that they are configured with. You can get around this problem by using a connection document on the client which specifies what name to expect.

Network Address Translation Characteristics of Lotus Notes

Lotus Notes RPC does not include embedded IP addresses and will work without modification through a network address translation system. It does include embedded hostnames, which may release information that you expected to be concealed by the network address translation system. However, those embedded hostnames must not be changed, since they are used as part of server authentication.

Summary of Recommendations for Lotus Notes

- If you need to pass Lotus Notes through your firewall, use a proxy server.
- If you are using Notes RPC across the Internet, set the server to use encryption on all traffic.
- Configure clients with maximum restrictions on LotusScript in unsigned documents and documents with unknown signatures.
- Follow normal recommendations for web browsers when configuring Notes as a web browser, and normal recommendations for web servers when configuring Domino as a web server.

Post Office Protocol (POP)

SMTP is used to exchange mail between servers. Sometimes, users access their mail as a file (directly, or using NFS or something similar) on the machine where it is delivered; however, there are often reasons to use a separate protocol to distribute mail from a server to an individual user.

POP is a client/server protocol for handling user electronic mailboxes. With POP, a user's mail spool (the actual file where that user's incoming email is held for later access) is kept on a server, rather than on the user's personal machine. The server is probably available to accept incoming mail more consistently than the user's personal machine is (particularly if the user's "personal machine" is a portable that is only sometimes connected to the network). Clients like Eudora, Z-Mail, or

Netscape use POP to transfer the mail to the personal machine when the user wants it.

Two major security issues are involved in using POP across the Internet. First, be aware that standard POP clients and servers send the user's POP password over the Internet in the clear, so that anyone snooping on the connection can capture and reuse it later. In most cases, the POP password is the same as the user's login password, so that someone who snoops on it can get all of the user's privileges— not just the user's electronic mail. More secure variants of POP support Kerberos (called KPOP) and a challenge-response system for authentication (called APOP), but these secure variants are not widely available or widely supported. You may have trouble finding a combination of clients and servers that supports these variants and that works for your site.

Second, regardless of the authentication issues, be sure to also consider the sensitivity of the email your users will be accessing over the Internet via POP. Whatever email your users access will be visible to anyone snooping on their POP sessions; you need to think about how sensitive email might be in your own environment. Many sites decide that, regardless of the authentication issues, their users' internal email is often too sensitive to risk being snooped on by someone monitoring their POP sessions. These sites decide to provide alternative access methods, such as dial-ups, that aren't as susceptible to snooping. If you provide your users with the ability to reach your network on the inside of the firewall (for example, using a VPN or with modems and PPP), you can give them POP access while they're traveling without allowing it to be snooped on the Internet.

Two different processes are being used to provide protection for POP. Currently, some servers and clients support the use of POP over SSL, encrypting the entire connection (this is sometimes called SecurePOP). This is an effective stopgap measure, but it requires the use of another port for POP over SSL. (SSL and TLS are discussed in Chapter 14, *Intermediary Protocols.*)

There is also a standard in progress that extends the POP protocol to allow clients and servers to negotiate the use of TLS on a normal POP connection. This is the preferred method for providing encryption for services, since it doesn't require a new port, and the supply of port numbers is limited. Unfortunately, the standard is not yet complete and support for it is not widespread.

Packet Filtering Characteristics of POP

POP is a TCP-based service. POP servers for the current version of the POP protocol (which is known as POP3 and is by far the most common version in use) use port 110. Servers for the older POP2 protocol use port 109. (POP1 was never in widespread use.) POP clients use ports above 1023. Servers providing POP3 over SSL use port 995.

Direction	Source Addr.	Dest. Addr.	Protocol	Source Port	Dest. Port	ACK Set	Notes
In	Ext	Int	TCP	>1023	110, 109[a]	b	Incoming POP connection, client to server
Out	Int	Ext	TCP	110, 109[a]	>1023	Yes	Incoming POP connection, server to client
In	Ext	Int	TCP	>1023	995	b	Incoming POP over SSL connection, client to server
Out	Int	Ext	TCP	995	>1023	Yes	Incoming POP over SSL connection, server to client
Out	Int	Ext	TCP	>1023	110, 109[a]	b	Outgoing POP connection, client to server
In	Ext	Int	TCP	110, 109[a]	>1023	Yes	Outgoing POP connection, server to client
Out	Int	Ext	TCP	>1023	995	b	Outgoing POP over SSL connection, client to server
In	Ext	Int	TCP	995	>1023	Yes	Outgoing POP over SSL connection, server to client

[a] Modern POP (POP3) servers use port 110; older POP2 servers use port 109.
[b] ACK is not set on the first packet of this type (establishing connection) but will be set on the rest.

An outgoing POP connection would allow your users to download their mail from other sites. This is no more dangerous than allowing outgoing Telnet, and you will probably want to allow such a POP connection if there is any demand.

Incoming POP connections are those that allow people at other sites to read mail delivered for them at your site. As discussed in the previous section, you probably don't want to allow incoming POP. If you do, you should certainly limit POP connections to a POP server running on a single host. There have been several problems with buffer overflows in POP servers, and if any new ones are found, you would like to be able to patch them on just one host, without worrying about all your internal hosts. This is easiest if you run POP on a dedicated bastion host.

You will also want to be sure that POP servers that serve incoming connections are configured so that POP does not use user accounts for authentication. Some POP servers use normal user accounts to authenticate connections. Since the POP server is a bastion host, you don't want users to be able to log in to it, particularly from the Internet. You should either use a POP server that supports an alternate source of authentication, or disable logins on the accounts that POP uses.

Proxying Characteristics of POP

POP is straightforward to proxy because it uses a single connection. Most commercial proxy systems include POP support. Many of the web browsers that also provide an email client support POP and will use SOCKS with POP. (Netscape Communicator and Microsoft's Outlook both support POP through SOCKS.) The older dedicated email clients are less likely to have SOCKS support.

Two POP proxies are available as add-ons to the TIS-FWTK. *pop-gw* is an inbound proxy for POP3. *pop3-gw* will do inbound or outbound proxying. For inbound proxying, you can configure it to run as a pass-through, passing all connections to a specific internal server. For outbound use, it uses modified procedures; the user specifies *user@server[:port]* as his or her username and connects to the proxy server. The proxy server will use APOP to speak to the real server if it is available and may be configured to refuse connections if APOP is not available; this will keep you from passing reusable passwords around via the proxy. Note that all data will still be transmitted unencrypted and will be interceptable.

Network Address Translation Characteristics of POP

POP does not use embedded IP addresses and will work with network address translation without problems.

Summary of Recommendations for POP

- Do not allow your users to transfer your site's mail over the Internet via POP, unless you can do so without revealing reusable passwords, and unless either you aren't concerned about the sensitivity of the mail itself or you have an encrypted channel to transfer it over.

- If you have users who wish to transfer mail from other sites via POP, allow it via packet filtering or by using *pop3-gw* (set to require APOP from the server).

Internet Message Access Protocol (IMAP)

IMAP,* like POP, is a protocol used by mail user agents to retrieve mail, for a specific user from a server. IMAP is a more recent protocol providing more flexibility, including support for multiple mailboxes for each user. POP is commonly used to transfer all messages in a single mailbox to the client from the server; IMAP is designed to store messages on the server, allowing them to be copied and manipulated by the client. IMAP is a much more capable protocol than POP and correspondingly is harder to implement securely.

Otherwise, the security implications of IMAP are much like the security implications of POP. IMAP does allow for nonreusable passwords, but not all IMAP servers and clients support them. Similarly, an Internet standard is evolving that will

---

* This acronym is sometimes also expanded to "Interim Mail Access Protocol".

allow IMAP to use TLS to support the encryption of messages as they pass between the server and client, but currently few servers and clients support this option. There is also an assigned port for IMAP over SSL, which is supported by a slightly larger number of clients and servers. Unless you control the IMAP servers and have configured them to require nonreusable passwords and data encryption, or you are restricting connections to IMAP over SSL, you should assume that IMAP is passing reusable passwords and unencrypted data.

Packet Filtering Characteristics of IMAP

IMAP uses straightforward TCP connections to port 143 and is therefore easy to allow through packet filters. IMAP over SSL currently uses port 993, but an earlier convention uses port 585. Several variants of IMAP are in use (you may see variants described as "v2" or "rev4", for instance), but all IMAP versions in wide distribution use the same port.

Direction	Source Addr.	Dest. Addr.	Protocol	Source Port	Dest. Port	ACK Set	Notes
In	Ext	Int	TCP	>1023	143	a	Incoming IMAP connection, client to server
Out	Int	Ext	TCP	143	>1023	Yes	Incoming IMAP connection, server to client
In	Ext	Int	TCP	>1023	993, 585[b]	a	Incoming IMAP over SSL connection, client to server
Out	Int	Ext	TCP	993, 585[b]	>1023	Yes	Incoming IMAP over SSL connection, server to client
Out	Int	Ext	TCP	>1023	143	a	Outgoing IMAP connection, client to server
In	Ext	Int	TCP	143	>1023	Yes	Outgoing IMAP connection, server to client
Out	Int	Ext	TCP	>1023	993, 585[b]	a	Outgoing IMAP over SSL connection, client to server
In	Ext	Int	TCP	993, 585[b]	>1023	Yes	Outgoing IMAP over SSL connection, server to client

a ACK is not set on the first packet of this type (establishing connection) but will be set on the rest.
b 993 is the current standard, but some older implementations use 585.

Proxying Characteristics of IMAP

IMAP is a straightforward protocol to proxy, since it uses a single TCP connection. There do not appear to be any IMAP-specific proxies available at this time, but generic proxies will work with IMAP (without providing any strong security guarantees).

Network Address Translation Characteristics of IMAP

IMAP does not use embedded IP addresses and will work with network address translation without problems.

Summary of Recommendations for IMAP

- Do not allow your users to transfer your site's mail over the Internet via IMAP, unless you have configured your IMAP server to require nonreusable passwords and encrypted data.

- If you have users who wish to transfer mail from other sites via IMAP, allow it via packet filtering, perhaps restricted to connections from specific sites or to specific hosts on your end.

Microsoft Messaging API (MAPI)

The Microsoft Messaging API (MAPI) is, as the name implies, an application programming interface (API) and not a network protocol at all. It is included here because for various reasons, including the uncanny resemblance of its name to "IMAP", it is often mistaken for a mail protocol. MAPI is used on Microsoft operating systems for applications to communicate with messaging systems. It is internal to a single machine; an application uses MAPI to communicate with MAPI drivers, which then communicate with mail and directory servers. A MAPI driver will use whatever protocol it needs to in order to communicate with mail and directory servers. This means that applications that are programmed with MAPI can be used with a variety of email servers without changes, by changing the MAPI drivers.

Knowing that an application uses MAPI does not allow you to predict what protocol will be used to communicate between a client and a server. Instead, you need to know what protocols the MAPI driver is using; usually the easiest way to determine this is to determine what kind of server is being used. Probably the biggest user of MAPI is the Microsoft Exchange client, which is provided with MAPI drivers that use Microsoft RPC to speak to Microsoft Exchange servers.

Network News Transfer Protocol (NNTP)

NNTP is the service generally used to transfer Usenet news across the Internet. A news server is the place where Usenet news flows into and out of your organization, and which your users access (via news clients) to read and post news. News servers generally speak NNTP among themselves so they can transfer news between sites. In addition, most news clients use NNTP to access news servers.

(Traditionally, Unix-based news clients read news from local files, and some sites may still be using older clients that do this.)

There are a number of freely available news servers, including B-News, C-News, and INN. There are also number of commercial servers, which claim to have better performance.

These days, not all sites choose to offer news. If you do not have your own news server, you may wish to allow your users to contact external NNTP servers. The risk involved is relatively low; although NNTP has been used to attack news servers, there are no known serious problems with the NNTP protocol for clients. NNTP does, of course, provide another way for information to flow into and out of your organization, where the inbound information may include undesirable things like viruses, illegitimate copies of copyrighted information, and data that is illegal to distribute in some jurisdictions (including hate speech and pornography), and the outbound information may include your organization's secrets. These are the same risks found in protocols like HTTP and SMTP, and an NNTP client is vulnerable to the same data-driven risks as an electronic mail client, including the risks associated with handling of MIME- and HTML-enhanced messages.

If you do choose to run your own news server, the best way to configure it is the same way that you configure SMTP; set up a server on a bastion host that talks to external sites, possibly sanitizing information in the process, and relays news to an internal server. Your internal clients then exchange news with the internal server. The external server needs only a minimal configuration, since the news will be stored on the internal server. This configuration gives you a maximum of security and control, but it is a significant amount of administrative overhead. In addition, even minimal news servers place a heavy load on machines, and it is advisable to put the externally visible news server on a dedicated bastion host.

If you are unable to use a configuration with two news servers, the next best option is to use a single news server on a bastion host. If you do this, you will be able to support only news readers that use NNTP; older Unix clients that expect to read files directly will not have access to the bastion host. In addition, you should not create private newsgroups that are intended to be internal to your organization if your news server is a bastion host. The probability that the newsgroups will leak to the outside universe is far too high.

Finally, you can use a single news server on your internal network and very carefully control which hosts can reach it. This is the most dangerous option, since you are letting external hosts make connections directly to your internal network. However, you can limit the connections to those servers you exchange news with, and this solution will let you have internal newsgroups and non-NNTP news readers. In this situation, you should try to use servers and feed sites that support NNTP authentication, so that you have some authentication besides the IP source address. NNTP authentication is not standard but is implemented in many servers.

Packet Filtering Characteristics of NNTP

NNTP is a TCP-based service. NNTP servers use port 119. NNTP clients (including servers transferring news to other servers) use ports above 1023. Some news servers (in particular, INN) allow you to specify other port numbers to use for server-server transactions, which can be useful for a number of reasons. In particular, it allows you to separate server-server transactions from server-reader transactions and put separate restrictions on them. This can be particularly useful on heavily loaded servers that may otherwise have difficulty receiving news during peak reading times.

Direction	Source Addr.	Dest. Addr.	Protocol	Source Port	Dest. Port	ACK Set	Notes
In	Ext	Int	TCP	>1023	119	a	Incoming news
Out	Int	Ext	TCP	119	>1023	Yes	Incoming news responses
Out	Int	Ext	TCP	>1023	119	a	Outgoing news, or internal client contacting external server
In	Ext	Int	TCP	119	>1023	Yes	Outgoing news responses, or external server responding to internal client

a ACK is not set on the first packet of this type (establishing connection) but will be set on the rest.

Proxying Characteristics of NNTP

NNTP is a store-and-forward protocol, capable of doing its own proxying. It is also easy to proxy as a straightforward single-connection protocol. TIS FWTK provides a generic proxy, *plug-gw*, which is frequently used with NNTP, as well as modified user procedures (the NNTP connection is directed to the proxy server, which redirects the connection based on the client address). It would be easy to modify clients to use a generic modified-client proxy like SOCKS. In addition, the clients provided with web browsers (including Netscape Navigator and Internet Explorer) are capable of using SOCKS.

Network Address Translation Characteristics of NNTP

NNTP does not use embedded IP addresses and will work with network address translation systems. However, NNTP servers may use the source IP address and port of connections as an authentication mechanism. In addition, news articles will contain hostname information, which may be either a name provided by the client that submits the article, or a name gotten by resolving the source IP address, or both. This may give away information that you don't want to make public. In addition, running NNTP through network address translation may cause the NNTP server to decide that you're lying about your host information (because the name provided by the client and the name gotten by resolving the source IP address don't match).

Summary of Recommendations for NNTP

- Use two NNTP servers—have your users read news from an internal NNTP server, and have the internal NNTP server exchange news with a bastion host that talks to external sites.

- Allow external NNTP connections only from the sites you exchange news with.

17

File Transfer, File Sharing, and Printing

Although files can be sent from one computer to another via electronic mail, email tends to be an inefficient way of transferring data, best suited for relatively small documents. Other protocols are better for moving large files around. These protocols come in two kinds: protocols designed for file transfer, and protocols designed for file sharing. In file transfer, a user copies a file to or from a server, so that one file is on the server and another copy of the file is on the client. In file sharing, the file remains on the server and is modified by the client, so that only one copy of the file exists. The file sharing model is particularly useful in situations where multiple people need to work on a file.

When using mobile computers, it is useful to have some sort of hybrid between these two options; a mobile computer may not be able to contact a file server to use a file that's located on the server, so local copies are desirable, but the mobile is unlikely to be reliably backed up and accessible to other people, so server-based files are desirable. Although there are various solutions to this situation, all of them involve using existing protocols designed for file transfer or for file sharing. The most common versions are programs like Microsoft's Briefcase, which use file sharing to synchronize files between a mobile computer and a server.

FTP is the de facto standard for file transfer on the Internet. In addition, some specialized protocols are used for applications where FTP is not suitable. TFTP is used by dedicated devices to transfer configuration files.

NFS is the de facto standard for file sharing under Unix, although AFS and DCE DFS are both used at some sites. CIFS/SMB and NetWare are used for file sharing under Microsoft network operating systems. AppleShare is the file sharing protocol for Apple Macintoshes. There are a wide variety of ways to mix and match these protocols (for instance, Unix machines can run SMB and NetWare, Microsoft and Apple machines can run NFS, and Microsoft servers can translate NetWare and AppleShare into SMB).

Printing is effectively a special case of file transfer, in which files are transferred to the printer. Not only does printing have most of the same security properties as file transfer, it is actually implemented as a special type of file transfer on many platforms, so we have included it here.

File Transfer Protocol (FTP)

FTP is used to transfer files from one machine to another. You can use FTP to transfer any type of file, including executable binaries, graphics images, ASCII text, PostScript, sound and video files, and more. The data provided by an FTP server is organized hierarchically, and the contents can be navigated interactively using Unix-like commands. There are two types of FTP access: user or authenticated FTP and anonymous FTP. *User FTP* requires an account on the server (in general, it is for users who already have accounts on the machine and lets them access any files they could access if they were logged in). *Anonymous FTP* is for people who don't have an account and is used to provide access to specific files to the world at large.

Anonymous FTP is by far the most common use of FTP on the Internet. Anonymous FTP servers are the standard mechanism for distributing source code, compiled programs, information, and other files that sites wish to make available to the Internet at large. If a site provides an anonymous FTP server, anyone on the Internet can initiate an FTP connection to the site, tell the FTP server that their login name is "anonymous", and access whatever files the server's owners have chosen to make available in a restricted area. This process is done automatically by most web browsers when they encounter a URL that begins "ftp:", so many people use FTP without being aware that they are doing so.

Packet Filtering Characteristics of FTP

FTP uses two separate TCP connections: one to carry commands and results between the client and the server (commonly called the *command channel*), and the other to carry any actual files and directory listings transferred (the *data channel*). The command channel uses port 21 on the server end and a port above 1023 on the client. FTP has two different ways to set up the data channel, called *normal mode* and *passive mode*. (Passive mode is also sometimes written as "PASV mode", after the command used to set it up.) In normal mode, the server uses port 20 for the data channel, while in passive mode, it uses a port above 1023. The client always uses a port above 1023 for the data channel.

To start an FTP session in normal mode, a client first allocates two TCP ports for itself, each of them with a port number above 1024. It uses the first to open the command channel connection to the server and then issues FTP's PORT command to tell the server the number of the second port, which the client wants to use for the data channel. The server then opens the data channel connection. This data channel connection is backwards from most protocols, which open connections from the client to the server. This backwards open complicates things for sites that are attempting to do start-of-connection packet filtering to ensure that all TCP connections are initiated from the inside, because external FTP servers will attempt to initiate data connections to internal clients, in response to command connections opened from those internal clients. Furthermore, these connections will be going to ports known to be in an unsafe range. Figure 17-1 shows this kind of FTP connection.

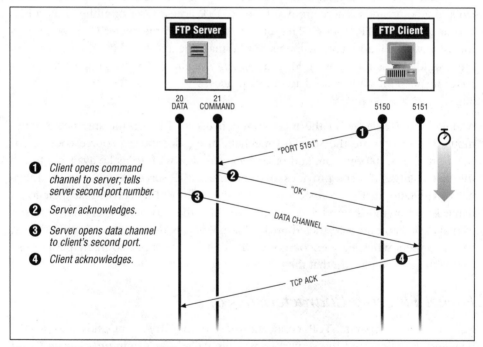

Figure 17-1. A normal-mode FTP connection

To start a connection in passive mode, an FTP client allocates two TCP ports for its own use and uses the first port to contact the FTP server, just as when using normal mode. However, instead of issuing the PORT command to tell the server the client's second port, the client issues the PASV command. This causes the server to allocate a second port of its own for the data channel (for architectural reasons, servers use random ports above 1023 for this, not port 20 as in normal mode; you couldn't have two servers on the same machine simultaneously listening for incoming PASV-mode data connections on port 20) and tell the client the number of that port. The client then opens the data connection from its port to the data port the server has just told it about. Figure 17-2 shows a passive-mode FTP connection.

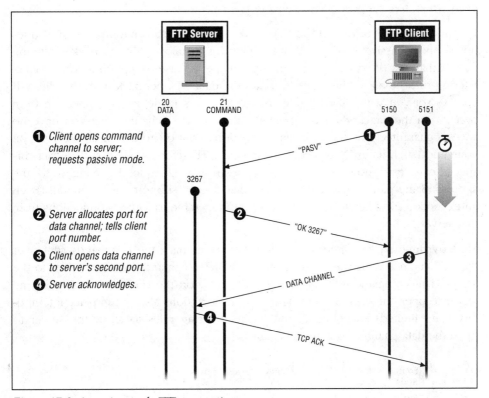

Figure 17-2. A passive-mode FTP connection

Passive mode is useful because it allows you to avoid start-of-connection filtering problems. In passive mode, all connections will be opened from the inside, by the client.

Most FTP servers in widespread use support passive mode, but not all FTP clients do. If a given client does support passive mode, it will usually be mentioned as a feature in the documentation or description. Some clients support both normal and passive modes and provide the user some way to specify which mode to use. If you're having trouble finding passive-mode clients, it's useful to know that the built-in FTP clients in most web browsers (Netscape Navigator, for example) use passive mode. Chances are, your users will want to have these browsers anyway for web access, and you can show them how to use the browsers as FTP clients as well.

Different FTP servers have different strengths and weaknesses. You may find that combinations of servers and clients that work well with normal-mode transfers hang periodically when you do passive-mode transfers, or vice versa. You may also find some FTP servers that have difficulty with web browsers as FTP clients, even when they support other clients in passive mode.

If your FTP client (or one of the FTP servers you wish to communicate with) does not support passive mode, and you still want to allow FTP via packet filtering (rather than via proxy), you'll have to put a special-case exception in your packet filtering rules to allow the server to open the data channel back in to the client. If you do so, you will still be vulnerable to attackers launching a connection from port 20 on the attacker's end (nominally the FTP data channel, but you have no way to guarantee that on a machine you don't control) to a port above 1023 on your end (such as an X server, for example). Therefore, you should restrict this special-case exception as much as possible—for example, by tying it to the address of the particular client or server that doesn't support passive mode. (Even an exception for a single server makes you vulnerable to forged connections from that server.)

Most dynamic packet filtering implementations monitor the commands sent over the FTP command channel and notice the PORT command the client sends to the server. This command tells the server on which port the client is listening for the server to open the data channel. These implementations also put in place a temporary (time-limited) exception in the packet filtering rules to allow the server to open the data channel back to the client.

Direction	Source Addr.	Dest. Addr.	Protocol	Source Port	Dest. Port	ACK Set	Notes
In	Ext	Int	TCP	>1023	21	a	Incoming FTP request
Out	Int	Ext	TCP	21	>1023	Yes	Response to incoming request
Out	Int	Ext	TCP	20	>1023	a	Data channel creation for incoming FTP request, normal mode
In	Ext	Int	TCP	>1023	20	Yes	Data channel responses for incoming FTP request, normal mode
In	Ext	Int	TCP	>1023	>1023	a	Data channel creation for incoming FTP request, passive mode
Out	Int	Ext	TCP	>1023	>1023	Yes	Data channel responses for incoming FTP request, passive mode
Out	Int	Ext	TCP	>1023	21	a	Outgoing FTP request
In	Ext	Int	TCP	21	>1023	Yes	Response to outgoing request
In	Ext	Int	TCP	20	>1023	a	Data channel creation for outgoing FTP request, normal mode
Out	Int	Ext	TCP	>1023	20	Yes	Data channel responses for outgoing FTP request, normal mode

Direction	Source Addr.	Dest. Addr.	Protocol	Source Port	Dest. Port	ACK Set	Notes
Out	Int	Ext	TCP	>1023	>1023	a	Data channel creation for outgoing FTP request, passive mode
In	Ext	Int	TCP	>1023	>1023	Yes	Data channel responses for outgoing FTP request, passive mode

a ACK is not set on the first packet of this type (establishing connection) but will be set on the rest.

Proxying Characteristics of FTP

Because of the problems with passive mode, and because of complications introduced in name service (the "double-reverse lookups" discussed in Chapter 20, *Naming and Directory Services*), proxying is a particularly attractive solution for outbound FTP. Using a normal-mode proxied client allows you to talk reliably to external servers without having to allow incoming TCP connections for the data channel to any host except the bastion host doing the proxying. For this reason, you may choose to proxy FTP even if you allow most other protocols directly through the firewall via packet filtering. Both modified-client and modified-procedure proxies are available for FTP.

The SOCKS package includes an FTP client for Unix that has been modified to use SOCKS. Because of the multiple simultaneous TCP connections involved in FTP, modifying other FTP clients yourself requires some work (more than modifying clients for straightforward single-connection protocols like SMTP and POP).

TIS FWTK provides a proxy FTP server that operates with modified clients or modified user procedures. It provides additional logging, operation denial, and user authentication features, giving you finer control than you can achieve with packet filters or SOCKS proxying.

If you want to use modified clients with the TIS FWTK FTP proxy server, you will need to do all of the modification yourself; the proxy server does not provide a modified client or even a client library. Using modified clients with the TIS FWTK FTP proxy server will also prevent you from running a standard FTP server on the machine you're using as the proxy server. Some versions of FWTK have had an FTP server that could act as a proxy server and a regular FTP server, but there have been some problems with it, and it's not clear that it will continue to be included with newer releases of the toolkit.

Some FTP clients are not sufficiently flexible to be used with modified user procedures involving the TIS FWTK FTP proxy server. The custom procedures users have to follow involve opening an FTP connection to the machine where the proxy server is running and then logging into the FTP proxy server as *anonymous@host.some.net*, specifying the name of the host they really want to connect to as part of the login. Some FTP clients have "anonymous" simply hardcoded in or limit the length of the login field to something too short to contain "anonymous@" plus a reasonably long hostname.

Any commercial proxying packages will almost certainly support outbound FTP proxying because FTP is such a commonly used protocol on the Internet.

Many sites use both proxy and packet filtering solutions for FTP. You can sometimes reduce the number of modified clients you need by using proxying to support normal-mode connections and packet filtering to support passive-mode connections. You can also use a combined solution for added security by using a proxy FTP server that uses passive mode to make external connections, regardless of the mode it uses to talk to the internal hosts; this converts all connections that cross the firewall to passive mode and allows you to tighten the packet filters that protect the host doing the proxying. On the other hand, it will prevent you from using servers that don't support passive mode.

Network Address Translation Characteristics of FTP

FTP uses embedded IP addresses to set up the data connection and will not work with network address translation unless the translator modifies the contents of packets. However, almost all network address translation systems are FTP-aware and will be able to make this change.

Providing Anonymous FTP Service

With anonymous FTP, a user logs in to the FTP server as "anonymous". The user is then asked for a password and is expected to enter his or her full email address in response. At most sites, this request is not enforced, however, and users can enter whatever they want, as long as it looks like an email address; even if the information is entered, it's usually just logged, not verified in any way beyond a superficial plausibility check (i.e., does it contain an "@" sign?). Many standard FTP servers, like the ones shipped with most versions of Unix, don't even log the information.

There are three main ways you can limit the risks of providing anonymous FTP service:

* Limiting access to only the information you want to make public
* Preventing people from using your FTP server to distribute their information
* Preventing people from using your FTP server to attack other machines

Limiting access to information

In setting up anonymous FTP, one precaution you can take is to limit what other information is available on the machine that's providing anonymous FTP service. In this way, even if attackers get "outside" the anonymous FTP area on the machine, nothing of interest to them is elsewhere on the machine (or reachable from the machine via NFS or some other mechanism).

Most Unix FTP servers perform a *chroot* to the anonymous FTP area before the FTP server starts processing commands from an anonymous user. Although Windows NT doesn't have a *chroot* mechanism, Windows NT FTP servers also provide a "virtual root", which is supposed to limit access given to anonymous users. To support both anonymous and user FTP, however, FTP servers need access to all files. This means that *chroot*, which is normally regarded as extremely safe, doesn't guarantee as much for an FTP server because the server is not always running in the *chroot*ed environment. On Windows NT, the restrictions are provided entirely by the FTP server (rather than the operating system), which is an even weaker guarantee (and indeed, a number of Windows NT FTP servers have had problems with people using pathnames that include ".." to escape the restricted area).

To deal with this problem under Unix, you can modify *inetd*'s configuration so that instead of starting the FTP server directly, it *chroots* (using something like the *chrootuid* program described in Appendix B, *Tools*) and then starts the FTP server. Normally, FTP runs with limited access only for anonymous users, and nonanonymous users have their normal access permissions. Doing the *chroot* before starting up the FTP server means that the nonanonymous users will also be limited; if you don't have any nonanonymous users of your FTP server (and you probably shouldn't), this is irrelevant.

Under Windows NT, you cannot get the operating system to enforce this sort of restriction. You should be sure that all filesystems on your FTP server are NTFS and use NTFS filesystem permissions to ensure that the account that is used for anonymous access does not have access to files that it should not be able to read. On the Microsoft FTP server that's part of the Internet Information Service and comes with Windows NT Server; that account is named IUSR_*computername*, and it is normally made part of the Guests group, which by default has almost universal read permissions. You should explicitly give Guests "No Access" to everything outside the anonymous FTP directories.

The details of setting up an anonymous FTP system vary depending on the operating system and the particular FTP daemon code in use. Start with the instructions (if any) in the manual pages for your FTP daemon; this should get you through most of the vendor-specific steps. Then, once you've performed all the steps there, if you are running Unix, obtain and follow CERT-CC Advisory 93:10 (for information on obtaining CERT-CC advisories, see Appendix A, *Resources*), which addresses setting up anonymous FTP servers to close the holes left by most of the vendor instructions.* (There doesn't seem to be an equivalent source of information for Windows NT FTP servers.)

Unfortunately, one of the most common ways that anonymous users get access to files they shouldn't be able to see is that an internal user innocently puts the files up for anonymous FTP, on the assumption that this is somehow safe. Usually, the internal user is relying on security through obscurity, assuming that nobody will notice the files. This does not work well. People do notice, especially if the names of the new files are meaningful. At popular FTP sites, curious people poke around randomly, and they notice new files almost immediately and may transfer them out of pure curiosity. On less-visited FTP sites, files may remain unnoticed until some service indexes them. Unless you have explicitly arranged to have your FTP site skipped, you should assume that it is being indexed.

It's best to avoid putting files up for anonymous FTP if you don't want the entire world to read them. Use other methods of file transfer if possible. If not, you may want to use a modified FTP server, like the *wuarchive* server, which allows semi-anonymous access that requires an anonymous user to provide an additional password to get access to certain directories. (No such server appears to exist for Windows NT.) You can also put up files in directories that allow people to read the files without being able to do a directory listing; under Unix, you give execute permission but not read permission on the directory, while under Windows NT, you give read permission but not list permission. Doing so will let people who know the names transfer the files, but won't let people look to see what files exist.

Whatever method you choose, be sure that everybody at your site who can put files in the anonymous FTP directories knows not to put confidential files where they're world-readable. An easy way to do this is to prevent your internal users from writing to the anonymous FTP directories and to require them to ask a system administrator to make a file available.

Preventing people from using your server to distribute their data

If you have an anonymous FTP server, you may want to use it to get data as well as to distribute data. For example, you might want to let customers upload crash dump files (which are too big to conveniently send through email) so you can do a crash analysis on them, or you might want to let people give you software they've written. One way to do this is to provide a writable area in your anonymous FTP server.

---

* Many vendors ship instructions containing critical problems, ranging from security holes to missing steps that disable parts of FTP's functionality.

Writable areas can be very useful, but they have a dark side. Such writable directories *will* (notice that we didn't say *may*) be found and used by "the underground" on the Internet as storage space and distribution areas for illicit material; this generally means pirated software packages or music and pornographic image files.

The folks who do this can be amazingly well organized and hard to track down. They have their own communication mechanisms for telling each other about new sites—places they've found to store their stuff—without revealing who they are. When they find a new site, they typically create a hidden subdirectory in which to store their files and images. They give the subdirectory an innocuous name such as ".. " (that's "dot dot space space"). When casually looking around an anonymous FTP area, you probably won't notice a name like this. It's particularly easy to miss on Unix systems because file and directory names beginning with "." are ignored by the Unix *ls* command, unless you give the command a special argument or run it as root.

On some sites in which intruders play this game, you can see a barter economy in operation. Someone leaves a note saying they're seeking a certain package or file and listing what they have to offer in exchange. A short time later, someone else comes along, uploads the requested files, and leaves another note telling the original poster what they want in return.

What's wrong with this misuse of your anonymous FTP areas? There are several problems:

- It consumes your resources, such as disk space and network bandwidth (particularly on your Internet connection), and it interferes with the legitimate use of those resources: it's a denial of service attack.

- It potentially exposes your site to legal action for assisting (even unwittingly) in copyright violations, software piracy, or perhaps sexual harassment, or even sexual exploitation of minors. Even if such actions are unlikely to succeed, your attorneys will probably tell you that they'd rather avoid the issue and not have to fight the battle in the first place.

- Even if no legal actions are undertaken, such an incident could generate significant negative publicity and embarrassment for your site or organization. Once your name has been linked to software piracy or child pornography in any way, you are in bad trouble regardless of how innocent your involvement was.

How can you protect your anonymous FTP areas from such misuse? The first question to ask yourself is this: do you really need to provide writable space in your anonymous FTP area? There are often other acceptable ways (electronic mail, for example) for folks to send files to you. If you decide that you must provide writable space in your anonymous FTP area, you can limit your vulnerability in a number of ways, as we describe in the following sections.

Making your incoming directory write-only. The most obvious approach is to make your "incoming" directory write-only. Under Unix, this is directory permissions 773 or 733—that is, "rwxrwx-wx" or "rwx-wx-wx". Make sure that the directory is owned by some user other than "ftp" (or whatever your anonymous FTP server runs as when doing anonymous FTP). If the mode is 773 instead of 733, then also make sure that the group of the directory is something other than the default group of the "ftp" login. Under Windows NT, set the directory so that the user used for anonymous FTP has Add permission on the directory and Write permission on files created in the directory. This shows up in the Permissions dialog as "(WX)(W)" and can be done by giving the Add permission and then going to Special File Permissions and giving Write permission.

The problem with this approach under Unix is that all you're doing is keeping people from being able to see what's in the top-level directory. They can still see what's in subdirectories, and they can still access files and directories they create in the top-level directory if they communicate exact filenames among themselves (and they can, via their mailing lists and other communications channels).

Under Windows NT, since you can specify the permissions that files are created with, you do not have this problem. On the other hand, the filesystem will allow the creator to change those permissions; you are relying on there being no way for an anonymous FTP user to take advantage of it. Microsoft's FTP server does not allow users to change permissions, so there is no automatic problem. However, if the anonymous user has any further access (for instance, a bug allows them to cause the FTP server to execute arbitrary code, even with the anonymous user's normal user permissions), it may be possible to make files readable.

Making anonymous read and anonymous write exclusive. One way to keep people from using your server as a distribution point is to prohibit the user "anonymous" from reading any file that was created by the user "anonymous", regardless of the filesystem permissions on the file. This won't interfere with normal operation of the server; users can still read files you are trying to distribute and transfer files to you, but they can't use you as a third-party distribution service. This feature is unfortunately not in most FTP implementations although the code to implement it in a BSD-derived FTP daemon is only a few lines long.

Disabling the creation of directories and certain files. Another approach is to disable the creation of directories and files with funny names (for example, files that begin with ".") in your anonymous FTP server. Depending on your server, you may be able to do this with a configuration file (for example, the *wuarchive* server lets you restrict anonymous users from deleting, overwriting, or creating certain types of files), or you may have to modify the server source code. (This is a non-trivial modification, which requires a reasonably competent C programmer.) Microsoft's FTP server doesn't provide this disable capability.

This approach doesn't keep people from uploading stuff to the writable directory you provide; it simply makes it more difficult for them to hide that stuff so that it escapes your notice. If you do this, you will still need to look at the writable area every day (and look at the contents of files, not just the names) to be sure everything is something that belongs there.

Uploading by prearrangement. Another approach is used frequently by sites that want people to be able to upload files but only by prearrangement. These sites take a page from the underground's own book by creating hidden writable subdirectories that you can access only if you know they're there. The attackers can't see them; they're unaware that there's a "there" there for their wares.

Here's what you do:

1. Make an "incoming" directory.
2. Make a subdirectory there with a "secret" name, chosen in much the same way you'd choose a password—that is, something unguessable.
3. Make the subdirectory with the secret name be writable.
4. Make the parent directory (the incoming directory) mode execute-only (under Unix, mode 111—that is, --x--x--x; under Windows NT the anonymous FTP user should have only the Execute permission on the directory and no permission on files in it, which is represented as "(X)(None)").

Users can now upload files to the writable directory only if they know (presumably because you've told them) its secret, password-like name. You can create as many of these secret subdirectories as necessary, and you can change or delete them as often as necessary. If your site creates a top-level index of your FTP area (such as a file containing the output of "ls -lr ~ftp"), you need to make sure that the hidden directories don't appear in the index. The easiest way to do that is to run the indexing command as the "ftp" user, so that it has the same permissions that someone using anonymous FTP would have.

Beware that some FTP clients with graphical user interfaces will only let a user access a directory that the FTP client can see; they don't provide a way for the user to jump blindly to a directory that doesn't appear in a directory listing. Such clients won't work with this scheme because, by design, the client can't see the names of the subdirectories containing the actual data. This is not usually a problem for people coming in from Unix machines, and there are publicly available clients for most platforms that do not have this problem, so you may be able to work around this limitation.

Removing the files. You might take one other approach on Unix, particularly if you find that your anonymous FTP area is already being abused and you're curious to see what people are uploading there. Basically, you run a program once a minute as a *cron* job that moves files from the writable incoming directory to another directory outside the anonymous FTP area. This will ensure that the intruders won't be able to see what's been uploaded. You may need to rename files when you move them to avoid overwriting files with the same name. Because the files aren't there to look at, it's easy for people to unintentionally create name conflicts (particularly if they're sending you crash dumps, which probably all start out having the same name).

Make sure that the new directory is on the same filesystem, so the operating system doesn't have to copy the data. Because of the way that the Unix filesystem works, this approach works even if the file is still being written when the "move" takes place, as long as the directory you're moving it to is on the same filesystem as the original directory ("moving" a file in such a case doesn't actually move the data; it merely renames the file). You should also be cautious about how you handle the original filename. People can create files with names that contain space, newlines, and other interesting characters that wreak havoc with carelessly written shell scripts.

This approach doesn't avoid denial of service attacks; people can still fill up your disk space. In fact, they may retry uploads multiple times (because the files keep mysteriously disappearing) and unintentionally fill up your disks.

This approach doesn't work as well on Windows NT because the FTP server opens files in a mode that does not allow any other process to access them. It's therefore impossible to move files while they are being written. On the other hand, people can't read them while they're being written, either, so you don't lose much by moving only files that are complete.

Preventing people from using your server to attack other machines

As we discussed earlier, a normal-mode FTP connection involves having the server open a connection to the client. In order to do that, it uses information provided by the client (an IP address and port number). A specially modified FTP client can send the server any IP address and port number it likes, and the FTP server will attempt to connect to that address and port number, and return information to the client about whether or not the attempt works. This allows clients to use the FTP server as a sort of port scanner.

Microsoft's FTP server by default requires the IP address to be the same as the source address on the data channel and allows the client to specify only the standard FTP data port, or a port number above 1023. Few Unix servers provide this kind of functionality. If you run a server that does not implement limits, you should be sure that packet filters prevent the machine from acting as a useful port scanner. It should not be able to create arbitrary connections to other machines.

In some cases, intelligent packet filters are also vulnerable to this kind of attack. If an attacker connects to an FTP server and issues the Port command, the packet filter will usually open a hole for the requested connection. This hole will exist regardless of whether or not the FTP server actually obeys the command.

Using the wuarchive FTP daemon

Many Internet sites—both major and minor—that provide anonymous FTP run the *wuarchive* version of the Unix FTP server, developed at Washington University (the "wu" in the name) in St. Louis, Missouri. This server provides a number of features that are especially useful for anonymous FTP servers. These include the following features and many others:

- Better and more complete logging. It can log uploads, downloads, or every command sent to it; it can also keep track of the number of accesses by user classes (e.g., by anonymous users).

- Per-directory message files; these are shown to a user who visits that directory to provide relevant information about the directory's contents (for example, "This version is now obsolete").

- The ability to define classes of users; based on the account they log in to the server with, and/or the host from which they access, you can determine what files they have access to and when they can log in.

- Restrictions on certain classes of users. For example, *wuarchive* can limit the number of simultaneous anonymous users who are accessing the server; the limit can vary by time of day and day of the week. By using these restrictions, you control the load generated by the FTP server.

- The ability to compress, tar, and otherwise manipulate files automatically as they are transferred.

- Nonanonymous *chroot*ed access, for users who need only limited access to your machines. This allows you to give a specific account access to files that are not accessible to "anonymous" without giving the account the ability to look around at everything on your disks.

For information about obtaining the *wuarchive* FTP daemon, see Appendix B, *Tools*. Make sure that you are installing the genuine, most recent version. This program has in the past been distributed by attackers with added trap doors, and older versions may have security problems that have since been fixed.

Be aware that one cost of the additional power and complexity offered by *wuar-chive* is a bigger potential for security problems. The bigger and more complex a program is, the more likely it is to contain bugs. If the program is security-critical (as the FTP server is), many of those bugs are likely to have security impacts. Some features of the *wuarchive* server may also interact badly with some clients (in particular, some poorly implemented clients do not deal well with the displayed messages and hang). Workarounds are available, but if a significant percentage of your users has these clients, you may want to avoid *wuarchive*.

Summary of Recommendations for FTP

- If you have FTP clients that properly support passive mode, then allow internal hosts to contact external FTP servers via packet filtering. This is safe only if you can filter on the TCP ACK bit, so that you can allow only outgoing TCP connections from ports above 1023 to ports above 1023.

- If you have FTP clients that don't support passive mode, then use an FTP proxy server such as the one in the TIS Internet Firewall Toolkit.

- Encourage users to use web browsers as FTP clients in order to get up-to-date FTP features and proxying support without having to distribute additional FTP clients.

- Consider providing FTP access via both packet filtering and proxies, supporting passive mode via packet filtering and normal mode via proxies.

- If you want to allow incoming FTP, use packet filters to allow incoming FTP only to your bastion host.

- If you allow incoming FTP (anonymous or user), use an up-to-date FTP server.

- If you allow anonymous FTP users to write files, protect the writable area so it can't be used to transfer files between third parties.

- Be careful about who within your organization can put up files for anonymous FTP, and make sure they understand what they're doing.

Trivial File Transfer Protocol (TFTP)

TFTP is a simplified file transfer protocol. It is simpler than FTP and is designed to be implemented in ROM for booting diskless systems like X terminals, diskless workstations, and routers. There is no authentication with TFTP; a TFTP client simply connects to the server and asks for a file, without saying who the file is for. If the file is one that the server can access, the server gives the client the file. For this reason, you need to be very careful about what your TFTP server (if you have one) can access, and what clients can access the server.

Generally, there's no reason at all to allow TFTP across your firewall, even if you use it internally. You do not want to boot diskless systems across the Internet, and people do not transfer files with TFTP.

Packet Filtering Characteristics of TFTP

TFTP is a UDP-based protocol. Servers listen on port 69 for the initial client-to-server packet to establish the TFTP session, then use a port above 1023 for all further packets during that session. Clients use ports above 1023.

Direction	Source Addr.	Dest. Addr.	Protocol	Source Port	Dest. Port	ACK Set	Notes
In	Ext	Int	UDP	>1023	69	a	Incoming TFTP request (first packet from client)
Out	Int	Ext	UDP	>1023	>1023	a	Response to incoming request
In	Ext	Int	UDP	>1023	>1023	a	Subsequent packets from client
Out	Int	Ext	UDP	>1023	69	a	Outgoing TFTP request (first packet from client)
In	Ext	Int	UDP	>1023	>1023	a	Response to outgoing request
Out	Int	Ext	UDP	>1023	>1023	a	Subsequent packets from client

a UDP has no ACK equivalent.

Intelligent packet filters may have difficulty supporting TFTP because the responses do not match normal criteria for responses. In general, a packet is considered a response only if its source and destination are reversed from a recently received packet. In TFTP, the response packet has a destination that matches a recent source, but the source is new. In order to support this, the packet filter needs to have special rules for TFTP, instead of using normal rules for supporting UDP-based protocols.

Proxying Characteristics of TFTP

TFTP does not lend itself well to proxying. Because TFTP clients are often implemented in hardware, with no users involved, neither modified clients nor modified user procedures are generally implementable. A transparent proxy could easily support TFTP, providing the same extremely minimal amount of security achievable if you allow TFTP through packet filters.

Network Address Translation Characteristics of TFTP

TFTP does not use embedded IP addresses and can work with network address translation systems. There are two possible problems. First, TFTP responses come from a different port from the one the original request is sent to. Some systems will consider this a new interaction and may not perform the appropriate translation to match the original request. Second, TFTP clients and servers pay attention to the source port of data. If the source port maps changes during an interaction, the transfer will be interrupted.

Summary of Recommendations for TFTP

*   Do not allow TFTP across your firewall.

Network File System (NFS)

The NFS protocol is designed to allow systems to access files across the network on a remote system, as conveniently as if the files were on directly attached disks. The NFS protocol itself was designed to be *stateless* for both server implementation simplicity and robustness. A stateless protocol is one where each transaction is handled separately; the server doesn't need to keep information about what clients have done previously. Being stateless allows an NFS server to reboot while clients are making requests and, once it returns to service, continue serving files to clients as if nothing had happened.

This may seem like a fairly simple concept, but it's quite difficult to make a protocol stateless when it deals with file access. A number of important features of most filesystems are inherently based on state. For instance, being able to maintain file locking requires keeping track of what process has locked the file. This design decision has had a major impact on security and the proliferation of system administrator jokes based upon the kernel message "NFS server not responding".

Machines may be NFS servers (exporting their disks for access by other machines), NFS clients (accessing disks exported by NFS servers), or both. Almost every Unix implementation uses NFS as the primary way to share files, and NFS client applications are available for most other popular operating systems. (NFS server applications for non-Unix machines are more rare.)

Two versions of NFS are currently in widespread use. NFS version 2 is the protocol people are usually referring to when they just mention the term *NFS*. It is usually run over UDP (although the specification allows the use of TCP, most implementations do not implement it). NFS version 3, frequently written as *NFSv3*, is a newer version with several improvements, including support for larger files, and almost every implementation allows it to be run over TCP as well as UDP.

From a security standpoint, there is little to distinguish between the two versions, so we use the term *NFS* to apply to both versions unless otherwise noted.

The NFS protocol itself is quite a straightforward RPC protocol, and all implementations and versions use a fixed port number (normally port 2049). A fixed port number is used so that an NFS client does not have to perform a portmapper query when a NFS server is restarted. However, in order to operate correctly, NFS relies upon a number of other services for initially mounting the filesystem, for file locking and for recovery after a system crash. These additional services are also based upon RPC but do not always use the same port numbers. This means that portmapper requests are needed to locate the services. For more information about RPC see Chapter 14, *Intermediary Protocols*.

Some vendors also support a version of NFS based on Secure RPC, which addresses many of the problems with authentication, providing better authentication both of the client machine and of the user. Secure RPC has several problems that also apply to NFS implemented on top of it:

- It is not widely supported; it is available almost exclusively on Suns.

- The process of exchanging keys between machines is difficult.

- It doesn't perform as well as standard RPC. (NFS is particularly performance-sensitive.)

- The sizes of the public keys are too small.

Secure RPC is discussed further in Chapter 14.

NFS Authentication

NFS was originally designed to be used within local networks for file sharing, and although it can be tuned to work over a network that has delays, it is unsafe to allow across a firewall for various reasons. NFS's main security problems are:

- The NFS server relies on the IP address to authenticate client hosts, making it vulnerable to address forgery.

- The NFS server relies on the client to authenticate the user, making it vulnerable to any user who has compromised a client machine.

- The NFS server doesn't recheck the client authentication on every request. The server assumes that if the client uses a valid file handle, the client is authorized to access that filesystem. An attacker with a forged or captured file handle can access the filesystem just as easily as a legitimate client can.

The primary problem with NFS is its weak authentication of requests. Access to a given NFS-exported filesystem is all or nothing; either a given client machine is trusted to access the filesystem, or it isn't. If the server trusts a given client machine, the server believes whatever the client tells it about who is trying to access which files. It then uses that information for authorization according to the standard Unix file protection mechanisms (i.e., user, group, and other permissions).

The server's trust in the client is established when the client mounts the filesystem from the server. To mount a filesystem a client sends a mount request containing the name of the filesystem to the *mountd* RPC service on the server and asks for permission to mount it. The *mountd* service checks whether or not the client is allowed to access that filesystem, using the source IP address of the request to identify the client. If the access is allowable, the *mountd* service gives the client a *file handle* (basically a magic set of credentials for the client), which the client then uses for all access to the filesystem.

Once the client has mounted the filesystem (and received a file handle from the server), the client sends a request using the NFS protocol to the server each time it wants to act on a file on that filesystem. The request describes the action the client wants to take and includes the file handle obtained from the server, so the server assumes that the client is authorized to request that action. Some NFS servers will log error messages when requests are received with invalid file handles, but many of them simply ignore them, which helps attackers who are trying to guess file handles. If you have the choice, choose an NFS server that will log requests with invalid file handles (this may not be the default configuration even on servers which support logging; check to make certain that you not only have the capability, but have actually enabled it).

This system has at least three problems. First, there are difficulties with the initial authentication. In addition to the usual problems with using forgeable source IP addresses for authentication, there is another way for attackers to authenticate illicitly. The RPC port location service offers a forwarding service where a client can send a request to a service via the location server. This request will show up to *mountd* as if it had been issued by the location service, which is running on the server. If *mountd* permits the server to mount its own filesystems, then an attacker can send a mount request using the forwarding feature in order to obtain a valid file handle. To deal with this, either the server should deny itself access, or the forwarding feature of the port location service should be disabled (and the best option is to do both).

The second problem with *mountd* authentication has to do with the use of the file handle as an authentication token. If an attacker can determine a valid file handle without help from *mountd*, the attacker can then use it without further authentication. Simply guessing randomly isn't going to work; NFS version 2 uses 32-byte file handles, and NFS version 3 uses variable-length file handles up to 64 bytes long. But attackers don't have to guess randomly because NFS implementations typically impose a structure to the file handles. Only a component of the file handle data is random, and that's the only part the attacker has to guess. Implementations vary on how much random data there is; early implementations are particularly bad about it, using file handles that are based on the time the filesystem was created, which is often easy to guess.

Modern implementations of NFS have addressed this problem, and patches are available for many older implementations. If you run NFS on a system where security is important, you should consult your vendor's documentation to make sure that you have an NFS server with reasonable randomness in the file handle generation, and that you have followed any special instructions for setting up filesystems (some file handle generation schemes require special initialization for filesystems to ensure unguessable file handles).

The third problem with file handles is that they're difficult to get rid of. An NFS server is required to be stateless; all it can do is look at a file handle and determine whether or not that file handle is any good. On most implementations, once a client has a file handle, the only way to keep the client from using it is to change the method for generating file handles so that all previous file handles are invalid, requiring every client to remount the filesystem and probably generating mass trauma.

Well-behaved clients don't save file handles and will contact *mountd* for a new file handle each time they mount a filesystem. This still means that a well-behaved client that already has a filesystem mounted can continue to use it if you change its access permissions, but it does give you some measure of control. Eventually, the client will have to remount the filesystem (and you may be able to force it to do so if you have some sort of access to it). Nothing requires an attacker to be this well behaved; a hostile client can simply save the file handle and reuse it without requiring *mountd*'s assistance. In general, the only way to change the validity of file handles and prevent this is to change the filesystem on the server (for instance, by changing where it is mounted on the server). Vendor documentation will usually tell you what operations change file handles (mostly to prevent you from accidentally changing file handles and interrupting operations on clients).

NFS and root

Under NFS, root may be treated differently from normal users. Some Unix NFS servers always treat root the same way they treat normal users: the client's root user gets the same access that the server's root user would have. Some of them always translate the client's root user to a UID known as "nobody" that is never used as a regular user; thus, this user will have only the permissions granted to the world. This "nobody" UID may be either the highest possible UID or a UID that translates to –1 (which might be written as –1, or as the highest possible UID plus

1). Just for additional complication, "nobody" is sometimes –2 instead of –1, and for some unknown reason, System V release 4 defines the highest possible UID as 60,000. On some Unix machines, more than one of these numbers (–1, –2, 60000, 60001, 65535, and 65536) are listed in the password file as "nobody". Most Unix NFS servers allow you to choose whether you wish to allow root access or translate it to "nobody" via an option in the */etc/exports* file. Non-Unix servers normally treat root as if it were any other user, but because that user is unlikely to have special privileges on the server, it isn't a problem.

Translating root to "nobody" is an extremely minor security improvement. Anybody who is capable of being root on the client is capable of pretending to be any user whatsoever on the client, and can therefore see and do anything any user can do. The translation hides only those files on the server restricted to access by root itself. You will still probably want to use translation wherever you can for the minimal protection it does give you, but you should not feel that it makes it safe to export filesystems to possibly hostile clients.

Better protection for the server is available by exporting the filesystem read-only. If the filesystem is exported purely read-only (no host is allowed to write it) you can be reasonably certain the data cannot be modified via NFS. If you allow any host to write it, you're vulnerable to forgery.

NFS Client Vulnerabilities

NFS clients may also be in danger from NFS servers. For example, an NFS-mounted filesystem may contain *setuid* programs; users on the client would be able to use those programs to become root. Device entries on an NFS-mounted partition are considered to apply to the client's devices, not the server's devices. Somebody with an account on an NFS client and root permission on an NFS server can use this to get unlimited, if inconvenient, read-write access to all data on the client.

Some NFS clients provide options to *mount* that can be used to disable devices and *setuid/setgid* on mounted filesystems. If *mount* is not available to users other than root, or if it always uses these options for users other than root, this will protect the client from the server. If these options are not available, even if only root can mount filesystems, you should consider mounting an NFS filesystem to be equivalent to granting the server machine root access to the client.

NFS clients may also be vulnerable to less obvious forms of attack from NFS servers. Mounting a filesystem is a privileged operation, so NFS clients run as root. A hostile server may be able to exploit buffer overflow errors in the NFS client, causing it to run arbitrary programs. In general, this is not transparent to the user (it interferes with the ability to use whatever filesystem the client was trying to get to), and it requires an attacker with a high level of control over the server machine. In traditional fixed NFS server environments, it's not a major threat. On the other hand, the use of automounters, which are discussed in a later section, can make it an effective attack.

File Locking with NFS

File locking allows one process to prevent other processes from accessing a file in specific ways. It is most often used to keep multiple processes from writing overlapping changes to a file, but it can also be used for other reasons (for instance, it may be advisable to keep other processes from even reading a file while it is being changed). NFS provides a voluntary file-locking mechanism. By default, there are no locks associated with a file, and any process can do anything with it. A process that wants a lock must explicitly ask for it.

File locks are a form of state; when you request a lock on a file, you change the state of the file, and that state has to be kept track of both by the server (so that it can enforce the lock) and the client (so that it can release the lock when it is no longer needed). This is problematic for NFS because it's a stateless protocol.

There are therefore two parts to the problem of implementing locking in NFS. First, you have to add the ability to keep any kind of state across server and client restarts, and then you have to track the locks themselves.

It's easy enough for any program to keep state internally; it's not even all that difficult for a server to save that state so that when the server restarts, it can pick up where it left off. However, that's not good enough for NFS locking because the state that is important also includes the programs that had requested the locks, and NFS clients will almost never regain this state when they restart. If a machine crashes while you are in the middle of editing a file, the editor is unlikely to resume where it left off. If the editor had a lock on the file you were editing, something needs to free that lock so that you can restart your editing session. If the editor itself crashes, this task is handled by other programs on the machine. If the entire machine crashes, however, there has to be some other mechanism that will handle the situation.

The problem of dealing with restarts is solved using an ancillary protocol called *statd*, which is responsible for tracking and reporting restarts on behalf of other protocols. *statd* handles two types of requests: programs on the local machine can ask *statd* to notify them when specific remote machines restart, and remote machines can ask *statd* to notify them when the local machine restarts. It's also possible to cancel these requests, and when things shut down cleanly, they will cancel all outstanding requests. *statd* keeps track of requests in files, so that its state is preserved across restarts. *statd* is voluntary in that it relies on the remote systems to honor requests for notification when they restart—for scalability reasons *statd* does not poll for status. When *statd* starts, it checks its files and notifies all remote machines that have requested notification.

statd is built on top of RPC and uses UDP. It is particularly problematic for fire-walls because it involves traffic initiated by the server. NFS clients will request restart notification from NFS servers. The original request for notification will go from the client to the server, but if the server reboots, the notification will come from the server to the client and will not normally be permitted.

Locking itself is implemented using *lockd*. *lockd* in turn relies heavily on *statd* to reestablish locking after a restart as it does not store any persistent state. When a client wishes to lock a file on an NFS filesystem, it contacts the remote *lockd* in order to lock the file and requests its own *statd* to monitor the server. When both the *lockd* and *statd* response are received, the client assumes that the file is locked. When it receives the *lockd* request, the server asks the server *statd* to monitor the client. At this point, one of the following can occur:

- The client releases the lock.
- The server restarts.
- The client restarts.

When the client releases the lock, the client sends an unlock request to the server *lockd*.

After a server restart, the server *statd* notifies all remote clients using locking of the event, which causes them to resubmit all lock requests. This can have unexpected results if more than one client was attempting to lock the same file. After a server restart, you can lose a lock. If the purpose of the lock was to prevent another sys-tem from making changes while a critical update was occurring, then this will usu-ally result in loss of data or file corruption. More correct locking semantics would suggest that the original client should regain the lock so that it could proceed with the critical update. This is one reason why NFS file locking cannot be relied upon.

After a client restart, *statd* notifies all servers of the event. This causes them to immediately release any locks the client may have been holding before the restart. If the purpose of the lock was to prevent another system from making changes while a critical update was occurring, then this will usually result in loss of data or file corruption. More correct locking semantics would leave the file locked so that a cleanup process could check the consistency of the file before allowing another client to make changes. This is another reason why NFS file locking cannot be relied upon.

lockd, like *statd,* is built on top of RPC and uses UDP, which makes it extremely difficult to safely pass through a firewall. Some stateful and proxy firewall systems can handle RPC, and so it may be possible to use NFS file locking across this type of firewall. You will need to be very careful; some systems will allow everything but the server-to-client restart notifications, in which case locking will appear to work, but lock consistency will be lost as soon as the server restarts. If file locking is not needed, then it is possible to run some systems without either *statd* or *lockd.* However, any application programs that try to use file locking on NFS filesystems are likely to fail in bad ways that are likely to involve loss or corruption of data (which presumably would not occur in the unlikely event that *lockd* and *statd* were working correctly).

Automounting

Originally, NFS filesystems were mounted by machines at boot time, which has some significant disadvantages. It means that at boot time, a machine has to decide what server it's going to get particular files from, and the only way to change that decision is to reboot. It also has to mount all the filesystems it might ever need. On a multi-user system, where different users want different files, this results in a lot of wasted communication as machines mount filesystems that they don't actually need. It can also result in major annoyances as machines wait around for crashed file servers, sometimes pointlessly.

The solution to this problem is to use an *automounter*, a program that mounts filesystems when there is some reason to and unmounts them when they are no longer in use. Most automounters will also allow you to configure things so that a given filesystem is available on multiple machines, and clients use the most appropriate copy.

Intuitively, automounters seem as if they ought to be free from network vulnerabilities. After all, they provide services only to the local host. They ought to have only the vulnerabilities that other NFS clients have, and those are relatively minimal.

Unfortunately, this is not the case. Automounters have two additional kinds of vulnerabilities. First, and most obviously, automounters often use other services to get lists of NFS servers. (For instance, many of them will use NIS maps for this purpose.) They will have all the vulnerabilities associated with those services, and if those services are insecure, it may be easy for an attacker to direct an automounter system to a hostile server. It may also be possible to attack the automounter directly with the information about which servers to use; for instance, if the automounter itself has buffer overflow problems, feeding it an overlength server name may give an attacker the ability to run arbitrary commands.

The more major source of vulnerabilities comes from the way automounters are implemented. For technical reasons, the most effective way for an automounter to work is for it to claim to be an NFS server. Client programs that want to access filesystems speak to this fake server, which then acts as a client to the genuine servers. This fake server needs to accept requests only from clients on the local machine, but the fact that it is an NFS server opens it up to a number of attacks. For instance, the attack that depends on forwarding requests through the port location service is particularly effective against automounters, which must accept local requests.

If you are using an automounter on a client, you should be aware that it could be vulnerable to NFS server, RPC server, and other network application vulnerabilities.

Packet Filtering Characteristics of NFS

NFS is an RPC-based service. As mentioned in Chapter 8, *Packet Filtering*, it's very difficult to handle RPC-based services with a packet filtering system because the servers normally don't use predictable port numbers. NFS is an exception to this rule, however. Although it is RPC-based, it uses port 2049 reliably, and as of NFS3, this standard is official.* In order to attempt to enforce some minor amount of authentication, many but not all implementations of NFS use privileged ports as client source ports.

NFS is provided over both TCP and UDP. Some clients and servers prefer TCP, and others prefer UDP. TCP-based NFS is relatively new, and not all clients or servers support it. Those that do often behave differently over TCP than over UDP. If a particular client-server combination behaves badly over one protocol, try it over the other.

In order to make use of NFS across a firewall, you will also need to make the port-mapper and *mountd* available; the portmapper is at port 111. *mountd* is an RPC protocol at a randomly chosen port number managed by the portmapper. As discussed earlier, you may need *lockd* and *statd* as well, and in that case, you will need to allow *statd* in both directions. *lockd* and *statd* are also RPC protocols at randomly chosen port numbers managed by the portmapper. See Chapter 14 for more information about packet filtering and RPC.

Direction	Source Addr.	Dest. Addr.	Protocol	Source Port	Dest. Port	ACK Set	Notes
In	Ext	Int	TCP/UDP	>1023	111	a	External NFS client to internal server, portmapper requests
Out	Int	Ext	TCP/UDP	111	>1023	Yes[b]	Internal NFS server to external client, portmapper responses

---

* Ironically, the version 2 protocol incorrectly predicts that while 2049 is an unofficial standard, "later versions of the protocol use the 'Portmapping' facility of RPC". Later versions of the protocol in fact just made 2049 official.

Direction	Source Addr.	Dest. Addr.	Protocol	Source Port	Dest. Port	ACK Set	Notes
In	Ext	Int	TCP/UDP	<1024[c]	2049	[a]	External NFS client to internal server, NFS requests
Out	Int	Ext	TCP/UDP	2049	<1024[c]	Yes[b]	Internal NFS server to external client, NFS responses
Out	Int	Ext	TCP/UDP	>1023	111	[a]	Internal NFS client to external server, portmapper requests
In	Ext	Int	TCP/UDP	111	>1023	Yes[b]	External NFS server to internal client, portmapper responses
Out	Int	Ext	TCP/UDP	<1024[c]	2049	[a]	Internal NFS client to external server, NFS requests
In	Ext	Int	TCP/UDP	2049	<1024[c]	Yes[b]	External NFS server to internal client, NFS responses

[a] ACK is not set on the first TCP packet (establishing connection) but will be set on the rest. UDP has no ACK equivalent.
[b] TCP only; UDP has no ACK equivalent.
[c] Some implementations may use ports >1023 instead.

Proxying Characteristics of NFS

RPC-based protocols are almost as unpleasant to proxy as they are to allow with packet filtering; they cannot be handled adequately with generic proxies. NFS is particularly difficult, because of the large number of protocols involved and the server-initiated transactions that are required to support locking. Some RPC-knowledgeable transparent proxy systems do support NFS, but it would be unwise to use them for critical or high-volume applications. NFS is particularly problematic for proxying because it is data-intense, exchanging large volumes of data in situations where delay is very noticeable to the user. A host doing NFS proxying is going to need to deal with multiple connections transferring large packets at high speeds.

Network Address Translation Characteristics of NFS

Although the NFS protocol itself does not contain embedded IP addresses and could function with address translation, you will have problems with *mountd* as it uses IP addresses for authentication. Some implementations of NFS use a *mountd* that issues different NFS file handles for each client, and the NFS server checks both the IP address and file handle for consistency; this is likely to fail if you are using address translation. If you have to run NFS through a translation system, use TCP to reduce the load on the translation system as far as possible.

File Sharing for Microsoft Networks

A number of protocols are involved in file sharing on Microsoft networks, and you will hear a significant number of names thrown around. The most recent and most standard is the Common Internet File System (CIFS), which is based on Server Message Block (SMB). Officially, CIFS is an SMB-based standard that extends Microsoft's current practice for using SMB; in practical terms, it's simply a new name for SMB. You will also see people refer to file sharing for Microsoft networks as SMB or SMB file sharing. Despite the word "file" in the name, CIFS, like SMB, provides a wide variety of features, not limited to file sharing. These are discussed further in Chapter 14, *Intermediary Protocols*.

You'll also see people using terms like "NetBEUI", "NetBIOS", "NetBT", or "LanManager" as if they were file sharing protocols. NetBEUI is a networking protocol used on local area networks; it operates at the same level that IP does. NetBIOS is a higher-level networking protocol originally run on top of NetBEUI. NetBT is a TCP/IP implementation of NetBIOS; a program that uses NetBIOS can use either normal NetBIOS over NetBEUI or NetBT over TCP/IP, without needing to know what's going on. LanManager is an older Microsoft protocol suite, still supported by SMB file sharing and CIFS in compatibility modes. All of these protocols tend to come together; normally, if you run SMB, you also run NetBIOS (in which case you must run either NetBEUI or NetBT), and if you run NetBIOS, you also run SMB, which is why there is so much confusion about which does what. These days, the association is getting looser (in particularly, running CIFS directly over TCP/IP is supported in Windows 2000). Figure 17-3 shows the protocol stack normally involved in running CIFS over TCP/IP.

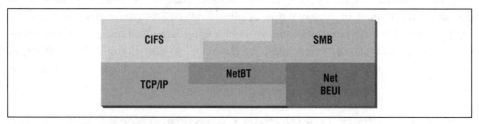

Figure 17-3. The CIFS protocol stack

CIFS file sharing is usually used with other members of a large protocol family and frequently is capable of using multiple different methods of achieving a given end. See Chapter 20, *Naming and Directory Services*, for information about WINS and NetBT Name Service, which are often used with CIFS. Chapter 21, *Authentication and Auditing Services*, discusses the user authentication protocols used with CIFS.

It is almost impossible to separate file sharing from the other services supported by SMB. CIFS is not actually a new protocol but simply a new name for a way of using SMB. As such, it provides all the capabilities of SMB, including a number of capabilities that are not normally thought of as part of a filesystem, including messaging, print service, and multiple methods of doing general-purpose transaction processing. This makes it much more risky than dedicated file sharing protocols.

It is worth noting that although the extra features in CIFS make it more risky than NFS, it does at least usually provide better authentication. CIFS filesystem transactions require the user to authenticate, instead of relying on the client host to provide user identification, the way most NFS servers do. CIFS can also provide message authentication to protect from hijacking. It does not provide data encryption, however.

Samba

The most popular program that provides SMB services on Unix machines is Samba, which is best known for its support of file services. It is an open source program, implemented without Microsoft's cooperation. Because Microsoft does not release details of all of their protocols, Samba is the source of the most detailed information about how SMB and related services actually work, as well as being one of the major tools used for Unix-NT integration. Historically, Microsoft relied upon their control of SMB clients for some of their security, and SMB servers were highly vulnerable to badly behaved clients (whether these were actively hostile or merely buggy). This led to Microsoft's denouncing Samba, the first widely available client that Microsoft did not control, as a "hacking tool" because it revealed weaknesses that had not previously been important. In fact, this is neither the purpose that Samba was designed for nor its most common use (although it is true that some people have modified Samba source code to use it to attack systems). However, it is nice to note that since Samba became widespread, Microsoft has significantly improved the security of its SMB servers.

The base of Samba is a file server; in order to effectively provide file service from a Unix machine without a Microsoft support structure, it also includes a WINS server and a browser server and is capable of acting as a domain controller to do user authentication. SMB clients are available for Linux and some Unix operating systems, and although they are not actually part of Samba, they are often distributed with Samba.

Samba itself is both more robust and more secure than most SMB file servers. Admittedly, much of its security derives from the fact that it doesn't offer all of the services you would get from an equivalent server on a Microsoft operating system (for instance, there's no need to worry about people using a Samba server to remotely access the Performance Monitor or the User Manager). Most security problems with Samba are caused by the fact that it bridges the Unix and Microsoft world and is often managed by people who are naive about one of the two. Samba provides authentication and file service and can give away all of your authentication information and files if you configure it incorrectly, just like any other program that provides these services. If you configure it poorly, you will not be protected just because it uses Microsoft protocols that are supposed to have well-behaved clients, and you should not blame unfortunate results on either Samba or Microsoft.

Distributed File System (Dfs)

Microsoft provides a system called the Distributed File System (Dfs*) that provides clients with a unified interface to multiple file servers. A Dfs server exports something that appears to be a standard directory structure, but which may contain files from many file servers. Dfs also allows you to have multiple servers with replicas of a file, and have clients balanced between the servers and rerouted if a server fails.

Dfs has been available for some time but is first becoming a standard part of installations in Windows 2000. Dfs is not actually a separate file sharing protocol. Instead, it uses standard file sharing protocols for actual file access (usually, this means CIFS, but a client can use any file sharing protocol it has available). Dfs clients use RPC to get information from a Dfs server about where to look for actual files.

Packet Filtering, Proxying, and Network Address Translation Characteristics of Microsoft File Sharing

Microsoft file sharing is based on CIFS, and the packet filtering, proxying, and network address translation characteristics of CIFS are discussed in Chapter 14, *Intermediary Protocols*. Dfs is based on CIFS and on RPC (RPC is also discussed in Chapter 14). Depending on your network and your needs, a full file sharing environment may also require any or all of WINS, the Browser, and domain authentication. WINS and the Browser are discussed in Chapter 20, *Naming and Directory Services*, while domain authentication is discussed in Chapter 21, *Authentication and Auditing Services*.

Summary of Recommendations for File Sharing

- Don't allow file sharing across your firewall via NFS or CIFS. Use a virtual private network or a protocol more suited to secure data transmission over wide area networks.

---

* Microsoft appears to prefer the capitalization "Dfs" instead of the more traditional "DFS".

Printing Protocols

One specialized form of file transfer is printing, where you are sending files to a printer instead of to another general-purpose computer. Although people tend to think of printing as relatively safe, in fact, it involves most of the same risks as other file transfer protocols, and printers have most of the capabilities of other computing devices.

You need to realize that many modern network printing devices respond to protocols other than the dedicated printing protocols discussed here. For instance, they may have administrative interfaces that use Telnet or HTTP; they may auto-configure interfaces with DHCP; they may accept file transfers via FTP; and they will certainly respond, not necessarily correctly, to at least some ICMP. These extra protocols may introduce entirely new classes of vulnerability. For instance, one plotter has a network interface that not only allows you to telnet to the plotter, but then allows you to telnet from the plotter to other hosts. (Apparently, the easiest way to get an intelligent interface was to simply take it, lock, stock, and barrel, from a network hub made by the same company—except that a network hub can reasonably be expected to do this sort of thing, while few people suspect a plotter of also having network management capabilities and a guest login.) You should carefully examine the network capabilities and protections of printing devices before putting them on unprotected networks.

Because modern PostScript printers can be intelligent Ethernet devices with their own disks, it is theoretically possible for a rogue print job to turn one into a network sniffing device. In practice, this is a baroquely complex approach; attackers aren't very likely to succeed at it. However, more mundane denial of service attacks on printers are eminently possible and in fact have been known to happen.

Some are merely annoying, such as simply printing page after page of garbage (or, better yet, something offensive to the victim or the victim's coworkers) until the printer runs out of paper. But a few of them are serious, and the nastiest of them are enabled by a security feature in PostScript. PostScript was designed to protect certain dangerous commands by requiring a password before they were executed. This password is stored in an EEPROM chip on the printer and is factory-set to "0" on every brand of PostScript printer. It's always the same because it *must* always be the same. Some of the commands that the PostScript designers considered dangerous are routinely used by standard PostScript drivers, and if you change the password, those drivers will no longer work. Because, in order to reset it, you need either the old password or a hardware method to override the EEPROM, a program that uses the well-known "0" password to reset the password to something unknown can make printers effectively unusable until new EEPROMs are sent from the factory. (Some printers will run without the EEPROM, with an effective password of 0.) Removing or replacing the EEPROM resets not only the password, but also the printer ID and the page count; if you have fonts licensed to the printer, they will have to be relicensed. Since the last wave of such attacks, licensing of fonts to individual printers has become uncommon, reducing the attack's popularity. On the other hand, there are likely to be other, equally annoying Post-Script attacks in the future.

The intelligence and vulnerability of PostScript devices makes it important to protect your printers from Internet access. Make sure you have blocked any remote printing protocols your machines and printers use. You will need to check every printer type and every machine type separately.

lpr and lp

The BSD *lpr* printing system is very similar to the BSD "r" commands (*rsh, rlogin, rcp, rdump*) discussed in Chapter 18, *Remote Access to Hosts.* Unlike the "r" commands, *lpr* authorizes hosts, not individual users, and it will accept jobs from hosts in */etc/printers.equiv* as well as */etc/hosts.equiv.*

There have been a number of security problems with *lpr* and its associated printing commands. Some of these are inherent in the design of *lpr*, which provides no user authentication and no data protection. Most of them, however, are implementation problems, including buffer overflows, printers, and spooling systems that crash on invalid or dubious input, and ways of using the printer system's administrative privileges to print out, overwrite, or delete files that would be otherwise inaccessible. Several *lpr* problems give remote attackers the ability to run any command as root. You should carefully limit access to *lpr* print servers and run current versions of the printing system.

The System V *lp* printing system doesn't really have a remote printing component. When it does remote printing, it usually does it by handing the job off to a BSD *lpr* printing system, or by using the BSD *rsh* command (which is often called *remsh* on System V systems because such systems have another program called *rsh* that does something else entirely).

When jobs are actually printed via *lp* or *lpr*, they are normally run through printer-specific filters, which translate the user-readable data into a format the printer will accept. Even when the printing system itself is secure, the printer filter can introduce new security problems. If you are accepting print jobs from possibly hostile sources, you should be extremely careful about the printer filters that you run and the permissions that they have.

LPRng

A freely available printing system called LPRng (for "*lpr* next generation"), originally designed by Patrick Powell, addresses a number of the problems with *lpr*. It adds support for both authentication and encryption of printer jobs, while still providing backward compatibility with *lpr*. It uses the same ports as *lpr*.

Packet filtering characteristics of lpr

lpr is TCP-based. Servers use port 515. Clients use random ports below 1024, just like the BSD "r" commands (for further information about the BSD "r" commands, see Chapter 18, *Remote Access to Hosts*). For historical reasons, some clients use ports only between 721 and 731 (this behavior is documented in the RFC that discusses *lpr*, but in practice few servers require it).

Direction	Source Addr.	Dest. Addr.	Protocol	Source Port	Dest. Port	ACK Set	Notes
In	Ext	Int	TCP	<1024[a]	515	[b]	Incoming *lpr*, client to server
Out	Int	Ext	TCP	515	<1024[a]	Yes	Incoming *lpr*, server to client
Out	Int	Ext	TCP	<1024[a]	515	[b]	Outgoing *lpr*, client to server
In	Ext	int	TCP	515	<1024[a]	Yes	Outgoing *lpr*, server to client

[a] May be restricted to 721–731.
[b] ACK is not set on the first packet of this type (establishing connection) but will be set on the rest.

Proxying characteristics of lpr

lpr is a store-and-forward protocol, capable of being configured to do its own proxying. You can simply run a standard *lpr* configuration on your proxy server and configure it to drive whatever printers you like or pass jobs to another server. This does not provide security improvements over direct *lpr*, but it will let it cross a nonrouting host.

Network address translation characteristics of lpr

lpr does not use embedded IP addresses and will work with network address translation systems without problems. However, print jobs will normally contain information about internal hostnames.

Packet filtering and proxying characteristics of lp

lp itself provides no remote printing support. It handles printing across the network by using either *rsh*, which is covered in Chapter 18 with the other BSD "r" commands, or *lpr*. To determine what your printer configuration is using, configure a remote printer and read its interface file (which is usually stored in */usr/spool/lp/interfaces/printername*). Some vendors also provide novel remote printing systems for use with *lp*; consult your vendor documentation for information.

Windows-based Printing

Windows operating systems use three main kinds of network-based printing protocols. Windows NT and Windows 95 and above are capable of using *lpr* as a network printing protocol. In addition, two Windows-native network printing
protocols are based on SMB, a LanMan version (which uses specialized printing
calls) and a CIFS version (which uses a named pipe into the spooler system and
general transaction calls). These protocols have some special security implications
in addition to the general issues with SMB. Most clients are set so that if a print
server claims to have an upgraded version of a printer driver, the client will accept
and run the new software. This is one of the few cases where a server can actually force a client to download and run arbitrary code via SMB without a user's
consciously asking for something to be executed. While *lpr* outbound (from an
internal client to an external print server) is relatively secure, outbound SMB printing is even less secure than inbound SMB printing.

Other Printing Systems

Given the deficiencies of both *lp* and *lpr*, many Unix vendors implement their own
solutions to remote printing. Other platforms may support *lp*, *lpr*, a separate protocol, or some combination. Because it has its own protocol, which is somewhat
easier to implement than *rsh*, *lpr* is more popular than *lp* on non-Unix systems, but
many of them have their own protocols. Some printers are network devices in
their own right, sometimes speaking *lp* or *lpr* directly, and sometimes (particularly
older printers) speaking a protocol developed by the printer manufacturer.

For the most part, the wide variety of other network printing protocols that are out
there share a common feature; they're no more secure than *lpr*. Most of them are
not even as secure as *lpr* (if you can reach the system with a print request in the
right protocol, it will print it).

The IETF is working on a protocol called the Internet Printing Protocol (IPP),
which is designed to be used across the Internet. This protocol is not yet in widespread use, although it is provided with Windows 2000 and is expected to become
more popular as Windows 2000 comes into use. IPP is based on HTTP and may
be run on the normal HTTP port or on port 631. IPP encryption is provided by
running it over HTTPS instead of HTTP. Authentication may be provided either by
using HTTPS with client certificates, or by using any HTTP authentication method.
See Chapter 15, *The World Wide Web*, for more information about HTTP and
HTTPS.

Hewlett-Packard printers also support a network printing interface that has
become a de facto standard, although it barely qualifies as a protocol. The printer
accepts printer jobs on TCP port 9100, much the same way it would over a serial

or parallel connection. Each TCP connection is a separate job, and the printer simply processes the data as it receives it, returning any error codes. This obviously provides no encryption or authentication.

Summary of Recommendations for Printing Protocols

* Do not permit printing protocols across your firewall.

Related Protocols

Under Unix, *rcp* is also frequently used for file transfer; it is discussed in Chapter 18, *Remote Access to Hosts*, with the rest of the Berkeley "r" commands. A more secure *rcp* replacement, *scp*, is also discussed in that chapter along with SSH, which *scp* is based on.

HTTP is actually also a file transfer protocol and can be used to transfer arbitrary files.

rsync, discussed in Chapter 22, *Administrative Services*, is normally used for synchronization but may also be used as a generalized file transfer protocol over wide area networks.

Microsoft's NetMeeting, discussed in Chapter 19, *Real-Time Conferencing Services*, also supports file transfer.

18

Remote Access to Hosts

Sometimes you want to use a network to run programs on a computer other than the one you're sitting in front of. You might want to run a program on a much faster computer, a computer with a hardware device you don't have (a CD writer, say), or a computer that runs an operating system you don't like enough to have on your desk but that has some important piece of software. You might also need to administer computers that it's inconvenient or impossible to get to physically.

You can do this a number of ways. For instance, if the remote computer supports terminals, you can connect to it over the network as if you were connecting to it via a terminal. You may also be able to send a single command to the remote computer for it to execute (remote execution). Finally, you may be able to get a connection that includes graphics. This chapter discusses the protocols used for these various kinds of connections.

Microsoft's Remote Access Service (RAS) provides remote access to a network, not to an individual host, and is not discussed in this chapter; instead, it is discussed in Chapter 14, *Intermediary Protocols*, along with other protocols used for connecting networks, including PPP and PPTP.

Terminal Access (Telnet)

Telnet allows a user to remotely access a command shell on another computer. Telnet is supported by most platforms on the Internet, including not only Unix and Windows NT,[*] but even some MS-DOS and Microsoft Windows systems (which provide access to a DOS shell via a Telnet server). The major exception is the

---

[*] Windows 2000 includes both the client and the server; Windows NT 4 includes only a Telnet client, but Telnet servers for it are available from third parties or as part of the Windows NT Resource Kit.

Macintosh operating system, which doesn't have a command line–oriented shell to give users access to, regardless of whether or not they're local (unless you install the Unix-style development environment, which gives you both the shell and the Telnet server).

Although remote terminal access is the most common use of Telnet, most Telnet clients support the specification of arbitrary port numbers to access text-based TCP services at other ports. This is useful if you have a service for which you don't want to distribute a dedicated client; for example, it's often used to give access to MUDs (Multi-User Domains) and MOOs (Multi-user domains, Object Oriented), which are multi-user environments for games, collaborative work environments, or chat areas. Telnet clients are also used fairly often for debugging protocols that are normally accessed by dedicated clients. For example, people will check SMTP servers or verify usernames by using *telnet hostname 25* to connect to the SMTP server directly on port 25 and type SMTP commands to it. It's important to understand that, although you may be using the program named *telnet* for these purposes, all it's doing is opening a simple TCP connection to the specified port number. The *telnet* program doesn't initiate the Telnet protocol (which provides for things like option negotiation between client and server, line-at-a-time and character-at-a-time modes, and so on) unless it is talking to a server on the standard Telnet port (port 23).* This section discusses only the use of Telnet clients to access Telnet servers.

Incoming and outgoing Telnet have very different security implications. Most sites want to allow their users access to outgoing Telnet service, so their users can get to command shells and information services provided via Telnet on remote systems on the Internet. (Figure 18-1 illustrates outbound Telnet.) On the other hand, most sites don't want to allow (or want to allow but very strictly control) incoming Telnet access to their site.

Regardless of whether the access is incoming or outgoing, Telnet is a cleartext protocol (just like most others). Whatever information your users access or provide over a Telnet session (for example, accessing sensitive data or providing their passwords for other systems) is going to be visible to someone snooping on the Telnet connection. The exception to this is Windows 2000 Telnet, which is discussed later in this chapter; in some circumstances, it protects the authentication information, but any other information on the connection will still be visible. Encrypting versions of Telnet are available, but none are widely deployed. Most sites that need encrypted terminal access use SSH instead. (See the "Secure Shell (SSH)" section, later in this chapter, for a discussion of SSH.)

---

* Although Telnet does not initiate negotiation except when talking to port 23, most Telnet clients will still respond to negotiation requests, which can be used by servers to detect people using Telnet instead of standard clients (for instance, people using Telnet to port 25 to attempt to forge email).

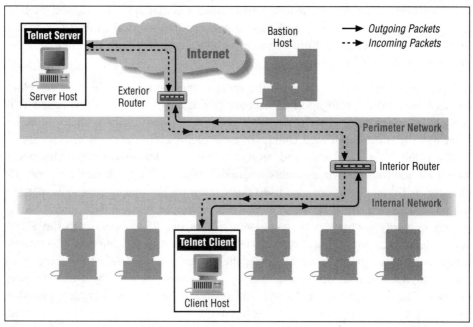

Figure 18-1. Outbound Telnet

Users should be warned to use different passwords on external hosts from those they use on your hosts. When they make outgoing Telnet connections, their passwords may be sniffed. (See Chapter 21, *Authentication and Auditing Services*, for more information about passwords and password sniffing.)

Windows 2000 Telnet

Windows 2000 provides some features that are not standard parts of Telnet but that make it somewhat more secure in a homogeneous Windows 2000 environment.

When both ends of the connection are running Windows 2000, and NTLM authentication is possible between them, Telnet can use NTLM authentication. In this case, authentication will take place outside the Telnet connection without passing cleartext password or username information. For more information about NTLM authentication, see Chapter 21. The Telnet server and client may be configured to always use cleartext authentication, to attempt NTLM authentication and fall back to NTLM authentication, or to require NTLM authentication.

In addition, the Windows 2000 Telnet server can be configured to allow only users with local accounts or to allow users with domain accounts.

Packet Filtering Characteristics of Telnet

Telnet is a TCP-based service. Telnet servers normally use port 23 (they can be set to use any port number but very rarely use any port but 23). Telnet clients use ports above 1023. (Telnet is used as an example in Chapter 8, *Packet Filtering*, so its filtering characteristics are discussed in more detail there.)

Direction	Source Addr.	Dest. Addr.	Protocol	Source Port	Dest. Port	ACK Set	Notes
In	Ext	Int	TCP	>1023	23	a	Incoming session, client to server
Out	Int	Ext	TCP	23	>1023	Yes	Incoming session, server to client
Out	Int	Ext	TCP	>1023	23	a	Outgoing session, client to server
In	Ext	Int	TCP	23	>1023	Yes	Outgoing session, server to client

a ACK is not set on the first packet of this type (establishing connection) but will be set on the rest.

Proxying Characteristics of Telnet

Telnet is well supported by proxies. SOCKS provides a modified Unix Telnet client; modifying clients on other platforms is relatively trivial. TIS FWTK provides a Telnet proxy server that requires modified user procedures. The SOCKS proxies should allow you to connect to ports other than the standard Telnet port, if such connections are OK according to your SOCKS server configuration file. Almost any commercial proxying package will probably provide Telnet proxying because Telnet is such a commonly used protocol on the Internet.

Network Address Translation Characteristics of Telnet

Telnet does not use embedded IP addresses and functions with network address translation without problems.

Summary of Recommendations for Telnet

- Restrict incoming Telnet as far as possible; most sites have little or no need for it.
- Outgoing Telnet can safely be allowed via packet filtering or proxying.
- If you're concerned about the sensitivity of the data accessed over Telnet sessions, consider using an encrypting version of Telnet, or use *ssh* instead.

Remote Command Execution

A variety of protocols exist primarily to allow users to execute commands on remote systems. This section describes the BSD "r" commands, *rexec* and *rex*.

BSD "r" Commands

The BSD "r" commands (*rsh, rlogin, rcp, rdump, rrestore,* and *rdist*) are designed to provide convenient remote access, without requiring the user to type a password, to services such as remote command execution (*rsh*), remote login (*rlogin*), and remote file copying (*rcp* and *rdist*).

These programs are extremely useful, but as we discuss later in this section, they are safe to use only in an environment in which all of the machines are more or less trusted to play by the rules. While it may be appropriate to use these services within a local area network, it's almost never appropriate to use them across the Internet. It's just too easy for someone to convince these services that they're OK and that the service should perform what's requested.

The difficulty with these commands is that they use address-based authentication. The server looks at the source address of the request and decides whether or not it trusts the remote host to tell it who the user is (this is controlled by the */etc/hosts.equiv* and *.rhosts* files on Unix systems).

An attacker who convinces one of these servers that a connection is coming from a "trusted" machine can essentially get complete and unrestricted access to your system. This can be done by impersonating a trusted machine and using its IP address, by confusing DNS so that DNS thinks that the attacker's IP address maps to a trusted machine's name, or by any of a number of other methods.

If the trusted host check described previously fails (that is, if the user is not coming from a trusted host), most of these services simply deny the client's request and disconnect. The *rlogind* server, however, will prompt the client for a password if the trusted host check fails. The password entered is sent in the clear over the net, just as with Telnet, so you have to worry about attackers capturing passwords from *rlogin* sessions, as they can from Telnet sessions. See Chapter 21, *Authentication and Auditing Services,* for a discussion of ways to address password sniffing attacks.

On some systems, it is possible to disable the trusted host checks with a command-line argument to the servers; even if your server doesn't provide a convenient switch to disable the checks, if you have (or can get) source code for the servers, it's usually a relatively simple fix. However, without the trusted host mechanism, the *rshd* server is completely pointless because it provides no way to prompt for a password or other authenticator if the trusted host check fails. The *rlogind* server is still somewhat useful without the trusted host check because it can ask for a password, but it's not much more useful than Telnet.

BSD "r" commands under Windows NT

Windows NT 4 provides clients for *rcp* and *rsh,* and the Windows NT 4 Server Resource Kit provides servers for all of the commands except *rlogin,* which requires a separate server from the rest. Although the Windows NT clients use a slightly different syntax from modern Unix clients, they have the same security implications.

The security implications for the server are somewhat worse in Windows NT than they are in Unix. The basic problem is the same; the server is relying on the client's information about the user. Most clients are not in the least trustworthy (there are a number of ways for somebody with control over a client to take on any identity they please). In addition, since the client is identified only by checking the source IP address, the server is vulnerable to IP address spoofing even if it only trusts carefully chosen clients.

Worse yet, there is a mismatch between *rsh* and Windows NT's security model. Under NT, a program cannot just assume a user's identity without a password. *rsh,* however, is incapable of providing a password. The *rsh* server has to find some way to bridge this gap. Some servers take the straightforward and completely inse-cure approach of not even trying to assume the user's identity, and running every-thing with the server's permissions. Others store a mapping between *rsh* users and Windows NT users, including the Windows NT password. This provides better security when the server is in use, but an attacker who gets access to the map-ping data has user and password information.

Because of these problems, running these servers is not advisable.

Packet filtering characteristics of the BSD "r" commands

The "r" commands are TCP-based services. For the server, they use well-known port 513 (*rlogin*) or 514 (*rsh, rcp, rdump, rrestore,* and *rdist*; these are just differ-ent clients for the same server). They are somewhat unusual in that they use ran-dom ports *below* 1024 for the client end.

Using ports below 1024 for the client end is an attempt at a security scheme that allows password-less access to these services as long as the requests come from a trusted host and user, as discussed earlier. The idea is that, if the request comes from a port below 1024 on the client end, then the request must be OK with root on the client machine; if it were not, the client never could have gotten the port below 1024 to use for the request. This notion is completely incorrect on Windows operating systems, where any user can use any port that is not already in use.

Further, some of the clients of the server on port 514 (*rsh,* for example) use a sec-ond TCP connection for error reporting. This second TCP connection is opened from a random port below 1024 on the server to a random port below 1024 on the client; that is, an outgoing *rsh* command involves an incoming TCP connection for the error channel.

Direction	Source Addr.	Dest. Addr.	Protocol	Source Port	Dest. Port	ACK Set	Notes
In	Ext	Int	TCP	<1024	513	a	*rlogin*, external client to internal server
Out	Int	Ext	TCP	513	<1024	Yes	*rlogin*, internal server to external client
In	Ext	Int	TCP	<1024	514	a	*rsh/rcp/rdump/rrestore/ rdist*, external client to internal server
Out	Int	Ext	TCP	514	<1024	Yes	*rsh/rcp/rdump/rrestore/ rdist*, internal server to external client
Out	Int	Ext	TCP	<1024	<1024	a	*rsh* error channel, internal server to external client
In	Ext	Int	TCP	<1024	<1024	Yes	*rsh* error channel, external client to internal server
Out	Int	Ext	TCP	<1024	513	a	*rlogin*, internal client to external server
In	Ext	Int	TCP	513	<1024	Yes	*rlogin*, external server to internal client
Out	Int	Ext	TCP	<1024	514	a	*rsh/rcp/rdump/rrestore/ rdist*, internal client to external server
In	Ext	Int	TCP	514	<1024	Yes	*rsh/rcp/rdump/rrestore/ rdist*, external server to internal client
In	Ext	Int	TCP	<1024	<1024	a	*rsh* error channel, external server to internal client
Out	Int	Ext	TCP	<1024	<1024	Yes	*rsh* error channel, internal client to external server

a ACK is not set on the first packet of this type (establishing connection) but will be set on the rest.

Proxying characteristics of the BSD "r" commands

The only one of the "r" commands that's widely used across the Internet is *rlogin*. TIS FWTK provides a proxy *rlogin* server that uses modified user procedures to provide outbound *rlogin*.

The other commands rely completely on address-based authentication, and don't allow the user to specify a password at all. They're used so seldom across the Internet that proxies for them are not widely available. All of them allow the user to specify enough data that's passed to the server that it would be possible to write modified-procedures proxies for them. Modifying the *rcmd()* and related functions in the standard Unix library allow you to create clients that use a generic proxy server.

Network address translation characteristics of the BSD "r" commands

For the most part, the BSD "r" commands will function with network address translation without problems. The *rsh* error channel, however, is set up from the server to the client, and the server gets the client's IP address from the *rsh* protocol. Most network address translation systems will not translate this embedded address, and error channel creation will fail, causing *rsh* to fail. Network address translation systems that change port numbers may also cause connections to fail if they move the client port above 1023.

Summary of recommendations for the BSD "r" command

- Don't allow any of the "r" commands across your firewall except outbound by proxy; they're unsafe. Use SSH or alternative protocols such as Telnet, FTP, and so on that can be made more secure.

- There is no way to safely provide outgoing *rsh* service using packet filters, because to do so you would have to allow incoming TCP connections to random ports below 1024 for the error channels.

- Because of the mismatch in security models, the *rsh* server is particularly dangerous on Windows NT; although Windows NT-based *rsh* clients are reasonably safe, Windows NT-based *rsh* servers are much more dangerous than Unix-based *rsh* servers.

- If you absolutely have to allow "r" commands, make sure that the trusted host mechanisms are strictly controlled (preferably by disabling that code in the server, which may require command-line options or modifying the source code).

- Beware disclosure of reusable passwords when using *rlogin*, just as when using Telnet.

rexec

rexec is a widely run but rarely used server. It's rarely used because almost no operating system provides both the client and the server. It is unclear to us why it is widely run, but almost every Unix system ships with *rexecd* enabled in */etc/inetd.conf*, apparently just in case somebody should be moved to write a local client for it. By contrast, Windows NT 4 machines ship with an *rexec* client but no daemon (in case you are running Unix machines, perhaps?). The only systems we know of which commonly ship with both a client and a server are Silicon Graphics machines running IRIX, which use *rexec* as the underlying protocol for the *inst* software installation program.

rexec is usually lumped in with the BSD "r" commands, but actually it has a slightly more secure design than the others. Rather than providing source-address authentication, it always requires the user to provide a username and password. This advantage is outweighed by the fact that it passes these across the network in the clear, so it has no security advantage over Telnet, for example. Worse yet, most *rexec* daemons provide no logging whatsoever. This makes *rexec* a favorite point of attack, since you are unlikely to notice the attackers at any point—while they're trying to break in, or even after they've gotten in.

Packet filtering characteristics of rexec

rexec is a TCP-based service. The server uses port 512. The client uses a random port above 1023.

Direction	Source Addr.	Dest. Addr.	Protocol	Source Port	Dest. Port	ACK Set	Notes
In	Ext	Int	TCP	>1023	512	a	Incoming *rexec*, client to server
Out	Int	Ext	TCP	512	>1023	Yes	Incoming *rexec*, server to client
Out	Int	Ext	TCP	>1023	512	a	Outgoing *rexec*, client to server
In	Ext	Int	TCP	512	>1023	Yes	Outgoing *rexec*, server to client

a ACK is not set on the first packet of this type (establishing connection) but will be set on the rest.

Proxying characteristics of rexec

Because very few platforms are widely available with both clients and servers for *rexec*, no proxies are widely available for it. If you had a client that did use *rexec*, it would not be terribly difficult to modify it to use a generic proxy like SOCKS. If the *rexec* clients on a given machine were always accessing the same server, you could also use a generic proxy server like the *plug-gw* program in TIS FWTK. It would be somewhat trickier, but by no means impossible, to write a dedicated proxy server that would use modified user procedures.

Network address translation characteristics of rexec

rexec does not use embedded IP addresses, and it will function with network address translation without problems.

Summary of recommendations for rexec

• Do not allow *rexec* across your firewall.

• Disable *rexecd* on all machines that do not need it to provide software packages via *inst*.

rex

rex is an RPC-based service for remote command execution. For an understanding of the problems RPC-based services pose for firewalls, see the discussion of RPC-based services in Chapter 14, *Intermediary Protocols*. There are worse problems with *rex*, however; in particular, it places all of its security checks in the client (which is a program named *on*), and anyone can use a modified client that bypasses these checks.

rex is a TCP Sun RPC service; for more information on the packet filtering, proxying, and network address translation characteristics of RPC services, see Chapter 14.

Summary of recommendations for rex

- Don't allow *rex* across your firewall; better yet, don't allow it at all because it's completely insecure even within a LAN environment.

Windows NT Remote Commands

For Windows NT 4, the Windows NT Resource Kit also provides three Windows NT-specific services that allow you to remotely execute commands. They are:

- Remote Command Line or REMOTE
- Remote Command or RCMD
- Remote Console or RCONSOLE

(For Windows 2000, this sort of functionality is handled by the Terminal Server, which is discussed later in this chapter.)

Despite their very similar names, these services do quite different things. RCMD is a fairly standard remote execution service; you start up the server, and clients that connect to it can then execute any command. REMOTE is more limited; you start the command to be run at the same time you start the server, and the client can control only the command you started. Commands that use graphics or complicated input and output methods will not work with either service (this includes a number of standard programs you might want to use from a command line, including most notably *edit*). Neither service encrypts information.

Remote Console provides more capabilities than either RCMD or REMOTE. It gives you a console on the remote machine exactly as if you were physically logged into the machine and had asked for a command prompt. It takes over video and all input and output, so that any program that normally works in a console window will work correctly. Remote Console does support encryption. By default, it encrypts authentication information. In addition, clients can request that an entire connection be encrypted (the server cannot require encryption). Authentication information is encrypted with DES. The details of the other encryption systems are not documented.

The services also use different security models. RCMD uses normal Windows NT authentication. The user who is running the client must have permission to log in to the server machine interactively, and the commands will run with that user's permissions. (Some early versions of RCMD do not actually correctly run the commands with the user's permissions; you should be sure to run the most recent version.) REMOTE does not by default do any authentication whatsoever, and the command is run with the permissions of the user who started the server. When you start a REMOTE server, it is possible to limit access to a particular group or user.

Remote Console uses its own authentication. By default, only members of the Administrators group can use Remote Console. It is possible to give this ability to other users by making them members of the group "RConsoleUsers"; if you do this, the users will automatically have the privilege "Log on as a batch file". When these users use Remote Console, they will get a console running with their normal permissions, as if they were physically logged in at the console (except that Remote Console does not check to see if they have the "Log on locally" permission that would let them do that).

REMOTE is of limited usefulness and is highly insecure. RCMD is more useful but still not very secure. If you need occasional command-line access to remote machines on a relatively secure network, Remote Console is a reasonable way to provide it. If you need full administration remotely, you will need a more powerful remote access solution; if you need to cross an insecure network, you will need a better protected one. In any case, if you are working remotely between NT machines, Remote Console is preferable to *rsh*, since Remote Console uses Windows NT user authentication, which is more secure than *rsh*'s source address authentication.

All of these services are based on SMB transactions; the packet filtering, proxying, and network address characteristics of SMB transactions are discussed in Chapter 14, *Intermediary Protocols*.

Summary of recommendations for remote commands

- Don't allow Remote Console, RCMD, or other SMB-based services, across your firewall.

- Don't run REMOTE at all.

Secure Shell (SSH)

The secure shell, or SSH, derives its name from one of the commands in the original implementation, which was written by Tatu Ylonen in 1995. SSH can be used as a secure replacement for the BSD "r" commands because it provides all of their functionality but uses strong authentication and encryption. On a Unix system it provides login (*slogin*), remote shell (*ssh*), and remote copy (*scp*) commands. In addition, SSH provides a built-in proxy mechanism that overcomes the problems of using remote X Windows clients (X Windows is discussed in more detail later in this chapter). SSH can also perform arbitrary "port forwarding", routing traffic received on one port on one machine to another port on another machine. Because SSH uses encryption, the port forwarding mechanism can be used as a very limited VPN capability.

SSH servers are widely available for Unix and Windows NT and may be available for other platforms that provide command-line interfaces. SSH clients are available for almost all platforms.

There is a good bit of confusion about the name "SSH". Originally there was a single program called *ssh*, but over time, several other entities have grown up. There is a package, including the *ssh* program and others, which is usually called SSH; there is a network communications protocol that the *ssh* program (and others) are based on, which is also usually called SSH; and there is a company called SSH Communications Security that has other products that use the SSH name.

Currently, two versions of the SSH protocol exist, SSH version 1 and SSH version 2. SSH version 1 is the original. Version 2 has a number of new features, including support for the TLS protocol, which is discussed further in Chapter 14, *Intermediary Protocols*. This protocol (at the time of writing) is not yet an IETF standard, and hence, SSH version 2 is still a work in progress. SSH version 2 is also in the process of becoming an IETF standard.

The original implementation, which is distributed primarily in source code form, has a generous license that makes it available free of charge for most noncommercial purposes. The reference implementation of SSH version 2 by SSH Communications Security is being supported and sold commercially (although it is available free of charge for very limited uses). Multiple programs based on the SSH protocols, some of them commercial and some of them freely available, are also developed by other people.

Because of the multiple implementations and the different licensing and legal restrictions, both versions are in widespread use, and this is expected to continue to be the case for some time. Unless otherwise noted, this discussion applies to both versions of the SSH Communications Security package.

Used correctly, SSH provides protection against a number of risks. Because it uses an encrypted connection for the entire conversation, including user authentication, it protects against eavesdroppers, whether they are looking for passwords or for data. The integrity mechanism that's used prevents session hijacking; an attacker cannot take over an existing connection because the attacker will not be able to correctly generate the integrity checksums.

SSH is a very popular tool for people who break into sites, as well as for administrators, and for many of the same reasons. Because SSH provides encrypted connections, administrators can't tell what information is moving across an SSH connection. Furthermore, SSH provides port-forwarding features (discussed later), which allow you to run all sorts of other protocols across an SSH connection, without any administrative control.

Since SSH is often used for remote administration, it's also a very useful command for attackers to booby-trap. Attackers will often install versions of SSH that function normally but send the attacker all authentication information, as well as the information needed to decrypt a connection (allowing them to snoop on it or hijack it). You should keep careful control over what machines can run SSH, and they should be protected bastion hosts where you will detect changes.

What makes SSH secure?

The security of SSH does not come purely from the fact that it uses a specific encryption algorithm, cryptographic hash, or public key cryptography, but from the way the algorithms are used. The important characteristics of a secure private communication session are discussed in Appendix C, *Cryptography*.

Both version 1 and 2 of SSH meet the characteristics of a secure private communication session because:

- The client and server negotiate encryption algorithms (in the case of SSH version 2, negotiation also determines which key exchange mechanism and integrity checksums are used).

- The identity of the server to which a client is connecting is always verified, and this identity check is performed before any client user authentication information is sent. This mechanism is discussed in the next section on server authentication.

- The key exchange algorithms that are used prevent man-in-the-middle attacks.

- At the end of the key exchange, a checksum exchange will detect any tampering with algorithm negotiation.

- The server checks the client identity in a number of ways; these mechanisms are discussed later in the section on client authentication.

- All data packets exchanged include message integrity checks. An integrity check failure causes a connection to be closed.

- An SSH server uses temporary authentication parameters that are discarded after a configurable time period (normally one hour) to prevent recorded sessions from being decrypted at a later time.

SSH server authentication

As mentioned earlier, SSH clients always verify the identity of an SSH server before sending any user authentication information—the ordering here is critical because it prevents a rogue server from impersonating a real server and capturing user authentication information. The server authentication mechanism does not rely on name service or IP address authentication. If you connect to a machine via Telnet, you are relying on your name service to give you the correct IP address information; if an attacker can feed you bad name service data, you will be connected to the attacker's machine and will happily give it your username and password information.

In both versions of SSH, public key cryptography is used to prove the identity of a server. The first part of checking the identity is to verify that you have a valid public key for the server that you wish to connect to. At the time SSH version 1 was developed, this was a very difficult problem because there was no standard interoperable global infrastructure for the purpose of distributing and verifying public keys. This situation is slowly improving, and SSH version 2 can use a certificate authority to verify a public key (this is one of the features provided by using TLS, which is discussed in Chapter 14, *Intermediary Protocols*). SSH version 2 also supports the mechanism developed for SSH version 1.

The solution SSH version 1 uses is novel; the client retrieves the public key from the server itself, checks to see if it already knows a key for a server having this name, and compares the keys. A mismatch in keys causes a warning to be printed. When the client doesn't already have a key, it also prints a warning and optionally stores the public key for the next time you connect to the server. This system makes the client vulnerable to a hostile server on the first connection, but it does provide significantly more security than having the client vulnerable to a hostile server on every connection.

It is also possible to provide a local system database of keys for servers that users might want to connect to. This protects clients against a hostile server but at the expense of maintaining the local database. Having a local database is effective only if it is possible to know in advance which servers clients are going to connect to.

After checking the validity of a key, SSH then checks the identity of the server by sending a message encrypted using the public key.* When the server proves that it successfully decrypted the message, and therefore knows the private part of the public key, the client believes it is talking to the correct server.

SSH client authentication

The SSH protocol supports a number of client authentication mechanisms:

rhosts

The *rhosts* authentication mechanism is exactly the same as for the BSD "r" commands. If the client is using a privileged port and the *.rhosts* file permits the login, then it is allowed. This mechanism is not enabled by default, and it is not recommended because it is not secure. This mechanism requires that SSH be installed so that it can use a privileged port.

rhosts with RSA authentication of the client host

This approach combines *.rhosts* with public key cryptography. The server first checks the identity of the client host. If the RSA public key for the client host is known to the server and the client can prove it knows the host private key, then *.rhosts* authentication is performed. Allowing this mechanism is the simplest way to replace the BSD "r" commands without forcing users to set up any new files. This mechanism also requires that SSH be installed so that it can use a privileged port and be able to read the client host private key.

RSA authentication of the user

This approach uses only public key cryptography. The client first sends the user's public key to the server. If the server is willing to accept the key, it responds with a challenge so that the client can prove that it knows the user's private key. This mechanism reads only user files and does not require SSH to use a privileged port. SSH can also use an "agent" to hold user private keys. SSH clients, when they need to use a private key, contact the SSH agent to perform cryptographic operations on their behalf. By default SSH clients will automatically set up forwarding to your SSH agent if you have one running. This means that you can chain together multiple SSH connections through several systems without having to copy your private key to multiple systems.

Kerberos v5 authentication and TIS authentication server

These modes work the same way as other applications that use these systems, which are described in Chapter 21, *Authentication and Auditing Services*.

---

* SSH version 2 does not always use public key algorithms for this. See the description of TLS in Chapter 14, *Intermediary Protocols*, for how server identity is determined.

Passwords

The final, and fallback authentication mode for SSH is to prompt for the user's normal login password. This is the same authentication used by programs like Telnet; the advantage is that at the point where SSH asks for the password, it has already established an encrypted connection, so the password is not passed in cleartext the way it is with Telnet or *rlogin*.

Additional SSH options for client control

An SSH server may accept or reject a connection based upon a number of conditions in addition to its client and user authentication, including:

- The source IP address of the connection
- The name of the host from which the connection is coming
- The groups of which the user is a member

SSH session hijacking protection

One of the important features of SSH is that it prevents session hijacking. Both versions of SSH use a message integrity mechanism to prevent hijacking. This makes it difficult for a third party to take over an open connection and use it because the third party must generate packets that both ends will accept. Versions 1 and 2 use different mechanisms, and each is believed to make it virtually impossible to hijack a session—no successful hijackings have ever been reported. However, the cryptographic techniques used in SSH version 2 (because it uses TLS) are considered to be superior.

Port forwarding

SSH has a facility called *port forwarding* that allows you to run other protocols across an SSH connection. There are two ways of doing port forwarding, "local" and "remote" (see Figure 18-2). Both kinds of forwarding are configured when the SSH client connects to the server, and both of them allow a connection made on one end of the SSH connection to go to the other end and then continue from there, possibly to a completely different host. Port forwarding stops when you close the SSH session to the server.

In local forwarding, the SSH client accepts connections and sends the data to the SSH server, which sends it on to the destination. In remote port forwarding, the server accepts the connections and sends the data to the client. In either case, whenever a connection is made to the listening port, a new TCP connection is made to the target system. Multiple, simultaneous connections are supported. Neither the connection to the listening port nor the connection from the SSH tunnel to the final destination is encrypted or authenticated. The tunnel can be used by

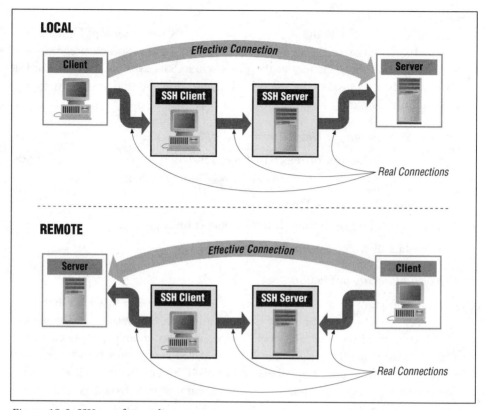

Figure 18-2. SSH port forwarding

other people, not just by the person who set it up; depending on exactly how the tunnel is created, it may be available to any user on the same machine that the listening port is on, or it may be available to any host that can reach the listening port.

Port forwarding is both a useful feature and a very dangerous one. It is useful, for example, if you want to create a simple virtual private network between two servers that you control. Allowing SSH with port forwarding can be an effective way to protect protocols like POP and IMAP that normally exchange unencrypted data.

Port forwarding is dangerous because it can be set up to forward external connections to an internal service, effectively bypassing your firewall. If this occurs, it will be difficult to detect by examining network traffic because the connections will be encrypted. For this reason, you should only allow incoming SSH connections to servers that you control, and you should consider turning off the general port forwarding features for incoming connections. Similarly, you should limit outgoing SSH connections to using SSH clients that you control, preferably with port forwarding turned off. Remote port forwarding will allow apparently outbound connections to carry inbound traffic.

Port forwarding does require some knowledge of how the protocols work and the port numbers that are used. It is therefore not useful to most users. If you receive requests to use port forwarding features, you may wish to consider implementing a real virtual private network. See Chapter 5, *Firewall Technologies*, for information on virtual private networking.

Both the client and the server provide ways to permanently turn off port forwarding; you can compile them without the port forwarding feature, or use a system configuration file to disable it. However, this will not prevent users from using their own clients (which may ignore the system configuration file).

Inbound port forwarding is configured at the start of an SSH session. SSH can set up forwarding for several different ports at the same time. However, an attacker can only exploit the ports that were set up at the start of a session; additional ports can only be attacked when new SSH sessions are started. For instance, if you set up port forwarding to an IMAP server, that may expose the IMAP server to attackers, but it doesn't allow access to any other services. It is possible to place default forwarding information into the per-user configuration file. This will cause ports to be forwarded automatically whenever an SSH session is started. You may want to disable inbound port forwarding on your SSH server to keep users from opening internal ports to attackers with this feature.

However, if an attacker can do port forwarding to a proxy server, and the proxy server can talk to the internal network, a single port forward can turn into extremely general access. For instance, if a port is forwarded from the outside to a web proxy, the attacker then has access to anything that the web proxy can reach. For various reasons, ranging from laziness to a desire to accommodate bad browser configurations, administrators often set up their external proxy systems so that they can reach internal servers. In this configuration, one single port forward can provide an attacker straightforward access to the entire internal web, and all the information and vulnerable servers that are on it. A SOCKS proxy server can give even more direct and widespread access.

If you allow incoming SSH connections and port forwarding, you should make sure that any firewall proxy services refuse and log connection attempts from those systems. In general, if you are using firewall proxy services, you should configure them to not allow connections to internal systems. This protects you from users using port forwarding on an incoming SSH server and using your proxy servers to access internal or external resources.

Remote X11 Window System support

SSH has a very useful feature that allows remote X11 Window System applications to be run. This is a special case of port forwarding, which also transparently handles X11 authentication cookies. For more information on the X11 Window System, see the X11 section later in this chapter. We recommend that you enable the X11 features only for systems on which you will be using it. The default setting can normally be made either globally or using individual user configuration files. The documentation for the version of SSH you are using should contain instructions on how to do this.

Packet filtering characteristics of SSH

SSH servers are at TCP port 22; SSH clients need to use a port 1024 below when using *.rhost*-based authentication methods, but use a port above 1023 when they are not.

Direction	Source Addr.	Dest. Addr.	Protocol	Source Port	Dest. Port	ACK Set	Notes
In	Ext	Int	TCP	Any[a]	22	[b]	Incoming SSH connection, client to server
Out	Int	Ext	TCP	22	Any[a]	Yes	Incoming SSH connection, server to client
Out	Int	Ext	TCP	Any[a]	22	[b]	Outgoing SSH connection, client to server
In	Ext	Int	TCP	22	Any[a]	Yes	Outgoing SSH connection, server to client

[a] SSH clients use a port below 1024 when using *.rhost*-based authentication methods, and a port above 1023 otherwise.
[b] ACK is not set on the first packet of this type (establishing connection) but will be set on the rest.

Proxying characteristics of SSH

It is easy to proxy SSH as it uses a single TCP connection from the client to the server. When not using *.rhosts* authentication, it does not rely on using a port below 1024 and IP addresses for authentication. A proxy cannot perform any content checks due to the use of encryption in SSH. Under Unix, SSH has compile-time support for either SOCKS v4 or SOCKS v5. Some clients for other platforms also support SOCKS.

Network address translation characteristics of SSH

SSH does not use embedded IP addresses and will work transparently with network address translation.

Summary of recommendations for SSH

- If you have to allow inbound connections, SSH is one of the safest ways.

- Avoid using the *.rhosts*-based authentication methods.

- Only allow inbound SSH connections to servers that you control.

- Consider turning off port forwarding.

- Only enable remote X11 support when you need it.

- Consider disallowing outbound SSH connections, because they can be used to tunnel inbound connections, and it is difficult to enforce port forwarding restrictions on them.

Remote Graphical Interfaces

The programs discussed in the previous sections give you text-based access to a machine, but these days, you're likely to want access to graphics as well. That's a different, and much more recent, problem with different solutions.

X11 Window System

Most window systems supplied by Unix vendors are either based on or very similar to X11—from a firewalls point of view, most of the considerations are the same—so this discussion of X11 applies to other window systems as well.

The X11 Window System poses a number of problems for a firewall system.

The first problem with X11 is that the client/server relationship is backwards from most other protocols. The X11 "server" is the display/mouse/keyboard unit, and the "clients" are the application programs driving windows or interacting with the mouse and keyboard on that server. Thus, the server is typically inside the firewall (sitting on the user's desk), and the clients are outside (running on whatever remote computers the user has accessed). Figure 18-3 shows an X server and client.

X11 servers have certain capabilities that make them a very tempting target for attackers. There are a number of things an attacker can do with access to an X11 server, including:

Getting screen dumps

Obtaining a copy of whatever information is being displayed on the screen at any given time.

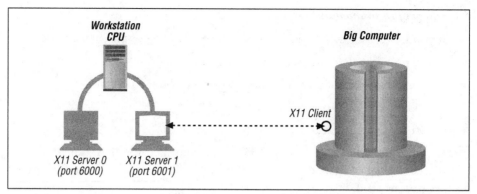

Figure 18-3. X Windows server and clients

Reading keystrokes

For example, reading a user's password as it is typed at the keyboard.

Injecting keystrokes as if they were typed by the user

This potentially allows the attacker to do all kinds of mean and nasty things, especially in a window where the user happens to be running a root shell.

Clients can do all of these things without doing anything that's visible to the user, which makes it difficult to detect if such a client is connected.

X11 has two security mechanisms; the first and original is called the *xhost* mechanism. This mechanism allows the user to tell the server which remote IP addresses the server should accept connections from. Users are supposed to authorize only specific hosts where they intend to run X11 clients. There are two problems with this:

- Users tend to forget to preauthorize the host before starting the clients, which are then refused access. After this happens a few times, many users disable the control altogether. For example, they issue an *xhost* + command to allow connections from any and all hosts in the name of convenience (so they can easily run programs on remote systems), without giving any thought to the security implications of their actions.

- There's no way for the *xhost* mechanism to determine whether or not any given connection from one of those machines is legitimate; any user on one of the allowed machines can run an X11 client and connect to the X11 server.

The second form of authentication, which is commonly referred to as the *magic cookie* security mechanism, relies on a secret shared between the server and legitimate clients; clients are allowed to access the server only if they can prove they know the secret. The required cookie is generated when the X server starts up. It is unpredictable, and it is different each time the server or a managed user session starts. The cookies for each server a user has access to are stored in a file and can be manipulated with the *xauth* program; for the Unix operating system, the file will be located in the user's home directory under the name "*.Xauthority*".

There are two security problems with the normal version of cookie authentication (which is known as "MIT-MAGIC-COOKIE-1"). First, the cookie is passed unprotected from the client to the server. Anybody who is snooping on the network can intercept the cookie and use it to start new connections. Second, no mechanism is provided to get the cookie to the client machine in the first place or to secure it once it gets there. It is not uncommon for sites to share the cookie (either intentionally or unintentionally) between machines with NFS. This transfers it in cleartext yet again.

The first problem can be dealt with by using a mechanism called "XDM-AUTHORIZATION-1", which uses the magic cookie as a key to encrypt other data and passes that data, instead of the cookie itself, across the network. Unfortunately, this still doesn't solve the problem of getting the cookie on both the client and the server securely. Furthermore, not all X servers and clients support this mechanism.

A small number of servers and clients support other authentication mechanisms. For instance, some of them use Secure RPC or Kerberos to identify users. These mechanisms avoid the problems with cookies.

SSH tunneling of X avoids some of the problems involved in using cookies with special handling of the authentication cookie. The SSH client generates a new authentication cookie and sends it to the SSH server. The SSH server uses this cookie and pretends to be an X server, setting an appropriate DISPLAY variable before running any commands. When an X client connects to the fake X server, the connection is forwarded back to the SSH client, which substitutes the real authentication cookie and makes a connection to the real X server. This means that the real X server authentication cookie is never copied and left on a remote system. Because the cookie sent to the SSH server is not the real cookie, remote X applications can be started only for the duration of the SSH session. We do recommend that you enable this SSH client feature only when you will need to run remote X applications. The default setting for this feature can normally be made either globally or using individual user configuration files. The documentation for the version of SSH you are using will contain instructions on how to do this.

Additional servers

Several additional protocols are often run in conjunction with X11, including the X Display Manager Control Protocol (XDMCP) and the X font server (which does not have an acronym).

Some X hosts are designed or configured to act as the modern equivalent of dumb terminals on time sharing systems. These limited-function hosts (commonly called

X displays or *X terminals*) are not full-fledged workstations, which provide services (such as login) and run applications locally; rather, they are simply input/output devices for services provided by other systems on the network. XDMCP provides a standard way for these X terminals to find and use login services provided by servers elsewhere on the local area network. When it starts or restarts, an X terminal tries to find an XDMCP server, either by using broadcast or by sending unicast packets to a preconfigured list of servers. One or more XDMCP servers will respond to this request, letting the X terminal know which server or servers can provide login services for that X terminal. An XDMCP server may generate broadcast requests on behalf of an X terminal and return the list of responding servers.

The XDMCP protocol is commonly implemented under Unix by a service called *xdm* (the X display manager), which will either provide a graphical login screen or run a chooser that allows one of a list of hosts be selected. Access control is performed using hostnames or IP addresses. *xdm* is often used to manage the login process on machines that are not providing services for remote displays and may be present and willing to accept network connections on any machine running X.

XDMCP has many vulnerabilities. First, it exchanges authentication information and can be used to attack the X server host. Second, it will generate broadcast traffic based on requests and can be used to magnify incoming traffic for denial of service attacks. In addition, there have been buffer overflow problems with *xdm*. XDMCP should never be allowed through a firewall. If an X-based graphical display is needed for a bastion host, the display manager service should be configured to refuse external connections and manage only a local display.

The X font server is designed to provide a centralized font storage service for X displays. (Fonts can take up a large amount of disk space, which may not be available on all X devices.) The X font server protocol allows a server to indicate alternative font servers if it is too busy. This redirect capability can specify arbitrary port numbers, allowing a hostile server to redirect a client to any host and port combination. The X font server protocol should never be allowed through a firewall. If an X-based graphical display is needed for a bastion host, then the fonts should be directly installed, and the X font server should be disabled.

Packet filtering characteristics of X11

X11 uses TCP port 6000 for the first server on a machine. This choice of ports presents another problem for packet filtering systems: the X11 ports are in the middle of the "above 1023" range of ports that most applications use for random client-side ports. Thus, any packet filtering scheme that allows in packets to ports above 1023 (in order to allow packets from remote servers to local clients) needs to be very careful not to allow in connections to X11 servers. It can do this either by totally blocking access to the range of ports used by these servers (which can be a tricky proposition because of the possibility of multiple servers per machine, as we discuss later in this chapter) or by using start-of-connection filtering (looking at the TCP ACK bit) to disallow inbound TCP connections to any ports.

Some machines run multiple X11 servers. The first server is at port 6000, the second at 6001, and so on. On a Unix system, the DISPLAY environment variable tells clients what X11 server to contact. This variable is of the form *hostname:n*, which tells clients to contact the server on port 6000+*n* on machine *hostname*.

Sometimes, such machines actually have multiple display/keyboard/mouse setups, but more often the multiple servers are *virtual* servers. There are several reasons for a machine to run a virtual X11 server. For instance, X11 is a very verbose, high-bandwidth protocol; it doesn't run well over dial-up links. One of the solutions that's been adopted (for example, by NCD's XRemote package) is to run a virtual X11 server on a well-connected machine (for example, linked by Ethernet to the machines the client programs are running on) and then to speak some other, more frugal protocol over the slow link between this virtual server and the real X terminal. SSH also uses a virtual X11 server to do X11 tunneling. This mechanism is illustrated in Figure 18-4 (SSH's virtual X11 server is usually at 6011 to allow for machine running multiple displays at lower numbers).

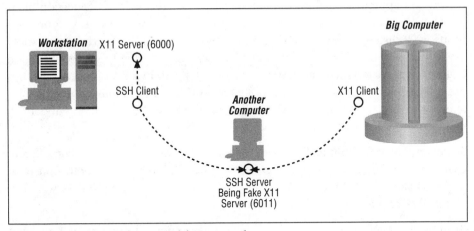

Figure 18-4. X11 virtual servers and SSH tunneling

Every machine running X11 will have a server at port 6000. A few will have servers at 6000 and 6001 or 6011. Only a very few machines (mostly those running virtual servers) will have more than that.

Thus, to block access to all these servers, assuming that you can't do start-of-connection filtering, you need to block access to ports 6000 through 6000+*n*, where *n* is some undetermined number. Ports 6000 to 6063 are officially registered for X

Windows, so that's one reasonable guess for n, although at most sites that's a larger block than you really need. Another possible guess is the one used by SSH when it looks for a free port to put a fake server on; it skips 6000–6010, assuming that it will miss most real servers that way (however, it will then pessimistically search up to 6999 to find a free port, so you can look at it as setting n to 10 or to 999). You don't want to make n too small because that might expose some of the virtual X11 servers to attack. On the other hand, you don't want to make it too big either, because you're blocking ports in the range of random ports that could be used by other application clients. You don't want to keep another protocol's client (e.g., Telnet or FTP) from working simply because it happened to pick as its random client port a port blocked to prevent X11 access.

You do have one thing going for you: the way most operating systems allocate such random ports. Generally, when a client application asks the operating system to allocate a random port for its use, the kernel allocates the next available port after the last one allocated (wrapping around to the beginning of the port number space when necessary). If a client happens to grab a port blocked because of X11, the client will fail. If the user tries to run the client again a few times, the client will get a new port each time and will eventually succeed when the port allocated moves beyond the blocked range.

A common approach (again, assuming that you can't do start-of-connection filtering to block external connections to internal servers) is to block, say, four ports (ports 6000 through 6003) on all hosts, and more ports on hosts where you know or suspect people will run lots of virtual X11 servers (e.g., the hosts people dial in to from their X terminals at home). A more straightforward approach is to use proxying to direct connections to a bastion host that is not running a window system. It can make outbound connections on any port without worrying about hitting the blocked range because it doesn't need a blocked range.

Some vendors provide modified or enhanced X11 servers with somewhat different characteristics; for example, Sun's OpenWindows server listens at both port 6000 (for X11) and port 2000 (for Sun's older NeWS window system protocol), with second servers at ports 6001 and 2001, and so on.

XDMCP uses UDP port 177 and, if the service is configured to do so, will respond to broadcast requests. The X font server uses TCP port 7100.

Direction	Source Addr.	Dest. Addr.	Protocol	Source Port	Dest. Port	ACK Set	Notes
In	Ext	Int	TCP	>1023	6000+n	a	Incoming X11 connection to nth server, client to server
Out	Int	Ext	TCP	6000+n	>1023	Yes	Incoming X11 connection to nth server, server to client
In	Ext	Int[b]	UDP	>1023	177	c	Incoming XDMCP

Direction	Source Addr.	Dest. Addr.	Protocol	Source Port	Dest. Port	ACK Set	Notes
Out	Int	Ext	UDP	177	>1023	c	XDMCP reply
In	Ext	Int	TCP	>1023	7100[d]	a	Incoming request to X font server
Out	Int	Ext	TCP	7100[d]	>1023	Yes	Reply from internal X font server
Out	Int	Ext	TCP	>1023	6000+n	a	Outgoing X11 connection to nth server, client to server
In	Ext	Int	TCP	6000+n	>1023	Yes	Outgoing X11 connection to nth server, server to client
Out	Int	Ext[b]	UDP	>1023	177	c	Outgoing XDMCP
In	Ext	Int	UDP	177	>1023	c	XDMCP reply
Out	Int	Ext	TCP	>1023	7100[d]	a	Outgoing request to X font server
In	Ext	Int	TCP	7100[d]	>1023	Yes	Reply from external X font server

[a] ACK is not set on the first packet of this type (establishing connection) but will be set on the rest.
[b] XDMCP may have a broadcast address as a destination.
[c] UDP has no ACK equivalent.
[d] The server may redirect the client to a different port and/or host.

Proxying characteristics of X11

X11 does not work well with generic proxy systems because it requires high performance and makes connections inbound instead of outbound. Dedicated X11 proxies are available, most of which are designed to provide added features, instead of added security. The most effective way to proxy X11 is to use SSH tunneling, which allows you to make the connection outbound and provides encryption and authentication.

Network address translation characteristics of X11

X11 itself does not use embedded IP addresses and will work without difficulty with network address translation systems. However, the reversed nature of X11 means that connections will usually be made from the outside to the inside. Since the network address translation system cannot set up translations automatically in this situation, you will need to have some sort of predefined translation in place to use X11 through a network address translation system.

In addition, the data that's used for the XDM-AUTHORIZATION-1 authentication mechanism normally includes the client's IP address. If you are using this form of authentication through a network address translation system, you will need to specially configure the client and server to use hostnames instead of addresses.

Summary of recommendations for XII

- Do not allow clients on the Internet to connect to X11 servers on your internal network.

- Use SSH to allow clients on the Internet to connect to your local display.

- If you cannot use SSH, use an X11 proxy server (such as the one in the TIS FWTK) running on a bastion host.

- Do not run an unrestricted XDMCP server on a bastion host.

- Do not allow XDMCP through a firewall.

- Do not run an X font service on a bastion host. If you need X, install the fonts locally.

Remote Graphic Interfaces for Microsoft Operating Systems

A wide variety of programs provide remote access to machines running Windows operating systems (to name a few at random, LapLink, RemotelyPossible, and pcANYWHERE). While most of these programs were originally designed to work with modems, many of them now work over networks as well, and those that do almost always support TCP/IP. Most of them use proprietary protocols; for details on port usage of such programs, you will need to contact the vendor of the particular program you are interested in using.

The security concerns with all of these programs are the same and fall into the following categories:

- Are remote and local users of the machine kept separate? Can the local user control what remote users can do, and are remote users protected from interference by local users who are at the physical machine at the same time?

- Is there secure and strong authentication of the remote user?

- Is data subject to interception between the remote user and the machine?

- What capabilities does the remote user have? Can a remote user reboot the machine or transfer files from it?

A remote user will have the same access to your network as does the computer he or she is attached to. You can therefore make a trade-off between the security of the protocol you are using and the capability of the machine people are accessing with it; the more secure the protocol is, the more access you can grant the machine. However, many of these programs use a single reusable password and an unencrypted connection to give a remote user complete access to the computer; allowing this to pass through your firewall is effectively equivalent to simply attaching the computer to the Internet and is extremely unlikely to be an acceptable option.

Remote control programs are one of the most common security problems in Microsoft-based networks. It doesn't matter how good the security of a machine is if you put an unprotected remote control program on it. At best, a remote control program will give a remote user the complete control that a local user has; at worst, it may give a remote user administrative control with more capabilities than a normal local user. This is much more dangerous than any other service you are likely to run and should be protected appropriately.

You should closely evaluate the security claims made by these programs. In particular, many of them provide improved security either on authentication, or on the data stream, but not both. This is basically pointless; an attacker who can authenticate doesn't need to eavesdrop, and vice versa. In addition, some of their "security enhancements" on authentication are extremely minimal.

For instance, many packages claim that using normal Windows domain authentication is a security improvement. It certainly makes administration more convenient and may slightly enhance security (since an administrator can enforce the use of relatively good passwords), but it is not a major advance in network security over having an equivalent-length local password. It may be no advance at all, since the domain authentication is going to occur on the local area network, between the computer and its domain controller; the password and username information has to get to the computer via whatever protocol the remote access program is using, which may be reusable or even unencrypted.

Note that even if passwords are passed across the network in a nonreusable form, they may be quite simply guessable—if you elect to allow this sort of access, you should be sure you are using strong passwords and that the program logs failures so that you can detect password-guessing attacks.

Independent Computing Architecture (ICA)

ICA[*] is a protocol developed by Citrix for remote display of Windows clients. It is the most widespread of the Windows remote access protocols, and clients are available for a number of platforms, including Unix and Macintoshes. There is also a Java-based client that will allow any Java device (for instance, most web browsers) to be an ICA display. ICA is available over a wide range of lower-level protocols, not just TCP/IP (this is one of its advantages over competing protocols). We will discuss only the TCP/IP implementation in this section.

ICA uses an obscured connection for user authentication. Although passwords are disguised, they are not strongly protected; programs that read passwords from an ICA authentication negotiation are readily available. A variant called Secure ICA actually uses encryption for authentication and is capable of using an encrypted connection for the data stream as well. It uses RC5 encryption with Diffie-Hellman key exchange, using a 128-bit key for the authentication. (For more information

---

[*] This protocol is also known as Intelligent Console Architecture and Intelligent Console Access; Citrix appears to have repeatedly changed opinions about the best way to expand the acronym.

about encryption algorithms and the implications of key length, see Appendix C, *Cryptography*.) Due to previous U.S. export restrictions, non-U.S. versions use a weaker 40-bit key on the data stream; U.S. versions may use 40-bit, 56-bit, or 128-bit encryption on the data stream. (Changes in the U.S. export restrictions will probably remove the distinction from future versions.) Packets from the server to the client consists of partial screen updates that are useful only if you have an entire data stream. Data going from the client to the server includes keystroke information that it would be relatively easy to reassemble into a usable form. However, doing so would still require an amount of time and effort to break the 40-bit key U.S. export version and likely be worthwhile only to a determined or highly motivated attacker.

Many security issues of remote access are outside the control of the protocol itself. For instance, although ICA uses an encrypted connection for authentication, it is up to the particular server software to do the authentication (and therefore to control how long passwords can or must be) and to do any authentication logging.

Packet filtering characteristics of ICA

There are two ICA protocols: one for client connections and one for browsing (looking for ICA servers). In TCP/IP, client connections are based at TCP port 1494; browsing is done via UDP broadcast to port 1604. Browsing is not critical to ICA functioning. If it is disabled, users will have to type machine names, instead of selecting them from a list (the list, when available, sometimes provides useful information about the relative load on the servers).

Direction	Source Addr.	Dest. Addr.	Protocol	Source Port	Dest. Port	ACK Set	Notes
In	Ext	Int	TCP	>1023	1494	a	Incoming ICA connection, external client to internal server
Out	Int	Ext	TCP	1494	>1023	Yes	Incoming ICA connection, internal server to external client
In	Ext	Int bcast[b]	UDP	>1023	1604	c	ICA browse request, external client to internal server
Out	Int	Ext	UDP	1604	>1023	c	ICA browse response, internal server to external client
Out	Int	Ext	TCP	>1023	1494	a	Outgoing ICA connection, internal client to external server
In	Ext	Int	TCP	1494	>1023	Yes	Outgoing ICA connection, external server to internal client
Out	Int	Ext bcast[b]	UDP	>1024	1604	c	ICA browse request, internal client to external server
In	Ext	Int	UDP	1604	>1023	c	ICA browse response, external server to internal client

[a] ACK is not set on the first packet of this type (establishing connection) but will be set on the rest.
[b] It is extremely unlikely that packets of this type will pass through intermediate routers, even if you choose to allow them through your routers.
[c] UDP has no ACK equivalent.

Proxying characteristics of ICA

As of this writing, Citrix did not know of any available dedicated proxies for ICA. However, the important part of ICA is a straightforward TCP connection, which can easily be proxied by any generic proxy system. Many commercial proxy systems provide instructions for proxying ICA.

Network address translation characteristics of ICA

ICA does not use embedded IP addresses and will work transparently through a network address translation system. However, the browsing system will attempt to communicate IP addresses. On recent clients and servers, you should be able to configure a static mapping, configure the server to know about the mapping as an alternate address, and configure the client to use the alternate address for connections.

Microsoft Terminal Server and Terminal Services

Microsoft's Terminal Server is a separate edition of Windows NT 4 but is simply a service in Windows 2000. This reflects changes in the underlying operating system to support multi-user operation. These changes were partly developed by Citrix but are now part of Microsoft's operating system development (this history is reflected in frequent rumors about Citrix, Microsoft, Terminal Server, and ICA, many of them incorrect).

By default, Terminal Services uses a Microsoft-developed protocol called the Remote Desktop Protocol (RDP), which is an extension of the International Telecommunications Union T.120 standard. (T.120 is discussed further in Chapter 19, *Real-Time Conferencing Services.*) It is also possible to buy ICA support from Citrix and add it to Terminal Server. ICA support provides some useful features that RDP does not; most notably, RDP support is available only on Windows platforms, while ICA is available for a wide range of operating systems.

RDP provides three levels of encryption: low, medium, and high. "Low" encryption encrypts only data sent from the client to the server, using 40-bit RC4. This includes the authentication data. "Medium" encryption encrypts all data but uses 40-bit RC4; "high" encryption encrypts all data using 128-bit RC4.

Packet filtering characteristics of RDP

RDP uses a straightforward TCP connection on port 3389.

Direction	Source Addr.	Dest. Addr.	Protocol	Source Port	Dest. Port	ACK Set	Notes
In	Ext	Int	TCP	>1023	3389	[a]	Incoming RDP connection, external client to internal server
Out	Int	Ext	TCP	3389	>1023	Yes	Incoming RDP connection, internal server to external client

Direction	Source Addr.	Dest. Addr.	Protocol	Source Port	Dest. Port	ACK Set	Notes
Out	Int	Ext	TCP	>1023	3389	a	Outgoing RDP connection, internal client to external server
In	Ext	Int	TCP	3389	>1023	Yes	Outgoing RDP connection, external server to internal client

a ACK is not set on the first packet of this type (establishing connection) but will be set on the rest.

Proxying characteristics of RDP

As of this writing, we do not know of any available dedicated proxies for RDP. However, RDP uses a straightforward TCP connection, which can easily be proxied by any generic proxy system.

Network address translation characteristics of RDP

RDP does not use embedded IP addresses and will work transparently through a network address translation system.

BO2K

BO2K is a controversial remote access tool. In its favor, it's a freely available tool with a variety of available extensions, including a wide range of encryption and communications methods that allow it to work securely across the Internet. However, it's written and distributed by people who break into computers and is often installed by means of a Trojan horse. It is designed to be concealed from the local user, even somebody with administrator privileges on the local machine (this is an advantage both for attackers trying to hide from system administrators and for system administrators trying to hide from attackers).

Because BO2K provides a system for adding extensions, it's hard to make absolute statements about its capabilities; people add new capabilities frequently.

BO2K provides the remote user with full Administrator access to the machine, and it can't be configured to provide more limited access. This makes it a dubious choice as a general-purpose remote access tool for users. On the other hand, it does provide some authentication of the remote user. The BO2K server, which runs on the machine to be controlled, has an embedded encryption password, and you must know that password in order to be able to control it. The password is recoverable from the server if you have access to the server binary, so you should protect the server binary the same way you would protect other files that can provide attackers with Administrator access.

Packet filtering characteristics of BO2K

BO2K supports UDP or TCP for communications, and a plug-in is available to support communication over ICMP. It can use any port number. By default, it tends to use UDP over port 31337, but this is extremely easy to reconfigure. In general, it's unwise to make any assumptions about what ports BO2K will use. If you are installing it for your own use, you can of course select whatever ports and protocols suit you.

Proxying characteristics of BO2K

As of this writing, there are no proxy-aware plug-ins for BO2K. Because the BO2K server runs on the machine to be controlled, connections are frequently made with the server inside the firewall and the client outside; this is a direction where proxy servers are not generally used.

Network address translation characteristics of BO2K

BO2K does not use embedded IP addresses and should work through network address translation systems without problems. On the other hand, the server runs on the machine to be controlled. If that machine is on the inside of the network address translation system, you will need to set up a static translation for it. Transactions will be initiated from the client, and inbound traffic cannot set up a dynamic translation.

Summary of Recommendations for Windows Remote Access

- In general, these protocols are highly insecure. Allowing them to pass through your firewall effectively opens the machines running the servers to the Internet (and running them with a modem effectively opens the machine to anybody who happens to call the phone number). Consider using virtual private networking or dial-up networking as a remote access method instead (see Chapter 20, *Naming and Directory Services*, for more information about these options).

19

Real-Time Conferencing Services

Services like the Web, electronic mail, and newsgroups allow people to send each other messages that will be read at later times, but what if you want to send an immediate message or have a discussion instead? Several services available on the Internet allow people to interact in real time on the Internet, ranging from "chat rooms" where people can send text messages to teleconferencing programs with video, audio, and whiteboard facilities.

Internet Relay Chat (IRC)

IRC is a multi-user text-based real-time conferencing system. Users run IRC client programs to connect to IRC servers. IRC servers can be arranged in a spanning tree and talk to each other to pass messages to all of the clients; these days, many IRC servers are independent and don't take part in a tree. Figure 19-1 shows how the IRC servers are connected. Clients might connect to any of these servers.

Most of the security problems with IRC are related to who uses it and how, not to the protocol per se. As we mentioned in Chapter 2, *Internet Services*, many clients allow servers far more access to local resources (files, processes, programs, etc.) than they should, and a malicious server can wreak havoc with a weak or poorly configured client. Further, some of the frequent users of IRC have a nasty habit of persuading new users to naively run commands that those users think will do neat things on their systems but instead trash these systems.

Many well-intentioned IRC users are simply naive about security. For example, they think it's really neat to distribute software by putting up a little server on their machine and advising people to "*telnet* myhost myport | sh" to have the software installed for them, which allows external users to install the software without inter-action from the user but would also let them run any command whatsoever on the

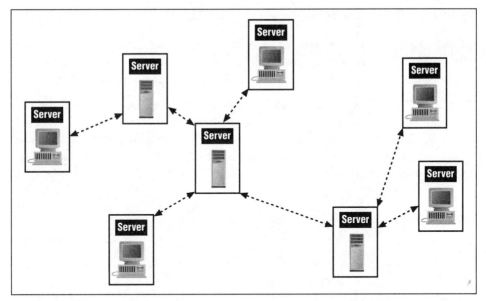

Figure 19-1. IRC server tree

internal user's host as that user. It's close to impossible to distinguish hostile people from naive ones, and users should be advised to never issue any command, in or out of their IRC client, just because somebody advised them to over IRC.

Although these problems are widespread on IRC, IRC is also a useful and popular way for people to talk to each other. Text-based, multi-user, real-time communication can be handy; it has many of the advantages of teleconferencing for a much lower price tag.

While IRC clients pose a risk, IRC servers are relatively safe. You should be able to safely run an IRC server in a restricted (*chrooted*) environment on a bastion host, but it would be somewhat bizarre to run a server without having any local clients that could access it, and a server that could access the Internet would probably not be safe for clients to talk to. You may want to run one inside your firewall for private IRC conferencing.

Many IRC clients support something called Direct Client Connections (DCC). DCC allows two IRC clients to negotiate and establish a direct TCP connection between themselves, bypassing all the servers except for the initial negotiation. Most IRC servers will attempt to use the Auth protocol to get information about the user. Some IRC servers will not accept connections if Auth doesn't work. See Chapter 21, *Authentication and Auditing Services*, for more information about Auth.

Packet Filtering Characteristics of IRC

IRC is a TCP-based service. Servers generally listen for incoming connections (from both clients and other servers) on port 6667, although some servers use other port numbers. Clients (and servers contacting other servers) use ports above 1023.

Clients use ports above 1023 to talk to other clients using DCC. To start, the calling client passes an invitation to the called client through the normal IRC server channels. The invitation includes a TCP port number where the calling client is listening for an incoming connection. The called client, if it chooses to accept the invitation, opens a TCP connection to that port.

Direction	Source Addr.	Dest. Addr.	Protocol	Source Port	Dest. Port	ACK Set	Notes
In	Ext	Int	TCP	>1023	6667[a]	b	External client or server contacting internal server
Out	Int	Ext	TCP	6667[a]	>1023	Yes	Internal server answering
Out	Int	Ext	TCP	>1023	>1023	b	DCC connection requested by external client; internal client answering invitation from external client
In	Ext	Int	TCP	>1023	>1023	Yes	DCC connection from external client
Out	Int	Ext	TCP	>1023	6667[a]	b	Internal client or server contacting external server
In	Ext	Int	TCP	6667[a]	>1023	Yes	External server answering
In	Ext	Int	TCP	>1023	>1023	b	DCC connection requested by internal client; external client answering invitation from internal client
Out	Int	Ext	TCP	>1023	>1023	Yes	DCC connection from internal client

[a] Although 6667 is the most commonly used port for IRC, some servers use other port numbers.
[b] ACK is not set on the first packet of this type (establishing connection) but will be set on the rest.

Proxying Characteristics of IRC

When all IRC servers were part of the same spanning tree, any IRC server could serve as a proxy server. These days, IRC servers tend to be independent, and users are likely to want to contact many different servers. It's therefore necessary to have true proxies. A SOCKS-aware IRC client, *mIRC*, is available for most Unix variants; so is a security-aware dedicated IRC proxy called *tircproxy*.

DCC connections will not work with *mIRC* through SOCKS but will with *tircproxy*, which intercepts and rewrites them. *tircproxy* is also capable of intercepting, denying, or sanitizing DCC and other dangerous requests, limiting the number of attacks that are possible. It also provides for user authentication on outgoing requests, either in the form of genuine authentication of individual users with user-name/password information (passed in cleartext) or in the form of quiz questions intended to let all human beings through while preventing people from using *bots*, programs that take part in IRC.

Network Address Translation Characteristics of IRC

Normal IRC connections do not include embedded IP addresses and work without problems through network address translation. Some servers will require access to an Auth server on the same apparent IP address, so you will need to provide a mapping that will allow inbound Auth to succeed. DCC connections are more complicated, since they require passing IP addresses and port numbers and allowing inbound connections. In order to allow DCC, the network address translation system will need to understand the IRC protocol, correctly modify the IP addresses and port numbers in DCC commands, and accept the incoming connections associated with them. Alternatively, you can use *tircproxy* in combination with network address translation and provide static translation for the host running *tircproxy. tircproxy* will do the work of intercepting the DCC commands.

Summary of Recommendations for IRC

- Although it's theoretically possible to proxy IRC, or to allow just IRC through filters, it's probably not a good idea because of the weaknesses of the clients. The best way to allow IRC is to put an untrusted victim machine with no confidential data on a perimeter network and let users log into that machine to run IRC.

- If you run an internal IRC server, be sure it is not part of a tree of external IRC servers; otherwise, it will effectively proxy for your IRC clients and for attacks against them from the outside.

ICQ

ICQ is a conferencing protocol developed by Mirabilis and run in conjunction with the conferences available on their servers. Although ICQ is a proprietary service, it is one of the more popular web-based chat services. Like IRC, ICQ is a popular place for attackers to look for targets, including computers that may be vulnerable and people who may be possible to manipulate with social engineering. Many people report that they notice an increased number of people probing their site when they use ICQ.

In addition to the significant indirect problems with ICQ, straightforward security problems have occurred with the ICQ client itself. These are mostly denial of service attacks where people can crash or hang the machine running the client, but some of them have been buffer overflow problems that could allow an attacker to run arbitrary commands. In addition, one version of the client set up a web server as well as the ICQ client. This is unpleasant for security no matter what web server it is (the vulnerabilities of a web server are quite a bit larger than those of a chat client) and was made worse by the fact that the particular web server that Mirabilis provided allowed any file on the machine to be transferred. Although these problems have been rapidly corrected by Mirabilis, the history of repeated problems is a cause for concern.

Packet Filtering Characteristics of ICQ

ICQ communicates via UDP on port 4000 to the server at *icq.mirabilis.com* and via TCP on a port above 1024 from the client to the server or between clients. The client can be configured to control which ports it uses; normally, it will choose ports between 3989 and 4000.

Direction	Source Addr.	Dest. Addr.	Protocol	Source Port	Dest. Port	ACK Set	Notes
Out	Int	Mirabilis	UDP	>1023	4000	a	Internal client to server
In	Mirabilis	Int	UDP	4000	>1023	a	Server to internal client
Out	Int	Mirabilis	TCP	>1023[b]	>1023	c	Internal client sending messages via server
In	Mirabilis	Int	TCP	>1023	>1023[b]	Yes	Server sending messages to internal client
Out	Int	Ext	TCP	>1023[b]	>1023	c	Internal client sending messages direct to external client
In	Ext	Int	TCP	>1023	>1023[b]	Yes	External client replying to internal client
In	Ext	Int	TCP	>1023	>1023[b]	c	External client sending messages direct to internal client
Out	Int	Ext	TCP	>1023[b]	>1023	Yes	Internal client replying to external client

[a] UDP has no ACK equivalent.
[b] The port range used for this purpose can be configured on the client.
[c] ACK is not set on the first packet of this type (establishing connection) but will be set on the rest.

Proxying Characteristics of ICQ

The ICQ client is SOCKS-aware and will speak to SOCKS4 or SOCKS5 servers. However, since ICQ uses both TCP and UDP, and SOCKS4 does not proxy UDP, using SOCKS4 is not a complete solution; you will also need to allow UDP to port 4000. ICQ will allow you to direct the UDP packets to the firewall to facilitate use of a UDP relayer or SOCKS5 UDP support.

Normally, ICQ clients will attempt to send messages directly to each other. If you are using a proxy server incoming connections will presumably fail, even when outgoing ones succeed, since the initiating client doesn't know that it should contact the proxy server. Therefore, if you tell your ICQ client that you are using a proxy server, it will route conversations through the ICQ server (via the proxy server) instead of directly to the other client.

Network Address Translation Characteristics of ICQ

ICQ uses embedded port number information to set up direct client-to-client communications. In general, this will not work through network address translation, and clients behind a network address translation system will be able to contact the servers at Mirabilis, and to send direct client-to-client messages, but not to receive them. However, if you set up static inbound mappings for the port numbers that ICQ uses, direct client-to-client communication will be possible.

Summary of Recommendations for ICQ

- Do not allow ICQ through your firewall.
- If you must run ICQ, consider using a victim machine to do it.

talk

talk is a text-based real-time two-person conferencing system; it allows two people to establish a "chat" session with each other. Each of their screens gets split into two sections; what one person types appears in one section; what the other person types appears in the other section.

talk is very convoluted in that it uses UDP to negotiate the connections between the two sites and then uses TCP to actually move the data back and forth between the participants. UDP is used between the calling client and the answering server, and again between the answering client and the calling server; TCP is then used between the two clients.

To further complicate matters, there are two incompatible versions of the *talk* protocol, commonly referred to as either *talk* and *ntalk* (for "new talk") or *otalk* (for "old talk") and *talk*, depending on who you ask. The earlier version depended on bytes being in a certain order in memory and only worked reliably between machines of the same CPU type. The later version fixes this problem but is incompatible with the earlier version.

The calling client contacts the answering server via UDP to announce the call. The answering server tells the user being called that someone is requesting a *talk* session and how the user should respond in order to accept the call. While waiting for the user to respond, the calling client also contacts the calling server to say that it's expecting an incoming call and to specify what TCP port it wishes to use for that call (somewhat like calling your secretary to say that you're expecting a call back from someone and that it should be put through to the extension you're currently at). When the answering user accepts, that user's client (the answering client) contacts the calling server via UDP to find out what port the calling client is waiting on; the answering client then contacts the calling client on that TCP port. Figure 19-2 shows how *talk* works.

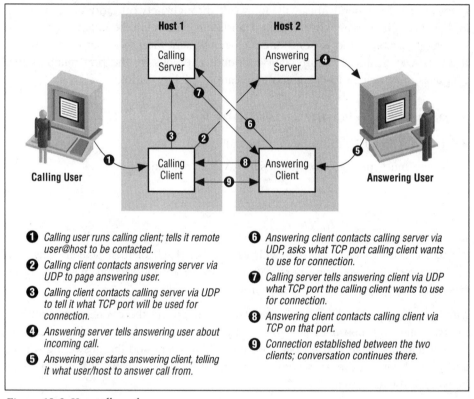

Host 1   **Host 2**

Calling User

Answering User

❶ Calling user runs calling client; tells it remote user@host to be contacted.

❷ Calling client contacts answering server via UDP to page answering user.

❸ Calling client contacts calling server via UDP to tell it what TCP port will be used for connection.

❹ Answering server tells answering user about incoming call.

❺ Answering user starts answering client, telling it what user/host to answer call from.

❻ Answering client contacts calling server via UDP, asks what TCP port calling client wants to use for connection.

❼ Calling server tells answering client via UDP what TCP port the calling client wants to use for connection.

❽ Answering client contacts calling client via TCP on that port.

❾ Connection established between the two clients; conversation continues there.

Figure 19-2. How talk works

Because of the incompatible *talk* protocols, *talk* fails relatively often even between sites that do no packet filtering, or between machines of different types within the same site. *talk* clients and servers are generally provided only on Unix machines.

Packet Filtering Characteristics of talk

talk servers (which broker connections between *talk* clients and then get out of the way) use either UDP port 517 (for old versions of *talk*) or UDP port 518 (for newer versions). *talk* clients use UDP ports above 1023 to interact with *talk* servers. *talk* clients also use TCP ports above 1023 to interact with each other. This means that, in order to allow *talk* across your firewall, you'd have to allow TCP connections where both ends are using arbitrary ports above 1023; this isn't safe because of vulnerabilities like X11 servers that use ports above 1023.

Direction	Source Addr.	Dest. Addr.	Protocol	Source Port	Dest. Port	ACK Set	Notes
In	Ext	Int	UDP	>1023	517 518[a]	[b]	External client contacting internal server
Out	Int	Ext	UDP	517 518[a]	>1023	[b]	Internal server answering external client
Out	Int	Ext	UDP	>1023	517 518 [a]	[b]	Internal client contacting external server
In	Ext	Int	UDP	517 518[a]	>1023	[b]	External server answering internal client
Out	Int	Ext	TCP	>1023	>1023	[c]	Internal client communicating with external client
In	Ext	Int	TCP	>1023	>1023	[c]	External client communicating with internal client

[a] Old versions of *talk* use port 517; newer versions use port 518.
[b] UDP has no ACK equivalent.
[c] ACK is not set on the first packet of this type (establishing connection) but will be set on the rest.

Proxying Characteristics of talk

No proxies are available for *talk*. It would theoretically be possible to write one. Because *talk* involves internal and external clients simultaneously, it would almost have to be a modified-procedure proxy server. (No generic server would handle it, in any case, because it involves both TCP and UDP.) Given the considerable difficulty of writing a *talk* proxy, and the extreme fragility of the process, it's unlikely that one will become available. *talk* has been almost altogether abandoned for cross-Internet conversations, in favor of things like IRC and ICQ, described previously.

Network Address Translation Characteristics of talk

Because of the way *talk* negotiates port numbers and opens connections, you would need a network address translation system that was aware of *talk* in order to make it work. The network address translation system needs to pay attention to the port number negotiation in order to set up the appropriate translation for inbound connections.

Summary of Recommendations for talk

- It is impossible to safely allow *talk* through filters or to proxy it, so you can't allow *talk* between the Internet and your internal machines. If, for some reason, you absolutely must allow *talk*, you will need to put a victim machine on your perimeter net that is untrusted and has no confidential data, and allow users to log into it and run *talk* from there.

Multimedia Protocols

Up to this point, we've been discussing methods of exchanging real-time messages in text. There are also real-time messaging systems that allow the exchange of other kinds of data; these include Internet telephones, video conferencing systems, and application-sharing systems. These types of data require a great deal more bandwidth than plain text and often have more security implications.

Multimedia protocols tend to have several common characteristics. First, they normally use more than one port. They use multiple data streams in order to separate data with different characteristics and in order to maximize the efficiency with which they use network resources. Thus, they normally separate audio data from video data and use different channels for data going in different directions. They also separate the actual data from administrative commands, so that the port used to send video is not the same as the port used to say "Stop sending me video, I can't take it any more"; this maximizes the chances that the administrative commands will actually get through. The administrative functions are normally known as *call control*.

Most multimedia protocols use different lower-level protocols for data and for call control. Data is almost always sent over UDP, while call control is almost always sent over TCP. This is because the data needs a maximum of speed. It's not important if some packets are lost, as long as all the packets that get through are used as soon as they arrive. The call control, on the other hand, happens less often but must not get lost; it's worth the higher overhead of TCP in order to be guaranteed that commands will arrive.

Multimedia protocols are very difficult to protect adequately with firewalls. It would be hard to support any protocol that involved a large number of channels, going in both directions, and using both connection-oriented and connectionless protocols, but multimedia protocols further complicate the picture by requiring very high performance.

T.120 and H.323

T.120 and H.323* are International Telecommunications Union (ITU) standards for conferencing. T.120 covers file transfer, chat, whiteboard, and application sharing;

---

* In case you're curious, the letters "T" and "H" are the designators for the ITU subcommittees that produced the standard, and subcommittee designators are just given out in alphabetical order. They're not short for anything.

H.323 covers audio and video conferencing. These are both higher-level standards that use a number of lower-level protocols for various purposes, and you will occasionally hear people talk about Q.931, G.711, H.245, H.261, and H.263 in particular as parts of H.323, and T.122 through T.127 as parts of T.120. For most purposes, you don't need to worry about these lower-level protocols, which are used in conjunction with the higher-level protocols.

Neither the H.323 nor the T.120 standard requires implementors to provide any security. H.323 is used to carry audio and video data that will be presented to the user. Although this presents a risk of information leaks, it's not directly dangerous to the client except in the ways all protocols are dangerous to clients. Because H. 323 sets up a large number of incoming data channels, both UDP and TCP, there's a significant risk that allowing H.323 will allow people to attack other, more vulnerable services.

T.120, on the other hand, is inherently dangerous. Both file transfer and application sharing are directly attackable applications.

Packet filtering characteristics of T.120

When running over TCP/IP, T.120 uses a straightforward TCP connection on port 1503. (This is actually specified by T.123, which is the transport standard associated with T.120.)

Direction	Source Addr.	Dest. Addr.	Protocol	Source Port	Dest. Port	ACK Set	Notes
In	Ext	Int	TCP	>1023	1503	[a]	External client contacting internal server
Out	Int	Ext	TCP	1503	>1023	Yes	Internal server answering external client
Out	Int	Ext	TCP	>1023	1503	[b]	Internal client contacting external server
In	Ext	Int	TCP	1503	>1023	Yes	External server answering internal client

[a] ACK is not set on the first packet of this type (establishing connection) but will be set on the rest.

Proxying characteristics of T.120

Because T.120 uses a single TCP connection on a well-defined port, it is quite easy to allow through proxies. However, since T.120 allows both relatively safe uses (chat and whiteboard) and dangerous uses (file transfer and application sharing), it would be wise to have a T.120-aware proxy to enforce some security. Such proxies do not appear to be available yet.

Network address translation characteristics of T.120

T.120 will work transparently with network address translation.

Packet filtering characteristics of H.323

H.323 uses at least three ports per connection. A TCP connection at port 1720 is used for call setup. In addition, each data stream requires one dynamically allocated TCP port (for call control) and one dynamically allocated UDP port (for data). Audio and data are sent separately, and data streams are one-way; this means that a normal video conference will require no less than eight dynamically allocated ports (a TCP control port and a UDP data port for outgoing video, another pair for outgoing audio, another pair for incoming video, and a final pair for incoming audio). Figure 19-3 shows the connections involved in a generic H.323 conference. Note that four of the dynamically allocated ports will be established from the outside to the inside (regardless of which side initiated the conversation).

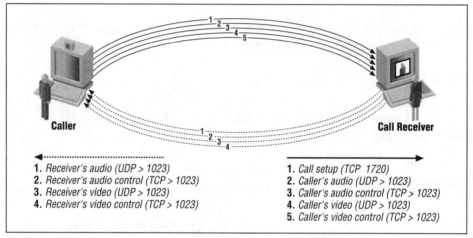

1. *Receiver's audio (UDP > 1023)*
2. *Receiver's audio control (TCP > 1023)*
3. *Receiver's video (UDP > 1023)*
4. *Receiver's video control (TCP > 1023)*

1. *Call setup (TCP 1720)*
2. *Caller's audio (UDP > 1023)*
3. *Caller's audio control (TCP > 1023)*
4. *Caller's video (UDP > 1023)*
5. *Caller's video control (TCP > 1023)*

Figure 19-3. An H.323 video conference, with audio

Direction	Source Addr.	Dest. Addr.	Protocol	Source Port	Dest. Port	ACK Set	Notes
In	Ext	Int	TCP	>1023	1720	a	External caller contacting internal callee
Out	Int	Ext	TCP	1720	>1023	Yes	Internal callee responding to external caller
Out	Int	Ext	TCP	>1023	1720	a	Internal caller contacting external callee
In	Ext	Int	TCP	1720	>1023	Yes	External callee responding to internal caller
Out	Int	Ext	TCP	>1023	>1023	b	Call control for data going internal to external
In	Ext	Int	TCP	>1023	>1023	Yes	Responses to call control for data going internal to external
In	Ext	Int	TCP	>1023	>1023	b	Call control for data going external to internal

Direction	Source Addr.	Dest. Addr.	Protocol	Source Port	Dest. Port	ACK Set	Notes
Out	Int	Ext	TCP	>1023	>1023	Yes	Responses to call control for data going external to internal
Out	Int	Ext	UDP	>1023	>1023	b	Data going internal to external
In	Ext	Int	UDP	>1023	>1023	b	Data going external to internal

a ACK is not set on the first packet of this type (establishing connection) but will be set on the rest.
b UDP has no ACK equivalent.

The extensive use of dynamically allocated ports makes H.323 very hard to deal with via packet filtering; in fact, Microsoft's instructions for NetMeeting (which is based upon H.323 and mentioned later) suggest allowing all UDP and TCP connections in either direction where both ends are above 1024. This configuration is extremely insecure, and we don't recommend it. However, it is the only way to allow H.323 through a nonstateful packet filtering firewall.

A stateful packet filter that can monitor the H.323 port negotiation would be capable of allowing only the needed data ports. Note that straightforward tricks like allowing only UDP responses will not work for H.323 because the incoming data streams from the remote host will not meet the normal criteria to be considered a response; the packet filtering must be H.323-aware. Unfortunately, H.323 is not particularly easy to parse, so H.323-aware packet filters are rare, although high-end packet filtering systems do offer them.

Because H.323 does not have any built-in authentication, allowing H.323 through a packet filter is not very secure, even if you use a dynamic packet filtering system that understands H.323. If you are concerned about transmitting confidential data, or about the security of your clients, you would be better off using a proxy that provides authentication features.

Proxying characteristics of H.323

H.323 has almost every characteristic that makes a protocol hard to proxy; it uses both TCP and UDP, it uses multiple ports, it uses dynamically allocated ports, it creates connections in both directions, and it embeds address information inside packets. The only good news is that the protocol provides a space where clients can specify a desired destination, making it easy for a proxy to figure out where connections should be directed.

One way of getting around the problems with proxying H.323 is to use what the standard calls a Multipoint Control Unit (MCU) and place it in a publicly accessible part of your network. These systems are designed primarily to control many-to-many connections, but they do it by having each person in the conference connect to them. It means that if you put one on a bastion-host network, you can allow both internal and external callers to connect to it, and only to it, and still get conferencing going. If this machine is well configured, it is relatively safe. However, it's not a true proxy. The external users have to be able to connect directly to the multipoint control unit; one multipoint control unit will not connect to another. The end result is that two sites that both use this workaround can't talk to each other. It works only if exactly one site in the conversation uses it. Several systems are available that provide this functionality, under various names.

It is also possible to get true H.323 proxies, which usually provide multipoint control and security features as well. In general, these are special-purpose products, not included with generic proxying packages. As we've pointed out, proxying H.323 is considerable work; it's not a minor modification to a normal proxy. However, vendors like Cisco and Microsoft that offer wide product ranges do offer H.323 proxying as part of specialized video conferencing products.

Network address translation characteristics of H.323

Because H.323 uses embedded IP addresses to set up the server-to-client connections, it will not work with straightforward network address translation. You will need a network address translator that is H.323-aware. These translators are rare because the IP address is not embedded in a fixed location; the network address translator has to actually parse the packets in order to be able to do the translation. This functionality is included in some of the H.323 proxies.

Summary of recommendations for T.120 and H.323

- Do not allow T.120 through your firewall.

- Use a special-purpose H.323 proxy that provides security features to allow H.323.

The Real-Time Transport Protocol (RTP) and the RTP Control Protocol (RTCP)

RTP is an IETF standard for transmitting real-time data (notably, audio and video). The most common use of RTP is actually as a lower-level protocol in conjunction with H.323. The standard for RTP actually details a pair of protocols; RTP transfers data, and RTCP is the control protocol. Some products that talk about RTP mean RTP in conjunction with RTCP, while others truly mean that they use RTP only, using some other protocol for control.

Packet filtering characteristics of RTP and RTCP

RTP and RTCP may use any underlying protocol. In TCP/IP implementations, they are normally UDP-based; they may use any pair of UDP ports, but RTP is supposed to use an even-numbered port with RTCP at the next higher port number. If

RTP is at an odd-numbered port, RTCP will use the next lower port number instead, so that they are always at two successive ports with the lower one being even numbered. RTP is assigned port number 5004 and RTCP 5005, but they also often use 24032 and 24033.

Direction	Source Addr.	Dest. Addr.	Protocol	Source Port	Dest. Port	ACK Set	Notes
In	Ext	Int	UDP	>1023	5004[a]	[b]	External RTP client to internal server
Out	Int	Ext	UDP	5004[a]	>1023	[b]	Internal RTP server to external client
In	Ext	Int	UDP	>1023	5005[c]	[b]	External RTCP client to internal server
Out	Int	Ext	UDP	5005[c]	>1023	[b]	Internal RTCP server to external client
Out	Int	Ext	UDP	>1023	5004[a]	[b]	Internal RTP client to external server
In	Ext	Int	UDP	5004[a]	>1023	[b]	External RTP server to internal client
Out	Int	Ext	UDP	>1023	5005[c]	[b]	Internal RTCP client to external server
In	Ext	Int	UDP	5005[c]	>1023	[b]	External RTCP server to internal client

[a] Or 24032, or any other port number, preferably even; see text for further explanation.
[b] UDP has no ACK equivalent.
[c] Or 24033, or any other port number, preferably odd; see text for further explanation.

Proxying characteristics of RTP and RTCP

RTP and RTCP are straightforward protocols, based on UDP. It would not be particularly difficult for a generic proxy system that supported UDP to allow them, but dedicated proxies for them are not widely available.

Network address translation of RTP and RTCP

RTCP may contain embedded hostnames and/or IP addresses as part of the sender description. This is not used to set up the connection but may reveal information that you wished to conceal. Aside from that, network address translation does not pose a problem for RTP or RTCP.

Summary of recommendations for RTP and RTCP

- You are unlikely to encounter RTP and RTCP being used by themselves; they are normally used in conjunction with other protocols as part of a larger package. They are not inherently terribly dangerous, so your approach to them will depend on your approach to the rest of the package.

NetMeeting

NetMeeting is Microsoft's conferencing program. It allows multiple people to connect for file transfer, chat, whiteboard, and application sharing, or two people to connect for audio/video conferencing.

NetMeeting is based on T.120 and H.323 but uses some extra protocols; Figure 19-4 shows a full-featured NetMeeting conference.

In addition to the normal security implications of T.120 and H.323, NetMeeting has had implementation problems, including buffer overflow bugs. However, most of the security concerns with NetMeeting involve the capabilities provided by T.120 and H.323. As NetMeeting has evolved, it has added more and more features to allow clients to place limits on what can be done. For instance, it is now possible for a client to allow audio/video conferencing without permitting file transfer or application sharing, and it is possible to require authentication. On the other hand, it is still extremely difficult for an administrator to force those controls on clients. There is no good way for an administrator to make sure that clients inside the firewall are safe from attack via NetMeeting.

Packet Filtering Characteristics of NetMeeting

NetMeeting uses T.120 and H.323, but in addition to their normal ports, it uses an extra audio call control connection at TCP port 1731, an LDAP-based locator service called the Internet Locator Service (ILS) at TCP port 389, and a proprietary locator service called the User Location Service (ULS) at TCP port 522. The connections involved are shown in Figure 19-4; the table shows only the ports that are special to NetMeeting.

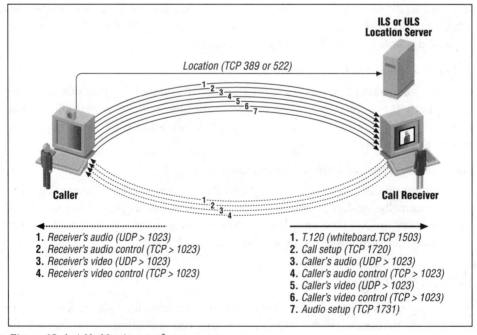

Figure 19-4. A NetMeeting conference

Direction	Source Addr.	Dest. Addr.	Protocol	Source Port	Dest. Port	ACK Set	Notes
In	Ext	Int	TCP	>1023	1731	a	External caller contacting internal callee, audio control
Out	Int	Ext	TCP	1731	>1023	Yes	Internal callee responding to external caller, audio control
In	Ext	Int	TCP	>1023	389	b	External client to internal ILS server
Out	Int	Ext	TCP	389	>1023	Yes	Responses from internal ILS server
In	Ext	Int	TCP	>1023	522	b	External client to internal ULS server
Out	Int	Ext	TCP	522	>1023	Yes	Responses from internal ULS server
Out	Int	Ext	TCP	>1023	1731	a	Internal caller contacting external callee, audio control
In	Ext	Int	TCP	1731	>1023	Yes	External callee responding to internal caller, audio control
Out	Int	Ext	TCP	>1023	389	b	Internal client to external ILS server
In	Ext	Int	TCP	389	>1023	Yes	Responses from external ILS server
Out	Int	Ext	TCP	>1023	522	b	Internal client to external ULS server
In	Ext	Int	TCP	522	>1023	Yes	Responses from external ULS server

a ACK is not set on the first packet of this type (establishing connection) but will be set on the rest.

Proxying Characteristics of NetMeeting

The protocols that NetMeeting uses in addition to T.120 and H.323 are relatively straightforward, so NetMeeting can be handled by any system that can proxy H.323 (as we discussed earlier, there are few such systems).

Network Address Translation Characteristics of NetMeeting

Because NetMeeting is based on H.323, it requires an H.323-aware proxy to handle the embedded IP addresses used for server-to-client connections. See the information earlier about H.323.

Summary of Recommendations for NetMeeting

- Do not allow NetMeeting across your firewall.

Multicast and the Multicast Backbone (MBONE)

As we discussed in Chapter 4, *Packets and Protocols*, IP supports three kinds of packets; *unicast* (addressed to a single host), *broadcast* (addressed to all hosts), and *multicast* (addressed to a group of hosts). Multicast IP packets look just like regular IP packets with destination addresses that are in the range 224.0.0.0 through 239.255.255.255. An individual address in this range (224.0.1.1, for instance) is called a *multicast group* (because it addresses a group of hosts).

Because of the nature of multicast, it makes sense only to multicast IP protocols that are not session oriented. One host cannot usefully set up a single session with multiple other hosts. Since TCP is session oriented, a TCP packet should never have a multicast destination address. Currently the only IP protocols that are normally seen with multicast destination addresses are UDP, IGMP, and OSPF. Similarly, multicast addresses are valid only as destination addresses, not as source addresses (a packet can't come from a group of hosts).

Multicasting is particularly useful when you're dealing with high-bandwidth loss-tolerant applications like audio and video conferencing. With such applications, you may have a number of stations all receiving the same stream of packets, and the stream may consume a significant fraction of the available network bandwidth. If a given stream consumes 10 percent of your available network bandwidth (which is not uncommon), you wouldn't want to unicast it to each interested host because each of these unicasts would consume another 10 percent of your bandwidth, limiting you to 10 participating hosts, and that assumes that you did nothing else with the network. You also wouldn't want to broadcast it to all hosts unless all (or almost all) of your hosts were actually interested in the stream because it places a significant load on each host to process a broadcast packet and then decide to ignore it.

Multicast groups are somewhat like cable television channels. A variety of channels (multicast groups), such as HBO, CNN, ESPN, and MTV, are available, but most homes (hosts) subscribe to only a few of the available channels. Some multicast groups are permanent; that is, certain addresses are reserved for certain uses, such as NTP, video conferencing of Internet Engineering Task Force (IETF) meetings, NASA Select video feeds (whenever the space shuttle is in orbit), and so on. Other multicast groups are transient: set up for a particular purpose or event and then shut down when they are no longer needed, to be reused for something else later on.

Multicasting is being used on the Internet today primarily for real-time conferencing services, including video, audio, and electronic whiteboard services. It's starting to be used for other services as well, such as transmitting Usenet news efficiently to a wide body of recipients.

Not all networks will pass multicast traffic. Some networks refuse to pass multicast in order to preserve network bandwidth, and others use routing hardware that doesn't understand multicast. In either case, it is possible to use multicast, while controlling the traffic that is passed, by using multicast *tunnels*.

A common approach to linking two multicast-capable networks (such as Ethernets) over a unicast-only network (such as a T1 leased line) is to create a *tunnel* over the unicast network, with multicast routers (often called *mrouters*) at either end of the tunnel. These *mrouters* take multicast IP packets, encapsulate them into unicast IP packets, and send them (via regular IP unicast) to the *mrouter* on the other end, which unencapsulates them to turn them back into multicast IP packets. By creating a web of *mrouters* and tunnels, you can create a virtual multicast network on top of a unicast backbone.

The MBONE is the ad hoc Multicast Backbone on the Internet and is just such a web of *mrouters* and tunnels. Its participants are sites that are interested in using IP multicasting for a variety of services on the Internet.

IP multicasting brings up several firewall issues. If a site uses tunneling to take part in the MBONE, what do the packets for the tunnels look like? What could be sent through the tunnels? If a site doesn't use tunnels, but uses IP multicasting directly, how will the site's packet filtering system deal with it? Can nonmulticast services (such as SMTP and NFS) be accessed by attackers via multicast, whether or not they're tunneled?

IP multicast tunneling is currently done with IP-in-IP encapsulation, which is discussed further in Chapter 4, *Packets and Protocols*. IP multicast tunnels used to be done with source-routed IP packets, but this practice caused a number of problems (not the least of which was upsetting folks who had firewalls), and it is no longer recommended.

To prevent a multicast tunnel from being used as a back door into or out of a network, the current publicly available *mrouter* code will only accept multicast packets through the tunnel; it won't accept unicast packets shoved through the tunnel in an attempt to bypass your firewall. If you're using a commercial multicast router, rather than the publicly available code off the Internet, you should verify that it will behave in a similar way.

If you have routers and a network topology that support multicast directly, without tunnels, you still have to worry about how any packet filtering system you use is going to cope with it. It shouldn't be too difficult, though, because from a packet filtering point of view, multicast packets look just like regular packets with somewhat unusual destination addresses (addresses in the range 224.0.0.0 through 239.255.255.255). Treat them just as you would anything else: block them all by default and allow the ones you understand and want to support. Keep in mind that each of these multicast addresses is going to apply to multiple internal machines, and that if you're accepting multicast packets from the outside world, then all of the internal machines that are accepting those packets will have to be protected against attack from the outside world—just as if you were accepting any other packets directly from the outside world. Multicast routing is handled by a special protocol called IGMP, which is discussed in Chapter 22, *Administrative Services.*

For a long time, multicast was used almost exclusively for multimedia, but there are now more and more uses of multicast for administrative protocols. This has made accepting multicast much more risky, since there are now vulnerable services (NIS under Unix, WINS replication under Windows NT) that support multicast.

Even if your tunnel is restricted to only multicast packets, or if you're using multicast directly without tunneling, and you have protected risky servers that support multicast, there is still the question of how your hosts will respond to multicast packets addressed to regular ports, such as your SMTP and NFS ports. Behavior varies from operating system to operating system, and even from release to release within the same operating system. If your operating system's code is based on release 3.3 or later of the "IP Multicast Extensions for BSD-Derived Unix Systems" from Xerox PARC and the University of Delaware, then your system should be safe against these kinds of attacks. Unless you installed the multicast extensions yourself, however, you could have a very difficult time determining what your operating system's multicast code is based on. (Your best bet is to ask your vendor, but don't be surprised if it's difficult to find anybody who knows.)

Summary of Recommendations for Multicast

- Block all traffic with multicast source addresses.

- Block all multicast traffic except for protocols you intend to support (usually just UDP).

- If you are tunneling multicast traffic, use tunnel software that will accept only multicast.

20

Naming and Directory Services

This chapter discusses services used to distribute information about machines, people and network addresses. This includes naming services, which translate hostnames to IP addresses (and vice versa) and more general directory services. The Internet standard for name service is the Domain Name System (DNS), but other protocols, including the Network Information Service (NIS) and the Windows Internet Name Service (WINS), are used to distribute this information within individual networks. In addition, this chapter discusses the Windows Browser, which is also used by human beings to find machines; the Lightweight Directory Access Protocol (LDAP), which is used for a wide range of directory information; the *finger* program, which provides information about people; and the *whois* program, which provides information about network ownership.

Domain Name System (DNS)

The Domain Name System (DNS) is an Internet-wide system for the resolution of hostnames and IP addresses. You will also see it called Domain Name Service. Unfortunately for the sanity of administrators, the Domain Name System and Microsoft Windows domains are different things. Microsoft Windows machines can and do use DNS (and it is required for Windows 2000), but a Windows domain is fundamentally a unit of authority that may or may not control the name of a machine. (Windows domains are discussed further in Chapter 21, *Authentication and Auditing Services*; they are also relevant to the Browser, which is discussed later in this chapter.)

DNS is a distributed database system that translates hostnames to IP addresses and IP addresses to hostnames (for instance it might translate hostname *miles.somewhere.example* to IP address 192.168.244.34). DNS is also the standard Internet mechanism for storing and accessing several other kinds of information about hosts; it provides information about a particular host to the world at large. For example, if a host cannot receive mail directly, but another machine will receive mail for it and pass it on, that information is communicated with an MX record in DNS.

DNS clients include any program that needs to do any of the following:

- Translate a hostname to an IP address

- Translate an IP address to a hostname

- Obtain other published information about a host (such as its MX record)

Fundamentally, any program that uses hostnames can be a DNS client. This includes essentially every program that has anything to do with networking, including both client and server programs for Telnet, SMTP, FTP, and almost any other network service. DNS is thus a fundamental networking service, upon which other network services rely. DNS service is a complicated subject, which we cannot discuss fully here. For more information about DNS, consult a DNS reference (for instance, *DNS and BIND* by Paul Albitz and Cricket Liu, O'Reilly & Associates, 1998).

Other protocols may be used to provide this kind of information. For example, NIS and WINS are used to provide host information within a network. However, DNS is the service used for this purpose across the Internet, and clients that need to access Internet hosts will have to use DNS, directly or indirectly. On networks that use WINS, NIS, or other methods internally, the server for the other protocol usually acts as a DNS proxy for the client. Many clients can also be configured to use multiple services, so that if a host lookup fails, it will retry using another method. Thus, it might start by looking in NIS, which will show only local hosts but try DNS if that fails, or it might start by looking in DNS and then try a file on its own disk if that fails (so that you can put in personal favorite names, for example). We'll discuss this later in this chapter. (One debugging tool that is very useful in this situation is *nslookup*, which is a pure DNS client. If the information you get from *nslookup* is not the same as the information you get when you try to resolve a hostname in another program, you know that the other program is not getting its information from DNS.)

In Unix, DNS is implemented by the Berkeley Internet Name Domain (BIND). On the client side is the resolver, a library of routines called by network processes. On the server side is a daemon called *named* (also known as *in.named* on some systems). In Microsoft Windows, the client-side libraries are less localized because of the complex possibilities for mixing native Microsoft protocols for name resolution with DNS. The server side is a server called Microsoft DNS Server, which is designed to be highly interoperable with BIND. BIND and Microsoft DNS Server are never perfectly interoperable—each one has its own special features and interpretations of the standards that are changed with each release—but they have a large overlap and are rarely actually incompatible.

DNS is designed to forward queries and responses between clients and servers, so that servers may act on behalf of clients or other servers. This capability is very important to your ability to build a firewall that handles DNS services securely.

How does DNS work? Essentially, the most common procedure goes like this: When a client needs a particular piece of information (e.g., the IP address of host *ftp.somewhere.example*), it asks its local DNS server for that information. The local DNS server first examines its own cache to see if it already knows the answer to the client's query. If not, the local DNS server asks other DNS servers, in turn, to discover the answer to the client's query. When the local DNS server gets the answer (or decides that it can't for some reason), it caches any information it got* and answers the client. For example, to find the IP address for *ftp.somewhere. example*, the local DNS server first asks one of the public root name servers which machines are name servers for the *example* domain. It then asks one of those *example* name servers which machines are name servers for the *somewhere.example* domain and then it asks one of those name servers for the IP address of *ftp. somewhere.example*.

This asking and answering is all transparent to the client. As far as the client is concerned, it has communicated only with the local server. It doesn't know or care that the local server may have contacted several other servers in the process of answering the original question.

The DNS protocol does not require servers to act like this. Servers do not have to maintain local caches, and they do not have to pass queries to other servers (they can refer the client to another server instead). In practice, however, all name servers in widespread use provide both caching and recursion (which is the term used in DNS circles to refer to the process where the server asks other servers if it cannot find the answer).

Packet Filtering Characteristics of DNS

There are two types of DNS network activities: lookups and zone transfers. *Lookups* occur when a DNS client (or a DNS server acting on behalf of a client) queries a DNS server for information—for example, the IP address for a given hostname, the hostname for a given IP address, the name server for a given domain, or the mail exchanger for a given host. *Zone transfers* occur when a DNS server (the secondary server) requests from another DNS server (the primary

---

* On some types of failures, some servers will cache the fact that the query failed. Others cache only information retrieved on a successful query.

server) everything the primary server knows about a given piece of the DNS naming tree (the zone). Zone transfers happen only among servers that are supposed to be providing the same information; a server won't try to do a zone transfer from a random other server under normal circumstances. You will sometimes see random zone transfer requests because people occasionally do zone transfers in order to gather information (which is OK when they're calculating what the most popular hostname on the Internet is, but bad when they're trying to find out what hosts to attack at your site). Some DNS servers allow access control lists to restrict which hosts can perform zone transfers. Adding an access control list doesn't really gain you very much; it might give you some protection against bugs in the implementation of zone transfers or may hinder an attacker using a script. However, the information can still be obtained by performing lots of individual DNS lookups.

For performance reasons, DNS lookups are usually executed using UDP. If some of the data is lost in transit by UDP (remember that UDP doesn't guarantee delivery), the lookup may be redone using TCP. There may be other exceptions (nothing actually requires clients to try UDP first or to ever try TCP at all). Figure 20-1 shows a DNS name lookup.

A DNS server uses well-known port 53 as its server port for TCP and UDP. It uses a port above 1023 for TCP requests. Some servers use 53 as a source port for UDP requests, while others will use a port above 1023. A DNS client uses a random port above 1023 for both UDP and TCP. You can thus differentiate between the following:

A client-to-server query
> Source port is above 1023, destination port is 53.

A server-to-client response
> Source port is 53, destination port is above 1023.

A server-to-server query or response
> At least with UDP on some servers where both source and destination port are 53; with TCP, the requesting server will use a port above 1023. Servers that do not use UDP source port 53 are indistinguishable from clients.

DNS zone transfers are performed using TCP. The connection is initiated from a random port above 1023 on the secondary server (which requests the data) to port 53 on the primary server (which sends the data requested by the secondary). In order to figure out when to transfer the zone, a secondary server must be able to do a regular DNS query of a primary server or to get a notification update (called a *DNS NOTIFY*) from the primary server. These notifications behave like normal server-server queries, except that they go from the primary to the secondary. Figure 20-2 shows a DNS zone transfer.

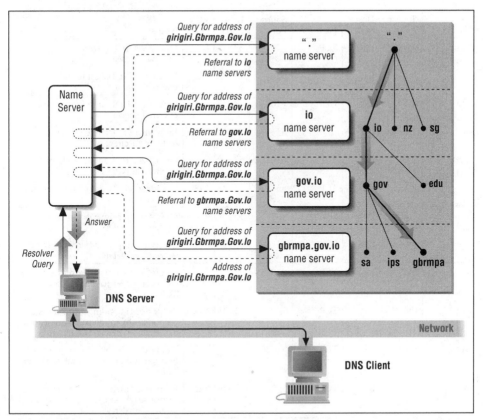

Figure 20-1. DNS name lookup

If your primary and secondary servers both support DNS NOTIFY so that the primary server can notify the secondary server of changes, you only need to allow TCP between them. DNS NOTIFY is required to be able to use TCP when UDP is unavailable, although it defaults to UDP. If you cannot use DNS NOTIFY, you may have to allow UDP between the two servers because the secondary server must be able to query the primary server and is not required to use TCP to do so. Most servers will fail over to TCP if UDP is unavailable, but the only way to be sure is to check what the servers you are running actually do. Note that DNS NOTIFY is a relatively recent addition and not all servers support it.

Direction	Source Addr.	Dest. Addr.	Protocol	Source Port	Dest. Port	ACK Set	Notes
In	Ext	Int	UDP	>1023	53	a	Query via UDP, external client to internal server
Out	Int	Ext	UDP	53	>1023	a	Response via UDP, internal server to external client

Direction	Source Addr.	Dest. Addr.	Protocol	Source Port	Dest. Port	ACK Set	Notes
In	Ext	Int	TCP	>1023	53	b	Query via TCP, external client to internal server
Out	Int	Ext	TCP	53	>1023	Yes	Response via TCP, internal server to external client
Out	Int	Ext	UDP	>1023	53	a	Query via UDP, internal client to external server
In	Ext	Int	UDP	53	>1023	a	Response via UDP, external server to internal client
Out	Int	Ext	TCP	>1023	53	b	Query via TCP, internal client to external server
In	Ext	Int	TCP	53	>1023	Yes	Response via TCP, external server to internal client
In	Ext	Int	UDP	53	53	a	Query or response between two servers[c] via UDP
Out	Int	Ext	UDP	53	53	a	Query or response between two servers[c] via UDP
In	Ext	Int	TCP	>1023	53	b	Query or zone transfer request from external server to internal server via TCP
Out	Int	Ext	TCP	53	>1023	Yes	Response (including zone transfer response) from internal server to external server via TCP
Out	Int	Ext	TCP	>1023	53	b	Query or zone transfer request from internal server to external server via TCP
In	Ext	Int	TCP	53	>1023	Yes	Response (including zone transfer response) from external server to internal server via TCP

[a] UDP has no ACK equivalent.
[b] ACK is not set on the first packet of this type (establishing connection) but will be set on the rest.
[c] Not all servers use 53 as a source port for UDP; some will use a port above 1023, like other clients.

Proxying Characteristics of DNS

DNS is structured so that servers normally act as proxies for clients. It's also possible to use a DNS feature called *forwarding* so that a DNS server is effectively a proxy for another server. The remainder of this DNS discussion describes the use of these built-in proxying features of DNS.

In most implementations, it would be possible to modify the DNS libraries to use a modified-client proxy. On machines that do not support dynamic linking, using a modified-client proxy for DNS would require recompiling every network-aware program. Because users don't directly specify server information for DNS, modified-procedure proxies seem nearly impossible.

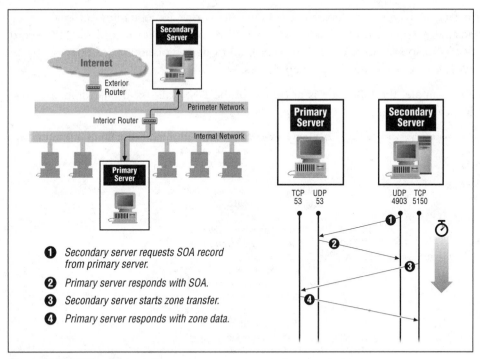

Figure 20-2. DNS zone transfer

DNS Data

DNS is a tree-structured database, with servers for various subtrees scattered throughout the Internet. A number of defined record types are in the tree, including the following.*

Record Type	Usage
A	Translates hostname to IP address
PTR	Translates IP address to hostname
CNAME	Translates host alias to hostname ("canonical" name)
HINFO	Gives hardware/software information about a host
NS	Delegates a zone of the DNS tree to some other server
SOA	Denotes start of authority for a zone of the DNS tree
MX	Specifies another host to receive mail for this hostname (a mail exchanger)

---

* For detailed information about DNS record types, what they mean, and how to use them, see the *DNS and BIND* book, referenced earlier in this chapter.

In fact, there are two separate DNS data trees: one for obtaining information by hostname (such as the IP address, CNAME record, HINFO record, or MX record that corresponds to a given hostname), and one for obtaining information by IP address (the hostname for a given address).

For example, the following is a sample of the DNS data for a fake domain *somebody.example*:

```
somebody.example. IN SOA tiger.somebody.example. root.tiger.somebody.example. (
                        1001        ; serial number
                        36000       ; refresh (10 hr)
                        3600        ; retry (1 hr)
                        3600000     ; expire (1000 hr)
                        36000       ; default ttl (10 hr)
                        )
                IN  NS      tiger.somebody.example.
                IN  NS      lion.somebody.example.
tiger           IN  A       192.168.2.34
                IN  MX      5 tiger.somebody.example.
                IN  MX      10 lion.somebody.example.
                IN  HINFO   INTEL-486 BSDI
ftp             IN  CNAME   tiger.somebody.example.
lion            IN  A       192.168.2.35
                IN  MX      5 lion.somebody.example.
                IN  MX      10 tiger.somebody.example.
                IN  HINFO   SUN-3 SUNOS
www             IN  CNAME   lion.somebody.example.
wais            IN  CNAME   lion.somebody.example.
alaska          IN  NS      bear.alaska.somebody.example.
bear.alaska     IN  A       192.168.2.81
```

This domain would also need a corresponding set of PTR records to map IP addresses back to hostnames. To translate an IP address to a hostname, you reverse the components of the IP address, append *.IN-ADDR.ARPA*, and look up the DNS PTR record for that name. For example, to translate IP address *1.2.3.4*, you would look up the PTR record for *4.3.2.1.IN-ADDR.ARPA*.

```
2.168.192.IN-ADDR.ARPA. IN SOA tiger.somebody.example.root.tiger.somebody.example.
(
                        1001      ; serial number
                        36000     ; refresh (10 hr)
                        3600      ; retry (1 hr)
                        3600000   ; expire (1000 hr)
                        36000     ; default ttl (10 hr)
                        )
            IN  NS  tiger.somebody.example.
            IN  NS  lion.somebody.example.
34          IN  PTR tiger.somebody.example.
35          IN  PTR lion.somebody.example.
81          IN  PTR bear.alaska.somebody.example.
```

DNS Security Problems

Some security problems with DNS are described in the following sections.

Bogus answers to DNS queries

The first security problem with DNS is that many DNS servers and clients can be tricked by an attacker into believing bogus information. Many clients and servers don't check to see whether all the answers they get relate to questions they actually asked, or whether the answers they get are coming from the server they asked. A machine that asks for the IP address of "malicioushost" and gets back the requested information plus a false IP address for "trustedhost", as well, may cache the extra answer without really thinking about it and answer later queries with this bogus cached data. This lack of checking can allow an attacker to give false data to your clients and servers. For example, an attacker could use this capability to load your server's cache with information that says that the IP address of a machine the attacker controls maps to the hostname of a host you trust for password-less access via *rlogin*. (This reason is only one of several why you shouldn't allow the BSD "r" commands across your firewall; see the full discussion of these commands in Chapter 18, *Remote Access to Hosts*.)

Later versions of DNS for Unix (BIND 4.9 and later) check for bogus answers and are less susceptible to these problems. Earlier versions, and DNS clients and servers for other platforms, may still be susceptible.

Some Unix DNS implementations will accept and cache answers even when they haven't made a query; some Microsoft implementations will crash if they receive an unrequested answer. Both of these behaviors are undesirable and have been eliminated by recent releases. Windows 2000 by default will only accept answers to queries but will accept those answers from any server. It can be configured to require the response to come from a queried server and should be on security-critical machines.

Malicious DNS queries

Not only are some DNS implementations vulnerable to hostile answers, some are vulnerable to hostile questions. In particular, some DNS servers have problems with buffer overflows and may crash or execute hostile code if a query is too long. (See Chapter 13, *Internet Services and Firewalls*, for more information about buffer overflow attacks.) If your log files show queries that contain very long "hostnames" containing control characters, people are probably attempting buffer overflow attacks.

Again, vendors have been working on eliminating these vulnerabilities, but you should check to make certain the appropriate patches have been made in the version you are running. There are known problems with versions of BIND 4 prior to 4.9.7 and BIND 8 prior to 8.1.2 (note that this does not guarantee that later versions don't also have problems that haven't been found yet).

Mismatched data between the hostname and IP address DNS trees

The attack that uses bad cached data to give you an apparently trustworthy hostname for an untrusted host points out the problem of mismatched data between the hostname and IP address trees in DNS. In a case like the one we've described, if you look up the hostname corresponding to the attacker's IP address (this is called a *reverse lookup*), you get back the name of a host you trust. If you then look up the IP address of this hostname (which is called a *double-reverse lookup*), you should see that the IP address doesn't match the one the attacker is using, which should alert you that something suspicious is going on. Reverse and double-reverse lookups are described in more detail later in this DNS discussion.

There are perfectly valid reasons for these checks to return inconsistent values; no rules require a forward and reverse lookup to return consistent information. In fact, when DNS is used for load balancing between servers, it is difficult to arrange for this consistency. In these situations, DNS is being used to determine the location of a service rather than the IP address of an individual host.

Any program that makes authentication or authorization decisions based on the hostname information it gets from DNS should be very careful to validate the data with this reverse lookup/double-reverse lookup method. In some operating systems (for example, SunOS 4.x and later), this check is automatically done for you by the *gethostbyaddr()* library function. In most other operating systems, you have to do the check yourself. Make sure that you know which approach your own operating system takes and that the daemons that are making such decisions in your system do the appropriate validation. (And be sure you're preserving this functionality if you modify or replace the vendor's *libc*.) Better yet, don't do any authentication or authorization based solely on hostname or even on IP address; there is no way to be sure that a packet comes from the IP address it claims to come from, unless some kind of cryptographic authentication is within the packet that only the true source could have generated.

Some implementations of double-reverse lookup fail on hosts with multiple addresses, (e.g., dual-homed hosts used for proxying). If both addresses are registered at the same name, a DNS lookup by name will return both of them, but many programs will read only the first. If the connection happened to come from the second address, the double-reverse will incorrectly fail even though the host is correctly registered. Although you should avoid using double-reverse implementations that have this flaw, you may also want to ensure that on your externally visible multi-homed hosts, lookup by address returns a different name for each address, and that those names have only one address returned when it is looked up. For example, for a host named "foo" with two interfaces named "e0" and "e1", have lookups of "foo" return both addresses, lookups of "foo-e0" and "foo-e1" return only the address of that interface, and lookups by IP address return "foo-e0" or "foo-e1" (but not simply "foo") as appropriate.

> For internal multi-homed hosts, you probably don't want to set things up in the way we've described; if you do, you may end up needing to list them by multiple names anywhere you want to give them permissions, such as in */etc/exports* files.

Dynamic update

It's very convenient for clients to be able to update DNS servers. For instance, at sites that use DHCP to dynamically assign addresses to computers, dynamic updates allow clients to have consistent names. When a client gets an address from DHCP, it can then register that address with the name server under the client's usual name. There is a standard for dynamic updates of DNS, but it isn't very widely used because it provides no kind of authentication. Some servers do provide authentication methods for dynamic updates (for instance, Windows 2000 allows you to integrate DNS with Active Directory and use Kerberos to authenticate update requests), but there is no widespread and interoperable standard for this.

Without authentication, dynamic update of DNS is extremely risky. You can't keep hostile clients from stealing addresses from each other or swamping the server in changes. Therefore, dynamic updates in DNS can be used only inside networks where there is a very high degree of trust.

Revealing too much information to attackers

Another problem you may encounter when supporting DNS with a firewall is that it may reveal information that you don't want revealed. Some organizations view internal hostnames (as well as other information about internal hosts) as confidential information. They want to protect these hostnames much as they do their internal telephone directories. They're nervous because internal hostnames may reveal project names or other product intelligence, or because these names may reveal the type of the hosts (which may make an attack easier). For example, it's easy to guess what kind of system something is if its name is "lab-sun" or "cisco-gw".

Even the simplest hostname information can be helpful to an attacker who wants to bluff his or her way into your site, physically or electronically. Using information in this way is an example of what is commonly called a *social engineering* attack. The attacker first examines the DNS data to determine the name of a key host or hosts at your site. Such hosts will often be listed as DNS servers for the domain or as MX gateways for lots of other hosts. Next, the attacker calls or visits your site, posing as a service technician, and claims to need to work on these hosts. The attacker will then ask for the passwords for the hosts (on the telephone) or ask to be shown to the machine room (in person). Because the attacker seems legitimate and seems to have inside information about the site—after all, the machine names are right—people will often grant access. Social engineering attacks like this takes a lot of brazenness on the part of the attacker, particularly if they're carried out in person, but you'd be amazed at how often such attacks succeed.

Besides internal hostnames, other information is often placed within the DNS—information that is useful locally but you'd really rather an attacker not have access to. DNS HINFO and TXT resource records are particularly revealing:

HINFO (host information records)
> These name the hardware and operating system release that a machine is running: it's very useful information for system and network administrators but also tells an attacker exactly which list of bugs to try on that machine.

TXT (textual information records)
> These are essentially short unformatted text records used by a variety of different services to provide various information. For example, some versions of Kerberos and related tools use these records to store information that, at another site, might be handled by NIS.

Attackers will often obtain DNS information about your site wholesale by contacting your DNS server and asking for a zone transfer, as if they were a secondary server for your site. You can prevent this either with packet filtering (by blocking TCP-based DNS queries, which will block more than just zone transfers) or by configuring your DNS server to control which hosts it is willing to do zone transfers to (although it will use the IP address to validate hosts and will be vulnerable to IP spoofing). The various versions of BIND control this in different ways (consult your BIND documentation for more information), while the Microsoft DNS server allows you to specify that only hosts that receive notifications may do zone transfers.

The question to keep in mind when considering what DNS data to reveal is, "Why give attackers any more information than necessary?" The following sections provide some suggestions to help you reveal only the data you want people to have.

Setting Up DNS to Hide Information, Without Subdomains

We've mentioned that DNS has a query-forwarding capability. By taking advantage of this capability, you can give internal hosts an unrestricted view of both internal and external DNS data, while restricting external hosts to a very limited ("sanitized") view of internal DNS data. You might want to do this for such reasons as the following:

- Your internal DNS data is too sensitive to show to everybody.

- You know that your internal DNS servers don't all work perfectly, and you want a better-maintained view for the outside world.

- You want to give certain information to external hosts and different information to internal hosts (for example, you want internal hosts to send mail directly to internal machines but external hosts to see an MX record directing the mail to a bastion host).

Figure 20-3 shows one way to set up DNS to hide information; the following sections describe all the details. This mechanism will work only for sites that use a single domain (all hosts are named something like *host.foo.example*, rather than *host.sillywalks.foo.example* and *host.engineering.foo.example*). If you have subdomains, you will need a more complicated configuration, which we discuss in the next section.

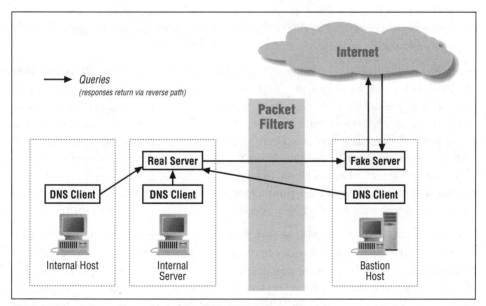

Figure 20-3. A firewall can be used to hide DNS information

Set up a "fake" DNS server on the bastion host
for the outside world to use

The first step in hiding DNS information from the external world is to set up a fake DNS server on a bastion host. This server claims to be authoritative for your domain. Make it the server for your domain that is named by the NS records maintained by your parent domain. If you have multiple such servers for the outside world to talk to (which you should—some or all of the rest may belong to your service provider), make your fake server the primary server of the set of authoritative servers; make the others secondaries of this primary server.

As far as this fake server on the bastion host is aware, it knows everything about your domain. In fact, though, all it knows about is whatever information you want revealed to the outside world. This information typically includes only basic hostname and IP address information about the following hosts:

- The machines on your perimeter network (i.e., the machines that make up your firewall).

- Any machines that somebody in the outside world needs to be able to contact directly. One example of such a machine is an internal Usenet news (NNTP) server that is reachable from your service provider. (See the section on NNTP in Chapter 16, *Electronic Mail and News*, for an example of why you might want to allow this.) Another example is any host reachable over the Internet from trusted affiliates. External machines need an externally visible name for such an internal machine; it need not be the internal machine's real name, however, if you feel that the real name is somehow sensitive information, or you just want to be able to change it on a whim.

In addition, you'll need to publish MX records for any host or domain names that are used as part of addresses in electronic mail messages and Usenet news postings, so that people can reply to these messages. Keep in mind that people may reply to messages days, weeks, months, or even years after they were sent. If a given host or domain name has been widely used as part of an electronic mail address, you may need to preserve an MX record for that host or domain forever, or at least until well after it's dead and gone, so that people can still reply to old messages. If it has appeared in print, "forever" may be all too accurate; sites still receive electronic mail for machines decommissioned five and ten years ago.

You can create a wildcard MX record that redirects mail for any hostname that there is no other record for. It looks like a normal MX record for a host named "*". However, you should be aware that wildcard MX records do not apply to names that have other records of their own. Any host that has an A record will require an individual MX record, even if there is a wildcard MX record; the same holds true for names of subdomains that have NS records.

You will also need to publish fake information for any machines that can contact the outside world directly. Many servers on the Internet (for example, most major anonymous FTP servers) insist on knowing the hostname (not just the IP address) of any machines that contact them, even if they do nothing with the hostname but log it. In the DNS resource records, A (name-to-address mapping) records and PTR (address-to-name mapping) records handle lookups for names and addresses.

As we've mentioned earlier, machines that have IP addresses and need hostnames do reverse lookups. With a reverse lookup, the server starts with the remote IP address of the incoming connection and looks up the hostname that the connection is coming from. It takes the IP address (for example, 172.16.19.67), permutes it in a particular way (reverses the parts and adds *.IN-ADDR.ARPA* to get *67.19.16. 172.IN-ADDR.ARPA*), and looks up a PTR record for that name. The PTR record should return the hostname for the host with that address (e.g., *mycroft.some-where.example*), which the server then uses for its logs or whatever.

How can you deal with these reverse lookups? If all these servers wanted was a name to log, you could simply create a wildcard PTR record. That record would indicate that a whole range of addresses belongs to an unknown host in a particular domain. For example, you might have a lookup for **.19.16.172.IN-ADDR.ARPA* return *unknown.somewhere.example*. Returning this information would be fairly helpful; it would at least tell the server administrator whose machine it was (*some-where.example*'s). Anyone who had a problem with the machine could pursue it through the published contacts for the *somewhere.example* domain.

There is a problem with doing only this, however. In an effort to validate the data returned by the DNS, more and more servers (particularly anonymous FTP servers) are now doing a double-reverse lookup and won't talk to you unless the double-reverse lookup succeeds. It is the same kind of lookup we mentioned previously; it's certainly necessary for people who provide a service where they use IP addresses to authenticate requests. Whether or not anonymous FTP is such a service is another question. Some people believe that once you put a file up for anonymous FTP, you no longer have reason to try to authenticate hosts; after all, you're trying to give information away. People running anonymous FTP servers that do double-reverse lookup argue that people who want services have a responsibility to be members of the network community and that requires being identifiable. Whichever side of the argument you're on, it is certainly true that the maintainers of several of the largest and best-known anonymous FTP servers are on the side that favors double-reverse lookup and will not provide service to you unless double-reverse lookup succeeds.

In a double-reverse lookup, a DNS client:

- Performs a reverse lookup to translate an IP address to a hostname
- Does a regular lookup on that hostname to determine its nominal IP address
- Compares this nominal IP address to the original IP address

The regular lookup can return different information from the original IP address in several situations. As we've discussed, they may return different information for legitimate reasons (the host is multi-homed or is using a wildcard PTR record) or because an attacker has provided illegitimate cached data. They may also be different if the attacker legitimately controls the name server with the PTR data in it but is returning other people's hostnames in the hope that services will use the results without checking them.

In order to make double-reverse lookups work, your fake server needs to provide consistent fake data for all hosts in your domain whose IP addresses are going to be seen by the outside world. For every IP address you own, the fake server must publish a PTR record with a fake hostname, as well as a corresponding A record that maps the fake hostname back to the IP address. For example, for the address 172.16.1.2, you might publish a PTR record with the name *host-172-16-1-2.some-where.example* and a corresponding A record that maps *host-172-16-1-2.some-where.example* back to the corresponding IP address (172.16.1.2). When you connect to some remote system that attempts to do a reverse lookup of your IP address (e.g., 172.16.1.2) to determine your hostname, that system will get back the fake hostname (e.g., *host-172-16-1-2*). If the system then attempts to do a double-reverse lookup to translate that hostname to an IP address, it will get back 172. 16.1.2, which matches the original IP address and satisfies the consistency check.

If you are strictly using proxying to connect internal hosts to the external world, you don't need to set up the fake information for your internal hosts; you simply need to put up information for the host or hosts running the proxy server. The external world will see only the proxy server's address. For a large network, this by itself may make using proxy service for FTP worthwhile.

Set up a real DNS server on an internal system for internal hosts to use

Your internal machines need to use the real DNS information about your hosts, not the fake information presented to the outside world. You do this through a standard DNS server setup on some internal system. Your internal machines may also want to find out about external machines, though (e.g., to translate the hostname of a remote anonymous FTP site to an IP address).

One way to accomplish this is to provide access to external DNS information by configuring your internal DNS server to query remote DNS servers directly, as appropriate, to resolve queries from internal clients about external hosts. Such a configuration, however, would require opening your packet filtering to allow your internal DNS server to talk to these remote DNS servers (which might be on any host on the Internet). This is a problem because DNS is UDP-based, and as we discuss in Chapter 8, *Packet Filtering*, you need to block UDP altogether in order to block outside access to vulnerable RPC-based services like NFS and NIS.

Fortunately, the most common DNS server (the Unix *named* program) provides a solution to this dilemma: the *forwarders* directive in the */etc/named.boot* server configuration file. The *forwarders* directive tells the server that, if it doesn't know the information itself already (either from its own zone information or from its cache), it should forward the query to a specific server and let this other server figure out the answer, rather than try to contact servers all over the Internet in an attempt to determine the answer itself. In the */etc/named.boot* configuration file, you set up the *forwarders* line to point to the fake server on the bastion host; the file also needs to contain a "slave" line to tell it to use only the servers on the *forwarders* line, even if the *forwarders* are slow in answering.

The use of the *forwarders* mechanism doesn't really have anything to do with hiding the information in the internal DNS server; it has everything to do with making the packet filtering as strict as possible (i.e., applying the principle of least privilege), by making it so that the internal DNS server can talk only to the bastion host DNS server, not to DNS servers throughout the whole Internet.

If internal hosts can't contact external hosts, you may not want to bother setting things up so that they can resolve external hostnames. SOCKS proxy clients can be set up to use the external name server directly. This simplifies your name service configuration somewhat, but it complicates your proxying configuration, and some users may want to resolve hostnames even though they can't reach them (for example, they may be interested in knowing whether the hostname in an electronic mail address is valid).

Figure 20-4 shows how DNS works with forwarding; Figure 20-5 shows how it works without forwarding.

Internal DNS clients query the internal server

The next step is to configure your internal DNS clients to ask all their queries of the internal server. On Unix systems, you do this through the *resolv.conf* file.* There are two cases:

---

* These days, clients may also keep DNS configuration information elsewhere—for instance, under IRIX 6.5 and above, DNS configuration parameters can also be put in the *nsswitch* file that will override the equivalent parameters in *resolv.conf.*

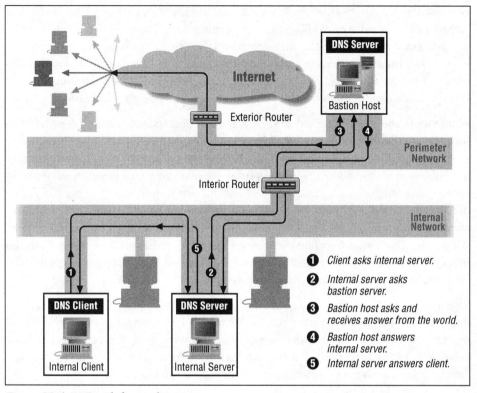

Figure 20-4. DNS with forwarding

- When the internal server receives a query about an internal system, or about an external system that is in its cache, it answers directly and immediately because it already knows the answers to such queries.

- When the internal server receives a query about an external system that isn't in its cache, the internal server forwards this query to the bastion host server (because of the *forwarders* line described previously). The bastion host server obtains the answer from the appropriate DNS servers on the Internet and relays the answer back to the internal server. The internal server then answers the original client and caches the answer.

In either case, as far as the client is concerned, it asked a question of the internal server and got an answer from the internal server. The client doesn't know whether the internal server already knew the answer or had to obtain the answer from other servers (indirectly, via the bastion server). Therefore, the *resolv.conf* file will look perfectly standard on internal clients.

In this arrangement special care is needed when configuring internal SMTP servers. Because such services have access to address information, they may try to deliver mail directly rather than through your mail gateway.

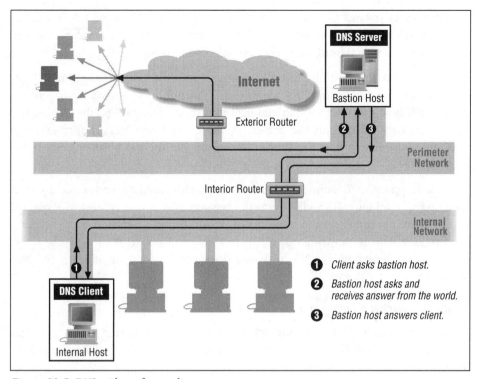

Figure 20-5. DNS without forwarding

Bastion DNS clients also query the internal server

The key to this whole information-hiding configuration is that DNS clients on the bastion host must query the internal server for information, not the server on the bastion host. This way, DNS clients on the bastion host (such as Sendmail, for example) can use the real hostnames and so on for internal hosts, but clients in the outside world can't access the internal data.

DNS server and client configurations are completely separate. Many people assume that they must have configuration files in common, that the clients will automatically know about the local server, and that pointing them elsewhere will also point the server elsewhere. In fact, there is no overlap. Clients never read */etc/named.boot*, which tells the server what to do, and the server never reads */etc/resolv.conf*, which tells the clients what to do.

Again, there are two cases:

- When a DNS client on the bastion host asks about an internal system, it gets the real answer directly from the internal server.

- When a DNS client on the bastion host asks about an external system, the internal DNS server forwards the query to the bastion DNS server. The bastion server obtains the answer from the appropriate DNS servers on the Internet and then relays the answer back to the internal server. The internal server, in turn, answers the original client on the bastion host.

DNS clients on the bastion host could obtain information about external hosts more directly by asking the DNS server on the bastion host instead of the one on the internal host. However, if they did that, they'd be unable to get the "real" internal information, which only the server on the internal host has. They're going to need that information because they're talking to the internal hosts as well as the external hosts.

Since it is possible to configure a DNS client with multiple server names, it is tempting to configure DNS clients on the bastion host to query both the internal and the external server, in the hope that they will try one and then try the other if the first one returns "host unknown". In fact, this will not work; a DNS client will try a second server only if the first one does not respond. It will accept "host unknown" as a valid answer.

What your packet filtering system needs to allow

In order for this DNS forwarding scheme to work, any packet filtering system between the bastion host and the internal systems has to allow all of the following (see the table for details):

- DNS queries from the internal server to the bastion host server: UDP packets from port 53 or ports above 1023 on the internal server to port 53 on the bastion host (rule A), and TCP packets from ports above 1023 on the internal server to port 53 on the bastion host (rule B)

- Responses to those queries from the bastion host to the internal server: UDP packets from port 53 on the bastion host to port 53 or ports above 1023 on the internal server (rule C), and TCP packets with the ACK bit set from port 53 on the bastion host to ports above 1023 on the internal server (rule D)

- DNS queries from the bastion host DNS clients to the internal server: UDP and TCP packets from ports above 1023 on the bastion host to port 53 on the internal server (rules E and F)

- Responses from the internal server to those bastion host DNS clients: UDP packets, as well as TCP packets with the ACK bit set, from port 53 on the internal server to ports above 1023 on the bastion host (Rules G and H)

Rule	Direction	Source Addr.	Dest. Addr.	Protocol	Source Port	Dest. Port	ACK Set	Action
A	Out	Internal server	Bastion host	UDP	53, >1023	53	a	Permit
B	Out	Internal server	Bastion host	TCP	>1023	53	Any	Permit

Rule	Direction	Source Addr.	Dest. Addr.	Protocol	Source Port	Dest. Port	ACK Set	Action
C	In	Bastion host	Internal server	UDP	53	53, >1023	a	Permit
D	In	Bastion host	Internal server	TCP	53	>1023	Yes	Permit
E	In	Bastion host	Internal server	UDP	>1023	53	a	Permit
F	In	Bastion host	Internal server	TCP	>1023	53	Any	Permit
G	Out	Internal server	Bastion host	UDP	53	>1023	a	Permit
H	Out	Internal server	Bastion host	TCP	53	>1023	Yes	Permit

a UDP has no ACK equivalent.

Setting Up DNS to Hide Information, with Subdomains

If your site has subdomains, you cannot simply set up a server for each subdomain and have it forward queries to a bastion host that has only external information. If you do this, a host in one subdomain will not be able to get information on hosts in other subdomains. When *host.sillywalks.foo.example* queries for *host. engineering.foo.example*, the name server for *sillywalks.foo.example* will notice that it does not have the information and will forward the query to the bastion host, which does not contain internal information and will not be able to respond to the query.

There are a number of solutions to this problem, which are discussed in detail in *DNS and BIND*, by Paul Albitz and Cricket Liu, referenced earlier in this chapter. None of them are perfect. One option is to set up every server so that it knows about every subdomain; this removes many of the advantages of having the subdomains in the first place. Another is to set up the bastion host so that it has correct internal information but refuses to give it out to external queriers (you use the *secure_zones* directive for this). This removes much of the security of having a separate bastion host name server.

You can also avoid the problem by avoiding query forwarding. If there is no forwarding, normal resolution will take place, and all of the subdomains will work. On the other hand, internal machines will not be able to resolve external hostnames to IP addresses and will need to have carefully configured proxying solutions to reach external hosts.

Setting Up DNS Without Hiding Information

The approach we've described in the previous section is not the only option. Suppose that you don't feel it's necessary to hide your internal DNS data from the world. In this case, your DNS configuration is similar to the one we've described previously, but it's somewhat simpler. Figure 20-6 shows how DNS works without information hiding.

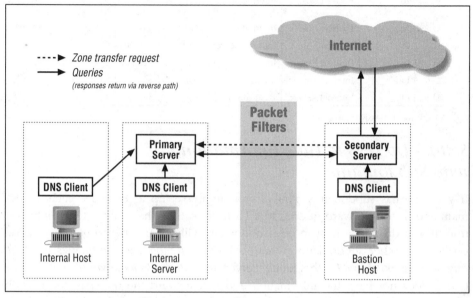

Figure 20-6. DNS without information hiding

With this alternate approach, you should still have a bastion host DNS server and an internal DNS server; however, one of these can be a secondary server of the other. Generally, it's easier to make the bastion DNS server a secondary of the internal DNS server and to maintain your DNS data on the internal server. You should still configure the internal DNS server to forward queries to the bastion host DNS server, but the bastion host DNS clients can be configured to query the bastion host server instead of the internal server.

You need to configure any packet filtering system between the bastion host and the internal server to allow the following (see the table for details):

- DNS queries from the internal DNS server to the bastion DNS server: UDP packets from port 53 or ports above 1023 on the internal server to port 53 on the bastion host (rule A), and TCP packets from ports above 1023 on the internal server to port 53 on the bastion host (rule B)

- Responses from the bastion DNS server to the internal DNS server: UDP packets from port 53 on the bastion host to port 53 or ports above 1023 on the internal server (rule C), and TCP packets with the ACK bit set from port 53 on the bastion host to ports above 1023 on the internal server (rule D)

If the bastion host is also a DNS secondary server and the internal host is the corresponding DNS primary server, you also have to allow the following:

- DNS queries from the bastion host DNS server to the internal DNS server: UDP packets from port 53 or ports above 1023 on the bastion host to port 53 on the internal server (rule E), and TCP packets from ports above 1023 on the bastion host to port 53 on the internal server (rule F)

- Responses from the internal DNS server back to the bastion DNS server: UDP packets from port 53 or ports above 1023 on the internal server to port 53 or ports above 1023 on the bastion host (rule G), and TCP packets with the ACK bit set from port 53 on the internal server to ports above 1023 on the bastion host (rule H)

- DNS zone transfer requests from the bastion host to the internal server: TCP packets from ports above 1023 on the bastion host to port 53 on the internal server (note that this is the same as rule F)

- DNS zone transfer responses from the internal server to the bastion host: TCP packets with the ACK bit set from port 53 on the internal server to ports above 1023 on the bastion host (note that this is the same as rule H)

Rule	Direction	Source Addr.	Dest. Addr.	Protocol	Source Port	Dest. Port	ACK Set	Action
A	Out	Internal server	Bastion host	UDP	53, >1023	53	a	Permit
B	Out	Internal server	Bastion host	TCP	>1023	53	Any	Permit
C	In	Bastion host	Internal server	UDP	53	53, >1023	a	Permit
D	In	Bastion host	Internal server	TCP	53	>1023	Yes	Permit
E	In	Bastion host	Internal server	UDP	53, >1023	53	a	Permit
F	In	Bastion host	Internal server	TCP	>1023	53	Any	Permit
G	Out	Internal server	Bastion host	UDP	53	53, >1023	a	Permit
H	Out	Internal server	Bastion host	TCP	53	>1023	Yes	Permit

a UDP has no ACK equivalent.

Windows 2000 and DNS

Windows 2000 uses DNS extensively; it is the primary method for name resolution, replacing Windows native modes of name resolution, which are supported only for older clients. Windows 2000 requires some DNS extensions that currently are in the standards process but are not yet accepted or widely used.

In particular, Windows 2000 consistently uses names that contain underscores. Traditionally, DNS names have been allowed to contain only letters, numbers, or hyphens (-). The underscore (_) has been forbidden by the standard. In practice, most name servers did not enforce these name restrictions. Although the underscore has been theoretically forbidden for many years, name servers that do not allow underscores became popular fairly late in the development of Windows 2000. At about the same time, a push to loosen the restrictions on allowable names began. This situation has not been resolved as of this writing; a standard under discussion would allow almost any character in a DNS name, but it has not yet been accepted. In the meantime, some servers enforce strict name rules and reject names with underscores; some servers follow tradition and accept almost any ASCII character; and some servers accept even more characters, including those outside the ASCII range (for instance, accented letters). Windows 2000 minimally requires a DNS server that will allow underscores. Windows 2000 allows machine names that use other characters outside the normally permitted types, and those names may create mysterious failures unless you use a DNS server that accepts them.

Windows 2000 also uses a record type, the SRV record, which has not yet been standardized. A number of DNS servers support SRV, including versions of BIND starting with 4.9.6 (and all versions of BIND 8).

Windows 2000 relies on the ability to do dynamic updates of DNS information. When machines boot, they need to be able to register names in the DNS server. Dynamic updates are supported by BIND 8 but not with the authentication mechanisms used by Windows 2000. Using BIND 8 to support Windows 2000 therefore requires using unsecured dynamic updates.

Windows 2000 DNS can use Active Directory as a storage and replication method. In this configuration, the DNS information is stored in Active Directory, and DNS is simply used as a method of accessing it. A DNS server that is integrated with Active Directory must be a primary server; it can send updates to other DNS servers via normal zone transfers but cannot accept them because it is not controlling the data. However, when Windows 2000 DNS is integrated with Active Directory, it supports secure dynamic update using Kerberos for authentication.

Network Address Translation Characteristics of DNS

There is no particular difficulty using network address translation with a DNS client that is having its address translated; the client's address is not embedded in the DNS transaction. Putting a DNS server behind an address translator is a different proposition. If the data in the server is about machines that are also behind the address translator, the address translator will need to operate on the data inside the DNS packets, not just on the source and destination addresses. Otherwise, the server will be handing out useless information. Some network address translation systems are capable of doing this, although some of them will translate only responses to queries, not zone transfers.

Summary of Recommendations for DNS

- Set up an external DNS server on a bastion host for the outside world to access.

- Do not make HINFO records visible to the outside world; either don't use them, or configure DNS for information hiding as described earlier.

- Use an up-to-date BIND implementation and double-reverse lookups to avoid spoofing.

- Consider hiding all internal DNS data and using forwarding and fake records; this doesn't make sense for all sites, but it might for yours.

- Disable zone transfers to anyone but your secondaries, using packet filtering or the mechanism supported by your DNS server. Even if you've chosen not to hide your DNS information, there's probably no valid reason for anyone but your secondaries to do a zone transfer, and disallowing zone transfers makes life a bit harder for attackers.

Network Information Service (NIS)

NIS* is a protocol primarily used under Unix and designed to provide distributed access to centralized administrative information (such as host tables, password files, site-wide email aliases, and so on) shared by machines at a site. The advantage of NIS over DNS for hostname resolution on a local area network is that NIS is a broadcast-based protocol; clients do not have to have all of the configuration information necessary for them to use DNS. In addition, having a unified mechanism that distributes all of the administrative information simplifies site administration.

The main problem with NIS is that its security isn't good enough to adequately protect some of the data it contains. In particular, a site's NIS servers generally contain the site's shared password file (equivalent to the */etc/passwd* file on a single system), complete with encrypted passwords. All you need to get data from an NIS server is the NIS domain name with which the data is associated. An attacker who can talk to a site's NIS server, and who can guess what the site has chosen as its NIS domain name (often the same as, or a derivative of, its regular Internet domain name), can request any information the server has. If the attacker gets the

---

* NIS was formerly known as Yellow Pages (YP), and some commands still preserve this abbreviation.

shared password file, these passwords can be cracked at the attacker's leisure. You therefore do not want to allow NIS requests inbound.

> NIS transfers may include the encrypted passwords even if the machines are configured to use shadow passwords and the encrypted passwords are not readable on the NIS server. If NIS transfers do not include encrypted passwords, they cannot be used for authentication, so implementations that close this hole simply do not allow you to use both NIS and shadow passwords.

There is no reason to allow NIS requests outbound because most of the information provided is local to an individual site, and most NIS servers will act as gateways to DNS for external hostname information when correctly configured.

A revised version of NIS, called NIS+, is available from some vendors. (It is the default version used on Suns.) NIS+ has not achieved wide acceptance, partly because of licensing and compatibility issues, but mostly because the majority of sites have managed to work around the deficiencies of NIS already, and therefore aren't motivated to switch to something new. NIS+ improves security only if it is configured so that it will not support NIS If you configure NIS+ to support NIS clients (and because few NIS+ clients are available, most NIS+ sites do use it in this mode), it is no more secure than original NIS.

A few NIS servers (notably Sun's) support a configuration file called *securenets*, which allows you to use IP address authentication to control which hosts your NIS server will release data to. This is an order of magnitude improvement in NIS security. It changes NIS attacks from guessing games (guess the domain name and the NIS server, and you get a free prize) to requiring you to do all the same guessing and then make a serious effort to determine what addresses the NIS server will respond to and forge packets from them. Unfortunately, an order of magnitude is probably not enough of an improvement for data as crucial as your encrypted passwords. While *securenets* (if you have it available) will protect you from casual attackers who want to get into any site they can, it will not protect you from an attacker who knows your site and who wants to attack it in particular. The trick, then, is to prevent an attacker from talking to your NIS servers.

NIS is an Sun RPC-based service, generally provided over UDP. Although NIS is an especially vulnerable service, it is otherwise the same as every other RPC-based service. We do not know of special proxies or packet filters for it. NIS+ may be provided over normal RPC, but this removes much of its extra security; by default, it's run over Secure RPC. The packet filtering, proxying, and network address translation characteristics of RPC and Secure RPC are discussed in Chapter 14, *Intermediary Protocols.*

NIS clients may also use additional means to find servers. Older clients will do this via broadcast; newer ones will use multicast instead. Whichever method is used by clients, if you want NIS to work through a firewall, you will need to either make certain that the relevant queries are passed to the server, or explicitly configure clients with a server name.

Summary of Recommendations for NIS

* Don't allow NIS across your firewall.

NetBIOS for TCP/IP Name Service and Windows Internet Name Service

NetBT name service is the NetBT service used to translate NetBIOS names to IP addresses. There are two ways to get name service under NetBT: a broadcast mechanism in which each machine keeps a database, and a unicast mechanism in which there is a designated server. In theory, that designated server is called a NetBT Name Server, or NBNS. However, Microsoft's NBNS implementation is called Windows Internet Name Service (WINS). It's rare to see the general term "NBNS" used outside of standards documentation, even for non-Microsoft servers, which are technically implementations of NBNS, not WINS.

In order to minimize the inevitable confusion, we will call broadcast-based NetBT name service "NetBT name service", and unicast-based service "WINS". This reflects common usage and is no more arbitrary and confusing than any other naming scheme.

A NetBIOS name is up to 15 characters long.* NetBIOS names are "unqualified" (according to Microsoft documentation) which means two things:

* They must be unique within a server's area of control.

* They cannot contain periods.

There is no notion of hierarchy in NetBIOS. Only one machine can be named "foo", and there is no way to indicate in a name what server is responsible for it. In order to reduce problems with name collisions, Microsoft provides the concept of a NetBIOS *scope*, which strongly resembles a NIS domain; this is a string that

---

* Technically speaking, all NetBIOS names are exactly 16 characters long, and Microsoft reserves the 16th character for administrative use. Short names are automatically and transparently padded to 16 characters. To the user, this is indistinguishable from having names up to 15 characters long.

defines a group of machines that talk to each other. If you are using NetBIOS scopes, a machine's name needs to be unique only within the scope. By default, machines use a null NetBIOS scope. The NetBIOS name and scope taken together can be up to 255 characters long (effectively limiting the scope to 240 characters), and the NetBIOS scope can contain periods.

NetBIOS scopes are much more limiting than NIS domains. Machines that are in different NetBIOS scopes cannot speak any NetBIOS protocols to each other, including file and printer sharing. On controlled networks, this can actually be an advantage, as it provides a small security improvement; the NetBIOS scope setting effectively acts as a password for network access. This is a protection from accidental misconfiguration, not from hostile action. The NetBIOS scope is passed in cleartext across the network as part of the NetBIOS hostname, and any attacker can simply read it from valid packets (it is particularly simple because it is sent in broadcast packets, so no special ability to snoop the network is required.)

It is important to keep in mind that WINS and NetBT name service are merely variants on the same service. Clients that use broadcast resolution run their own name servers, and although they expect only broadcast-based queries, they will respond to unicast queries. Do not assume that you are safe from remote requests just because you have avoided running WINS; normal NetBIOS clients are still running name servers that will feed their own data and any other data that they have cached to anybody who asks them. As we will see later, even machines that use WINS exclusively must have servers running that will respond to unicast name queries in order to have full WINS functionality. This is one of the things that the "Server" service normally does on clients.

Even though these services are tightly interrelated, the same machine may run both servers, in which case the WINS server will get unicast packets and the NetBT name server will get broadcast packets (Unix aficionados will probably find this upsetting). This means that the two services will run completely independently and may have different data on them. A WINS server will not provide data gathered by WINS to a NetBT name service client, or data gathered by NetBT name service to a WINS client, even though the servers are running on the same port on the same computer. (Therefore, a machine that runs a WINS server but is not configured as a WINS client won't advertise its own services via WINS!)

Name Resolution Under Windows

For historical reasons, Microsoft provides multiple methods of name resolution. Windows 2000 uses DNS wherever possible, but other Microsoft Windows machines may use numerous methods to translate a name to an address, depending on their configurations. They may try multiple methods to translate the same name, attempting various things until something succeeds.

For this purpose, there are two kinds of names: possible NetBIOS names and non-NetBIOS names. A genuine NetBIOS name is one known to the NetBIOS name service, but a possible NetBIOS name is any name that is up to 15 characters long. (In theory, a name with a period in it is not a possible NetBIOS name, but in fact, it will be treated as one under some versions of Windows NT.) Names that are not possible NetBIOS names (that is, ones that are over 15 characters long) must be resolved via DNS. The methods recent Windows machines can use for possible NetBIOS names are:

- Do a local NetBIOS broadcast and see if a machine by that name answers.
- Check a local file named *lmhosts* or *hosts* for an entry with the relevant name.
- Do a WINS query.
- Do a DNS query.

In addition, they may have the information cached and therefore not need to look it up at all. Windows NT 4 machines that are WINS and DNS clients by default try these options in the following order:

1. Look in the machine's cache of name information; this includes information for machines that have been looked up recently and information from *lmhosts* that has been marked #PRE, and it may include information about hosts on the local network that have booted recently.
2. Do a WINS query.
3. Check a local *lmhosts* file.
4. Do a NetBIOS broadcast.
5. Check a local *hosts* file.
6. Do a DNS query.

Various configuration options will change this order (most notably, if DNS support is not configured, DNS and *hosts* will not be checked). Other operating systems prefer other orders. In particular, older operating systems may try broadcasting before doing a WINS query or may not support any method except broadcasting.

Microsoft has a complicated naming scheme for describing these options; a machine that does only broadcast is a b-node, one that only does WINS queries is a p-node ("p" for "point-to-point"), one that does broadcast and then WINS is an m-node ("m" for "mixed"), and one that does WINS first and then broadcast is an h-node ("h" for "hybrid"). This naming scheme is useful mostly for understanding Microsoft documentation, since knowing what kind of node a machine is does not tell you where in the process it consults DNS or *lmhosts*. However, you may wish to remember that "m-node" and "b-node" both mean a "machine that generates lots of annoying broadcast packets". As you can determine by careful reading of the definitions and the preceding steps, Windows NT machines configured to use WINS are normally h-nodes.

Clients may get DNS data without making DNS queries; WINS servers can act as gateways into DNS, and other machines may cache DNS data and return it in answer to NetBIOS queries. In some configurations, this will result in a puzzling situation where the clients cannot reach hosts with names over 15 characters long. Since these are not valid NetBIOS names, clients must speak DNS directly in order to resolve them.

Just to further confuse matters, Microsoft DNS servers are capable of acting as gateways to WINS servers, making WINS queries to try to resolve DNS queries. This has two advantages; it obviously simplifies DNS administration for sites that are already using WINS, by making it nearly nonexistent. More importantly, WINS supports dynamic host registration. When a host comes up, it tells the WINS server what its name and network address are. By contrast, standard DNS provides no way for a host to give this information to the server; the server must be preconfig-ured with the name-address mapping. (DNS and dynamic update are discussed earlier.) Forwarding DNS queries to WINS provides dynamic DNS registration with-out modification of DNS.

The *nbtstat* command will show you information about NetBT names on a machine. Using *nbtstat* to check NetBT naming information and *nslookup* to check DNS naming information will often help you straighten out questions about where information is coming from (and therefore what to fix in order to get things to work correctly).

NetBIOS Names

NetBT name service is used to resolve more than just hostnames. There are two basic types of NetBT names: unique names and group names. A unique name maps to exactly one IP address, while a group name may map to multiple IP addresses. Each of these has multiple subtypes, used for different purposes. For instance, one type of group name is used to indicate a multihomed host; another type is used to indicate an administrative group (all the printers, for instance); and a third type is used for showing domain and workgroup membership. Different types of unique names are used for different services. The sixteenth byte of a Net-BIOS name is used to indicate the type, and this byte is typically shown in hexa-decimal notation when names are displayed (you may see type 03 displayed as "0x03", "<03>", or "03h").

If you actually look at packet traces, particularly if you are using a packet trace system that is not aware of NetBT, you may see NetBIOS names in mangled form.

NetBT is based on DNS packet formats. DNS names are longer than NetBIOS names but can't contain the arbitrary hexadecimal values NetBIOS uses for type indicators. In order to make NetBIOS names fit into DNS name fields, NetBT applies a system that converts each byte of the NetBIOS name into two uppercase ASCII characters, which results in eye-catching, if incomprehensible, name strings. They are made even more noticeable by the fact that the mangling algorithm converts spaces, which are used for padding, into "CA", so that almost every name ends in "CACA". Many English speakers (including presumably the engineer who designed the algorithm) attach no special meaning to this string, but the repeating pattern is still very striking. For details of the name-mangling algorithm, see RFC 1001. If you are on a Microsoft machine, most packet sniffing programs will unmangle the names for you; if you are on a Unix machine, the Samba package contains name mangling and unmangling routines. See Appendix A, *Resources*, for information on how to get Samba.

When a computer boots, it registers multiple names of different types. These names are not necessarily based on the hostname of the machine; they are chosen according to the purpose the name will be used for. For instance, one of the NetBT names that machines normally register is a unique name for the Messenger service. This service is used to send messages, and if a user is logged in to the console of the machine, the Messenger service will be registered under the user's name as well as under the computer's name. This is designed to allow you to send messages to people by name (human beings rarely want to talk to computers, after all), but it means that NetBT name registrations will contain not only hostnames, but also usernames, and in many cases will let you figure out whether or not somebody is logged in to a machine.

A machine will also register a group name for the workgroup or domain it is part of. This does not make the machine a valid member of a domain; machines may register as parts of domains they don't belong to, and it will not have any security implications. For clients, there is no difference between the registration for a domain and a workgroup. Domain controllers will make some extra registrations; there is a group name for all of the domain controllers and a unique name for the primary domain controller.

In addition, machines that are running the Windows Browser server will register a number of special names used by this service. These name registrations are sometimes treated specially. See the section on the Windows Browser, later in this chapter, for more information about these names and their registration.

Group names can contain large numbers of hosts, which makes them expensive to maintain. As a result, WINS servers are allowed to skip a lot of the verification they do on hostnames when they're dealing with group names, and invalid group names may remain registered for long periods of time.

NetBT Name Service Operations

DNS is a simple question-and-answer system. NetBT name service, because it's dynamic, is nowhere near as straightforward. Clients and servers interact in numerous ways, in order to register names, refresh and release them, and look up other names. The details of this process are quite intricate, and despite the daunting amount of detail here, a number of special cases and possible interactions have been glossed over.

General principles of NetBT operations

There are some generalizations about how NetBT name service works:

- Queries may be broadcast or unicast, but responses are always unicast to the host that made the query.

- WINS servers respond to all requests with positive or negative answers (in fact, if a query takes any significant amount of time to process, they will return an intermediate answer called a *wait acknowledgment* or WACK). NetBT name servers dealing with broadcast requests, however, answer only if they have something to say.

- Clients will always repeat a query if there is no answer (even if it is a broadcast query to which no answer was expected).

Name registration

When a client starts up, it registers the names it wants to answer to, starting with a name registration request. Under NetBT name service, it does this by broadcasting the registration request; with WINS, the request is sent directly to the WINS server. In either case, it may turn out that some other machine already has a name the client wants, which will set off a procedure of name conflict resolution that's discussed later. A WINS server will always answer the request, while NetBT name servers will answer name registration requests only in order to dispute them. If the name is not already taken, the client will send out a name announcement that confirms that it has the name to the same place or places it sent the original request.

For a normally configured Windows NT machine that's trying to register the non-conflicting name "unique" and is configured with a WINS server address, the process looks like this:

1. The machine sends a name registration request for "unique" to the WINS server.

2. The WINS server updates its database and sends a positive response containing a time-to-live (TTL).

3. The machine broadcasts a name registration request for "unique" and gets no response.

4. The machine broadcasts another three name registration requests for "unique", just in case, and still gets no response.

5. The machine sends a name announcement to the broadcast address.

6. All machines that receive the broadcast cache the information temporarily, overwriting any previous entry they had for that name.

Name refresh

In order to keep WINS server databases free of old junk data, WINS servers hand out limited-time registrations. Clients need to send a name refresh request before the TTL given to them with the name registration expires. If they don't send a name refresh, the WINS server will eventually remove the name. This process is not particularly fast. Windows NT normally gives out registrations with six-day TTLs, so a client that goes away may still be visible in the database for up to six days if nobody tries to release or register the name.

Clients may also send out name refresh requests for reasons of their own (for instance, a client that changes its configuration to use WINS will send a name refresh request to the WINS server).

Name resolution

When a client wants to map a name to an IP address, it sends out a name query request, either by broadcast or to the WINS server. Every machine that has a mapping for the name will reply with that mapping. A WINS server will reply to the request even if it doesn't have the answer. Suppose "unique" wants to talk to "stupid", which is a misconfigured client on the local network that doesn't use WINS and didn't boot recently. The procedure will look like this:

1. "unique" checks its cache but doesn't find "stupid" there (if "stupid" had just booted, it would have worked).

2. "unique" sends a name query request to the WINS server.

3. The WINS server sends a negative response.

4. "unique" broadcasts a name query request.

5. All machines that know where "stupid" is, including "stupid" itself and every machine that's connected to it recently, return responses. "unique" believes the first answer it gets.

Name release

When a client shuts down or changes its name, it sends a name release request to the WINS server and/or the broadcast address to give notice that the name is now available. As usual, the WINS server will always respond, while other servers will respond only if they have something to say (in this case, if they reject the name release). A client that is trying to release its own name will consider a name released and continue if it receives any response to the name release request (positive or negative). If it gets no answer, it will try again before continuing.

Name release requests may also be sent by machines other than the client that registered the name. This is supposed to allow a machine to correct invalid data. A machine that receives a response from the server, but gets no response at that address, can send a name release request for the name. The WINS server will then do a name query request and release the name if it fails. Other servers will respond to name release requests only for names that they own, for which they will return negative responses. A client that tries to release somebody else's name pays attention to the contents of the response and does not release a name for which it gets a negative response.

Conflict management

What happens if a machine tries to register a name as a unique name, but it's already in use, or tries to refresh a name that some other host has registered? Using broadcasts, when a machine sends out the name registration request, the machine that already has the name registered will respond with a negative response. Machines that have conflicting cached data will not respond.

A WINS server has a somewhat more complicated task. It can't be sure that the existing record it has is for a machine that's still running—in fact, there's a significant chance that the existing record is actually for the same machine, and it's just been moved from one network to another. Therefore, the WINS server will check to see if the record is correct by sending a name query request for the name to the address it's registered at. If the host is still there, it will answer, and the WINS server will send a negative response to the new registration.

There's an important subtlety to note here. Machines that are not WINS servers normally receive name query requests only via broadcast; unicast name queries are the business of WINS. But name query requests used for conflict resolution and verification of third-party release requests are unicast, so non-WINS servers must answer them. Machines that don't run name servers cannot defend against conflicting name registrations, even if they otherwise use WINS.

Conflict management is one case where groups have a special exemption. If a host tries to register an existing group name as a unique name, the WINS server is not required to check that the group registration is still valid; it can simply reject the attempt.

WINS Server-Server Communication

As well as picking up information from clients as they boot, WINS servers can also exchange information with other WINS servers. This approach is used to provide redundancy and to allow name information to be propagated across large networks.

Unlike DNS servers, WINS servers have no hierarchical structure and do not normally forward queries from one server to another.* WINS servers that talk to each other are trying to cause both servers to have identical databases. The replication protocol uses several tricks to try to distribute only updates rather than entire databases between servers, but there is nothing like a DNS zone that would allow them to subdivide the database.

WINS server replication is a complicated topic, involving numerous options (for instance, WINS servers need not replicate symmetrically). The details are beyond the scope of this book but are covered in most references about Windows NT network administration (for instance, in Microsoft's *Windows NT Server Networking Guide*, Microsoft Press, which is part of the Windows NT Server Resource Kit). From a firewall point of view, the interesting points about WINS server replication are:

- WINS servers speak to each other over TCP port 42.

- WINS servers attempt to locate replication partners via multicast and will send out IGMP packets to register multicast addresses for this purpose. IGMP is discussed in Chapter 22, *Administrative Services*.

- No matter what kind of WINS replication you establish, a pair of replicating WINS servers will make connections in both directions (you cannot set up replication so that only one of the two servers needs to be able to initiate a connection).

WINS servers may have "push" or "pull" partners, but in fact, data is transferred between them only when the receiving machine requests it. A machine that tries to "push" data will simply inform the other machine that new data is available, and the other machine will then request the data.

By default, WINS servers will send data only to machines that are configured as replication partners. It can be reset via the WINS Manager or the registry. It should be left in the default mode to help prevent attackers from pretending to be replication partners and pulling the entire WINS database with all of its information about valid hostnames and usernames.

---

* The protocol allows a WINS server to answer a query by directing the client to query another server, but this facility does not appear to be used in practice; in any case, there is no direct server-server forwarding.

The WINS Manager

It is possible to control and configure WINS servers on remote machines with the WINS manager, which uses Microsoft RPC. The security implications of Microsoft RPC are discussed in Chapter 14, *Intermediary Protocols.*

Security Implications of NetBT Name Service and WINS

NetBT Name Service and WINS are very vulnerable and are much more sensitive than DNS. The information they provide is valuable to attackers; it's not just the hostname data DNS provides, which is already useful, but also information about what usernames are valid and whether anybody is logged in, plus structural information about what machines provide what services. This information gives all sorts of leads to further possible attacks.

In addition, these services modify their databases and take other actions based on information from clients, which vastly magnifies the risks. An attacker who can send packets to a WINS server can cause the WINS server to send packets other places, using it as an amplifier to spread denial of service attacks and as a gateway to get those attacks to networks that may not be directly vulnerable to the attacker. It's also easy for an attacker to contaminate NetBT name service and WINS databases with bad data, which is relatively difficult in DNS.

The protocols are more complex than DNS. The extra protocol layers and headers are all opportunities for implementors to introduce bugs that can become denial of service attacks. Some of these problems have already been found by accident by people implementing these protocols on other platforms and are fixed in recent versions; others are presumably lurking, waiting for malicious people to run out of easier targets.

Finally, DNS servers are relatively rare. Any given site has a handful. NetBT name servers are everywhere. Every machine that uses NetBT name service must also be a NetBT name server. For an attacker who is going after quantity, rather than quality, NetBT name service is a very tempting target; it has information-rich servers everywhere accepting queries and data from arbitrary hosts.

Packet Filtering Characteristics of NetBT Name Service

NetBT name service uses TCP and UDP port 137. Almost all NetBT name service traffic will be UDP; clients normally use TCP only if they issue a query via UDP and get a truncated response because the response is too long to fit into a single

UDP packet. However, servers will respond to any query via TCP. Microsoft implementations use port 137 for queries as well as responses. Some older versions will return UDP responses to port 137 regardless of the port the query was made from. Given that most requests are UDP, and both ends are at port 137, it is basically impossible to allow service in a single direction. (Since server-initiated queries are part of conflict resolution, it wouldn't help much anyway.)

Clients that do not use WINS will send queries to the broadcast address; responses always are unicast, as are WINS queries. WINS servers will try to use multicast to contact replication partners and will therefore generate IGMP packets (see Chapter 22, *Administrative Services*, for packet filtering details of IGMP). WINS server replication uses TCP port 42.

Direction	Source Addr.	Dest. Addr.	Protocol	Source Port	Dest. Port	ACK Set	Notes
In	Ext	Broadcast	UDP	137, >1023	137	a	Incoming NetBT name service query via UDP, client to server
In	Ext	Int	UDP	137, >1023	137	a	Incoming WINS query via UDP, client to server
Out	Int	Ext	UDP	137	137, >1023	a	Answer to incoming UDP query, server to client
In	Ext	Int	TCP	137, >1023	137	b	Incoming query via TCP, client to server
Out	Int	Ext	TCP	137	137, >1023	Yes	Answer to incoming TCP query, server to client
Out	Int	Broadcast	UDP	137, >1023	137	a	Outgoing NetBT name service query via UDP
Out	Int	Ext	UDP	137, >1023	137	a	Outgoing WINS query via UDP
In	Ext	Int	UDP	137	137, >1023	a	Answer to outgoing UDP query
Out	Int	Ext	TCP	137, >1023	137	b	Outgoing query via TCP, client to server
In	Ext	Int	TCP	137	137, >1023	Yes	Answer to outgoing TCP query, server to client
Out	Int	Ext	TCP	>1023	42	b	WINS server replication request from internal server to external server
In	Ext	Int	TCP	42	>1023	Yes	WINS server replication reply
In	Ext	Int	TCP	>1023	42	b	WINS server replication request from external server to internal server
Out	Int	Ext	TCP	42	>1023	Yes	WINS server replication reply

a UDP has no ACK equivalent.
b ACK is not set on the first packet of this type (establishing connection) but will be set on the rest.

Proxying Characteristics of NetBT Name Service and WINS

Microsoft provides something called a *WINS proxy service*, which turns broadcast NetBIOS name resolution requests into WINS requests, in order to allow non-WINS clients to use a WINS server. This is a form of proxying, although it also is changing the protocol in use.

It would be perfectly possible to do more traditional firewall proxying of WINS, but there do not appear to be any implementations available.

Network Address Translation Characteristics of NetBT Name Service and WINS

Because these protocols are attempting to maintain mappings between names and IP addresses, they frequently contain embedded IP addresses. Furthermore, these addresses are often deep in the content of the packet (not simply in the NetBT destination headers used by many other NetBT-based protocols). A network address translator would have to be aware of the details of the protocol in order to successfully translate all of the embedded addresses. In any case, you cannot save address space by using a network address translator if you run the name service through it, since all hosts will attempt to register their names and addresses.

Summary of Recommendations for NetBT Name Service and WINS

- Do not allow WINS queries or server replication across your firewall.
- Bastion hosts that are configured not to respond to name requests will be unable to defend themselves from other hosts that try to take over their names via NetBT. These machines should be statically configured into WINS servers or accessed via 16-character names that cannot be resolved with NetBT. See Chapter 10, *Bastion Hosts*, for more information.

The Windows Browser

The information that Windows machines display in the Network Neighborhood and in other places where you can pick a computer from a list comes from a server known as the Windows Browser. This is a separate service from name resolution and is not just dependent on name resolution, but also intertwined with it. In particular, machines use special names to locate Browser servers, and those names are sometimes registered and resolved exceptionally. The Browser service is responsible for most of the mysterious broadcast packets to port 138 that you will see on Windows networks, and a significant number of the mysterious headaches suffered by Windows administrators. The headaches are greatly magnified by the fact that very few people understand exactly what Browser service is supposed to do, let alone how it does it.

The Browser service is responsible only for maintaining lists of computers so that human beings can pick them from the list instead of having to be able to type the computer's name. The Browser does not list the resources actually available on the computer; it isn't part of WINS, much less the same thing as WINS; and it isn't involved in any direct interactions between servers and clients. It's not at all unusual for a machine to be visible via the Browser but not actually accessible, and this is not a problem with the Browser. If it is accessible but unintentionally invisible, that's a Browser problem but not a surprise.

Originally, Windows Browser service was entirely broadcast-based. A number of complicated changes have been made to allow it to work across routers, so that in theory if a network stays the same for long enough, and contains enough Windows NT machines, browsing information will stabilize and propagate across the entire network. For a complex network, this process may take a considerable amount of time and in fact will often take longer than the average delay between network changes.

Domains and Workgroups

Every machine on a Windows network must be part of some domain or workgroup. A *workgroup* is simply a collection of machines that share the same workgroup registration; there are no controls over what machines can be in a workgroup. Being a member of a workgroup is like being a sports fan; if you say you're part of the group, then you are.

A *domain* is an administrative entity where there is a centralized source of information (a domain controller). Joining a domain is like joining an exclusive club; you have to be admitted by the administration. Unfortunately, it is possible to create a workgroup with the same name as a domain.

The Browser service was created before domains, and as a result, it is not fully aware of the distinction between workgroups and domains. It treats them identically and pretends that they are domains (both by calling them domains and by assuming that every group of workstations that it knows about has a contactable domain controller).

Windows Browser Roles

A Browser server contains information about a single domain, which it gathers by listening to the registrations broadcast by machines at boot time. Since the Browser is primarily broadcast-based, many things about the Browser apply to the set of machines that are reachable by broadcast. For convenience, we'll call this set of machines a *subnet*, although depending on how you configure your network it may not technically be a subnet.

Most machines that know about Browser service are capable of being Browser servers, and it is perfectly legitimate for multiple machines on the same subnet to be Browser servers for the same domain or workgroup. These machines will use broadcast to elect a master browser. There will always be exactly one master browser per subnet per domain or workgroup. A single subnet may have multiple master browsers for different domains or workgroups, and a single domain or workgroup may have multiple master browsers on different subnets. Figure 20-7 shows a network with multiple subnets and multiple domains and the resulting browser configuration.

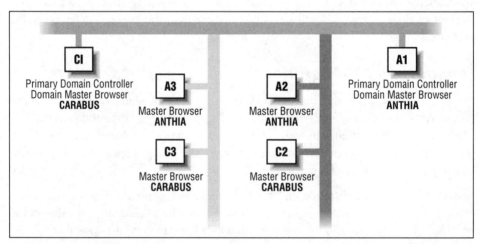

Figure 20-7. Master browsers in a network with multiple domains and multiple subnets

In general, users don't care about subnet boundaries; they want to know about all the machines in a domain or workgroup, regardless of what subnet they're on. Since Browser servers collect data via broadcast, it requires some mechanism for master browsers on different networks to synchronize information. In a workgroup configuration, there is simply no way for this to occur. Workgroups have no centralized structure. In a domain configuration, however, there is a central source of information (the domain controller), and the master browsers for a domain will all synchronize to it. The domain controller's centralized Browser server is called a *domain master browser.*

Browser servers do not initiate transactions to individual hosts by their normal names. Instead, the Browser sends out broadcast packets or unicast packets to special hostnames. The Browser does not need to know how to find other servers; it simply tries to send packets to the name that the server would be using if it existed. If no server is there, name resolution will fail (for unicast packets), or the broadcast will be ignored (for broadcast packets). The Browser simplifies things still further by not even attempting name resolution for most group names and simply sending out broadcasts with a destination NetBIOS name set. Hosts that are not part of the group will ignore the broadcasts.

The following sections describe the browser roles and the names associated with them.

Domain master browser

The domain master browser registers a unique name with the name of the domain and the type 1B. It is always the primary domain controller. Because it is a domain controller, it also registers a group name with the name of the domain and the type 1C. Aside from registering the name, the domain master browser takes no special actions. Other master browsers will initiate connections to it for synchronization. (This will be true whether or not there is an actual domain master browser, since the Browser assumes that everything is a domain. If there is no domain master browser, or it is unreachable, the amount of name resolution traffic will be significant as master browsers try to resolve the 1B and 1C names.)

Master browser

A master browser registers a unique name with the name of the domain and the type 1D. This represents a problem for WINS because WINS spans multiple subnets. It's legal for more than one master browser to exist, as long as they're on different subnets, but if they're all talking to the same WINS server, they shouldn't be able to register the name as a unique name. This is dealt with by having WINS treat the type 1D as special. WINS servers will return success for any attempt to register a unique name with type 1D, and failure for any attempt to resolve such a name. This allows the broadcast-based NetBT name service to handle uniqueness and resolution for master browsers.

A master browser also registers the group name _MSBROWSE_, which is used to distribute information among master browsers so that each one has the full list of available domains and workgroups.

Master browsers collect information from broadcasts to build up a list of all hosts in the domain or workgroup that they are responsible for, and to build up a list of other domains and workgroups and their master browsers.

Master browsers initiate four types of communication:

- They broadcast their lists of hosts and domains to the backup browsers (using the group with the name of the domain and the type 1E).

- They broadcast their domain and name to the other master browsers (using the group _MSBROWSE_).

- They synchronize their lists of hosts and domains with their domain master browser (using the unique name with the name of the domain and the type 1B or, if that fails, the group name with the name of the domain and the type 1C).

- They tell machines that are potential browsers to become backup browsers (using a packet that is an IP unicast but has a NetBT destination of the group name with the name of the domain and the type 1E).

In addition, master browsers get requests from clients and return lists of backup browsers.

Backup browsers

Backup browsers have two functions: they take requests from clients and return actual data, and they participate in elections to select a master browser. Backup browsers register a group name with the name of the domain and the type 1E.

Potential browsers

Potential browsers register a group name with the name of the domain and the type 1E. They participate in elections, but otherwise do nothing unless they are promoted to backup browsers.

Browseable server

Any machine that has a service that should show up in the browser sends an announcement every 12 minutes to a group with the name of the domain and the type 1D.

Browser client

A client that's in the domain "netherworld" and wants to look up a browse list for the domain "limbo" goes through the following steps:

1. Sends a GetBackupListRequest via a NetBT message at UDP port 138 to the special unique name "netherworld<1d>" (this is sent as an IP broadcast and is processed only by the local master browser).

2. Sends a GetBackupListRequest to the unique name "netherworld<1b>" (this is sent as an IP unicast because it's a unique name, and it goes to the domain master browser, which is also the primary domain controller).

3. Gets back two lists of servers, which contain computer names.

4. Selects three of the servers listed in the browser lists provided to it and saves them for future browsing.

5. Asks one of those three servers for a list of domains and workgroups; this comes back with the names of the domains or workgroups and the computer name of the local master browser for each one. This is a NetBT session conversation at TCP port 139.

6. Sends a name resolution query for the name "limbo<1d>" via broadcast to UDP port 137 (NetBT name service). This is a special query that is done over broadcast even on a machine that would otherwise try WINS before broadcast.

7. If step 6 succeeded, sends a request for a list of members to the machine "limbo<1d>". This is once again a NetBT session conversation at TCP port 139.

8. If there was no response to the previous request, resolves the computer name listed as the master browser for domain "limbo" by the machine's standard name resolution procedure and connects to it over NetBT session for a list of members.

If the client wanted a member list for its own domain, it would send that request at step 5. If there is no response to the initial GetBackupList requests, both requests are retried up to three times, and if there is still no response, the client starts an election. The client starts an election only if both GetBackupList requests fail.

Browser Elections

Elections are one of the best-documented parts of the Browser protocol; for the details on how they work, consult almost any book on Microsoft networking (for instance, Microsoft's *Windows NT Server Networking Guide,* mentioned earlier). In outline, the procedure is that a machine that wants an election to occur sends a packet to the IP broadcast address with the NetBT destination of the group with the name of the domain and the type 1E. This packet includes several parameters that indicate the machine's qualifications to be master browser. Each browser that gets the packet compares those qualifications to its own and sends another election packet if it is more qualified. A machine that sends out an election packet without getting a response from a more qualified machine will send out three more; once a machine has sent out four election packets without seeing a response from a more qualified machine, it will consider itself elected and send out a master browser announcement.

Because master browsers are important for the speed with which browsing works, elections are designed to prefer more stable machines. Election qualifications include a parameter that depends on the machine's operating system version (Windows NT Server is better than Windows NT Workstation is better than Windows 95), plus a parameter specific to the browser, which you can think of as an indication of how much the machine wants to win, and a parameter that depends on the machine's uptime (longer uptime wins). Master browser announcements include information about some of these parameters (in particular, the operating system type and part of the browser-specific information).

There are two situations in which machines will decide to call elections:

- A client will call an election if it tries to find a master browser and cannot. In this case, it will send out an election packet that is guaranteed to lose (all the parameters are set to zero). This is called an *election force*. If the client is also a potential browser server, it will not send out its real election packet unless it gets one from a less-qualified candidate, or it gets no response to repeated election force attempts.

- A browser server will call an election if it receives a master browser announcement from a less qualified machine. This should normally happen only when a more qualified machine boots onto a network (for instance, when a machine running Windows NT Server comes onto a network of machines running Windows 98). However, you may see less qualified machines boot and immediately claim to be master servers, thereby forcing elections on otherwise stable networks.

Security Implications of the Windows Browser

Obviously, the Windows Browser gives out security-critical information (valid hostnames). Less obviously, it has many fewer security implications than WINS does. The Browser provides information in bulk, unlike WINS, but it provides only hostname information, while WINS coincidentally provides much more sensitive information about valid usernames and current logins. Various sorts of denial of service and network flooding attacks can be carried out via the Browser, but the Browser has no equivalent of a WINS server that can be used as a magnifier and distributor to carry attacks to networks that the attacker is not connected to. You can spread misinformation via the Browser, but doing so is merely confusing; unless the misinformation is actually in NetBT name service as well, connections will simply fail.

This is all highly theoretical, however, since making the Windows Browser work requires making all of NetBT work. You can't allow the relatively safe Windows Browser without also allowing the highly unsafe NetBT name service. If you do allow all of NetBT, adding the Windows Browser is a relatively small decrease in security. (From a purely practical standpoint, as opposed to a security standpoint, we advise against it; while the security problem is small, the administrative problem is extremely large, and the Browser almost never works well, or even predictably, in complex networks.)

Packet Filtering Characteristics of the Windows Browser

The Windows Browser depends on NetBT name service at port 137 (UDP and TCP, broadcast and unicast), NetBT datagram service at port 138 (UDP, broadcast, and unicast), and NetBT session service at port 139 (TCP, unicast only). Packet filtering characteristics of NetBT session and datagram service are discussed in Chapter 14, *Intermediary Protocols*; NetBT name service is discussed earlier in this chapter.

Proxying Characteristics of the Windows Browser

Because the Browser is strongly based on broadcasts, standard proxying systems will not work with it. It is possible to use router configurations to forward broadcasts, but this is not terribly effective with the Browser because of the large amount of traffic involved and the multiple port numbers used.

Network Address Translation Characteristics of the Windows Browser

Not only does the Browser use NetBT (which has embedded IP addresses), it also relies on many-to-many communication via broadcasts. This is not a promising situation for network address translation. In particular, it is not possible to conserve address space using network address translation and the Browser, since all hosts must be able to speak to all other hosts. Furthermore, unlike many NetBT-based protocols, the Browser actually uses the embedded IP addresses in some situations and will need them to be correct.

Summary of Recommendations for the Windows Browser

- Do not allow access to the Windows Browser across your firewall.

Lightweight Directory Access Protocol (LDAP)

The Lightweight Directory Access Protocol (LDAP) is used to maintain directory databases. For instance, it is frequently used to distribute public key certificates, address book information, and user authentication information. It is rarely used directly by users; instead, it is a utility protocol that other programs use to look up information.

LDAP itself is believed to be a relatively secure protocol. However, LDAP servers frequently contain security-critical information (for instance, authentication information, which at best will allow an attacker to determine what account names are valid, and at worst may provide a password to use with them). Therefore, you normally do not want to make internal LDAP servers accessible to the Internet. LDAP servers pass information unencrypted, so snooping is possible.

LDAPS

In order to provide security, LDAP can also be run over TLS, providing encryption and server-client authentication. This is called LDAPS and is assigned to port 636. TLS is discussed in Chapter 14, *Intermediary Protocols*.

Packet Filtering Characteristics of LDAP

LDAP is a TCP-based service. Servers use port 389 (or port 636 for LDAPS). Clients use ports above 1023. Windows 2000 Active Directory Service uses an extra server, the global catalog server, that also uses LDAP but uses port 3268 for unsecured access and 3269 for SSL-secured access.

Direction	Source Addr.	Dest. Addr.	Protocol	Source Port	Dest. Port	ACK Set	Notes
In	Ext	Int	TCP	>1023	389[a]	[b]	Query, external LDAP client to internal server
Out	Int	Ext	TCP	389[a]	>1023	Yes	Response, internal server to external LDAP client
In	Ext	Int	TCP	>1023	636[c]	[b]	Query, external LDAPS client to internal server
Out	Int	Ext	TCP	636[c]	>1023	Yes	Response, internal server to external LDAPS client
Out	Int	Ext	TCP	>1023	389[a]	[b]	Query, internal LDAP client to external server
In	Ext	Int	TCP	389[a]	>1023	Yes	Response, external server to internal LDAP client
Out	Int	Ext	TCP	>1023	636[c]	[b]	Query, internal LDAPS client to external server
In	Ext	Int	TCP	636[c]	>1023	Yes	Response, external server to internal LDAPS client

[a] 3268 for active directory service global catalog.
[b] ACK is not set on the first packet of this type (establishing connection) but will be set on the rest.
[c] 3269 for active directory service global catalog.

Proxying Characteristics of LDAP

A large number of programs are available that claim to be LDAP proxies, but they are not all the sort of proxies that you normally think of in conjunction with firewalls. Many of them take LDAP queries and turn them into queries of other directories, using LDAP to give a unified view on complex information systems or providing transition service. Some proxies are intended to provide additional security, allowing you to use a single LDAP server for both internal and external service, by having the external users contact the proxy server.

Surprisingly, the Netscape Web browser does not use SOCKS when connecting to an LDAP server. LDAP is a perfectly straightforward protocol and can be used with SOCKS without problems.

Network Address Translation Characteristics of LDAP

LDAP does not use embedded IP addresses and will work through a network address translation system without problems. However, LDAP servers may give out referrals, recommending that clients contact other servers, and those referrals may contain IP addresses. If you intend to place an LDAP server behind a network address translation system, you should be careful not to configure the server to make referrals that are impossible for clients to follow.

Summary of Recommendations for LDAP

- If you provide LDAP service to the Internet, use a dedicated LDAP server that does not contain confidential information or a proxy that will control access to data.

Active Directory

Active Directory is the directory service used in Windows 2000. Windows 2000 uses DNS for its usual purposes (for instance, resolving hostnames to IP addresses) and Active Directory for information specific to Windows 2000 domain objects (for instance, information about user accounts). This can be confusing because Windows 2000 requires the DNS structure and the Active Directory structure to use the same names. A computer that is part of a Windows 2000 domain must have a DNS record that gives its IP address and an Active Directory record that holds the authentication information the computer uses to join the domain. These two records will normally have the same name.

Active Directory uses both DNS and LDAP to communicate with clients. Clients use DNS to find Active Directory servers and LDAP to query those servers. (As discussed previously, the DNS used with Active Directory may be an independent server or may be integrated with Active Directory.) In addition, Active Directory uses Kerberos for authentication (for instance, when authenticating clients in order to perform dynamic updates).

To distribute information between servers, Active Directory can use either RPC or SMTP. RPC is the default mechanism, and it is used for all communications within a single site. SMTP can only be used between sites (partly because it is not allowed in situations where both servers can modify the same information; in updates that occur between sites, each piece of information is owned by one end of the transfer, whereas in updates within a site, there is normally information that can be modified by either machine). Regardless of the mechanism that's used to distribute information, servers must have access to each other's certificate information in order to communicate because information is transferred in encrypted form.

Active Directory uses valid electronic mail messages when it is transferring data via SMTP. There is no need for the replicating servers to communicate to each other directly; the messages can be routed like any other electronic mail. SMTP is not a particularly efficient or rapid method of transferring the data, but it is extremely flexible, and it is easier to provide securely through a firewall than RPC. Active Directory does try to maximize efficiency on links between sites (no matter which transport is in use) by transmitting only changes and compressing data.

The firewall characteristics of DNS and LDAP are discussed earlier in this chapter, Kerberos is discussed in Chapter 21, *Authentication and Auditing Services*, RPC is discussed in Chapter 14, *Intermediary Protocols*, and SMTP is discussed in Chapter 16, *Electronic Mail and News*.

Information Lookup Services

The *finger* and *whois* services are very specialized sorts of directory services; they look up information about users and sites on the Internet and provide it in a human-readable format. They are relatively little used these days.

finger

The *finger* service looks up information about users. This information may include the person's real name, username, and information about when they most recently logged in and where they logged in from. *finger* can also be used to show the list of all users currently logged into a host. *finger* is designed to allow people to find each other, but it gives out more information than you probably want to make available. Intruders find it invaluable; it will tell them what the valid usernames on the host are, which of them are not in use, and when people are logged in who are likely to notice their activity.

We recommend that you limit incoming *finger* requests to a bastion host and that you run a replacement *finger* server on that host. Chapter 11, *Unix and Linux Bastion Hosts*, discusses how to construct and install a replacement *finger* server.

Outgoing *finger* requests are also mildly problematic. The *finger* protocol has no command channel to the client, so command channel attacks are nonexistent, but data-driven attacks are possible. Many *finger* clients do no filtering on the data they receive from the server (although the standards strongly suggest that clients should allow only printable ASCII characters). The attacks possible through this data channel are mostly annoyances; the nasty *finger* server sends back immense amounts of data or makes your terminal beep 400 times and start displaying black letters on a black background. Some of them are more serious. Some terminals are programmable with control characters, so that a *finger* server can send back data that reprograms the "e" key so that it executes the command "rm -rf/*" or a command that mails your password file. Such terminals are not particularly widespread these days (the most popular terminal emulators don't support this kind of thing), but they still exist, and so do terminal emulators that are overly faithful and reproduce these behaviors. If you are using intelligent terminals, or terminal emulators set up to emulate mainframe terminals with programmable function keys, you may be vulnerable.

In general, data-driven attacks on *finger* are not a major concern, but if your users frequently use *finger* to external sites—particularly universities, which have lots of people who still think making your terminal beep 400 times is amusing—you may want to run a replacement *finger* client that filters out control characters and limits the amount of returned data it will accept.*

A modified *finger* with an extended protocol is available from the GNU Project. This version of *finger* supports some useful features for large sites (for example, it lets one machine keep track of the most recent login times for an entire network so that users are not constantly complaining that they're incorrect), but it does not include any security enhancements on either the server or the client ends. Several pieces of information it makes available are clearly undesirable to provide to attackers (for example, it will provide a list of machines that are idle and/or have no users logged in). The security implications of the extended protocol it uses are unclear.

---

* This will prevent you from appreciating the cleverness of people who have managed to put animations in their *.plan* files using only VT100 control sequences, but that's not a major loss.

Packet filtering characteristics of finger

finger is a TCP-based service. Servers use port 79. Clients use ports above 1023.

Direction	Source Addr.	Dest. Addr.	Protocol	Source Port	Dest. Port	ACK Set	Notes
In	Ext	Int	TCP	>1023	79	a	Query, external client to internal server
Out	Int	Ext	TCP	79	>1023	Yes	Response, internal server to external client
Out	Int	Ext	TCP	>1023	79	a	Query, internal client to external server
In	Ext	Int	TCP	79	>1023	Yes	Response, external server to internal client

a ACK is not set on the first packet of this type (establishing connection) but will be set on the rest.

Proxying characteristics of finger

SOCKS provides a modified *finger* client for Unix, and *finger* clients on other platforms should be easy to modify to use SOCKS. Some *finger* servers support the notation *finger user@host@proxying-host*, which sends the request to the proxying host and from there to the destination host. If this form of proxying is available, however, it will work equally for external and internal users. External users will be able to use it to reach your internal hosts, which you may find undesirable.

Network address translation characteristics of finger

finger does not use embedded IP addresses and can be used with network address translation without problems.

Summary of recommendations for finger

- Limit incoming *finger* requests to a bastion host.
- Run a replacement *finger* service on the bastion host.
- Permit outgoing *finger* requests but consider running a replacement *finger* client.

whois

whois is another information-lookup protocol, much like *finger*. It is commonly used to obtain public information about hosts, networks, domains, and the people who manage them from various Network Information Centers (NICs), such as *whois.internic.net*. Sites generally don't provide their own *whois* server; they merely access the *whois* servers at the NICs. People don't expect other sites to run *whois* servers. *whois* clients are available for almost every platform and are sometimes embedded into other tools.

The data that is available via *whois* is not necessarily of much interest to normal users. It is really useful only as a way of tracking down what IP addresses belong to what organizations, and it's no longer easy to use even for that purpose, because many addresses have been allocated to service providers that then distribute them to their clients. In addition, there used to be only one NIC, which held all the information for the Internet. Now there are multiple NICs, and it may be necessary to query multiple ones before you find the one that holds the information of interest. Older *whois* clients do not do this automatically. At most sites, the only people who have any use for *whois* are system and network administrators. Many NICs also make the same data available via other methods, such as the World Wide Web.

On the other hand, there have been no known security problems with *whois* clients, and any that occurred would have to be data-driven. (All that a *whois* server can do to a client is to return data.) Because *whois* is almost never used with arbitrary servers, in order to do any real damage, somebody who manages to find a data-driven bug in a *whois* client would have to compromise, subvert, or forge packets from the most frequently used and most secure machines on the Internet. Furthermore, while *finger* shows data that was entered by random users, *whois* pulls its information from a central database. Therefore, if your users want to use *whois* clients, there's no reason to prevent them. If they don't have any particular desire to use *whois*, there's no reason to make it available.

Packet filtering characteristics of whois

whois is TCP-based. Servers use port 43. Clients use ports above 1023.

Direction	Source Addr.	Dest. Addr.	Protocol	Source Port	Dest. Port	ACK Set	Notes
Out	Int	Ext	TCP	>1023	43	a	Query, internal client to external server
In	Ext	Int	TCP	43	>1023	Yes	Response, external server to internal client

a ACK is not set on the first packet of this type (establishing connection) but will be set on the rest.

Proxying characteristics of whois

SOCKS does not provide a modified *whois* client, but such clients are available. Because *whois* is a straightforward single-connection protocol with plenty of user-specified data, it is trivial to modify *whois* clients for SOCKS, and relatively simple to write a modified-procedure proxy server for it.

Network address translation characteristics of whois

whois does not use embedded IP addresses and will function with network address translation without problems.

Summary of recommendations for whois

- You don't need to run an externally visible *whois* server.

- Don't allow incoming *whois* queries unless you put a server up.

- If you have *whois* clients available, allow outgoing *whois* queries from the machines your system and network administrators are likely to use. Otherwise, use web services to look up this data.

21

Authentication and Auditing Services

Services can get information about how to identify users, and what users are allowed to do, from various sources. For instance, they can keep local files (this is what Unix web servers do when they use "basic" authentication), or they can use the operating system's normal methods (this is what Windows NT web servers do when they use "Windows NT Challenge/Response" authentication). However, there is now a third popular option, a centralized authentication service that is independent of the specific service and the specific computer the service is running on. That service makes up part of something often referred to as an *AAA server*.

An AAA server (sometimes spoken as "Triple A server") provides authentication, authorization, and auditing services:

Authentication
> The process of obtaining verified, proven identification. Authentication determines who somebody or something is.

Authorization
> The process of determining what somebody can do. Don't confuse authentication and authorization. Authentication is a prerequisite for authorization (unless everybody is authorized to do something, such as anonymous FTP).

Auditing
> Provides information on when authentication and authorization was granted or denied.

Authentication services attempt to prove identity, to ensure that you know what person you are dealing with. This task can be very easy if it doesn't matter very much and you are in an environment you trust, or very difficult if people may be trying to deceive you. In many contexts, you'll accept someone's business card as an authentication. If you're suspicious, you may want something better, or you may want to check up on the information on the card. You might call the phone number on the card, for instance (but the person carrying the card certainly can control where that phone number goes). If you were really worried, you might get a phone number from an external source and call it.

Similarly, authentication services can be relatively simple when they're used on internal, trusted networks but are quite complex when they can't assume a basic level of trust. What happens if you're trying to verify that business card, but the person carrying it actually controls your telephone system, so no matter what number you call, that person can answer the telephone? That's effectively the situation you face when you're trying to authenticate somebody over an untrusted network connection.

Normal Unix password systems, and older Microsoft systems, use authentication methods equivalent to simply accepting business cards and trusting what they say. They use reusable tokens, and any time you give one out, somebody might be storing it away to use later while pretending to be you. Strong authentication services go to considerable lengths to ensure that what is transmitted over the network cannot be used to impersonate you at some point in the future.

Some services that are also sometimes used for authentication have been covered earlier in this book. For information on NIS and LDAP, see Chapter 20, *Naming and Directory Services*.

What Is Authentication?

Usually, people think of authentication in terms of passwords. Although passwords are frequently used for authentication, there are actually a variety of authentication mechanisms. These mechanisms can generally be categorized as verifying one or more of the following:

Something you are
> This is the field of biometrics, including techniques such as fingerprint scans, retina scans, voiceprint analysis, and so on.

Something you know
> This is a traditional password system.

Something you have
> This includes mechanisms such as challenge-response lists, one-time pads, smart cards, and so on.

Some systems combine these approaches. For example, a smart card that requires the user to enter a personal identification number (PIN) to unlock it is a combination of something you have (the card) and something you know (the PIN). In theory, it is considered a good idea to combine at least two mechanisms because people can steal either one: the thing you have is susceptible to ordinary theft, and the thing you know is compromised by sniffing if it passes over the Internet; but it's rare for somebody to be able to get both at once. Automatic teller machines use this combination. However, ATMs also demonstrate the flaw in the theory: when you are authenticating (standing at the ATM), you reveal what you have (your card) and what you know (your PIN) simultaneously, making yourself vulnerable to a thief who watches you use the machine to capture your PIN, then steals your card as you leave, or to a fraudulent ATM machine, which can pick up your PIN and your card at the same time.

Something You Are

Many types of biometric systems are in use or under development today; they test such diverse personal characteristics as your voice, your fingerprint or handprint, your retina, your signature, and your typing patterns. Biometric systems are extremely attractive because they get around the problems associated with using things that can be stolen or revealed. (Even the horror movie scenario of hacking off somebody's thumb to use in the fingerprint scanner is taken into account; most scanners insist that a pulse be present.) Unfortunately, biometric systems are not practical for normal Internet applications.

Most computers do not come with devices capable of reading fingerprints, much less retinas. Voiceprint technology is more tempting; it's not unusual for machines these days to have microphones. But it's not universal, either, and you can't guarantee that every machine you'll want to log in from has the high quality microphone, free disk space, and available network bandwidth required for this approach. Finally, if the biometric information has to be communicated from where you are to where it can be checked, you run the risk of an attacker's capturing it and replaying it later, unless you have some way of encrypting or otherwise protecting it.

Even if every machine had all the capabilities it needed, reliable voiceprint identification is surprisingly hard to accomplish. Many people wish to use their computers even when they have head colds, which throw off many voice-recognition systems. You can't use a fixed phrase as a password, or you would be vulnerable to a literal playback attack involving a tape recorder. (These problems have been addressed in dedicated systems, but no authentication systems widely available for general-purpose computers can deal with them, and it's not at all trivial to develop one.) You can't use a different phrase every time because voiceprint comparison on arbitrary text is not a real-time operation—unless you have a spare super-computer lying around to do it. Almost everybody wants to log in with a delay measured in seconds, at worst; getting back to the user with an answer in a few hours is not going to work.

Keystroke timing, used to characterize someone's typing pattern, is a surprisingly reliable biometric identification system and requires no special hardware. The computer provides a phrase to type and then times the gaps between characters as you type it. On a phrase of reasonable length, people type in an identifiable pattern, and imitating it is much harder than it looks. Like voiceprints, keystroke timings may change for environmental reasons; in the case of keystroke timings, colds aren't a problem, but people have great difficulty authenticating while drunk (which is not necessarily a disadvantage, of course). The genuine disadvantage is that keystroke timings can be gathered only at the machine to which the keyboard is attached. That means that use of this method across the Internet requires modified clients. In addition, some people, mostly poor typists, have trouble ever authenticating because their typing patterns are inconsistent.

Biometric solutions are slowly improving over time; the cost of the add-on hardware is dropping, and the effectiveness of the software is increasing. However, manufacturers have been promising that biometrics are going to be universally accepted Real Soon Now for many years, and there is no sign that they are likely to overcome the hurdles any time soon. If you have special security needs that warrant adding hardware to every machine that people may need to authenticate from, a biometric solution may be appropriate, but for most sites, biometrics are still in the distant future.

Something You Know

If the long-lost heiress to a fortune turns up in a novel, you can bet that fingerprints aren't going to be available to do biometric authentication. Instead, the claimant is probably going to try to prove that she is who she says she is because she knows the name of the stuffed animal she slept with at age three. This is authentication by knowledge, just like the traditional Unix password system. (And, just like traditional Unix passwords, the claimant's answers can be faked if she's a good guesser and gets enough tries.)

Authentication that depends on something you know relies on that something's being both hard to guess and secret. In order for you to authenticate reliably, you have to know the secret reliably, too. This isn't as easy as it sounds. Most people are bad at making up and remembering unguessable things, and they're worse at keeping secrets. If you use short keys, it's easy to guess them; if you use long keys, it's hard to remember them. If you write them down, you're basically converting to a different type of authentication; now, it's something you have.

System administrators who unblushingly tell their users never to write down passwords probably have a few stashed in their wallets anyway; this is a combination of "what you know" and "what you have". "What you know" is how to read your own handwriting, and which slip of paper contains the passwords, rather than last week's lunch order. "What you have" is the slip of paper itself.

Despite all of the risks of "what you know" systems, it is still practical to use them as long as you aren't revealing the secret to everybody in the near vicinity every time you authenticate. There is a reason why passwords are so popular: they're fast, they're cheap, and, in practice, people don't forget them or lose the pieces of paper all that often. However, it is absolutely impractical to pass them across the Internet in any form that can be used safely.

Is there any way to use a "what you know" system safely on the Internet? Yes— use passwords but make sure that they are nonreusable (one-time) passwords.

There are two ways to make traditional, memorized passwords nonreusable. One is to include an *encrypted timestamp*—this is the method that Kerberos uses. As long as you can't modify the timestamp without knowing the password, it prevents playback. Unfortunately, it requires two things:

- Special client software that knows how to timestamp the password.

- Synchronized time between the client and the server. If the server and the client have different times, the password will be either invalid already or not yet valid when it arrives.

The other way to make traditional, memorized passwords nonreusable is to use a *challenge-response system*. With such a system, the password you give depends on a prompt that the server gives you. Challenge-response is the traditional method for identifying yourself at a speakeasy, entering a military camp, or meeting fellow spies in art museums. It may seem to be an impractical approach, because in order to be reasonably safe from playback attacks, you need a wide variety of challenges, each with a separate response. If you have trouble remembering one password, you certainly aren't going to remember 47 of them.

In fact, however, challenge-response systems for computers are designed so that instead of memorizing the response to each challenge, you memorize a rule for converting the challenge into a response. This concept has yet to become popular as a pure "what you know" option because it's difficult to apply to a large number of people. A rule like "reverse the first three letters, capitalize the fourth, delete the fifth, and uppercase the rest of them" is easy to program, but it's not necessarily easy to represent so that you can have a different rule for each user. Even if you can remember your own rule, you're apt to follow along the challenge with a finger, muttering the rule to yourself while you try to implement it; someone watching over your shoulder can pretty easily determine the rule.

Some systems that present standard password prompts to the user then use challenge-response systems internally. This is what Windows NT challenge-response authentication does; the user gets a standard password prompt and provides a fixed password, but the dialog between the server and the client uses a challenge-response system.

Both Windows NT challenge/response and Kerberos are vulnerable to password-guessing attacks. If you use this type of system across the Internet, you will need to have both passwords that are hard to guess and good auditing systems to catch attempts to guess them. On most operating systems, including Windows NT and most versions of Unix, you will need additional software to force users to pick good passwords.

Something You Have

In practice, the most successful authentication systems for Internet use today are based on the third type of authentication: "something you have". What you have may be a printed list of single-use passwords or an electronic card; it's usually, but not always, combined with "something you know".

The use of electronic cards makes it practical to use challenge-response or time-based encryption. For challenge-response, you encode in the card itself the rule that converts the challenge to the response. For time-based encryption, you encode in the card both the time source and the encryption smarts. Either way, you can do authentication without needing modified clients or users with trick memories.

Using printed lists of passwords is generally referred to as using *one-time passwords*. This confuses people because all nonreusable passwords are good only one time, by definition. Printed password lists are called that because they resemble a spy device called a *one-time pad* that consists of a pad of paper with different instructions on each page. You encrypt one message with each page, so that the opposite side doesn't get multiple chances to break the code.*

Passwords

Since many authentication mechanisms depend on passwords, it's important to understand how passwords can be compromised. There are three ways of getting around a requirement for a fixed password:

*   Find a way to get the system to tell you the password.

---

* In fact, printed one-time password lists resemble one-time pads so closely that it's inadvisable to bring one to the attention of a customs agent when travelling internationally.

- Find a way to authenticate without knowing the password.

- Guess what the password is.

Systems like Telnet, where the password is passed across the network in cleartext, make it easy for attackers to get the actual password. So do systems where the password is stored on the computer in some way where it can be decrypted (this is common in third-party applications for Windows NT). Although this sort of problem is regrettably common, it's a pretty obvious design flaw, and systems designed with any regard for security usually manage to avoid it. Authentication that involves a cleartext or decryptable password is unacceptably poor for most purposes.

Systems that pass a hashed password around, but use the same hashed password each time, give attackers a way to authenticate without knowing the password. They can simply grab the hashed string and use it. This is not as convenient as knowing the actual password, since you can't use normal client programs and you usually don't get more than one kind of access, but it's still quite sufficient to do damage. Authentication that uses reusable tokens is also unacceptably poor for most purposes.

These days, most systems avoid these pitfalls, leaving attackers to guess what the password is. The only way to actually prevent password guessing is to use true one-time passwords where the password is different every time. However, it is possible to make it much more difficult by making the passwords relatively unpredictable and by making it hard to check the accuracy of guesses.

The first step in making passwords unpredictable is to make certain that there are a large number of possible passwords. This means allowing a wide variety of different characters and as many characters as possible. The mathematics are not intuitive to many people, who have a habit of thinking that if you double the size of the character set or the length of the password, you will double the number of possible passwords. Actually, you do much better than that. Suppose that you have a one-character password, and it can be any lowercase letter. In that case, there are 26 possible passwords. Adding a second character gets you 26 squared, or 676. If you allow both upper- and lowercase, that doubles the one-character case (there are now 52 possibilities), but it brings two characters up to 52 squared, or 2,704.

A standard Unix password is 8 characters long. The size of the character set it uses is a matter of some dispute; theoretically, any ASCII character, including control characters, is acceptable, giving roughly 127 characters. Most of them are difficult to type at best and frequently impossible to get typed in rather than interpreted. In practice, it's more reasonable to assume that the possible characters are limited to the ones actually on a keyboard, which leaves 84 characters. This gives roughly $2.47 * 10^{15}$ possibilities (247 trillion in the United States, 247 billion elsewhere).* The algorithm used to produce the strings stored in Unix password files adds two additional "salt" characters. The "salt" makes it more difficult (by a factor of 4,096) to create a dictionary or index that could be used to look up the results of the algorithm to find the password.

Standard Windows NT passwords are 14 characters long, again with a possible character set of about 84 characters. In theory, that would allow for $8.70 * 10^{26}$ possible passwords (87 septillion in the United States, and 87 quadrillion elsewhere). This is much larger than the number of possible Unix passwords, but Windows NT passwords are often stored and transmitted using an old format known as *LanMan*, which is also the name of many other things. The LanMan format greatly decreases the number of possible passwords. First, LanMan is case-insensitive; it uppercases all letters, so it uses only 68 characters. With only 68 characters, this would theoretically give $4.52 * 10^{25}$ possibilities for a 14-character password. Second, it splits the password into two 7-character halves and hashes them independently. This is a terrible error because it turns the 14-character Lan-Man password into two independent 7-character passwords. Each 7-character password only has $6.72 * 10^{12}$ possibilities. This means that it is much easier to create a lookup dictionary for 14-character LanMan format passwords than it is for an 8-character Unix password.

Many people figure that splitting the password into two halves means that there are half as many possibilities to search, but the truth is much worse than that. In general, when a 14-character password is hashed correctly it has a theoretical 6 trillion times (6 billion times, outside the United States) as many possibilities as a 7-character password and is therefore this many times more difficult to create a lookup dictionary or search. Because of the split, a 14-character password in Lan-Man format has only twice as many possibilities as a 7-character password, and this is a very large reduction in security.

Windows NT also has a newer hash format that hashes all 14 characters at the same time, forcing attackers to search the entire space of possible passwords. However, if a Windows NT machine is willing to support clients that use LanMan hashes for authentication, it will store passwords in the older format unless they contain characters that are illegal in LanMan passwords.

The reason that storage formats are important is that attackers have to check the validity of their guesses. It's impractical to try large numbers of possibilities by try-

---

* The United States and other English-speaking countries use different names for large numbers. Since English-speakers in general are not able to convert the names easily and may be unaware of the problem, we provide both.

ing to log into machines. It is relatively slow to start with, and operating systems intentionally slow down responses when multiple failed attempts are made to log in to the same account. Furthermore, even the least attentive system administrator is apt to notice something wrong after the first million or so attempts. Most methods of trying to authenticate take at least a second, and at that rate, it's over 11 days to try a measly million possibilities. On the other hand, an attacker who has the password in its stored form can generate the stored form for each guess and compare them, without the delay or the risk of interacting with the system under attack. Depending on the particular stored form in use and the technology that the attacker is bringing to bear, it may be as slow as hundreds of attempts per second or as fast as millions of attempts per second. Ideally, you would like to prevent people from getting the stored form at all, but you would also like the stored form to be as difficult as possible to compare things against.

It would be possible to build a specialized Unix password cracker similar to the machine "Deep Crack",[*] which could start with a Unix password hash and find the matching password in less than one day by brute force (meaning that every possible password would be tried). It is also possible to do it with a general-purpose computer, but it would take longer. LanMan hashes are much easier to crack; modern, general-purpose computers can brute-force them in a week. Windows NT password hashes, on the other hand, are significantly more difficult than Unix password hashes.

Unfortunately, all this talk about brute force password cracking, password lengths, and encryption formats misses the important problem with most password systems; people pick really bad passwords. Regardless of the trillions of possible passwords that people could be using, at most sites anywhere from 30 to 70 percent of the passwords can be guessed using only thousands of possibilities (common words and women's names, in general). Few people will voluntarily use special characters or passwords of any significant length. Most of them, left to their own devices will use something they find highly memorable (supposing that they don't just use "password", of course), probably their own name or the name of somebody they love.

Automatically generated passwords may be better, or they may be worse. Systems that generate passwords for users also tend to work in a relatively small range (they have to, to get things that people will remember instead of writing down), and an attacker who knows the algorithm used will be able to search only the possible passwords the generator could come up with. Packages that provide an administrative account with a randomly generated password often do even worse,

---

[*] "Deep Crack" is a machine for searching for DES keys; it was built by the Electronic Frontier Foundation and described in the book *Cracking DES: Secrets of Encryption Research, Wiretap Politics, and Chip Design*, by the Electronic Frontier Foundation (O'Reilly & Associates, 1998).

choosing something that's dependent on the machine they're installed on, or a hexadecimal representation of some number (with only 16 possible letters, it doesn't matter how impeccably random your data is, there still aren't very many different passwords to search).

Authentication Mechanisms

In order to use any of the methods of authentication we've outlined earlier, you need hardware or software to implement them. This section discusses some of the commonly available hardware and software authentication mechanisms that are at the heart of authentication systems (in particular, it discusses those supported by TIS FWTK, which is the most widely available system). The most popular of the full-blown systems are discussed later in this chapter.

One-Time Password Software

There are two ways a one-time password system may work:

- The list can be generated randomly, and a copy kept by the user and the system.

- The list (or, more likely, a specific entry from the list) can be generated on demand by the user and validated by the system.

The problem with keeping a list on the system is that if the system is compromised, so is the list, and the list could then be used for future access. This is as bad as having someone snoop on a reusable password while you use it.

An IETF standard addresses this problem; it's a system called OTP (for one-time password), which is based on S/Key, originally designed by Leslie Lamport and developed by Bellcore. While it allows a system to reliably authenticate a user, nothing on the system compromises the user's password if the system itself is compromised. The system has the ability to validate a user's current response but does not have the ability to predict what that user's *next* response will be.

OTP works by iteratively applying a cryptographically secure hash algorithm, starting with some initial seed value. A cryptographically secure hash algorithm is one that takes arbitrary-sized input and produces a much smaller output (something like a checksum) that has two special properties:

- The input cannot be regenerated from the output; thus, it's not simply a compression or encryption algorithm.

- The probability of two different inputs (particularly two different inputs of the same size) producing the same output is vanishingly small.

OTP can use a variety of different algorithms for this purpose. All OTP systems must support MD5, and they are encouraged to also support SHA and MD4. (The original S/Key used only MD4.) Cryptographic checksum algorithms are discussed further in Appendix C, *Cryptography*.

OTP works by starting with a seed (which is either provided by the user or generated randomly) and applying the chosen hash algorithm iteratively to get a sequence of keys. It applies the hash algorithm to the seed to get the first key, applies the hash algorithm to the first key to get the second key, applies the hash algorithm to the second key to get the third key, and so on. In order to validate a user, the system has to know some key (call it key number *n*) in the sequence. The system prompts the user for the previous key (key *n*–1), applies the hash algorithm to the user's answer (supposedly key *n*–1), and checks to see if the result is the key *n* that it knows. If the result is the key *n*, the user must have supplied the correct key *n*–1.

OTP can encode each key into a series of short words, so they are easier for a user to read and type, rather than simply generating a random-looking jumble of characters. Figure 21-1 shows how OTP works.

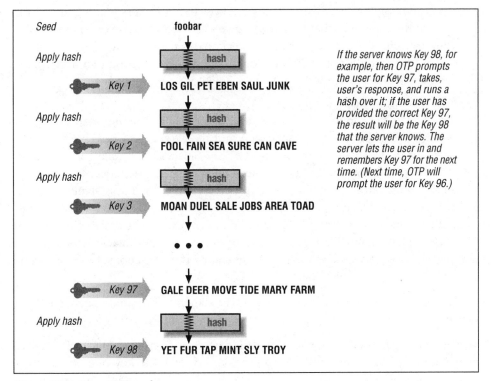

Figure 21-1. How OTP works

Because cryptographic hashing is nonreversible (you can't determine the input given the output), the system can't easily figure out what key *n*–1 is, even though it knows key *n*. All the server can do is to verify that key *n*–1 (when presented by the user) is the key that generates key *n*. This means that even if an attacker can somehow obtain key *n* (for example, by snooping on a user's login session), he won't be able to easily figure out the next key (key *n*–1).

OTP isn't absolutely invulnerable to attack. Several attacks are possible:

Brute force attacks

> Attackers could try a whole series of possibilities for key *n*–1 until they found one that translated to key *n*. However, this type of attack is very unlikely to succeed. Because of the size of the key space (the number of possible keys) and the computation requirements of cryptographic hashing, a brute force approach of this kind is considered to be computationally infeasible for all but the most serious and well-financed attackers. (It would probably take a significant amount of supercomputer time before they found the right key.)

Dictionary attacks

> If the user provides the initial seed (rather than having the initial seed be generated randomly), dictionary attacks are possible. Attackers could guess at the seed in the same way that they might guess at reusable passwords; they'd typically try things like words from the dictionary, names, places, etc. To these words, they would apply the cryptographic hashing algorithm an appropriate number of times to see if it generates a key they've seen used.

Modified sniffing attacks

> An attacker can run a packet sniffer and collect the beginning of an OTP password (all but the last few characters) and then try all the possible combinations for the last characters, before the user finishes. This relies on extremely delicate timing, but in Telnet connections, user input is frequently sent keystroke by keystroke as it is generated. This creates a lag that is significant for a computer. An attacker probably won't be able to try all possible combinations but may be able to try all possible combinations that make English words. OTP implementations are required to try to prevent this attack, which is usually done by preventing multiple simultaneous connections from the same user.

There are two ways for users to use OTP: either keys can be generated on demand, or the user can be supplied with a printed list of keys.

To generate OTP keys on demand, the user needs a computer and a program to generate them. That user will have to provide the seed, the key number, and the cryptographic algorithm to be used, and the program will iterate the algorithm that many times to generate the key desired. The seed will have to be either entered by the user or read from a file on the computer. If the seed is entered by the user, the user would probably pick a seed the same way he or she would pick a password. Because users are notoriously poor at picking passwords, this makes the system subject to dictionary attacks, as we've described earlier. If the seed is read from a file, it can be more random (and therefore less guessable) than something the user would provide, but you have to worry about the risks—probably low—of the computer or file being stolen.

The alternative way to use OTP is to have the system generate and print a list of keys, enough keys to last the user for a reasonable period of time. In this case, the system randomly generates the initial seed, thus protecting itself against dictionary attacks. The printout should simply be a numbered list of keys, with no further identification or explanation. It is possible that the list could be stolen from a user, but you have to decide which you think is more likely: that the list will be stolen (and that the thief will know what it is and what to do with it), or that the user's session will be snooped on. If your users are generating keys on demand, they're probably using a seed that's subject to dictionary attack (otherwise, they would find it too hard to remember the seed); if one of their sessions is snooped on, their keys can be attacked.

We think that using a seed that's subject to dictionary attack is a greater risk than having a list of keys stolen, so we prefer using printed lists of keys to using keys generated on demand.

One-Time Password Hardware

There are also systems for generating nonreusable passwords in hardware. The systems in common use are small cards, about the size of miniature calculators. You install software and/or hardware on the computer, and a user who wants to log in uses information generated by the card as part of the process. In order to prevent attackers from simply stealing the card, there is usually a "something you know" component, which is either a fixed password used to unlock the card itself, or a fixed password added to the generated information as part of the login process.

These systems use a variety of different ways to generate passwords. Some of them vary the password based on the time; some of them work their way through a one-time password list; and some of them use a challenge-response system, where the computer provides a challenge that the user types into the card, and the card provides a response for the user to give the computer.

Although the card-based systems have different strengths and weaknesses, they share the same general advantages and disadvantages. On the good side, they provide a guaranteed level of protection without requiring special reader hardware; on the bad side, there are considerable hardware costs for the cards, and you have to alter login software on the machines that you want to protect. Most authentication systems now contain support for the popular cards, but you will still need to install vendor libraries.

Card-based tokens are something of a hassle for their users, who have to carry the device, type things into it, read things from it, and protect a small and expensive object from being damaged or lost. Printed one-time password lists also present a certain number of user annoyances; there's nothing like turning over your list to discover that the print has worn off the next password you need.

Other hardware "something you have" options avoid many of these problems. For instance, smart cards, which put a small amount of information into a chip suitable for embedding in a credit card–sized object, are cheaper, easier to carry, and don't have keypads or readouts to fiddle with. The "secret encoder ring", which puts a small transmitter into a device that will pass for a chunky ring or a smallish ornament for your keys, is still a small, valuable object that you have to protect, but it doesn't have a keypad or a readout, and it's emotionally very satisfying. However, all of these options require reader hardware at the location where the user needs to authenticate. Smart card readers are becoming more prevalent, and smart cards are the most likely of these options to be practical for widespread use. While it's unlikely that Internet cafes and terminals in airports will provide smart card readers soon, it's relatively easy to get them for laptop computers.

You can also use hand-held computers like Palm Pilots and Windows CE machines to generate one-time passwords. It is very convenient for people who already have these devices, but it is not as secure as using devices that are designed to be security tokens. General-purpose hand-held devices do not provide hardware protection (they can be taken apart, so that people have access to the data). Most of them don't provide significant software protection, either; you can set a password, but it's generally easy to guess, and if you back the device up to a larger computer, the data is usually completely unprotected on the larger computer. If you use these devices for one-time passwords, you should consider adding additional access protection beyond that provided with the device.

Modular Authentication for Unix

Traditionally, programs wishing to authenticate a user (such as the *login* program or the *ftpd* daemon) have had to know *how* to authenticate a user; they have had to understand and implement whatever authentication method or methods were to be used. In a Unix system, this means that these programs have to do all of the following to authenticate a user:

1. Prompt the user for a login name.

2. Look up that login name and obtain its encrypted password.

3. Prompt the user for a password.

4. Use the user-provided password and the first two characters from the encrypted password to encrypt a known string (eight bytes of nulls).

5. Check to see if the result of this encryption matches the encrypted password for the user.

If you want to add a second authentication mechanism (for example, the S/Key mechanism, which we discussed earlier), you have to modify all of these programs to understand this second mechanism as well as, or instead of, the standard Unix password mechanism. And if you later want to add a third authentication mechanism (for example, support for the SecurID cards), you have to modify the programs yet again; and so it would go for each additional authentication mechanism. Each time you modify these programs, you're making them bigger and more complex and increase the chances that you've introduced some kind of bug that's going to result in a security problem. (This is a serious risk because these are very security-critical programs—they control access to your system.)

Modular authentication takes a different approach. With it, you modify all the authenticating programs (e.g., *login, ftpd*) once, to make them talk to an authentication service instead of doing the authentication themselves. All of the details of the authentication mechanism—for example, what to prompt the user with, how to validate the user's response, etc.—are then handled by the authentication service. When you want to add or modify authentication methods, you do so by changing the authentication service (which is modular and designed to accommodate such changes), not by changing the individual authenticating programs.

The TIS FWTK Authentication Server

The authentication server in TIS FWTK is a modular solution for authenticating users coming in from the Internet. The server implements a variety of authentication mechanisms, such as standard reusable passwords (not recommended), S/Key, Security Dynamics SecurID cards, and Digital Pathways SNK-004 cards. In addition, the server is modular and extensible, and is designed so that new authentication mechanisms can easily be integrated.

A single authentication server can handle any number of client machines and programs, and any number of different authentication methods; different users within the same server can use different authentication methods. For example, some might use S/Key while some might use the Digital Pathways SNK-004 cards.

When a client program (such as *login* or *ftpd*) wishes to authenticate someone using the TIS FWTK authentication server, it has to go through the following steps:

1. Prompt the user for a login name.

2. Contact the authentication server and tell it who is trying to log in.

3. Receive a response from the authentication server that tells it what to prompt the user with.

4. Display the prompt specified by the authentication server.

5. Collect the user's response and send it to the authentication server.

6. Receive either an OK or an error message from the authentication server.

7. Allow the user access (if OK) or display the error message.

This whole process is carried out with a single TCP connection between the client and the authentication server, so that the server knows it's talking to the same client and the client knows it's talking to the same server throughout the authentication process.

The authentication server consults its databases to determine how to authenticate that user and determines the appropriate prompt for the authentication mechanism for that user. For example:

- If traditional passwords are being used as the authentication method, the prompt will be a simple "Password:" prompt.

- If the authentication method is S/Key, the prompt will be the number of the key the user is to respond with.

- If the authentication method is the Digital Pathways SNK-004 card, the prompt will be a randomly generated challenge number.

Figure 21-2 shows how the TIS FWTK authentication server works.

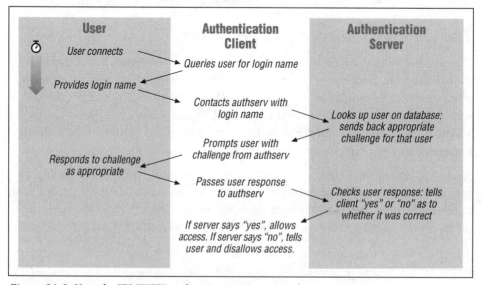

Figure 21-2. How the TIS FWTK authentication server works

TIS FWTK includes a number of programs (such as *ftpd*) that, in addition to other modifications and enhancements for security, have already been modified to use the authentication server. Converting an existing program to use the authentication server, rather than traditional Unix passwords, is pretty straightforward. It typically involves only 20 or so lines of C code, examples of which are given in the toolkit.

The toolkit also includes some programs to support binary-only systems where you don't have the source to modify. For example, for systems in which you don't have the source code to the *login* program available for modification, the toolkit includes a program you can use as the user's shell (which is specified for each user in the */etc/passwd* file) instead of one of the normal shells (e.g., */bin/csh* or */bin/sh*) This replacement shell authenticates the user with the authentication server, and if the user passes, starts his or her real shell.

Problems with the authentication server

The major problem in running an authentication server is getting secure communication between the client and the server. An attacker who can convincingly pretend to be the authentication server can authenticate as anybody.

Some configurations may have additional problems; for example, using shell replacement can produce problems because not all programs deal well with situations in which a user's shell environment variable and the entry for that user in the */etc/passwd* file do not match.

Pluggable Authentication Modules (PAM)

PAM is a more recent system for providing modular authentication, which uses an even more flexible mechanism than the TIS FWTK authentication server. The basic principle is much the same; programs that need to do authentication are modified to use the PAM system, after which you can completely control what kind of authentication they use through PAM, without making further changes to the individual programs. PAM differs from the authentication server in that it is a local service; PAM operates by dynamically loading authentication modules into applications that have been configured to use them. Authentication modules execute with the same privileges as the application that loaded them.

A program can ask PAM to authenticate a user or to change a password. The password change feature saves users from having to learn a new password change mechanism for each new authentication mechanism.

An administrator can configure PAM to do extra work in addition to authenticating the user. For instance, it can grant or deny access based on criteria other than whether or not the user authenticated properly. This allows you to control what time of day people can use a service, or how many simultaneous users there can be, or whether or not they're accessible from the machine's console. PAM can also set up the environment that the service will execute in, by setting environment variables or by running programs (for instance, it can use *chroot* to limit the parts of the filesystem that the service has access to).

Authentication modules can be stacked up, either to allow for fail-over (if you can't authenticate one way, try another) or to enforce complicated rules (allow George to log in only at the console and only between 3:00 and 5:00 in the morning, but allow everybody else to log in from the local network with reusable passwords, or from the Internet with a one-time password). It's also easy to add new authentication modules, but you should use new modules with caution. When you trust a piece of code to authenticate users, you are trusting it with the security of your system; that's not something you should do lightly.

PAM is an extraordinarily flexible system, and as a natural consequence, it can be hard to configure. Configuration errors will often result in an unusable computer, but it's also easy to accidentally produce a configuration that has unexpected insecurities. The module-stacking features, for instance, provide any number of ways to accidentally allow access that you intended to deny. Effectively, they give you an entire programming language with obscure and varying syntax, and an error as simple as using the keyword "required" instead of "requisite" can have unfortunate consequences.

Like any powerful tool, PAM should be used with caution:

*   Because relatively minor errors have the potential to disable all access to the machine, you should know how to boot your machine into single-user mode before you start to configure PAM. Access to single-user mode is not controlled by PAM, so it will give you a way to re-enable access to the rest of the machine.

*   Because all of PAM's files are security-critical (an intruder can easily install back doors by modifying any part of PAM), you should use it in conjunction with a checksumming system that will detect unauthorized changes (see Chapter 11, *Unix and Linux Bastion Hosts*, for more information on such systems).

*   Because PAM configuration is tricky, you should test your configurations before relying on them. When you are deciding how to configure a service, make a list of the important cases when it should allow access and when it should deny access. Once you have written the configuration, test each of these cases to make sure there are no surprises.

In most installations, PAM will allow you to use one single configuration file that contains the configuration for all services, or a directory with a separate file for each service. You should use a separate file for each service; it will help keep configuration errors for one service from propagating to others.

No matter how you set up the configuration files, you will need to specify a default behavior for the service called "other", which will be used if there is no specific information for a PAM-enabled service. You should set this up so that it denies access and logs this fact; this way, if you accidentally install a PAM-enabled service without installing configuration information for it, you will not grant access to it. Of course, if you accidentally remove the configuration for an existing service, you will turn off all access to it. This is unpleasant, but not as unpleasant as a compromised machine.

Kerberos

Kerberos was developed at MIT by Project Athena (the same folks who developed the X Window System). It is designed to provide authentication and encryption services through modified versions of standard clients and servers (e.g., Telnet clients and servers).

Kerberos provides strong authentication in a distributed environment, and it is widely available. It is the primary source of authentication in Windows 2000. Some other vendors also provide Kerberos support with their operating systems; MIT has freely available implementations for many versions of Unix; and the code is freely available if you wish it to port it to an operating system that does not yet have an implementation.

Kerberos attempts to solve the problem where a client wants to talk to a server over an untrusted network. The client and the server don't have to trust each other or the network, but they have to trust the Kerberos server (it is the trusted third party). Imagine a courier attempting to deliver gems to a jewelry store. The jewelry store doesn't want to let in a fake courier who might be a robber; the courier doesn't want to give the gems to a fake jeweler who might be a robber. If both of them trust a third party, that person can verify the identity of both sides of the transaction.

There have been two official releases of Kerberos, version 4 and version 5. Version 5 was released in 1993 and fixed a number of problems. We do not recommend using Kerberos version 4. MIT's Unix code is freely available under license (see Appendix A, *Resources*), but Kerberos is not in the public domain. Because Kerberos needs to be integrated into everything that uses authentication data, implementing Kerberos in your environment can be tricky. Several companies and operating systems vendors offer commercial versions of Kerberos where some or all of this work has been done for you.

Windows 2000 uses some extensions to Kerberos version 5. As a result, not all operations are possible when you combine Windows 2000 with other implementations of Kerberos. In particular, there is a high degree of interoperability for authentication, but Windows 2000 also transfers Windows-specific data used for authorization. Other implementations of Kerberos will not have the authorization data available, so that authentication may succeed while authorization fails. While this is not technically a Kerberos interoperability problem (Kerberos is an authentication protocol, and the authorization is not part of it), the net result is that a Windows 2000 user who attempts to use a non-Windows 2000 Kerberos server will probably be unable to get access to Windows 2000 resources. On the other hand, other platforms do not normally transfer authorization data this way, so a Windows 2000 Kerberos server can usually serve clients on other platforms. (As we discuss in the section on packet filtering characteristics of Kerberos, Windows 2000 uses TCP for some Kerberos transactions, and other platforms do not; this can result in authentication failures, particularly if the user is a valid Windows 2000 user with a full set of Windows 2000 authorization information.)

Microsoft's implementation of Kerberos uses Microsoft-specific names for many Kerberos concepts. This is intended to ease the transition to Kerberos for experienced Microsoft administrators by making the names similar to the old names for similar functions, and in some cases, the names may in fact be more intuitive. However, it may confuse experienced Kerberos administrators. We use standard Kerberos terminology, but when we introduce a term, we also give the Microsoft-specific name where applicable.

How It Works

Kerberos provides secure authentication for clients and servers across an untrusted network, as long as the Kerberos authentication servers themselves are protected from tampering. Figure 21-3 shows the basic requirements for a Kerberos network to be secure. Note that the trust relationships shown are the only important ones. The application server can be completely insecure, without being able to compromise anything. Similarly, the user can be hostile and try to attack the authentication server or the application server, without compromising security. The authentication server must be protected, and the client software must do what the user expects it to do. If either of these fails, security will be compromised. If the time is not synchronized, security may be compromised, but it's more likely that users will just be unable to authenticate.

Kerberos uses slightly different terminology from most authentication systems. The area of authority of a Kerberos installation is called a *realm*. A realm is equivalent to a Windows NT or NIS domain, and in fact Windows 2000 uses *domain* instead of realm. All versions of Kerberos refer to the parties involved in a transaction as

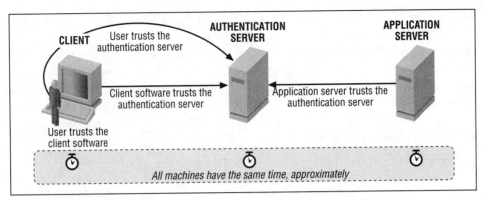

Figure 21-3. Kerberos requirements

principals. A principal is an entity that needs to be authenticated. In most cases, a transaction involves a user talking to a server (for instance, somebody trying to pick up mail with POP), and therefore principals are normally users and services. In some cases, something else may need to be authenticated. For instance, the principals in the transaction when a machine transfers files for diskless booting are a host and a server instead of a user and a server.

The authentication server is also known as a *Key Distribution Center*, or KDC. In Windows 2000, every domain controller is also an authentication server.

Every principal has a secret that is shared with the authentication server. These secrets are known only by the principal and the authentication server, and they are never passed around the network unencrypted. However, principals identify each other every time they interact. Every time a user makes a request of a server that uses Kerberos, an identifier called a *ticket* is handed to the server. That ticket is specific to the user and to the server that the user is trying to use.

This could be a nasty problem for the user. The secret that a user shares with the authentication server is a password, and every time that password is needed, the user has to type it in. (Having software store the password is a major security risk.) Nobody wants to type in a password every time he or she reads a file on a file server, prints a file to a printer, or checks mail. The need to type in passwords is reduced two ways. First, you don't need a new ticket every time you interact with a service; tickets are all-day passes, typically good for eight hours. Second, you don't always have to give a password to get a ticket. Most services will accept tickets given out by a *ticket-granting service*. The ticket-granting service itself takes tickets (but it will accept only ones given out directly by the authentication server).

Suppose that you want to use a Kerberized POP server to read your mail, and you haven't done anything else with Kerberos in the last eight hours. When you ask to use the POP server, you will be asked for your password. The client will ask the authentication server for a ticket to the ticket-granting service and use the password to complete the process. It will then present that ticket to the ticket-granting service and ask for a ticket to the POP server. Finally, it will present this second ticket to the POP server. If you check your mail again, the client will give the same ticket to the POP server. If you decide to print a piece of mail to a Kerberized printing system, the client will take the ticket for the ticket-granting service and ask for a ticket to the print server, all without asking you for your password again. Figure 21-4 shows the initial process for speaking to the first application server.

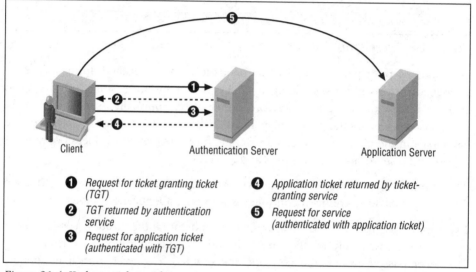

Figure 21-4. Kerberos ticket exchange

In standard Kerberos terminology, the master ticket you get from the ticket-granting service is called a *ticket granting ticket*, or TGT. In Windows 2000, it is called a *user ticket*. The ticket that is handed to an application is called a *session ticket* in standard Kerberos and a *service ticket* in Windows 2000.

Not all services will take a ticket that's given out by the ticket-granting service; for that matter, not all services will let you reuse a ticket. It's up to the service to decide how paranoid to be. Services that let you change your password, for instance, will normally require a ticket direct from the authentication service. If you leave to get a cup of tea, somebody at your keyboard will still be able to get tickets from the ticket-granting service, but not from the authentication service, because getting a ticket from the authentication service always requires providing a password.

In most Kerberos implementations, the password that the user types in as part of the authentication process is a fixed password. This password never crosses the network in the clear (so it can't be sniffed). On the other hand, nothing prevents an attacker from simply guessing the password. Kerberos goes to some lengths to avoid storing the password, even in encrypted form, where an attacker can get at it to optimize guessing attacks, but attackers are still free to try guessing the hard way (simply trying out passwords to see if they work). Some implementations support one-time password systems to prevent these attacks.

Extending Trust

Kerberos realms can trust each other, so that users who authenticate in one Kerberos realm can use resources in another. This is accomplished by using inter-realm tickets, which allow a ticket-granting service in one realm to issue tickets for another. Trust between Kerberos realms is transitive; if the chemistry department's realm trusts the realm run by the college of physical science, and so does the physics department, chemistry and physics trust each other.

When a service gets a ticket from outside the service's realm, the ticket includes information about the realm that originally issued the ticket, and all the realms that the ticket has gone through. In the preceding example, when a user in chemistry sends a ticket to a service in physics, the service will see that the ticket was issued in chemistry and passed through the college of physical science. The service can then use this information to decide what privileges the user should have.

Inter-realm trusts don't particularly change the firewall issues with using Kerberos. A firewall that's between two realms will see the same sorts of traffic as a firewall that's between two parts of the same realm, except for initial authentication.

Packet Filtering Characteristics of Kerberos

Kerberos v5 uses the assigned port 88 for ticket request operations. Although the Kerberos protocol specifies the use of UDP, Windows 2000 may also use TCP for some requests. This is because Windows 2000 tickets contain more information than standard Kerberos tickets and therefore may be larger than will fit in a single 1,500-byte UDP packet. When this happens, the client will make an initial request over UDP, receive a truncated answer, and repeat the request over TCP. (This is a standard mechanism in several UDP-based protocols, including DNS and WINS, which allows most requests to use low-overhead UDP, while falling back to the more expensive TCP as an easy means to accommodate occasionally larger data transfers.)

Direction	SourceAddr.	Dest. Addr.	Protocol	Source Port	Dest. Port	ACK Set	Notes
In	Ext	Int	UDP	>1023	88	a	Request to internal KDC
Out	Int	Ext	UDP	88	>1023	a	Response from internal KDC
Out	Int	Ext	UDP	>1023	88	a	Request to external KDC

Direction	SourceAddr.	Dest. Addr.	Protocol	Source Port	Dest. Port	ACK Set	Notes
In	Ext	Int	UDP	88	>1023	a	Response from external KDC
In	Ext	Int	TCP	>1023	88	b	Over-length request to internal KDC
Out	Int	Ext	TCP	88	>1023	Yes	Over-length response from internal KDC
Out	Int	Ext	TCP	>1023	88	b	Over-length request to external KDC
In	Ext	Int	TCP	88	>1023	Yes	Over-length response from external KDC

a UDP has no ACK equivalent.
b The ACK bit will not be set on the first packet but will be set on all subsequent packets.

All packets contain authenticators and integrity checksums. In order to start a conversation with a Kerberos server, you need to have previously arranged to share a secret with the server. This means that it is likely that you will be able to detect attempts by foreign machines to obtain Kerberos credentials. On the other hand, it means that you will need to have a set of processes and procedures so that you can add and remove systems from your Kerberos realms.

Proxying and Network Address Translation Characteristics of Kerberos

Kerberos authenticator packets include the IP addresses of the originating system. These addresses are supposed to be checked against the source IP address (although it does not appear that all implementations actually make this check) to prevent the packet from being sniffed and replayed from a different IP address. This makes it difficult to use Kerberos with proxies or network address translation because the IP address in the packet will be the address of the internal host, while the source address will be the proxy server or the translated address.

One solution, which requires modifications to the Kerberos sources,* is to have the internal systems add the external IP addresses to all Kerberos packets. This effectively disables the IP address checking performed by remote systems. It also means that the internal systems are trusting not only the Kerberos server, but also the proxy or address translation system, which is capable of masquerading as any internal host. This significantly raises the risk; Kerberos servers are highly protected machines, but proxy and address translation servers are extremely exposed.

Since Kerberos is UDP-based, there are also the usual problems with UDP proxying; the proxy machine has to keep track of the state in order to know what pack-

---

* The modification was written by Ken Hornstein and is available at *ftp://ftp.ncsa.uiuc.edu/aces/kerberos/ misc_patches/patch.app-proxy.*

ets are responses to what requests. This can cause difficulties in situations where there are lots of transactions or where packets are being lost.

It's worth noting that Kerberos also has a concept of *proxy tickets*. These are tickets that allow a server to act on behalf of another principal (for instance, a print service may use them to access a user's files). They don't have anything to do with proxying in the firewall sense.

Summary of Recommendations for Kerberos

- If you use Kerberos internally and wish to allow machines to authenticate from the Internet, you can allow inbound authentication, but you should use one of the one-time password add-ons to prevent password guessing.

- Allowing internal machines to authenticate to external Kerberos servers requires permitting dangerous amounts of UDP traffic. If you must allow it, restrict it to individual hosts and treat those machines as bastion hosts, or use proxying. Neither solution scales well.

- You must be able to completely trust the security of any Kerberos server you use for authentication. Even if you allow hosts to authenticate against external Kerberos servers, don't accept externally controlled authentication for internal services.

NTLM Domains

NTLM domains provide user and group authentication for Windows machines. It is not clear exactly what "NTLM" stands for, although presumably it's something like "NT Logon Manager". Until Windows 2000, these were simply called *domains*.

The term *domain* is used in an unfortunately large number of contexts in the networking world. There are DNS domains, NIS domains, NTLM domains, and now Kerberos domains, all of them similar (in that they indicate regions of administrative control) and yet distinctively different. NTLM domains, like NIS domains and Kerberos realms, control information about users and groups. They are not tied to machine names but are a source of authentication and authorization information.

Under Windows NT, domain means an NTLM domain. Under Windows 2000, domain by default means a Kerberos realm. However, Windows 2000 machines are able to authenticate in NTLM domains, and Windows 2000 domain controllers can be configured to provide both Kerberos and NTLM services (for instance, to allow older operating systems to authenticate).

The computers that hold the information are called *domain controllers*. An NTLM domain has one computer that is a primary domain controller and may have one or more computers that are backup domain controllers. Any domain controller can do user authentication, but database changes (password changes, user additions or deletions, changes to group membership) all take place on the primary domain controller and are distributed from there to the backup domain controllers.

When a user wishes to log in to a computer that is part of an NTLM domain using a user account that is in a NTLM domain, the user provides a username, a password, and the name of a domain. The computer passes the provided information to the computer's domain controller. If the domain controller is able to authenticate the user with that information, it returns a security identifier; if not, it returns an error. The computer then checks the access permissions of the security identifier to see if that security identifier is permitted to log in, and if so, continues the login process. Note that this procedure separates authentication from authorization; it is possible to authenticate correctly and still be unable to log in because there is no authorization to do so.

If authentication is successful, the client will cache the information locally. If a user tries to log in and no domain controller is available, the client will use the cached information. If a domain controller is available, the cache will not be consulted. Most clients cache 10–15 sets of credentials (the default is 10, but it is modifiable). If you remove a user account from a domain, the user will still be able to log into any computer they have recently logged into, as long as they first disconnect it from the network. In addition, anybody with Administrator access to the machine can read the cached credentials. Because the cached credentials are stored in a doubly hashed form, standard password crackers will not work against them; on the other hand, it would be possible to write a cracker for them, and presumably somebody eventually will. In security-critical environments, you should disable credential caching; in Windows NT 4, it can be done by setting the following registry key to 0:

```
HKEY_LOCAL_MACHINE\Software\Microsoft\Windows NT\CurrentVersion\winlogon\
Cached Logons Count
```

Normally, the domain controller will authenticate the user locally. However, there are two cases where the domain controller will ask another domain controller for information. First, if the domain the user wants to authenticate in is not the one controlled by the domain controller, the domain controller may be able to forward the request to an appropriate domain controller. Second, if the domain controller is a backup domain controller and authentication fails, the backup domain controller will forward the request to the primary domain controller just in case there's been an update that has not yet been distributed.

In order for a domain controller to forward an authentication request into another domain, the two domains must have a pre-existing relationship called a *trust relationship*. If you are willing to accept another domain's authentication, you trust that domain. Trust relationships are one-way; if the domain "sheep" decides to trust the domain "wolves", it does not require "wolves" to trust "sheep".* In NTLM domains, trusts are also nontransitive: if "sheep" trusts "wolves", and "wolves" trusts "lions", it does *not* mean that "sheep" trusts "lions". (Windows 2000 domains are Kerberos realms, and Kerberos trust relationships are transitive.)

Finding a Domain Controller

There are two ways to find a domain controller: broadcast and WINS (for more information about NetBIOS naming and WINS, see Chapter 20, *Naming and Directory Services*). Clients that are configured to use broadcast name resolution will also use broadcast to find domain controllers, although the broadcasts are different (they are sent to the NETLOGON name). Clients that are configured to use WINS for name resolution will use WINS name resolution to find domain controllers by looking up the NetBIOS group with the name of the domain and the type 1C (for the domain "sheep", it would be "SHEEP<1C>"). Once a client has used WINS to get a list of domain controllers, it sends a directed packet to each domain controller in the list. Regardless of the way that a client looks for domain controllers, it selects the first domain controller to respond.

The Logon Process

There are two ways for the actual logon process to occur: one based on SMB and one based on Microsoft RPC. Most machines use the SMB-based process; machines running Windows NT Server use the Microsoft RPC process. In the SMB-based process, once a machine has identified a domain controller, it makes an SMB connection to the domain controller, using standard SMB authentication of the user, and connects to the IPC$ share. It then uses remote API calls to finish the process of getting a security token for the user. The Microsoft RPC process is similar; it sets up a secure channel (described in the next section) and then uses remote API calls across it.

Regardless of which way the initial logon is done, the machine will connect to the domain controller with SMB to look for a policy file. In fact, this will be done even if the user is authenticated locally, without involving the domain controller at all.

Secure Channel Setup

Each Windows NT server that is part of a Windows NT domain sets up a secure channel to a domain controller when the computer starts up. In addition, at startup time, each backup domain controller sets up a secure channel to its primary

---

* You will hear "bidirectional trusts" mentioned; this is actually just a convenient shorthand for a pair of trusts.

domain controller. A secure channel is also used for the communication between domains that have a trust relationship. A secure channel is simply an authenticated connection over Microsoft RPC where the two ends have a shared secret that can be used to encrypt data. Depending on the service pack that is installed and the configuration of the machine, some or all of the information sent across the secure channel will be encrypted with the shared secret.

The username and password information is passed across the secure channel in a decryptable form. No challenge-response and no hashing is used; the domain controller will decrypt the password and use it in cleartext form. If the domain controller is compromised, the intruder will be able to log passwords. (Note that a compromised domain controller already gives the intruder control of the site; it is a minor addition to the thousands of horrible things that somebody can do when they control the domain.)

In some implementations, when a server initially joins a domain, it uses a well-known password to set up the first secure channel. An attacker who can eavesdrop on this initial conversation can decrypt it and can read all the information in it, including the password change to a new password that will be used for future secure channels. At this point, the attacker can decrypt all information in the secure channel, including passwords, until there is a password change that they don't manage to eavesdrop on. It is critical to protect this initial secure channel from eavesdroppers (for instance, by putting the server and the domain controller on a switched network where other machines cannot see the traffic); the secure channel is believed to be reasonably secure as long as the password is unknown and is changed with reasonable frequency, but once a password is compromised, the channel is completely insecure. Service Pack 6 for Windows NT 4 addresses this problem, which is also fixed in Windows 2000.

SMB Authentication

When an SMB client connects to an SMB server, the client and server negotiate which dialect of SMB they are going to use. This negotiation mainly controls the method used to exchange authentication data. There are four ways to exchange user authentication data (listed here in order from oldest to newest, which is also from weakest to strongest):

Cleartext
> The client sends the server the username and the unencrypted password (an ASCII string up to 24 characters long).

LanMan 1.2
> Challenge-response, using LanMan password hashing. The server sends a challenge; the client takes an ASCII password, uppercases it, converts it to exactly

14 characters (truncating or padding with spaces as necessary), uses the result as a key to encrypt a fixed 8-byte string, appends five nulls, uses the result as a key to encrypt the challenge, and returns that value.

NT LM 0.12

Challenge-response, using Windows NT password hashing and verifying only the client. The server sends a challenge; the client takes the password, represented in Unicode,[*] calculates a 16-byte MD4 message digest of it, appends five nulls, uses the result as a key to encrypt the challenge, and returns the value. The server calculates the same value and verifies the user if they match.

NT LM++

Challenge-response, using Windows NT encryption with mutual verification. The server sends a challenge; the client sends back its own challenge, and the server's challenge, encrypted with a value derived from the password. The server calculates the same result and verifies the user if they match. The server then calculates a different value based on the password, encrypts the client's challenge with it, and returns it to the client, which can then verify that the server also knows the password.

Not all servers and clients will support all of these methods. Some of the servers and clients were written before all of the methods had been developed and therefore do not support the newer, safer methods; others refuse to support older methods for security reasons. For instance, if a malicious server can negotiate the use of cleartext passwords, clients will simply send all their authentication data to it in a form suitable for reuse. Less obviously, there's a smaller risk to a server that allows a client to negotiate cleartext passwords. Not only are the passwords open to password sniffing, but a malicious client that can negotiate cleartext passwords has a much easier time attempting to guess passwords, since it doesn't have to waste CPU time encrypting the guesses. You should be sure that both servers and clients are configured to refuse to use cleartext passwords.

Accessing Other Computers

A user may want to access a computer other than the one he or she originally logged into (for instance, to use a printer, access files remotely, or use a program like the Event Viewer). When this happens, a Windows NT machine will usually try four ways of authenticating on the remote computer, in order:

---

[*] Unicode is a system for representing text that allows a larger character set than the ASCII encoding normally used for English text. Although this authentication method would theoretically allow for passwords in Unicode, vastly increasing the available characters that could be used in passwords, most systems will allow only users to enter ASCII characters. This may be different in clients designed for languages that do not have adequate ASCII representations.

1. Provide the username, password, and domain information the user originally used. This will work only if the remote computer is a member of the same domain or a trusting domain.

2. Provide the username and password without the domain information. This will work if the remote computer has an account with the same username and password.

3. Ask the user for a new password and provide the original username with the new password. This will work if the remote computer has an account with the same username but a different password.

4. Request guest access to the remote computer.

This means that it is possible to accidentally grant access to remote users if you happen to create an account with a username and password that matches one in use in another domain.

In some circumstances, you will be able to specify username, password, and domain information explicitly. In particular, you can usually specify this information when accessing files but not when running programs.

Alternate Authentication Methods

Windows NT machines are not required to use NetLogon to authenticate users. The authentication process is handled by a module called the Graphical Identification and Authorization (GINA) module, and other modules can be used instead of the normal NetLogon process. (Note that this is authentication for local resources only; using resources from other servers will require reauthentication.) The most common use of it in mixed Windows NT-Unix networks is something called NIS-GINA, which allows Windows NT machines to use NIS for authentication.

An attacker who has Administrator access to a Windows NT machine can use this feature to install additional authentication modules. It is particularly easy to write a module that saves the provided username and password information for the attacker's future use.

If the relevant registry keys do not have the correct permissions, it may be possible for an attacker to install additional authentication modules without first having Administrator access. As shipped, these keys are protected, but it's important to make sure that protection is maintained if you change anything, particularly on the following key:

```
HKEY_LOCAL_MACHINE\System\CurrentControlSet\Control\Lsa
```

Controller-to-Controller Communication

Domain controllers speak to each other for a number of purposes:

Communication within domains

Primary domain controllers replicate information to backup domain controllers; they transfer authentication information via NetLogon and profiles and policies via directory replication.

At startup, backup domain controllers establish a secure channel to the primary controller, used for pass-through authentication and for replication.

Communication between domains

The secure channel is used for pass-through authentication between trusted domains.

In addition, once a week, the primary domain controller contacts the primary domain controller for each trusted domain controller to change the password used to establish secure channels with that domain.

The User Manager

Changing user information (adding and removing users, changing passwords and rights) needs to be done via different protocols from those used for authentication. Administrators manage accounts using the User Manager for Domains, which connects to the primary domain controller using SMB transactions.

Packet Filtering, Proxying, and Network Address Translation Characteristics of NTLM Domain Authentication

Windows NT domain authentication is based on SMB and Microsoft RPC, which are discussed in Chapter 14, *Intermediary Protocols*, and on Microsoft name services, which are discussed in Chapter 20, *Naming and Directory Services*. We will call machines that use domain authentication but not secure channels *domain participants*; this includes machines running Windows 98, for instance. Machines that use the secure channel are full-fledged domain members; this is what Windows NT machines usually are.

If a firewall is between a domain participant and its domain controller, it needs to provide:

• A way to find the controller (either by having a working WINS configuration or passing NetLogon broadcasts)

• SMB to the domain controller

A firewall that's between a domain member and its domain controller needs to provide:

- A way to find the controller (either by having a working WINS configuration or passing NetLogon broadcasts)
- SMB to the domain controller
- Microsoft RPC to the domain controller

A firewall that's between a secondary domain controller and a primary domain controller needs to provide:

- SMB between the controllers
- Microsoft RPC between the domain controllers

A firewall that's between two domains that have a trust relationship needs to provide:

- A way to find the controllers (either by having a working WINS configuration or passing NetLogon broadcasts)
- Microsoft RPC between the domain controllers

Summary of Recommendations for NTLM Domain Authentication

- Do not allow authentication through your firewall.

Remote Authentication Dial-in User Service (RADIUS)

RADIUS is a protocol normally used to authenticate dial-in users. It provides both authentication and accounting data and is widely supported by dial-in terminal servers and other devices designed to support remote access over telephone lines.

When you are using RADIUS, a user dials up or otherwise contacts some sort of server that is giving out connections. That server is a RADIUS client; it holds a dialog with the user and passes information back and forth to a RADIUS client. Remember that it is the terminal server that is the RADIUS client, not the remote machine. The remote machine won't be able to join the network until after the RADIUS dialog is complete. Figure 21-5 shows the pattern of connections involved in RADIUS.

RADIUS encrypts password data but sends all other information unencrypted. This includes information about usernames and associated capabilities that you do not want hostile people to be able to read. RADIUS protects the data from tampering

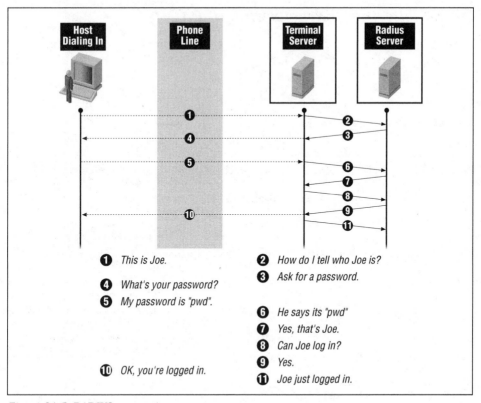

Figure 21-5. RADIUS connections

by including an authenticator that is an MD5 hash of the RADIUS data and a secret that is shared by the server and the client. (See Appendix C, *Cryptography*, for more information about cryptographic hashing and MD5.) This provides integrity protection, client authentication, and server authentication.

This system makes life difficult for proxying and network address translation systems. The RADIUS server has a different secret for each client, and it uses the source IP address of the RADIUS packet to choose which secret to add to the data before hashing. Similarly, if a client can talk to more than one server, it will use the source IP address to choose the secret to put into the hash at its end. This means that there must be a reliable one-to-one mapping between source IP addresses and RADIUS speakers; you cannot put multiple clients or servers behind the same proxy, or the server will not be able to tell them apart. For the same reason, you cannot put clients or servers behind a network address translation system unless they are statically mapped so that they will always appear with the same distinct source address.

Packet Filtering Characteristics of RADIUS

RADIUS authentication uses UDP port 1812, while accounting uses UDP port 1813. Early implementations of RADIUS used ports 1645 and 1646, but that usage is obsolete.

Direction	Source Addr.	Dest. Addr.	Protocol	Source Port	Dest. Port	ACK Set	Notes
In	Ext	Int	UDP	>1023	1812[a]	b	Authentication query, external client to internal RADIUS server
Out	Int	Ext	UDP	1812[a]	>1023	b	Authentication response, internal RADIUS server to external client
In	Ext	Int	UDP	>1023	1813[c]	b	Accounting notification, external client to internal RADIUS server
Out	Int	Ext	UDP	1813[c]	>1023	b	Accounting response, internal RADIUS server to external client.
Out	Int	Ext	UDP	>1023	1812[a]	b	Authentication query, internal client to external RADIUS server
In	Ext	Int	UDP	1812[a]	>1023	b	Authentication response, external RADIUS server to internal client
Out	Int	Ext	UDP	>1023	1813[c]	b	Accounting notification, internal client to external RADIUS server
In	Ext	Int	UDP	1813[c]	>1023	b	Accounting response, external RADIUS server to internal client.

[a] Early implementations may use 1645.
[b] UDP has no ACK equivalent.
[c] Early implementations may use 1646.

Proxying Characteristics of RADIUS

There are numerous RADIUS proxy servers. However, the term is used to refer to two different kinds of server. One of them is a standard RADIUS server speaking to another authentication server (for instance, a RADIUS server that uses NIS or Windows NT domain authentication to determine whether or not users can actually be authenticated). The other is a RADIUS server that will actually route requests via RADIUS to other RADIUS servers.

As we discussed earlier, the way that RADIUS authenticates clients and servers means that RADIUS will not work straightforwardly through generic proxy systems. RADIUS servers that do proxying do not pass the original authentication through; instead, the client and the proxy server authenticate each other, and then the proxy server recalculates the authenticator and separately authenticates to the next server. A generic proxy system cannot do this; if you need to proxy RADIUS, you should use a dedicated RADIUS proxy server.

Network Address Translation Characteristics of RADIUS

As mentioned, RADIUS uses source IP addresses as part of its authentication scheme and will not work if either the client or the server has a variable IP address. In order to use RADIUS through a network address translation system, you will need to set up static mappings, and make sure that the shared secret is assigned to the mapped address instead of the real address.

Summary of Recommendations for RADIUS

- Do not use RADIUS across untrusted networks; too much information is distributed unencrypted.

TACACS and Friends

TACACS might be an acronym for Terminal Access Controller Access Control System, or then again, it might not; its origins have been lost. TACACS is an old protocol. There are several newer versions of it, including XTACACS and TACACS+; TACACS+ currently appears to be the most popular.

All of these protocols, like RADIUS, are designed to provide authentication, authorization, and auditing services for dial-up users.

TACACS and XTACACS send all data, including usernames and passwords, in cleartext. TACACS+ uses MD5 to avoid sending passwords and usernames in a reusable form and normally also encrypts all data. Basically, this makes TACACS and XTACACS less secure than RADIUS, and TACACS+ more secure than RADIUS.

In order to support encryption, TACACS+ requires a secret key shared between the server and the client. This key must be stored on both the server and the client, and an attacker who has access to the key will be able to impersonate the server and to decrypt all data. This will not actually give the attacker access to passwords (the passwords are not sent in any decryptable form). Nonetheless, you should take reasonable steps to protect this key.

Packet Filtering Characteristics of TACACS and Friends

TACACS uses UDP port 49; it can also use TCP but does not necessarily use port 49 when using TCP. XTACACS uses UDP port 49. TACACS+ uses TCP port 49.

Direction	Source Addr.	Dest. Addr.	Protocol	Source Port	Dest. Port	ACK Set	Notes
In	Ext	Int	UDP	>1023	49	a	Request, external client to internal TACACS/XTACACS server
Out	Int	Ext	UDP	49	>1023	a	Response, internal TACACS/XTACACS server to external client.
In	Ext	Int	TCP	>1023	49b	c	External client connecting to internal TACACS/TACACS+ server
Out	Int	Ext	TCP	49b	>1023	Yes	Internal TACACS/TACACS+ server responding to external client
Out	Int	Ext	UDP	>1023	49	a	Request, internal client to external TACACS/XTACACS server
In	Ext	Int	UDP	49	>1023	a	Response, external TACACS/XTACACS server to internal client
Out	Int	Ext	TCP	>1023	49b	c	Internal client connecting to external TACACS/TACACS+ server
In	Ext	Int	TCP	49b	>1023	Yes	External TACACS/TACACS+ server responding to internal client.

a UDP has no ACK equivalent.
b This may be any port for TACACS.
c ACK will not be set on the first packet (establishing connection) but will be set on the rest.

Proxying Characteristics of TACACS and Friends

TACACS+ is a straightforward TCP-based protocol that is well suited for use with generic proxy systems. However, note that TACACS+ supports encryption using a secret key shared between the server and the client, and there is no standard way to determine which key to use if different clients have different keys. Some implementations may use the source address to determine the encryption key, requiring a dedicated proxy that has its own encryption key.

TACACS and XTACACS are both normally UDP-based, so they require proxies that can deal with UDP. However, they have no additional complexities and should work with any generic proxy that supports UDP.

Network Address Translation Characteristics of TACACS and Friends

TACACS and XTACACS do not use embedded IP addresses and will work without modification through network address translation systems. TACACS+ should also work, but just as with proxying, you should note that TACACS+ supports encryption using a secret key shared between the server and the client, and there is no standard way to determine which key to use if different clients have different keys. Some implementations may use the source address to determine the encryption key, requiring static address mappings.

In addition, TACACS+ supports the negotiation of IP addresses for PPP clients. In the unlikely event that you construct a network configuration where a network address translation system is modifying TACACS+ packets that are eventually used to set remote IP addresses, you should be careful to configure the TACACS+ server so that the addresses it provides are valid. The network address translation system will not be able to modify those embedded addresses.

Summary of Recommendations for TACACS and Friends

- Do not use TACACS or XTACACS across insecure networks (they transmit cleartext usernames and passwords); use TACACS+ instead.

Auth and identd

Auth is a protocol used to identify a remote user that generated a connection. The protocol is also sometimes referred to as *identd*, which is the name of a popular Unix daemon that implements it. Auth is used with protocols that do not identify a remote user that is generating a connection. When you make a connection with one of these protocols, the server you're talking to makes a connection back to your Auth server to get the information. For instance, HTTP requests don't include information about the user that made the request, so HTTP servers may use Auth to try to get that information to make log files more useful. SMTP and IRC requests do include information about the user, but that information is directly controlled by the user, who might be lying, so SMTP and IRC servers often use Auth to attempt to get more trustworthy information. Both attackers and network administrators also use Auth for more general information-gathering purposes.

Auth is really useful only if you can trust the remote server. If the people who're trying to lie to you control the Auth server, you're not going to get good information out of it. This means that Auth information may be interesting, but it's rarely trustworthy.

Furthermore, the information that normal Auth servers give out is information that's useful to attackers. The standard implementations of Auth simply give out usernames, and you don't want attackers to know what usernames are valid at your site. Some versions of *identd* and other Auth servers give out a unique per-user value that is not the username. This is useful to HTTP servers (all they want to know is how many different people are talking to them) and can be useful in tracking back attacks (if you log the value, an administrator at the attacking site can connect it to a username). It can be annoying for SMTP and IRC, which will normally display the value for human beings to look at.

Packet Filtering Characteristics of Auth

Auth is a TCP-based service. Servers use port 113. Clients use ports above 1023.

Direction	Source Addr.	Dest. Addr.	Protocol	Source Port	Dest. Port	ACK Set	Notes
In	Ext	Int	TCP	>1023	113	a	Query, external client to internal server
Out	Int	Ext	TCP	113	>1023	Yes	Response, internal server to external client
Out	Int	Ext	TCP	>1023	113	a	Query, internal client to external server
In	Ext	Int	TCP	113	>1023	Yes	Response, external server to internal client

a ACK is not set on the first packet of this type (establishing connection) but will be set on the rest.

We do not recommend discarding packets to port 113. If you choose not to permit this protocol, we suggest that you reject the packets with an error response or reset the connection. If you drop packets, you will experience delays when connecting to sites that insist on performing Auth lookups, and this may significantly slow down your electronic mail in particular. See Chapter 8, *Packet Filtering*, for more information about ways of responding to packets that you do not wish to accept.

Proxying Characteristics of Auth

A number of Auth proxy servers are available, mostly designed to let people use IRC servers that require Auth without giving away too much information. They are not traditional proxy servers; instead of proxying for internal clients, allowing them to make outbound Auth queries, they proxy for external clients, allowing them to make inbound Auth queries. Furthermore, they rarely complete the proxying process by forwarding the queries to the internal host, but reply to the queries immediately, usually with randomly chosen information.

For instance, Microsoft Proxy Server includes a service called "Identd Simulation service" that responds to Auth queries with randomly chosen identifiers. This sort of service is preferable to genuine proxying of Auth queries, which would leak information you probably do not want external hosts to have.

Network Address Translation Characteristics of Auth

Auth does not use embedded IP addresses, but it does contain port numbers. Auth will work transparently through network address translation systems, as long as they are changing only the host address and not the port number. On the other hand, Auth connections usually go in the opposite direction from the connections that caused them. That is, an outgoing SMTP or IRC connection will result in an inbound Auth connection; if the network address translation system is mapping ports instead of entire hosts, there will be no mapping for that inbound translation. You may therefore need to do special mappings to get Auth to work. For instance, you may want to direct all inbound Auth connections, regardless of their original destination, to an Auth proxy.

Summary of Recommendations for Auth

- Do not allow Auth through your firewall, but answer Auth queries with ICMP errors or TCP resets rather than simply dropping them, in order to speed up connections to servers that use Auth.

- If you decide to run an Auth server, choose one that does not return valid usernames.

- If you make Auth queries, don't trust the answers.

22

Administrative Services

This section describes a number of protocols that are used by people and programs to manage and maintain networks and machines. These include informational protocols like *syslog* and the Simple Network Management Protocol (SNMP), routing protocols like RIP and OSPF, system configuration protocols like *bootp* and Dynamic Host Configuration Protocol (DHCP), and ICMP and NTP. Where appropriate we also discuss tools that use these protocols, such as *ping* and *traceroute*.

System Management Protocols

These protocols are used to manage devices on the network, either by simply conveying information about their status or by actually controlling remote devices.

syslog

syslog is used to manage log messages in a centralized way. *syslog* got its start as a way of centrally recording messages for a set of Unix machines, but many network devices (routers, hubs, etc.) now use *syslog* to report status and usage information. Such devices often don't even have a way to record this information locally, because they don't have any writable storage media; if you want to know what they're reporting, something has to be listening to their *syslog* messages.

Microsoft operating systems do not provide *syslog* support; instead, they use a combination of a local log manager and SNMP for remote event reporting. It is possible to get implementations of *syslog* for such systems.

Attackers will often attempt to flood a site's *syslog* server in order to cover their tracks, so that the server runs out of disk space and stops logging new messages, or so that the evidence of their activities is lost in the noise. Recent versions of *syslog* often have the ability to turn off listening from the network, while still keeping the ability to send messages to remote servers; some of them also provide the ability to accept remote messages only from specific source addresses.

Packet filtering characteristics of syslog

syslog is a UDP-based service. *syslog* servers (which record messages logged by other systems) listen on UDP port 514. *syslog* clients generally (but not always) use ports above 1023 to talk to servers. *syslog* servers never send messages back to clients. *syslog* servers can be configured to pass messages along to other *syslog* servers; in such cases, the sending server generally uses port 514 as the client port. There are TCP-based variants of *syslog* available, but there is no standard yet.

Direction	Source Addr.	Dest. Addr.	Protocol	Source Port	Dest. Port	ACK Set	Notes
In	Ext	Int	UDP	>1023[a]	514	[b]	External client contacting internal *syslog* server
In	Ext	Int	UDP	514	514	[b]	External *syslog* server passing message to internal *syslog* server
Out	Int	Ext	UDP	>1023[a]	514	[b]	Internal client contacting external *syslog* server
Out	Int	Ext	UDP	514	514	[b]	Internal *syslog* server passing message to external *syslog* server

[a] Some *syslog* clients sometimes use ports below 1024.
[b] UDP has no ACK equivalent.

Proxying characteristics of syslog

syslog is a self-proxying protocol; that is, *syslog* servers can generally be configured to simply pass messages they receive on to other *syslog* servers. Although *syslog* would be straightforward to proxy with a proxy system that knows about UDP, there do not appear to be implementations available that provide this facility.

Network address translation and syslog

Although *syslog* does not use embedded IP addresses, the log entries *syslog* makes include information derived from the source IP address; using network address translation may make it hard to figure out where messages are from.

Summary of recommendations for syslog

- Do not allow *syslog* in from the outside world. In this way, you'll prevent attackers from attempting to flood your *syslog* servers.

- If your *syslog* daemon supports it, turn off the ability to receive external syslog requests.

Simple Network Management Protocol (SNMP)

SNMP is a standardized remote monitoring and management mechanism for network devices like hubs, routers, and bridges, as well as servers and workstations. The theory is that any SNMP-capable management station should be able to monitor and control any SNMP-capable network device.

Normally, SNMP management stations act as clients, contacting SNMP servers in the various network devices to request information or to issue commands. Sometimes, network devices act as SNMP clients to contact special SNMP servers (known as *trap* servers) on management stations to report critical information that can't wait until the next time the management station polls the device. SNMP trap servers are separate from regular SNMP servers so that a given machine can run both—that is, can be both an SNMP server (and thus be manageable via SNMP) and an SNMP trap server (and thus be a management station and receive traps from other devices).

In general, you don't want someone from the outside to be able to manage your network via SNMP. Therefore, you shouldn't allow SNMP to cross your firewall, and you should carefully configure (or disable) SNMP on your systems that are outside your firewall so that attackers can't use it to change that configuration. See Chapter 10, *Bastion Hosts*, Chapter 11, *Unix and Linux Bastion Hosts*, and Chapter 12, *Windows NT and Windows 2000 Bastion Hosts*, for more information on how to properly configure bastion hosts.

The SNMP version in widest use, which is SNMPv2, does support some rudimentary security; when information is requested, the requester needs to specify a *community* that it's in. Different communities can be shown different information, and in some implementations, a reusable password can be required for certain communities. At its best, this security is quite primitive; anybody who's doing packet sniffing can easily discover a community name and password. Since relatively few implementations support passwords, and almost all implementations provide a default community called "public", it's very rare to find things at their best. At least one implementation not only comes with the "public" community but does not provide any permanent way to disable access for this community!

SNMP can be an extraordinarily dangerous protocol. The minimal information most devices will give out includes operating system details and precise traffic loads and destinations, which is already information you don't want attackers to have. Many implementations add even more critical information (for instance, Microsoft's SNMP server will list all valid account names on the machine and most of the services running on it). In addition, it is possible for a remote machine not only to request information but to set variables. Since SNMP is intended for network management, and an SNMP client is expected to be a network management console, these variables usually give you full control of at least the machine's network configuration, and often more than that. For instance, you can often reboot a remote machine via SNMP, and Microsoft systematically attempts to make all the functionality of service control panels available over SNMP. Routers can often be completely controlled via SNMP.

In general, the default "public" community is able only to read information, but it is often able to read all the available information, which in several implementations from large router vendors includes a listing of all the communities and their capabilities, so that anybody can read the information about how to get write access.

On machines that are running multiple SNMP-enabled services (for instance, machines that have an operating system SNMP agent and are also running Oracle), SNMP servers may be at unexpected ports. If multiple SNMP agents need to run on the same machine, only one of them can be at SNMP's normal port. One way to deal with it is to have a master agent at that port and move some or all of the other SNMP agents to other ports (normally above 1024, since that's where free ports are likely to be). The master agent then speaks SNMP to the other agents (commonly referred to as *sub-agents*), which don't have to be aware that there's anything unusual happening. This is a very flexible approach, but it is yet another service that may be vulnerable if you open up connections above 1024.

SNMP version 3

Implementations of SNMPv3 are just becoming available. SNMPv3 provides greatly enhanced security, including user authentication, encrypted communications, and time-stamped digital signatures that prevent attackers from intercepting and resending packets. Gateways that translate between SNMPv3 and earlier versions of SNMP are available, allowing you to use SNMPv3 across insecure links to manage older devices as long as there is some secure link between the gateway and the managed device.

Packet filtering characteristics of SNMP

SNMP is a UDP-based service. SNMP servers (in network devices) listen on UDP port 161. (TCP port 161 is also reserved for use by SNMP but has been used only experimentally.) SNMP trap servers (in management stations) listen on UDP port 162. SNMP clients generally use ports above 1023 to talk to both regular and trap servers. By convention, SNMP sub-agents are at port 1161, but they might be anywhere.

Direction	Source Addr.	Dest. Addr.	Protocol	Source Port	Dest. Port	ACK Set	Notes
In	Ext	Int	UDP	>1023	161	a	Query from external management station to internal SNMP device
Out	Int	Ext	UDP	161	>1023	a	Response from internal SNMP device to external management station
Out	Int	Ext	UDP	>1023	161	a	Query from internal management station to external SNMP device
In	Ext	Int	UDP	161	>1023	a	Response from external SNMP device to internal management station
In	Ext	Int	UDP	>1023	162	a	Trap from external SNMP device to internal management station
Out	Int	Ext	UDP	>1023	162	a	Trap from internal SNMP device to external management station

a UDP has no ACK equivalent.

All versions of SNMP use the same port numbers, so you will not be able to tell what version you are allowing through your packet filters. Since different versions have very different levels of security, you will probably want to limit access to those devices that you know are appropriately secure.

Proxying characteristics of SNMP

SNMP is not commonly used across the Internet (although Internet service providers frequently use it), and proxies are not widely available. You may be able to modify network management stations to use proxies for SNMP gets, but in many cases, you will not be able to do traps through proxies. This is because the SNMP agent has to generate the trap, and it is often running on a device where neither the software nor the procedures are particularly modifiable.

Network address translation and SNMP

SNMP does not use embedded IP addresses directly, and SNMP itself will function without problems through network address translation systems. However, the information that's distributed through SNMP will almost always include IP addresses that will not be translated. This may leak information that's considered confidential and will certainly cause problems if any person or program tries to use the information. A number of network management programs will use the address information inside the SNMP data to make subsequent connections to managed machines, which will not work.

System Management Server (SMS)

Microsoft's System Management Server is a suite of programs used to manage Windows computers. It is not a single service, and the exact services that are included change with different releases of SMS. The basic functions of SMS are:

- Hardware and software inventory
- Software distribution
- Shared application management
- Remote control

In addition, SMS normally includes a variety of utilities intended to help system administrators, including:

- An enhanced network monitor
- SNMP tools to convert events to traps and receive traps
- Database tools to clean databases and produce reports

SMS also depends on having a SQL server available to store data in and uses directory replication to distribute some of its information. Most of these services, including directory replication and the default configuration for the SQL server, are based on SMB transactions, which are discussed in Chapter 14, *Intermediary Protocols*.

SMS has very serious security implications. The SMS hardware and software inventory provide detailed information about machines, and the software distribution mechanism allows any command to be executed with full Administrator permissions. All client machines are completely at the mercy of the SMS servers. In addition, an SMS system normally involves multiple server machines (for instance, one running the database server, one running software distribution, and one storing the shared applications), and those servers all trust each other. If any of the machines involved is compromised, the attacker will have control of all of the servers and, through them, of all of the clients.

Several of the utilities included in SMS are useful in a firewall environment; the network monitor, for instance, is an important diagnostic tool, and there is a tool for turning events into SNMP traps. The primary functions of SMS (hardware and software inventory, software distribution, and shared application management) are all risky and should not be run through a firewall or to firewall machines.

Performance Monitor and Network Monitor

Under Windows NT, the two most frequently used tools for diagnosing system problems and tracking usage are Performance Monitor and Network Monitor. Both of these programs allow you to access remote machines and get data from them. They are based on SMB transactions, which are discussed further in Chapter 14, *Intermediary Protocols.*

Performance Monitor and Network Monitor both provide information that's useful to attackers. Performance Monitor is the less interesting of the two; it provides performance and utilization data that will tell an attacker some useful data about the machine configuration, the amount of work needed to produce a denial of service, and the likelihood that anybody will notice if the attacker starts using the machine, but it doesn't give out anything of immediate use in breaking into the machine.

Network Monitor, on the other hand, comes with an agent that will let an attacker use the machine as a remote network sniffer. The version of Network Monitor that comes with Windows NT shows only packets sent to and from the machine it's running on (including broadcast and multicast packets), but that's plenty of data for an attacker to do damage with. If you have installed the full-featured version that comes with System Management Server, it will show all traffic that comes to the port, regardless of the machine that the traffic was sent to. Depending on your network configuration, this may make no difference (for instance, on a switched network, hosts will normally receive only their own traffic), or it may be all the traffic on the network segment (for instance, if you're using simple hubs or classic Ethernet bus-style cabling).

Because they are based on SMB transactions, Network Monitor and Performance Monitor are different to secure through a firewall, and you should not allow them. Because the Network Monitor Agent and Performance Monitor are extremely useful management tools, you may want to allow them on machines that make up your firewall. In this situation, you should be sure that they are not running on interfaces that can be reached from the Internet. It would be better yet to run Network Monitor and Performance Monitor locally on the firewall machine and disable SMB over the network altogether.

Summary Recommendations for System Management

- Do not allow any system management protocols across or into your firewall from the Internet. (This may require special SNMP configurations on your packet filtering routers, which are probably themselves SNMP-capable devices.)

- If you need to use SNMP remotely, use SNMPv3.

Routing Protocols

Routing protocols are used to distribute information about where packets should be directed. Any given device can pass a packet only to another device on the same local area network. If the packet's destination is on a different local area network, the device must know what machine can move it to the next network, on the way to its destination. Most desktop machines have very little use for routing protocols—usually, a desktop machine has a single network interface and attaches to a network with only one cross-connection to other networks. Thus, a desktop machine needs to know only "If the packet isn't bound for a machine on this network, hand it to that address over there". However, bastion hosts and Internet-connected gateways may be keeping track of much more complex situations, involving multiple network interfaces, and multiple connections from those networks to others.

Routing protocols in general are dangerous. Attackers who can send you bad routing information not only have an easy way of performing a denial of service attack (if you route your packets the wrong places, you can't talk to anybody), but also have a much easier time of intercepting data (they can get you to send data to them so they can read it on the way past). Furthermore, routing protocols tend to be old. Many of the routing protocols in use today were designed when the Internet was a kinder, gentler, and smaller place, and the idea that people might intentionally lie to you about routes had never occurred to anybody, so there is no provision for preventing it.

It's actually quite difficult to design a routing protocol that's secure and is still usable for routing on the Internet backbone, since the protocol needs to move quite large amounts of data, including frequent changes, between hosts that are already busy. Because the backbone routers are specialized devices, not general-purpose computers, and because routing problems on the backbone can cause widespread disruption, changes to backbone routing protocols have to be made very slowly and carefully.

Fortunately, the routing protocols currently used on the backbone are different from the protocols used within individual sites. We do not discuss protocols that are used between distinct entities across the backbone because these protocols do not usually cross firewalls. Instead, we discuss the protocols most commonly used for routing within networks (often called *interior gateway protocols*), which you may need to use across internal firewalls.

Routing Information Protocol (RIP)

RIP is the oldest routing protocol on the Internet. In fact, it predates IP; it was taken almost verbatim from the older Xerox Network Services (XNS) system. It is also still a very commonly used routing protocol on local area IP networks. Routers (including general-purpose machines with multiple interfaces that can act as routers) use RIP to periodically broadcast which networks they know how to reach and how far away those networks are. By listening to these broadcasts, a router or host can determine what networks are reachable and choose the best (shortest) path to each. RIP servers generally just broadcast this information every 30 seconds or so for anyone interested to hear, but a RIP client can request a special update from a RIP server, which will cause the server to reply directly to the client with the information requested.

By default, RIP is completely insecure; clients simply accept any data they are sent. RIP does not provide any place in the protocol for authentication. There have been security problems with RIP clients because it is possible for RIP packets to contain not only routing information, but also the request to turn on logging to a specified file. Some Unix RIP clients were willing to accept such requests; since routing daemons have to run as root, they were then willing and able to overwrite any file on the system with a log of routing updates, which is not a useful substitute for most system files. RIP clients are no longer routinely configured to accept such requests.

Many RIP implementations will allow you to configure a RIP client with slight security improvements; for instance, they will allow you to specify that you are willing to accept RIP updates only from certain IP source addresses, and/or they will allow you to declare that certain routing information cannot be modified by RIP updates. This is usually sufficient to protect clients from local misconfigurations but not sufficient to protect against active hostile acts.

A modified version of RIP, called RIP-2, provides several improvements to the routing information that's distributed and also allows for the use of passwords. Unfortunately, the normal method of using passwords is to put the same 16-character password in every packet. Again, this is sufficient to protect clients from local misconfigurations (you're unlikely to get the right password by accident) but not against hostile acts (any attacker can read the password out of any valid RIP broadcast and use it). It is easier to maintain than a list of valid IP source addresses. RIP-2 implementations that support MD5 authentication are becoming more widely available, and this authentication actually provides a reasonable amount of protection.

RIP-2 and RIP implementations can interoperate, but RIP implementations won't verify or attach the password. As a result, if you're using RIP-2 with passwords, routers that implement RIP can receive routing updates but cannot successfully send them.

Packet filtering characteristics of RIP

RIP is a UDP-based service. RIP servers listen on port 520 for broadcasts from other servers and requests from clients. RIP servers generally send their broadcasts from port 520. RIP clients generally use ports above 1023.

Direction	Source Addr.	Dest. Addr.	Protocol	Source Port	Dest. Port	ACK Set	Notes
In	Ext	Int	UDP	>1023	520	a	Request, external client to internal server
Out	Int	Ext	UDP	520	>1023	a	Response, internal server to external client
Out	Int	Ext	UDP	>1023	520	a	Request, internal client to external server
In	Int	Ext	UDP	520	>1023	a	Response, external server to internal client
In	Ext	Broad-cast	UDP	520	520	a	Update, external server to internal servers
Out	Int	Broad-cast	UDP	520	520	a	Update, internal server to external servers

a UDP has no ACK equivalent.

Open Shortest Path First (OSPF)

OSPF is a more recent protocol than RIP that uses a completely different approach to distributing routing information. The main difference between the two protocols involves the kinds of routing information they distribute, but there are also significant differences in the ways they use the network. RIP is based on UDP, while OSPF is based directly on IP; RIP uses unicast and broadcast, while OSPF uses unicast and multicast.

OSPF supports authentication, which could theoretically be quite secure—the protocol allows for cryptographic message digests. However, the cryptographic message digest algorithm is not specified by the standard, so in practice OSPF authentication is restricted to eight-character cleartext passwords or the same degree of authentication as RIP-2. This will protect from accidental misconfigurations but not from hostile attacks.

Packet filtering characteristics of OSPF

OSPF is layered directly on IP, not on TCP or UDP, and is IP protocol 89. OSPF uses both multicast and unicast packets. OSPF uses two special multicast groups, AllSPFRouters (224.0.0.5) and AllDRouters (224.0.0.6). OSPF does not have port numbers but does distinguish between different messages with a packet type identifier.

Direction	Source Addr.	Dest. Addr.	Protocol[a]	Packet Type[b]	Notes
In	Ext	224.0.0.5	89	1	Router hello, announcing its existence and neighbors
Out	Int. Router	224.0.0.5	89	1	Internal router hello, announcing its existence and neighbors
In	Ext	Int Router	89	2	External router database description, giving an external router's link state database
Out	Int. Router	Ext	89	2	Internal router database description
In	Ext	Int Router	89	3	External router link state request, asking for information about a particular link
Out	Int. Router	Ext	89	4	Internal router link state update for a particular link in response to a request.
Out	Int. Router	Ext	89	3	Internal router link state request
In	Ext	Int Router	89	4	External router link state update
In	Ext	224.0.0.5	89	4	External router link state update, flooding all link states, from a designated router
Out	Int. Router	224.0.0.6	89	5	Internal router link state acknowledgment response from a nondesignated router
In	Ext	224.0.0.6	89	4	External router link state update, from a nondesignated router
Out	Int. Router	224.0.0.5	89	5	Internal router link state acknowledgment from a designated router
Out	Int. Router	224.0.0.5	89	4	Internal router link state update from a designated router
In	Ext	224.0.0.6	89	5	External router link state acknowledgment from a nondesignated router
Out	Int. Router	224.0.0.6	89	4	Internal router link state update, from a nondesignated router
In	Ext	224.0.0.5	89	5	External router link state acknowledgment from a designated router

[a] OSPF is layered directly on IP, not on TCP or UDP.
[b] OSPF does not have source and destination ports, but messages are distinguished by type.

OSPF multicast packets are not intended to be forwarded and will be sent with a TTL of 1, which means that the packets will not go through a router. If you are doing packet filtering that is not completely transparent, and for some reason you still want to do OSPF through the packet filter, you have two choices. The preferred option is to preconfigure the routers that need to pass routing updates through the packet filter so that they know about their neighbors. This will usually remove the need to pass multicast packets. If that is unacceptable, and the packet filter is sufficiently flexible, you may be able to configure the packet filter so that it does not decrease the TTL on OSPF packets and will pass them on. This is an extremely eccentric network configuration and is rarely advisable; any packet filter capable of this sort of trickery is probably on a machine capable of simply speaking OSPF directly, which would be preferable.

Internet Group Management Protocol (IGMP)

IGMP is used to manage multicast groups. See Chapter 19, *Real-Time Conferencing Services*, for more information about multicast. Multicasting is also increasingly being used by administrative protocols; for example, it's used for WINS server replication.

Multicast routers do not forward all multicast packets to all networks; they forward multicast packets only to places where hosts are listening for them. In order to make this decision, a multicast router has to keep track of the multicast groups in use. Since multicast packets go to all the hosts on a network segment that want them, the router doesn't need to identify all the hosts that are in a group, but it does need to know, for each network segment, what groups are of interest. IGMP is the protocol that hosts and routers use to communicate this information.

Multicast routers receive all multicast packets, regardless of the multicast address they are sent to. Hosts that use multicast receive packets only for groups they subscribe to, but all of them subscribe to a group called AllSystems (224.0.0.1). All IGMP packets are sent out with a TTL of 1, which means that they will not be forwarded through a router. This makes sense because the purpose of IGMP is to configure a router's information about a particular, directly attached network segment.

There are two parts to the IGMP process: first, hosts send out notifications, called *membership reports*, when they join any group other than AllSystems (and in some versions, when they leave those groups as well). Second, routers can send out periodic queries asking about group membership. A router can ask for information either about all groups, or about a particular group. In either case, hosts respond with membership reports, just like the ones they send when they initially join groups. The protocol is designed so that only one host per group will respond. All the router needs to know is whether or not there is interest in the group; it doesn't need to know how many hosts are interested.

Packet filtering characteristics of IGMP

IGMP is based directly on IP and is protocol 2. IGMP does not have port numbers; IGMP packets are distinguished by packet types. IGMP is a datagram protocol that does not have an ACK bit or its equivalent. All IGMP packets are sent with a TTL of 1 and will not pass through a packet filter unless it is completely transparent or is specially configured to pass IGMP without decreasing the TTL. You would pass IGMP through a packet filter only if the packet filter was between a multicast router and the hosts it serves, and the packet filter was also going to pass all other multicast. In this situation, it would probably be better to either tunnel multicast or configure the packet filter to be a multicast router.

Source Addr.	Dest. Addr.	Protocol	Packet Type	Notes
Router	224.0.0.1	2 (IGMP)	0x11	Host membership query
Host	Multicast[a]	2 (IGMP)	0x12	Version 1 host membership report
Host	Multicast[a]	2 (IGMP)	0x16	Version 2 host membership report
Host	224.0.0.1	2 (IGMP)	0x17	Leave group

[a] This will be addressed to the multicast group that it is reporting about.

Router Discovery/ICMP Router Discovery Protocol (IRDP)

Router discovery, also known as ICMP Router Discovery Protocol (IRDP), is not actually a routing protocol. It is a mechanism that hosts can use to find routers, independent of any routing protocol. Router discovery allows a host to ask what routers are on its network, using something called a *router solicitation*, and get back an answer from each router. The routers can also provide information about relative desirability. That is, each router sends a number indicating how good it thinks it is, configured by the administrator who set up the router. The host can then use this information to pick a router. That's all the information the host gets from the router; there's no information about what networks the router is connected to, for instance.

In addition to responding to requests from hosts, routers send out the same information periodically. Whether or not it's been requested, it is called a *router announcement*, and hosts are supposed to treat unsolicited announcements the same way they treat announcements they've asked for.

Router discovery is a useful way for hosts to find default routers without needing to implement complicated routing protocols. However, it contains no authentication information at all, allowing attackers to send out router announcements that will divert traffic. If the attacker is on the network being attacked, those announcements could divert traffic to where the attacker could read or modify it. If the attacker doesn't have a point of presence on the network, there's less benefit to the attacker. Denial of service attacks are certainly possible, and in a few cases, an attacker might be able to divert traffic to another network that the attacker was present on.

Router discovery is not widely implemented, and most hosts that use it do so as a supplement to other ways of configuring routing. You may therefore have hosts that are using router discovery without knowing it. These hosts will already have routes configured by some other means (using RIP announcements, DHCP, or simply having some human type them in somewhere). How these hosts treat router announcements is entirely implementation dependent. Many of them will use announced routers instead of routers they knew about from other sources; others will apply a ranking based on the information in the announcement; and some of them will prefer preconfigured routers to announced routers.

There is absolutely no reason for router discovery to ever go through a router. Router discovery is intended only to convey information about the local network. It is therefore safe and advisable to filter it out in all packet filtering routers. You will also want to turn off router discovery on bastion hosts, in order to be sure that they are not going to pay attention to invalid announcements if other bastion hosts are compromised.

Packet filtering characteristics of router discovery

Router discovery is based on ICMP. Router discovery is supposed to be multicast-based, but it is allowable (although strongly discouraged) for hosts to use broadcast instead of multicast.

Direction	Source Addr.	Dest.Addr.	Protocol	Message Type[a]	Notes
In	Ext	Broadcast, 224.0.0.2	ICMP	10	Incoming router solicitation
Out	Int	Ext, Broadcast, 224.0.0.1	ICMP	9	Outgoing router announcement
Out	Int	Broadcast, 224.0.0.2	ICMP	10	Outgoing router solicitation
In	Ext	Int, Broadcast, 224.0.0.1	ICMP	9	Incoming router advertisement

[a] ICMP messages do not have source or destination port numbers; they have a single ICMP message type field instead. ICMP has no ACK equivalent.

Proxying Characteristics of Routing Protocols

Because routing protocols are used by a host to develop routing tables that are specific to where that host is in the network, it doesn't make any sense to proxy routing protocols to hosts elsewhere in the network.

Network Address Translation Characteristics of Routing Protocols

Routing protocols transfer information that's highly dependent on network addresses and is certain to be pointless if it passes through a network address translator. It doesn't make any sense to run network address translation on routing protocols.

Summary of Recommendations for Routing Protocols

- Do not allow routing protocols (RIP or otherwise) across your firewall to or from the Internet. Routing on the firewall is generally very simple and is accomplished best with static routes. Simply configure the firewall to direct packets bound for internal source addresses to an internal router and to direct all other packets to your Internet connection.

- Configure routing on bastion hosts carefully, in order to provide depth of defense against problems with the firewall or other bastion hosts and some level of protection against local misconfiguration.

Protocols for Booting and Boot-Time Configuration

These protocols are used to provide information to machines while they are booting. For instance, these protocols are used to bring up diskless clients, to configure portable machines that move from network to network and need to discover information, and frequently to configure network devices like routers and printers that generally do not have persistent storage to keep complex configuration information locally. TFTP, which is discussed in Chapter 17, *File Transfer, File Sharing, and Printing*, is also a critical part of this process in many cases.

bootp

bootp is a broadcast-based protocol used by clients to get configuration data and other boot-time information, particularly IP addresses. A client that comes up with no configuration data may use link-layer broadcasts and its MAC address to get basic data from a server. Because *bootp* is broadcast-based at the link layer, it will not cross a router unless the router has been specifically configured to pass it (for instance, using an "IP helper address" on a Cisco). However, most *bootp* servers will accept unicast packets, so you should not rely on this to protect *bootp* servers from attack.

Dynamic Host Configuration Protocol (DHCP)

DHCP is an extension of *bootp* (and uses the same network port numbers). *bootp* supports a one-to-one mapping from MAC addresses to TCP/IP addresses. DHCP is a more complex protocol that allows for multiple servers, dynamic address allocation, automatic name registration, and passing client-specific configuration parameters. Dynamic addresses are "leased" to clients that must periodically request continued ownership. DHCP is used for machines that can boot themselves but still require network configuration information to work on a network. It's particularly useful with mobile machines, since their network configurations change often, but it's also used to make permanent machines easier to configure.

Bastion hosts should have permanent addresses that are configured on the machine itself; it is unwise to use DHCP to configure them, and we strongly recommend against doing so. Using DHCP makes bastion hosts dependent on the DHCP server.

DHCP requires both broadcast and unicast requests in order to function correctly. Putting a normal router in place will prevent a DHCP server from doing anything useful for clients on the far side of the router without actually protecting the DHCP server from attackers.

Packet Filtering Characteristics of DHCP and bootp

bootp is UDP-based; *bootp* clients use port 68, and *bootp* servers use port 67. UDP does not use ACK bits. Although it is not specified in the standard, DHCP servers and/or clients frequently also use ICMP echo sent to the address that a client will be offered, or an ARP request to determine whether the address is actually free or is in use.

Direction	Source Addr.	Dest. Addr.	Protocol	Source Port	Dest. Port	Notes
In	Ext[a]	Broadcast	UDP	68	67	External client request to internal server
Out	Int	Ext[b]	UDP	67	68	Internal server positive response to external client
Out	Int	Broadcast	UDP	67	68	Internal server negative response to external DHCP client
In	Ext[b]	Broadcast	UDP	68	67	External client accepting DHCP offer
Out	Int	Ext[b]	UDP	67	68	Internal server acknowledging DHCP lease
Out	Int[a]	Broadcast	UDP	68	67	Internal client request to external server
In	Ext	Int[b]	UDP	67	68	External server positive response to internal client
In	Ext	Broadcast	UDP	67	68	External server negative response to internal DHCP client

Direction	Source Addr.	Dest. Addr.	Protocol	Source Port	Dest. Port	Notes
Out	Int[b]	Broadcast	UDP	68	67	Internal client accepting DHCP offer
In	Ext	Int[b]	UDP	67	68	External server acknowledging DHCP lease

[a] This address need not be a valid address; the destination machine is assumed not to be fully configured, and the packet will actually be delivered based on lower-level data, not on the apparent destination address. The lower-level data may have a broadcast or unicast address depending on client capabilities.

[b] This is now the valid, agreed-upon address.

Proxying Characteristics of bootp and DHCP

Because *bootp* and DHCP are broadcast-based, they are normally limited to a single LAN segment. In most networks, it is inconvenient to put servers on every LAN segment and then attempt to keep the configuration data synchronized between them. *bootp* proxies are therefore extremely common (and since DHCP is *bootp*-based, it proxies it as well). Almost any machine with a *bootp* or DHCP implementation will also have a proxy. In addition, many routers can be configured to forward some or all broadcast packets to other broadcast or unicast addresses; this can function as a crude proxy.

None of these proxy mechanisms is particularly configurable; these are not security-oriented proxies likely to do protocol checking, authorization, or logging.

Network Address Translation Characteristics of Booting and Boot-Time Configuration

Because these protocols give out information about network addresses, it's hard to conceive of a configuration where it would be a good idea to run them through a network address translator.

Summary of Recommendations for Booting and Boot-Time Configuration

- Do not allow these protocols across your firewall. You should not trust external hosts to provide you with booting information, and you do not want to help external hosts boot with your information.

- Do not configure bastion hosts to use DHCP; they should use permanently assigned addresses determined by their configuration files.

ICMP and Network Diagnostics

The ICMP and network diagnostic protocols and programs are mostly used by network administrators to debug networks. They are the network administration equivalent of a carpenter's hammer and saw: the most basic, simple, and critical tools, ancient in design but nonetheless indispensable.

Because they are widely accepted low-level protocols, they are also frequently exploited for attacks. A number of denial of service attacks are based upon malformed ICMP packets, and a number of Trojan horses use ICMP to send information out of compromised sites. In addition, forged or inaccurate ICMP packets are often used as part or all of attacks on systems. For instance, an attacker can send an ICMP "destination unreachable packet" for a host that is actually reachable; this will interfere with communications to the attacked destination.

Many packet filtering systems let you filter ICMP packets in much the same way as TCP or UDP packets: by specifying the ICMP message type code instead of the TCP or UDP source or destination port number. If your packet filtering system has this capability, its documentation should include a list of the ICMP numeric codes or keywords that the packet filtering system understands. You may not want to filter all ICMP because it will prevent path MTU discovery from functioning, and this may cause problems (see Chapter 4, *Packets and Protocols*, for more information about path MTU discovery).

ping

The *ping** program checks network connectivity. The *ping* application generates an ICMP "echo request" packet. The destination system responds with an ICMP "echo response" packet. ICMP is typically implemented in the kernel, so it's the kernel that generates the "echo response" packet; there is no separate server for ICMP on most systems. (On some machines, the echo response is actually generated in the network interface itself, not in the operating system, and the machine need not even be fully running to respond to *ping*.) *ping* is not the only program that uses ICMP echo; others include *spray* and almost any dedicated network management tool.

ping is a useful network troubleshooting tool, and it is reasonably safe. You'll probably want to allow *ping* outbound from at least the machines your network operations staff uses and inbound from at least the network operations center machines of your network service provider.

---

* *ping* is not an acronym. Mike Muus, who wrote the original program, confirms that he named it after the noise sonar makes.

Because of where it is implemented, it is almost impossible to disable replies to *ping* on individual hosts; packet filtering is the only way to control it.

There are multiple dangers in allowing ICMP echo:

- It can be used for a denial of service attack—that is, to flood your network. Although any protocol you accept can be used in this way, ICMP echo is particularly tempting because commonly available programs designed for network testing (including some versions of *ping*) let you flood networks with simple command-line options.

- Anybody who can send ICMP echo requests to and receive ICMP echo responses from your network can discover how many machines you have and what network addresses they're at; this increases the efficiency of any further attacks. That's why you want to limit requests to machines that have a legitimate reason to be probing your network.

- Malformed ICMP echo requests may have unfortunate effects on weak implementations of IP. This is true of all protocols, but ICMP is easily overlooked and therefore tends to have hastily written implementations that are particularly vulnerable.

- The data portion of ICMP echo requests and responses are unimportant to the protocol and may legally contain anything. This makes ICMP echo a particularly useful way to smuggle information through a firewall.

Packet filtering characteristics of ping

To allow the *ping* program to operate outbound (i.e., *ping*ing remote hosts), you'll have to allow ICMP echo request packets outbound and ICMP echo response packets inbound. To allow inbound *ping* (i.e., a remote host *ping*ing a local host), you'll have to allow ICMP echo request packets inbound and ICMP echo response packets outbound. If possible, you will also want to limit the acceptable size of ICMP echo request packets. Limiting the inbound size is a self-protection measure, designed to protect against denial of service attacks; limiting the outbound size is a matter of politeness.

Direction	Source Addr.	Dest. Addr.	Protocol	Message Type[a]	Notes
In	Ext	Int	ICMP	8	Incoming *ping*
Out	Int	Ext	ICMP	0	Response to incoming *ping*
Out	Int	Ext	ICMP	8	Outgoing *ping*
In	Ext	Int	ICMP	0	Response to outgoing *ping*

[a] ICMP messages do not have source or destination port numbers; they have a single ICMP message type field instead. ICMP has no ACK equivalent.

If you have a stateful packet filtering system, it is wise to configure it so that you allow responses only if you have seen a matching request. This is particularly important if you only allow requests in one direction, since the responses will be going in the direction where requests are denied. Unsolicited responses are always hostile, whether they are actual attacks or being used as covert channels to smuggle information.

Proxying characteristics of ping

SOCKS5 provides a modified-client proxy system for *ping*. Because *ping* is neither TCP- nor UDP-based, it won't work with most generic proxy servers for modified-client proxying. Because *ping* transmits no user-supplied data to the destination host, modified-procedure proxying for *ping* is not possible. Modified-procedure proxying also relies on the ability of the proxy server to intercept the request before the machine it's running on generates a reply, which is difficult with *ping*. In a pure modified-procedure proxying environment, *ping* will have to be provided by letting users connect to the proxying host (for instance, with a special web page) and run *ping* from there, as discussed in Chapter 9, *Proxy Systems*. Several systems that use packet interception to do proxying supply *ping* proxies.

When proxying *ping*, it is a good idea to sanitize the packet bodies. Instead of passing the original data portion of the response or request, the proxy should replace it with an equivalent length of data generated by the proxy. This will prevent the use of *ping* as a covert channel. In a few cases, it will also interfere with debugging (some network problems are dependent on particular data patterns triggering bugs in networking hardware). Fortunately, this kind of debugging rarely needs to cross the Internet.

Network address translation and ping

ping does not use embedded IP addresses and should work without problems through any network address translation system that supports ICMP.

traceroute

traceroute (also known as *tracert* on Microsoft systems) is an application that shows you the route that packets take to a particular IP destination. Because no system typically knows the full path to the destination (merely the next step towards the destination), this is a neat trick.* *traceroute* works by carefully constructing special packets. The destination address of the packets is the remote host; depending on the implementation, the packets are either ICMP echo packets or UDP packets where the destination port is an unused (or so we hope, as we'll

---

* *traceroute* is, fundamentally, a "cool hack".

discuss later) port on the remote host. The really special thing about the packets, though, is that the time to live (TTL) fields are set very low (starting at 1), so that the packets will be rejected by intermediate routers as if they were looping in the network. By looking where the rejections (ICMP "time to live exceeded" messages) come from, *traceroute* can determine who the intermediate routers are.

TTL is a field in the header of every IP packet. It normally isn't of interest from a firewall point of view. The name is somewhat misleading; it might be more intuitively called "hops to live". When a packet is first created, its TTL field is set to some value (typically 16, 30, or 255). Every router that handles the packet along its journey decrements the TTL field by 1. If the TTL field ever reaches 0, the packet is assumed to be in some sort of a loop; it is encapsulated within an ICMP "time to live exceeded" message and is returned to the source address.

Thus, the first router that handles the first of *traceroute's* specially constructed packets (which has a TTL of 1) will decrement the TTL field, see that it's 0, and return an ICMP "time to live exceeded" message, telling *traceroute* the IP address of the first router (the IP source address in the ICMP message).

traceroute then constructs another packet, this time with a TTL of 2, and sends it out. This packet gets to the second router before TTL gets decremented to 0, and *traceroute* knows that the router that returns the ICMP "time to live exceeded" for that packet is the second router along the path to the destination. *traceroute* then constructs a packet with a TTL of 3, then 4, and so on, to determine the path to the destination.

traceroute knows it's finished when it gets back an ICMP "echo reply" or ICMP "destination unreachable" message, rather than an ICMP "time to live exceeded" message from some intermediate router.

Most versions of *traceroute* will also note and display relevant ICMP "host unreachable", "network unreachable", and other ICMP messages received.

If *traceroute* can't reach the destination host (or can't get anything back from it), it eventually times out.

Packet filtering characteristics of traceroute

To allow *traceroute* outbound through your packet filters (i.e., someone running *traceroute* from the inside, to an external destination), you have to allow the constructed UDP or ICMP packets outbound, and the relevant ICMP response packets inbound (particularly "time to live exceeded" and "destination unreachable").

To allow *traceroute* inbound, you have to allow the constructed UDP or ICMP packets inbound, and the relevant ICMP messages back outbound. You may wish to limit this capability to the *traceroute* machines used by the network operations center of your network service provider, in order to keep a tight rein on the UDP packets allowed through your firewall. Limiting UDP protects RPC-based services (like NFS and NIS) and keeps attackers from using *traceroute* to discover which addresses at your site are actually assigned to hosts. The issues with ICMP echo, and the characteristics of echo and echo reply packets, are discussed earlier in the section about *ping*.

Some versions of *traceroute* that use UDP can be told (via a command-line or a compile-time option) which range of UDP ports to use for the destination. You may need to establish a convention for your site of what port(s) will be allowed through the packet filters for use by *traceroute*. You don't want to allow any more latitude in your packet filters for *traceroute* than absolutely necessary (particularly for incoming *traceroute*). Because *traceroute* is UDP-based, an attacker could potentially take advantage of the UDP-based rules in your packet filtering that are there to allow *traceroute* in order to attack other UDP-based services like NFS and NIS.

Direction	Source Addr.	Dest. Addr.	Protocol	Source Port[a]	Dest. Port[a]	Message Type[a]	Notes
Out	Int	Ext	UDP	b	b	a	Outgoing UDP *traceroute* probe
Out	Int	Ext	ICMP	a	a	8	Outgoing ICMP *traceroute* probe
In	Ext	Int	ICMP	a	a	0	ICMP echo response (answering probe)
In	Ext	Int	ICMP	a	a	11	Incoming "time to live exceeded"
In	Ext	Int	ICMP	a	a	3	Incoming "destination unreachable"
In	Ext	Int	UDP	b	b	a	Incoming UDP *traceroute* probe
In	Ext	Int	ICMP	a	a	8	Incoming ICMP *traceroute* probe
Out	Int	Ext	ICMP	a	a	0	ICMP echo response (answering probe)
Out	Int	Ext	ICMP	a	a	11	Outgoing "time to live exceeded"
Out	Int	Ext	ICMP	a	a	3	Outgoing "destination unreachable"

a UDP packets have source and destination ports; ICMP packets have only message type fields. UDP or ICMP have no ACK equivalent.

b *traceroute* probe packet UDP source/destination ports vary by implementation, invocation, and/or command-line arguments. They are generally >32768, but that's about the only generalization you can make about them. Specific implementations (particularly in routers and on non-Unix platforms) may vary. Destination ports, in particular, are usually in the range 33434 through 33523. (Why this is the case is somewhat complicated, and you should read the comments in the Unix *traceroute* source code if you're perversely curious.)

Proxying characteristics of traceroute

Like *ping, traceroute* could easily be supported by an ICMP-knowledgeable modi-fied-client proxy server. An appropriate server and client are provided as part of the SOCKS5 package. Modified-procedure proxying is not possible with *trace-route,* although it is easy to use a web page to give people access to run *trace-route* on a bastion host.

Network address translation and traceroute

Since *traceroute* is intended to determine the network addresses that packets go through, using it with a network address translation system will often create confu-sion. If the network address translation statement is aware of ICMP, there is no reason for the *traceroute* to actually fail, but the information it returns to the user will include the translated addresses. For somebody running *traceroute* from a translated address, this should not be a problem. On the other hand, running a *traceroute* to a translated address may produce unpredictable results. There often will simply be no relevant mapping, and the *traceroute* will fail.

Other ICMP Packets

A number of ICMP message types used for network management don't have pro-grams associated with them. These are automatically generated and interpreted by various programs and network devices.

ICMP message types may also have codes, which contain more information. For instance, there are a number of codes under "destination unreachable", including "service unavailable", "communication administratively prohibited", and "fragmen-tation required and Don't Fragment set". In most cases, the codes within "destina-tion unreachable" are the only ones of interest; none of the other widely used ICMP types actually use codes this way

What to do with ICMP messages depends on the message and the direction it's going in. We've already talked about "echo request", "echo reply", "destination unreachable", and "time to live exceeded" messages. The other ICMP message types you probably want to allow, both inbound and outbound, are "source quench" (used by a receiver to tell a sender to "slow down" because it's sending data too fast) and "parameter problem" (which is sort of a catch-all code to return when a problem with packet headers can't be reported any other way).

Many other ICMP message types have the potential to change local information on your hosts (for example, "redirect" causes changes to a host's routing tables), so you probably don't want to allow such messages inbound through your packet filters.

Even "destination unreachable" can be problematic. Some attackers send out false "destination unreachable" messages, which may cause hosts to cut off communications in progress. (This is a popular attack against people using IRC.) There is no way to tell a valid "destination unreachable" from an invalid one, in general, because a "destination unreachable" can be sent by any machine in the path between the two hosts. However, most "destination unreachable" messages can legitimately be sent only at the beginning of a connection, and it is reasonable for hosts to ignore "destination unreachable" messages that are not plausible responses to packets that have been sent.

In general, you want to allow ICMP outbound only when it has the chance of doing you some good. Both "source quench" and "parameter problem" are used to get the sending host to be nicer to you and are worth allowing outbound. Any of the ICMP types that indicate that the connection can't be made ("destination unavailable", "network unavailable", "service unavailable", "destination administratively unavailable", or "network administratively unavailable", for example) will help an attacker probe your network without giving you much benefit, and you may want to block these outbound.

There are two exceptions to this rule. First, you may find it expedient to return some sort of error (either an ICMP error or a TCP reset) to Auth* queries if you are not going to allow them, in order to speed up mail transmission. This is discussed further in Chapter 21, *Authentication and Auditing Services*. Second, you will want to return "fragmentation required and Don't Fragment set" from any host that can be directly reached with TCP from the Internet, in order to support path MTU discovery. This is discussed further in Chapter 4, *Packets and Protocols*. In both these cases, the rules that you really want to implement are impossible to specify on most packet filtering systems; they don't allow you to specify that an ICMP type is allowable only in response to a specific port, or to specify specific codes within a type. You may be able to use other workarounds discussed in the detail sections on these issues.

Packet filtering characteristics of ICMP

As we've said earlier, ICMP packets do not have source or destination port numbers but have a single ICMP message type field instead. Many packet filtering systems will let you filter ICMP packets based on that field in the same way they allow you to filter TCP or UDP packets based on the source and destination port number fields. The following table lists some common ICMP message types and how you should handle them (whether you should allow them through your firewall or block them).

---

* The Auth protocol is also known as *identd* after a popular Unix daemon that implements it.

Message Type	Description	Permit/Deny
0	Echo reply (reply to *ping*).	See *ping* section earlier.
3	Destination unreachable. May indicate host unreachable, network unreachable, port unreachable, or other.	See *traceroute* section earlier.
4	Source quench (somebody telling destination "slow down; you're talking too fast").	Should usually be allowed in both directions.
5	Redirect (somebody telling destination to change a route); is supposed to be ignored by your systems unless it comes from a directly connected router. In particular, make sure the routers that are part of your firewall ignore it.	Should usually be blocked inbound. Definitely block to routers that are part of your firewall.
8	Echo request (generated by *ping*).	See *ping* section earlier.
9	Router announcement (used by router discovery).	Should be blocked in both directions (see router discovery section earlier).
10	Router selection (used by router discovery).	Should be blocked in both directions (see router discovery section earlier).
11	Time to live exceeded (packet appears to be looping).	Should usually be allowed in both directions.
12	Parameter problem (problem with a packet header).	Should usually be allowed in both directions.

Summary of Recommendations for ICMP

• Allow ICMP echo requests outbound but limit incoming ICMP echo requests to those that are coming from machines with a legitimate need to probe your network (such as your network service provider's network operations center) and are bound to hosts known to have hardened network stacks. Allow ICMP echo responses either way, but only if they match recent requests.

• Allow *traceroute* outbound, but limit incoming *traceroute* requests to those coming from machines with a legitimate need to probe your network and limit the port range used.

• Look for a router that will allow you to sanity-check ICMP packets, and reject obviously malformed or malicious packets regardless of their source and destination.

• Allow only safe ICMP message types, as described previously.

Network Time Protocol (NTP)

NTP allows you to set the clocks on your systems very accurately, to within 1 to 50 ms of the time on a central server. Knowing the exact time is extremely important for certain types of applications and protocols:

- It's much easier to correlate information from multiple machines (log files, for example, when analyzing a break-in attempt) when all the clocks on those machines are synchronized. It's helpful to know exactly who was attacked, and in what order, if you're going to understand what the attacker was after— and what might be coming next.

- Some security protocols depend on an accurate source of time information in order to prevent "playback" attacks. Such protocols tag their communications with the current time, so that those same communications (e.g., a login/password interaction or even an entire communication) can't be replayed at a later date as part of an attack. This tagging can be circumvented if the clock can be set back to the time the communication was recorded.

NTP servers communicate with other NTP servers in a hierarchy to distribute clock information. The closer a system is to a reference clock (an atomic clock, radio clock, or some other definitive clock), the higher it is in the hierarchy. Servers communicate with each other frequently to estimate and track network delay between themselves, so that this delay can be compensated for. NTP clients can track network delay the same way servers do or can simply ask servers for the current date and time without worrying about compensating for communication delays.

NTP is provided with several vendors' versions of Unix; a few vendors (notably Silicon Graphics) include services based on the older Time protocol instead of or in addition to NTP. NTP is not provided with Windows NT but is supported by *timeserv*, which is part of the Server Resource Kit.

By default, NTP does not include any authentication; as a result, it's easy for an attacker to forge packets with incorrect time settings. It's possible to use authentication starting in NTPv3, and you should do so.

Packet Filtering Characteristics of NTP

NTP is a UDP-based service. NTP servers use well-known port 123 to talk to each other and to NTP clients. NTP clients use random ports above 1023. As with DNS, you can tell the difference between the following:

An NTP client-to-server query
  Source port above 1023, destination port 123

An NTP server-to-client response
  Source port 123, destination port above 1023

An NTP server-to-server query or response
  Source and destination ports both 123

Unlike DNS, NTP never uses TCP, and NTP has no analog to the DNS zone transfer operation.

NTP servers may also talk to each other using broadcast or multicast; the multicast address 224.0.1.1 is reserved for this purpose.

Direction	Source Addr.	Dest. Addr.	Protocol	Source Port	Dest. Port	Notes
In	Ext	Int	UDP	>1023	123	Query, external client to internal server
Out	Int	Ext	UDP	123	>1023	Response, internal server to external client
Out	Int	Ext	UDP	>1023	123	Query, internal client to external server
In	Ext	Int	UDP	123	>1023	Response, external server to internal client
In	Ext	Int	UDP	123	123	Query or response between two servers
Out	Int	Ext	UDP	123	123	Query or response between two servers
In	Ext	224.0.1.1	UDP	123	123	Multicast query or response from an external server
Out	Int	224.0.1.1	UDP	123	123	Multicast query or response from an internal server

Figure 22-1 shows how packet filtering works with NTP.

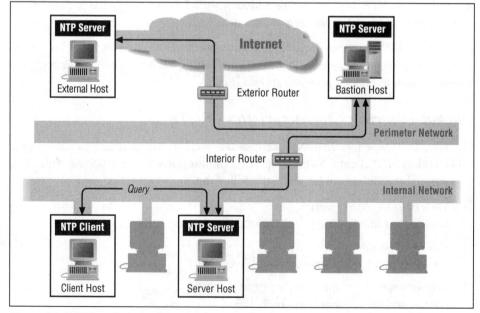

Figure 22-1. NTP with packet filtering

Proxying Characteristics of NTP

As a UDP-based application, NTP can't be proxied by SOCKS4 but can be used with the UDP Packet Relayer or SOCKS5. Because NTP employs a hierarchy of servers, it can be configured to run on a bastion host without using explicit proxying, as shown later in this chapter.

Network Address Translation Characteristics of NTP

NTP does not use embedded IP addresses and will work transparently with network address translation.

Configuring NTP to Work with a Firewall

Do you really need to configure NTP to work with a firewall? That's your first decision. You may not need to if either of the following cases is true at your site:

- If you have an accurate source of time within your internal network—for example, a radio clock receiving time signals from the National Bureau of Standards atomic clocks on one of their radio stations (or the equivalent from non-U.S. standards organizations), or a satellite clock receiving data from the Global Positioning System (GPS) satellites.

- If you're more worried about having time be consistent *within* your network than *between* your network and the outside world.

In either of these cases, you don't need to run NTP across your firewall; you can simply run it internally.

If you do want to run NTP across your firewall, the best way is to set up an NTP server on a bastion host that talks to multiple external NTP servers and another NTP server on some internal host that talks to the bastion host. (You want the bastion host to talk to multiple external NTP servers because it increases accuracy and makes it harder to fool.) Next, configure internal NTP clients and other internal NTP servers to talk to the internal server that talks to the bastion server. You need to configure any packet filtering system between the internal server and the bastion host to allow the following:

Queries from the internal NTP server to the bastion host NTP server
UDP packets from port 123 on the internal server to port 123 on the bastion host

Answers from the bastion host NTP server to the internal NTP server
UDP packets from port 123 on the bastion host to port 123 on the internal host

Summary of Recommendations for NTP

- Consider running NTP purely internally.

- If you run NTP to the Internet, use an NTP server on a bastion host as a proxy for an internal server.

File Synchronization

Strictly speaking, protocols that synchronize files between two computers are file transfer programs. However, they are primarily used for administrative purposes, so we cover them here. These services are intended to make files identical on two computers. They are usually used to synchronize multiple servers that are supposed to be interchangeable or to make certain that all the machines in a group have the same application versions.

Some systems use normal file transfer protocols to do synchronization—for instance, to synchronize laptops to servers when they are present on a network. To figure out how to use such systems with a firewall, first figure out what file transfer protocol they're using and then look up the details of that protocol in Chapter 17, *File Transfer, File Sharing, and Printing*.

rdist

rdist is the best known of the Unix programs for file synchronization. Two versions are in widespread use: version 5 (sometimes known as *ordist*) and version 6. Version 6 is not compatible with version 5, but most version 6 servers will fall back to using the version 5 executables if they are available. *rdist* version 5 uses *rsh* to communicate between machines; *rdist* version 6 can use either *rsh* or SSH. The characteristics of *rsh* and SSH (for packet filtering, proxying, and network address translation) are discussed in Chapter 18, *Remote Access to Hosts*, and are not changed by using them for *rdist*.

While *rdist* is an incredibly useful system administration tool, it also has a long and sad history of security problems, mostly related to its use of *setuid* to run as root, sometimes at inappropriate moments. This is only made worse by using *rsh* as its base. You should not use *rdist* version 5 through a firewall or to any bastion host; use SSH-based *rdist* version 6 or *rsync* instead (see the next section for more information about *rsync*).

rsync

rsync is a synchronization protocol that uses checksums to determine differences (instead of relying on modification dates) and does partial file transfers (transferring only the differences instead of the entire files). *rsync* was developed by Andrew Tridgell and Paul Mackerras.

rsync may either be run like *rdist* on top of a remote shell protocol (preferably *ssh* but *rsh* is also possible), or use its own daemon, *rsyncd*. *rsyncd* does authentication but does not encrypt the data being transferred. *rsyncd* is useful if you are interested in using *rsync* to distribute publicly available files; it allows you to use *rsync* like FTP, without allowing remote shell access to the Internet. It is arguably more secure than FTP (it provides less functionality) and will certainly be more efficient in situations where people need to transfer updated files repeatedly. If you are transferring confidential data, you should use *rsync* over SSH instead of using *rsyncd*.

Packet filtering characteristics of rsync

rsync is generally run over SSH, although it is possible to run it over *rsh* if you are not concerned with security. Packet filtering characteristics of SSH and *rsh* are discussed in Chapter 18, *Remote Access to Hosts*. The dedicated *rsync* daemon, *rsyncd*, uses TCP port 873.

Direction	Source Addr.	Dest. Addr.	Protocol	Source Port	Dest. Port	ACK Set	Notes
In	Ext	Int	TCP	>1023	873	a	Request, external client to internal server
Out	Int	Ext	TCP	873	>1023	Yes	Response, internal server to external client
Out	Int	Ext	TCP	>1023	873	a	Request, internal client to external server
In	Int	Ext	TCP	873	>1023	Yes	Response, external server to internal client

a ACK will not be set on the first packet (establishing connection) but will be set on the rest.

Proxying characteristics of rsync

rsync is normally run over SSH or *rsh*; proxying characteristics of these protocols are discussed in Chapter 18. The *rsync* client provides support for using an HTTP proxy for *rsync* connections, as long as the HTTP proxy is willing to connect to port 873. (For more information about HTTP proxies, see "Proxying Characteristics of HTTP" in Chapter 15, *The World Wide Web*.) *rsync*'s own protocol is straightforward to proxy and could also easily be used with SOCKS, for instance. However, since *rsyncd* is not terribly widespread, proxies for it are not available. You will need to set them up yourself.

Network address translation characteristics of rsync

rsync is normally run over SSH or *rsh*; network address translation characteristics of these protocols are discussed in Chapter 18, *Remote Access to Hosts. rsync's* own protocol does not use embedded IP addresses and should function through a network address translation system without problems.

Windows NT Directory Replication

Directory Replication (also known as LMRepl) is used to automatically copy information from machines running Windows NT Server to machines running Windows NT 4 or OS/2. Windows 2000 does not support this service. It is used to copy login scripts and policy information between domain controllers and package information between SMS servers in the same site; it can also be used to copy whatever other information administrators want to distribute.

In Directory Replication, there is an exporting computer and at least one importing computer. Each machine has a special account that is used for replication. These accounts have the permissions for the "Backup Operators" group, which will allow them to read and write any file on the computer, regardless of its permissions. Furthermore, the accounts have to be effectively equivalent on the exporting and importing computer (either by having them actually be the same account, as part of a domain, or by giving them the same username and password). This means that two machines that replicate directories effectively trust each other completely; if either one of them is compromised, the other one will be too.

Windows NT Directory Replication is based on SMB transactions; see Chapter 14, *Intermediary Protocols*, for a discussion of the packet filtering, proxying, and network address translation characteristics of SMB.

Because Directory Replication is based on SMB transactions, it is difficult to allow it securely through a firewall. Because it involves extensive trust, it is a bad idea to use it to or from machines that make up part of a firewall.

Windows 2000 File Replication Service (FRS)

In Windows 2000, the service that's used to automatically synchronize files is the File Replication Service (FRS). Like directory replication, FRS is used routinely as part of the process of synchronizing information among domain controllers, but it can also be used explicitly to maintain replicas of other files. When FRS is used to synchronize information among domain controllers, it is referred to as SYSVOL replication.

Directory replication is a single master system, where one machine maintains the master copy and propagates it to other machines. Files can be changed only on the machine with the master copy. FRS is a multiple master system, where files can be changed on any machine, and the changes will be propagated to the other systems.

FRS uses authenticated RPC calls to distribute information between replicas. For more information about the firewall characteristics of RPC, see Chapter 14, *Intermediary Protocols*.

Summary of Recommendations for File Synchronization

- Do not allow file synchronization across your firewall. (You may wish to make an exception for *rsyncd* if you are distributing information to the public with it.)

Mostly Harmless Protocols

A handful of protocols are widely implemented for no apparent reason except that:

- They're easy to implement.
- They're standards.
- They might come in handy every so often for testing something.

These include *chargen, echo,* and *discard. chargen* (character generator) is a server that babbles. When you connect to it, it produces characters in an endless stream until you go away again (if you send it UDP, it sends you back a single UDP packet with random characters in it). *echo* simply echoes back any data you send it; *discard* even more simply discards all data you send it. It's easy to see that these might in fact be useful for administrative and testing purposes, but in practice they don't come up much. They sat around for years being apparently harmless if pointless curiosities, enabled by default on almost all Unix machines and used on rare occasions for network testing. Then various people found interesting ways to pervert them (forge a packet from one machine's *echo* server to another, creating a vicious circle, for instance), and they became noteworthy. It has never been advisable to allow them (if you don't need services, don't turn them on—and you don't need any of these), but now it's actually important to turn them off.

Interestingly, not long after *echo* became dangerous, it started to be used for relatively benign purposes as well. Web sites (most notably, the advertisement servers at *doubleclick.net*) periodically attempt to use *echo* to determine round-trip times and choose the closest server to a given client. TCP-based *echo* is used instead of the ICMP echo used by *ping* in order to get responses more like those that TCP-based HTTP will get. Although these attempts are benign, there is no reason to allow them; they are not required in order for services to work. You do need to be aware that you will probably see logs of discarded *echo* traffic, which do not indicate hostile acts.

Given that *chargen, echo,* and *discard* are ancient and rarely used, you might expect that Microsoft's relatively modern implementation of TCP/IP services would omit them, but in fact these services are all bundled as part of the "Simple TCP/IP Services" service on Windows NT. This also includes the equally unused *daytime* and *quotd* services. *daytime* produces a human-readable date and timestamp; *quotd* (quote of the day) produces a quote (in Windows NT's case, from an extremely small quotes file). They are both genuine and widely implemented services but are even less used than the others.

Many of these services are provided by the operating system on Cisco routers as well and should be disabled as part of router configuration.

Packet Filtering Characteristics of Mostly Harmless Protocols

All of these services work on both TCP and UDP. *chargen* is at port 19, *echo* is at port 7, *discard* is at port 9, *daytime* is at port 13, and *quotd* is at port 17.

Direction	Source Addr.	Dest. Addr.	Protocol	Source Port	Dest. Port	ACK Set	Notes
In	Ext	Int	UDP	>1023	19, 7, 9, 13 or 17	a	Request, external client to internal server
Out	Int	Ext	UDP	19, 7, 9, 13, or 17	>1023	a	Response, internal server to external client
Out	Int	Ext	UDP	>1023	19, 7, 9, 13 or 17	a	Request, internal client to external server
In	Int	Ext	UDP	19, 7, 9, 13, or 17	>1023	a	Response, external server to internal client
In	Ext	Int	TCP	>1023	19, 7, 9, 13, or 17	b	Request, external client to internal server
Out	Int	Ext	TCP	19, 7, 9, 13, or 17	>1023	Yes	Response, internal server to external client

Direction	Source Addr.	Dest. Addr.	Protocol	Source Port	Dest. Port	ACK Set	Notes
Out	Int	Ext	TCP	>1023	19, 7, 9, 13, or 17	b	Request, internal client to external server
In	Int	Ext	TCP	19, 7, 9, 13, or 17	>1023	Yes	Response, external server to internal client

a UDP has no ACK equivalent.
b ACK will not be set on the first packet (establishing connection) but will be set on the rest.

Proxying Characteristics of Mostly Harmless Protocols

While it would be theoretically quite easy to proxy most of these protocols (the proxy for *discard* is particularly simple to write), the sheer pointlessness of doing so means that proxies for them are not widely available. In particular, on the rare occasions when *chargen*, *echo*, and *discard* are used, they're used to gather data about network performance, which will be obscured if a proxy is in the transaction.

Network Address Translation Characteristics of Mostly Harmless Protocols

None of these protocols include embedded IP addresses; they will all work with straightforward network address translation.

Summary Recommendations for Mostly Harmless Protocols

- "Mostly harmless" is not good enough; do not allow any of these protocols through your firewall.

23

Databases and Games

This chapter discusses two categories of protocols that didn't fit in other chapters—the protocols used to talk to databases and the protocols used to play games remotely.

Databases

At most sites, much of the site's most security-critical information is stored in databases. At companies, they store inventory and ordering data; at universities, they store student information, including grades; at research institutes, they store personnel information and (usually on different machines) research data. Originally, these databases were protected mostly by restricting access to them, but that's no longer practical. People have become accustomed to mobile, distributed computing, where they can make instant updates to their own information, and that requires giving them the ability to reach databases. In addition, databases are being used for more and more purposes, as a way of storing and sharing information.

This means that network access to databases is now critical, particularly for electronic commerce applications where database servers and web servers need to exchange data. We have discussed issues about locating database servers and web servers in Chapter 15, *The World Wide Web*. Here, we will discuss the protocols used to provide network access and their security implications.

Locating Database Servers

Most database protocols are deeply insecure and difficult to pass through a firewall. Nonetheless, you are likely to want to let an externally available web server talk to your database servers in order to provide data to your customers (for instance, to enable web-based order tracking). There are fundamentally four options:

- Put the web server and the database on the same perimeter network (possibly even on the same machine). No database traffic will have to pass through the firewall in normal operation. (You will still need to figure out how to load the data onto the perimeter database and restrict access to the database.)

- Put the web server and the database both on the internal network. No database traffic will have to pass through the firewall; on the other hand, HTTP requests will. You are relying on the security of the web server.

- Put the web server on the perimeter network and the database server on the internal network, and use the database's native protocol to connect them. You are relying on your ability to configure the firewall and the database appropriately to secure the protocol; you must let database traffic through.

- Put the web server on the perimeter network and the database server on the internal network, and use a custom-written protocol to connect them. You are relying on your ability to construct a secure protocol that enables the transactions you need.

All of these approaches can be successful; putting the database on the perimeter network provides the most protection for your internal network, and putting the web server on the internal network provides the least. Using a custom protocol to connect a web server on the perimeter to a database server that's internal provides the best balance between protecting the internal network and protecting the data, but it's the hardest solution to maintain.

Putting both the web server and the database on the perimeter network

If you choose to put both the web server and the database on the perimeter network, as shown in Figure 23-1, you have two primary concerns. First, you need to be sure that the database contains only data that you are actually willing to have accessed from the Internet. You do not get any significant security benefit from putting the database on the perimeter network if it contains all the private data people could get by breaking into the internal network! Second, in most cases you are still going to need to move and synchronize data between the external database and the internal database, and you will need to develop a secure means of doing it. It will be complicated by the first problem (it's unlikely that the external database will be a simple, straightforward copy of the internal database). In general, it's possible to do this copy with a scheduled job that exports data from the two servers, transfers it across the firewall using a secured remote copy mechanism, sanity-checks it, and imports the appropriate data onto each server.

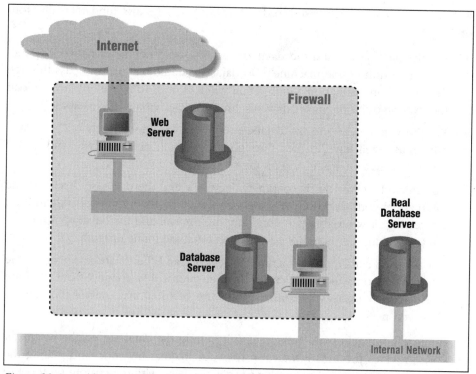

Figure 23-1. A web server using a database server on a perimeter network

Using a scheduled job to export data provides high performance between the web server and the database. However, it is not appropriate if data is going to need to move frequently between the internal and the external database server; that transfer can be quite slow. It also complicates the procedures for internal users who need to see the external data (for instance, support people answering customer calls about the web site). This method might be appropriate for a web-based catalog listing but is less appropriate for e-commerce applications where orders are going to need to be moved briskly to the internal databases, and order status will need to be frequently updated in the other direction.

Putting both the web server and the database on the internal network

If you choose to put the web server and the database both on the internal network, as shown in Figure 23-2, you are allowing external traffic to go to the internal network. This is a highly risky configuration, and we do not recommend it. However, if you are extremely confident about the security of the web server you are using, it may be more secure to pass HTTP through the firewall than to try to pass any of the database communication protocols. In this situation, consider passing connections through a proxy that can verify the HTTP; this will be more secure than using straightforward packet filtering.

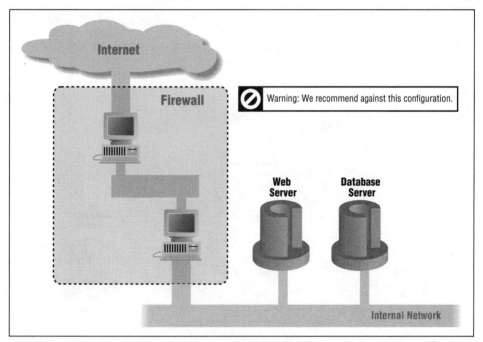

Figure 23-2. A web server and a database server on an internal network

Using the database's protocols to connect to a perimeter web server

Putting the web server on the perimeter network and then using normal database remote access methods to connect to an internal database, as shown in Figure 23-3, is the most straightforward method of providing web access to the database. In this situation, the web server effectively proxies the request to the database server, so external commands do not arrive directly on the internal network. However, you are still vulnerable to any security problems in the remote access provided by the vendors, and you still need to get the database requests across to the internal network without opening up other vulnerabilities. Depending on the database and the firewall you are using, this can be quite difficult.

Your internal database will also be vulnerable if the perimeter network is compromised. If any machine is compromised, it may be vulnerable to sniffing attacks; if the web server is compromised, an intruder will have the full power of the remote database access mechanism available (note that any required passwords are likely to be stored on the web server and used automatically).

You can reduce this vulnerability by carefully configuring the access that the web server has. You should use all of the access controls that your database server provides to make certain that the web server can do only things that it's supposed to be able to do. Don't use a generic database account that has many permissions. Instead, set up the web server to use a specific database account that can access

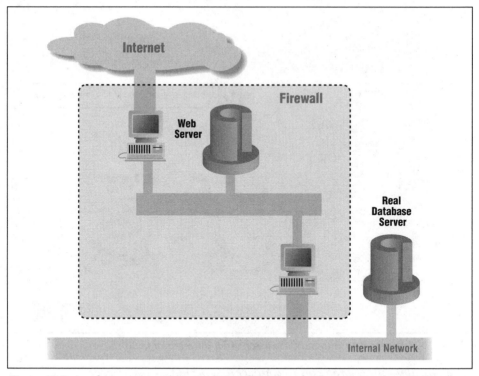

Figure 23-3. A web server on a perimeter network using a database server on an internal network

only necessary data. If at all possible, set it up to use stored procedures so that it does not have access to the arbitrary database commands but can only do pre-defined operations that are stored as part of the database.

The amount of additional security you can get this way depends a great deal on what the web site is supposed to do. If web users are only able to read data, you may be able to get pretty good protection from the database security. On the other hand, if the web site allows people to order things, cancel their orders, or otherwise modify data, an attacker who compromises the web server is going to be able to really make you suffer, no matter what the database security is like.

Using a custom protocol to connect to a perimeter web server

Using a locally designed custom method to connect a perimeter web server to an internal database leaves the architecture the same as the one shown in Figure 23-3; it just changes the protocols used to connect the web server to the database. This configuration provides real-time access to the internal data, while giving you complete control over both the protocol and port numbers and the capabilities accessible by the web server. For instance, if the web server needs to read only data, your program can support only data read queries; even if the web server is compromised, the intruder will not be able to write data into the database. Note that if you add security features such as strong authentication and encryption, your solution may be slower than using the vendor mechanisms.

We recommend building your protocol on top of an existing message-passing mechanism, but only if it provides the necessary access controls. It may be tempting to use HTTP, but we recommend against it for a number of reasons. First of all, HTTP is connectionless, which makes it difficult to build something that is transaction based and robust. Second, it means that you will have to run CGI or an equivalent on an internal HTTP server. This then makes it equivalent to an architecture we recommend against.

Building a custom protocol is not always practical. It assumes that you have local programming talent sufficient to write a small but secure client/server application. Creating a secure client/server application is not easy, so implementing the communications yourself may simply introduce different security problems from those you would have been exposed to if you'd used the database vendor's communication package. Implementing it yourself also has long-term maintenance ramifications. Nevertheless, on balance this method has significant advantages.

Open Database Connectivity (ODBC) and Java Database Connectivity (JDBC)

Open Database Connectivity (ODBC) is a Microsoft-developed applications programming interface (API) that allows applications developers to write software that connects to a variety of database servers. ODBC is not a protocol at the network level. Instead, it's a set of libraries that may use other network-level protocols. A program that uses the ODBC API will eventually end up talking to the database server through whatever that server's native communication protocol is. Therefore, knowing that an application uses ODBC tells you nothing useful about what network transactions it will make; you need to know what database driver ODBC is calling, which is determined by what type of database is running on the database server.

There is a great deal of confusion about ODBC. If you are on a machine that uses ODBC and you are trying to configure the machine to talk to a database across a network, you will usually go through the process of configuring something called an ODBC *driver*. This causes many people to believe that the driver is actually part of ODBC and that ODBC controls what options are in it, which is not the case. The ODBC driver is specific to the database you are talking to, not to ODBC; it is the driver that makes ODBC talk to your database, and it is provided by the database vendor. ODBC itself does not control the network communications and has no firewall characteristics. ODBC applications do not have to use the network at all; ODBC may be used to talk to a database running locally on the same machine.

JDBC™ is simply the Java analog to ODBC, a Java API that will connect to any of a variety of vendor database drivers. Because JDBC is based on Java, which is designed to be dynamically loaded, it allows clients to dynamically load the needed drivers, while in ODBC, they have to be explicitly installed. As usual, this increases convenience at the cost of security.

If you are asked to allow ODBC or JDBC through a firewall, you should ask what database is being used and research the network characteristics of that particular database. ODBC and JDBC by themselves will not change those characteristics. (Occasionally, databases that offer multiple connection options may not offer ODBC or JDBC drivers for all the options. Again, this is determined by the data-base developer and is not inherent to ODBC or JDBC.) If you have no further information to work from, assume that people who ask for ODBC really want to use Microsoft SQL Server, since it is the database most closely associated with plat-forms that run ODBC.

Oracle SQL*Net and Net8

SQL*Net is Oracle's SQL network interface for Oracle7, and Net8 is its successor for Oracle8. Both SQL*Net and Net8 perform complex network manipulations; depending on server and client configurations, connections may use unpredict-able port numbers or may be restarted or initiated from the server to the client. This makes most SQL*Net and Net8 implementations extremely difficult to pass through a firewall that is not specially aware of Oracle.

SQL*Net and Net8 are both based on Oracle's Transparent Network Substrate (TNS) and will attempt to speak to a server known as a *TNS listener*. Oracle's net-work situation is further complicated by the fact that it provides its own naming service, Oracle Names, which has its own server. Some proxying services are pro-vided by Oracle Connection Manager in Oracle8 and the Oracle Multiprotocol Interchange server in Oracle7.

Security implications of SQL*Net and Net8

Both the TNS listener and Oracle Names will accept commands on the same port they normally provide service over. You can password-protect commands that are considered dangerous (for instance "start" and "stop") but not commands Oracle considers safe (for instance, "status" or "show" to show variable settings). By default, there is no password protection. Even when password protection is on, passwords may be stored unprotected in server or client configuration files. In addition, there have been reports that at least the Oracle8 TNS listener is quite vulnerable to denial of service attacks from unexpected commands, which may cause it to consume large amounts of CPU resources.

Encryption is actually handled by TNS, but Oracle doesn't provide TNS versioning information. In the TNS version built into SQL*Net v1, nothing is encrypted, not even user authentication. Passwords are sent across the network not only reusable but unprotected and in the clear. As of SQL*Net v2, user authentication and TNS listener control passwords are protected but reusable when passed across the network. As of Net8/Oracle8, Oracle Names uses a protected control password as well.

The Oracle Advanced Networking Option (ANO) provides data stream encryption (via 40-bit RC4 or DES internationally, 56-bit RC4 or DES or 128-bit RC4 within the United States) and MD5 message digests. It also provides support for nonreusable passwords. Oracle also has a separate Security Server product that is used to provide an API for explicit data signing and signature verification at the application level—a normal Oracle application cannot control whether or not the client and server are using Advanced Networking's encryption features. An Oracle server, however, may choose to require encryption and/or checksumming on all connections.

Oracle has had many security problems with their server installations. Most of these problems have involved ways to turn access to the server machine into root access or Oracle administrator access, using Oracle tools. However, some problems (like the denial of service problems previously mentioned) were exploitable from the network.

Packet filtering characteristics of SQL*Net and Net8

Oracle uses entirely TCP ports over 1024.* These ports can be configured, and there are multiple defaults depending on the version of Oracle you are running. In what appears to be the most common default configuration, the TNS listener is at 1521, the Oracle Multiprotocol Interchange listener is at 1526, Oracle Names is at 1575, and Oracle Connection Manager is at 1600. Client-to-server connections will normally start out going to 1521 or 1600 but may not remain there. It is not at all uncommon for hosts to run multiple TNS listeners at different ports, and Oracle's own documentation also shows alternate defaults (for instance, Oracle Names is often shown at 1521 and the TNS listener at 1526). You will need to know the details of your configuration.

---

* People are often confused by the IANA registrations for ports 66 and 140, which have "sql" and "net" in their names but are not used by Oracle. They are historical curiosities left over from previous theories about networked SQL.

Direction	Source Addr.	Dest. Addr.	Protocol	Source Port	Dest. Port	ACK Set	Notes
In	Ext	Int	TCP	>1023	1575[a]	[b]	Name lookup, external client to internal server
Out	Int	Ext	TCP	1575[a]	>1023	Yes	Name response, internal server to external client
In	Ext	Int	TCP	>1023	1600[c]	[b]	Request, external client to internal server (using Connection Manager)
Out	Int	Ext	TCP	1600[c]	>1023	Yes	Response, internal server to external client (using Connection Manager)
In	Ext	Int	TCP	>1023	1521[d]	[b]	Request, external client to internal server (using TNS)
Out	Int	Ext	TCP	1521[d]	>1023	Yes	Response, internal server to external client (using TNS)
In	Ext	Int	TCP	>1023	1526[e]	[b]	Request, external client to internal server (using Multiprotocol Interchange)
Out	Int	Ext	TCP	1526[e]	>1023	Yes	Response, internal server to external client (using Multiprotocol Interchange)
In	Ext	Int	TCP	>1023	>1023[f]	[b]	Redirected request, external client to internal server
Out	Int	Ext	TCP	>1023[f]	>1023	Yes	Response to redirected request, internal server to external client
Out	Int	Ext	TCP	>1023	1575[a]	[b]	Name lookup, internal client to external server
In	Ext	Int	TCP	1575[a]	>1023	Yes	Name response, external server to internal client
Out	Int	Ext	TCP	>1023	1600[c]	[b]	Request, internal client to external server (using Connection Manager)
In	Ext	Int	TCP	1600[c]	>1023	Yes	Response, external server to internal client (using Connection Manager)
Out	Int	Ext	TCP	>1023	1521[d]	[b]	Request, internal client to external server (using TNS)
In	Ext	Int	TCP	1521[d]	>1023	Yes	Response, external server to internal client (using TNS)

Direction	Source Addr.	Dest. Addr.	Protocol	Source Port	Dest. Port	ACK Set	Notes
Out	Int	Ext	TCP	>1023	1526[e]	[b]	Request, internal client to external server (using Multiprotocol Interchange)
In	Ext	Int	TCP	1526[e]	>1023	Yes	Response, external server to internal client (using Multiprotocol Interchange)
Out	Int	Ext	TCP	>1023	>1023[f]	[b]	Redirected request, internal client to external server
In	Ext	Int	TCP	>1023[f]	>1023	Yes	Response to redirected request, external server to internal client

[a] 1575 is a popular default, but this may be set to any port number.
[b] ACK will not be set on the first packet (establishing connection) but will be set on the rest.
[c] 1600 is a popular default, but this may be set to any port number.
[d] 1521 is a popular default, but this may be set to any port number.
[e] 1526 is a popular default, but this may be set to any port number.
[f] This port is dynamically assigned by the server.

*Proxying characteristics of SQL*Net and Net8*

Oracle has proxy code for SQL*Net, but the company has chosen to make it available to firewall manufacturers, and in binary format for limited operating systems. Therefore, although several commercial firewalls provide proxying support for SQL*Net, it may not be available on all platforms even within a given manufacturer's product line. Also, while the proxy code does know about SQL*Net's port number negotiation, there is no way of knowing how much protocol enforcement it does, and given Oracle's history of being naive about security, it is reasonable to assume that it does not do much.

Oracle provides a product called Oracle Connection Manager that will provide proxying, among other things, for SQL*Net and Net8 clients. Oracle Connection Manager provides extremely limited control over what clients can connect; you can accept or deny based on the following:

- Source host or IP address
- Source port
- Destination host or IP address
- Destination port
- Destination database name

Wildcards are allowed, but they must be for entire components of a name or IP address; for instance, you can permit all hosts in *somedomain.example* or all hosts in 192.10, but not all hosts that begin with "ora" in *somedomain.example* or all hosts in 192.10.47.128/28.

*Network address translation characteristics of SQL*Net and Net8*

SQL*Net and Net8 both use embedded IP address and port number information and may start up connections from the server to the client. They will not work through a network address translation system unless it has special facilities for dealing with them. Since Oracle doesn't release protocol details, this means that network address translation for SQL*Net and Net8, like proxying, will have to be provided by Oracle. As of this writing, Oracle has not provided such a module.

*Summary of recommendations for SQL*Net and Net8*

- If at all possible, avoid running SQL*Net or Net8 across your firewall. If you must run it, use a proxy server that supports it (either Oracle Connection Manager or one of the commercial firewall products that has Oracle's proxying code).

Tabular Data Stream (TDS)

TDS is a database protocol used by both Sybase and Microsoft SQL Server, among other products, for network communications. It is a proprietary protocol, owned by Sybase. Sybase offers relatively liberal access to the protocol specification, but their license specifically forbids distribution of information about the protocol specification, so the only people who really know how the protocol works aren't allowed to say.

TDS is a straightforward TCP-based protocol, in which the client starts up a single connection to the server. No fixed port is used by TDS, and different implementations default to using different port numbers. In its simplest form, TDS transmits all data, including usernames and passwords, unprotected and in the clear. However, some TDS implementations use encryption to protect all or part of the data. All in all, knowing that a product uses TDS tells you relatively little about its security and firewalling implications, although the information does tend to suggest that it will be relatively straightforward to pass through a firewall (it does not tell you whether or not that would be a good idea, since TDS may be cleartext or encrypted).

Sybase

Sybase takes an open approach to network communications. It supports multiple different protocols, including TDS, IIOP, and HTTP. Security can be provided by running IIOPS or HTTPS. (TDS is discussed in the previous section; IIOP is related to CORBA and is discussed in Chapter 14, *Intermediary Protocols*; HTTP is discussed in Chapter 15, *The World Wide Web*.)

Packet filtering characteristics of Sybase

Sybase can use TDS, HTTP, HTTPS, IIOP, or IIOPS for network communications. All of these by default use TCP connections from the client to the server with both ends at a port above 1023. The port that the server will use is defined when the database server is configured and can be set to any unused port. Sybase defaults to using 7878 for TDS, 8080 for HTTP, 8081 and 8082 for HTTPS, 9000 for IIOP, and 9001 and 9002 for IIOPS. If the server has the necessary privileges and no other web server is already using them, HTTP and HTTPS may be moved to their normal reserved ports (80 and 443, respectively). HTTP and HTTPS are discussed in Chapter 15; IIOP and IIOPS are discussed in Chapter 14.

Direction	Source Addr.	Dest. Addr.	Protocol	Source Port	Dest. Port	ACK Set	Notes
In	Ext	Int	TCP	>1023	7878[a]	[b]	Request, external client to internal server (using TDS)
Out	Int	Ext	TCP	7878[a]	>1023	Yes	Response, internal server to external client (using TDS)
In	Ext	Int	TCP	>1023	8080[c]	[b]	Request, external client to internal server (using HTTP)
Out	Int	Ext	TCP	8080[c]	>1023	Yes	Response, internal server to external client (using HTTP)
In	Ext	Int	TCP	>1023	8001, 8002[d]	[b]	Request, external client to internal server (using HTTPS)
Out	Int	Ext	TCP	8001, 8002[d]	>1023	Yes	Response, internal server to external client (using HTTPS)
In	Ext	Int	TCP	>1023	9000[e]	[b]	Request, external client to internal server (using IIOP)
Out	Int	Ext	TCP	9000[e]	>1023	Yes	Response, internal server to external client (using IIOP)
In	Ext	Int	TCP	>1023	9001, 9002[f]	[b]	Request, external client to internal server (using IIOPS)
Out	Int	Ext	TCP	9001, 9002[f]	>1023	Yes	Response, internal server to external client (using IIOPS)
Out	Int	Ext	TCP	>1023	7878[a]	[b]	Request, internal client to external server (using TDS)
In	Ext	Int	TCP	7878[a]	>1023	Yes	Response, external server to internal client (using TDS)
Out	Int	Ext	TCP	>1023	8080[c]	[b]	Request, internal client to external server (using HTTP)

Direction	Source Addr.	Dest. Addr.	Protocol	Source Port	Dest. Port	ACK Set	Notes
In	Ext	Int	TCP	8080[c]	>1023	Yes	Response, external server to internal client (using HTTP)
Out	Int	Ext	TCP	>1023	8001, 8002[d]	b	Request, internal client to external server (using HTTPS)
In	Ext	Int	TCP	8001, 8002[d]	>1023	Yes	Response, external server to internal client (using HTTPS)
Out	Int	Ext	TCP	>1023	9000[e]	b	Request, internal client to external server (using IIOP)
In	Ext	Int	TCP	9000[e]	>1023	Yes	Response, external server to internal client (using IIOP)
Out	Int	Ext	TCP	>1023	9001, 9002[f]	b	Request, internal client to external server (using IIOPS)
In	Ext	Int	TCP	9001, 9002[f]	>1023	Yes	Response, external server to internal client (using IIOPS)

a 7878 is the default, but this may be set to any port number.
b ACK will not be set on the first packet (establishing connection) but will be set on the rest.
c 8080 is the default, but this may be set to any port number.
d 8001 and 8002 are the defaults, but this may be set to any port number.
e 9000 is the default, but this may be set to any port number.
f 9001 and 9002 are the defaults, but this may be set to any port number.

Proxying characteristics of Sybase

HTTP proxies are widespread and can be used with Sybase's HTTP support. In addition, a number of firewall vendors provide TDS proxies. Note that none of these proxies will significantly increase security, so you should carefully protect your databases.

Network address translation characteristics of Sybase

Both TDS and HTTP run without problems through network address translation systems, so you should have no difficulty configuring your server to work with a network address translation system.

Summary of recommendations for Sybase

- If possible, avoid running Sybase through a firewall. If you need to support Sybase through a firewall, consider using IIOPS or HTTPS.

Microsoft SQL Server

Microsoft's SQL Server, like Sybase, can use TDS for communications (it refers to this as the TCP/IP network library). On TCP/IP networks, it also supports the use of Microsoft RPC either directly (via the Multiprotocol network library) or over SMB (via the Named Pipes network library). See Chapter 14, *Intermediary Protocols*, for more information about RPC and SMB.

Microsoft SQL offers multiple options for user authentication. If you set it to use SQL authentication over TDS, it passes authentication data over the network in cleartext. If you set it to use Windows NT authentication over TDS, the username and password data is obscured. (It is not clear what this is, but it appears to be reversible encryption rather than challenge-response.) SQL authentication over TDS does not protect username and password data and should never be used in an insecure environment.

You should be careful about what accounts you use for SQL access. They should have the minimum necessary permissions on the SQL database and under Windows NT. They should not be accounts that are used for logins or file sharing under Windows NT.

Note that if a client attempts to use SQL authentication across an insecure network, and the server is set up to use Windows NT authentication, the authentication will fail, but the account will still be compromised. The client will send the cleartext username and password, which can be intercepted, and there is no way for the server to prevent it.

Some versions of Microsoft SQL Server support database replication only over SMB; more recent versions will allow database replication over TDS, but it is less efficient.

Packet filtering characteristics of Microsoft SQL Server

Microsoft SQL Server normally uses TCP port 1433 for TDS but can be configured to use any port. Packet filtering characteristics of SMB named pipes and Microsoft RPC are discussed in Chapter 14.

Direction	Source Addr.	Dest. Addr.	Protocol	Source Port	Dest. Port	ACK Set	Notes
In	Ext	Int	TCP	>1023	1433[a]	[b]	Request, external client to internal server
Out	Int	Ext	TCP	1433[a]	>1023	Yes	Response, internal server to external client
Out	Int	Ext	TCP	>1023	1433[a]	[b]	Request, internal client to external server
In	Ext	Int	TCP	1433[a]	>1023	Yes	Response, external server to internal client

[a] 1433 is the default, but this may be set to any port number.
[b] ACK will not be set on the first packet (establishing connection) but will be set on the rest.

Proxying characteristics of Microsoft SQL Server

TDS is easy to proxy with generic proxies. You should ensure that clients are using Windows NT domain authentication, not SQL authentication, in order to avoid disclosing username and password information. Proxying characteristics of SMB and Microsoft RPC are discussed in Chapter 14, *Intermediary Protocols*.

Network address translation and Microsoft SQL Server

TDS works transparently with network address translation, so there should be no problem configuring Microsoft SQL Server to run through a network address translation system. Network address translation characteristics of SMB and Microsoft RPC are discussed in Chapter 14.

Summary of recommendations for Microsoft SQL Server

- Avoid passing Microsoft SQL Server through a firewall if possible.
- If you need to use Microsoft SQL Server through a firewall, use TDS but use Windows NT authentication instead of SQL authentication in order to ensure that username and password information is protected.

Games

Internet games are a lot of fun. Unfortunately, game designers are rarely security experts, and many of the same people who attack computer systems are attracted to Internet games. That's not to say that Internet gamers are inherently bad people; most of them are fine upstanding citizens. On the other hand, the primary audience for Internet shoot-em-ups is the same crowd of adolescents with computers and free time that attackers come from, and it would be a miracle if there weren't a lot of overlap between the two cultures. If you take an application that wasn't designed for security, put it on a network, and hand it over to people who like to attack computer systems, the result is predictable and not very pretty.

Furthermore, the design constraints for Internet games in general make easy-to-secure connections undesirable. Persistent TCP connections to known ports are just not suitable for most game-playing situations. Well-documented protocols are easier for players to interfere with, which game manufacturers rarely want, and in any case, game manufacturers are generally busy turning out documentation for users who just bought their first computer, and the manufacturers don't have much time to spare to document technical details so people can configure firewalls. (The most common firewall advice in game documentation is "You must not be behind a firewall.")

It is impossible to document the firewall characteristics of games in any detail. Games go in and out of favor rapidly, and even those that are persistent favorites change frequently. For instance, knowing that you want to play Quake doesn't predict what ports or even what protocols you will need; some versions of Quake require both TCP and UDP, while others use only one or the other.

A networked game is always a client, usually of a protocol with unknown features and security implications. One that can be a controller for a multiplayer game is a server of some sort as well. Many games always provide both client and server features when they are running in a multiplayer mode. This means that running networked games may create vulnerabilities even if you do not connect to external players (if the game brings up a server, that server may be vulnerable to attack even if you don't initiate connections). Machines that run networked games should be protected from incoming Internet connections.

Running plug-ins and extensions to games may change their security characteristics by adding new capabilities. If you have a game that you trust, don't upgrade it or change it without re-evaluating its security.

Quake

Quake, in its many and varied versions, is one of the most popular Internet games. It also has a long and sad history of security problems, particularly in its Unix versions. You should not run any Quake binaries as root, regardless of what the documentation says; Quake servers are susceptible to remote attacks, and Quake clients running as root can be exploited by local users.

When Quake was originally written, the game developer, ID, put in a special feature allowing the developer to run commands on all Quake servers. These commands are not logged, and they don't have to be normal Quake commands (Quake can run external programs). On all platforms, you should be careful to run an up-to-date Quake server and/or to refuse packets from ID's corporate network (192.246.40.0/24) because the back door will allow attackers who forge packets from that network to run arbitrary (and unlogged) commands with the permissions of the Quake server.

Summary of Recommendations for Games

- Don't allow games through your firewall if you have a choice. It may seem cruel to block harmless amusements, but they carry real dangers.

- If you want to run a game server, use a victim machine with nothing else on it that you care about.

- For popular games, you may be able to get dedicated proxies, some of which offer security features. They are usually produced by third parties and are rarely polished, commercial-level products. They're not appropriate for highly secure environments or naive users, but may be sufficient to support dedicated players in an environment that doesn't require a great deal of security.

- Install games with great care. It is almost never safe to run either servers or clients as a privileged user.

24

Two Sample Firewalls

In this chapter, we describe two sample configurations for basic firewalls. Almost any real firewall is going to be more complex than those described in this chapter, but this presentation should give you some idea of the tasks involved in building a firewall and how the various pieces fit together.

> We want to emphasize that these examples are just that: examples. You shouldn't blindly implement one of these examples without first taking the time to understand your own needs, your environment, and the implications and complications of the services you want your firewall to provide.

The services that we're going to provide through these sample firewalls are just the basics: the World Wide Web, terminal access, file transfer, electronic mail, Usenet news, and DNS.

Screened Subnet Architecture

The screened subnet architecture, described in Chapter 6, *Firewall Architectures*, and shown in Figure 24-1, is probably the most common do-it-yourself firewall architecture. This architecture provides good security (including multiple layers of redundancy) at what most sites feel is a reasonable cost.

There are two-router and single-router variations of the screened subnet architecture. Basically, you can use either a pair of two-interface routers or a single three-interface router. The single-router screened subnet architecture works about as well as the two-router screened subnet architecture and is often somewhat cheaper. However, you need to use a router that can handle both inbound and

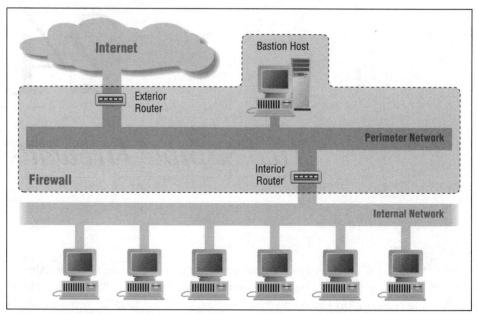

Figure 24-1. Screened subnet architecture

outbound packet filtering on each interface. (See the discussion of this point in Chapter 8, *Packet Filtering.*) We're going to use a two-router architecture as our example in this section because it is conceptually simpler.

This type of firewall includes the following components, presented originally in Chapter 6, *Firewall Architectures*:

Perimeter network

Isolates your bastion host from your internal network, so a security breach on the bastion host won't immediately affect your internal network.

Exterior router

Connects your site to the outside world. If possible, the exterior router also provides at least some protection for the bastion host, interior router, and internal network. (This isn't always possible because some sites use exterior routers that are managed by their network service providers and are therefore beyond the site's control.)

Interior router

Protects the internal network from the world and from the site's own bastion host.

Bastion host

Serves as the site's main point of contact with the outside world. (It should be set up according to the guidelines in Chapter 10, *Bastion Hosts.*)

In addition to the machines that make up the firewall itself, assume there are machines on the internal network (internal hosts) that fulfill the following roles (note that any given internal machine might fill any, or even all, of these roles):

- Mail server

- Usenet news server

- DNS server

- Client for various Internet services

Each of these internal services is provided directly (via packet filtering) or indirectly (via proxy servers running on the bastion host).

We're going to assume (at least for the purposes of this example) that internal users in our system are trusted not to actively try to circumvent the firewall, and that there is no particular need to monitor or log their Internet activities.

We're also going to assume that you are using properly assigned and routed IP addresses (that is, addresses assigned to your site and properly routed and advertised to the rest of the Internet by your service provider) for your internal and perimeter networks. If you aren't, you have to use proxies or network address translation because you can't allow packets with those unassigned IP addresses onto the Internet; even if you did allow them, replies would have no way to come back to you.

Finally, we're going to assume you're using separate network numbers for your perimeter net and internal net, so that you can detect forged packets easily. (See the discussion in "Risks of Filtering by Source Address" in Chapter 8, *Packet Filtering*.)

Service Configuration

Given the architecture we've just described, how do we provide the basic Internet services?

HTTP and HTTPS

We will want to provide two kinds of HTTP service. We'll want to allow our users to access other people's web sites, and we'll want to put up our own web site.

For outgoing HTTP and HTTPS (letting our users access other sites), we can use either packet filtering or proxy servers. Packet filtering will allow our users to access HTTP and HTTPS servers only on standard ports; proxying will allow them to reach all HTTP and HTTPS servers. Which approach should we take?

Standard browsers support HTTP and HTTPS proxying, so we don't need to worry about using customized clients with either approach. Proxying will increase configuration overhead, but that price seems fair for the increased abilities it offers.

On the other hand, we could simply allow internal hosts to create connections to port 80, port 443, and any port at or above 1024. That will allow access to almost any HTTP or HTTPS server and will also be useful for supporting FTP. It does add a significant amount of risk; internal users will be able to use any protocol above 1024, with no control from the firewall. If these users are ill intentioned or even careless, they could expose the site to all sorts of dangers. In addition, any Trojan horse programs they bring in will easily be able to send out data. However, we originally chose to trust the users, so this is not an issue. Using pure packet filtering this way would lose us only servers at nonstandard ports below 1024, and those ports are all supposed to be reserved anyway.

If we use a caching proxy server, we significantly improve HTTP performance for all of the following:

HTTP clients

> They obtain pages from the cache over the internal network, rather than from the original server over our Internet connection, which is probably much slower.

Non-HTTP clients

> The HTTP clients won't be using so much of the bandwidth of our Internet connection, leaving more of it for other clients to use.

HTTP servers at other sites

> They will get only one request from our site for a given page, rather than multiple requests.

HTTPS connections can't be cached because the encryption means that pages are different every time they're accessed, but a caching proxy server won't interfere with HTTPS service; it will simply act like a normal proxy.

Most caching servers will also allow us to provide HTTP service to external sites, so we can take advantage of that to publish our site's own public web pages. This configuration is not particularly secure; the security requirements for proxying and publishing are different, and ideally we would want to separate the two. However, in a configuration with only one bastion host, we can't provide much separation in any case.

Combining the proxying and publishing wouldn't be acceptable if we wanted to provide popular pages, or if we needed much security for the pages we were providing (for instance, if the web pages are used for electronic commerce). In either of those situations, we'd separate the outgoing cache from the public web server, putting them not only on different pieces of software but also on different computers. In fact, we might well choose to have the public web server on somebody else's network altogether, using a commercial web hosting service.

HTTP and HTTPS proxying is also trivial to add once you have other things proxied via SOCKS or TIS FWTK. If we had SOCKS running, it would be very tempting to simply proxy through it because SOCKS is one of the systems that many of the browsers support. On the other hand, it's a lot of trouble to install SOCKS just for HTTP and HTTPS; it's probably not worth it unless we have other applications that will use it. If we used the TIS FWTK HTTP proxy, we'd have to get the users to modify URLs they use. In this case, the users wouldn't be able to cut and paste out of their electronic mail when people tell them about cool new things. Neither SOCKS nor TIS FWTK makes an attractive option in this situation.

However, both proxying (through a proxying server) and packet filtering appear to be attractive and reasonable choices. Proxying is definitely preferable if we aren't going to provide passive-mode FTP directly (which gives our users the ability to talk to servers on any TCP port above 1023). On the other hand, packet filtering would definitely be preferable if we wanted to use clients that didn't come with built-in support for proxying, or if we wanted not to provide an HTTP server and had no other services being proxied.

For this example, we're going to assume that we're providing HTTP and HTTPS service to internal clients via a proxy server running on the bastion host, and that we're using the same server to publish our public web pages to the world. We will take special care to make sure that the proxy component is configured to prevent external users from using the proxy to access either our internal network or other external servers. Our reasons for using a proxy server are based mostly on the added efficiency, although it's also useful to make sure that users can reach HTTP and HTTPS servers on nonstandard ports below 1023.

SMTP

There aren't many options for SMTP in any configuration. We want all external SMTP connections to go to a single machine with a secured SMTP server, and we don't trust random internal machines to have safe SMTP servers. That means we'll put a secured SMTP server on the bastion host and use DNS MX records to direct all incoming mail to the bastion host, which will then pass all the incoming mail to a single secured internal SMTP server.

What other options do we have? We could put a secure SMTP server on the internal mail server and direct incoming mail to it, but if that SMTP server were compromised, the entire internal net would then be at risk. Alternatively, we could have the bastion host send mail directly to machines on the internal network, but once again, we'd be increasing our vulnerability if the SMTP server on the bastion host were compromised. The compromised bastion host would be speaking to untrustworthy internal SMTP servers, and compromise of the internal net would quickly follow. If the bastion host can speak only to the internal mail server, that narrows the possible attacks it can make; the internal mail server can run a secured SMTP server. Furthermore, by making this choice, messy maintenance tasks are transferred from the security-critical bastion host to the less vulnerable internal mail server.

How about outgoing mail? It would probably be safe to allow internal machines to send mail directly to the outside world, but doing so creates a maintenance headache. (You have to watch the mail configuration on all the internal machines.) Besides, doing this opens another direct connection between the internal and external networks. There aren't any known ways for an SMTP server to attack an SMTP client, but stranger things have happened.

Allowing internal machines to send mail directly to the outside world doesn't seem to bring much advantage either. The only difference it makes is that we'd be able to send mail (but not receive it) when the bastion host is down.

No matter what decision we make, we'll have to configure our mail clients. (Unlike FTP and Telnet, SMTP does not work as installed without modifying configuration files.) In addition, the work to direct the mail to a server is less than the work to correctly send it to the external universe.

The only real question is whether to direct the outgoing mail from the internal machines to the internal mail server or to the bastion host. Directing it to the internal mail server has the same advantages as for incoming mail and keeps internal information away from the bastion host. Mail between internal users should not go through the bastion host.

We'll set up SMTP, as outlined in Chapter 16, *Electronic Mail and News*, with the bastion host acting as a middleman for incoming and outgoing mail. Here's what to do:

- Publish DNS MX records that direct incoming mail for the site to the bastion host.

- Configure internal machines to send all outgoing mail to the internal mail server.

- Configure the bastion host to send all incoming mail to a single internal mail server and to send outgoing mail directly to its destination.

For this example, we're going to assume that there is a single internal mail server for incoming and outgoing mail.

Telnet

Outgoing Telnet could be provided through packet filtering or through proxies. Which approach should we use?

Proxying will require either modified clients or modified user procedures; either one will be tedious to implement. Proxying would allow us to restrict or monitor Telnet usage by user by forcing our users to authenticate to a proxy server before completing their requests. However, remember that we have decided to assume that internal users are trustworthy, so there is no need for authentication. Proxying would be necessary if we were using unassigned or unadvertised IP addresses internally, but that's not the case here either. Because we have trustworthy users and proper IP addresses, proxying for Telnet doesn't provide any advantage over packet filtering, and it's more difficult to set up and maintain. Therefore, for this example, we're going to provide outgoing Telnet via packet filtering.

Incoming Telnet is considerably more difficult to provide safely and conveniently. If it were necessary, incoming Telnet could be provided on the bastion host using extra authentication. However, for a site that is looking for a simple configuration, the reasonable thing to do is to disallow incoming Telnet altogether, replacing it with SSH. That's what we'll do for this example.

SSH

Although incoming Telnet is unsafe, it's useful to be able to allow some form of remote access. The safest way to do so is to allow SSH. One way would be to allow SSH inbound to the bastion host only, forcing users to log into the bastion host and then go from there to their internal destination; this is effectively a form of proxying. Another option would be to allow SSH inbound to any host.

Forcing SSH to a single bastion host allows us to make sure that what's coming in is genuinely SSH and that the SSH server is safely configured. On the other hand, it requires us to have user accounts configured on the bastion host. If only a few users need to use SSH, it may be the best way to provide the service. However, with only a single bastion host, significant risks are involved in having user accounts around.

Allowing SSH inbound to all hosts avoids the problem with user accounts on the bastion host but opens up the possibility of having hosts running SSH servers that will do port forwarding, or running other servers altogether on the SSH port. As we discuss in Chapter 18, *Remote Access to Hosts*, port forwarding across SSH is a significant risk, which may make your site vulnerable to people who are attacking the client. We will allow SSH inbound to all hosts (we're already trusting internal users).

For a more secure configuration, we would limit the hosts that were accessible via SSH, either by adding another bastion host on the screened network or by treating some internal hosts as screened hosts and allowing SSH to just those hosts.

Since we are allowing incoming SSH, we should also allow outgoing SSH; it would be unjust to ask people to use SSH to access our site but require our users to use insecure Telnet to access other sites. However, we will want to warn our users about the risks of remote port forwarding. Unlike outgoing Telnet, outgoing SSH opens us up to incoming attacks if port forwarding is turned on. (See Chapter 18, *Remote Access to Hosts*, for more information about the risks of SSH port forwarding.) For more security, we might want to limit even outgoing SSH to a machine where we could control the clients in use and disallow remote port forwarding. Note that even when SSH is limited to a single machine, it is significantly difficult to prevent users from providing their own SSH clients.

FTP

Unlike Telnet, FTP doesn't lend itself to a pure packet filtering solution. Because normal-mode FTP requires an incoming connection to an arbitrary port over 1023, trying to allow it without doing anything else gives attackers access to all kinds of services running on our internal systems. That leaves us two choices:

• Support passive mode via packet filtering

• Support normal mode via proxies

In either case, the standard FTP clients shipped with Unix operating systems, and most of the popular, publicly available clients for personal computers, won't work the normal way. If we use the TIS FWTK *ftp-gw* proxy gateway (described in Chapter 9, *Proxy Systems*), we can use unmodified clients, but at the cost of teaching the users to follow special procedures. Some popular FTP clients—the ones built in to Web browsers like Netscape Navigator or Internet Explorer—do use passive mode without being modified, but then again, not all servers support it well.

A reasonable compromise would be to use both packet filtering and proxies, using a proxying gateway like *ftp-gw* from TIS FWTK that doesn't require modification of the clients. Clients that support passive mode will work via the packet filters. On platforms where we can easily replace the provided clients, we can provide passive-mode clients; on platforms where we can't easily replace the clients, we can modify user procedures instead.

As we've said, if we wanted to monitor FTP usage, we'd have to use proxying exclusively, but that's not the case here. If we were using an unassigned or unrouted network number, we'd have to do either proxying or network address translation. We also might want to use proxying exclusively if we decided to hide

DNS data—it would save us the trouble of faking data for double-reverse lookups by using a published address with an advertised reverse mapping—but hiding DNS data is more trouble than it's worth. In a situation where proxying is used exclusively, we'd have to reconsider which proxy server to use. The proxy server we've selected requires users to modify their procedures, which makes sense in the configuration we're discussing because there are no other options. The balance might come out differently if everybody were proxying.

Be aware that in order to use the TIS FWTK *ftp-gw* proxy server on your bastion host, your packet filtering will have to allow TCP connections from ports above 1023 on your bastion host to ports above 1023 on internal hosts, and from port 20 on external hosts to ports above 1023 on your bastion host, for FTP data channels. (See the discussion of FTP in Chapter 17, *File Transfer, File Sharing, and Printing*.) This means that someone who breaks in to the bastion host could easily connect to any server on any internal host that uses a TCP port above 1023 (for example, an X11 server on port 6000). Further, any servers that are using such ports (that is, TCP ports above 1023) on the bastion host itself are also vulnerable. For this reason, if you allow these FTP data connections at all for proxying, you probably want to explicitly block access to internal systems to TCP ports above 1023 where you know, or have good cause to suspect, that servers might be listening. At the very least, the ports you want to block probably include 6000 through around 6003 (assuming four or fewer real or virtual X11 servers per machine; see the discussion of X11 in Chapter 18, *Remote Access to Hosts*). Since we're allowing SSH, we also need to protect the virtual X11 servers that SSH creates, which start at 6010, so we'll extend this port range to 6020.

Keep in mind, however, that blocking specific ports, rather than blocking all ports by default and then allowing specific ports, is generally a dangerous strategy. It's hard to develop and maintain a complete list of ports that need to be blocked at your site. It would be better to block everything by default and then allow only specific ports, but you can't do that with standard (nonpassive) FTP because of the way it works.

Allowing passive-mode FTP with packet filtering is a fairly liberal approach because it allows pretty much any connection to go through as long as it is initiated by the inside. The number of servers above port 1023 is very large. This has some advantages (it lets users access nonstandard HTTP servers, for example), but it may also allow users to access all kinds of services that are unsafe. In allowing it, we're assuming that our users are not only well intentioned, they're also capable of telling the difference between a safe and an unsafe connection, or at least avoiding the temptation to do unexpected things.

Because we've denied incoming Telnet, it makes sense to deny incoming user FTP as well. Both services require approximately the same security measures, and making one of them available would make configuring the other trivial.

Incoming anonymous FTP is a different matter, and we'll provide it. Because we're not a major Internet service provider, and because we're using TIS FWTK already anyway, we can go for security over features and use the TIS FWTK anonymous FTP server. If we were going to provide major anonymous FTP, we'd probably want to use the more feature-filled *wuarchive* FTP server (see Chapter 17, *File Transfer, File Sharing, and Printing*, for a description of its capabilities) and run it on a machine that was not the main bastion host but that was still a bastion host on the perimeter network. Using another bastion host avoids overloading the main bastion host with risky and interacting services.

NNTP

As we've discussed in Chapter 16, *Electronic Mail and News*, the most practical way to set up NNTP across a firewall is to allow your NNTP service provider(s) to talk directly to your internal Usenet news host, and vice versa. We'd need an overwhelming reason to do something else, and it's hard to imagine one. Even if we didn't have an existing internal news host, building one isn't any harder than building a news server on the bastion host, and it's safer by a vast margin. News servers fail with dreary regularity; while the problems usually aren't security-related, you still don't want to install anything requiring high maintenance on a bastion host.

For this example, we're going to assume a single external NNTP newsfeed.

DNS

As discussed in Chapter 20, *Naming and Directory Services*, DNS is best provided across a firewall with a pair of servers: one on the bastion host, the other on an internal host. Like NNTP, DNS presents a situation in which the number of rational solutions is clearly limited. We need to decide whether to use separate internal and external servers to do information hiding, or whether we should allow the external world to see all of our host data. By deciding to allow direct passive-mode FTP, we've already made that decision indirectly. Direct passive-mode FTP would require intricate DNS setup to support information hiding and still provide valid data for the internal hosts that are FTP clients.

For this example, we're going to assume that the DNS server on the bastion host is a secondary server for our domain, and that the primary server is on an internal host. We're not going to do any DNS information hiding.

Packet Filtering Rules

Based on the configuration decisions we've made in the previous sections, let's look at the packet filtering rules necessary to support this configuration. We assume an "ideal" router (as discussed in "Choosing a Packet Filtering Router" in Chapter 8, *Packet Filtering*). If our router were less than ideal in terms of capabilities, we'd need to modify these rules accordingly, probably at the cost of security. We might have to rethink several crucial decisions entirely. For example, if we couldn't filter on the ACK bit, direct outbound passive-mode FTP would no longer be acceptably safe, and a lot of our other decisions have used that as a major factor. (See Chapter 8 for a full discussion of packet filtering capabilities and the implications of not having particular capabilities.)

In the packet filtering rules presented in the following table, we assume that the filtering system:

- Can distinguish between incoming and outgoing packets

- Can filter on source address, destination address, packet type (TCP or UDP), source port, and destination port

- Can filter on whether or not the ACK bit is set (for TCP packets)

- Applies rules in the order listed

In the following table, directions are shown relative to the site, as they have been in previous tables.

Interior router

The purpose of the interior router is to protect the internal network from the Internet and from your own bastion host. The interior router needs the following rules to support the outlined configuration. Explanations of each rule follow the table.

Rule	Dir.	Source Address	Dest. Address	Protocol	Source Port	Dest. Port	ACK Set	Action
Spoof-1	In	Internal	Any	Any	Any	Any	Any	Deny
Spoof-2	Out	External	Any	Any	Any	Any	Any	Deny
HTTP-1	Out	Internal	Bastion	TCP	>1023	80	Any	Permit
HTTP-2	In	Bastion	Internal	TCP	80	>1023	Yes	Permit
Telnet-1	Out	Internal	Any	TCP	>1023	23	Any	Permit
Telnet-2	In	Any	Internal	TCP	23	>1023	Yes	Permit
SSH-1	Out	Internal	Any	TCP	Any	22	Any	Permit

Rule	Dir.	Source Address	Dest. Address	Protocol	Source Port	Dest. Port	ACK Set	Action
SSH-2	In	Any	Internal	TCP	22	Any	Yes	Permit
SSH-3	In	Any	Internal	TCP	Any	22	Any	Permit
SSH-4	Out	Internal	Any	TCP	22	Any	Yes	Permit
FTP-1	Out	Internal	Any	TCP	>1023	21	Any	Permit
FTP-2	In	Any	Internal	TCP	21	>1023	Yes	Permit
FTP-3	Out	Internal	Any	TCP	>1023	>1023	Any	Permit
FTP-4	In	Any	Internal	TCP	>1023	>1023	Yes	Permit
FTP-5	Out	Internal	Bastion	TCP	>1023	21	Any	Permit
FTP-6	In	Bastion	Internal	TCP	21	>1023	Yes	Permit
FTP-7	In	Bastion	Internal	TCP	Any	6000-6020	Any	Deny
FTP-8	In	Bastion	Internal	TCP	>1023	>1023	Any	Permit
FTP-9	Out	Internal	Bastion	TCP	>1023	>1023	Yes	Permit
SMTP-1	Out	Internal SMTP server	Bastion	TCP	>1023	25	Any	Permit
SMTP-2	In	Bastion	Internal SMTP server	TCP	25	>1023	Yes	Permit
SMTP-3	In	Bastion	Internal SMTP server	TCP	>1023	25	Any	Permit
SMTP-4	Out	Internal SMTP server	Bastion	TCP	25	>1023	Yes	Permit
NNTP-1	Out	Internal NNTP server	NNTP feed server	TCP	>1023	119	Any	Permit
NNTP-2	In	NNTP feed server	Internal NNTP server	TCP	119	>1023	Yes	Permit
NNTP-3	In	NNTP feed server	Internal NNTP server	TCP	>1023	119	Any	Permit
NNTP-4	Out	Internal NNTP server	NNTP feed server	TCP	119	>1023	Yes	Permit
DNS-1	Out	Internal DNS server	Bastion	UDP	53	53	[a]	Permit
DNS-2	In	Bastion	Internal DNS server	UDP	53	53	[a]	Permit
DNS-3	Out	Internal DNS server	Bastion	TCP	>1023	53	Any	Permit
DNS-4	In	Bastion	Internal DNS server	TCP	53	>1023	Yes	Permit
DNS-5	In	Bastion	Internal DNS server	TCP	>1023	53	Any	Permit
DNS-6	Out	Internal DNS server	Bastion	TCP	53	>1023	Yes	Permit
Default-1	Out	Any	Any	Any	Any	Any	Any	Deny
Default-2	In	Any	Any	Any	Any	Any	Any	Deny

[a] UDP has no ACK equivalent.

Here is some additional information about each set of rules in this table:

Spoof-1 and Spoof-2

Spoof-1 blocks incoming packets that claim to come from internal IP addresses (that is, forged packets presumably sent by an attacker). Spoof-2 blocks outgoing packets that claim to come from external IP addresses (these reflect either bad misconfiguration of machines or an attacker's operating inside your network). Spoof-2 may be difficult to implement on some packet filtering systems because it can be easily written only if you can use negation on source addresses (to specify addresses that are not in the internal range). It would be acceptable to omit it in this situation; it is mostly there to protect other people, not to protect your site.

HTTP-1 and HTTP-2

Allow internal HTTP clients to connect to the HTTP proxy server on your bastion host. Clients can use their HTTP connection to the proxy server to request services with any protocol the proxy server will support; the connection from the client to the proxy server will be over port 80, while the connection from the proxy server to the destination server will be over the appropriate port for the desired protocol. Therefore, these rules will support HTTPS as well as HTTP.

Telnet-1 and Telnet-2

Allow outgoing Telnet connections.

SSH-1 and SSH-2

Allow outgoing SSH connections. We have the client port set to "Any" (instead of ">1023" like most of the other protocols) because some forms of authentication require SSH clients to use ports at or below 1023.

SSH-3 and SSH-4

Allow incoming SSH connections. We have the client port set to "Any" (instead of ">1023" like most of the other protocols) because some forms of authentication require SSH clients to use ports at or below 1023.

FTP-1 and FTP-2

Allow outgoing command-channel connections to FTP servers, for use by passive-mode internal clients that are interacting with those servers directly.

FTP-3 and FTP-4

Allow the FTP data channel connections from passive-mode internal clients to external FTP servers. Note that these rules actually allow all connections from internal TCP ports above 1023 to external TCP ports above 1023. That may be more than you want to allow, but there's no way to cover passive-mode FTP with anything less broad, and connections are at least restricted to those opened from the inside.

FTP-5 and FTP-6

Allow normal (nonpassive-mode) internal FTP clients to open an FTP command channel to the proxy FTP server on the bastion host. Note that these rules are actually redundant if you have rules FTP-1 and FTP-2 in place earlier in the list because "Bastion" as a source or destination (covered by rules FTP-5 and FTP-6) is a subset of "All" (covered by rules FTP-1 and FTP-2). Having these redundant rules is going to impose a slight performance cost but makes the rule set easier to understand. It also makes it possible to change rules FTP-1 and FTP-2 (e.g., if you decide you don't want to support passive-mode clients) without accidentally breaking normal-mode client access to the proxy server.

FTP-7 through FTP-9

Allow FTP data connections from the proxy server on the bastion host to non-passive internal clients. The FTP-7 rule prevents an attacker who has gained access to the bastion host from attacking internal X11 servers via the hole created by rules FTP-8 and FTP-9. If you have other servers internally listening for connections on TCP ports above 1023, you should add similar rules for them. Note that trying to list things that should be denied (as in rule FTP-7) is generally a losing proposition because your list will almost always be incomplete somehow (e.g., because you overlooked or didn't know about some internal service, or because the service was added after the filters were established). However, it's the best you can do in this situation to support normal-mode FTP clients.

SMTP-1 and SMTP-2

Allow outgoing mail from your internal mail server to the bastion host.

SMTP-3 and SMTP-4

Allow incoming mail from the bastion host to your internal mail server.

NNTP-1 and NNTP-2

Allow outgoing Usenet news from your news server to your service provider's news server.

NNTP-3 and NNTP-4

Allow incoming Usenet news from your service provider's news server to your news server.

DNS-1

Allow UDP-based DNS queries and answers from the internal DNS server to the bastion host DNS server.

DNS-2

Allow UDP-based DNS queries and answers from the bastion host DNS server to the internal DNS server.

DNS-3 and DNS-4

Allow TCP-based DNS queries from the internal DNS server to the bastion host DNS servers, as well as answers to those queries. Also allow zone transfers in which the bastion host DNS server is the primary server and the internal DNS server is the secondary server.

DNS-5 and DNS-6

Allow TCP-based DNS queries from the bastion host DNS server to the internal DNS server, as well as answers to those queries. Also allow zone transfers in which the bastion host DNS server is the secondary server and the internal DNS server is the primary server.

Default-1 and Default-2

Block all packets not specifically allowed by one of the preceding rules.

How you translate these abstract rules into specific rules for your particular filtering system depends on the syntax used by your system. Some systems allow you to enter the rules as a single table, much as we show here in this table. Other systems require you to specify rules for incoming and outgoing packets in separate rule sets. Splitting these rules between incoming and outgoing packets is not a problem, as long as you preserve the order for rules of each type; that is, as long as all the incoming rules stay in the same order relative to each other, and all the outgoing rules stay in the same order relative to each other.

Exterior router

The purpose of the exterior router is twofold:

- To connect the perimeter net (and thus your site) to the outside world

- To protect the perimeter net and the internal net against the outside world

In many circumstances, only the former purpose is possible because the exterior router is often provided and managed by your network service provider. That provider may be unable or unwilling to set up and maintain packet filtering rules on the exterior router (and unable or unwilling to let you do it yourself).

The differences between the rules for the interior router and the exterior router all have to do with the bastion host. That's because the bastion host sits "outside" of the interior router (i.e., on the side of the interior router towards the Internet), but it sits "inside" of the exterior router (i.e., on the side of the exterior router away from the Internet).

If you can set up filtering on the exterior router, it's a good idea to do so. If nothing else, it can serve as a backup to some of the filtering on the interior router. For this example, you would need to establish the following rules.

Rule	Dir.	Source Address	Dest. Address	Protocol	Source Port	Dest. Port	ACK Set	Action
Spoof-1	In	Internal	Any	Any	Any	Any	Any	Deny
Spoof-2	In	Perim.	Any	Any	Any	Any	Any	Deny
Spoof-3	Out	External	Any	Any	Any	Any	Any	Deny
HTTP-1	Out	Bastion	Any	TCP	>1023	Any	Any	Permit
HTTP-2	In	Any	Bastion	TCP	Any	>1023	Yes	Permit
HTTP-3	In	Any	Bastion	TCP	>1023	80	Any	Permit
HTTP-4	Out	Bastion	Any	TCP	80	>1023	Yes	Permit
Telnet-1	Out	Internal	Any	TCP	>1023	23	Any	Permit
Telnet-2	In	Any	Internal	TCP	23	>1023	Yes	Permit
SSH-1	Out	Internal	Any	TCP	Any	22	Any	Permit
SSH-2	In	Any	Internal	TCP	22	Any	Yes	Permit
SSH-3	In	Any	Internal	TCP	Any	22	Any	Permit
SSH-4	Out	Internal	Any	TCP	22	Any	Yes	Permit
FTP-1	Out	Internal	Any	TCP	>1023	21	Any	Permit
FTP-2	In	Any	Internal	TCP	21	>1023	Yes	Permit
FTP-3	Out	Internal	Any	TCP	>1023	>1023	Any	Permit
FTP-4	In	Any	Internal	TCP	>1023	>1023	Yes	Permit
FTP-5	Out	Bastion	Any	TCP	>1023	21	Any	Permit
FTP-6	In	Any	Bastion	TCP	21	>1023	Yes	Permit
FTP-7	In	Any	Bastion	TCP	Any	6000-6020	Any	Deny
FTP-8	In	Any	Bastion	TCP	20	>1023	Any	Permit
FTP-9	Out	Bastion	Any	TCP	>1023	20	Yes	Permit
FTP-10	In	Any	Bastion	TCP	>1023	21	Any	Permit
FTP-11	Out	Bastion	Any	TCP	21	>1023	Yes	Permit
FTP-12	Out	Bastion	Any	TCP	20	>1023	Any	Permit
FTP-13	In	Any	Bastion	TCP	>1023	20	Yes	Permit
FTP-14	In	Any	Bastion	TCP	>1023	>1023	Any	Permit
FTP-15	Out	Bastion	Any	TCP	>1023	>1023	Any	Permit
SMTP-1	Out	Bastion	Any	TCP	>1023	25	Any	Permit
SMTP-2	In	Any	Bastion	TCP	25	>1023	Yes	Permit
SMTP-3	In	Any	Bastion	TCP	>1023	25	Any	Permit
SMTP-4	Out	Bastion	Any	TCP	25	>1023	Yes	Permit
NNTP-1	Out	Internal NNTP server	NNTP feed server	TCP	>1023	119	Any	Permit
NNTP-2	In	NNTP feed server	Internal NNTP server	TCP	119	>1023	Yes	Permit
NNTP-3	In	NNTP feed server	Internal NNTP server	TCP	>1023	119	Any	Permit
NNTP-4	Out	Internal NNTP server	NNTP feed server	TCP	119	>1023	Yes	Permit
DNS-1	Out	Bastion	Any	UDP	53	53	a	Permit

Rule	Dir.	Source Address	Dest. Address	Protocol	Source Port	Dest. Port	ACK Set	Action
DNS-2	In	Any	Bastion	UDP	53	53	a	Permit
DNS-3	In	Any	Bastion	UDP	Any	53	a	Permit
DNS-4	Out	Bastion	Any	UDP	53	Any	a	Permit
DNS-5	Out	Bastion	Any	TCP	>1023	53	Any	Permit
DNS-6	In	Any	Bastion	TCP	53	>1023	Yes	Permit
DNS-7	In	Any	Bastion	TCP	>1023	53	Any	Permit
DNS-8	Out	Bastion	Any	TCP	53	>1023	Yes	Permit
Default-1	Out	Any	Any	Any	Any	Any	Any	Deny
Default-2	In	Any	Any	Any	Any	Any	Any	Deny

a UDP has no ACK equivalent.

Here is some additional information about each set of rules in this table:

Spoof-1 and Spoof-2

Block incoming packets that claim to have internal or perimeter net source IP addresses—that is, forged packets presumably sent by an attacker. Rule Spoof-1 is the same as the Spoof-1 rule on the interior router; rule Spoof-2 is unique to the exterior router.

Spoof-3

Block outgoing packets that claim to have external source IP addresses. These are either forged packets from an attacker on your network or symptoms of bad network misconfigurations. Spoof-3 may be difficult to implement on some packet filtering systems because it can be easily written only if you can use negation on source addresses (to specify addresses that are not in the internal range). It would be acceptable to omit it in this situation; it is mostly there to protect other people, not to protect your site.

HTTP-1 and HTTP-2

Allow the bastion host HTTP proxy server to connect to the HTTP and HTTPS servers on any machine on the Internet. Actually, these rules allow any TCP client program on the bastion host using a port above 1023 to contact any server program on any host on the Internet using any port. This is done so that the HTTP proxy server can contact HTTP servers on nonstandard port numbers (i.e., other than port 80). As broad as these rules are, it's important that they allow only outgoing connections, by examining the ACK bit.

HTTP-3 and HTTP-4

Allow external clients to contact the bastion host HTTP server. There are no equivalent rules on the interior router because no HTTP servers are on the internal network that external clients can access.

Telnet-1 and Telnet-2

Allow outgoing Telnet connections. These are identical to the corresponding rules on the interior router (as are all rules on the exterior router that involve internal and external hosts but nothing on the perimeter net).

SSH-1 and SSH-2

Allow outgoing SSH connections. We have the client port set to "Any" (instead of ">1023" like most of the other protocols) because some forms of authentication require SSH clients to use ports at or below 1023. These are the same as the corresponding rules on the interior router.

SSH-3 and SSH-4

Allow incoming SSH connections. We have the client port set to "Any" (instead of ">1023" like most of the other protocols) because some forms of authentication require SSH clients to use ports at or below 1023. These are the same as the corresponding rules on the interior router. If there is a need to allow administrators to reach the bastion host with SSH for remote administration, we will need to add another pair of rules. As it is, administrators can use SSH to an internal host and then connect from there to the bastion host, but this is somewhat fragile (if the interior router is down, there will be no way to administer anything remotely).

FTP-1 through FTP-4

Allow outgoing passive-mode FTP connections and are identical to the corresponding rules on the interior router.

FTP-5 and FTP-6

Allow the FTP proxy server on the bastion host to open an FTP command channel to FTP servers on the Internet. Note that, unlike the corresponding rules on the interior router, these rules are *not* redundant if you have rules FTP-1 and FTP-2 in place earlier in the list. Why? Because "Bastion" as a source or destination (covered by rules FTP-5 and FTP-6) is not a subset of "Internal" (covered by rules FTP-1 and FTP-2).

FTP-7 through FTP-9

Allow FTP data connections from external FTP servers to the proxy server on the bastion host. The FTP-7 rule prevents an attacker from attacking X11 servers on the bastion host via the hole created by rules FTP-8 and FTP-9. If other servers on the bastion host are listening for connections on TCP ports above 1023, you should add similar rules for them. Note that trying to list things that should be denied (as in rule FTP-7) is a losing proposition because your list will almost always be incomplete (e.g., because you overlooked or didn't know about some service or because the service was added after the filters were established). However, it's the best you can do in this situation if you must support normal-mode FTP.

FTP-10 through FTP-15

Allow passive- and normal-mode FTP from external clients to the anonymous FTP server on the bastion host. There are no equivalent rules on the internal router because no FTP servers are on the internal network that external clients can access.

SMTP-1 and SMTP-2

Allow outgoing mail from the bastion host to the outside world.

SMTP-3 and SMTP-4

Allow incoming mail from the outside world to the bastion host.

NNTP-1 to NNTP-4

Allow Usenet news both ways between your Usenet news server and your service provider's news server. These rules are identical to the corresponding rules on the interior router.

DNS-1

Allows UDP-based DNS queries and answers from the bastion host DNS server to DNS servers in the outside world.

DNS-2

Allows UDP-based DNS queries and answers from Internet DNS servers to the bastion host DNS server. Note that rule DNS-2 (which allows server-to-server communication) is redundant if rule DNS-3 (which allows client-to-server communication) is present.

DNS-3 and DNS-4

Allow external UDP-based DNS clients to query the DNS server on the bastion host and it to answer them.

DNS-5 and DNS-6

Allow TCP-based DNS queries from the bastion host to DNS servers on the Internet, as well as answers to those queries. Also allow zone transfers in which the bastion host DNS server is the secondary server and an external DNS server is the primary server.

DNS-7 and DNS-8

Allow TCP-based DNS queries from the outside world to the bastion host DNS server, as well as answers to those queries. Also allow zone transfers in which the bastion host DNS server is the primary server and an external DNS server is the secondary server.

Default-1 and Default-2

Block all packets not specifically allowed by one of the preceding rules, just as the corresponding rules do on the interior router.

Other Configuration Work

In addition to setting up the packet filtering rules, we need to do various other kinds of configuration work, as follows:

On all of the internal machines

Configure electronic mail so that outgoing mail gets sent to the internal mail server. We're also going to need to install passive-mode FTP clients if they're available. We may want to install SSH clients and servers, configured to disable port forwarding.

On the internal mail server

Install a trusted SMTP server.

On the internal (primary) name server

Put in an MX record for every A record, pointing incoming mail to the bastion host; further MX records may be necessary for the internal mail server to direct the traffic internally. We also need to configure the bastion host as a recognized secondary name server, and remove any TXT or HINFO records we don't want the external world to see (i.e., pretty much any records the external world could possibly make any sense of).

On the bastion host

Do all the standard bastion host configuration tasks (removing unused servers, adding logging, and so on), as discussed in Chapter 10, *Bastion Hosts.* We need to install TIS FWTK and configure FTP proxying, a trusted SMTP server, and anonymous FTP service from it. We also need to install the HTTP server and configure it to do proxying, as well as to serve the HTTP pages we want to show the outside world.

Analysis

Just how good a firewall is this one we've configured? Let's consider it in relation to the strategies and principles discussed in Chapter 3, *Security Strategies.*

Least privilege

The principle of least privilege is that an object (a program, a person, a router, or whatever) should have the minimum privileges necessary to perform its assigned task and no more. A corollary of this principle is that systems should be configured so they require as little privilege as possible. You can see this principle in action in several places in this setup. For example, configuring SMTP so that outgoing mail goes out via the bastion host (rather than directly to remote systems) is an application of least privilege because it lets you control more tightly how internal systems connect to external systems. (In this case, it makes it unnecessary for internal systems to talk directly to external systems in order to provide this service.)

Defense in depth

The principle of defense in depth is something else that you can see in the setup we've described. For example, internal hosts are protected from the outside world by the exterior and interior routers. Similarly, the bastion host is protected against attack both by its own careful configuration and by the exterior router.

Several times, we've explicitly made decisions to increase the depth of defense. For example, that's one of the main purposes of using an internal mail server between the bastion host and the internal clients. The interior and exterior routers often deny the same packets. Defense in depth is almost the only reason for having the interior router deny packets that it supposedly can't receive (because they've already been denied by the exterior router).

Choke point

The principle of a choke point is clearly applied in our setup because everything between internal clients and the Internet comes through the perimeter net. Further, much of it comes through the bastion host via proxies. Only Telnet, SSH, and FTP are provided in ways that leave them relatively open. These services could have been better choked by using proxies everywhere.

Weakest link

There is no single obvious weak link to attack in this configuration. Probably the weakest link is the bastion host, but even a completely compromised bastion host isn't going to help an attacker much when it comes to attacking the internal systems; not that many connections are allowed from the bastion host to internal systems. Some of the weakest links you can see remaining in this setup include incoming SSH, proxy FTP, combining a public HTTP server with the outgoing caching proxy server.

Allowing inbound SSH to every host is another candidate for the weakest link; it is the point where we put the most trust in the users. Users who choose poor passwords or set up SSH tunnels can easily undermine the security of the firewall. This could be strengthened significantly by restricting SSH to a dedicated bastion host, which could help enforce password and tunneling restrictions. Users could still connect from that host to internal hosts.

The proxy FTP setup we've described would allow an attacker who has compromised the bastion host to attack servers on ports above 1023 (if there are any) on internal hosts. How can you address this vulnerability? Obtain and use only passive-mode FTP clients internally, don't run proxy FTP, and remove the rules allowing proxy FTP from the filters.

Combining incoming and outgoing HTTP service has several drawbacks. First, the server program itself is more complicated; it is trying to enforce different restrictions for internal and external users, and bugs or misconfigurations may inappropriately mix the two, allowing external users to use the server to attack internal machines or third parties. Second, public HTTP servers attract attackers, who you do not want to concentrate on a machine that is important to your site's functioning. You could address this problem by moving the public HTTP server to a dedicated machine, or even using an outside web hosting service to remove it from your site altogether.

As discussed in Chapter 3, *Security Strategies*, there are two reasons for knowing what the weakest links in your firewall are. The first reason is so that you can fix them, if possible; we've already talked about things you might change in this firewall to strengthen some of the weak links. The second reason is so that you can monitor those links which you cannot eliminate for one reason or another. For instance, to address the risks posed by allowing SMTP from the bastion host to the internal mail server, you can't practically disallow incoming SMTP; that would cut off incoming mail from the outside world, which probably isn't appropriate. Since you can't eliminate that weak link, you should instead monitor it closely to make sure that an attacker doesn't take advantage of it (i.e., you should monitor the internal mail server for attacks from the bastion host via SMTP, by monitoring the SMTP logs and reports on the internal mail server).

You can keep playing the game of thinking "If I were an attacker, what would I do?" and then addressing the problems you discover ad nauseam, or until you run out of time or money. At some point, though, you (or your management) will probably decide you've done enough (based on your own site's definition of "enough").

Fail-safe stance

You can see the principle of a fail-safe stance applied through the packet filtering rules. In general, the rules specify what you're going to allow and deny everything else by default. This is a fail-safe approach because if something unanticipated comes along (a new service, for example), it won't be allowed through your firewall, unless, of course, it mimics or is tunneled through some other service you do allow. The redundant router rules also provide a fail-safe against failure of one router or the other. If filtering accidentally or temporarily gets turned off on one router (causing it to pass all packets), the other still does most of the same filtering, at least as far as the outside world is concerned.

Universal participation

If this is our site's only connection to the Internet, we have involuntary universal participation; everybody has to go through the firewall to get to the Internet. Of course, we'd be much better off with voluntary universal participation, but that may require some user education about the goals of and the need for the security measures we're adopting.

To some extent, we're relying on voluntary universal participation. We've granted free Telnet, SSH, and FTP access, and in the process, we've allowed any outbound connection to ports at or above 1024 (which is plenty of rope for the users to hang us with). FTP is by no means the only service above 1024.

In particular, we've assumed that this is your sole connection to the Internet and that internal users aren't just going to bypass the firewall entirely by setting up their own Internet connections. All it takes is one joker with a modem, a PPP software package, and an outside phone line, and you too could have an unprotected back door into your network.

Diversity of defense

There are opportunities in this configuration to apply the principle of diversity of defense (e.g., using routers from different vendors for the interior and exterior packet filtering systems). Most sites will probably conclude that such an approach is not worth the hassle. However, even if you use similar or identical hardware, you still might get some diversity by having different people do at least the initial configuration of the different filtering systems, and then having them cross-check each other's work.

Using different SMTP servers on the internal mail server and the bastion host would be a fairly major advance in this configuration because that's one of the main weak points of this setup. Even a less secure but different SMTP server on the internal mail server is arguably better than one that's going to yield to the exact same attack that just succeeded on the bastion host. The more vulnerable the SMTP server you're using, the more important an issue this is.

Simplicity

Simplicity is another important security strategy. This particular firewall configuration provides simplicity by separating components so that each component is as simple and comprehensible as possible. We've made a number of decisions specifically to simplify the configuration; for example, the decision to use separate interior and exterior routers (rather than a single three-interface router) simplifies the packet filtering rules and makes them easier to understand.

Conclusions

A lot of advantages are offered by a scheme such as the one we've described in the previous sections. The main potential disadvantages we can see are cost and complexity; but we don't think that the configuration we've presented is too expensive for most sites, and we think that it presents the minimum necessary level of complexity.

What if you really need to save some money? It would be feasible to construct a screened subnet architecture using a single three-interface router, instead of the pair of two-interface routers we've described. The solution would be a little more complex because you'd have to merge the two separate filtering sets described previously, but doing so shouldn't be too difficult.

It would also be relatively easy to construct a more secure configuration with the same basic architecture. A less trusting site would force all Telnet, SSH, and FTP through proxies, which would allow much better logging and remove the nagging holes created by allowing every outbound connection to ports above 1024. Once you force the extra protocols through proxies, you'd also find that DNS information hiding would be both more practical and more reasonable. However, the price of this increased security would be a more complex and fragile configuration, and one that presents more annoyance to the users.

It would also be possible to increase the services offered without major architecture changes. For example, incoming Telnet and incoming user FTP could be supported relatively easily for a few users on the bastion host or on a dedicated host on the screened network. Serious anonymous FTP service or HTTP service could be provided by configuring extra machines on the screened network. Similarly, you could scale up the firewall to support a second Internet connection or redundant bastion hosts to provide more reliable service or service for a much larger internal network.

Merged Routers and Bastion Host Using General-Purpose Hardware

The merged interior and exterior router architecture, described in Chapter 6, *Firewall Architectures*, and shown in Figure 6-10, is a lower security, lower cost alternative to the screened subnet architecture discussed in the previous section. It can be a very useful architecture for small sites that are facing significant cost constraints, particularly when it is built around a general-purpose computer that can provide not only routing but also flexible packet filtering and proxying. Figure 24-2 shows this architecture.

This architecture is typical of commercial single-box firewalls, where the perimeter network is often referred to as the *services net*.

In this example, there is a perimeter net but no interior and exterior routers. One machine provides routing and filtering and some normal bastion host functions as

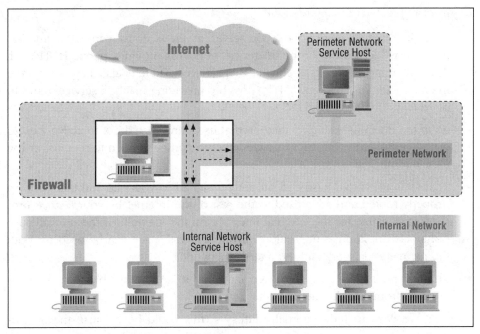

Figure 24-2. Merged routers using general-purpose hardware

well. The perimeter net provides only external services, and there are no connections from the perimeter net into the internal network.

This architecture obviously reduces the cost of the firewall by requiring one router instead of two, but it provides other advantages as well. For instance, it requires only one assigned Internet-visible address; the merged router's external interface must be a legitimate address, but if the merged router can do network address translation, all the other addresses can be selected from private address space. This architecture also makes a clean separation between the firewall and the perimeter services host, allowing them to be managed by different people with different attitudes towards security and only minimal interaction with each other.

Although this architecture closely resembles a condensed version of the previous one, the constraints are significantly different. Because you are putting all the functions on the same machine, there are limits on what you can expect that machine to do. You're going to need to move all noncritical functionality off the firewall itself. On the other hand, you have much more flexibility in what you do on the perimeter services host because it is not critical to the security of the internal hosts (in the screened subnet architecture, the bastion hosts on the perimeter network were security-critical for internal hosts).

In this example, we're going to assume:

- That the firewall is not the only server at the site. In particular, another machine is located on the perimeter network that provides public HTTP and, if the filtering software is adequate, FTP services. There is also a system on the internal network to accept SMTP (possibly providing mailbox services) and to provide internal network DNS service.

- As in the previous example, that internal users are trusted not to actively try to circumvent the firewall, and that we have no particular need to monitor or log their Internet activities.

- That an address that has been properly assigned to your site and that is being properly routed and advertised to the rest of the Internet by your service provider is available for the external interface on the firewall. (If the firewall supports network address translation, private address space can be used for both the perimeter network and the internal network.)

- That the perimeter net is untrusted, and that it is unacceptable to make connections from it to the internal net.

- That we wish to hide internal addresses (this could be because they're private, unroutable addresses or just because we're paranoid).

- That we do not want internal machines to be dependent on the firewall for anything except Internet access; the internal network should continue to function if the firewall stops working.

Service Configuration

How do we provide the basic Internet services with this architecture?

HTTP and HTTPS

We have several options for providing internal users with access to the Web:

- We could simply allow them to go out directly, using packet filtering.
- We could run a simple proxy server.
- We could run a caching proxy server.

As we discussed earlier, using packet filtering means either limiting the servers that people can access or permitting almost all outbound connections. It's an acceptable choice but places a lot of trust in the users. Running a simple proxy server, like SOCKS, on the firewall itself would give us extra logging and control without significantly limiting what users can do or putting a large load on the firewall. Running a caching proxy server on the firewall itself would probably be a mistake. Caching proxy servers are relatively complex, and they require disk space for the caching. However, caching proxy servers provide a lot of benefits, and we could safely put one on the internal services host.

By contrast, we don't want to publish web pages on an internal services host, which is full of our internal data. We don't want to publish them directly from the firewall either because a web server will add both significant risk and significant load. Publishing web pages will require a separate server on the perimeter network.

Therefore, we will use an HTTP server on the perimeter network to provide service to the Internet. For internal users accessing the Internet, we will use a caching proxy server on the internal services host. Packet filtering on the firewall will allow the caching proxy server to make requests.

We could use the perimeter net web server for HTTPS as well as HTTP; this would require only small changes to the filtering rules. On the other hand, there's no reason to do HTTPS on a simple, noninteractive web server, and a complex server that required HTTPS (e.g., a server that supported e-commerce) would almost certainly require other support services as well (e.g., a database). Since we aren't configuring those other servers in this example, there's no apparent reason to allow HTTPS to the perimeter net, and we will leave it disabled.

SMTP

Here we have two reasonable choices. First, we could choose to use a dual-server setup like the one discussed previously, with a security-oriented SMTP server on the firewall and a mail server on the services host inside. This will require disk space on the firewall to spool the mail, as well as the CPU power to process it. Second, for more performance at slightly more risk, we could simply pass SMTP to the services host. (We could use an SMTP server on the perimeter net, but we don't consider that a reasonable choice because it would require the perimeter net to create connections to the internal net, which we don't want to allow.)

In order for SMTP to go directly to the services host, either the firewall needs to do network address translation, or the services host needs to have a valid externally visible address.

We will assume that the firewall has disk space and enough CPU power and run a security-oriented SMTP server on the firewall. All incoming mail will be directed (via DNS MX records) to the firewall, which will then pass mail to the internal services host. Similarly, outgoing mail will be sent from the internal services host to the security-oriented SMTP server on the firewall. As we've discussed previously, it's never advisable to let incoming mail go directly to all of your internal machines. Also, once you're directing incoming mail through a single point, it's actually easier—not to mention safer—to route outgoing mail through there than to send it direct.

Telnet

We allow only outgoing Telnet from the internal network to the Internet through packet filtering; incoming Telnet is too risky to allow at all. Instead, we will support incoming connections via SSH.

SSH

We can improve security somewhat over the screened subnet architecture by limiting inbound and outbound SSH to just the internal network services host. This will allow us to control the SSH servers and clients that people use, preventing the use of SSH tunneling.

We will also allow SSH from the internal network to the perimeter network, so that it can be used to administer servers there. It is the only connection between the internal network and the perimeter network, and it is a one-way connection (the perimeter network cannot create it). It is therefore a reasonably safe way to give people administrative access to servers. File transfer protocols like *scp* and *rsync* that can use SSH for transport can be used to load files on the server.

FTP

As in the screened subnet architecture, outgoing passive-mode FTP can be safely and conveniently provided via packet filtering from the internal network. Normal-mode FTP cannot because you would have to allow incoming connections. If you want to use normal-mode FTP, you will need an FTP proxy. That proxy should not run on the internal services host because in order to support the proxy there, we'd still need to allow incoming connections to a machine on the internal network. However, we could run an FTP proxy on the firewall, and many systems suitable for this kind of firewall will supply appropriate proxies.

For the sake of example, we'll assume that we don't have FTP proxying software on the firewall, and we'll use packet filtering to allow outgoing FTP, but only in passive mode. Since most FTP comes from web browsers, which use passive mode by default, this is unlikely to be a problem.

Incoming FTP is more difficult. Supporting incoming passive-mode FTP with pure packet filtering would require allowing all TCP connections from all Internet hosts on any port >1023 to the perimeter services host on any port >1023. For this architecture, it is an unacceptable risk to the perimeter services host. It is possible to safely support normal-mode FTP to the perimeter network, but as we mentioned previously, most FTP comes from web browsers, which will default to using passive mode and will not work. Unless the packet filtering system we are using supports a transparent proxy for FTP, we will not be able to offer FTP services to the Internet.

If the packet filtering system does support a transparent FTP proxy, then you could configure it to direct connections to a server on the perimeter net. We will assume that it does not and that we will not be providing incoming FTP service.

NNTP

At most sites this size, the best option (assuming that NNTP service is important) is to purchase NNTP from an external server and allow clients to connect directly to that server. Many Internet service providers will provide this service for a small surcharge. It would be possible to provide NNTP internally if we wanted to dedicate an internal machine to be an NNTP server. It would be unwise to make either the internal services host or the firewall an NNTP server; instead, we'd need to dedicate another internal services host. We will assume that an external Internet-based NNTP service will be used.

Unfortunately, this will keep us from having private newsgroups that are visible only to internal users, unless we set up a separate internal news server for only those groups. Many news clients (particularly those that are part of web browsers) can easily access newsgroups from multiple servers.

DNS

Because we wish to hide the internal addresses, we will need to have two DNS servers: one for the Internet and one for the internal users. The Internet-visible DNS server could go on the firewall or on the perimeter services host (the two places we put externally visible services). The internal DNS server could go on the firewall or on the internal services host (the two places we put internally visible services).

Putting the Internet-visible DNS server on the perimeter services host is not a good idea. The perimeter is an untrusted network, but DNS is critical to the functioning of the Internet connection. The Internet-visible DNS server should therefore be on the firewall.

The internal DNS server, on the other hand, should not be on the firewall for two reasons. First, putting it on the firewall will make internal hosts dependent on the firewall for otherwise internal functions, which we want to avoid. Second, we've already got the external DNS server there, and it's going to be complicated to administer them both on the same machine.

We'll assume the following configuration:

- The firewall is the primary external DNS server for your domain.

- You have an external DNS secondary server for your domain, (e.g., one of your service provider's machines).

- The internal services host is the primary internal DNS server.

Packet Filtering Rules

Let's look at the packet filtering rules necessary to support the configuration we've described in the previous sections. As in the first example of the screened subnet architecture, we're going to assume an "ideal" router. In this case, because we're providing services on the firewall itself and to a perimeter network, we need to consider the interfaces separately, so we have an extra column indicating which of the network interfaces the rule applies to. "Ext" is the interface to the external world, "Int" is the interface to the internal network, and "Pmtr" is the perimeter network.

"Internal" and "Perimeter" mean the range of IP addresses for those networks. "Int Service" and "Pmtr Service" are the IP addresses of the internal network and perimeter network services machines, respectively, while "Firewall Ext" is the firewall's external interface, "Firewall Int" is the firewall's internal interface, and "Firewall Pmtr" is the firewall's perimeter interface.

Because this firewall has multiple interfaces, we need to specify slightly different information from what we've been providing. On a two-interface firewall, it's clear exactly what happens to a packet that's going "In"; it goes from the Internet to the internal network. On a three-interface firewall, there are two possible routes for such a packet: it could be going from the Internet to the internal network, or from the Internet to the perimeter network. These two options need different rules.

In order to deal with this situation, we have to specify a direction for each interface, not for the whole firewall. A packet that crosses the firewall will go in on an interface and out on an interface, regardless of the direction it is traveling. Packets that come from the Internet to the internal network will be going "Inward" on the external interface and "Outward" on the internal interface; packets that go from the internal network to the Internet will go "Inward" on the internal interface and "Outward" on the external interface.

In general, when looking at the following table, you will notice that the "Inward" filtering rule for one interface will be identical to an "Outward" rule for another interface. This pairing of rules and interfaces ensures that the filtering rules are not dependent on packet routing decisions.

In the following table, directions are relative to the specific interface, not to the firewall as a whole. This is different from the other tables in the book, which do not show individual interfaces.

The firewall needs the following rules to support the configuration we've outlined:

Rule	Interface	Relative Dir.	Source Address	Dest. Address	Protocol	Source Port	Dest. Port	ACK Set	Action
Spoof-1	Ext	Inward	Internal	Any	Any	Any	Any	Any	Deny
Spoof-2	Ext	Inward	Perimeter Net	Any	Any	Any	Any	Any	Deny
Spoof-3	Int	Inward	External	Any	Any	Any	Any	Any	Deny
Spoof-4	Int	Inward	Perimeter Net	Any	Any	Any	Any	Any	Deny
Spoof-5	Pmtr	Inward	External	Any	Any	Any	Any	Any	Deny
Spoof-6	Pmtr	Inward	Internal	Any	Any	Any	Any	Any	Deny
Cross-1	Ext	Inward	Any	Firewall Int	Any	Any	Any	Any	Deny
Cross-2	Ext	Inward	Any	Firewall Pmtr	Any	Any	Any	Any	Deny
Cross-3	Pmtr	Inward	Any	Firewall Int	Any	Any	Any	Any	Deny
HTTP-1	Ext	Inward	Any	Pmtr Services	TCP	>1023	80	Any	Permit
HTTP-2	Ext	Outward	Pmtr Services	Any	TCP	80	>1023	Yes	Permit
HTTP-3	Pmtr	Outward	Pmtr Services	Any	TCP	>1023	80	Any	Permit
HTTP-4	Pmtr	Inward	Any	Pmtr Services	TCP	80	>1023	Yes	Permit
HTTP-5	Int	Inward	Int Services	Any	TCP	>1023	Any	Any	Permit
HTTP-6	Int	Outward	Any	Int Services	TCP	Any	>1023	Yes	Permit
HTTP-7	Ext	Outward	Int Services	Any	TCP	>1023	Any	Any	Permit
HTTP-8	Ext	Inward	Any	Int Services	TCP	Any	>1023	Yes	Permit
Telnet-1	Int	Inward	Internal	Any	TCP	>1023	23	Any	Permit
Telnet-2	Int	Outward	Any	Internal	TCP	23	>1023	Yes	Permit
Telnet-3	Ext	Outward	Internal	Any	TCP	>1023	23	Any	Permit
Telnet-4	Ext	Inward	Any	Internal	TCP	23	>1023	Yes	Permit
SSH-1	Int	Inward	Int Services	Any	TCP	Any	22	Any	Permit
SSH-2	Int	Outward	Any	Int Services	TCP	22	Any	Yes	Permit
SSH-3	Ext	Outward	Int Services	Any	TCP	Any	22	Any	Permit

Rule	Interface	Relative Dir.	Source Address	Dest. Address	Protocol	Source Port	Dest. Port	ACK Set	Action
SSH-4	Ext	Inward	Any	Int Services	TCP	22	Any	Yes	Permit
SSH-5	Ext	Inward	Any	Int Services	TCP	Any	22	Any	Permit
SSH-6	Ext	Outward	Int Services	Any	TCP	22	Any	Yes	Permit
SSH-7	Int	Outward	Any	Int Services	TCP	Any	22	Any	Permit
SSH-8	Int	Inward	Int Services	Any	TCP	22	Any	Yes	Permit
SSH-9	Int	Inward	Internal	Pmtr Services	TCP	Any	22	Any	Permit
SSH-10	Int	Outward	Pmtr Services	Internal	TCP	22	Any	Yes	Permit
SSH-11	Pmtr	Outward	Internal	Pmtr Services	TCP	ANY	22	Any	Permit
SSH-12	Pmtr	Inward	Pmtr Services	Internal	TCP	22	Any	Yes	Permit
SMTP-1	Int	Inward	Int Services	Firewall Int	TCP	>1023	25	Any	Permit
SMTP-2	Int	Outward	Firewall Int	Int Services	TCP	25	>1023	Yes	Permit
SMTP-3	Int	Outward	Firewall Int	Int Services	TCP	>1023	25	Any	Permit
SMTP-4	Int	Inward	Int Services	Firewall Int	TCP	25	>1023	Yes	Permit
SMTP-5	Ext	Outward	Firewall Ext	Any	TCP	>1023	25	Any	Permit
SMTP-6	Ext	Inward	Any	Firewall Ext	TCP	25	>1023	Yes	Permit
SMTP-7	Ext	Inward	Any	Firewall Ext	TCP	>1023	25	Any	Permit
SMTP-8	Ext	Outward	Firewall Ext	Any	TCP	25	>1023	Yes	Permit
SMTP-9	Pmtr	Inward	Pmtr Services	Firewall Pmtr	TCP	>1023	25	Any	Permit
SMTP-10	Pmtr	Outward	Firewall Pmtr	Pmtr Services	TCP	25	>1023	Yes	Permit
NNTP-1	Int	Inward	Internal	NNTP server	TCP	>1023	119	Any	Permit
NNTP-2	Int	Outward	NNTP server	Internal	TCP	119	>1023	Yes	Permit
NNTP-3	Ext	Outward	Internal	NNTP server	TCP	>1023	119	Any	Permit
NNTP-4	Ext	Inward	NNTP server	Internal	TCP	119	>1023	Yes	Permit
DNS-1	Ext	Inward	Any	Firewall Ext	UDP	Any	53	a	Permit
DNS-2	Ext	Outward	Firewall Ext	Any	UDP	53	Any	a	Permit

Rule	Interface	Relative Dir.	Source Address	Dest. Address	Protocol	Source Port	Dest. Port	ACK Set	Action
DNS-3	Ext	Inward	Any	Firewall Ext	TCP	Any	53	Any	Permit
DNS-4	Ext	Outward	Firewall Ext	Any	TCP	53	Any	Yes	Permit
DNS-5	Int	Inward	Int Services	Firewall Int	UDP	Any	53	a	Permit
DNS-6	Int	Outward	Firewall Int	Int Services	UDP	53	Any	a	Permit
DNS-7	Int	Inward	Int Services	Firewall Int	TCP	Any	53	Any	Permit
DNS-8	Int	Outward	Firewall Int	Int Services	TCP	53	Any	Yes	Permit
DNS-9	Pmtr	Inward	Pmtr Services	Firewall Pmtr	UDP	Any	53	a	Permit
DNS-10	Pmtr	Outward	Firewall Pmtr	Pmtr Services	UDP	53	Any	a	Permit
DNS-11	Pmtr	Inward	Pmtr Services	Firewall Pmtr	TCP	Any	53	Any	Permit
DNS-12	Pmtr	Outward	Firewall Pmtr	Pmtr Services	TCP	53	Any	Yes	Permit
FTP-1	Int	Inward	Internal	Any	TCP	>1023	21	Any	Permit
FTP-2	Int	Outward	Any	Internal	TCP	21	>1023	Yes	Permit
FTP-3	Ext	Outward	Internal	Any	TCP	>1023	21	Any	Permit
FTP-4	Ext	Inward	Any	Internal	TCP	21	>1023	Yes	Permit
FTP-5	Int	Inward	Internal	Any	TCP	>1023	>1023	Any	Permit
FTP-6	Int	Outward	Any	Internal	TCP	>1023	>1023	Yes	Permit
FTP-7	Ext	Outward	Internal	Any	TCP	>1023	>1023	Any	Permit
FTP-8	Ext	Inward	Any	Internal	TCP	>1023	>1023	Yes	Permit
Default-1	All	Outward	Any	Any	Any	Any	Any	Any	Deny
Default-2	All	Inward	Any	Any	Any	Any	Any	Any	Deny

aUDP has no ACK equivalent.

Here is some additional information about each set of rules in this table:

Spoof-1 and Spoof-2

Block packets from the Internet that claim to have source IP addresses that you are using at your site—that is, forged packets, presumably sent by an attacker.

Spoof-3 and Spoof-4

Block packets from the internal network that claim to have source addresses on an external network or the perimeter network. Spoof-3 may be difficult to implement on some packet filtering systems because they can be easily written only if you can use negation on source addresses (to specify addresses that are not in the internal range). It would be acceptable to omit them in this situation; they are mostly there to protect other people, not to protect your site.

Spoof-5 and Spoof-6

Block packets from the perimeter network that claim to have source addresses on an external network or the internal network. Spoof-5 may be difficult to implement on some packet filtering systems because they can be easily written only if you can use negation on source addresses (to specify addresses that are not in the internal range). It would be acceptable to omit them in this situation; they are mostly there to protect other people, not to protect your site.

Cross-1 through Cross-3

Block packets sent from the outside world to the firewall's internal and perimeter interfaces. These addresses would otherwise be considered legitimate addresses in the ranges for the internal and perimeter networks, and rules that were meant to allow traffic to these networks would also allow the firewall to be attacked on those ports. Rather than excluding the interfaces explicitly for each rule that allows traffic to those networks, we will make a blanket exclusion for traffic that's trying to cross the firewall. Should the perimeter network services host be compromised, there is a rule that prevents it from being used to attack the internal interface of the firewall. (If the internal network is compromised, it can be used to attack the perimeter network; since the internal network is more security-critical than the perimeter network, this is not a major problem, but you could easily add a Cross-4 to prevent it.)

HTTP-1 through HTTP-4

Allow incoming HTTP to the perimeter network services host. These rules allow traffic from the Internet to the site's public HTTP service. Because each interface has a separate default deny rule, we need to explicitly permit the traffic on each interface that it crosses. HTTP-1 and HTTP-3 both permit the same incoming traffic, while HTTP-2 and HTTP-4 are both required to permit the responses.

HTTP-5 through HTTP-8

Allow outgoing HTTP and HTTPS from the internal services host. These rules allow the HTTP proxy to contact any Internet host on any port. Depending on the HTTP proxy server, this could allow users to circumvent firewall rules preventing direct TCP connections (for example, direct delivery of SMTP mail). Some HTTP proxy servers can be configured to prevent the connection to certain port numbers.

Telnet-1 through Telnet-4

Allow outgoing Telnet from any internal host.

SSH-1 through SSH-4

Allow outgoing SSH connections from the internal network services host. We have the client port set to "Any" (instead of ">1023" like most of the other protocols) because some forms of authentication require SSH clients to use ports at or below 1023.

SSH-5 through SSH-8

Allow incoming SSH connections to the internal network services host. We have the client port set to "Any" (instead of ">1023" like most of the other protocols) because some forms of authentication require SSH clients to use ports at or below 1023.

SSH-9 through SSH-12

Allow outgoing SSH connections from the internal network to the perimeter network for administration.

SMTP-1 through SMTP-4

Allow electronic mail between the firewall and the internal services host. SMTP-1 and SMTP-2 permit mail to the firewall, while SMTP-3 and SMTP-4 permit mail from the firewall.

SMTP-5 through SMTP-8

Allow electronic mail between the firewall and the Internet.

SMTP-9 and SMTP-10,

Allow electronic mail only from the perimeter network to the firewall host. We do not allow mail to be delivered to the perimeter network services host.

NNTP-1 through NNTP-4

Allow your clients to reach your service provider's news server.

DNS-1 through DNS-4

Allow external UDP- and TCP-based DNS clients to query the DNS server on the firewall host, and it to answer them. In the process, they also permit the server-to-server queries, which are always from port 53 to port 53. These rules also allow the DNS server on the firewall host to make DNS queries to the Internet and to support secondary DNS servers to perform zone transfers.

DNS-5 through DNS-8

Allow the internal services host to make UDP- and TCP-based DNS queries to the firewall DNS server. The DNS service on the internal services host is configured as a forwarder to the firewall host.

DNS-9 through DNS-12

Allow the perimeter network services host to make UDP- and TCP-based DNS queries to the firewall DNS server. The DNS service on the perimeter network services host is configured as a forwarder to the firewall host.

FTP-1 through FTP-8

Allow outgoing passive-mode FTP connections. The FTP-1 through FTP-4 rules allow the command channel, and the FTP-5 through FTP-8 rules allow the data channel. In fact, FTP-5 through FTP-8 allow any TCP connection to be opened from the internal machines to any host on the Internet, as long as the port numbers used on both ends are above 1023.

Default-1 and Default-2

Block all packets not specifically allowed by one of the preceding rules.

Other Configuration Work

If you are using Linux and *ipchains* as your packet filtering system, you will also need to add rules for the FORWARD chain so that the system will forward packets between the interfaces. You could add a single allow rule to the FORWARD chain and rely on the specified interface rules to protect you. For a more secure but harder to maintain configuration, you could duplicate all the rules that pass traffic from one interface to another in the FORWARD chain.

In addition to setting up the packet filtering rules, we need to do various other kinds of configuration work, as follows:

On all of the internal machines

Configure electronic mail so that it gets sent to the internal services host. We're also going to need to install passive-mode FTP clients, if they're available, and configure web browsers to use the proxy server on the internal services host.

On the internal services host

Configure the mail server to send mail to the firewall. Set up a caching HTTP proxy server. Set up the internal DNS server.

On the firewall

Set up the externally visible DNS server.

On the perimeter services host

Set up the externally visible web server.

Analysis

Just how good a firewall is this? It's not great, but it's functional. Let's consider it in relation to the strategies and principles discussed in Chapter 3, *Security Strategies*, and in comparison to the screened subnet architecture we configured in the first example.

Least privilege

You can see the principle of least privilege in action in some places in this setup. For example, configuring SMTP so that outgoing mail goes out via the internal network services host rather than directly to remote systems is an application of least privilege. Why? Because it lets you control more tightly how internal systems connect to external systems. (In this case, it makes it unnecessary for internal systems to talk directly to external systems in order to provide this service.)

Similarly, we've very carefully applied least privilege to the perimeter network, giving it the minimum access needed to provide web services to external hosts. On the other hand, merging the interior and exterior routers clearly fails to enforce least privilege, particularly when the resulting host also provides services like DNS and SMTP. In order to perform all of these functions, the routing host ends up with a very large number of privileges. To some extent, we've moved privilege from the perimeter to the firewall host.

We've also created an internal services host with multiple levels of privilege; it's providing several services, and it's sitting on the internal network, which is a kind of privilege in itself. This host is a second place where least privilege is violated.

The screened subnet architecture we described earlier in this chapter does a somewhat better job of applying the principle of least privilege than the architecture described in this section.

Defense in depth

The principle of defense in depth is almost missing from this setup. Internal hosts are protected from the outside world by the firewall host and the internal services host, but nothing protects them from the firewall host; if that one host is compromised, all of the internal hosts are compromised. A small amount of defense in depth is present in the separation between the services hosts and the router; the router protects the internal services host from the Internet and protects the internal hosts from the perimeter services host. However, the defense of the internal services host isn't all that good.

The screened subnet architecture we described earlier in this chapter does a much better job of applying the principle of defense in depth.

Choke point

The principle of a choke point is clearly applied in this example because everything between internal clients and the Internet comes through at least the firewall host. Further, most of it comes through the internal services host via proxies.

The screened subnet architecture described earlier in the chapter does a slightly better job of applying the principle of a choke point, but not by much.

Weakest link

The obvious weak link to attack in this architecture is the firewall host; the internal services host runs a close second because we allow incoming SSH. If either of these hosts is compromised, it is going to severely affect the security of the rest of the internal hosts because they are on the same network as the internal hosts and because nothing protects the internal hosts from them. With the screened subnet architecture, on the other hand, the interior router protects the internal hosts from the bastion host.

The screened subnet architecture presents a much stronger weakest link to an attacker.

Fail-safe stance

You can see the principle of a fail-safe stance applied through the packet filtering rules specified for the merged routers architecture. In general, the rules specify what you're going to allow and deny everything else by default. This approach is fail-safe because if something unanticipated comes along (for example, a new service), it won't be allowed through your firewall, unless, of course, it mimics or is tunneled through some other service that you do allow.

However, the design of the architecture itself is not fail-safe. If the firewall or internal services hosts are compromised, your whole site's security is severely compromised. The screened subnet architecture is much better at implementing a fail-safe stance.

Universal participation

If this is your site's only connection to the Internet, you've got involuntary universal participation: everybody has to go through the firewall to get to the Internet. Voluntary universal participation would be better, but it would require some user education concerning the goals of and the need for your security measures.

In terms of the universal participation principle, there really isn't much difference between the first and second sample architectures.

Diversity of defense

There are few opportunities here to apply the principle of diversity of defense because you pretty much have only one of everything: there is only one firewall host and only one internal services host.

Simplicity

Although this firewall initially appears simpler than our first example, it actually adds complexity by combining functions. In particular, the packet filtering rules are more complex because we have chosen to use a single three-interface router and filtering system. For example, rather than being able to simply think about "in" and "out" relative to the site, we have to think about "inward" and "outward" relative to each of three interfaces; for packets inbound to the site, we have to set up an inbound filter on one interface and an outbound filter on another, which is tedious and error-prone. Another example of complexity is the decision to implement packet filtering, proxy servers, and application servers all on the same firewall host; there may be unexpected interactions and dependencies between these services, which an attacker can take advantage of. On the other hand, putting the external server on a perimeter network and preventing it from talking to the internal network significantly simplifies the configuration of that bastion host.

Conclusions

The merged router architecture can be cheaper to implement than the screened subnet architecture, but it's less secure. There is little or no redundancy in the design, and it's not really fail-safe. On the other hand, it provides an effective way to use a single Internet address to provide reasonably safe and full-featured access to and from the Internet.

It may be cheaper than the screened subnet architecture, but not by much. The screened subnet architecture requires a minimum of three dedicated machines (two routers and a bastion host). This architecture really also requires a minimum of three dedicated machines (one firewall and two services hosts). One advantage of this architecture is that you can use similar hardware for the firewall host and the internal and perimeter network hosts. It is possible to build all of these systems using spare PC equipment and freely available software.

If you don't need to provide web service to external clients (for instance, if you choose to out-source your web site to a web hosting service), you could make this architecture significantly cheaper and simpler by eliminating the perimeter network altogether. Or, if you don't need to keep the price down, you could combine this architecture with the screened subnet architecture; to do so, you would put a perimeter network on a third interface on the external router in the screened subnet architecture. This extra network would be the untrusted network that handled services for clients on the Internet.

IV

Keeping Your Site Secure

This part of the book describes how to establish a security policy for your site, maintain your firewall, and handle the security problems that may occur with even the most effective firewalls.

25

Security Policies

The word "policy" makes many people flinch because it suggests impenetrable documents put together by unknowledgeable committees, which are then promptly ignored by everyone involved (except when they make a good excuse or weapon). That's not the kind of policy we're discussing in this chapter.

The policy we're talking about here is like a nation's foreign policy. It might be discussed in documents—of varying amounts of legibility—but its primary purpose is to establish a direction, a theory of what you're trying to achieve. People sometimes confuse the words "policy", "strategy", and "tactics". A *policy* is what determines what wars you're going to fight and why. A *strategy* is the plan for carrying out the war. A *tactic* is a method for carrying out a strategy. Presidents determine policy; generals determine strategies; and anybody down to a foot soldier might determine a tactic.

Most of this book is about tactics. The tactics involved in building a firewall, the nitty-gritty details of what needs to be done here, are complex and intricate. However, no matter how good your tactics are, if your strategy and policy are bad, you can't succeed. In the 1800s, an American named William Walker set out to conquer Nicaragua for the United States. His strategy and tactics were, if not impeccable, certainly successful: he conquered Nicaragua. Unfortunately, there was a fatal flaw in his plan. The United States did not at the time want Nicaragua, and when he announced that he had conquered it, the U.S. government was completely uninterested in doing anything about it. Walker ended up ruling Nicaragua very briefly before he was killed in a popular uprising. This was the result of getting the strategy and the tactics right but completely botching the policy.

Your Security Policy

Most technical computer people consider a single, unified, published security policy to be desirable in the abstract but believe—with a strong basis in personal experience—that attempting to come up with one is going to be extremely painful. For example, ask any system administrator about users and passwords, and you are almost guaranteed to be rewarded with a rant. Everybody has a story about the apparent insanity of people faced with passwords, one of the simplest and most comprehensible security issues: the professor who explained that he was too important to need a good password; the mathematician who was told that he couldn't use a password because it was in an English dictionary (and who replied that he wasn't using the *English* word that was spelled that way, he was using the *Russian* word that was spelled that way, and nobody had told him not to use Russian words). This kind of experience is apt to convince system administrators that their user community is incapable of dealing intelligently with security issues.

Putting together a security policy undoubtedly is going to be a long, involved process, and it's the exact opposite of the types of tasks most technical people enjoy. If you like to program, you are unlikely to enjoy either the meetings or the bureaucracy involved in policy making. On the other hand, putting together a security policy is a great deal more amusing than dealing with the side effects of not having a policy. In the long run, you'll spend less time in meetings arguing about security if you get it out of the way ahead of time.

Developing a security policy also doesn't need to be as bad as you may be expecting. Many of the problems with security policies are caused by people who are trying to write a security policy that sounds like a security policy, which is to say that it's written in big legal and technical words and says threatening things about how users had better behave themselves. This doesn't work. It's also the most unpleasant way to do things because it involves hostility and incomprehension all around. It's true that your organization may at some point need a security policy that's written in big legal words (to satisfy some big legal requirements). In that case, the security policy you write shouldn't contradict the legalistic document, but the policy you write doesn't need to be that legalistic one.

Another problem people have in trying to write security policies is that they have a strong feeling about what the policy ought to be, and they're uncomfortable that the actual policy they enforce does not meet that standard. A great deal of lip service is paid to the notion that security should be absolute: you should have a site that nobody could ever break into; where every user has exactly one account, and every account has exactly one user; and where all the passwords are excellent, and nobody ever uses anybody else's password for anything.

In the real world, nobody's site is like that, a fact that is well known and well accepted. That doesn't keep people from claiming that they want to make their site like that, sometimes in big words on many pieces of paper that they call a "security policy". Every time, without exception, these policies are not followed by anybody.

It's unlikely that your policy is one that emphasizes security at all costs. Such a policy would be irrational. It is reasonable to value other things highly enough to be willing to compromise security.

Most houses would be more secure with bars over all the windows. Few people are willing to put bars over their windows, despite a desire to protect themselves. People have a number of reasons for compromising their security in this way. To start with, bars are expensive, and they interfere with using the windows for many of their normal purposes (e.g., seeing out of, climbing out of in an emergency). But people are willing to go to equal expense and inconvenience to apply other security solutions, and they may avoid barring windows even when it's the cheapest and most convenient solution, because it looks bad and makes them feel oppressed.

This is entirely reasonable, and it's entirely reasonable to make the same type of decision about your computer security. You may not want the best security money can buy or even the best security you can afford.

What do you want? You want the best security that meets your requirements for:

Affordability
How much money does the security cost?

Functionality
Can you still use your computers?

Cultural compatibility
Does it conflict with the way people at your site normally interact with each other and the outside world?

Legality
Does it meet your site's legal requirements?

Don't pretend that you want to be absolutely secure, if only you could afford it. You don't live your life with the most perfect security money could buy. For the same reasons, it's extremely unlikely that your institution can maintain the characteristics that are important to it if it also installs the most perfect security money could buy. People don't like learning or working in a hostile environment; because they won't do it, you'll either lose the security or lose the organization.

Sometimes a small concession to insecurity can buy a large payoff in morale. For example, rulemakers reel at the idea of guest accounts, but a guest account for a spouse can make a big difference in how people feel about work. And there are sometimes unexpected results. One university computer center was asked why its student employees were allowed to hang around at all hours, even after the labs were closed, doing random activities of dubious value to the computer center; it seemed insecure at best. The answer was that several years before, an operator who was typing his girlfriend's term paper in a lab after hours had discovered and responded to a critical emergency. Because he had saved the facility from what seemed likely to be a million dollars worth of uninsured damage (insurance companies have a nasty tendency to consider floods in windowless third-floor computer rooms to be acts of God, and thus uninsurable), the computer facility management figured that all the computer time the operators wanted had already been paid for.

On the other hand, if you have too little security, you can lose the organization to lawyers or attackers, and what matters there is what you do, not what you write down. Writing down marvelous policies that don't get enforced certainly won't save you from people who are trying to break into your computer, and it generally won't save you from lawsuits either. The law counts only policies that you make some attempt to enforce. If you don't do anything, that's bad; but if you write it down, and then you don't do it, that's worse. You've proved that you knew you were supposed to do it.

What Should a Security Policy Contain?

First and foremost, a security policy is a way of communicating with users and managers. It should tell them what they need to know to make the decisions they need to make about security.

Explanations

It's important that the policy be explicit and understandable about why certain decisions have been made. Most people will not follow rules unless they understand why they're important. A policy that specifies what's supposed to be done but not why is doomed. As soon as the people who wrote it leave, or forget why they made those decisions, it's going to stop having any effect.

Everybody's responsibilities

A policy sets explicit expectations and responsibilities among you, your users, and your management; it lets all of you know what to expect from each other. It's a mistake to distribute a policy that concentrates entirely on what users need to do to make the site secure (it seems hostile and unfair) or entirely on what system administrators need to do (it encourages the users to believe that somebody else will handle it, and they don't have to worry about it).

Regular language

Most people are not lawyers, and they're not security experts. They're comfortable with casual descriptions. You may be afraid to write a policy that way because it may seem uncomfortably casual and too personal. But it's more important to make your security policy friendly and understandable than to make it precise and official looking. Write it as if you were explaining it to a reasonably bright but nontechnical friend. Keep it a communication between peers, not a memo from Mount Olympus. If that's not acceptable in your organizational culture, write two separate policy descriptions.

You will not get people to comply unless they understand the document and want to comply with it, and that means they have to at least be willing to read it. If they shut their brains off in paragraph two because the document sounds legal and threatening, you lose. You also lose if they decide that you think they're stupid, or if they decide that you don't care. Don't get so informal that you seem condescending or sloppy. If necessary, get a technical writer to clean up the grammar, punctuation, and spelling.

Writing in legalese will not make a document more legally binding, particularly if it's not written by a lawyer. Lawyers write the way they do because they are trying to achieve very precise meanings. Using a legal-sounding term slightly wrong just confuses the situation; it might have its legal meaning, in which case your document very accurately says something you didn't mean, or it might have no meaning, in which case your document is no more accurate than it would be if you just wrote it in casual language.

Enforcement authority

Writing down the policy is not the point; living by it is. That means that when the policy isn't followed, something should happen to fix the situation. Somebody needs to be responsible for making those corrections happen, and the policy needs to specify who that's going to be and the general range of corrections. Here are some examples of what a security policy might specify:

- Managers of certain services have the authority to revoke access.
- Managers of employees will be asked to take care of some kinds of transgressions.
- The people who run the corporate network may cut off facilities that don't meet certain standards.

The policy should specify who is going to decide and give some indication of what kinds of penalties are available to them. It should not specify exactly what will happen when; it's a policy, not a mandatory sentencing law.

Provision for exceptions

No policy is perfect. You can't cover every possible future event, and the policy will be unreadable and unusable if you even try. Therefore, you need to specify what process will be used to make exceptions. Is there a person with that authority? Is it a committee? How is the reader going to make contact? How long is it going to take?

Provision for reviews

You can't expect to set up a policy once and forget it. The needs of your site will change over time, and policies that were perfectly sensible may become either too restrictive or too lax. Sometimes change is obvious: if you work for a startup company that goes from 6 people to 6,000 people, it will probably occur to you that things are different in important ways (but you still may not get around to redoing the security policy if you didn't set up a mechanism for that in advance). If you work for a 200-year old university, however, you may not expect much change. However, even if the organization appears to be doing its best to fossilize, the computers change, the external networks change, and new people come in to replace ones who leave. You still need to review and update your policies on a regular basis.

Discussion of specific security issues

Because of the differences between organizations, it's hard to be specific about issues without writing an entire book just about security policies. However, here are some common issues to consider when you are writing a policy:

- Who is allowed to have an account at your site? Do you have guest accounts? What do you do about contractors, vendors, and clients?

- Can accounts be shared among multiple people? What about a secretary who uses an executive's account to process that person's electronic mail? What about joint projects? What about family members? Is it sharing an account if you let somebody else borrow a window on your machine really quickly?

- When do people lose the privilege of having an account, and what do you do about it? What happens if people leave or are denied access?

- Who can set up dial-in modems? Is it OK for other people to set up dial-out modems? Is there anything special about PPP, SLIP, or ISDN lines?

- What do people need to do before they connect a computer to the main network?

- How secure do computers need to be before they get services from centrally maintained machines?

- How secure do computers need to be in order to connect to a network with unprotected access to the Internet?

- How is financial data going to be protected?

- How is confidential information about people going to be protected? Are other, perhaps foreign, offices covered by different laws regarding the handling of this type of information?

- What do individual users need to do to protect themselves and the site? What kinds of passwords should they have, and when should they change them?

- What can people do on the Internet? Should they be importing random executables and running them?

- What precautions do you need to take against viruses on personal computers?

- Who can connect your site to external networks, and what's an external network? Is it OK for a project manager to connect your site to another specific site? What about connections to business partners? How about other connections to the Internet?

- How are home computers going to be secured? How are they going to get secure access to your network?

- How are people who are traveling going to get access to the network?

- What are the requirements for systems performing electronic commerce?

- What information is considered company confidential? How is it going to be protected? Can it be sent outside the site via electronic mail?

- If you have remote sites, how are they going to get secure access to your main network?

What Should a Security Policy Not Contain?

Some pieces of information don't belong in your site's security policy, as we discuss in this section.

Technical details

The security policy needs to describe what you're trying to protect and why; it doesn't necessarily need to describe the details of how. It's much more useful to have a 1-page document that describes *what* and *why* in terms that everyone in your organization can understand than a 100-page document that describes *how,* but that nobody except your most senior technical staff can understand.

For example, consider a policy that includes a requirement that says:

> Nonreusable passwords shall be used to authenticate all incoming connections from the outside world, in order to prevent potential attackers from being able to capture reusable passwords by monitoring such connections.

This requirement is much more useful than a policy that says:

> OTP* will be used for all incoming connections.

Why? Because the first policy describes *what* is to be protected and *why,* and it leaves *how* open so the technical staff can select the best implementation.

A policy that says the following is better yet:

> Regular passwords are often stolen and reused when they pass across networks. We won't use passwords that can be reused across networks our company doesn't control.

This policy communicates the same information without the legal-style language. It also clarifies some other points. For example, in the original language does the "outside world" include companies that have special relationships with yours? It may seem obvious to you that it does, but it probably doesn't seem obvious to the managers who are arranging to work with those companies. The reworded language makes it clear what the criterion is (although you may still end up arguing about what networks meet it).

Policy can guide you in selecting and implementing technology, but it shouldn't be used to specify it. It's often much easier to get management to buy into, and sign off on, an overall policy than on a specific technology.

Somebody else's problems

Every site's security policy is different. Different sites have different concerns, different constraints, different users, and different capabilities; all of these lead to different policies. Further, a site's policy may change over time, as the site grows and changes. Don't assume that you need to do things the way they've always been done, or that you can borrow somebody else's policy and simply change the names in it.

---

* OTP is the IETF standard for one-time passwords. It is based upon S/Key.

Problems that aren't computer security problems

People displaying obscene pictures on their computer screens aren't a computer security problem; they're a human resources problem (and a legal problem, if somebody decides to sue for harassment). People playing computer games all day aren't a computer security problem, either; they're a management problem. These issues should be adequately covered by existing policies. If they aren't, you have problems far too large to try to handle with a computer security policy. If they are, trying to cover them again risks setting up a conflict between the two policies. Furthermore, computer security policies cover enough complex and emotional territory without adding yet more.

Putting Together a Security Policy

Once you know what you want in a security policy, how do you put one together?

What Is Your Security Policy?

The first step towards putting together a working security policy for your site is to decide what your personal opinion is. If you've been administering a site or making any decisions about security, you've been enforcing an implicit theory about security, even if you've never articulated it. You're going to need to come to a clear and explicit understanding of what that implicit policy is before you can discuss policy issues with other people in order to produce a written policy for your site.

With that in mind, look at the decisions you've made about security and decide what you think your site's security goals should be. That may not be the policy that your site ends up with, but it's an important first step.

What Is Your Site's Security Policy?

The second step towards putting together a working security policy for your site is to determine what everybody else's security policy is. What do the users and managers expect security to do for them? What do they think of the way security is handled currently? What are other computer facilities doing and why?

Every site has at least one security policy. The problem is that most sites have more than one, all the way up to as many as there are people involved with the site's computers. Sometimes this proliferation of policies is purely unconscious; different computer facilities within the same site may be doing radically different things without even realizing it. Sometimes it's an open secret; administrators may be trying to maintain a security policy that they believe is necessary, even though the user population does not agree with them. Sometimes it's out-and-out war.

Generally, people think of universities as the main place where computer users and computer administrators are engaged in open security warfare, but in fact many companies spend large amounts of time fighting about security issues (for example, administration and the engineers are often at odds).

Some of the security policies for a site may be written down already, but most are likely to be implicit and unpublicized. The only way to find out about them is to ask. Be sure to ask managers, system administrators, and users. Then look at the actual computers and see what's really going on. It's unlikely that anybody will actually lie to you. However, they may be telling you what they think is going on, or what they wish was going on, or what they know is supposed to be going on, instead of reporting the actual state of affairs.

Managers who are used to dealing with computers that have been secured may believe that computers are automatically secure; the shipped configuration will be reasonably safe if it is connected to a network. This is not true. In fact, the truth is almost the exact opposite. The default configuration that machines are shipped with is usually laughably insecure, and it requires considerable expertise to arrive at a secure configuration. Therefore, a manager who says that all of the computers are perfectly secure may be completely incorrect, without having the least intention of deceiving you.

If you ask questions that have clear "right" answers, most people will tend to try to give you those answers. Other people will become defensive. Try to ask neutral questions that don't have a clear bias. For example, don't ask people if they think security is important; instead, ask which is more important to them, security or a cooperative work environment, and then get them to expand on that answer.

When you talk to people, make it extremely clear why you're asking. Asking about security policies tends to give people the impression that you're trying to check up on them. Some people will try to get a good grade, rather than discussing reality. Others will become hostile (after all, why should you be checking up on them?). If you get either of these reactions, stop asking questions about security policies (there's no point in it if they're not going to give useful answers) and go back to trying to explain what you're doing and why. If they never believe you, ask somebody else.

External Factors That Influence Security Policies

Your site isn't completely independent. Issues outside of a computer facility influence security policy. These include legal requirements, contractual obligations, and existing organizational policies.

Let's look first at legal issues. In the United States, a publicly traded company has a legal responsibility to its shareholders to protect its assets. This means that if you work for such a company, even if everybody at the company agrees that you ought to remove all of the passwords and let the Internet in, you can't choose that as a security policy. Your security policy must show evidence that you are safeguarding the company's computers and information. What's required is "due diligence", an attempt in good faith to take normal precautions. "Normal precautions" limit what you need to do; you don't have a legal responsibility to require retinal scans before people can touch the computers!

Regardless of the type of institution you work for, in most places in the United States, there is also a legal responsibility to safeguard certain types of information about employees. Employee reviews are generally legally protected, and so are straightforward personnel records of information like home addresses. Universities have legal responsibilities to safeguard student records, right down to the information about which students attend the university. Data about individuals has even more legal protection in some European countries. If you do not work for Human Resources or Student Records, you may think you don't have to worry about protecting this kind of information, but you're probably wrong. Every manager or supervisor usually has confidential employee data to deal with; similarly, the information used to maintain accounts at universities contains confidential student data (e.g., whether or not the student is enrolled, and what classes the student is taking).

Your organization may also have contractual obligations to protect data. If you have customer or client data on your systems, your contracts probably require you to protect it. (This may apply to research contracts at universities as well.) If you have source code or prerelease software, you almost certainly have a license that requires you to protect it.

Your organization may also have existing policies that influence security policies. These are often policies about the protection of data (usually written to meet the many and varied legal obligations discussed previously), but there may be policies requiring that people have access to data, especially at universities and public institutions.

If your organization has a legal department, consult it. Don't ask the people in the legal department to write a policy; just ask them to explain the institution's legal obligations or to join the team that writes the policy. If your organization does not have a legal department, consult a senior manager. In any case, find any existing written policies and wade through them to see what they say that's relevant to security. Going through these written policies will also give you a good idea for what works and doesn't work in a written policy. If you like the existing policies, base your new ones on them. If you hate the existing policies, resist the temptation to make your new ones like them just because they're the way they've always been written before.

Many people resist determining their legal responsibilities out of a hope that they won't have to actually meet them if they don't know what they are. You may have an uneasy feeling that it's probably not legal to keep employee reviews on an unprotected machine, but you don't want to have to deal with it. You may also suspect that the law is going to require you to do something insanely difficult. The bad news is that ignorance of the law is no excuse, and you simply must find out what the legal responsibilities are and make a good-faith effort to meet them. (It is inadvisable to find out what they are and then spend all your time trying to figure out how to avoid them. It will not protect you from legal problems, and it will annoy the judge.) The good news is that it is actually quite rare for the law to require you to do anything incredibly difficult. If your lawyer says it does, check out other legal opinions and other institutions' practices.

Getting Strategic and Policy Decisions Made

Strategic decisions need to be understood and made by top-level management, or they will never be successfully implemented. If you don't have top-level management support for security, you aren't going to have security; it's that simple. Why wouldn't you have support from top-level managers? Probably because you haven't addressed their concerns in ways they understand. Here are some things to consider in making your case.

Enlist Allies

You don't need to do all of this alone. In fact, you probably can't. You will need an executive sponsor (somebody high up in the organization—a vice president or the equivalent, at least). If you don't talk to people that high up on a regular basis, you need somebody at an intermediate level who can help you figure out who to talk to and how. It need not be anybody in your management chain; anybody you can trust who passionately wants a security policy will do. The most likely people are people in security (yes, the same people who do locks on doors), legal, accounting, internal audit, and quality certification. If anybody has suffered real pain from a security incident recently, try that department—it may include sales or marketing if you had a publicized incident.

It's also often highly effective to bring in consultants. A consultant has the authority of a certified Expert and has both more patience and more skill at the necessary meetings than most technical staff. The consultant also doesn't have the complicated existing relationships with people and can afford to cheerfully be a scapegoat for things people don't like forever after. In this situation, you want a consultant whose strengths are politics and authority, not necessarily the most technical person you can find.

Involve Everybody Who's Affected

You may be the person with the best understanding of the technical issues, but you aren't necessarily the person with the best understanding of the institution's needs as a whole. Strategic and policy decisions must be made by people working together. You can't just come up with a policy you like, take it around to a lot of people, and have them rubber-stamp it. Even if you manage to get them to do it—which may well be more difficult than getting them to help make intelligent decisions—they won't actually follow it.

One major computer manufacturer had a policy forbidding dial-in modems. Unfortunately, the company's centralized dial-in access didn't satisfy all of their programmers. Although the programmers couldn't request modem lines, some of them figured out that they could unplug the telephone lines from fax machines, connect them to modems, go home at night, and dial up their work computers. Even more unfortunately, a programmer in one of the groups with this habit was fired and proceeded to break into the site. He systematically tried all the phone numbers in the range the company had assigned to fax machines until he connected to one of the redirected ones and got a login prompt from an unsecured machine inside the corporate firewall. The former employee did significant damage before he was detected and shut out. He was able to gain a lot of time because the people trying to shut him out didn't know the modems existed. When they did figure out that modems were involved, the process of getting rid of them all proved to be tedious and prolonged, because lines were diverted only when people planned to use them.

That whole incident was the result of the fact that management and system administrators had a policy that ignored some genuine needs of the people using the computer facility. The official policy required dial-in access to be so secure it was almost completely unusable, and the unofficial policy required dial-in access to be so usable that it was almost completely insecure. If a policy that allowed moderately insecure dial-in access had been in place, the break-in might have been avoided, and it certainly would have been easier to detect and stop. It would also have been avoided if the programmers had agreed that security was more important than dial-in access, but that kind of agreement is much harder to achieve than a compromise.

In fact, there wasn't much actual disagreement between the parties involved in this case. If the managers had been asked, they would have said that letting people work from home was important to them; they didn't understand that the existing dial-in system was not providing acceptable service. If the programmers had been asked, they would have said that preventing people from maliciously deleting their work was important to them; they didn't understand the risks of what they were doing. But nobody thought about security and usability at the same time, and the result was pure disaster.

Accept "Wrong" Decisions

You may find that the security policy you come up with is one you don't particularly like. If this happens because the people who made it don't understand what they've done, then you should fight strongly to get it fixed. If, on the other hand, people understand the risks, but they don't share your priorities, put your objections down in writing and go ahead with the policies. Yes, this will sometimes lead to disasters. Nonetheless, if you ask a group to make a decision, you can't insist that it be your decision. You also can't be sure that your way is the only right way.

Sometimes managers have a genuine willingness to accept risks that seem overwhelming to system administrators. For example, one computer manufacturer chose to put one of their large and powerful machines on an unprotected network and to give accounts on the machine to customers and prospective customers upon request. The system administrator thought it was a terrible idea and pointed out that the machine was fundamentally impossible to secure; there were a large number of accounts, changing rapidly, with no pattern, and they belonged to people the company couldn't control. Furthermore, the reason the company was giving out test accounts was that the machine was a fast parallel processor, which also meant that it might as well have been designed as the ultimate password-cracking machine. To the system administrator, it seemed extremely likely that once this machine was broken into (which was probably inevitable), it was going to be used as a tool to break into other machines.

A battle ensued, and eventually, a compromise was reached. The machine was made available, but extra security was employed to protect internal networks from it. (It was a compromise because it interfered with employees' abilities to use the machine, which they needed to do to assist the outsiders who were using it.) Management chose to accept the remaining risk that the machine would be used as a platform to attack other sites, knowing that there was a potential for extremely bad publicity as a result.

What happened? Sure enough, the machine *was* compromised and was used to attack at least the internal networks. The attacks on the internal networks were extremely annoying and cost the company money in system administrators' time, but the attacks didn't produce significant damage, and there was little or no bad publicity. Management considered this expense to be acceptable, however, given the sales generated by letting people test-drive the machine. In this case, conflicting security policies were resolved explicitly—by discussion and compromise— and the result was a policy that seemed less strong than the original, but that provided sufficient protection. By openly and intentionally choosing to accept a risk, the company brought it within acceptable limits.

Present Risks and Benefits in Different Ways for Different People

You need to recognize that different people have different concerns. Mostly, these concerns are predictable from their positions, but some are personal. For example, suppose that:

- Your chief financial officer is concerned about the cost of security, or the cost of not having enough security.

- Your chief executive officer is concerned about the negative publicity a security incident involving your site could bring, or about potential loss or theft of intellectual property via the Internet or other network connectivity.

- A department chair is concerned that tenure reviews will be revealed.

- A mid-level manager is concerned employees are squandering all their time reading Usenet news or surfing the Web.

- Another mid-level manager is concerned employees are importing virus-infected PC software from the Internet.

- Still another mid-level manager is concerned how best to provide technical support to customers over the Internet.

- A professor on sabbatical is concerned his or her data won't be accessible from other institutions.

- An instructor is concerned that students are stealing answers from each other or tests from instructors.

- Users are concerned about the availability of Internet services they feel are vital for their jobs.

- Users are concerned they won't be able to work together if there are too many security issues.

- Students are concerned they won't be able to play with the computers, which is a part of how they learn.

- Graduate students and project managers are concerned that security measures are going to slow down projects with strict time lines.

You need to take the time to discover all of these different, legitimate concerns and address them. You may also decide that these various people *should* be worried about some things, but aren't because they don't know any better; you have to educate them about those issues. This means you need to take the time to understand their jobs, what they want to accomplish with the network, and how well they appreciate the security issues.

Talk to each of these people in terms they care about. This requires a lot of listening, and probably some research, before you ever start talking. To managers, talk about things like probable costs and potential losses; to executives, talk about risk versus benefit; and to technical staff, talk about capabilities. Before you present a proposal, be prepared with an explanation that suits your audience's point of view and technical level. If you have trouble understanding or communicating with a particular group, you may find it helps to build a relationship with someone who understands that group and can translate for you.

Be prepared to think about other people's issues in other people's terms, which means that you're going to give different explanations to different people. You're not trying to deceive anybody. The basic information is the same, no matter who you're talking to. On the other hand, if a particular decision saves money and makes for a more enjoyable working environment, you don't go to the chief financial officer and say "We want to do it this way because it's more fun", and then go the programmers and say "We want to do it this way because it's cheaper".

If you are a technical person, you may initially despair at the idea that you need to discuss security in terms of money. In particular, you may feel that you can't possibly come up with the "right" answer. You don't need to come up with the right answer. Nobody could possibly actually say how much a given security policy costs—hardware and software costs are usually easy, but then you have the time to set it up, the management meetings to argue about it, the maintenance, the extra five minutes a day for every programmer to log in, the changes to other systems. Saying how much money it saves is even worse; generally, the worst-case possibility is utter disaster, costing any amount of money your imagination can dream up or your organization can dredge up from the bottom of its pockets. However, that's so implausible you can't use it, so you have to guess how much more mundane incidents will cost you and how. Will people sue you? Will you lose customers? Will you lose control of a valuable asset? This process is not going to come up with answers that will make a technical person happy. That's OK. Come up with a method of estimating that you find plausible and that gives the results you want, attach equally plausible numbers to it, chart them, and present them. You can be perfectly honest about the fact that they're imprecise; the important thing is that you have numbers, and that you believe the justification for those numbers, no matter how accurate (or inaccurate) you think the result is. In general, you're not expected to produce absolute truth.

Avoid Surprises

When it comes to security, nobody likes surprises. That's why you need to make sure that the relevant people understand the relevant issues and are aware of, and agree with (or at least agree to abide by), the decisions made concerning those issues.

In particular, people need to know about the consequences of their decisions, including best, worst, and probable outcomes. Consequences that are obvious to you may not be obvious to other people. For example, people who are not knowledgeable about Unix may be quite willing to give out root passwords. They don't realize what the implications are, and they may be very upset when they find out.

People who have been surprised often overreact. They may go from completely unconcerned to demanding the impossible. One good break-in, or even a prank, can convert people from not understanding all the fuss about passwords to inquiring about the availability of voiceprint identification and machine gun turrets. (It's preferable to get them to make decisions while they are mildly worried, instead of blindly panicked!)

Condense to Important Decisions, with Implications

When you're asking a top manager to decide issues of policy, present only the decision to be made and the pros, cons, and implications of the various options— not a lot of extraneous decisions. For example, you shouldn't waste your CEO's time by asking him or her to decide whether you should run Sendmail or Microsoft Exchange as your mailer, or whether you should use NetBEUI or TCP/IP as the primary transport on internal networks; those decisions are primarily technical and should be resolved by the relevant technical staff and managers. On the other hand, you may need to call upon your CEO to decide strategic issues regarding mail, such as whether or not everyone in the organization is to have email access, or only certain people (and if it's to be limited, to whom).

Don't offer people decisions unless they have both the authority and the information with which to make those decisions. You don't want somebody to get attached to a decision, only to have it overruled from higher up (or worse yet, from somebody at their level but with the appropriate span of control). Always make it clear why they're being asked to decide (instead of having the decision made somewhere else).

In most cases, you want to avoid open-ended questions. It's better to ask "Should we invest money in a single place to be a defense, or should we try to protect each machine individually?" than "What do you think we should do about Internet security?" (The open question gives the replier the option of saying "nothing", which is probably not an answer you're going to be happy with.) In most cases, it's better yet to say "Should we spend about $5,000 on a single defensive system, or $15,000 on protecting each machine individually?"

Justify Everything Else in Terms of Those Decisions

All of the technical and implementation decisions you make should follow from the high-level guidance you've obtained from your top managers and executives. If you don't see which way you should go with a technical issue because it depends on nontechnical issues, you may need to request more guidance on that issue. Again, explain clearly the problem; the options; and the pros, cons, and implications of each option.

When you explain policies or procedures, explain them in terms of the original decisions. Show people the reasoning process. If you find that you can't do so, either the original decisions didn't cover some issues that are important to you (maybe so important you didn't think they needed to be mentioned), or the policies and procedures are unfounded and possibly unreasonable.

Emphasize that Many Issues Are Management and Personnel Issues, not Technical Issues

Certain problems, which some people try to characterize or solve as technical problems, are really management or personnel problems. For example, some managers worry that their employees will spend all their time at work reading Usenet news or surfing the Web. However, this is not a technical problem but a personnel problem—the online equivalent of employees spending the day at their desks reading the newspaper or doing crossword puzzles.

Another common example of misdirected concern involves managers worrying that employees will distribute confidential information over the Internet. Again, this usually isn't a technical problem; it's a management problem. The same employee who could email your source code to a competitor could also carry it out the door in his pocket on an zip disk (generally far more conveniently and with less chance of being caught). It is irrational to place technological restrictions on information that can be sent out by email unless you also check everybody's bags and pockets as they leave the premises.

Don't Assume That Anything Is Obvious

Certain things that seem obvious to a technical person who is interested in security may not be at all obvious to nontechnical managers and executives. As we've mentioned, it's obvious to anyone who understands IP that packet filtering will allow you to restrict access to services by IP addresses, but not by user (unless you can tie specific users to specific IP address). Why? Because "user" is not a concept in IP, and nothing in the IP packet reflects what "user" is responsible for that packet. Conversely, certain things that seem obvious to managers and executives are not at all obvious to technical staff—for example, that the public's perception (which is often incomplete or simply incorrect) of a problem at your company is often more important than the technical "truth" of the matter.

What If You Can't Get a Security Policy?

What do you do if, despite your best efforts, you can't get a security policy written down? The safest answer is this: document, document, document. Write down what you're doing, and why, and what the existing policies are, and what you tried, and why you think the situation is bad. Print it out on paper, sign it, and deliver it—at least to your manager, if not to several managers above your manager. File a paper copy with your signature and the dates you gave it to people.

Every year, or every time there is a significant change in the situation, try to get the policy created again. If it doesn't work, repeat the entire documentation process. Be sure to edit the document; it's tempting to just change the date and resend it, but it probably won't be quite right any more, and it weakens your position.

Doing what we recommend is fairly confrontational behavior, and it can look as if you're more interested in making certain that you're safe than in making certain your site is safe.* It's worth working a long time on getting your document to say exactly what you want it to say. Don't fall into the trap of feeling that you have to use formal language. If what you want to say is "I understand that we're an informal company and we don't do written policies, but I think this issue is so important that we still need to have something written down", just say exactly that.

---

* This may be true, but nobody else is going to fix anything in order to make you feel safer.

26

Maintaining Firewalls

If you've done a good job of designing a firewall that fits the needs of your organization, maintaining that firewall should be fairly straightforward. What does it mean to maintain a firewall? Maintenance tasks fall into three major categories:

- Housekeeping
- Monitoring your system
- Keeping up to date

Once you've designed and built your firewall, it really shouldn't take a great deal of effort to keep it going, especially because much of the maintenance work can be automated.

Housekeeping

Housekeeping is the eternal round of small tasks that need to be done to keep your firewall clean and safe. There are three main tasks you'll need to deal with again and again:

- Backing up your firewall
- Managing your accounts
- Managing your disk space

Backing Up Your Firewall

Make sure to back up all parts of your firewall. That means not only the general-purpose computers you may be using as bastion hosts or internal servers, but also the routers or other special-purpose devices. Rebuilding router configurations usually isn't easy, and your security depends on having your routers configured correctly.

Put your general-purpose machines on a regular, automated backup system. Preferably, that system should produce confirmation mail when it is running normally and distinctly different messages when it sees errors.

Why not produce mail only when errors occur? If the system produces mail only on errors, you won't notice the system if it fails to run at all. (Silence is not necessarily golden, as any parent of small children knows. If they aren't making noise, they're probably making mischief.)

Why distinctly different messages? If the system produces even vaguely similar messages when it is running normally and when it fails, people who are accustomed to ignoring the success messages will also ignore the failure messages. Ideally, a separate program should check to make sure that the backups have run and to produce messages when they haven't.

Special-purpose machines like routers change much less often and probably don't need an automated backup system. (This is fortunate because such machines rarely support them.) When you do make changes, take advantage of any means available to record the configuration. Most systems write their configuration to flash memory and can transfer configurations via FTP. Some of them also have floppy drives. If you can write the configuration to floppy, do so, and store a floppy separate from the machine. Make backups even if you have downloaded the configuration with FTP; you don't want the router to be completely dependent on another machine. If you didn't download the configuration with FTP, make an FTP copy as well as the floppy disks. Why? Sometimes it's easier to find files than to find small physical objects like floppy disks, and sometimes the floppy drive dies when the rest of the router still works. If you cannot write a floppy disk or another backup that the router can read directly, you should at least be sure that the necessary files for FTP are available from multiple places.

 The design of backup systems is outside the scope of this book. This description (along with the section in Chapter 27, *Responding to Security Incidents*, called "Backing Up Your Filesystems") provides only a summary. If you're uncertain about your backup system, you'll want to look at a general system administration reference. See Appendix A, *Resources*, for complete information on additional resources.

Managing Your Accounts

Account management—adding new accounts, removing old ones, changing passwords, etc.—is one of the most often neglected housekeeping tasks. On firewall systems, it's absolutely crucial that new accounts be added correctly, old accounts removed promptly, and passwords changed appropriately. (See your own system's documentation for how to do all this.)

Establish a procedure for adding accounts; wherever you can, use a program to add them. Even though there shouldn't be many users on your firewall systems, every one of them is a possible danger, and it's worth the effort to ensure they're set up correctly every time. People have an unfortunate tendency to leave out steps or to pause for a few days in the middle of a process. If that gap leaves an account that has no password, you're creating open invitations to intruders.

Make sure your account creation procedure includes dating the account and that accounts are automatically reviewed every few months. You don't need to automatically turn them off, but you do need to automatically inform somebody that they've timed out. It's relatively easy to do on a general-purpose computer; it may be harder on other systems, particularly dedicated systems like routers. If possible, set things up so that the accounts can be watched by an automated system. This can be done by generating account files on a general-purpose computer and then transferring them to the other machine, or by generating the accounts on the machine itself, but automatically copying the account files to a general-purpose computer and examining them.

If your devices support reasonably secure protocols that will allow you to centrally maintain accounts, you should consider using them. However, doing user authentication via NIS or Windows domain authentication on firewall machines is not advisable for security and reliability reasons.

You should also arrange to get termination notices from the appropriate authorities whenever someone leaves your organization. Most companies are able to send notices for full-time employees, and most universities can provide graduation notification for students. It may be much harder to keep track of contractors and students who drop out, so you shouldn't rely on official notifications to tell you about everybody who has left. You may also need to confirm notifications: for example, you may get termination notices for people who are actually converting to contract status, or graduation notices for people who are continuing as graduate students or junior faculty. These people are going to be annoyed if you get rid of all their files (although it's probably acceptable to temporarily disable their accounts if their status is in doubt).

If you can, set up all accounts on the firewall to have nonreusable passwords (see Chapter 21, *Authentication and Auditing Services*, for more information on nonreusable password systems). This will prevent people from either guessing or sniffing passwords and may help limit people's ability to share passwords with each other.

If you are using reusable passwords, or nonreusable passwords with a fixed component, encourage people to change them regularly to help prevent guessing and limit the usefulness of password sniffing. If your operating system supports password aging, you may want to turn it on. Use a relatively long time period—perhaps three to six months. If you time out passwords more frequently (e.g., every month), users will be willing to go to great lengths to circumvent the timeout, and you probably won't see any real gain in security. Similarly, if your password aging doesn't guarantee that the user will see a notification before the account becomes unusable, don't turn it on. Otherwise, you will annoy your users, and you will run the risk of accidentally locking out administrators who have a critical need to use the machine.

If password aging on your system is going to require users to change their password as they are logging in, you need a password program that strictly enforces good passwords. If you don't do this, people will choose simple passwords in the heat of the moment, honestly intending to change them to better ones later. All in all, you may find it more effective to simply send people notices on a regular basis, even though you'll get less compliance that way.

Managing Your Disk Space

Data always expands to fill all available space, even on machines that have almost no users. People dump things in odd corners of the filesystem "just for now", and they build up there. This causes more problems than you may realize. Aside from the fact that you may want that disk space, this random junk complicates incident response. You'll end up asking yourself:

> Is that a program that you left lying around last time you needed to install a new version, or did an intruder put it in?

> Is that truly a random data file, or does it have some deep meaning to an intruder?

Unfortunately, there is no automatic way to find junk; human beings, particularly system administrators who can write anywhere on the disk, are too unpredictable. Another person needs to look around on a regular basis. It's particularly effective to send every new system administrator on a tour of the disks; they'll notice things the old hands have become accustomed to.

Auditing programs like Tripwire, discussed in Chapter 10, *Bastion Hosts*, will tell you about new files that appear in supposedly static areas, and this information will help you keep things straight. You will still need to check all the areas where you intentionally allow changes, and you should periodically go back and re-check the static areas. You will probably get the alert while you still know why you put that file in that place, and that knowledge may wear off over time.

Aside from accumulating junk, your main disk space problem will be logs. These can and should be rotated automatically, and you may want to compress, encrypt, or digitally sign them as well. A program like _trimlog_ (see Appendix B, _Tools_) can help automate the process. You should also consider making a copy of the files on another system.

It is very important to correctly rotate or truncate logs. If a program is trying to write to a log file while you're trying to move or truncate it, you're obviously going to have problems. In fact, you may run into difficulties even if a program is simply holding the file open in preparation for writing to it later; notably, you may later discover that the program is still logging to the file you renamed.

Under Unix the normal convention for rotating log files is as follows:

1. Rename the log file.

2. Create a new and empty file using the original name (and the same file per-missions).

3. Signal the program writing the logs in some way.

Signaling could involve sending a Unix signal or creating a dummy file that the program checks for.

Most Windows NT programs use the Event Logger to deal with logging. As we discussed in Chapter 12, _Windows NT and Windows 2000 Bastion Hosts_, the Event Logger provides no way to rotate logs, which means that it has to be done by hand or with third-party software. The situation with programs that keep their own logs is not so clear; you will normally need to use a special accompanying tool to rotate a program's log files or configure the program to rotate the logs based upon some point (for instance, weekly or when a particular size has been reached).

Under both operating systems, it is unfortunately sometimes necessary, particularly when using add-on products, to stop programs or cause them to suspend logging while you truncate or move logs.

Monitoring Your System

Another important aspect of firewall maintenance involves monitoring your system. Monitoring is intended to tell you several things:

- Has your firewall been compromised?

- What kinds of attacks are being tried against your firewall?

- Is your firewall in working order?

- Is your firewall able to provide the service your users need?

In order to answer these questions, you'll need to know what the normal pattern of usage is.

Special-Purpose Monitoring Devices

You'll do most of your monitoring using the tools·and the logging provided by the existing parts of your firewall, but you may find it convenient to have some dedicated monitoring devices as well. For example, you may want to put a monitoring station on your perimeter net so you can be sure only the packets you expect are going across it. You can use a general-purpose computer with network snooping software on it, or you can use a special-purpose network sniffer.

How can you make certain that this monitoring machine can't be used by an intruder? In fact, you'd prefer that an intruder not even detect its existence. On some network hardware, you can disable transmission in the network interface (with sufficient expertise and a pair of wire cutters), which will make the machine impossible to detect and extremely difficult for an intruder to use (because it can't reply). If you have the source for your operating system, you can always disable transmission there; however, in this case, it's much harder to be certain you've been successful. In most cases, you'll have to settle for extremely cautious configuration of the machine. Treat it like a bastion host that needs to do less and be more secure.

In particular, you should note that Microsoft's Network Monitor registers a special NetBIOS name when it starts up. It is a blatant advertisement of the fact that you are monitoring the network. The only way to stop it from happening is to unbind NetBIOS from the network interface you're monitoring, which will also make it impossible to use the Network Monitor Agent on it (not to mention most other Microsoft-native network applications!).

Other forms of network sniffing are more subtle, but also often detectable. Most obviously, network sniffers tend to do a lot of name service requests, in order to find hostnames for the IP addresses. Less obviously, a machine that is accepting all packets often slightly changes the way it handles incoming requests. A group called The L0pht (pronounced "loft") released an anti-sniffer-sniffer to detect network sniffers, which has led to an arms race, with people developing less and less detectable sniffers, not to mention an anti-sniffer-sniffer-sniffer. These technologies are rapidly evolving; we advise that you deploy the most up-to-date, least detectable sniffer technology available and an anti-sniffer-sniffer on critical networks to help you find sniffers installed by attackers. (Information about getting The L0pht's anti-sniffer-sniffer can be found in Appendix B, *Tools.*)

Clever attackers will assume that you are intercepting packets and will take steps to conceal traffic, whether or not they can actually find your monitoring system. There's nothing you can do but stay alert.

Intrusion Detection Systems

An intrusion detection system is a piece of special-purpose software designed to figure out if somebody has broken into your site. Intrusion detection systems can range from relatively simple, passive programs that read log files and look for bad things, to extremely complex systems that use special-purpose monitoring devices spread out across a large network, inject fake traffic into the network to see if anybody uses the information, and/or employ sophisticated artificial intelligence techniques to detect subtle forms of abnormal behavior.

Intrusion detection is a big subject, and we can't cover it fully here. More information can be found in other places (for instance, Stephen Northcutt's *Network Intrusion Detection: An Analyst's Handbook*, New Riders, 1999).

There are two basic techniques for intrusion detection; either systems can know what kind of behavior is bad and set off alarms when it happens, or they can know what kind of behavior is good and set off alarms when anything else happens. Relatively speaking, it's easier to recognize bad behavior than good behavior. Unfortunately, it's more effective to recognize good behavior.

Systems that recognize bad behavior use *attack signatures,* information about what particular attacks look like. For instance, this sort of system would recognize a port scan as an attack because it would know that a series of attempts to contact different ports on the same host was a sign of an attack.

Systems that recognize good behavior use *usage profiles,* information about what normally happens. For instance, this sort of system would recognize a port scan as an attack because it would know that normally, when somebody connects to a port, the next thing that happens is that they use that port for its normal purpose. In a port scan, the attacker will connect, get a response, and immediately disconnect and try another port. This behavior is outside of the normal pattern and therefore will be detected as an attack.

The difficulty with recognizing attack signatures is that the system can detect only attacks that it knows about. When new attacks are created, the system won't know about them until a signature is created and added. In addition, it's often possible to disguise signatures. For instance, the signatures for port scans used to look for multiple connections to different ports from the same source host, so attackers now use multiple collaborating source hosts.

Systems that rely on usage profiles have problems with what are called "false positives", or cases where they think an attack is occurring but it isn't. Usage of systems changes over time, and any profile that's specific enough to catch any significant number of attacks will set off a large number of alarms. Good systems now have false positive rates in the range of about 1–3 percent; unfortunately, that's 1–3 percent of the events they look at, which in the case of a network usually means 1–3 percent of packets. Since many sites have millions of incoming packets a day, this apparently small error rate can still result in thousands of false alarms a day, which is rarely acceptable.

Intruders also have ways of hiding attacks that will defeat almost all intrusion detection systems. For instance, a patient intruder can scan a network very slowly; most intrusion detection systems look at a few minutes', or maybe a few hours', worth of context at a time. An impatient intruder can bury an attack in a large amount of network traffic, and few systems will be able to keep up.

Similarly, some techniques can be used that defeat almost all attempts at hiding attacks. The most powerful and popular of these is the *honeypot,* the tempting bait with nothing but a trap behind it. For instance, if you put a machine on your perimeter network that you don't use for any services, you know that any attempt to connect to it is an attack. It doesn't matter whether or not it matches an attack signature, or whether or not it fits a normal usage pattern. It's just obviously wrong.

How much an intrusion detection system can do for you depends mostly on how much time, money, and development effort you can invest in the system. Although intrusion detection is theoretically a very effective technology, actually making it work in practice is not an easy proposition, and it requires constant maintenance and attention. There is no point in having an intrusion detection system unless you have the personnel to keep it up to date and to deal with the alarms that it produces.

What Should You Watch For?

In a perfect world, you'd like to know absolutely everything that goes through your firewall—every packet dropped or accepted and every connection requested. In the real world, neither the firewall nor your brain can cope with that much information. To come up with a practical compromise, you'll want to turn on the most verbose logging that doesn't slow down your machines too much and doesn't fill up your disks too fast; then, you'll want to summarize the logs that are produced.

You can improve the disk space problem by keeping verbose logs offline, on some form of removable media (for instance, tapes, writable CDs, or writable

DVDs). Tapes are cheap and hold a lot of data, but they have some drawbacks. They're not particularly fast under the best circumstances, and log entries are generally too short to achieve maximum performance. They're also annoying to read data from. If you're interested in using them, write summary logs to disk and write everything to tape. If you find a situation where you need more data, you can go back to the tape for it. A tape drive can probably keep up with the packets on an average Internet connection, but it won't keep up with an internal connection at full LAN speeds or even with a T-1 connection to the Internet that's at close to its maximum performance. CD and DVD writers are even slower, but they're much easier to read data from. If you have large amounts of disk space to use as temporary storage, they may be an effective solution.

No matter what you are using to write logs to, you should protect the logs. The data that's in them may be useful to attackers, and it may be confidential for other reasons. For instance, if you log the contents of packets, you may well be logging encrypted sensitive information. Even if you don't log packet contents, the information about what packets went where may be private; it's one thing to log the 434 times that somebody tried to go to an embarrassing web site, and another to have it become public knowledge.

No matter how you're storing logs, you want to log the following cases:

- All dropped or rejected packets, denied connections, and rejected attempts

- At least the time, protocol, and username for every successful connection to or through your bastion host

- All error messages from your routers, your bastion host, and any proxying programs

For security reasons, some information should never be logged where an intruder could possibly be able to read it. For example, although you should log failed login attempts, you should not log the password that was used in the failed attempt. Users frequently mistype their own passwords, and logging these mistyped passwords would make it easier for a computer cracker to break into a user's account.

Some system administrators believe that the account name should also not be logged on failed login attempts, especially when the account typed by the user is nonexistent. The reason is that users occasionally type their passwords when they are prompted for their usernames. If invalid accounts are logged, it might be possible for an attacker to use those logs to infer people's passwords.

What are you watching for? You want to know what your usual pattern is (and what trends there are in it), and you want to be alerted to any exceptions to that pattern. To recognize when things are going wrong, you have to understand what happens when things are going right. It's important to know what messages you get when everything is working. Most systems produce error messages that sound peculiar and threatening even when they're working perfectly well. For example, in the sample *syslog* output in Example 26-1, messages 10, 14, and 17 all look vaguely threatening, but are in fact perfectly OK.* (Although these examples are taken from a Unix *syslog*, exactly the same phenomena can be seen in the Windows NT Event Log; information about setting up logging can be found in Chapter 10, *Bastion Hosts*, Chapter 11, *Unix and Linux Bastion Hosts*, and Chapter 12, *Windows NT and Windows 2000 Bastion Hosts*.)

If you see those messages for the first time when you're trying to debug a problem, you're likely to leap to the conclusion that the messages have something to do with your problem and get thoroughly sidetracked. Even if you never do figure out what the messages are and why they're appearing, just knowing that certain messages appear even when things are working fine will save you time.

Example 26-1. A Sample syslog File (Line Numbers Added)

```
1:  May 29 00:00:58 localhost wn[27194]: noc.nca.or.bv - - [] "GET
    /long/consulting.html HTTP/1.0" 200 1074   <Sent file: >
2:  May 29 00:00:58 localhost wn[27194]: <User_Agent: Mozilla/1.0N
    (X11; SunOS 4.1.3-KL sun4m)> <Referrer: http://www.longitude.example/>
3:  May 29 00:02:38 localhost ftpd[26086]: 26086: 05/29/95 0:02:38
    spoke.cst.cnes.vg(gupta@) retrieved
    /pub/firewalls/digest/v04.n278.Z(15788 bytes)
4:  May 29 00:15:57 localhost ftpd[27195]: 27195: 05/29/95 0:01:52
    client42.sct.io connected, duration 845 seconds
5:  May 29 00:18:04 localhost ftpd[26086]: 26086: 05/29/95 23:26:32
    spoke.cst.cnes.vg connected, duration 3092 seconds
6:  May 27 01:13:38 mv-gw.longitude.example user: host
    naismith.longitude.com admin login failed
7:  May 27 01:13:47 mv-gw.longitude.example last message repeated 2 times
8:  May 27 01:15:17 mv-gw.longitude.example user: host
    naismith.longitude.example admin login succeeded
9:  May 27 01:19:18 mv-gw.longitude.example 16 permit: TCP from
    192.168.20.35.2591 to 172.16.1.3.53 seq 324EE800, ack 0x0, win
    4096, SYN
10: May 29 02:20:09 naismith sendmail[27366]: CAA27366: SYSERR(root):
    collect: I/O error on connection from atx.eb.cm, from=<<Mailer-
    Daemon@eb.cm>: Connection reset by peer during collect
    with atx.eb.cm
11: May 29 02:30:28 naismith named[79]: sysquery: server name mismatch
```

---

* Message 10 is a common network failure that will result in a retry, and how good do you expect your connection to Cameroon to be? 14 is *traceroute* running. 17 says there are no synonyms defined, which you presumably already know.

Example 26-1. A Sample syslog File (Line Numbers Added) (continued)

```
        for [172.16.8.25]: (sun.nhs-relay.ac.cv != nhs-relay.ac.cv) (server
        for cus.ox.ac.cv)
12: May 29 02:31:00 naismith named[79]: sysquery: server name mismatch
        for [172.16.8.25]: (nhs-relay.ac.cv != sun.nhs-relay.ac.cv) (server
        for PANSY.CSV.WARWICK.AC.CV)
13: May 29 02:47:04 naismith named[79]: sysquery: server name mismatch
        for [172.16.8.25]: (nhs-relay.ac.cv != sun.nhs-relay.ac.cv) (server
        for LUPUS.CNS.UMIST.AC.CV)
14: May 29 07:50:59 mv-gw.longitude.example  8 deny: UDP from
        192.168.69.250.33072 to 192.168.20.34.33467
15: May 29 08:06:16 naismith popper: (v1.831beta) Servicing request
        from "penta.longitude.example" at 192.168.20.36
16: May 29 08:06:56 naismith popper: (v1.831beta) Ending request from
        "penta.longitude.com" at 192.168.20.36
17: May 29 10:04:02 localhost waisserver1[28430]: -2: Warning: couldn't open
        wais-sources/firewalls-digest.syn - synonym translation
        disabled
18: May 29 16:26:46 mv-gw.longitude.example  8 deny: UDP from
        192.168.186.11.20 to 192.168.20.34.1937
```

Most of your logging will probably be done via the Unix *syslog* facility or some other similar file-based log mechanism. You'll need to develop log-scanning scripts to analyze each of these log files on a regular basis. Some firewall packages, such as TIS FWTK, come with scripts to analyze and summarize their own logs. You could use these scripts as templates for your own logging, or you could write your own scripts from scratch in *awk, perl,* or some other suitable language.

As you can see, the log file is verbose and not particularly readable (even with better linebreaks inserted). An unimportant error condition on a distant host (the server name mismatch on *nhs-relay.ac.cv*) is producing multiple error messages (11, 12, and 13, in this highly condensed version). The log file is also in chronological order which is not particularly the order of importance.

Example 26-2 shows a report based on a log file, with messages arranged in a more useful order and somewhat summarized.

Example 26-2. A Report Based on a syslog File

```
May 27 06:42:07 localhost ftpd[10159]: securityalert: refused passwd
        file to chen@calm.example from chen.dialup.zarf.net
May 27 06:42:10 localhost ftpd[10159]: securityalert: refused passwd
        file to chen@calm.example from chen.dialup.zarf.net
-----------------------------------------------------------------
May 26 12:33:39 localhost su: nxn to root on /dev/ttyp1
May 27 01:23:17 naismith su: bart to root on /dev/ttyp3
-----------------------------------------------------------------
May 26 12:29:44 naismith kernel: uid 31 on /naismith_b: file system full
May 26 12:31:33 naismith kernel: uid 31 on /naismith_b: file system full
-----------------------------------------------------------------
May 26 02:49:03 naismith named[79]: Malformed response from
```

Example 26-2. A Report Based on a syslog File (continued)

```
    [192.168.192.2].53 (ran out of data in answer)
--------------------------------------------------------------------
May 26 12:14:36 mv-gw.longitude.example 16 deny: UDP from 192.168.69.1.58899
    to 192.168.20.35.33459
May 26 12:15:15 mv-gw.longitude.example 16 deny: UDP from 192.168.69.1.58962
    to 192.168.20.35.33459
May 27 01:24:05 mv-gw.longitude.example 16 permit: TCP from
    192.168.20.34.2637 to 192.168.54.72.23 seq BE793A01, ack 0x0, win
    4096, SYN
May 27 01:24:11 mv-gw.longitude.example 16 permit: TCP from
    192.168.20.34.2637 to 192.168.54.72.23 seq BE793A01, ack 0x0, win
    4096, SYN
--------------------------------------------------------------------

FTP:    Connections: 240
        Files: 733
        Bytes: 32,747,429 (31.23  M)
        Seconds: 92,787 (25.77  hours)
```

In general, it's safer to write scripts to filter out messages to be ignored (leaving unusual stuff), rather than writing scripts to identify the unusual stuff directly. The reason for this is that you seldom know all of the different messages your firewall might produce. It's easier to ignore the benign messages than to recognize the dangerous ones.

Log messages fall into three categories:

Known to be OK

> For example, "login succeeded for user smith". You would like to ignore these messages. Message 3 in Example 26-1 is clearly in this category.

Known to be dangerous

> For example, "bad disk block at location 0x47c7a8". You would like these messages to cause some action to happen; it may be anything from sending someone email, to submitting a trouble ticket, to paging you.

Unknown

> You would like these messages to be sent for a human to examine. Message 18 in Example 26-1 is an example; why is someone sending UDP packets from port 20 to an arbitrary port above 1024? That doesn't match any common protocol.

Setting up the criteria is an iterative process; once a human has examined a mystery message, future examples of that message can probably be classified as either OK or dangerous without being examined again. You'll change the rules as time goes on.

Log entries often must be considered in context. A message that's mildly mysterious if it occurs once is cause for serious worry if it occurs every minute. For example, "login succeeded for user smith" is good, unless it's preceded by three "login failed" messages for every user above "smith" in your password file; in that case, it's very bad indeed. In Example 26-1, message 9 shows an unexceptional outbound TCP connection, logged just on general principles. It wouldn't be at all worrying if it weren't preceded by messages 6 through 8. In context, you know that someone made three failed tries at logging in as "admin", finally succeeded, and then immediately started an outbound connection. This looks extremely suspicious. Message 7 doesn't mean anything at all without context.

In a large system, getting context may require correlating log files from multiple hosts. This is one reason for keeping consistent time settings; it is also a reason why people use intrusion detection systems. If you have high volumes of traffic, a complex firewall, or a requirement for strict security, you will probably need an intrusion detection system to help you with the log analysis.

The Good, the Bad, and the Ugly

Once you go beyond the obvious (for example, it's OK for users to log in; it's not OK for the disk to be bad), how can you tell when you're in trouble? Some rules of thumb:

Once is an accident; twice is coincidence; three times is enemy action
> One user who tries to log in at 2 A.M. and fails is up too late and can't type. Two users who try to log in at 2 A.M. may have been at the same party, but you're certainly going to be curious about the incident. Three or more attempts to log in at 2 A.M., and someone is trying to break in. This rule of thumb applies mostly to attempts on separate accounts; stubborn repeated attempts by the same user to do the same thing that doesn't work probably merely indicates that the user is single-minded—and wrong.

Accidents don't try to cover themselves up
> If your log files are missing, if entries have been deleted, or if there is any other evidence that somebody has been covering his or her tracks, you probably have a break-in. If not, you have some other serious problem. (Either something is broken, or somebody administering the machine is deleting things or rotating the logs inappropriately.)

Most mysteries don't mean anything
> For everybody who sets out to track down a mysterious problem or a strange log entry and finds an intruder, there are 99 people who set out to track down a mysterious problem or a strange log entry and find an annoying but trivial bug. You should still try to track these things down, but there's no need to panic.

Straightforward explanations are usually correct

It's possible that you were broken into at the same time you had another known problem, but it's not likely. If you know that you had a hardware failure, or a person wandering around doing misguided things, you'll want to spend some time ruling out side effects of the known problem before you decide that you also have an intruder. On the other hand, if your files are mysteriously disappearing and nothing is apparently wrong with your disk, somebody is probably deleting them, and you'll want to spend a very long time ruling out an intruder before you decide that your filesystem code is buggy.

You're going to end up classifying suspicious events into several categories:

- You know what caused it, and it's not a security problem.

- You don't know what caused it, you're probably never going to know what caused it, but whatever it was, it's not happening anymore.

- Somebody was trying to break in but not very hard; this is a *probe*.

- Somebody made a serious attempt to get in; this is an *attack*.

- Somebody actually broke in.

The boundaries between these categories are vague. Unless you're dealing with messages from the first category (i.e., a known nonproblem), it's going to come down to a judgment call most of the time. It's impossible to provide an exhaustive list of the symptoms of any of these situations, but here are some generalizations that may help.

You should suspect that someone's been probing your site if you see:

- A few attempts to access services at insecure ports (e.g., attempts to contact *portmapper* or an X server).

- Attempts to log in with common account names (e.g., "guest" or "lp"; most attempts to log in as "anonymous" are mistakes).

- Requests to TFTP files or to transfer NIS maps.

- Somebody feeding the *debug* command to your SMTP server.

- Packets sent to the same ports on every IP address in a range.

You should be more concerned if you see any of the following; an attack may be going on:

- Multiple failed attempts to log in to valid accounts on your machines, particularly accounts that are used across the Internet, or attempts on accounts in the order in which they appear in your password file.

- Unusual accepted packets or commands whose purpose you don't understand.

- Packets sent to every port in a range.

- Successful logins from an unexpected site.

- Sudden increases in incoming or outgoing traffic.

You should suspect a successful break-in if you see:

- Deleted or modified log files.

- Programs that suddenly omit expected information (this suggests that they have been replaced with versions that ignore the intruder's files and programs). On Unix machines, the most frequent victims are *login, ls, ps, netstat,* and *ifconfig.*

- New log files containing password information or packet traces that you can't explain.

- Directories that contain more administrative entries than they should. For example, on Unix machines, directories should contain two entries with names made out of periods ("." and "..", indicating "this directory" and "parent directory"), but there should not be more than two such entries (for instance, "..." or ".. "). If it looks as if there is more than one entry for each, the extra entry probably has spaces in it and is being used to conceal the file or directory from casual observation.

- Unexpected logins as privileged users (for example, root) or unexpected users who are suddenly able to become privileged users.

- Services running that you have not intentionally turned on.

- Apparent probes or attacks coming from your own machines.

- Extra processes with names that are variants of common system processes (for example, both *sendmail* and *Sendmail* are running, or *init* and *initd*; this is another trick for sneaking things in where you won't notice them).

- An unexpected change in the login behavior of your machine or for other machines you reach from yours. This indicates that the program you use to log in has been modified.

Responding to Probes

Inevitably, you're going to detect apparent probes of your firewall—packets sent to services you don't offer to the Internet, attempts to log in to nonexistent accounts, and so on. Probes are the Internet equivalent of someone walking down a line of doors and checking every door knob to see if it's locked. Probers generally try one or two things, and if they don't get an interesting response, they move on. If you're inclined to do so, you can spend a lot of time chasing down such incidents, attempting to figure out where the probes are coming from and who is behind them. However, in most situations, it probably isn't worth the effort. The novelty of chasing down probes of this kind fades quickly. If you're getting persistent probes from some site, you might contact the management of that site to let it know what's going on (in general, it has been broken into and needs to know), but that's usually about as far as folks need to go in responding to these probes.

It's unfortunate that on the Internet today, probes are so frequent that the laissez faire attitude we've described is often an appropriate one. In good neighborhoods, people don't get away with trying door knobs. You have a right to be unhappy with people who behave this way and trying to get them to stop is perfectly reasonable. However, you do need to decide where you're going to spend your energy. Save extreme responses for extreme situations. Treating probers with maximum harshness is just going to convince people that you are unreasonable.

Some people amuse themselves by setting up firewall machines to lead on people who try common probes. For example, they put a password file in the anonymous FTP area that appears to contain user account data. However, if the prober breaks the encrypted passwords, he or she sees a snide message. This is a harmless way to spend your spare time and provides a satisfactory feeling of revenge, but it doesn't actually improve your security much. It simply annoys attackers, and doing so may cause them to take a personal interest in breaking into your site.

Some people and some firewalls prefer a more active approach to probes, engaging in counter-attacks. A fairly wide variety of things are sold as counter-attacks (firewall marketers find the concept extremely sexy). They range from attempts to find out further information about where the probes are coming from (giving you a start on tracking them down), to automatically configuring the firewall to reject all connections from the probing site, to actual counter-attacks. Regardless of their often remarkably aggressive marketing material, no commercial firewall does anything that can reasonably be described as a counter-attack, for obvious reasons involving liability. This is good because misidentification, loops, and bad feelings often result from even mild automated responses.

For instance, a forged probe purporting to be from a site that does information-gathering when it gets probes and aimed at another such site is almost guaranteed to suck the site administrators into a "Yeah, but you hit me first!" argument. Why would somebody forge such a packet? Because they did something and were annoyed at the response they got. A little forgery can bring a lot of community pressure to bear on somebody who has an overly vigorous probe response. A notable example occurred with somebody whose response to anonymous FTP attempts was to send mail threatening to sue; a widely broadcast email contained a URL that attempted anonymous FTP to the site, causing both resource problems and publicity problems.

Different sites have different opinions about what constitutes a probe, and what constitutes a full-fledged attack. Most people call something a probe as long as they know it's not going to work, even if it is determined and drawn out. For example, somebody who determinedly tries every possible combination of lower-case alphabetic characters as your root password is not going to succeed and can probably be ignored as a probe until you get tired of reading the log messages. (That kind of attack won't succeed, no matter how many combinations are tried.) However, if you have the time and the energy, it's probably worth pursuing people who are making determined attempts, even when you know they'll fail.

Responding to Attacks

If your logs show that someone is making a determined attack against your system (see the rules of thumb we presented in the "The Good, the Bad, and the Ugly" section, earlier in this chapter), you probably want to do a little more than sit back and watch. Chapter 27, *Responding to Security Incidents*, describes in detail how you should respond to a real security incident.

Keeping up to Date

The final important aspect of firewall maintenance involves keeping up to date. You obviously need to keep your system up to date, but before you can do so, you need to keep yourself up to date.

Keeping Yourself up to Date

The hardest part of firewall maintenance is staying abreast of the continuous developments in the field. New things are happening every day: new bugs are being discovered and exploited; new attacks are being carried out; new patches and fixes for your existing systems and tools are being made available; and new tools are becoming available. Staying up to date with all these changes can easily be the most time-consuming part of a firewall maintainer's job.

How do you stay up to date? Well, primarily by staying involved. Find a set of mailing lists, newsgroups, web sites, and professional forums you feel comfortable with and follow them carefully. This section describes the most important ways you can keep involved. Appendix A, *Resources*, provides a more complete list, along with contact information.

Mailing lists

Several mailing lists might be of interest to anyone who maintains a firewall; instructions for subscribing to them are included in Appendix A. The most important list for folks interested in firewalls is the Firewalls mailing list. This list hosts discussions of the design, installation, configuration, maintenance, and philosophy of Internet firewalls of all types. The main drawback of the list is that it can be very busy; sometimes more than 100 messages per day are posted to the list. To address the problem of volume, a Firewalls-Digest version of the list is also available; Firewalls-Digest subscribers receive all of the same messages that subscribers to the main Firewalls list receive, but the messages are bundled into "digest" format (usually 10 to 20 messages are in a digest).

Another list you should almost certainly subscribe to is the CERT-Advisory mailing list. This is the list to which CERT-CC posts its new security advisories. If you are served by a response team other than CERT-CC (e.g., one of the other teams in FIRST, described in Appendix A, *Resources*), check to see if that team has its own advisory list and subscribe to that one as well as to the CERT-CC list. Your team will probably mirror most of CERT-CC's advisories and may produce advisories of its own that are relevant to its constituency (you) that aren't mirrored by CERT-CC.

Beyond the Firewalls and CERT-Advisory mailing lists, the choices are less clear. There are several geographic or industry-specific firewalls lists (e.g., the Firewall-Developers, Academic-Firewalls, and Firewalls-UK lists). A mailing list called Bugtraq provides detailed discussions of network security holes; if you can wade through the seemingly perpetual flame wars, you can occasionally find some gems there. The Windows NT-oriented list NT-Bugtraq is particularly useful.

There are also product- and package-specific lists for many firewalls products and packages; for example, there are lists for Livingston, Telebit, and Cisco routers and the TIS FWTK. If you are using (or contemplating using) a particular product or package, you should probably subscribe to the list for that product or package, if there is one. Lists of this kind are often an invaluable source of technical support, particularly during widespread security incidents.

Many operating system vendors also have special mailing lists used for distributing security information. Check with your vendor for information about lists they maintain and how to subscribe to them.

Newsgroups

In addition to the various mailing lists you might subscribe to, a variety of newsgroups are directly or indirectly relevant to firewalls. Many of these parallel the mailing lists mentioned in the previous section. For example, CERT-CC advisories are posted to the *comp.security.announce* group, and there are newsgroups for a variety of commercial and noncommercial network products. There is also a newsgroup dedicated to firewalls, *comp.security.firewalls*. Unfortunately, it is an extremely high-volume newsgroup and contains a large number of absolute beginners asking the same questions over and over again, and an almost equal number of firewall vendors either trying to push their products, or complaining that other people are trying to push products.

Web sites

The Web changes so rapidly that it's almost senseless to put the names of web sites in print. There are a wide variety of security and system administration sites, ranging from sites put up by attackers (that appear and disappear extremely rapidly) through subscription-only sites run by magazines. Your best bet is to use a web search engine to look for information about the topics that interest you. You usually will get better information from using a variety of sources found this way than from any single site.

Professional forums

Many professional forums are available for your participation. They include conferences, vendor user groups, local user groups, professional societies (such as IEEE and ACM special interest groups), and so on. Many people find attending these events invaluable, not so much for the formal programs presented, but for the contacts they make with other people who have solved problems similar to those they are currently facing.

At this point, one of the best conferences for Internet firewall builders and maintainers is the USENIX Security Symposium (generally held annually). If you are a Unix system administrator, one of the best possible ways you can spend a week each year is at the USENIX LISA* conference; Windows NT–only system administrators would be better off at the USENIX LISA-NT conference. You can find more information about all of these conferences and about USENIX in general in Appendix A, *Resources*.

Local user and special interest groups are also a great way to keep in touch between conferences; most meet monthly or bimonthly.

Keeping Your Systems up to Date

If you take care to keep yourself up to date, then keeping your system up to date is a fairly straightforward job. You just need to deal with whatever new problems you hear about, as you hear about them.

You should be able to collect enough information from the sources described in the previous section to decide whether or not a new problem is a problem for

---

* LISA used to mean "Large Installation System Administration", back in the days when a large installation meant having more than a dozen machines; today, most sites would qualify under that definition, and the focus of the conference has widened to include all types of Unix system administration—but the name lives on.

your site in particular. Be aware that you may not be able to determine instanta-
neously whether a problem applies to your site; it may take a few hours or days
for the information you need to become available to you. You may need to make
a judgment call about what to do about a particular problem in the absence of
solid information, with only vague reports about the problem and its consequences to go on. Which way you err—towards caution or convenience—is going
to be dictated by your particular circumstances. These circumstances include the
potential problem involved, what you can realistically do about it, how much your
site cares about security versus availability and convenience, and so on. Caution
would dictate blocking the problem if it's at all possible that it applies to you. Convenience, on the other hand, would dictate waiting to take action until you're
fairly sure that the problem does apply to you.

Keep in mind the following principles when you are deciding what fixes to apply
and when:

Don't be in a hurry to upgrade

> Don't be in too big a hurry to install a patch or a fix unless you have reason to
> believe that the problem is being, or could be, exploited against you. It's
> always better to let somebody else go first, to discover what new problems the
> patch or fix creates. We're not suggesting you should delay very long in
> installing a relevant patch, but it's often wise to wait at least a few hours or a
> couple of days to see if the patch blows up on anybody else.

Don't patch problems you don't have

> You don't want to apply patches for problems you don't have. If you do apply
> patches in this way, you run a great risk of introducing new problems. If a
> patch applies only to a particular piece of software or a particular release, and
> you don't use that software or that release, don't install the patch. If it applies
> to features that you don't use in programs that you do use, apply it anyway;
> you may start using the features in the future, and at that point, you won't
> remember whether or not you patched it.

Beware of interdependent patches

> While you generally shouldn't apply patches for problems you don't have, be
> aware that patches for problems you do have may depend on previous
> patches for problems you don't have. With any luck, the documentation for
> the patch you want to apply says what other patches (if any) are prerequi-
> sites, but this isn't always the case. Sometimes you just have to make your best
> guess. In such situations, it really helps to be tied in to the support mailing
> lists and newsgroups concerning your platform; you can ask there and see if
> anybody else has already figured this out.

How Long Does It Take?

As we've said, the hardest part of maintaining your firewall is keeping yourself up to date. How long does it take to keep up to date? If you're a novice at this, just getting started and at the hardest part of the learning curve, keeping up to date can easily occupy you full time. After you've been at it for a few weeks or months, and you've learned the fundamentals of what you need to know, your time requirement can drop off to just an hour or so a day to follow the various mailing lists, newsgroups, magazines, and other sources that you've decided to track.

Most of this time will be devoted to maintaining your own knowledge, not maintaining the firewall itself. Monitoring the firewall itself should take only minutes a day—long enough to scan the daily log summaries and make sure that nothing unusual or noteworthy has happened.

Obviously, you're occasionally going to have to devote more time to the firewall when it's time to fix something, upgrade something, or add new functionality. How long this takes depends on how complex the fix, upgrade, or addition is. The better job you've done anticipating your site's needs and designing and building the firewall in the first place, the less time you're going to spend adapting your firewall to changes. Many sites find that they need to update their firewall only about once every few months. The rest of the time, it sits in the corner just humming along.

When Should You Start Over?

One of the most important things to recognize about maintaining a firewall is that the older it is, the more maintenance it's going to require. At some point, you simply need to say "enough" and start over with a new firewall. At the rate the firewall arena is changing today, we generally tell people that if they build the best firewall they can today, they should probably plan on replacing it in 18 to 36 months. Lots of things that affect firewalls are changing very fast, including the attacks they're subjected to, the tools for building them, and the services their users demand.

Here are a few examples of how quickly things can change on the Internet. Between the first and second editions of this book:

- Windows NT became a viable platform for providing Internet services.

- The World Wide Web went from being a promising application that computer people knew about to being the most important technology on the Internet and an indispensable part of any advertising campaign for anything.

- Linux went from being one person's eccentric hobby to being something between a major operating system and a social uprising.

In another two years, we're going to be facing a whole new series of attacks, have a whole new set of tools at our disposal, and be dealing with a whole new set of services demanded by our users. Nobody knows for sure what these attacks, tools, and services will be, but you can safely predict that the Internet will be significantly different from what it is today. Of course, that's true for just about any two-year period in the history of the Internet that you care to examine. The one constant about the Internet is constant change—constant growth, a constant stream of new services and new tools, and so on.

27

Responding to Security Incidents

The CERT Coordination Center (CERT-CC) reports that, despite increased awareness, the first time many organizations start thinking about how to handle a computer security incident is *after* an intrusion has occurred. Obviously, this isn't a great approach. You need a plan for how you're going to respond to a computer security incident at your site, and you need to develop that plan well before an incident occurs.

There isn't room here to detail everything you need to know to deal with a security incident: attacks are many and varied and change constantly; responding to them can involve a byzantine assortment of legal and technical issues. This chapter is intended to give you an outline of the issues involved and the practical steps you can take ahead of time to smooth the process. Appendix A, *Resources*, provides a list of resources that may provide additional help.

Responding to an Incident

This section discusses a number of steps you'll need to take when you respond to a security incident. You won't necessarily need to follow these steps in the order they're given, and not all of these steps are appropriate for all incidents. But, we recommend that you at least contemplate each of them when you find yourself dealing with an incident.

In the "Planning Your Response" section, later in this chapter, we'll look again at each of these steps and help you figure out how to work them into the overall response plan that you should develop before an incident actually occurs.

Rules for Incident Response

In their book *Practical UNIX & Internet Security*, Simson Garfinkel and Gene Spafford provide two excellent, overriding rules for incident response. Keep these rules in mind as you read this chapter and during any real-life incident response:

- Rule 1: Don't Panic!
- Rule 2: Document!

Evaluate the Situation

The first step in responding to a security incident is to decide what response, if any, needs to be made immediately. Ask these questions:

Has an attacker succeeded in getting into your systems?
> If so, you have a genuine emergency on your hands, whether or not the attacker is currently active.

Is the attack currently in progress?
> If so, you need to decide how you're going to react right now. If the attack isn't currently in progress, you may not be in such a hurry.

If the incident looks like an aggressive attack on your system, you probably want to take strong steps quickly. These steps might include shutting down the system or your Internet connection until you figure out how to deal with the situation.

On the other hand, if the incident is a less aggressive one—perhaps someone has just opened a Telnet connection to your machine and is trying various login/password pairs—then you may want to move more slowly. If you're reasonably confident that the attack won't succeed (e.g., you can see that the attacker is trying passwords that consist of all lowercase letters, and you know for certain that no account on the system has such a password), you might want to leave things alone and just watch for a while to see what the attacker does. This may give you an opportunity to trace the attack. (However, see the "Pursuing and Capturing the Intruder" section, later in this chapter, for a discussion of the issues involved in tracing an attack.)

Whatever you do, remember Rule 1: Don't panic!

Start Documenting

As soon as you determine that you actually have a problem that you need to respond to, start documenting what's going on. You don't need to get fancy at this point (you don't have time to, until you've taken the next step), but you should at least start a log by making a note of what time it is.

Disconnect or Shut Down, as Appropriate

Once you've evaluated the situation, your next priority is to give yourself the time to respond without risking your systems further. The least disruptive alternative is usually to disconnect the affected machine from all networks; this will shut down any active connections. Shutting down active connections may make it harder to trace the intruder, but it will allow the rest of the people at your site to continue to do their work, and it will leave the intruder's programs running. This may help you to identify who the intruder might be.

If you're afraid that other machines have been compromised or are vulnerable to the same attack, you'll probably want to disconnect as many machines as you can as a unit. This may mean taking down your connection to the Internet, if possible. If your Internet connection is managed elsewhere in your organization, you may need to detach just your portion of the network, but you'll also need to talk to other parts of your organization as soon as possible to let them know what's happening.

In some situations, you may want to shut down the compromised system. However, this action should be a last resort for a number of reasons:

- It destroys information you may need.

- You won't be able to analyze or fix the machine while it's down; you'll have to disconnect it from the network eventually anyway to bring it back up again.

- It's even more disruptive to legitimate users than removing the network connection.

- It protects only one machine at a time. (It's much easier to cleanly disconnect a set of systems than to cleanly shut them down.)

Even if you're responding to an incident that has already ended, you still might want to disconnect or shut down the system, or at least close it to users, while you analyze what happened and make any changes necessary to keep it from happening again. This will keep you from being confused by things users are doing, and it will prevent the intruder from returning before you're done.

Analyze and Respond

Your next priority is to start to fix what's gone wrong. The first step in actually correcting the problem is to relax, think for a while, and make sure you really understand what's happening and what you're dealing with. The last thing you want to do is make the situation worse by doing something rash and ill considered. Whatever corrective actions you're contemplating, think them through carefully. Will they really solve the problem? Will they, in turn, cause other problems?

When you're working in an unusual, high-stress situation like this, the chances increase of making a major error. Because you're probably going to be working with system privileges (for example, working as root on a Unix system), the consequences of an error could be serious.

There are several ways you can reduce the chances of making an error. One good way is to work with a partner; each of you can check the other's commands after they're typed but before they're executed. Even if you're working alone, many people find that reading commands aloud and checking the arguments in reverse order before executing them helps avoid mistakes. Resist the temptation to try to work fast. You will go home sooner if you work slowly and carefully.

Try not to let your users get in the way of your response. You may want to give someone the specific job of dealing with user inquiries so the rest of your response team can concentrate on responding to the incident.

Also, try to keep your responders from tripping over each other. Make it clear which system managers and investigators are working on which task, so they won't step on each other's toes (or wind up unintentionally chasing each other as part of the investigation!).

Make "Incident in Progress" Notifications

You're not the only person who needs to know what's going on. A number of other people—in a number of different places—have to be kept informed.

Your own organization

Within your own organization are people who need to know that something is happening: management, users, and staff. At the very least, let them know that you are busy responding to an incident and that you may not be available to them for other matters. They usually need to know why they're being inconvenienced and what they should do to speed recovery (even if the only thing they can do is to go away and leave you alone).

It is particularly important that management and other staff know what's going on. Otherwise, you risk having them act in opposition to you. For instance, if you've disconnected the Internet connection, the chances are high that somebody's going to notice the service outage and try to fix it. That's a problem if it's another staff member, but it can be a disaster if it turns into a management requirement.

If people call management to complain about some side effect of your response, and the manager they get has been briefed about what's going on, the chances are that the manager will defend your need to make a response. At worst, the manager will make a reasoned decision about the importance of incident response versus other needs of the company. However, if the manager doesn't know what's going, he or she will probably respond the same way the manager would to any other network outage: "Gee, that's terrible, we'll fix it as soon as possible." The manager has then promised the user something, and the chances are very small that the manager will go back on that promise. Instead, your response will be curtailed by the need to restore service as soon as possible.

Depending on the nature of your site and the incident in question, you may also need to inform your legal, audit, public relations, and security departments. You will always want to contact the security department if:

- You want to involve law enforcement agencies.

- You suspect an insider is involved.

- You suspect physical access is involved.

If multiple computer facilities are at your site, you'll need to inform the other facilities as soon as possible; they are likely sources and future targets for similar attacks.

CERT-CC or other incident response teams

If your organization is served by an incident response team such as CERT-CC, or has its own such team, let them know what's going on and try to enlist their aid. (For instructions on how to contact CERT-CC or another response team, see Appendix A, *Resources*.) What steps response teams can take to help you will depend on the charter and resources of the response team. Even if they can't help you directly, they can tell you whether the attack on your site looks as if it is part of a larger pattern of incidents. In that case, they may be able to coordinate your response with the responses of other sites.

Vendors and service providers

You might want to get in touch with your vendor support contacts or your Internet service provider(s) if you think they might be able to help or should be aware of the situation. For example, if the attackers appear to be exploiting an operating system bug, you should probably contact the vendor to see if they know about it and have a fix for it. At the very least, they'll be able to warn other sites about the bug. Similarly, your Internet provider is unlikely to be able to do much about your immediate problem, but they may be able to warn other customers. There is also a possibility that your Internet provider has itself been compromised, in which case, they need to know immediately. Your vendors and service provider may have special contacts or procedures for security incidents that will yield much faster results than going through normal support channels.

You may get little or no visible response when you make these reports. This might be because you're being ignored or because companies are putting self-defense before the interests of their customers. On the other hand, it's often due to sensible precautions that are intended to make certain that problems are not publicized before fixes are available (jeopardizing places not yet under attack), that the fixes that are made are appropriate to the problem, and that attackers don't get valuable information by pretending to be sites under attack. You might as well give your suppliers the benefit of the doubt, since it's almost impossible to tell which of these is going on.

Other sites

Finally, if the incident appears to involve other sites—that is, if the attack appears to be coming from a particular site, or if it looks as if the attackers have gone after that site after breaking into yours—you should inform those other sites. These sites are usually easy to identify as the sources or destinations of connections. It's often much harder to figure out how to find an actual human being with some responsibility for the computer in question, who is awake and reachable and has a common language with you.

Once again, you may get little or no apparent response for any number of different reasons, some of them annoying and reprehensible, and some of them perfectly sensible. The other site may not care whether their users are attacking you, or they may care desperately but have no way of telling you about it without revealing information to the attackers. While it's always nice to get somebody who makes an immediate, visibly effective response and thanks you promptly for the information, don't expect it and don't be upset when you don't get it.

If you don't know who to inform, talk to your response team (or CERT-CC). They will probably either know or know how to find out, and they have experience in calling strangers to tell them they have security problems.

Snapshot the System

Another early step to take is to make a "snapshot" of each compromised system. You might do so by doing a full backup to tape or by copying the whole system to another disk. In the latter case, if your site maintains its own spare parts inventory, you might consider using one of the spares for this purpose, instead of a disk that is already in use and might itself turn out to have been compromised.

The snapshot is important for several reasons:

- If you misdiagnose the problem or blow the recovery, you can always get back to the time of the snapshot.

- The snapshot may be vital for investigative and legal proceedings. It lets you get on with the work of recovering the system without fear of destroying evidence.

- You can examine the snapshot later, after you're back in operation, to determine what happened and why.

Because the snapshot may become important for legal proceedings, you need to secure the evidence trail. Here are some guidelines:[*]

- Uniquely identify (label) the snapshot media and put the date, time, your name, and your signature on it.

- Write-protect the media—permanently, if possible.

- Safeguard the media against tampering (for example, put it in a locked container) so that if and when you hand it over to law-enforcement or other authorities, you can tell them whose custody the media has been in and why you're certain it hasn't been tampered with since it was first created.

It's a good idea to set aside an adequate supply of fresh media just for snapshots because you never know when you're going to need to produce one. It's very frustrating to respond to an incident, and be ready to do the snapshot, only to discover that the last blank tape got used for backups the day before and the new order hasn't come in yet.

Restore and Recover

Finally, you're at the point of actually dealing with the incident. What do you do? It depends on the circumstances. Here are some possibilities:

- If the attacker didn't succeed in compromising your system, you may not need to do much. You may decide not to bother reacting to casual attempts. You may also find that your incident was actually something perfectly innocent, and you don't need to do anything at all.

- If the attack was a particularly determined one, you may want to increase your monitoring (at least temporarily), and you'll probably want to inform other people to watch out for future attempts.

---

[*] See *Computer Crime: A Crimefighter's Handbook,* by David Icove, Karl Seger, and William VonStorch (O'Reilly & Associates, 1995), for a detailed discussion of labeling and protecting evidence.

- If the attacker became an intruder (that is, he or she actually managed to get into your computers), you're going to need to at least plug the hole the intruder used, and check to make certain he hasn't damaged anything or left anything behind.

At worst, you may need to rebuild your system from scratch. Sometimes you end up doing this because the intruder damaged things, purposefully or accidentally. More often, you'll rebuild your system because it's the only way to ensure you have a clean system that hasn't been booby-trapped. Most intruders start by making sure they'll be able to get back into your system, even if you close their initial entry point. As a result, your systems may be compromised even if the intruder was present for only a short time.

 Always assume that intruders have created back doors into your system so that they can get back in again easily. It's one of the first things many intruders do when they break in to a system.

If you need to rebuild your system, first ensure that your hardware is working properly. You want to make sure it passes all relevant self-tests and diagnostics; you don't want to restore onto a flaky system. A reinstall may reveal previously unnoticed hardware problems. For instance, a disk may have bad spots that are in unused files. When you reinstall the operating system, you will attempt to write over the bad parts, and the problem will suddenly become apparent.

Next, make sure you are using trusted media and programs, not necessarily your last backup, to restore the system. Unless you are absolutely sure that you can accurately date the first time the intruder accessed your system, you don't know whether or not programs had already been modified at the time the backups happened. It's often best to rebuild your system from vendor distribution media (that is, the tapes or CD-ROM your operating system release came on) and then reload only user data (not programs that multiple users share) from your backup tapes.

If you need programs you didn't get from your vendor (for instance, packages from the Internet), then do one of the following:

- Rebuild and reinstall these programs from a trusted backup (one you're absolutely positive contains a clean copy).
- Obtain and install fresh copies from the site you got the packages from in the first place.

Do not recompile software until you've reinstalled the operating system, including the compiler; you don't know whether the compiler itself, and the libraries it depends on, have been compromised.

This implies that if you're heavily customizing your system or installing a lot of extra software beyond what your vendor gives you, you need to work out a way of archiving those customizations and packages that you're sure can't be tampered with by an attacker. This way, you can easily restore those customizations and packages if you need to. One good way is to make a special backup tape of new software immediately after it's installed and configured, before an attacker has a chance to modify it.

You may have programs that were locally written, and in these cases, you may not be able to find even source code that's guaranteed to be uncontaminated. In this situation, someone—preferably the original author—will need to look through the source code. People rarely bother to modify source code, and when they do, they aren't particularly subtle most of the time. That's because they don't need to be; almost nobody actually bothers to look at the source before recompiling it.

In one case, a programmer installed a back door into code he expected would run on only one machine, as a personal convenience. The program turned out to be fairly popular and was adopted in a number of different sites within his university. Years after he wrote it, and long after the original machine was running a version without the back door, he discovered that the back door was still present on all the other sites, despite the fact that it was clearly marked and commented and within the first page of code. You can't make a comprehensive search of a large program, but you can at least avoid humiliation by looking for obvious changes.

Document the Incident

Life gets very confusing when you're discovering, investigating, and recovering from a security incident. A good chain of communication is important in keeping people informed and preventing them from tripping over each other. Keeping a written (either hardcopy or electronic) record of your activities during the incident is also important. Such a record serves several purposes:

- It can help keep people informed (and thereby help them to resolve the incident more quickly).

- It tells you what you did and when, in responding, so that you can analyze your response later on (and maybe do better next time).

- It will be vital if you intend to pursue any legal action.

From a legal standpoint, the best records are hardcopy records generated and identified at the time of occurrence. Just about anything else (particularly anything kept online) could be tampered with or falsified fairly easily—or at least a judge and jury could be convinced of that. You need to produce records on pieces of paper, label, date, and sign them. Furthermore, unless the pages are actually bound together, so that pages can't be inserted or removed without indication, you'll need to date and sign every page. (And you thought continuous tractor-feed paper was useless these days!)

You need to have legal documentation even if you aren't completely certain you're going to need it. An incident that initially looks fairly simple may turn out to be serious. Don't assume it isn't going to be worth bringing in the police.

For both legal and practical reasons, it's useful to put in exact times when things occurred. Legally, this helps to show that entries were being made in order. Practically, it's extremely helpful when you need to correlate multiple sources of information (for instance, when you need to compare your logs against event logs on computers or against somebody else's actions).

Here are several useful documentation methods you might want to consider:

- Notebooks—carbon copy lab notebooks are especially useful because you can write a note, tear it out and give it to someone and still have a copy of the note. Another benefit is that the pages are usually numbered, so you can determine later on whether any pages have been removed or added.

- Terminals running with attached printers or old-fashioned printing terminals.

- A shell running under the Unix *script* command, with the resulting typescript immediately printed and identified.

- A personal computer terminal program running in "capture" mode, with the resulting typescript immediately printed and identified.

- A microcassette recorder for verbal notes.

You will probably want to use multiple methods, one to record what's happening online and one to record what's happening outside of the computer. For example, you might have a typescript of the commands you were typing, but a handwritten log for phone calls.

It's easy to decide what to record online; you simply record everything you do. Remember to use the terminal or session that's being recorded. (With some methods, like *script*, you can record every session you've got going; just make sure you record each session in a separate file.) It's harder to decide what to record of the events that don't just get automatically captured. You certainly want to record at least this much:

- Who you called, when, and why.

- A summary of what you told them.

- A summary of what they told you. (That summary may end up being "see above" some of the time, but you still want to be able to figure out who you were talking to, and when and why.)

- Meetings and important decisions and actions that aren't captured online (e.g., the time at which you disconnected the network).

In addition to the journal, a log of time spent for everyone working on an incident can be invaluable. You may need to justify some level of "loss" in order for some law enforcement agencies to be able to open an investigation, and if the intruder didn't do any damage to the machines, the time that was spent cleaning up is the main loss.

Time logs may also be useful if you are having difficulty in convincing management that the organization needs to allocate additional resources to be prepared to deal with incidents. It's a way of showing how much these incidents cost. It's particularly helpful if you can show which areas could have been anticipated and mitigated by planning.

What to Do After an Incident

There are a variety of things you'll need to take care of after you finish responding to an incident. Don't relax just yet.

First and foremost, you want to figure out what happened and how to keep it from happening again. Now is the time to examine the snapshot you made of your system before you started the recovery process. When you've figured out what happened, you obviously want to take steps to keep it from happening again. You also need to think about anything you or others did during the response (for example, enabling or disabling certain software) that now needs to be undone, fixed, or documented and made permanent.

In addition to analyzing the incident, this is the time to analyze your response to the incident. In this phase, it's important to concentrate on critiquing the response, not on assigning blame for the original incident. Don't be confrontational but talk to any folks involved with, or affected by, the response. With them, try to determine what you did right, what you did wrong, what worked and didn't work, what other tools or resources would have helped, how to respond better next time, and what you've all learned from the experience.

If you made "incident in progress" notifications to various people and organizations, now is probably the time to tell them that the incident is over. Be sure to follow up with appropriate information about what happened, how you responded, and how you plan to keep it from happening again.

Pursuing and Capturing the Intruder

If you discover a security incident—particularly one in progress—you're going to be tempted to go gunning for the bad guys who are invading your system.

Going after the bad guys has a certain emotional appeal, but it's generally not very practical. There are a variety of approaches you can take, but there are also a variety of technical and legal hurdles.

For an appreciation of the problems involved in hunting down an intruder, see Cliff Stoll's book, *The Cuckoo's Egg* (Doubleday, 1989). In the late 1980s, Cliff was a system manager at Lawrence Berkeley Labs. While tracking down a minor inconsistency in the accounting system LBL used for computer time billing, he discovered evidence that an intruder had broken in over the Internet. He spent many months on an odyssey trying to chase down the attackers. Although Cliff succeeded admirably (and wrote an entertaining and useful book to boot), few of us are going to be able to emulate his feats. Most sites just don't have the time and resources to track their attackers the way Cliff did; most are going to have to be satisfied with simply getting them off their systems.

Tracking down intruders for legal action is always a long and involved process. Having it take months is actually unusually fast! In general, the process of prosecuting an intruder, or group of intruders, takes a year or more. Be prepared for a long and frustrating process. It can be extremely educational—you may learn more about the legal system and the phone system than you really wanted to know. It also can be a complete let-down; you call three law-enforcement agencies, two of which can't figure out how to do anything about a computer break-in, and the third of which says something noncommittal and takes down contact information. This might mean, as you will probably suspect, that they don't care and are going to ignore you, or it might mean that they are already nine months into an investigation of this intruder with the help of other sites and don't want to give you any information that might somehow get back to the intruder. You might find out when they call back and ask you to testify or to estimate damages. You might find out in the newspaper. It is worth doing your best to report these incidents anyway, but don't expect much from the experience.

There are two main problems in tracking down intruders: one is technical and the other is legal. The first problem is that tracking an attack back to its ultimate source is usually technically difficult. It's usually easy to tell what site an attack came from (simply by looking at the IP addresses the attacker's packets are coming from), but once you find the apparent source of the attack, you usually find out that the attack isn't really being carried out by a user from that site. Instead, it's very likely that the site has itself been broken into, and it's being used as a base by the person who attacked you.

If that site traces its own break-in, it will usually discover the same thing: the attacker isn't wherever the attacks appear to be coming from. Moreover, where the attacks appear to be coming from is simply another site in the chain that's been broken into. Each link in the chain between the attacker and you involves more sites and more people. There is a practical limit to how far back you can trace someone in a reasonable period of time. Eventually, you're probably going to run into a site in the chain that you can't get in touch with, or that doesn't have the time or expertise to pursue the matter, or that simply doesn't care about the attack or about you. As Figure 27-1 illustrates, these are many links in any network connection.

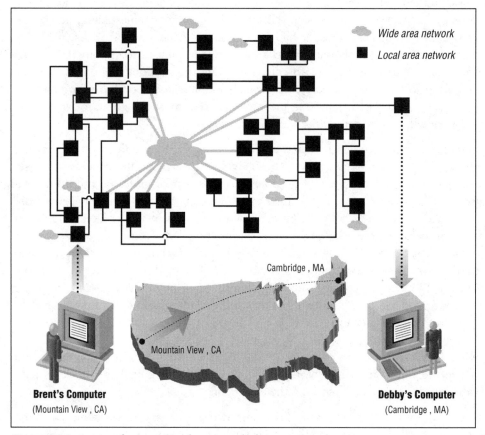

Figure 27-1. A network connection has many links

Furthermore, at some link in the chain, you are likely to discover that the attacker is coming in over a telephone line, and tracing telephone calls involves whole new realms of technical and legal problems.

You may well find the same attacker coming in from multiple sites. In one incident, responders kept correcting each other, until they realized that nobody was confused; one set of people was referring to SFU (Simon Fraser University, in Canada) and the other to FSU (Florida State University). The similarity of the abbreviations had momentarily concealed the fact that two separate sites, physically distant from each other, were being concurrently used by the same attacker. The attacker had not started from either of them, and when SFU and FSU closed down access, identical attacks starting occurring from other sites.

Be wary when using email or voicemail to contact administrators at other sites when tracking down an intruder. How do you know it's really the administrator that's receiving and responding to your messages and not the intruder? Even if you're sure that you're talking to the administrator of a site, maybe the intruder *is* the administrator.

The second problem is legal. You might contemplate leaving your site "open", even after you're aware of the attack, in hopes of tracking down the attackers while they're using your site. This may seem like a clever idea; after all, if you shut down your system or disconnect it from the Internet, the attackers will know they've been discovered, and it will be much harder for you to track them down.

The problem is this: leaving your site open doesn't just risk further loss or damage at your own site. What the attacker is probably doing at your site is using it as a base to attack other sites. If you're aware of it, and do nothing to prevent it, those other sites might have grounds to sue you and your organization for negligence or for aiding the attacker.

If you're dealing with someone who's attacking your system unsuccessfully, there's less risk. It's polite to inform the site that the attacker is apparently coming from, so the system administrators there can do their own checking. It also lets you straighten out people who aren't really trying to break in, but are just very confused. For example, attempts to log in as "anonymous", even extremely persistent ones, usually come from people who have confused FTP with Telnet and simply need better advice. Most sites are grateful to be told that attacks are coming from them, but don't be surprised if universities seem somewhat bored to hear the news. Although they will usually follow up, large universities see these incidents all the time.

You'll also find that the occasional site is uninterested, hostile, or incapable of figuring out what you're talking about, and it's not worth your time to worry about it unless the attacks from the site are persistent, determined, and technically competent enough to have a chance of succeeding. In this case, you should enlist the assistance of a response team.

Planning Your Response

All of the actions we've outlined in the previous sections sound fine in theory, but you can't actually do any of them reliably without an incident response plan. You may personally be able to mount a sensible response to an attack, but you aren't necessarily going to be the person who discovers one. You may not even be available at the time. How will your organization react if someone attacks your system? Unless you have an incident response plan in place, the people involved will waste valuable time trying to figure out what to do first.

If you already have a plan in place for disaster or emergency response of any kind (e.g., fire, earthquake, electrical problems), you're probably not going to have to change it significantly to meet your security needs. If you don't have such a plan already, you can probably use your security incident response plan with only minor modifications for most emergencies.

Your incident response plan need not be an elaborate document, but you need to have *something*, even if it's only an email message that records and confirms the details you've all worked out over lunch at the local sushi bar. You'll be better off than many sites even if you do nothing more than think about the issues and discuss them with the relevant people.

What's in your plan?

The response plan is primarily concerned with two issues: authority and communication. For each part of the incident response, the plan should say who's in charge and who they're supposed to talk to. Although you'll specify a few steps people will take, incidents vary so much that the response plan mostly specifies who's going to make decisions, and who they're going to contact after they've decided— not what they're going to decide. This section summarizes the different parts of a response plan.

Planning for Detection

An incident starts when somebody detects an intruder or attacker. That person might be a system administrator, but more often it's someone with no official responsibility. If you've properly educated the people who use your computers, they know they're supposed to report weird events. Somebody then needs to sort run-of-the-mill peculiarities from a security incident in progress. Who are the users going to report to? Who are those people going to report to if they're still not sure? What are they authorized to do if they are sure?

The two cases you really want to plan for are these:

- Somebody notices a real security incident in progress at 3 A.M.

- Somebody notices one of your perfectly legitimate users who happens to be doing vital work from halfway across the globe at 3 A.M. local time. (In Australia, where the user is consulting at the moment, it's a reasonable 5 P.M.)

In the first case, you need a procedure that is going to reliably start a full incident response immediately. Don't waste any time. It's going to be embarrassing and expensive if you don't actually get around to doing anything until your senior security person arrives in the next morning, takes in enough caffeine to become able to think, and gets around to looking at some report. (And that's if there is a report in the first place; without a response plan, it may be weeks before anyone actually tells someone who can begin to do something about the situation.)

In the second case, it's going to be embarrassing and expensive if you disconnect the network and get five people out of bed, all to prevent somebody from doing the work they're paid to do.

Either way, it's not a decision you probably want made by a night operator, or by a user acting alone because he or she can't figure out how to call somebody who knows how to tell a real incident from a false alarm.

At a small site, you might want to simply post a number that users can call to get help outside of office hours (for instance, a pager number). Users might be encouraged to shut down personal machines if they suspect an attack and know how to shut the machine down gracefully. You want to be very cautious about this, however, because an ungraceful shutdown, particularly of a multi-user machine, may be more damaging than an intruder.

At a larger site, one that has on-site support after hours, you should instruct the on-site support people to call a senior person if they see a possible security incident. They should be told explicitly not to do anything more than that unless circumstances are extreme, but to keep trying to contact senior personnel until they get somebody who can take a look at what's going on.

Planning for Evaluation of the Incident

Who's going to decide that you don't just have a suspicious situation—you actually have a security problem? You need to designate one specific person who will have responsibility for making the important decisions. It's tempting to pick one specific person in advance and put his or her name in your plan. But, what if that person isn't available in the event of an actual incident? Who, then, will have the responsibility?

Teamwork is great, but emergencies call for leadership. You don't want to have everybody doing their own thing and nobody in charge, and you certainly can't afford to stand around arguing about it. If your senior technical person is absent, do you want someone less senior but more technical to do the evaluation, or do you want someone more senior but less technical? How much time are you going to spend searching for the senior technical person when you have an emergency to deal with, before proceeding to your next candidate for the hot seat?

At a small site, you may not have a lot of options; if only one person has the skills necessary to do something about an attack, your policy will simply list that person as the one in charge in case of a security incident. If that person is unavailable, authority should go to somebody levelheaded and calm who can take stopgap actions and arrange for assistance (for example, from a relevant response team). In this situation, technical skills would be nice, but resourcefulness and calm are more important.

At a larger site, probably more than one person could be in charge. Your plan may want to say that the most senior will be in charge by default or that whoever is specified as being on call will be in charge. Either way, the plan should state that if the default person in charge is unavailable, the first of the other possible people to respond is in charge. Specifying what order they're going to be contacted in is probably overkill; let whoever is trying to reach these people use his or her knowledge of the situation. If none of those people are available, you'll usually want to work up the organizational hierarchy rather than down. (A manager, particularly a technical one, is probably better equipped to cope than an operator.)

In a small organization, you will pick your fallback candidates by name. In a large one, you will usually specify fallbacks by job title. If job title is your criterion, it's important to base your decision on the characteristics of the job, not of the person currently in it. Don't write into your plan that the janitor should decide, on the theory that the current janitor also is the most sensible and technical of those who aren't system administrators. The next janitor might be an airhead with a mop.

Planning for Disconnecting or Shutting Down Machines

Your response plan needs to specify what kind of situation warrants disconnecting or shutting down, and who can make the decision to do it. Most importantly, as we've discussed in "Pursuing and Capturing the Intruder", are you ever willing to allow a known intruder to remain connected to your systems? If you're not, are you going to take down the system, or are you going to disconnect from the network altogether?

If you are at a site with multiple computer facilities, do you want to take the entire site off the Internet if one facility has been compromised, or is it better (or even possible) to take just that facility off the Internet?

At most sites, the reasonable plan is to disconnect the site as a whole from the network as soon as you know for sure that you have an intruder connected to your systems. You may have a myriad of internal connections, with a triply redundant, diversely cabled, UPS-protected routing mesh, which can make "disconnecting" a daunting prospect (the system keeps "fixing" itself). On the other hand, you probably have only one (or a small handful) of connections to the outside world, which can be more easily severed.

Your plan needs to say how to disconnect the network, and how the machines should be shut down. Be very careful about this. You do not want to tell people to respond to a mildly suspicious act by hitting the circuit breakers and powering off every machine in the machine room. On the other hand, if an intruder is currently removing all the files on the machine, you don't want them to give that intruder a 15-minute warning for a graceful shutdown.

This is one case in which you need clear, security-specific instructions in your plan. Here's what we recommend you do:

- In most security emergencies, the correct way to shut down the machine is to do an immediate but graceful shutdown, with no explanations or warnings sent. Your plan should state that and specify the appropriate commands to issue.

- If the intruder is actively destroying things, you want people to shut the machine down by the fastest method possible. If they are physically near the machine, cutting off the power to the machine or the disk drive is completely appropriate, despite the damage it may cause. This implies that the relevant power switches must be easy to locate; a master switch for each machine is a good idea.

Whoever is going to disconnect the network needs to know how to do that. The safest and easiest way often is to unplug cables and clean up the side effects afterwards. With networks, this tends to result in voluminous error messages but to cause no actual damage. You do have to unplug the *relevant* cables, however, and the voluminous error messages may make it difficult to determine whether or not the cables that were unplugged were actually the correct ones. Your plan needs to tell people what to unplug and how to make things functional afterwards.

Planning for Notification of People Who Need to Know

Your incident response plan needs to specify who you're going to notify, who's going to do the notification, when they're going to do it, and what method they're going to use. As we described earlier in this chapter, you may need to notify:

- People within your own organization

- CERT-CC or other incident response teams

- Vendors and service providers

- People at other sites

Your own organization

To start with, you need to notify the people who are going to be involved in the response. You'll have an urgent need to get hold of them, so you need telephone and pager numbers. Be sure you have all the relevant phone numbers; in addition to home and work numbers, check to see if people have mobile phones at which they might be reached. This list includes anybody who manages computers within your site and anybody who manages those people, plus anybody else who might be needed to provide resources (to sign off on emergency purchases or to unlock doors, for example). Ideally, the list—or at least the key portions of it—should be reduced down so it's small enough to carry easily (for example, it might be laser-printed onto business card–sized stock). Obviously, the list isn't much use unless it's kept up to date.

If many people must be notified, you may wish to use a phone tree or an alert tree. In such a tree, shown in Figure 27-2, each person notifies two or three other people; it is a geometric progression, so a large number of people can be rapidly notified with relatively little work to any one person. Everybody should have a copy of the entire tree, so that if people are unavailable, their calls can be taken over by someone else (usually the person above them on the tree). It's best to set it up so that as many calls as possible are toll-free, and so that people are notifying other people they know relatively well (which increases their chances of knowing how to get through). There's no need for an alert tree to reflect an organizational chart or a chain of command.

Next, you're going to notify other people within your organization who need to know, starting with the users of your computer facility. For that, you'll use whatever your organization normally uses for relatively urgent notifications to everybody, whether that's memos or electronic mail. Your plan should specify how to do it (system administrators rarely send memos to all personnel and may not know how).

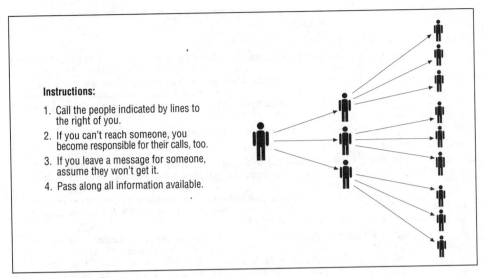

Figure 27-2. An alert tree

Your plan should also show a sample notification message for the users of your systems, which can sometimes be tricky. Your message needs to contain enough information so that legitimate users understand what's happening. They need to know:

- What has been taken out of service

- Why you're making their lives miserable

- Exactly which things that they normally do aren't going to work

- When service will be restored

- What they're supposed to do (including leave you alone so that you can concentrate on the response)

- That you realize you're making life unpleasant for them

- That you're doing everything possible to improve matters

- That you're going to tell them the details later

Things that are obvious to you may not be obvious to your users (e.g., they might not even understand why it's so bad to have an intruder). Writing an appropriate message (see Figure 27-3) is not easy, particularly if you're busy and tired.

For the remaining people within your organization—people from other computer facilities, legal, audit, public relations, or security—the plan needs to specify who gets notified. Do you need to call the legal department? If so, who should you talk to? Who are the administrators for other sites within your organization? During the Morris worm incident in 1988, at least one large government lab was reduced to

```
From: Anastasia Administrator

To: All Users of the Big and Cool Computer Facility

Because of a security incident in progress, The Big and Cool computer facility
is not currently connected to the Internet, and the machines big and cool
are not available for use. This means that you will not be able to send mail
offsite, FTP files, use Netscape to external hosts, or read news, until the
situation has been resolved. In addition, the following services are provided
from big and cool, and won't work:

Database access (including the coolness forecasting reports)

Mail service for personal computers

We appreciate that this represents a major inconvenience, and will prevent
people from getting work done. We took these steps because we had reason
to believe that there was imminent risk that confidential data would be
destroyed or released to the outside world. We are working to restore service
as fast as possible. Big and cool should be available by 10 A.M.; we expect
to restore Internet connectivity by noon.

You can assist us by reporting any anomalies, but otherwise contacting system
staff for emergencies only until service has been restored. At that time
we'll be glad to discuss the incident with everybody. Right now, the entire
staff is occupied in working on restoring service as fast as is safe.
```

Figure 27-3. A notification message

having the guards hand out flyers at the gate to people as they came to work, asking "Are you a system administrator?" because they had no idea who all the system administrators were, much less how to contact them.

Think about *how* you are going to send your message. If you send it via electronic mail, remember that the intruder may see it. Even if you know that your own systems are clean, don't assume that other people's are. Don't say anything in your message that you don't want the attacker to know. Even better yet, use a telephone.

Some sites use a simple code phrase to announce a system attack that they can include in electronic mail. This can rapidly degenerate into bad spy fiction, but if you have an agreed-upon phrase that isn't going to alert an intruder (and isn't going to cause people who don't know it or don't remember it to give the game away by asking what on earth you're talking about), it can be effective. Something like "We're having a pizza party; call 3-4357 to RSVP" should serve the purpose.

Should you contact your organization's security department? At some organizations, the security department is responsible only for physical security. You'll want to have a contact number for them in case you need doors unlocked, for example, but they are unlikely to be trained in helping with an emergency of this kind, so you probably won't need to notify them routinely of every computer security incident. However, if a group within your organization is responsible for computer security, you are probably required to notify that group. Find out ahead of time when the members of the group want to be notified and how, and put that information in the plan. Even if that group cannot help you respond to your particular type of incident (perhaps because they may be personal computer specialists or government security specialists), it's advisable to at least brief them on the incident after you have finished responding to it.

CERT-CC and other incident response teams

Your plan should also specify what emergency response team, if any, you're served by and how to contact them. CERT-CC and many teams in the FIRST have 24-hour numbers, and they prefer to be called immediately if a security incident occurs.

Vendors and service providers

Your plan should also contain the contact numbers for your vendors and Internet service providers. These people probably do not need to be called immediately, unless you need their help. However, if you have any reason to suspect that your Internet provider itself has been compromised, you should contact them immediately.

Many vendors and service providers have special contact procedures for security incidents. Using these procedures will yield much faster results than going through normal support channels. Be sure to research these procedures ahead of time and include the necessary information in your response plan.

Other sites

You will not ordinarily need to talk to other sites as part of the immediate incident response. Instead, you'll call them after the immediate emergency is over, when you have time to work without needing everything written down in the plan. In addition, no plan could cover all the information needed to find out what other sites were involved and to contact them. Therefore, your plan doesn't need to say much about informing other sites.

If you are providing Internet service for other sites, however, or have special network connections to other sites, you should have contact information in the plan and should contact them promptly. They need to know what happened to their service and to check that the attacker didn't reach them through your site.

Planning for Snapshots

Your incident response plan should specify how you're going to do snapshots of the compromised system. Make sure that your plan contains the answers to these questions:

- Where are the necessary supplies and what program are you going to use?

- How should the snapshot be labeled and where should it be stored?

- How should snapshots be preserved against tampering, for possible later use in legal proceedings?

Planning for Restoration and Recovery

Different incidents are going to require different amounts of recovery. Your response plan should provide some general guidelines.

Reinstalling an operating system from scratch is time consuming, unpleasant, and often exposes underlying problems. For example, you may discover that you no longer know where some of your programs came from. For this reason, people are extremely reluctant to do it. Unless your incident response plan says explicitly that they need to reinstall the operating system, they probably won't. The problem is, this leads to situations where you have to get rid of the same intruder over and over again because the system hasn't been properly cleaned up. Your response plan should specify what's acceptable proof that the operating system hasn't been tampered with (for instance, a comparison against cryptographic checksums of an operating system known to be uncompromised). If you don't have those tools, which are discussed in Chapter 10, *Bastion Hosts*, or if you can't pass the inspection, then you must install a clean operating system, and the plan should say so.

The plan should also provide the information needed to reinstall the operating system; for example:

- Where are the distribution media kept?

- How do you find out how to install the operating system?

- Where are the backups, and how do you restore from them?

- Where are the records that will let you reconstruct third-party or locally written programs?

Planning for Documentation

Your plan should include the basic instructions on what documentation methods you intend to use and where to find the supplies. If you might pursue legal action, your plan should also include the instructions on dating, labeling, signing, and protecting the documentation. Remember that you aren't likely to know when you start out whether or not there will be legal action, so you will always need to document if you ever want to be able to take legal steps; this is not something you can go back and "fix" later on.

Periodic Review of Plans

However solid your security incident response plans may seem to be, make sure to review them periodically. Changes—in requirements, priorities, personnel, systems, data, and other resources—are inevitable, and you need to be sure that your response plans keep up with these changes. The right question to ask about each item isn't "Has it changed?," but *"How* has it changed?"

A good time to review your incident response plan is after a live drill, which may have exposed weaknesses or problems in the plan. (See the "Doing Drills" section at the end of this chapter.) For example, a live drill may uncover any of the following:

- That you've changed all your storage since the plan was written
- That you can't actually restore your operating system from scratch
- That your plan relies on the ability to use the network to reach external sites, but at the same time instructs you to disconnect the network

Being Prepared

The incident response plan is not the only thing that you need to have ready in advance. You need to set up a number of practices and procedures so that you'll be able to respond quickly and effectively when an incident occurs. Most of these procedures are general good practice; some of them are aimed at letting you recover from any kind of disaster; and a few are specific to security incidents.

Backing Up Your Filesystems

Your filesystem backups are probably the single most important part of your recovery plan. Before you do anything else (including writing your response plan), make sure that your site's backup plan is a solid one and that it works. Don't assume that it's OK just because you haven't had a problem yet. It is entirely possible to go for months without noticing that you have no backups at all, and it may take you years to notice that they're only partially broken. Unfortunately, when you do notice, it's often when you need the backups most, and the outcome is likely to be disastrous.

Backups are vital for two reasons:

- If your site suffers serious damage and you have to restore your systems from scratch, you will need these backups.
- If you aren't sure of the extent of the damage, backups will help you to determine what changes were made to a system and when.

Every organization needs a backup plan and not just for security reasons. If you don't have one, that's probably a sign that your current backup system is *not* OK. When you are doing incident response planning, however, pay special attention to your backup plan.

For your security-critical systems (e.g., bastion hosts and servers), you might want to consider keeping your monthly or weekly backups indefinitely, rather than recycling them as you would your regular systems. If an incident does occur, you can use this archive of backup tapes to recover a "snapshot" of the system as of any of the dates of the backups. Snapshots of this kind can be helpful in investigating security incidents. For example, if you find that a program has been modified, going back through the snapshots will tell you approximately when the modification took place. That may tell you when the break-in occurred; if the modification happened before the break-in, it may tell you that it was an accident and not part of the incident at all.

If you're not sure whether or not you should be worried, try testing your backup system. Play around and see what you can restore. Ask these questions:

- Can you restore files from all of your tapes?

- Can you do a restore of an entire filesystem?

- If you pick a specific file, can you figure out how to restore it?

- If you have a corrupt file and want a version from before it was corrupted, can you do that?

- If all of your disks died (or were trashed by an attacker) simultaneously, would you be able to rebuild your computer facility?

Even the best backup system won't work if the backup images aren't safeguarded. Don't rely on online backups and keep your media in a secure place separate from the data they're backing up.

 The design of backup systems is outside the scope of this book. This description, along with the description in Chapter 26, *Maintaining Firewalls*, provides only a summary. If you're uncertain about your backup system, you'll want to look at a general system administration reference. See Appendix A for complete information on additional resources.

Labeling and Diagramming Your System

As organizations grow, they acquire hardware; they configure networking in different ways; and they add or change equipment of various kinds. Usually only one or two people really know what a site's systems look like in any detail.

Information about system configuration may be crucial to investigating and controlling a security incident. While you may know exactly how everything works and fits together at your site, you may not be the person who has to respond to the incident. What if you're on vacation? Think about what your managers or coworkers would need to know about each system in order to respond effectively to an incident involving that system.

Labels and diagrams are crucial in an emergency. System labels should indicate what a system is, what it does, what its physical configuration is (how much disk space, how much memory, etc.), and who is responsible for it. They should be attached firmly to the correct systems and easily legible. Use large type sizes and put at least minimal labels on the back as well as the front (the front of a machine may have more flat space, but you're probably going to be looking at it from behind when you're trying to work on it). Network diagrams should show how the various systems are connected, both physically and logically, as well as things like what kind of packet filtering is done where.

Be sure that labels are kept up to date as you move systems around; wrong labels are worse than no labels at all. It's particularly important to label racked equipment and equipment with widely scattered pieces. There's nothing more frustrating than turning off all the equipment in a rack, only to discover that some of it was actually part of the computer in the next rack over, which you meant to leave running.

Information that's easily available when machines are working normally may be impossible to find if machines are not working. For example, you'll need disk partition tables written down in order to reformat and reinstall disks, and you may need a printed copy of the host table in order to configure machines as they're brought back up.

Keeping Secured Checksums

Once you've had a break-in, you need to know what's been changed on your systems. The standard tools that come with your operating system won't tell you; intruders can fake modification dates and match the trivial checksums most operating systems provide. You will need to install a cryptographic checksumming program (these are discussed in Chapter 10, *Bastion Hosts*), make checksums of important files, and store them where an intruder can't modify them (which generally means somewhere offline). You may not need to checksum every system separately if they're all running the same release of the same operating system, although you should make sure that the checksum program is available on all your systems.

Keeping Activity Logs

An activity log is a record of any changes that have been made to a system, both before an incident and during the response to an incident. Normally, you'll use an activity log to list programs you've installed, configuration files you've modified, or peripherals you've added. During an incident, you'll be doing a lot more logging.

What is the purpose of an activity log? A log allows you to redo the changes if you have to rebuild the system. It also lets you determine whether any of the changes affect the incident or the response. Without a log, you may find mystery programs; you don't know where they came from and what they were supposed to do, so you can't tell whether or not the intruder installed them, if they still work the way they're supposed to, or how to rebuild them. Figure 27-4 shows a sampling of routine log entries and incident log entries.

There are a variety of easy ways to keep activity logs, both electronic and manual; email, notebooks, and tape recorders can also be used. Some are better for routine logs (those that record your activities *before* an incident occurs). Others may be more appropriate for incident logs (those that keep track of your activities *during* an incident).

Email to an appropriate staff alias that also keeps a record of all messages is probably the simplest approach to keeping an activity log. Not only will email keep a permanent record of system changes, but it has the side benefit of letting everybody else know what's going on as the changes are made. The email approach is good for routine logs, whereas manual methods are likely to work more reliably during an incident. During an actual security incident, your email system may be down, so any messages generated during the response may be lost. You may also be unable to reach existing online logs during an incident, so keep a printed copy of these email messages up to date in a binder somewhere.

Notebooks make a good incident log, but people must be disciplined enough to use them. For routine logs, notebooks may not be convenient because they may not be physically accessible when people actually make changes to the system. Some sites use a combination of electronic and paper logs for routine logs, with a paper logbook kept in the machine room for notes. This works as long as it's clear which things should be logged where; having two sets of logs to keep track of can be confusing.

Pocket tape recorders make good incident logs, although they require that somebody transcribe them later on. They're not reasonable for routine logging.

Routine Entries

Date 1/12/95
From: Bartholomew

Installed gnutar in /usr/local/bin; source is in /usr/source/local.

Date 4/8/95
From: Clementine

Modified /etc/fstab to mount /dev/dsk/c0d1s3 on /scratch.

Incident Entries

Date: 4/15/95 10:37 pm
From: Desmond

Noticed unusual login activity from a machine at Whatsamatta University.

Initiated planned incident response; attempted to contact Bartholomew to evaluate situation, but he was unavailable, so contacted Clementine instead.

Clementine said she'd log in from home and check things out, and would take responsibility for any further response.

Date: 4/15/95 10:41 pm
From: Clementine

Logged in from home to investigate report from Desmond. Crackers working from Whatsamatta University seem to have broken into machine "big"; not sure how yet, or how far they've gotten.

Called Desmond to tell him to shut down network connection per response plan, and to start contacting other members of response team, also per plan, while I drive in to work.

Date: 4/15/95 10:52 pm
From: Desmond

Disconnected from external net per response plan, on instructions from Clementine.

Date: 4/15/95 11:33 pm
From: Clementine

Arrived on site. Verified network disconnection and that other response team members had been notified and were on their way. Made incident in progress modifications to VP of Engineering and CERT, per plan.

Beginning to analyze how attackers got in and what they've done.

Figure 27-4. Activity logs

Keeping a Cache of Tools and Supplies

Well before a security incident, collect the tools and supplies that you are likely to need during that incident. You don't want to be running around, begging and borrowing, when the clock is ticking.

Here are some of the things you'll need in order to respond appropriately to an incident. (Actually, you ought to have these things around at all times; they come in handy in all sorts of disasters.)

- Blank backup tapes and possibly spare disks as well.

- Basic tools; you'll need them if you disconnect your system from the external network, or if you need to rewire the internal network to disconnect compromised hosts. Make sure you have a ladder if your site uses in-ceiling cabling or tall equipment racks.

- Spare networking equipment—at least cables.

Set aside basic supplies (e.g., a full backup's worth of media, networking cables, the most critical tools, notebooks or tape recorders for incident logs) in a cache to be used only in case of disaster. This cache should be separate from your normal stock of spare parts and tools.

Testing the Reload of the Operating System

If a serious security incident occurs, you may need to restore your system from backups. In this case, you will need to load a minimal operating system before you can load the backups. Are you equipped to do this?

Make sure that you:

- Understand your system's operating system installation procedures
- Understand the procedures for restoring from backups
- Have all the materials (distribution media, manuals, etc.) available to restore the system
- Test your reload plans and procedures before you really need them

Testing your ability to reload the operating system is a good idea, and too few organizations ever do it. You can learn a lot by doing this. While you're trying to reload a dead system is not a good time to discover that you've got a bad copy of the distribution media. It's also not a good time to discover that the people who have to do the reload can't figure out how to do it. The best way to test is to designate the least experienced people who might have to do the work, and let them try out the reload well ahead of time.

Most organizations find that the first time they try to reinstall the operating system and restore on a completely blank disk, the operation fails. This can happen for a number of reasons, although the usual reason is a failure in the design of the backup system. One site found that people were doing their backups with a program that wasn't distributed with the operating system, so they couldn't restore from a fresh operating system installation. (After that, they made a tape of the restore program using the standard operating system tools; they could then load the standard operating system, recover their custom restore program, and reload their data from backups.)

Doing Drills

Don't assume that responding to a security incident will come naturally. Like everything else, such a response benefits from practice. Test your own organization's ability to respond to an incident by running occasional drills.

There are two basic types of drills:

- In a paper (or "tabletop") drill, you gather all the relevant people in a conference room (or over pizza at your local hangout), outline a hypothetical problem, and work through the consequences and recovery procedures. It's important to go through all the details, step by step, to expose any missing pieces or misunderstandings.

- In a live drill, you actually carry out a response and recovery procedure. A live drill can be performed, with appropriate notice to users, during scheduled system downtimes.

You might also test only parts of your response. For example, before configuring a new machine, use it to test your recovery procedures by recovering an existing machine onto it. If you have down time scheduled for your facility, you may be able to use it to test what happens when you disconnect from the network. Run your checksum comparison program before and after you install changes to the operating system to see what changes it catches when you think everything's the same, and what it does about the things you know have changed. Coordinate with another site to see what messages are logged when various types of attacks occur (pick someone you know and trust and who'll reliably tell you exactly what they did, or do it yourself). Try taking down all of your central machines at the same time and see whether they'll all come back up in this situation. (Do this when you have a few hours to spare; if it doesn't work, it often takes a while to figure out how to coax the machines past their interdependencies.)

This is all a lot of trouble, but a certain amount of perverse amusement can be had by playing around with fictitious disasters, and it's much less stressful than having to improvise in a real disaster.

V

Appendixes

This part of the book consists of three appendixes: a list of places you can go for further information and help with Internet security; a list of the firewall tools we have referred to and how to get them; and background information on cryptography.

Resources

This book can't hope to tell you everything you need to know about firewalls and the broader issues of network and Internet security. In this appendix, we have pulled together references to what we think are the most useful additional resources. These include both electronic and offline resources: web pages, FTP sites, mailing lists, newsgroups, emergency response teams, other types of organizations, papers, conferences, and books. This list is not exhaustive. Because there are so many resources, and because technologies and publications change so rapidly, there is no way we can keep completely up to date. However, this list should point you in some useful directions.

Web Pages

You'll find these web pages particularly informative.

Telstra

http://www.telstra.com.au/info/security.html

This outstanding web page is maintained by Telstra Corporation (formerly known as Telecom Australia). It is very useful as a jumping-off point to other web pages and Internet resources related to network security.

CERIAS

http://www.cerias.purdue.edu/

CERIAS is the Center for Education and Research in Information Assurance and Security. CERIAS describes itself this way:

The Center for Education and Research in Information Assurance and Security, or CERIAS, is the world's foremost University center for multidisciplinary research and education in areas of information security. Our areas of research include computer, network, and communications security as well as information assurance.

CERIAS provides an excellent collection of security resources. CERIAS has taken over many of the research efforts formerly handled at Purdue by COAST. The COAST FTP archive is still available directly from the CERIAS home page.

The Linux Documentation Project

http://www.linuxdoc.org/

The Linux Documentation Project is an attempt to pull together all the documentation you could ever need for Linux. They describe themselves this way:

> The Linux Documentation Project is working on developing free, high quality documentation for the GNU/Linux operating system. The overall goal of the LDP is to collaborate in all of the issues of Linux documentation. This includes the creation of "HOWTOs and Guides". We hope to establish a system of documentation for Linux that will be easy to use and search. This includes the integration of the manual pages, info docs, HOWTOs, and other documents.

The Linux Router Project

http://www.linuxrouter.org

The Linux Router Project is a specialized version of Linux for networking. The web page describes it this way:

> A networking-centric micro-distribution of Linux. LRP is small enough to fit on a single 1.44MB floppy disk, and makes building and maintaining routers, access servers, thin servers, thin clients, network appliances, and typically embedded systems next to trivial.

FTP Sites

These two sites are an excellent source of tools, papers, security patches, and other Internet security resources.

cerias.purdue.edu

ftp://cerias.purdue.edu/

This archive is maintained by the CERIAS computer and network security laboratory at Purdue University (see the earlier description under the CERIAS web page) under the direction of Gene Spafford. It contains a large collection of software and papers, collected from all over the world, related to Unix and network security.

info.cert.org

ftp://info.cert.org/

This site contains all of the Computer Emergency Response Team Coordination Center (CERT-CC) past advisories (see the discussion of CERT-CC under "Organizations", later in this appendix), as well as a small collection of tools and papers.

Mailing Lists

It's hard to stay up to date because technologies and approaches for firewalls and other Internet security mechanisms change so rapidly. You'll find these mailing lists helpful in keeping informed.

Firewalls

The Firewalls mailing list, which is hosted by GNAC, is the primary forum for folks on the Internet who want to discuss the design, construction, operation, maintenance, and philosophy of Internet firewall security systems. Send a message to *majordomo@lists.gnac.net* with "subscribe firewalls" in the body of the message to subscribe to the list.

The Firewalls mailing list is fairly high volume (sometimes as many as 100 messages per day, though usually more like 10 to 20 per day). To accommodate subscribers who don't want their mailboxes flooded with lots of separate messages from Firewalls, a Firewalls-Digest mailing list is also available. Subscribers to Firewalls-Digest receive daily (more frequent on busy days) digests of messages sent to Firewalls, rather than each message individually. Firewalls-Digest subscribers get all the same messages as Firewalls subscribers; that is, Firewalls-Digest is not moderated, just distributed in digest form.

Further information about the Firewalls mailing list is available from:

http://lists.gnac.net/firewalls/

Firewall Wizards

The Firewall Wizards mailing list is a moderated mailing list for firewall developers. To subscribe, send a message to *majordomo@nfr.net* with "subscribe firewall-wizards" in the body of the message. More information is available at:

http://www.nfr.net/forum/firewall-wizards.html

FWTK-USERS

The FWTK-Users mailing list is for discussions of problems, solutions, and other issues among users of the TIS Internet Firewall Toolkit (FWTK). Subscribe to it by sending mail to *majordomo@ex.tis.com* with "subscribe fwtk-users" in the body of the message.

BugTraq

The BugTraq list describes itself as follows:

> BugTraq is a full disclosure moderated mailing list for the *detailed* discussion and announcement of computer security vulnerabilities: what they are, how to exploit them, and how to fix them.

To subscribe, send a mail message to *listserv@securityfocus.com* with a message body of:

```
SUBSCRIBE BUGTRAQ Lastname, Firstname
```

More information about BugTraq is available in the "Forums" section at:

> *http://www.securityfocus.com*

NTBugTraq

The NTBugTraq mailing list describes itself as follows:

> In the tradition of Aleph One's BugTraq mailing list, this list has been created to invite the free and open discussion of Windows NT Security Exploits/Bugs or *SEBs* as I call them. This list is not intended to be a forum to discuss "how to" issues, but instead should be used to report reproducible SEBs which you have personally encountered with Windows NT or its related BackOffice products.

More information is available at:

> *http://www.ntbugtraq.com/*

CERT-Advisory

New CERT-CC advisories of security fixes for Internet systems are posted to this list. Send to *cert-advisory-request@cert.org* for subscription requests.

Archived past advisories are available from *info.cert.org* via the Web:

> *http://www.cert.org/advisories*

RISKS

RISKS is officially known as the ACM Forum on Risks to the Public in the Use of Computers and Related Systems. It's a moderated forum for discussion of risks to society from computers and computerization. Send electronic mail subscription requests to RISKS-*Request@csl.sri.com*. Back issues are available from *crvax.sri. com* via anonymous FTP:

> *ftp://crvax.sri.com/risks/*

RISKS is available on the Web at:

> *http://catless.ncl.ac.uk/Risks*

RISKS is also distributed as the *comp.risks* Usenet newsgroup.

Newsgroups

You might find a variety of Usenet newsgroups to be interesting sources of information on network security and related topics:

comp.security.announce
> Computer security announcements, including new CERT-CC advisories

comp.security.unix
> Unix security

comp.security.misc
> Miscellaneous computer and network security

comp.security.firewalls
> Firewalls issues only

alt.security
> Alternative discussions of computer and network security

comp.admin.policy
> Computer administrative policy issues, including security

comp.protocols.tcp-ip
> TCP/IP internals, including security

comp.unix.admin
> Unix system administration, including security

comp.unix.wizards
> Unix kernel internals, including security

Response Teams

These organizations are particularly helpful if you experience a break-in or any kind of security incident at your site. They are also sources of useful general information about Internet security and incident response.

CERT-CC

> *http://www.cert.org/*
> *ftp://info.cert.org/pub/cert_faq*

From the Computer Emergency Response Team Coordination Center's (CERT-CC) Frequently Asked Questions (FAQ) document:

> The CERT Coordination Center is the organization that grew from the computer emergency response team formed by the Defense Advanced Research Projects Agency (DARPA) in November 1988 in response to the needs exhibited during the Internet worm incident. The CERT-CC charter is to work with the Internet community to facilitate its response to computer security events involving Internet hosts; to take proactive steps to raise the community's awareness of computer security issues; and to conduct research targeted at improving the security of existing systems.
>
> CERT-CC products and services include 24-hour technical assistance for responding to computer security incidents, product vulnerability assistance, technical documents, and seminars. In addition, the team maintains a number of mailing lists (including one for CERT-CC advisories) and provides an anonymous FTP server: *info.cert.org*, where security-related documents, past CERT-CC advisories, and tools are archived.

The CERT-CC FAQ, and other information about CERT-CC are available from *info. cert.org* via anonymous FTP.

You can contact CERT-CC:

- By telephone: +1 412 268-7090 (24 hours a day, seven days a week)
- By email: *cert@cert.org*

FIRST

> *http://www.first.org*

From the FIRST web page:

> This coalition, the Forum of Incident Response and Security Teams (FIRST), brings together a variety of computer security incident response teams from government, commercial, and academic organizations. FIRST aims to foster cooperation and coordination in incident prevention, to prompt rapid reaction to incidents, and to

promote information sharing among members and the community at large. Currently FIRST has nearly 70 members.

If you're not sure if you are served by an incident response team, contact FIRST; they can probably tell you. You can contact FIRST:

- By telephone: +1 301-975-3359
- By fax: +1 301 948-0279
- By email: *first-sec@first.org*

NIST CSRC

http://csrc.ncsl.nist.gov/

From the U.S. National Institute of Standards and Technology CSRC web page:

You are currently accessing the NIST Computer Security Resource Clearinghouse. The Clearinghouse is a National Performance Review (NPR) action. The Clearinghouse project at NIST is on-going; its goals are to

- Unify computer security-related information
- Ensure the information is complete and accurate
- Make the information easily searchable and convenient to obtain
- Keep the information current
- Make the Clearinghouse self-documenting; a model for how to do it

The main focus is on crisis response information; information on computer security-related threats, vulnerabilities, and solutions. At the same time, the Clearinghouse strives to be a general index to computer security information on a broad variety of subjects, including general risks, privacy, legal issues, viruses, assurance, policy, and training.

Other Organizations

Various other organizations also offer information and services relevant to firewalls.

Internet Engineering Task Force (IETF)

http://www.ietf.org/

The Internet Engineering Task Force is the primary network standards body for the Internet. For example, the RFC (Request For Comments) documents that are the primary technical standards for the Internet are all created and managed by the IETF. From the IETF web page:

The Internet Engineering Task Force (IETF) is a large open international community of network designers, operators, vendors, and researchers concerned with the evolution of the Internet architecture and the smooth operation of the Internet. It is open to any interested individual.

World Wide Web Consortium (W3C)

http://www.w3c.org/

From the W3C web page:

The World Wide Web Consortium was created in October 1994 to lead the World Wide Web to its full potential by developing common protocols that promote its evolution and ensure its interoperability....W3C is financed primary by its Members and, to a lesser extent, by public funds. W3C Membership is available to all organizations.

By promoting interoperability and encouraging an open forum for discussion, W3C commits to leading the technical evolution of the Web....To meet the growing expectations of users and the increasing power of machines, W3C is already laying the foundations for the next generation of the Web. W3C's technologies will help make the Web a robust, scalable, and adaptive infrastructure for a world of information.

USENIX Association

http://www.usenix.org/

From the USENIX web page:

Since 1975 the USENIX Association has brought together the community of engineers, scientists, and technicians working on the cutting edge of the computing world. The USENIX Conferences and Technical Workshops have become the essential meeting grounds for the presentation and discussion of the most advanced information on the developments of all aspects of computing systems.

USENIX and its members are dedicated to:

- Problem-solving with a practical bias
- Fostering innovation and research that works
- Communicating rapidly the results of both research and innovation
- Providing a neutral forum for the exercise of critical thought and the airing of technical issues

USENIX serves its members and supports professional and technical development through a variety of on-going activities, including:

- Annual technical conference.
- Frequent specific-topic conferences and symposia.

- A highly regarded tutorial program covering a wide range of topics, introductory through advanced.

- Numerous publications, including a book series, in cooperation with MIT Press, on advanced computing systems; proceedings from USENIX symposia and conferences; the quarterly journal *Computing Systems*; and the biweekly newsletter.

- Participation in various ANSI, IEEE, and ISO standards efforts.

- Sponsorship of local and special technical groups relevant to the Unix environment. The chartering of the System Administrators Guild as a Special Technical Group within USENIX is the most recent.

- *comp.org.usenix*, the association's newsgroup.

USENIX sponsors a variety of conferences and symposia, many of which are related to or touch on network and system security. The proceedings of past events are also available. You can contact USENIX:

- By telephone: +1 510 528 8649

- By email: *office@usenix.org*

System Administrators Guild (SAGE)

http://www.usenix.org/sage

From the SAGE web page:

SAGE stands for the Systems Administrators Guild (don't ask what happened to the E). It is a subgroup of the USENIX Association. SAGE is devoted to the Advancement of System Administration as a distinct profession, within the realm of computer science but with similarities to facilities management and other service industries.

SAGE answers the widely felt need for an organization dedicated to advancing the profession of systems administration. SAGE brings together system administrators to:

- Recruit talented individuals to the profession

- Share technical problems and solutions

- Establish standards of professional excellence while providing recognition for those who attain them

- Promote work that advances the state of the art or propagates knowledge of good practice in the profession

SAGE cosponsors the annual LISA and LISA-NT conferences. For more information about SAGE, contact the USENIX office:

- By telephone: +1 510 528 8649

- By email: *office@usenix.org*

System Administration, Networking, and Security (SANS) Institute

http://www.sans.org

From the SANS web page:

> The SANS (System Administration, Networking, and Security) Institute is a cooperative research and education organization through which more than 62,000 system administrators, security professionals, and network administrators share the lessons they are learning and find solutions for challenges they face. As a part of this effort, SANS offers a series of exceptional educational conferences featuring up to eight days of in-depth courses and multi-track technical conferences focusing on user experiences and problem solving. SANS also produces a series of cooperative research reports, electronic digests, posters of authoritative answers to current questions, and cooperatively-created software.

Conferences

Although there are many other conferences, these are the ones you will probably find the most interesting from a firewalls and Internet security point of view.

USENIX Association Conferences

http://www.usenix.org/events/

The USENIX Association and SAGE sponsor a number of worthwhile conferences every year, including the USENIX Security Symposium, the USENIX System Administration (LISA) Conference, and the USENIX Technical Conferences. For information about any of them, contact USENIX:

*   By telephone: +1 510 528-8649
*   By email: *office@usenix.org*

USENIX Unix Security Symposium

The USENIX Unix Security Symposium is one of the best venues for learning about practical solutions to Unix and network security issues. From the announcement for the 1995 symposium:

> The goal of this symposium is to bring together security practitioners, researchers, system administrators, systems programmers, and others with an interest in computer security as it relates to networks and the UNIX operating system.

USENIX System Administration (LISA) Conference

Jointly sponsored by SAGE and USENIX, the USENIX System Administration (LISA) Conference is the premier conference for Unix system and network administrators. It covers a wide range of topics, including host and network security. If you are a Unix system or network administrator, and you get to go to only one conference a year, this should be it. From a LISA conference announcement:

> The USENIX Systems Administration (LISA) Conference is widely recognized as the leading technical conference for system administrators. Historically, LISA stood for "Large Installation Systems Administration," back in the days when having a large installation meant having over 100 users, over 100 systems, or over one gigabyte of disk storage. Today, the scope of the LISA conference includes topics of interest to system administrators from sites of all sizes and kinds. What the conference attendees have in common is an interest in solving problems that cannot be dealt with simply by scaling up well-understood solutions appropriate to a single machine or a small number of workstations on a LAN.

USENIX Large Installation System Administration of Windows NT (LISA-NT) Conference

The LISA-NT conference is like the LISA conference but focused specifically on the Windows NT environment. From a LISA-NT conference announcement:

> The Large Installation System Administration of Windows NT conference, LISA-NT, is a forum to bring system administration professionals together to discuss workable solutions to the issues of administering and scaling all versions of the NT environment.

USENIX Technical Conferences

The main USENIX Technical Conferences are less focused on practical security issues than the Security or LISA conferences, but you can still learn a lot and make many valuable contacts there. If you have an opportunity to attend one, you should certainly consider it.

Unix System Administration, Networking, and Security (SANS) Conference

http://www.sans.org/

According to the conference documentation, this annual event:

> ...is a technical conference offering system administrators, security administrators, and network managers a unique forum in which to gain up-to-date information about immediately useful tools and techniques, in addition to sharing ideas and experiences and network with peers.

For information, contact the conference office:

- By telephone: +1 719/599-4303

- By email: *info@sans.org*

Internet Society Symposium on Network and Distributed System Security (SNDSS)

http://www.isoc.org/

The Internet Society sponsors an annual symposium on network security. From the 1995 symposium announcement:

> The symposium will bring together people who are building software and/or hardware to provide network and distributed system security services. The symposium is intended for those interested in the more practical aspects of network and distributed system security, focusing on actual system design and implementation, rather than on theory. We hope to foster the exchange of technical information that will encourage and enable the Internet community to apply, deploy, and advance the state of the available security technology.

For more information, contact the Internet Society:

- By telephone: +1 703/648-9888

- By email: *membership@isoc.org*

Papers

This section contains a list of papers about firewalls, security attacks, and related topics. It is by no means an exhaustive list, but it does contain references to some of the papers that we find the most interesting. To get most of them, as well as many other papers, consult the extensive collections available from the Telstra and CERIAS web pages described earlier in this appendix.

The following list does not include papers that describe topics that are adequately described in this book, nor does it include papers that simply describe software (such as Tripwire, TCP Wrapper, etc.) that are mentioned in this book and cited in Appendix B, *Tools*; up-to-date papers about tools are ordinarily included with the tools themselves. The published versions of the papers are out of date, so you will do better to get the papers or documentation distributed with the software.

Bellovin, Steve, *smb@research.att.com*. "Packets Found on an Internet". *Computer Communications Review.* 23(3): 26–31. July 1993.

> Describes some of the stranger and more malevolent packets seen by one of AT&T's gateways.

> *ftp://ftp.research.att.com/dist/smb/packets.ps*

Bellovin, Steve, *smb@research.att.com*. "There Be Dragons". *Proceedings of the Third USENIX Unix Security Symposium*. USENIX Association. Baltimore. September 14–16, 1992.

This paper describes some of the probes and attacks against one of AT&T's gateways.

ftp://research.att.com/dist/internet_security/dragon.ps

Cheswick, Bill, *ches@research.att.com*. "An Evening with Berferd in Which a Cracker Is Lured, Endured, and Studied". *Proceedings of the Winter 1992 USENIX Technical Conference*. USENIX Association. San Francisco. January 20–24, 1992.

Describes AT&T's experiences with one particular cracker who walked right into a trap and never knew he was the mouse being toyed with by the cat. The best part of the story isn't in the paper, however: how they got him to finally go away. The cracker was in the Netherlands, and they were sure they knew who it was, but there were no diplomatic channels through which they could get the Dutch police to do anything about it (what the cracker was doing wasn't illegal in the Netherlands, at least not at the time). Finally, one of the Dutch system administrators they'd been working with throughout the investigation got frustrated, called the cracker's mother, and the problem went away.

ftp://research.att.com/dist/internet_security/berferd.ps

Eichlin, Mark W., and Jon A. Rochlis, "With Microscope and Tweezers: An Analysis of the Internet Virus of November 1988". *Proceedings, IEEE Symposium on Research in Security and Privacy*. Pages 326–45. Oakland, CA. May 1989.

A detailed dissection of the Morris Internet worm (this paper's authors prefer "Internet virus") of 1988: what it was, how it worked, what it did, and so on, as well as a discussion of the response.

ftp://athena-dist.mit.edu/pub/virus/mit.PS

Farmer, Dan, and Wietse Venema. "Improving the Security of Your Site by Breaking into It."

A guide from the authors of COPS and SATAN (Dan) and TCP Wrapper, *portmap*, and *chrootuid* (Wietse) to testing your own security before attackers do it for you.

ftp://ftp.porcupine.org/pub/security/admin-guide-to-cracking.101.Z

Fraser, B. RFC 2196: *Site Security Handbook*. September 1997.

This RFC is a guide to establishing a security policy for your site. From the introduction:

This handbook is a guide to setting computer security policies and procedures for sites that have systems on the Internet. This guide lists issues and factors that a site must consider when setting their own policies. It makes some recommendations and gives discussions of relevant areas.

http://www.ietf.org/rfc/rfc2196.txt

Note that the RFCs ("Requests for Comments") are the defining documents for almost all Internet protocols and services. Start with file *rfc-index.txt*; this is the index to the rest of the documents:

http://www.ietf.org/rfc.html

Ranum, Marcus, and Matt Curtin (maintainers), "Internet Firewalls Frequently Asked Questions (FAQ)."

It is updated and posted to the Firewalls mailing list (*firewalls@greatcircle. com*) on a regular basis.

http://www.interhack.net/pubs/fwfaq/

Books

This section describes a number of books that are useful as references or for further understanding of particular topics.

Albitz, Paul and Cricket Liu. *DNS and BIND.* Third Edition. Sebastopol, CA: O'Reilly and Associates, 1998.

This book provides an explanation of the details of how Internet name service works on Unix systems.

Albitz, Paul, Matt Larson, and Cricket Liu. *DNS on Windows NT.* Sebastopol, CA: O'Reilly and Associates, 1998.

This version of the book provides an explanation of the details of how Internet name service works on Windows NT.

Cheswick, Bill and Steve Bellovin. *Firewalls and Internet Security.* Reading, MA: Addison-Wesley, 1994.

This was the first book published on firewalls, describing the authors' experiences building a series of firewalls for AT&T Bell Labs. The book tends to be strong on theory and background but weak on implementation details; it tells you how they build firewalls, but you probably can't duplicate their tools and methods without the same kind of backing they have (AT&T Bell Labs). Even so, it's a classic in the field.

Comer, Douglas E. *Internetworking with TCP/IP Volume I: Principles, Protocols, and Architecture.* Third Edition. Englewood Cliffs, NJ: Prentice Hall, 1995.

This book provides a helpful introduction to the nuts and bolts of TCP/IP networking. It discusses the basics about what packets look like and how routing works, etc. Later volumes include introductions to some of the higher-level protocols such as SMTP and FTP.

Garfinkel, Simson. *PGP: Pretty Good Privacy.* Sebastopol, CA: O'Reilly & Associates, 1994.

This is an excellent guide to the very popular program, PGP, which lets you encrypt and apply digital signatures to your messages. In addition to technical details, it contains the fascinating, behind-the-scenes stories of Phil Zimmermann's development of PGP, electronic privacy, and cryptography export and patents in the United States.

Garfinkel, Simson and Gene Spafford. *Practical UNIX & Internet Security.* Second Edition. Sebastopol, CA: O'Reilly & Associates, 1996.

This is a very good guide to Unix host security. Simson Garfinkel is also the author of *PGP: Pretty Good Privacy.* Gene Spafford is now one of the principals of the CERIAS center at Purdue University.

Hunt, Craig. *TCP/IP Network Administration.* Second Edition. Sebastopol, CA: O'Reilly & Associates, 1998.

This book provides an excellent system administrator's overview of TCP/IP networking. It focuses on Unix systems and includes a very useful reference to major Unix networking services and tools such as BIND (the standard Unix DNS server) and Sendmail (the standard Unix SMTP server).

Hunt, Craig, and Robert Bruce Thompson. *Windows NT TCP/IP Network Administration.* Sebastopol, CA: O'Reilly & Associates, 1998.

This book provides an excellent system administrator's overview of TCP/IP networking. It focuses on Windows NT systems.

Nemeth, Evi, Garth Snyder, Scott Seebass, and Trent R. Hein. *Unix System Administration Handbook.* Second Edition. Englewood Cliffs, NJ: Prentice Hall, 1995.

This is the standard reference guide to practical Unix system administration issues. It includes good, real-world coverage of thorny issues like backups.

Schneier, Bruce. *Applied Cryptography: Protocols, Algorithms, and Source Code in C.* Second Edition. New York: John Wiley & Sons, 1995.

This is an extremely comprehensive book about cryptography algorithms and techniques. It covers the Data Encryption Standard (DES), the RSA algorithm, and all of the other private and public key algorithms, with mathematical details for all of them. Source code is available.

Stevens, Richard W. *TCP/IP Illustrated, Volume 1: The Protocols.* Reading, MA:
Addison-Wesley, 1994.

This is a good guide to the nuts and bolts of TCP/IP networking. Its main
strength is that it provides traces of the packets going back and forth as the
protocols are actually in use and uses them to illustrate the discussions of the
protocols.

Stoll, Cliff. *The Cuckoo's Egg.* Garden City, NJ: Doubleday, 1989.

This is a fascinating true story about a hunt for crackers on the Internet. It
gives you an appreciation of the time and effort it takes to track an attack
against your site, and it also includes a good chocolate chip cookie recipe.

B

Tools

This appendix describes some of the tools and packages available on the Internet that you might find useful in building and maintaining your firewall. Many of these tools are mentioned in this book. Although this software is freely available, some of it is restricted in various ways by the authors (e.g., it may not be permitted to be used for commercial purposes or be included on a CD-ROM, etc.) or by the U.S. government (e.g., if it contains cryptography, it can't ordinarily be exported outside the United States). Carefully read the documentation files that are distributed with the packages.

Although we have used most of the software listed here, we can't take responsibility for ensuring that the copy you get will work properly and won't cause any damage to your system. As with any software, test it before you use it.

Many packages have verifiable digital signatures; the software supplier provides a cryptographic checksum for the package that has been encrypted with the supplier's private key. You can verify that you have the correct package by decrypting the checksum with the supplier's public key and calculating the checksum on the package yourself, and making sure that they match. We encourage you to take the trouble to use these signatures when you are dealing with security-sensitive software. Many people have distributed booby-trapped versions of popular software packages.

Authentication Tools

The tools in this category provide support for various types of authentication. See Chapter 21, *Authentication and Auditing Services*, for information about different authentication approaches.

TIS Internet Firewall Toolkit (FWTK)

ftp://ftp.tis.com/pub/firewalls/toolkit/

The TIS Internet Firewall Toolkit (TIS FWTK), from Trusted Information Systems, is a very useful, well-designed, and well-written set of programs you might find useful for authentication and other purposes. It includes:

- An authentication server that provides several mechanisms for supporting nonreusable passwords (described in Chapter 21)

- An access control program, *netacl* (described in Chapter 11, *Unix and Linux Bastion Hosts*)

- Proxy servers for a variety of protocols (FTP, HTTP, Gopher, *rlogin*, Telnet, and X11) (described in Chapter 9, *Proxy Systems*)

- A generic proxy server for simple TCP-based protocols using one-to-one or many-to-one connections, such as NNTP (described in Chapter 9)

- A wrapper (the *smap* package) for SMTP servers such as Sendmail to protect them from SMTP-based attacks (described in Chapter 16, *Electronic Mail and News*)

- A wrapper for *inetd*-started servers such as *telnetd* and *ftpd* to control where they can be contacted from (much like the TCP Wrapper package described later in this appendix and in Chapter 11)

The toolkit is designed so that you can pick and choose only the pieces you need; you don't have to install the whole thing. The pieces you do install share a common configuration file, however, which makes managing configuration changes somewhat easier.

Some parts of the toolkit (the server for the nonreusable password system, for example) require a Data Encryption Standard (DES) library in some configurations. If your system doesn't already have one (look for a file named *libdes.a* in whatever directories code libraries are kept on your system), you can get one from:

ftp://ftp.psy.uq.oz.au/pub/Crypto/DES/

TIS FWTK maintains a mailing list for discussions of improvements, bugs, fixes, and other issues among people using the toolkit; Send email to *fwall-users-request@tis.com* to subscribe to this list.

Kerberos

ftp://athena-dist.mit.edu/pub/kerberos/
ftp://coast.cs.purdue.edu/pub/tools/unix/kerberos/

Kerberos was developed by Project Athena at the Massachusetts Institute of Technology. From the Kerberos Frequently Asked Questions (FAQ) file:

> Kerberos is a network authentication system for use on physically insecure networks, based on the key distribution model presented by Needham and Schroeder. It allows entities communicating over networks to prove their identity to each other while preventing eavesdropping or replay attacks. It also provides for data-stream integrity (detection of modification) and secrecy (preventing unauthorized reading) using cryptography systems such as DES.

Analysis Tools

The tools in this category let you audit your system. Some perform audits and check for well-known security holes; others establish databases of checksums of all of the files in a system (to allow you to watch for changes to those files); some do both.

COPS

> *ftp://coast.cs.purdue.edu/pub/tools/unix/cops*

COPS, by Dan Farmer, is the Computer Oracle and Password System, a system that checks Unix systems for common security problems (such as unsafe permissions on key files and directories).

Tiger

> *ftp://coast.cs.purdue.edu/pub/tools/unix/tiger*

Tiger, by Doug Schales of Texas A&M University (TAMU), is a set of scripts that scan a Unix system looking for security problems, in the same fashion as Dan Farmer's COPS. Tiger was originally developed to provide a check of Unix systems on the A&M campus that users wanted to access from off campus. Before the packet filtering in the firewall could be modified to allow off-campus access to the system, the system had to pass the Tiger checks.

Tripwire

> *ftp://coast.cs.purdue.edu/pub/COAST/Tripwire*

Tripwire, by Gene H. Kim and Gene Spafford of CERIAS at Purdue University, is a file integrity checker: a utility that compares a designated set of files and directories against information stored in a previously generated database. Added or deleted files are flagged and reported, as are any files that have changed from their previously recorded state in the database. Run Tripwire against system files on a regular basis. If you do, the program will spot any file changes when it next runs, giving system administrators information to enact damage control measures immediately.

SATAN

http://www.fish.com/~zen/satan/satan.html

SATAN, by Wietse Venema and Dan Farmer, is the Security Administrator Tool for Analyzing Networks. (If you don't like the name, it comes with a script named *repent* that changes all references from SATAN to SANTA: Security Administrator Network Tool for Analysis.) It was the first well-publicized scanning tool but is not being actively maintained.

SAINT

http://www.wwdsi.com

SAINT is a security scanning tool aimed at system administrators; it is an update to SATAN. According to the authors:

> SAINT is the tool for System Administrators who are well versed in information security and want to maintain and configure security assessment tools within their own network environments.

Packet Filtering Tools

These tools allow you to add packet filtering to a Unix system.

ipfilter

http://coombs.anu.edu.au/~avalon

ipfilter is a TCP/IP filtering system for Unix, which works on a variety of Unix systems. It is discussed in Chapter 8, *Packet Filtering*.

Proxy Systems Tools

The tools in this category let you add proxy capabilities to your system. See the discussion in Chapter 9.

TIS Internet Firewall Toolkit (FWTK)

See the discussion of TIS FWTK in the "Authentication Tools" section, earlier in this appendix.

SOCKS

http://www.socks.nec.com

SOCKS is a proxy-building toolkit that allows you to convert standard TCP client programs to proxied versions of those same programs. There are two parts to SOCKS: client libraries and a generic server. Client libraries are available for most Unix platforms, as well as for Macintosh and Windows systems. The generic server runs on most Unix platforms and can be used by any of the client libraries, regardless of their platform. SOCKS was originally freely available; freely available and commercial versions, with somewhat different features, are now available from NEC.

UDP Packet Relayer

ftp://coast.cs.purdue.edu/pub/tools/unix/udprelay-0.2.tar.gz

This package, by Tom Fitzgerald, is a proxy system that provides much the same functionality for UDP-based clients that SOCKS provides for TCP-based clients.

tircproxy

http://www.mmedia.is/~bre/tircproxy/

tircproxy is an IRC proxy that provides intelligent proxying to increase the safety of IRC while making it work through a firewall. It is discussed in Chapter 19, *Real-Time Conferencing Services.*

Daemons

When you are building your firewall, you may wish to replace your standard daemons with the daemons described in the following sections.

wuarchive ftpd

ftp://ftp.wustl.edu/packages/wuarchive-ftpd/
ftp://ftp.uu.net/networking/archival/ftp/wuarchive-ftpd/

The *wuarchive* FTP daemon offers many features and security enhancements, such as per-directory message files shown to any user who enters the directory, limits on number of simultaneous users, and improved logging and access control. These enhancements are specifically designed to support anonymous FTP.

GateD

http://www.gated.merit.edu

GateD is a routing daemon that provides multi-protocol support and filters routes based on their source. GateD used to be freely available but is now a commercial product.

Zebra

http://www.zebra.org

Zebra is an open source routing daemon that provides multi-protocol support and filters routes based on their source.

Postfix

http://www.postfix.org

Postfix, by Wietse Venema, is a security-oriented Unix mailer daemon; it is discussed in Chapter 16, *Electronic Mail and News*.

qmail

http://www.qmail.org

qmail, by Dan Bernstein, is a security-oriented Unix mailer daemon; it is discussed in Chapter 16.

smail

ftp://ftp.planix.com/pub/Smail/

smail is also a replacement Unix mailer daemon, discussed in Chapter 16.

portmap

ftp://coast.cs.purdue.edu/pub/tools/unix/portmap.shar

portmap, from Wietse Venema, is a *portmapper* replacement that offers access control in the style of the TCP Wrapper program, described in the "Utilities" section, later in this appendix.

Andrew File System (AFS)

http://www.transarc.com

AFS is a network filesystem that is more suitable for use across wide area networks such as the Internet than traditional LAN-oriented network filesystem protocols such as NFS. From the AFS document:

> AFS is a distributed filesystem that enables cooperating hosts (clients and servers) to efficiently share filesystem resources across both local area and wide area networks.

> AFS is marketed, maintained, and extended by Transarc Corporation.

> AFS is based on a distributed file system originally developed at the Information Technology Center at Carnegie-Mellon University.

rsync

http://rsync.samba.org/rsync

rsync is a synchronization protocol that uses checksums to determine differences (instead of relying on modification dates) and does partial file transfers (transferring only the differences instead of the entire files). *rsync* was developed by Andrew Tridgell and Paul Mackerras. The *rsync* daemon, *rsyncd*, provides an efficient and secure way to make files available to remote sites.

Samba

http://www.samba.org

Samba is an open source package for Unix and related systems that provides SMB/CIFS service, including file and printer sharing. It allows a Unix system to act as a server for PCs. In addition, the Samba source is an effective form of documentation of how SMB/CIFS works and provides a number of tools that may help you in debugging Microsoft networks.

ssh

http://www.ssh.org

ssh is a secure remote login program, available for both Unix and Windows NT. It is discussed in Chapter 18, *Remote Access to Hosts*.

BO2K

http://www.bo2k.com

BO2K is a remote control program for Microsoft Windows systems. It is discussed in Chapter 18.

mIRC

http://www.mirc.com/

mIRC is an IRC client. It is discussed in Chapter 19, *Real-Time Conferencing Services.*

Utilities

A number of additional utilities provide services you'll find useful when you build and maintain your firewall.

TIS Internet Firewall Toolkit (FWTK)

See the discussion of the TIS FWTK in the "Authentication Tools" section, earlier in this appendix.

TCP Wrapper

ftp://coast.cs.purdue.edu/pub/tools/unix/tcp_wrappers/

With this package, from Wietse Venema, you can monitor and filter incoming requests for servers started by *inetd*.

chrootuid

ftp://coast.cs.purdue.edu/pub/tools/unix/chrootuid

chrootuid, from Wietse Venema, makes it easy to run a network service at a low-privilege level and with restricted filesystem access. The program can be used to run Gopher, HTTP, WAIS, and other network daemons in a minimal environment: the daemons have access only to their own directory tree and run under a low-privileged *userid*. The arrangement greatly reduces the impact of possible security problems in daemon software.

inzider

http://ntsecurity.nu/toolbox/

inzider, written by Arne Vidstrom, is a Windows NT tool that shows what processes are listening on what ports. It is a useful tool for understanding what network services are doing on a Windows NT machine.

MRTG

http://ee-staff.ethz.ch/~oetiker/webtools/mrtg/mrtg.html

The Multi Router Traffic Grapher (MRTG) is a tool that generates web pages with graphs of data about your network. Originally, it was designed to show data from routers, gathered with SNMP, but it is easy to use it to show any data that can be gathered via SNMP, and only slightly harder to adapt it for other ways of getting numeric values. It provides historical data (that is, it shows values over time), but it updates the web pages in real time, as information comes in. These graphs are very useful for recognizing patterns and trends in network usage.

NOCOL

http://www.netplex-tech.com/software/nocol/

NOCOL is a system and network monitoring system that runs on Unix systems and can poll many kinds of devices, using a variety of methods. It can watch *syslog*, use SNMP, and test machines with ICMP, for instance. Additional monitors can easily be added; there are C and *perl* APIs to help you write them.

NetCat

http://www.l0pht.com/~weld/netcat/

NetCat is a utility, available for Unix and Windows NT, that allows you to read and write data using arbitrary TCP and UDP ports. It is invaluable in debugging and in otherwise investigating network services.

NetSaint

http://www.netsaint.org

NetSaint is a network monitoring program that checks the status of services and notifies you when there are problems with them. It can use electronic mail or a pager for notification. NetSaint is written in C and is designed to run under Linux (and most other Unix variants) as a background process, intermittently running checks on various services that you specify. The actual service checks are performed by separate programs that return the status of the checks to NetSaint. Several CGI programs are included with NetSaint to allow you to view the current service status, problem history, notification history, and log file via the Web.

PGP

http://www.pgp.com

PGP, by Phil Zimmerman, is a suite of encryption tools, available for both Unix and Windows NT, that provides encryption for electronic mail and suitable file encryption for protecting binaries that you intend to leave on bastion hosts but don't want intruders to have access to.

trimlog

> *ftp://coast.cs.purdue.edu/pub/tools/unix/trimlog*

trimlog, by David A. Curry, is a program that helps you manage log files. It reads a configuration file to determine which files to trim, how to trim them, how much they should be trimmed, and so on. The program helps keep your logs from growing until they consume all available disk space.

AntiSniff

> *http://www.l0pht.com/antisniff/*

AntiSniff is a tool for detecting computers that are running network sniffers. It is discussed in Chapter 26, *Maintaining Firewalls.*

tcpdump

> *ftp://coast.cs.purdue.edu/pub/tools/unix/tcpdump/*

tcpdump is a Unix tool for collecting network traffic. It can be used for network monitoring and debugging and is the basis for a number of other tools that deal with packet-level information.

C

Cryptography

Cryptography is surrounded in myths, politics, and passionate opinions. This appendix is intended to help you sort them out to the extent necessary to build a firewall. It is not a complete introduction to cryptography; instead, it's a rapid tour of the essentials you'll need to understand the rest of this book. In particular, we avoid going into details on how cryptographic algorithms actually work, focusing instead on their general properties. A number of books focus on cryptography; we particularly recommend Bruce Schneier's *Applied Cryptography*, 2nd edition (John Wiley & Sons, 1995).

This appendix starts by discussing general issues in cryptography, then describes types of cryptographic algorithms and their uses, and finishes with some information about specific algorithms.

What Are You Protecting and Why?

For the most part, people use cryptography to protect information. Sometimes they are trying to keep something secret; sometimes they are trying to keep something from being changed; sometimes they are trying to ensure that the person responsible for something is clearly identifiable. But very few people use cryptography just for the amusement value.

In order to determine what you need from cryptography, you have to first know what you need to protect and what you're trying to protect it from. For instance, suppose you are attempting to keep some piece of information secret. That might be a trivial piece of information that's going to change again soon (for instance, what present you picked out for a friend's birthday next week), or it might be an important piece of information that can be turned into cash any time in the next several years (for instance, the number of the credit card you just got). It might be the press release you're going to make public next week, which commercial competitors may be actively trying to discover but will be pointless to conceal as soon as it appears in the newspaper, or it might be your government's nuclear bomb plans, which professional spies are actively trying to discover and will still destroy the world no matter when they're used.

Clearly, you're going to want different things from the algorithms you use to protect these pieces of information. If you're keeping the birthday present a secret, you want something that's fast and easy to use; you don't care much if it's easy to figure out (unless your friend is a cryptographer who hates surprises). If you're keeping a credit card number secret, you mostly care about how secure it is, but most of the time, people won't be trying to find it out. If you're keeping a press release secret from competitors, you only need to protect it until you release it; if you're keeping nuclear bomb plans secret, you need to protect them forever.

Similarly, cryptography can be used to prove your identity (this is discussed later in this appendix). You may use cryptography to prove who you are when sending a note to a friend, when approving an expensive purchase at work, or when releasing a piece of software to the world. These things require different levels of certainty, last for different amounts of time, and require different kinds of infrastructure.

If you're sending a note to a friend, the friend probably doesn't need to be all that certain who it's from; if somebody else pretends to be you, it will probably all get sorted out in the end, even if a certain amount of comedy or unpleasantness results. The friend needs to be able to verify your identity only when the message arrives. If the verification data isn't good months later, that's OK; the message is probably of purely sentimental value by then. You and the friend can set up a system between the two of you for verifying your identity; you don't need a way that will work on a large scale. Finally, all your friend needs to know is that the message is from you. Presumably, anybody you consider a friend already knows who you are and why they want to read messages from you.

If you're authorizing a purchase at work, there are legal requirements to be fulfilled. Those legal requirements demand a higher level of certainty. If somebody else pretends to be you, the company's money is at stake, and the consequences include prosecution for fraud or incompetence. The legal requirements also demand that the information be verifiable for a longer period of time; not only does somebody need to be able to verify your identity when the purchase is made, they need to be able to verify it again during a later query or audit. Practical requirements also mean that there needs to be a consistent company-wide architecture for verifying your identity. It can't be done differently for every employee, so an infrastructure of some sort is required. That infrastructure has to include not only identity data ("This is how you know it's from Ethelraeda

Perkins"), but also authorization data ("This is how you know Ethelraeda Perkins is allowed to authorize purchases up to $20,000").

If you're releasing software to the Internet, things change again. If somebody pretends to be you and releases destructive software in your name, your reputation can be permanently damaged, and the consequences include things like your name ending up on the front page of newspapers worldwide. You need a high level of certainty about identities, and you need that level of certainty for a long time (one of the authors still periodically receives questions about relatively obscure software distributed over 10 years ago). This has to be provided with a worldwide infrastructure, accessible to everybody you want to distribute software to, and that infrastructure must provide enough information so that people can readily tell not only who you are, but why they trust you enough to run programs you're distributing.

Key Components of Cryptographic Systems

Cryptography is used for multiple things, and cryptographic systems are built out of multiple parts. Encryption is the best-known and most obvious technique, but in order to understand how cryptography is used, you need to understand several other techniques as well, including those used for cryptographic hashing, integrity protection, and the generation of random numbers.

Encryption

Encryption is the process of reversibly hiding information. When you encrypt something, you take a piece of data (called the *plaintext*) and apply a process that produces another piece of data (called the *ciphertext*). There must also be a process for turning the ciphertext back into plaintext.

It's not practical to think up a new algorithm every time you want to encrypt something. Useful encryption algorithms therefore use an extra piece of data called a *key*. In order to decrypt data, you need not only the decryption algorithm, but also the key; this means that you can use the same algorithm to encrypt different things and share them with different people. If an encryption algorithm doesn't use a key, then as soon as you know the decryption algorithm, you can decrypt all the things encrypted with the algorithm.

Cryptographic wisdom considers an encryption process secure when the only way to recover a plaintext message from ciphertext is to know or discover the key. Furthermore, this rule should still be true even if every other detail about the encryption process is known. In fact, cryptographers become very concerned about the security of an algorithm when more than a key must be kept secret (for instance, when the algorithm or an important part of it is not disclosed).

There are some things that encryption cannot do. When you encrypt something, you conceal its content, which doesn't necessarily conceal everything useful about it. Attackers may be able to gain important information by looking at the lengths of messages, or the times they're sent, or the senders and receivers; none of that will be changed by encryption.

Furthermore, encrypting something does not protect it from being changed. Somebody who has access to the ciphertext can change it. They won't be able to predict exactly what plaintext you'll get, but it will almost certainly be different. This sort of tampering is normally easy for a human to detect in text but not so if the plaintext was binary data. Since computers are unable to comprehend text, they cannot detect tampering by inspection as humans can. In order to protect a message from modification, and in a way that a computer can detect, you must use integrity protection, which we will discuss. Although some integrity protection systems use encryption, encryption by itself does not provide integrity protection.

Kinds of encryption algorithms

There are two main families of encryption algorithms: symmetric and public key. A *symmetric algorithm* uses one key for both encryption and decryption. A *public key algorithm* uses two matching keys; when you encrypt with one of the keys, you use the other one to decrypt.

The primary characteristic of an encryption algorithm is its strength, which is the amount of effort it takes for somebody to turn the ciphertext into plaintext without having the key. There's no absolute measure of the strength of an encryption algorithm. It's possible to say that some algorithms are very weak (for instance, replacing every letter with the letter three characters later in the alphabet, so that "b" becomes "e" and "c" becomes "f", is definitely a very weak algorithm), and it's possible to say that some algorithms have no known weaknesses. When we discuss particular algorithms, we will mention algorithms that are known to be attackable, or weak. A wide range of algorithms are available that don't have known weaknesses, and in most circumstances, you can and should choose one of them.

In the real world, strength is not the only important characteristic of an encryption algorithm. Some algorithms are much faster to execute than others, for instance, and the speed may depend on the kind of processor you have available. Some algorithms require more memory than others. Some algorithms have legal restrictions on their use, which are different in different countries. Some algorithms are patented and are expensive or difficult to license.

Public key and symmetric algorithms differ on all of these fronts (most notably, symmetric algorithms are much faster than public key algorithms), but the most important difference between them comes from the extra capabilities of public key algorithms. With a symmetric key algorithm, anybody who can encrypt a message can also decrypt the message, and it is therefore important to keep the one key secure so that it is known only by the parties who are trying to communicate. With a public key algorithm, you can make one key public while keeping the other one completely private, so that only you know it.

Having a public key and a private key opens up a number of new uses of cryptography. For instance, if you encrypt something with your private key, you don't keep the data secret (anybody who has the public key can read it), but you do prove that you encrypted it (because only you have the private key). This is called *signing*. Digital signatures are discussed in detail later in this appendix. Anybody who wants to send you something secret can encrypt it with your public key, and be sure that only you can read it. In fact, some ways of using public key technology don't actually allow you to conceal data; you can only use them for authentication; some public key algorithms are not encryption algorithms.

Just as there are differences between public key algorithms and symmetric algorithms, there are differences among symmetric algorithms. Some work on fixed-sized chunks of data and are called *block ciphers*. Others, called *stream ciphers*, work on an arbitrary sequence of bits or bytes. There are various ways, called *modes*, to extend a block cipher so that it can encrypt more than just a single block of data. Stream ciphers are naturally designed to handle an arbitrarily sized stream of data.

The encryption of variable amounts of data is usually called *bulk encryption*. In this case, anything bigger than about 64 bits is considered "bulk". Almost all bulk encryption is done with symmetric algorithms because of the speed difference between symmetric and public key encryption. It is frequently desirable to use bulk encryption in situations where the communicating parties don't already have a common symmetric encryption key. An extremely common way to solve this problem is to combine public key cryptography with symmetric key cryptography. For instance, the PGP package, commonly used for bulk encryption of electronic mail, uses a symmetric key algorithm to encrypt the body of a mail message, and then uses public key encryption to encrypt the symmetric key and sends the encrypted symmetric key with the message.

Encryption algorithms and key length

One of the important ways algorithms differ is in the keys they use. As we've discussed before, in order to decrypt something that was encrypted with a strong algorithm, you have to know what the key is. Therefore, one way that people attack encryption algorithms is to try to figure out the key. There are obviously many ways to go about this, most of which are not under the control of the encryption algorithm (for instance, you can go around looking for places where the key is recorded and not adequately secured).

However, some ways of figuring out keys are based on how the algorithm works. With a symmetric key algorithm, the easiest way to figure out a key is to try all the possible keys until you find the correct one (knowing you have found the correct key is a separate, and tricky, problem). The more possible keys there are, the harder it is. With a public key algorithm, you can try to calculate a private key based on the public key using existing mathematical techniques if you know that you have a fast enough computer with enough memory, or you can invent a new mathematical theory for solving the equations used in the public key algorithm. Either of these methodologies will be easier than trying all possible private keys.

For any given algorithm, the longer the key is, the harder it is to find it out. On the other hand, you can't directly compare key lengths between different kinds of algorithms because the ways that they can be attacked are different. A 128-bit key is a pretty strong key for a symmetric algorithm but a pretty weak one for most public key algorithms. This is because 128 bits is a lot of keys to search but not large enough to prevent mathematical attacks on public key algorithms. Since different public key algorithms use different relationships between the private key and the public key, key lengths can't always be compared even between different public key algorithms.

If you know that trying all possible keys is the only way to find a key, you can be reasonably confident about your security; the speed of light imposes a theoretical limit on how fast computations can be performed, so if the key is big enough, nobody can be sure to find it within the estimated lifetime of the universe. (It's always possible to get lucky when you're trying keys, but you're much more likely to win a lottery.) The key length required to be big enough is surprisingly short; it's under 128 bits.

The situation with public keys is not as simple. Currently known techniques for finding private keys are difficult on today's computers, but it has yet to be proven that there are no faster techniques.

It's important to distinguish between key length and block length when discussing block ciphers. These are often but not always the same, and the block length is the length most often given. When somebody refers to a "64-bit block cipher", that is the length of the block, and not necessarily the length of the key. This can be horribly confusing, since for other ciphers the key length is the only thing normally specified in bits like that. Pay close attention to which length is being specified; a "64-bit public key algorithm" has a 64-bit key, while a "64-bit block cipher" might have any key length at all.

Cryptographic Hashes, Checksums, and Message Digests

A checksum is a number calculated on a given set of data that is designed to detect changes or errors in communication of that data. This is useful for a communications channel; if a sender calculates a checksum as data is being sent and a receiver does the same as it is being received, the two can simply compare checksums to see if the data arrived intact or if an error occurred during transmission. Another use might be to store the checksum and then repeat the calculation at a later time. If the two checksums are different, then something changed in the data.

A checksum is usually just several bytes long and will take up much less space than the original data. While this makes them easier to store, it also means that there must be situations where a checksum will give the same answer for two different pieces of data. This is called a *collision*, and checksum algorithms are designed to make collisions unlikely to occur for the differences they are designed to detect. Checksum algorithms for communications are designed to detect random bursts of errors or chunks of missing data because they are the kinds of differences that you often get on a telephone line or a radio transmission (to humans listening, these errors sound like clicks or pops).

What if the error was not random and a deliberate change was intended? If so, is it possible to make a deliberate change and keep the checksum the same? For many checksums, this is certainly possible because the checksums are not designed to make this difficult. There are ways to design checksum algorithms so that it is impossibly difficult to make a deliberate change and still have the checksum match. Algorithms designed this way are called *cryptographic hash functions, cryptographic checksums*, or *message digest functions*.

Note that the terminology used for the different techniques and uses of cryptographic hashes is confusing and overlapping. As a result, terms are not used very consistently; about the best you can say is that any term involving *integrity, digest*, or the acronym *MAC* (Message Authentication Code) probably refers to some process that uses some kind of hash. If you care about the details, investigate them, rather than trusting that terms are used consistently from one document to another.

The term *hash* comes from another situation where it is useful to have a short fixed-length string that you can generate consistently from a larger string and that has large changes in the output as a result of small changes to the input. Hash algorithms and checksum algorithms are not always used for the same purposes, but if you extend either concept for cryptographic security, you reach the following set of conditions for a cryptographic hash:

- It must be practically impossible to deliberately create data that has a hash value that matches another. This can be achieved by designing the algorithm so that it cannot be reversed and run backwards (you can't start with a hash value and use a method to create data that computes to the same hash).

- The hash must be of a large enough size so that you cannot create a list of files, one for each value the hash can have, and match a given hash that way. In practical terms, this means that a useful hash should be at least 128 bits and preferably 160 bits or more in size.

- If you change something only very slightly in the data, the hash will change by a large amount. Changing one bit in the data should change about half the bits in the hash. This makes it hard for people to slowly adjust individual bits in the data to achieve a desired hash value.

There are two principal uses for cryptographic hashes. First, they are used to detect changes in data. If you have a cryptographic hash for a piece of data and the hash is kept secure, you can be sure that if you recalculate the hash and it is the same, then the data hasn't been modified. This is the basis for digital signatures, which are discussed later in this appendix.

Cryptographic hashes are also frequently used in authentication systems. In most cases, passwords are not encrypted, but hashed. If you use encryption on a password, it is possible to decrypt it and get back the password, which an attacker could then use somewhere else. This makes storing and sending encrypted passwords dangerous. Instead, secure systems store a hash of the password and, when a user wants to authenticate to the system, compute a hash of the password provided by the user. If the hashes match, the user must know the correct password.

This technique does not help if a user can directly provide the hash, instead of the password (for instance, if the user is logging in over a network and what the system actually receives is the hash). If the hash is sent around, it simply becomes another fixed and reusable password. (This is discussed further in Chapter 21, *Authentication and Auditing Services.*) For this reason, good network authentication systems use a random piece of data that changes on every transaction, often called a *nonce.* Adding this changing value into the information that gets hashed and exchanged prevents eavesdroppers from reading and reusing the hashes.

It is possible to use a block cipher in a special way to calculate a cryptographic hash. When a cipher is used like this, the resulting checksum may be called a Message Authentication Code (MAC), a Message Integrity Code (MIC), or a Message Digest Check (MDC).

The use of block ciphers for calculating cryptographic hashes is often seen in older cryptographic protocols. In particular, they frequently use the Data Encryption Standard (DES) to produce 64-bit values. Most modern cryptographic protocols explicitly use cryptographic hash algorithms. One reason is that cryptographic hash algorithms tend to produce results that are 128 to 160 bits in size. This significantly reduces the chances of being able to come up with a different piece of data that produces the same hash value.

Integrity Protection

One of the most important uses of cryptographic hashes is to provide integrity protection. A cryptographic hash can be used to verify that no changes to data have been made, but this won't work if you include the hash value with the data. All someone wishing to change the data would have to do is replace the hash value with a new value computed from the changed data. Some way is needed to protect the cryptographic hash from being changed to the desired new value.

One way is to encrypt the cryptographic hash using a public key algorithm; this is essentially a digital signature, as we discuss later. Because of the slowness of public key encryption, it is not always a usable solution. Alternatives have been developed that are based on the calculation of cryptographic hashes, which include a secret key as part of the calculation. Without that key, someone wishing to change the data cannot recalculate a new and valid checksum. Many recent Internet protocols use a method called HMAC* for combining a key with a cryptographic hash. The HMAC technique can be used with any cryptographic hash function that produces at least 128 bits of output. HMAC is described in RFC 2104.

Random Numbers

Many parts of cryptography depend on being able to generate random numbers, or at least numbers that can't be predicted. For instance, if you need to send authentication information across the network in a form that's not reusable, you will want an unpredictable changing value to add in with the information. If an attacker can figure out what that value is, the attacker may be able to use the value to authenticate or to figure out the authentication data for later use.

Computers are very bad at being random because they are designed to be able to repeatedly calculate the same answer if given the same data to work with. If you have an algorithm for giving you random numbers, you will get the same list of random numbers whenever you run it. This is why random number generators on

---

* HMAC, although it is capitalized like an acronym, does not have an official expansion in the standard. In the paper originally describing the algorithm, it stood for "Hash-based Message Authentication Code".

computers are called *pseudo-random.* Knowing the algorithm and the starting information, and having a faster computer, would allow you to predict what the numbers were going to be. Truly random numbers cannot be predicted.

So where can a source of acceptable random numbers come from? It is easy if the computer has some hardware to generate random numbers; if not, then some random information can be obtained from peripheral devices attached to the computer. It has to be done very carefully because it is easy to overestimate how random some sources of information are. Sampling a fast running clock is not really a good way to get random numbers because typically only a small number of bits will change each time the clock is sampled.*

Several free Unix operating systems, including Linux, have special code as part of the low-level device drivers, which continuously collects random input events from the keyboard and other hardware devices and allows applications to obtain a source of random data.

Combined Cryptography

The basic building blocks (encryption, cryptographic hashes, and random numbers) can be put together to create various larger systems that meet needs beyond simply hiding data. These include digital signatures and certificates.

Digital Signatures

What is a *digital signature*? It is the digital equivalent of putting your signature on a document. When you sign a paper document, you are permanently attaching something that identifies you with a particular piece of information. The assumption is that only you can create your signature and your signature cannot be transferred to another document.

Normal signatures are relatively easy to work around. For instance, somebody can forge your signature, photocopy your signature, and stick it on another document, or change the document after you've signed it. Over the years, people have developed a number of systems to help prevent these kinds of attacks, with varying amounts of success. This includes ways of telling originals of documents from photocopies (ranging from the simple trick of signing in a pen that's not black† to complicated ways of making documents that don't photocopy well), systems where you sign and date every page of a document to keep people from substitut-

---

* RFC 1750 is an excellent source of information about random numbers for use in security applications.

† This is true only because good color photocopiers are not in widespread use in offices.

ing pages, and ways of physically protecting multiple copies so that nobody can modify them all. None of these systems is foolproof.

Digital signature algorithms try to provide a much more consistent set of guarantees, with mixed success. Digital signature technology combines public key cryptography and cryptographic hashing; public key cryptography provides a way to prove your identity, and cryptographic hashing provides a way to guarantee that the information to which you attached your identity has not been modified.

Tampering is prevented by using a cryptographic hash function to generate a hash of the document or data. The hash is then combined with the private key using the digital signature algorithm to produce something that can be produced only by you and is bound to a particular piece of data.

When you sign something, you use your private key; when recipients get the signature, they use your public key to verify it. This means that recipients must have access to a reliable data source that includes your public key information. This is identical to the paper versions. Organizations that are serious about signatures (banks, for instance) keep a sample of your signature on record so that they can make comparisons. Anybody who can replace that sample can authenticate as you.

A private key is an important authenticator, like a physical credit card. If you lose control of your credit card, there is a possibility that somebody else will use it, and you will need to make that credit card invalid. If you destroy the credit card accidentally, you need to get a new card, but there's no particular need to make the old one invalid.

The only person who should have the key you use to make signatures is you—there should not be any copies of the key. Somebody who has a copy of the key can pretend to be you. On the other hand, if you lose the ability to use your key, it does not prevent already signed documents from being verified, and nothing prevents you from generating and using a new key.

In order to be successful, a digital signature system not only has to provide an algorithm that lets you sign something, it also has to provide the infrastructure that lets people verify that signature. That infrastructure has to support a number of operations. You need to be able to generate a new key if you can't use the old one, and you need to be able to cancel a key if you lose control over it. The process of canceling a key is called *revocation*, and it is one of the hardest parts of successfully designing a digital signature system.

Certificates

What is a *certificate*? A certificate is a digitally signed piece of binary data that contains a set of public keys, some attributes and values, and an expiration date. Some of the values are designed to be displayed to humans, and others are intended for use by programs. Humans are interested in things such as names, the organization you work for, or your telephone number. Programs may be interested in things like your public key, your employee number, or the identifier of your manager. Sometimes values like an electronic mail address are useful to both humans and programs.

A certificate has similarities to a driver's license or a passport. These physical documents are deliberately made to be difficult for ordinary people to duplicate or alter because they are often used when you need to prove your identity. The authorities or organizations that create these documents usually go to some length to make sure they are given to the right people. This is because the organization ends up being a common point of trust between you and whomever you show the documents to.

There is one crucial and very important distinction between a signed digital certificate and a physical document such as a driver's license or a passport. The digital signature on a certificate is designed so that it cannot be forged; it doesn't matter how good you are with computers or with guessing numbers; your chances of being able to fool someone with a made up or altered certificate are impossibly small. There are, of course, ways to trick people into issuing real documents containing bogus information, and just as in the real world, it is possible with digital certificates. If the cryptography is sound, then it is really a problem with people or the processes used to create digital certificates, not a flaw in the certificate itself.

So who digitally signs a certificate? As in the real world, it is useful for a common point of trust to digitally sign a certificate. This might be the organization you work for or some externally recognized authority, depending on who you want to communicate with. In order for a certificate to be useful, the receiver has to be able to verify that it's valid.

In order to perform this verification, the receiver has to establish a connection from some certificate that the receiver knows is OK to the certificate in question. There may be additional certificates that must be checked in order to go from the entity who the verifier trusts to the certificate being checked. The connection between the common point of trust and the certificate being checked is called the *trust path*, and the collection of all the certificates is called the *certificate chain*. If all of the certificates in the trust path are valid, then the certificate verifier will trust the certificate.

This kind of process goes on with physical documents as well, but it's much slower, and the responsibility is all on the certificate holder. For instance, if you want to write a check to the grocery store, you will be asked for identification. Most grocery stores won't accept out-of-state driver's licenses for identification; they can't verify the validity of the license. But if you want to get a local driver's license, the license bureau will accept your out-of-state driver's license, allowing you to build up a certificate chain that lets you successfully authenticate to the grocery store.

What can a certificate be used for? A certificate can be used to provide information about your identity to someone you have not previously arranged to share information with. Certificates are often used as a way to verify public keys, for example. But they will work only if there is a common point of trust between you; everybody involved has to trust a common *certificate authority*.

In order to potentially be able to use a digital certificate to communicate with anyone alive, you need to have a common standard and a global infrastructure that supports certificates. There are currently two certificate standards being proposed for use on the Internet. One is called Simple Public Key Infrastructure (SPKI), and the other is called Public-Key Infrastructure X.509 (PKIX).

These certificate formats have some things in common. One common value in the contents of a certificate is an expiration date. An expiration date means that a certificate has a lifetime, and beyond that point, you will no longer believe that the contents of the certificate are valid. If a key is to be used beyond that point, the certificate will have to be re-signed.

Another thing in common between the design of the two infrastructures is a way to handle the situation when a certificate becomes invalid. This is the same problem we discussed previously for digital signatures; there needs to be a way to make a certificate unusable. For instance, certificates that contain public keys need to be made unusable if you want to tell people to stop using a public key, either because the private key is no longer available (so that messages encrypted with the public key are no longer readable), or because somebody other than the original holder has access to the private key and it can no longer be trusted. A certificate authority might also want to get rid of a certificate for other reasons (the authority might discover that the certificate holder lied about some of the information in the certificate or that the certificate holder's check bounced).

In all of these situations, you no longer want the certificate to be thought of as valid, but if this occurs before the certificate expires, there must be a way to get rid of it, which is called *revoking the certificate*. You cannot just get rid of the copy of the certificate that is at the certificate authority because anyone with a local copy will still use the certificate, without knowing that there's something wrong with it. What usually happens is that the key is placed on a special list, and for PKIX, this list is called the *Certificate Revocation List* (CRL). When someone wants to use a certificate, he or she first checks to see if it is on the CRL. If it isn't, then the certificate can be used. A revoked certificate needs to remain on this list until the certificate expires.

The CRL creates a problem; if you give a certificate a short lifetime, you will need to keep regenerating certificates, but if the lifetime is too long, you may need to keep a large CRL. The parameters for these things will depend entirely on the use of certificates. If you were a university, then you might wish to issue certificates with a lifetime of a year if you didn't want to continually sign certificates. On the other hand, you might choose to expire certificates at the end of each session of classes if you thought that lots of people will lose their certificates or need them revoked. An additional problem with CRLs is that they must be available when performing authentication. This can be difficult if, for example, your network is not working, and you are trying to authenticate the instructions to fix it.

Certificate Trust Models

A trust model defines the ways in which certificate authorities build up a chain of trust, so that two widely separated entities can find a common trusted authority. There are two basic certificate trust models. One is strictly hierarchical, and the other is a mesh.

The *hierarchical model* is like a chain of command and is frequently represented as a tree (this is a tree as in the data structure used in computer science). If you pick any two parts of the tree, it is always possible, by going upwards in the tree, to find a point where the two parts join. It is a very simple algorithm, and it always works. It is the model used by the PKIX standard.

To implement such a model globally you would need quite a large amount of infrastructure, not to mention dealing with the political wrangling for who wants to be at the top. For this reason, the PKIX standard allows a number of separate trees to be joined (which is called *cross certification*). This means that there can be a number of trees. However, the top of each tree is then made to be part of every other tree (making a full mesh between the tree tops!). This means that if the trees are joined, there will always be a certificate chain to reach anyone else, although it may be a very long chain.

The other model is a mesh and is sometimes called a *web of trust*. In this model, connections can be made voluntarily between any two certificate authorities. If any two parts of a web of trust are chosen, there may or may not be a way that they are connected. This model is used by PGP. In fact, PGP normally uses a model in which individuals are themselves the certificate authorities, choosing which other keys they will sign, and which keys they will trust based on who has signed them.

In theory, a web of trust is not as reliable as a hierarchical model. In reality, when certificates are used to identify individual human beings, it is not usually a problem. People rarely spontaneously wish to communicate with strangers. Most interactions are between a known group of people. If a web already exists between these people and a new person joins, there will be a way for the new person to communicate with the rest of the group.

Key Distribution and Exchange

Before you can communicate any data using a symmetric key algorithm, you have to make sure that all participants have the same symmetric key. You can't just send out that key the same way you're going to send the encrypted data because then anybody who's watching that channel will have the key (and if you don't think anybody's watching the channel, you don't need to encrypt the data in the first place). If you're using a public key algorithm, you have a different problem; you need to be sure that you have the correct public key for the entity you want to encrypt things for. These kinds of problems are called *key distribution* problems.

There are three common ways for symmetric keys to be distributed. The first method is called *manual keying*, which simply means that there is no defined way for the key to be distributed and some human being has to get it in. The assumption is that the human will get the key via some reasonably secure method that can't be compromised by the same techniques that would compromise the encryption system itself (so, for instance, if the encryption system is for a network protocol, the key will be sent via fax, not over the network).

Manual keying is regrettably common in systems that use long-lived keys and is bearable only in such systems; if you have to change keys frequently, having people involved is unusably slow and error prone. In addition, people frequently compromise manual keying systems (for instance, by sending keys in unencrypted electronic mail or by leaving the fax of the key lying around where attackers can find it).

Symmetric keys may also be distributed using *public key cryptography*; this simply changes the problem to one of public key distribution, which we'll discuss later. In systems that do this, one party decides on a symmetric key and encrypts it using the other party's public key. As long as the public key information is trustworthy, only the desired other party can read the symmetric key.

Finally, symmetric keys may be distributed using a *key exchange algorithm*. Key exchange algorithms are a special class of public key algorithms that don't encrypt data but do allow two sides of a transaction to figure out the same unpredictable number. The basic principle behind current algorithms is that each side picks a random number, performs a calculation on it, and sends the other side the result. Each side then performs another calculation, still using its original random number, on the other side's initial result, and the two sides come out with the same answer, which is used as a secret key. In order for this to be secure, it must be difficult for an eavesdropper who has the two intermediate results to calculate the final result.

Because public keys are not secret, they are in some ways easier to distribute than symmetric keys; you can send them around without trying to hide them. On the other hand, you need some way to verify that a public key is the correct public key for the entity you want to communicate with. If an attacker can convince you that the attacker's public key belongs to a friend of yours, you will cheerfully encrypt all the data you want to send to your friend so that the attacker can read it (but your friend can't).

There are two common ways to verify a public key. First, you can use a certificate authority (certificates are described earlier). Second, you can use external means to verify the key. One way, which was made popular by PGP, is to verify a key's *fingerprint*. A fingerprint for a key is usually a hexadecimal representation of a cryptographic hash of the public key. External verification of public keys, like manual exchange of symmetric keys, is flexible but clunky. In practice, keys that require external verification are almost never verified. It is also important to verify a fingerprint independently from the source used to obtain the public key. For instance, if your software vendor prints the fingerprint of a public key on the CDs they send out, then a suitably able attacker could produce similar CDs using a fake public key and print the bogus fingerprint on the CD.

What Makes a Protocol Secure?

The encryption algorithm is not the only thing that determines how secure a transaction is. Knowing what encryption algorithm is being used is like knowing what kind of safe somebody owns; it doesn't tell you anything about how secure the information actually is. You can have a completely burglar-proof safe but never bother to put documents in it, or put documents into it without locking the safe, or put documents into it and lock the safe using a combination that lots of people know or can guess.

Just as many people buy expensive and secure safes and use them badly, many people take good encryption algorithms and build them into insecure systems.

In order for a client and a server to have an authenticated and secure private communication session, the following are needed:

- The client and server must agree on what cryptographic algorithms they wish to use.

- The client must be able to tell it is talking to the right server, and the server must be able to tell what client it is talking to.

- The client and server must share a secret that nobody else can know or independently determine.

- The client and server must be able to tell if someone has altered any messages (particularly during the initial stages of communication).

- At the end of the session, the shared secret must be destroyed, and there should not exist a way for it to be recreated.

Selecting an Algorithm

In a perfect world, it would be possible to select the perfect encryption algorithm for clients and servers to use once, and no negotiation would be necessary. The real world doesn't work this way. Sometimes it's necessary for some clients or servers to use relatively weak encryption (either because they have computational limits and can't do stronger encryption fast enough to keep up, or because legal or licensing restrictions control what kind of encryption they can do). In this situation, you don't want to hold back all connections to the lowest common denominator, so you need to support negotiation.

Even when this kind of negotiation isn't needed, most protocols support negotiation in order to allow future implementations to change the encryption algorithm that is used. New encryption algorithms are frequently discovered, and so are new problems with old encryption algorithms. You don't want to be stuck using an encryption algorithm that somebody has figured out how to decrypt easily, or an algorithm that's half the speed of the newest and best thing. Once again, you need to be able to negotiate.

Safe negotiation is difficult. It should be possible for each end of the connection to specify what algorithms are acceptable. If one end can convince the other to negotiate little or no security, a hostile client or server can force connections that will leak information. Even more importantly, it should not be possible for any third party to influence the negotiation. You do not want an attacker to be able to select the encryption that's easiest to break!

A secure protocol uses a negotiation that:

- Allows each side to specify an ordered list of algorithms (from the most desirable to the least desirable)

- Always selects the most desirable possible algorithm

- Fails altogether if no algorithm is acceptable to both sides

- Uses message integrity protections to prevent third-party tampering (see the earlier discussion for more information on message integrity)

Mutual Authentication

In general, when people worry about authentication, they worry about client authentication; how does the server tell that it is offering services to the right client? In a secure protocol, it is also important for the client to be sure about what server it is talking to. The client is going to offer authentication data to the server. That authentication data is valuable to an attacker, and you don't want to blindly hand it out to anybody that asks.

A secure protocol therefore provides for mutual authentication; the server authenticates itself to the client, and the client authenticates itself to the server. There are various ways of doing this, most of them based on the same trick where each side proves that it can decrypt a value with a secret that only the authentic participant could know. This secret could be a key used with a symmetric algorithm, or it could be the private half of a public key/private key pair; it makes a difference in configuring the servers and clients but doesn't change the basis for the authentication. In either case, each side sends the other an unpredictable value and gets it back in a form that proves the other side could decrypt it.

Sharing a Secret

As we've mentioned before, public key cryptography is slow. Very few network protocols can rely on public key cryptography to protect data simply because it takes too long. Protocols therefore need to have a shared secret that can be used for symmetric encryption. That secret can be something they both know already, but there are a number of reasons why it is convenient to use a temporary key (sometimes known as a *session key*) for most transactions, and to discard the key when the transaction is over:

- In general, the more ciphertext that uses the same key that is available to an attacker, the easier it is for the attacker to discover the plaintext (this is particularly true of one of the fastest classes of encryption algorithms).

- The longer a key is in existence, the more likely it is to be inadvertently disclosed.

For these reasons, secure protocols negotiate a key to be used for symmetric encryption for a single transaction. This key needs to be unpredictable, so some random numbers need to be involved in the process.

Identifying Altered Messages

Encryption by itself will not keep people from altering data. A secure protocol needs to add something that will. In general, it will be some form of message integrity checksum, as discussed earlier in this appendix in the section about integrity protection.

Destroying the Shared Secret

Once you have decided to use a temporary shared secret, it is also important to destroy the secret when you are done with it. If there is a way to recreate the secret, then someone who recorded the session could, once they had the right information, decrypt it. If there is no way to recreate the secret, even with unlimited access to the computers on both sides of the communication, then you have achieved a cryptographic property called *perfect forward secrecy.*

Perfection is normally difficult or expensive to obtain, and perfect forward secrecy is no exception. In general, temporary keys are generated using information that is available to one or both sides of the transaction, and there are also usually situations where one side or the other is not sure whether or not the transaction has completed, and needs to keep the key around until the situation is clarified. For practical reasons, most systems implement *partial perfect forward secrecy,* where there is some period of time during which it is possible to recreate the shared secret. After this time period, things are reset, and the secret is destroyed.

Information About Algorithms

In this book, we frequently refer to specific cryptographic algorithms. This section is intended to give you some information about the specific algorithms that are frequently used in firewalls and network protocols, allowing you to make some comparisons between them. It is by no means an exhaustive listing of cryptographic algorithms that you may encounter, or of all the interesting information about the listed cryptographic algorithms.

Encryption Algorithms

These algorithms are designed to be used for encryption (reversibly obscuring information). As we've mentioned, it is often possible to use encryption algorithms for other purposes, and many of these algorithms are also used for digital signatures and/or for cryptographic hashing.

Rivest, Shamir, and Adleman (RSA)

RSA is a public key cipher that can use varying key sizes (which are theoretically unlimited). Typical key sizes are 512, 768, 1024, and 2048 bits. Because the algorithm is expensive to compute, the smaller key sizes tend to be seen in smart cards and smaller devices. A 1024-bit key is considered suitable both for generating digital signatures and for key exchange when used with bulk encryption. A 2048-bit key is sometimes used when a digital signature must be kept secure for an extended period of time. One such use is for a certificate authority key.

RSA was developed in 1978 by Ronald Rivest, Adi Shamir, and Leonard Adleman. Mathematically, it is arguably one of the simplest public key algorithms to understand and implement. The RSA algorithm obtains its strength from the belief that it is difficult to factor large numbers. The RSA algorithm is patented, although the last patent that is believed to cover the algorithm runs out on 20 September 2000. When implemented in software, RSA with 1024-bit keys is about 100 times slower than DES and gets much slower as the keys get larger.

The Data Encryption Standard (DES) and Triple DES

DES is a symmetric 64-bit block cipher that uses a 56-bit key. It has been demonstrated* that it is possible, with a modest investment, to build a specialized piece of hardware that can break a 56-bit DES key in about 24 hours. A group of individuals using a large number of general-purpose computers was able to break a 56-bit DES key in about three months. This size key is probably too short for protecting anything of significant value.

Triple DES (3DES) is a way of combining three uses of single DES with two keys, making the key size 112 bits. Because of the increase in key size, 3DES is believed to be much more secure than ordinary DES. 3DES runs about three times slower than single DES.

The DES algorithm was developed by IBM in the 1970s and was standardized by the U.S. National Bureau of Standards and Technology (the organization is now called the National Institute of Standards and Technology or NIST). It was intended for encrypting unclassified data. Some of the development process for this algorithm is shrouded in mystery, and the NSA had input into the design process that resulted in a number of modifications. The fact that nobody has been able to show that DES has significant weaknesses suggests that the influence of the NSA actually increased the strength of the cipher. It is not clear that the designers intended for the algorithm to be released to the public.

---

* See the book *Cracking DES: Secrets of Encryption Research, Wiretap Politics and Chip Design*, by the Electronic Frontier Foundation (O'Reilly & Associates, 1998).

RC2 and RC4

RC2 is a variable key length symmetric 64-bit block cipher; RC4 is a variable key length stream cipher. The key size for either algorithm can be anywhere from 1 to 2048 bits long. The algorithms are typically used with 40-bit and 128-bit keys. A 40-bit key is too small to protect anything of any value but is widely used due to previous U.S. export rules, which prevented the export of products using longer keys.

These algorithms were developed by Ronald Rivest and are trade secrets of RSA Data Security. The RC4 algorithm was disclosed by a 1994 anonymous Usenet posting; RC2 met the same fate in 1996. Both algorithms seem to be reasonably strong. When implemented in software they are about ten times faster than DES.

Skipjack

Skipjack is a symmetric 64-bit block cipher. The key size is 80 bits long. Skipjack was originally developed as part of a U.S. government encryption standard that was designed to make it easy for law enforcement agencies to decrypt data (which requires using Skipjack in conjunction with a protocol called the Key Exchange Algorithm, or KEA).

Skipjack was initially available only in a hardware implementation called the Clipper chip. The algorithm was declassified in 1998 and can now be implemented in software (in this form, it does not necessarily include the provisions for law enforcement access). Research into the strength of Skipjack itself is inconclusive, but it has been shown that a slightly modified version of Skipjack can be broken without using an exhaustive key search. Skipjack does not seem to be a very popular algorithm to implement, possibly because of its history, and as such there is little comparative timing data.

International Data Encryption Algorithm (IDEA)

IDEA is a symmetric 64-bit block cipher that uses a 128-bit key.

IDEA was invented by Xuejia Lai and James Massey and released in 1992. It has undergone some extensive cryptanalysis and seems to be a strong cipher. The IDEA algorithm is patented in Europe and the United States and must be licensed for commercial use. IDEA is the symmetric block cipher used in Phil Zimmerman's original PGP, one of the most widespread programs for exchanging arbitrary encrypted data across the Internet. There are no problems with the key size. When implemented in software, IDEA runs at about half the speed of DES, but one and a half times the speed of 3DES.

Blowfish

Blowfish is a symmetric 64-bit block cipher with a variable-length key. The key can be from 32 to 448 bits in size.

Blowfish was invented by Bruce Schneier and released in 1994. The algorithm appears to be strong. It is designed to be used on 32-bit microprocessors using simple mathematical operations. It does have larger memory requirements than other algorithms, which makes it less attractive for use in smart cards and other small devices. Blowfish is not patented, and implementations in C are in the public domain. When implemented in software, Blowfish runs at about five times the speed of 3DES.

Advanced Encryption Standard (AES)

The Advanced Encryption Standard is being set by the U.S. NIST organization, and the aim is to choose "a Crypto Algorithm for the Twenty-First Century". AES is intended to replace DES as a U.S. government standard. Having learned from the problems with DES, NIST has chosen to use a public process to develop the standard and to include algorithms designed outside the United States. At the time of writing, a standard has not yet been set, but the following five algorithms are being considered: Mars, RC6, Rijndael, Serpent, and Twofish. Comparison data for all of these algorithms is available from NIST; they all appear to be strong algorithms. In order to meet the requirements of the standard, they are all 128-bit block ciphers, and they all support 128 and 256 bit keys.

Digital Signature Algorithms

Digital signature algorithms were discussed earlier; they provide a way to combine public key encryption and cryptographic checksums so that a piece of information is attached to a specific identity:

Rivest, Shamir, and Adleman (RSA)

See the discussion earlier in the "Encryption Algorithms" section.

Digital Signature Algorithm (DSA) and the Digital Signature Standard (DSS)

The DSA is a public key algorithm that can be used to generate digital signatures. The key size is between 512 and 1024 bits (in 64-bit increments). A key size of 512 bits is too small for long-term security, but 1024 is acceptable.

The DSS is a U.S. NIST standard, issued in 1994, that standardizes the use of DSA; in an official sense, the DSA and the DSS are separate objects (one of them is an algorithm, and the other is an official U.S. government document), but in practice, the terms are often used interchangeably. The DSA is between 10 and 40 times slower to verify signatures than RSA. Some elements of the design of the DSA make it difficult to use for encryption, but it is possible with a full implementation of the algorithm.

The patent situation in regard to implementations using the DSA is unclear; there is some possibility that parts of it are patented and thus cannot be used without paying license fees. The U.S. government has indicated that they would indemnify companies that were sued by possible patent holders, but only if they were implementing the DSS as part of a government contract.

Elliptic Curve

Elliptic curve algorithms are discussed later, in the section on key exchange. They can also be used for digital signatures.

Cryptographic Hashes and Message Digests

Cryptographic hashes and message digests were discussed earlier; they are designed to take a long piece of data and generate a shorter value, in a way that makes it easy to detect changes to the long piece of data:

MD4

MD4 is a cryptographic hash algorithm that calculates a 128-bit number from an input of any length.

This algorithm was designed by Ronald Rivest and released in 1990 as RFC 1186. In 1996 some significant flaws in MD4 were discovered. As a result, MD4 should not be used.

MD5

MD5 is a cryptographic hash algorithm that calculates a 128-bit number from an input of any length.

This algorithm was designed by Ronald Rivest as an improvement to MD4 and was released in 1992 as RFC 1321. Research on MD5 has indicated that one of the design goals of a cryptographic hash (collision resistance) has been violated. A general way to generate collisions has not been found, but the research is troubling. Current cryptographic wisdom also suggests that the size of a cryptographic hash function should be at least 160 bits in size in order to be resistant to birthday* attacks. Given these issues, MD5 should probably be avoided in situations where long-term digital signatures are required.

SHA and SHA-1

SHA and SHA-1 are cryptographic hash algorithms that calculate a 160-bit number from an input of any length.

The SHA algorithm is a U.S. NIST standard and was first issued in 1992 for use with the DSA. In 1995 NIST released a technical update to SHA called SHA-1. This update supersedes the previous version and is thought to address a colli-

---

* A birthday attack is based on probability and is related to the question: How many people have to be in a room for there to be two people with the same birthday? The surprising answer to this is that there is more than a 50 percent chance of having two people with the same birthday if there are at least 23 people in the room. This footnote is too small to contain an explanation, but we encourage you to look this up in any good book on probability.

sion problem similar to the one discussed previously in MD5. SHA-1 should now be used instead of SHA. As this algorithm calculates a 160-bit value, it is more resistant to birthday attacks.

HMAC

HMAC is a method for combining a cryptographic hash algorithm with a key. It will work with any cryptographic hash that produces at least 128 bits of output. HMAC is described in RFC 2104.

Key Exchange

Key exchange algorithms are used to allow two parties to agree on a shared secret across an unsecured network. They are occasionally more correctly called *key agreement algorithms*:

Diffie–Hellman

Diffie-Hellman is a key exchange algorithm that can use varying key sizes (theoretically unlimited).

This algorithm was invented by Whitfield Diffie and Martin Hellman in 1976. It uses exponentiation and modular arithmetic as the basis of its calculations; this is known to be secure, but it involves very large numbers and relatively slow calculations. One of the most important features of Diffie-Hellman is that it can be used to generate a secret that has perfect forward secrecy. Diffie-Hellman was patented, but the patent expired in 1997 so the algorithm can now be freely used.

Diffie-Hellman is a pure key exchange algorithm, which cannot be used to encrypt data. People who claim to be using Diffie-Hellman to encrypt data are extremely confused (unfortunately, because Diffie-Hellman is commonly used for key exchange with bulk encryption schemes, such people are not as rare as one would hope).

Elliptic Curve

A new class of algorithms, called elliptic curve algorithms, is based on the mathematics of polynomial equations. (Ellipses are related to elliptic curve algorithms extremely indirectly; elliptic curves use the kinds of polynomials that are also used to calculate facts about ellipses.) Elliptic curve cryptography uses very simple calculations and very complex mathematics (unlike Diffie-Hellman, which uses complicated calculations and elegant mathematics), and the resulting keys are faster to generate and smaller than Diffie-Hellman keys at the same apparent level of security.

Elliptic key algorithms are much newer than Diffie-Hellman, which gives them two significant drawbacks. First, the mathematical foundations, including the cryptographic strengths and weaknesses, are not as well understood. Second, elliptic key algorithms are still subject to patent protection (and there are significant arguments about who owns what patents). As of this writing, elliptic curve algorithms are still considered a relatively risky choice; this may change as more mathematical results are found (it is beginning to look as if they may become a widely accepted choice, but it is also possible that they will become unusable, if there turns out to be a general solution to the problem that makes them difficult to solve).

RSA

RSA, the all-purpose cryptographic algorithm, can also be used for key exchange. Like Diffie-Hellman, it is secure but slow and memory-intensive for this purpose.

Key Sizes and Strength

Table C-1 gives our recommendations for acceptable algorithm types and key lengths. This sort of information is volatile; weaknesses are continually being discovered in algorithms; new algorithms are being developed; and both the speed and memory capacity of computers is increasing all the time. However, these are what we were willing to use at the time this book was published. We don't think it will ever be a good idea to use these algorithms with shorter keys than those shown.

Table C-1. Acceptable Cryptographic Algorithim and Key Lengths

Purpose	Size (in bits)	Acceptable Algorithms
Symmetric encryption	128	IDEA Blowfish RC4
	112	3DES
Cryptographic hashes	160	SHA-1
	128	MD5
Key exchange	1400	Diffie-Hellman
	1024	RSA
Digital signatures	1024	RSA DSS

Evaluating Other Algorithms

Evaluating the strength of a cryptographic algorithm can be extremely difficult. It's not unusual for people to find problems with algorithms that have been examined before by multiple professional cryptographers. However, this sort of analysis is needed only for new cryptographic algorithms. In general, a reasonably educated and suspicious person can do an adequate job of figuring out whether a cryptographic product is appropriately secure without delving into any of the details of the algorithms involved. A good resource is the "Snake Oil FAQ", published regularly on the *sci.crypt* newsgroup.

In fact, in most cases, all you need is the suspicion. Cryptography is a difficult business: it's hard to come up with good cryptographic algorithms; there are trade-offs between the speed of an algorithm, the memory requirements of an algorithm, and the strength of an algorithm; and no algorithm is perfectly unbreakable. Therefore, any product that advertises a magic new algorithm that runs really fast on small devices and can never be broken is at best over-optimistic and at worst fraudulent.

If you need to evaluate an algorithm, here are some questions you should ask:

- Has the algorithm been published? If not, has it been independently evaluated by multiple professional cryptographers? Independent evaluation is absolutely required to be sure that an algorithm is strong (algorithms are like arguments; everybody finds their own unassailable). Furthermore, a strong algorithm is not weakened by being made public. You should be suspicious of unpublished algorithms, and you should not accept algorithms unless there are independent evaluations of them.

- Is the algorithm being used for its intended purpose? It is possible to use hashing algorithms for encryption, and vice versa, but most algorithms work best when used for what they were designed.

- Is the algorithm being used exactly as designed? Apparently small changes in algorithms (optimizations in how values are calculated, changes in constants, differences in the values used to pad out odd-sized values to the block size needed for block-mode algorithms) can make big changes in the security of the algorithm. All such changes need independent evaluation.

- Are the key sizes being used acceptable? As we've discussed, key sizes mean different things to different algorithms. This makes it hard to decide what key length is long enough. On the other hand, you can often identify cases where a key is too short. It is extremely improbable that a 40-bit key, or even a 56-bit key, will ever again be long enough to protect data with a useful lifetime of more than a day. Present-day symmetric algorithms make maximum use of the available key length, and there is no such algorithm that will hold out against a determined attacker for more than a day with a 56-bit or shorter key.

- How new is the technology? It takes several years to develop enough experience with new techniques to give cryptographers confidence in them.

If you can get good answers to these questions, the algorithms are probably acceptable for most purposes. If you are trying to conceal highly important secrets, you may want to hire a cryptographer to do the analysis for you.

Meanwhile, good luck with your firewall.

Index

About the Authors

Elizabeth D. Zwicky is a director at Counterpane Internet Security, a managed security services company. She has been doing large-scale Unix system administration and related work for 15 years, and was a founding board member of both the System Administrators Guild (SAGE) and BayLISA (the San Francisco Bay Area system administrators group), as well as a nonvoting member of the first board of the Australian system administration group, SAGE-AU. She has been involuntarily involved in Internet security since before the 1988 Morris Internet worm. In her lighter moments, she is one of the few people who makes significant use of the *rand* function in PostScript, producing PostScript documents that are different every time they're printed.

Simon Cooper is a computer professional currently working in Silicon Valley. He has worked in different computer-related fields ranging from hardware through operating systems and device drivers to application software and systems support in both commercial and educational environments. He has an interest in the activities of the Internet Engineering Task Force (IETF) and USENIX, is a member of the British Computer Conservation Society, and is a founding member of the Computer Museum History Center. Simon has released a small number of his own open source programs and has contributed time and code to the XFree86 project. In his spare time, Simon likes to play ice hockey, solve puzzles of a mathematical nature, and tinker with Linux.

D. Brent Chapman is a networking professional in Silicon Valley. He has designed and built Internet firewall systems for a wide range of organizations, using a variety of techniques and technologies. He is the founder of the Firewalls Internet mailing list, and creator of the Majordomo mailing list management package. He is the founder, principal, and technical lead of Great Circle Associates, Inc., a highly regarded strategic consulting and training firm specializing in Internet networking and security. Over the last 15 years, Brent has worked in a variety of consulting, engineering, and management roles in information technology, operations, and technology marketing for a wide range of employers and clients, including the Xerox Palo Alto Research Center (PARC), Silicon Graphics, Inc. (SGI), and Covad Communications Company.

Colophon

The illustration on the cover of *Building Internet Firewalls* is of a doorway of Gothic design, topped by a crenelated parapet. The period of Gothic architecture is often said to have begun in the mid-12th century, when the church of Saint-

Denis was built, in Paris in 1144. The architect of that church is unknown. Although Gothic architecture was mainly used in the building of churches, by the late 13th century it was used for secular purposes also, including fortifications. The structure of the merlons (the raised portions of the parapet) in this illustration gives information about the date and place of construction. The oblique sides of the merlons suggest that the doorway was built in the 14th century, and the plain but sloping top suggests that it was built in England or France.

Merlons were designed to provide defense to those inside the fortification, while crenels (the recessed portions between the merlons) let them shoot projectiles at attacking enemies. Given the size of this door, and the relatively low merlons, this may have been a postern, a doorway used by foot travellers to avoid lowering the main gate.

Madeleine Newell was the production coordinator for this book. Nancy Crumpton provided all editorial and production services and wrote the index. Mike Sierra provided FrameMaker technical support. Nancy Kotary and Jane Ellin provided quality control.

Edie Freedman designed the cover of this book, using a 19th-century engraving from *Heck's Pictorial Archive of Art and Architecture*. The cover layout was produced by Emma Colby with QuarkXPress 3.3 using the ITC Garamond font. Whenever possible, our books use RepKover™, a durable and flexible lay-flat binding. If the page count exceeds RepKover's limit, perfect binding is used.

The inside layout for this second edition was adapted by Alicia Cech and David Futato from a design created by Nancy Priest, Edie Freedman, and Jennifer Niederst, and was implemented by Mike Sierra in FrameMaker 5.5.6. The text and heading fonts are ITC Garamond Light and Garamond Book. Chris Reilley created the figures for the first edition of this book; Robert Romano and Rhon Porter adapted those figures and created new figures for this second edition using Adobe Photoshop 5 and Macromedia Freehand 8. This colophon was written by Clairemarie Fisher O'Leary.

How to stay in touch with O'Reilly

1. Visit Our Award-Winning Web Site

http://www.oreilly.com/

★ "Top 100 Sites on the Web" —*PC Magazine*
★ "Top 5% Web sites" —*Point Communications*
★ "3-Star site" —*The McKinley Group*

Our web site contains a library of comprehensive product information (including book excerpts and tables of contents), downloadable software, background articles, interviews with technology leaders, links to relevant sites, book cover art, and more. File us in your Bookmarks or Hotlist!

2. Join Our Email Mailing Lists

New Product Releases
To receive automatic email with brief descriptions of all new O'Reilly products as they are released, send email to:
listproc@online.oreilly.com
Put the following information in the first line of your message (*not* in the Subject field):
subscribe oreilly-news

O'Reilly Events
If you'd also like us to send information about trade show events, special promotions, and other O'Reilly events, send email to:
listproc@online.oreilly.com
Put the following information in the first line of your message (*not* in the Subject field):
subscribe oreilly-events

3. Get Examples from Our Books via FTP

There are two ways to access an archive of example files from our books:

Regular FTP
- ftp to:
  ftp.oreilly.com
  (login: anonymous
  password: your email address)
- Point your web browser to:
  ftp://ftp.oreilly.com/

FTPMAIL
- Send an email message to:
  ftpmail@online.oreilly.com
  (Write "help" in the message body)

4. Contact Us via Email

order@oreilly.com
To place a book or software order online. Good for North American and international customers.

subscriptions@oreilly.com
To place an order for any of our newsletters or periodicals.

books@oreilly.com
General questions about any of our books.

software@oreilly.com
For general questions and product information about our software. Check out O'Reilly Software Online at **http://software.oreilly.com/** for software and technical support information. Registered O'Reilly software users send your questions to: **website-support@oreilly.com**

cs@oreilly.com
For answers to problems regarding your order or our products.

booktech@oreilly.com
For book content technical questions or corrections.

proposals@oreilly.com
To submit new book or software proposals to our editors and product managers.

international@oreilly.com
For information about our international distributors or translation queries. For a list of our distributors outside of North America check out:
http://www.oreilly.com/www/order/country.html

5. Work with Us

Check out our website for current employment opportunites:
www.jobs@oreilly.com
Click on "Work with Us"

O'Reilly & Associates, Inc.
101 Morris Street, Sebastopol, CA 95472 USA
TEL   707-829-0515 or 800-998-9938
      (6am to 5pm PST)
FAX   707-829-0104

International Distributors